Drafting Wills
in Scotland

Drafting Wills in Scotland

Alan R Barr
MA, LLB, NP, TEP
Director of the Legal Practice Unit,
The University of Edinburgh

John M H Biggar
WS, LLB, NP, TEP
Partner, Tods Murray WS

Andrew M C Dalgleish
WS, LLB, NP, TEP
Partner, Brodies WS

Hugh J Stevens
WS, LLB, NP, TEP
Partner, Brodies WS

Butterworths
Law Society of Scotland

Edinburgh   1994

United Kingdom	Butterworth & Co (Publishers) Ltd, 4 Hill Street, EDINBURGH EH2 3JZ and Halsbury House, 35 Chancery Lane, LONDON WC2A 1EL
Australia	Butterworths, SYDNEY, MELBOURNE, BRISBANE, ADELAIDE, PERTH, CANBERRA and HOBART
Canada	Butterworths Canada Ltd, TORONTO and VANCOUVER
Ireland	Butterworth (Ireland) Ltd, DUBLIN
Malaysia	Malayan Law Journal Sdn Bhd, KUALA LUMPUR
New Zealand	Butterworths of New Zealand Ltd, WELLINGTON and AUCKLAND
Puerto Rico	Butterworths of Puerto Rico Inc, SAN JUAN
Singapore	Butterworths Asia, SINGAPORE
South Africa	Butterworth Publishers (Pty) Ltd, DURBAN
USA	Butterworth Legal Publishers, CARLSBAD, California, and SALEM, New Hampshire

Law Society of Scotland
26 Drumsheugh Gardens, EDINBURGH EH3 7YR

A CIP Catalogue record for this book is available from the British Library.

ISBN 0 406 17940 9

Typeset by Phoenix Photosetting, Chatham, Kent
Printed and bound in Great Britain by
Redwood Books, Trowbridge, Wiltshire

For our respective wives –
Penny, Gill, Sheila and Margaret
(see paragraph 6.06)

PREFACE

This book has had a long gestation period. The patience of those who have maintained their wish to obtain it over this time is much appreciated by the authors. However, no-one is more pleased than the authors themselves to see its publication at last.

Although four people were involved in the actual writing, we wish to thank a number of others who were involved at different stages. For involvement in the book's conception, thanks to Richard Girdwood. For typing and word-processing above and beyond the call of duty, thanks to Pat Hay, Julia Tod and Yvonne Forrest at Brodies, Diane Begbie at Tods Murray, Betty Hayter and Jane Mackenzie at the University of Edinburgh, and Penny Barr. For efforts in various libraries, thanks to Susan Mansfield at Tods Murray and Alexander Elles, the last financed by a small grant from the Lindsay Bequest Committee at the University of Edinburgh. For reading and commenting on certain sections of the text, thanks to Professor Emeritus Ken Mason at the University of Edinburgh, Professor Michael Meston at the University of Aberdeen, Willie Young, Deputy Registrar, Capital Taxes Office and Chris Docker, Executive Secretary, VESS. For preparing the index, thanks to Alex Gerver. For illustrating Spotty the Dog, thanks to Doreen Fisher. For tolerance in awaiting the manuscript and diligence in editing it, thanks to Butterworths.

We have attempted to state the law as at 1 November 1994.

ARB
JMHB
AMCD
HJS
Edinburgh
November 1994

Disclaimer

While this book and in particular the Styles are designed to be used in practice, and whilst every care has been taken to ensure the accuracy of the contents, no responsibility can be accepted by the publishers, authors or their firms or employer for actions taken or not taken as a result of the material published. Expert professional advice should always be sought.

CONTENTS

TABLE OF STATUTES

TABLE OF CASES

BIBLIOGRAPHY

Anton

A E Anton and P R Beaumont *Private International Law* (2nd edn, W Green, Edinburgh, 1990)

Chapman

A L Chapman *Inheritance Tax* (8th edn by T J Lyons, Longman, London 1989)

Clive

E M Clive *The Law of Husband and Wife in Scotland* (3rd edn, W Green, Edinburgh, 1992)

Currie

J G Currie *The Confirmation of Executors in Scotland* (7th edn by A E M McRae, W Green, Edinburgh, 1973)

Dobie

W J Dobie *Manual of the Law of Liferent and Fee in Scotland* (W Green, Edinburgh, 1941)

Elder

A H Elder *Forms of Wills* (W Green, Edinburgh, 1947)

Gretton & Reid

G L Gretton and K G C Reid *Conveyancing* (W Green, Edinburgh, 1993)

Halliday

J M Halliday *Conveyancing Law and Practice* (W Green, Edinburgh, 1985–1990)

Henderson

R C Henderson *The Principle of Vesting in the Law of Succession* (2nd edn, W Green, Edinburgh, 1938)

Jones & Mackintosh

M H Jones and S A Mackintosh *Revenue Law in Scotland* (Butterworths, London, 1986)

Laidlow

P Laidlow *Tolley's Tax Planning for Post-death Variations* (Tolleys, Croydon, 1993)

McCutcheon

B D McCutcheon *Inheritance Tax* (3rd edn, Sweet & Maxwell, London, 1988)

Macdonald

R Macdonald, *An Introduction to the Scots Law of Succession* (W Green, Edinburgh, 1990)

Mackenzie Stuart

A Mackenzie Stuart *The Law of Trusts* (W Green, Edinburgh, 1932)

McLaren

J McLaren *The Law of Wills and Succession* (3rd edn, Bell and Bradfute, Edinburgh, 1894, with Supplement by D O Dykes, W Green, Edinburgh, 1934)

Menzies

A J P Menzies *The Law of Scotland Affecting Trustees* (2nd edn, W Green, Edinburgh, 1913)

Meston

M C Meston *The Succession (Scotland) Act 1964* (4th edn, W Green, Edinburgh, 1993)

Norrie & Scobbie

K McK Norrie and E M Scobbie *Trusts* (W Green, Edinburgh, 1991)

Phillips

A Phillips *Professional Ethics for Scottish Solicitors* (Butterworths, Edinburgh, 1990)

Pugh

John Pugh (editor) *The Administration of Foreign Estates* (Sweet & Maxwell, London, 1988)

Stair

Institutions of the Law of Scotland

Stair Memorial Encyclopaedia

The Laws of Scotland: Stair Memorial Encyclopaedia (Law Society of Scotland/ Butterworths, Edinburgh, 1987–)

Wilkinson & Norrie

A B Wilkinson and K McK Norrie *The Law Relating to Parent and Child in Scotland* (W Green/Sweet & Maxwell, Edinburgh, 1993)

Wilson & Duncan

W A Wilson and A G M Duncan *Trusts, Trustees and Executors* (W Green, Edinburgh, 1975)

ABBREVIATIONS

AC	Law Reports, Appeal Cases (House of Lords and Privy Council) 1890–
All ER	All England Law Reports 1936–
Ch	Law Reports, Chancery Division 1890–
D	Dunlop's Session Cases 1838–62
EG	Estates Gazette 1858–
F	Fraser's Session Cases 1898–1906
FC	Faculty Collection (Court of Session) 1725–1825
F (HL)	House of Lords Cases in Fraser's Session Cases 1898–1906
GWD	Green's Weekly Digest 1986–
LR Eq	Law Reports, Equity 1865–75
LT	Law Times Reports 1859–1947
M	Macpherson's Session Cases 1862–73
M (HL)	House of Lords Cases in Macpherson's Session Cases 1862–73
Macq	Macqueen's House of Lords Reports 1851–65
Mor	Morison's Dictionary of Decisions (Court of Session) 1540–1808
Pat	Paton's House of Lords Appeal Cases 1726–1821
R	Rettie's Session Cases 1873–98
R (HL)	House of Lords Cases in Rettie's Session Cases 1873–98
S	P Shaw's Session Cases 1821–38
SC	Session Cases 1907–
SC (HL)	House of Lords Cases in Session Cases 1907–
SLT	Scots Law Times 1893–1908, and 1909–
SLT (Notes)	Notes of Recent Decisions in Scots Law Times 1946–81
SLT (Sh Ct)	Sheriff Court Reports in Scots Law Times 1893–
SN	Session Notes 1925–48
STC	Simon's Tax Cases 1973–
Sh App	P Shaw's Scotch Appeals (House of Lords) 1821–26
WLR	Weekly Law Reports 1953–
W & S	Wilson & Shaw's House of Lords Cases 1825–34

CHAPTER 1

INTRODUCTION

AIMS OF THIS BOOK

1.01 We have aimed to produce a set of Style wills in a comprehensible modern form having substantial common elements.

The Styles have been prepared as a set. The general layout and form of each is the same. Many clauses are common to a number of Styles. This consistency is not merely because it facilitates commenting on them, but is to assist in comprehension and to show how even complicated wills are built up using similar parts. Care must always be taken when adding parts of a number of Styles together to form a single draft but it is hoped that the Styles presented here can have various elements moved between Styles, without causing serious internal conflicts in the final draft, between the various assembled parts. It is, therefore, to some extent possible to 'pick and mix' parts from a number of Styles. There are references in the text to some likely rearrangements, but in every case the drafter must ensure that the product is internally consistent.

The Styles are intended to be as readable, comprehensible and simple as the circumstances allow. There are of course limits to what can be done, but we have tried to advance usage in this area. Some clauses may appear somewhat novel. It is hoped that these will be more understandable than more traditional for-mulations. We have, for example, spent much time on the provisions for dealing with funds for young children to ensure that executors have wide powers to deal with matters flexibly. The provisions may appear similar to usual formulations, but they are wider in a number of areas.

We have also spent considerable time in producing effective accumulation and maintenance trusts. This effort has been encouraged by the Age of Legal Capacity (Scotland) Act 1991, which reduced the age at which children may claim funds from executors. The full form of accumulation and maintenance trust (Style S7), while providing that all of the beneficiaries should share the funds equally, is about as flexible as it is possible to be and still qualify as an accumulation and maintenance trust for inheritance tax purposes. Because of the length of deed such flexibility demanded, we decided to produce a short, simple form of accumulation and maintenance trust (Style S8) which may suit other situations. We regard this as quite an important innovation; this Style has been seen by and received tentative approval from the Capital Taxes Office as being effective for inheritance tax purposes.

1.02 We are clear that it is vital that the testator should understand as much as possible of the terms of the will. Many testators expect any legal document to contain a mass of text which they will not understand. In relation to pension trust deeds the Goode Committee commented:

'Although the formal documentation sets out the entire basis upon which the scheme is to function, in practice it is unlikely to be of much value to the average member. The documents will be prepared by lawyers; they will usually be long and difficult to understand, with extensive use of technical terminology. This is not to criticise those who have drafted trust deeds, merely to point to their obvious deficiency as a source of comprehensible information for members[1].'

Wills are shorter documents and we think that they should be a source of comprehensible information for testators and beneficiaries. Many items in a will relate to matters to which the testator has given no thought or knows nothing about, but if expressed simply the testator should be quite able to see the need for them. It is accepted that there are many areas, particularly in relation to trusts, where few testators will want to discuss the full details or implications of a particular clause. Nevertheless, it is important that there is a general understanding of its effects. Although the testator will not be directly concerned when the will comes into operation, it is quite likely that a spouse's will may be similar, so that the original testator's spouse may require further explanation. Such a surviving spouse will not be impressed by some unforeseen consequence of a will drafted on the basis of insufficient instructions or otherwise.

Where possible we have tried to make the Styles explicable and to remove the mystique associated with legal documents. This is not always easy and often attempts to meet the conflicting demands of combining detail with brevity result in the production of 'text which is masterly in its conciseness and almost wholly unintelligible'[2]. Nevertheless we have attempted to be both concise and intelligible. We believe that this is to the benefit of both the testator and the draftsman.

As well as trying to make the will comprehensible to the testator, we want to ensure that the Styles are fully understood by the practitioner. If the practitioner does not understand the terms of a will then the testator cannot be expected to either. The practitioner cannot advise on its terms nor assess whether it really meets the client's concerns from which instructions can be taken. We do not regard it as a counsel of perfection to say that the practitioner should fully understand the terms of the will – we regard it as essential. The practitioner should be able to explain and justify all of the clauses in the will. He should not resort (if pressed) to saying that they are technical legal matters not intelligible to the layman – that should not be the case.

STYLES

1.03 The Styles are based on those in common currency within the profession in Scotland. They began as the styles used by the authors, which themselves had

---

1 Report of the Pension Law Review Committee, CM2342–1, September 1993, para 4–12–19.
2 Ibid, para 4–1–24.

developed over the years and were based on older styles. The older published sources of styles are the *Encyclopaedia of Scottish Legal Styles* (1939), *The Scots Style Book* (1904) and in particular *Elder's Forms of Wills* (1947) for which work we have a great and continuing regard.

A more recent line of styles exists, based on the Law Society of Scotland Workshop series in the 1970s, the Law Society's Post Qualifying Legal Education courses on Wills and in the will styles for the Diploma in Legal Practice. The authors have had a close involvement with many of the styles in this line. There are various other published styles to which reference may be made[1]. There are inevitably many similarities between all of those styles, as there are between them and the Styles presented here. We have built on the work of others, in that new styles are evolutionary rather than revolutionary. Practice indicates which styles are preferable and this is the basis on which we have prepared the Styles presented here.

1.04 As mentioned, one of our aims has been to simplify styles and to make them more understandable. To this end we have removed Latin words and phrases from the Styles. Often a Latin tag provides a very short reference to a situation or event and as between lawyers may provide a very simple form of reference. It will not, however, usually be understandable by testators. We think that wills can be drafted without reference to Latin. We admit to having had very great difficulty when we tried to remove the reference to division between issue as being *per stirpes*. The result is longer and may be no clearer (see, for example, S3.6) and we provide a more traditional formulation in the text (see para 5.12). We have tried not to use obscure technical terms for the same reasons.

We use no Roman numerals in denoting paragraph clauses. We use Arabic figures rather than written numbers in addresses and dates where there can be no confusion. However, we retain numbers written as words in the case of pecuniary legacies as there might be scope for unauthorised alteration. We also retain numbers as words in numbering the various purposes of the Styles. This has been done in the interests of breaking up the text but could equally well be effected by using bold type if word processing considerations permit this.

We have limited the use of capital letters in the Styles to the initial letter of each purpose or paragraph. We use initial capital letters for words which are specifically defined, such as 'my Trustees' in S5.2, but not in 'my executors' in S1.2 where there is no definition. There are very few words defined in this way and so we have provided the definition following the first use of the term in the text and not provided a separate definition purpose.

We have tried to limit the use of the word 'said', to refer back to some previous use, to situations where it seems unavoidable without considerable expansion of the text.

We have had problems with references to sex. While it may be preferable to refer to 'he or she', there is no doubt that this would have broken the flow and

---

1 For example, Burns *Conveyancing Practice* (4th edn, 1957); Halliday *Conveyancing Law and Practice in Scotland* IV.

occasionally caused genuine awkwardness and confusion. The bulk of primary references are thus to the masculine and we rely on the terms of the Interpretation Act 1978 for this to include the feminine. No differentiation between the sexes is intended. There are very few differences between men and women in the area of succession. We generally refer to 'the liferenter' throughout, using it as a word referring to a beneficiary of either sex. Although there is a specific feminine term we do not use it, nor do we intend the reference to be changed in a Style referring to a female liferenter, as for example S5.8. The individual drafter may decide whether to adhere to this, as also whether to adopt the specific feminine term for executor. On occasion in Styles when referring to a child we refer to 'its parent' (for example, S3.6) as this seems to reflect current verbal practice and to be simpler than alternatives.

1.05   We believe that breaking up the text aids comprehension. We disapprove of a will being drafted all as one sentence with no physical gaps in the text, which was at one time regarded as normal. While the leaving of gaps at the end of lines can be seen as leaving a will open to alteration and fraud, we think that that risk can be reduced by proper punctuation and, in any event, the aim of comprehensibility seems to us to be preferable to attempting to prevent some limited forms of unlikely fraud.

We have therefore divided the text of each Style into numbered purposes in the form (ONE). Where necessary, these purposes are divided into numbered paragraphs in the form (1) and occasionally further divided into lettered clauses in the form (a). We encourage the drafter to lay out the text in a readable manner so that, for example, a list of individual bequests will show each beneficiary separately on a new line.

We also believe in extensive punctuation as an aid to comprehension. While views differ and, for example, in English wills punctuation seems to be viewed with horror and generally omitted, we think that properly used it assists in conveying meaning. It breaks up text into intelligible parts and is generally to be encouraged. We have used full stops liberally within each Style and sometimes within each purpose. We also use commas, colons, semi-colons and brackets. We have tried to be consistent, but we do not propose to justify particular usage in detail.

Each Style has side headings for each purpose and for main numbered paragraphs within each purpose. They have been omitted where there are merely numbered declarations within a purpose. We believe that side headings should be included in a draft will presented to a testator and in the engrossed will thereafter. The objects of these side headings are to make the will quicker to understand and to help navigate through it. While we have side headings it may be that some word-processing systems find them difficult to cope with, so that a heading above each purpose could be considered as an alternative. In relation to the numbered paragraphs within each purpose, a sub-heading in the body of text does not work as well.

1.06   Each of the Styles is provided with a précis. It is hoped that this enables the general gist of the will to be appreciated before reading the will itself. This may help the drafter in selecting a suitable Style. We believe that the précis has a further, more important, use. Particularly in relation to the longer wills, we suggest that a précis should be prepared relating to a draft will and that both should then be presented to the testator for consideration. For this purpose the précis should show the names of the executors, details or a summary of significant bequests and any particular alterations to the information set out in the basic précis. We have found that clients appreciate receiving a précis of a complicated will. They can concentrate on the main points and be sure that they have at least grasped them, if not the full detail presented in the will.

If the précis is used in this way, it is then suggested that once the will has been signed, a version of the précis including the date of the will is then both given to the testator with a copy of his completed will and also filed with the principal will, so that in the event of the testator's death there is available a simple summary to present to beneficiaries.

The précis is intended, therefore, to be of use to the drafter, to the testator and to the beneficiaries under the will.

HOW TO USE THE BOOK

1.07 The book consists of two main parts, the Styles themselves on the one hand and the text on the other.

The text includes detailed commentary on the Styles, but also includes more general discussion on drafting wills, together with alternative clauses which may be considered for substitution in the Styles.

Similar points may come up in a number of Styles and these are considered together in the text. The individual parts of each Style are all considered somewhere in the text, but the text has been written as a whole and so it will not necessarily conform to the arrangement of any of the Styles.

The Styles part of the book consists of fourteen full Styles. Each Style has a précis for use as discussed above (see para 1.06). Each Style is followed by a reference sheet. We considered incorporating reference numbers in the body of the text of each Style, but decided that this would detract from the appearance of the Styles. The reference section following each Style therefore notes each purpose and gives references to the text. It is hoped that this method will enable comment and alternatives on any point in the Styles to be found readily. There is in addition a traditional index which we hope is sufficiently comprehensive to be helpful.

Alternative clauses appear in the text. There is, however, one alternative purpose which because of its length and complexity has been placed in the Styles and given the designation S7A. This treatment makes it easier to incorporate in a précis and also to include textual references in the reference section.

It should be noted that in the alternative clauses in the text we have not included a reminder that parties should always be designed, for example 'A (design)'. This omission is simply to avoid excessive repetition; it is obviously vital to include a designation on the first reference to any person in a will or trust.

1.08 Styles are numbered and are referred to in the form Style S1 for the first Style. Each purpose is numbered. In the Styles the number of a purpose appears in the form of, for example, (ONE), while in the text the reference to that provision would be S1.1. A reference in the latter form also appears in the margin of the Styles, but this reference is only for use in this book and it is not suggested that it appear in a will. Where there are numbered paragraphs in a purpose, these are referred to in the form, for example, S5.12(2) which is the investment powers clause (2) of the powers purpose 12 of Style S5.

It may be tempting to pick out a Style for use in a particular case, but we cannot emphasise too strongly that the Styles are intended to be used in conjunction with the text and not regardless of it. This is akin to saying that a drafter should not draft a will if he does not understand the intention and effect of all of the clauses in it.

While commentary on all provisions in the Styles is included within the text, the majority of the Styles are also dealt with as complete draft documents, in relation to the specific aims of each formulation. Slight exceptions to this are found in relation to the first four Styles (S1 – S4). While references to every part of these Styles are included in the commentary, Styles S1 – S4 are intended to be examples of rather more basic wills which can be adopted and adapted for use in a large number of relatively simple situations. However, references to the relevant text are just as important in relation to the provisions of these Styles as with the rather more complex examples which follow them.

Chapter 9 mentions some common situations faced by practitioners and offers some suggestions for dealing with them. This may be a more suitable place to start selecting a Style than by looking at the Styles in isolation.

MAIN REASONS FOR HAVING WILLS

1.09 When drafting any will, it is not sufficient just to pick a Style which appears appropriate. The drafter should be clear as to the testator's intentions, as to the possibilities which may exist for carrying out those intentions and as to how those intentions are to be carried out. Only then should the drafter look for a suitable Style. Before considering detailed matters in relation to wills, it is worth looking at the main reasons why a person should make one. There follows a list of the more important objectives.

(1) To determine beneficiaries. To the extent that there is no will then the rules on intestacy will determine who the beneficiaries are.

(2) To appoint executors. Again if there is no will, then the beneficiaries on intestacy will generally be the people entitled to act as executors. If there are only children involved then it may be necessary to appoint a judicial factor, if they have no guardian.

(3) To make provision for children or other persons with special requirements. Where there are young children, the testator may want to arrange that funds for such beneficiaries are held until they attain full capacity at 16, or

perhaps longer. Beneficiaries may be mentally incapable and special provision may require to be made for them.

(4) To give proper powers to executors to administer funds. Where no powers are given to executors, then in investment matters they will be restricted to the Trustee Investments Act 1961 and their powers may be limited in other ways. This will be particularly significant in relation to funds held for children.

(5) To make ancillary provisions. A will is often used to deal with ancillary matters which are not concerned with the testator's estate. These might include funeral or burial arrangements, the appointment of guardians or the exercise of a power of appointment under a trust.

(6) To achieve tax planning aims. The possibilities here are numerous and change rapidly, but there is a lot of scope for planning. Tax planning considerations are discussed incidentally, but this book is not intended to be principally on this subject.

(7) To reassure a testator that his affairs are in order. This is partly an aspect of the previous objects but is often important on its own.

Not all of these objectives will be required in every case. It is possible to have only one aim intended. It is thus feasible to have a will determining beneficiaries but providing nothing else, or appointing executors but leaving no bequests. The possible objectives in making a will are discussed throughout the text which follows.

CHAPTER 2

GENERAL MATTERS

INTRODUCTION

2.01 This chapter considers some general matters in connection with the drafting of wills. The areas considered do not relate specifically to the Styles included in this book, nor (for the most part) to problems arising from drafting. However, the matters under consideration will require to be addressed (at least in the background) whenever wills are drafted. Consideration of some items covered will be absolutely crucial for certain testators, while those involved in drafting wills should at least be aware of possible problems which may arise in appropriate circumstances.

CAPACITY TO MAKE A WILL AND GROUNDS FOR REDUCTION

Full age

2.02 A person of sound mind and full age has testamentary capacity. The term 'full age' has taken on a new meaning following the Age of Legal Capacity (Scotland) Act 1991. Section 2(2) of that Act states that 'a person of or over 12 years shall have testamentary capacity including legal capacity to exercise by testamentary writing any power of appointment'. This section amends previous law by introducing a common age limit of 12 for both boys and girls at which time they attain testamentary capacity.

Section 3 of the same Act allows for the possibility of setting aside a transaction entered into while the young person was of, or over, the age of 16 but under the age of 18 years and which is a prejudicial transaction as defined by the Act. However, section 3(3) specifically *excludes* the exercise of testamentary capacity by way of a testamentary writing or testamentary exercise of a power of appointment from this relief. It is suggested that this exclusion was made because a simpler alternative remedy would be the making of a new will or document exercising the power of appointment.

Sound mind

2.03 The lawyer taking instructions must be satisfied that the testator is of sound mind. This does not have to be a permanent state of mind and a will has been sustained where it was made during a lucid interval[1].

If there is some doubt over whether the testator has sufficient capacity and medical advice is taken in advance, that view will normally prevail. It is not unusual for doctors and nurses to be asked to act as witnesses, in an attempt to ensure that would-be challengers will reflect carefully before raising an action of reduction. However, such a procedure will not necessarily guarantee validity. A respected member of the medical, and in particular psychiatric, profession, the late Professor Kenneth Macrae, expounded on this subject in his *Edinburgh Textbook on Psychiatry (Companion to Psychiatric Studies)*. In that book he advises the clinician to make sure that the patient:

'(1) understands the nature of the act of making a will and its effects;
 (2) has a reasonable knowledge of the extent of his property;
 (3) knows and appreciates the claims to which he ought to give effect;
 (4) is not influenced in making his dispositions by any abnormal emotional state or by any delusions.'

It has been suggested in correspondence with psychiatrists that where someone is quite mentally disturbed they may still manage to cope with points (1), (2) and (3) above. If this is the case then the testator's wishes should not be easily brushed aside just because of the presence of some degree of mental disorder.

If the testator was not of either the required age or sound mind and attempted to make a will, the purported will would of course be null and void from the outset. If he suffered from delusions at the time of making the will or was incapacitated by drink, drugs or in some other way unable to understand what he was doing, that will is ineffective, but an effective will could be made at another time[2].

Facility and fraud or circumvention

2.04 If the requirements of full age and sound mind were apparently met, it might still be possible to have the will reduced on the grounds of facility and fraud or circumvention.

These grounds for reduction are available where firstly there is no insanity, ie no incapacity to test, but there is weakness in the testator which exposes him to influence and requests of interested parties. The testator may be old, ill or merely naturally disposed to such advances.

Secondly, there must be either fraud or circumvention, ie undue influence perpetrated in addition to the facility. It is sometimes forgotten that there are two grounds to be satisfied in this situation, namely facility of the testator

---

1 *Nisbet's Trustees v Nisbet* (1871) 9 M 937.
2 *Laidlaw v Laidlaw* (1870) 8 M 882; *Hope v Hope's Trustees* (1898) 1 F (HL) 1; *Sivewright's Trustees v Sivewright* 1920 SC (HL) 63; *Gibson's Executor v Anderson* 1921 SC 774.

followed by circumvention in the form of fraud or undue influence. The greater the facility the less evidence which is needed for fraud or undue influence[1]. The standards required to establish circumvention are less than those generally necessary to establish fraud[2].

The influence on the testator may take the form of the testator being frightened or coerced or misled by people close to him or in whom he trusted.

The question arises as to the point at which facility becomes total incapacity. In the case of *Gibson's Executor v Anderson* above, the testator left certain holograph writings making bequests to his sister-in-law, with his son being the sole intestate heir. The son sought to reduce the holograph writings on the basis of *either* total incapacity *or* facility and circumvention. A jury found for him on the basis of the latter grounds and there was a subsequent petition for a new trial on the basis that the verdict was contrary to the evidence. No re-trial was granted, but it was interesting that the Lord Justice-Clerk dissented from the views of his fellow judges, on the grounds that the evidence led in the original trial was insufficient to allow the finding of reduction due to facility and circumvention, but could have allowed a finding of total incapacity. In that case medical men, a banker and several other witnesses gave evidence as to the total incapacity of the testator, although the jury in that case chose to find and allow reduction on the grounds of facility and circumvention.

While it would be dangerous to draw the conclusion that facility must be approaching total incapacity to allow a successful application for reduction, Scottish case law is not exactly littered with successful applications for reduction of a will on the grounds of facility and undue influence[3]. On being approached by someone who wishes to consider the possibility of the reduction of another person's will on the basis of facility and undue influence most solicitors react by saying that this is an extremely difficult matter on which to satisfy the court and such a reaction seems entirely correct in looking at some recent cases on the matter.

2.05   In the outer house case of *Brogan v Rennie*[4] an elderly lady executed a will in 1981 in which she had as her residuary beneficiary a niece with whom she had had a close relationship. In 1985 a nephew arranged for a doctor to visit the lady who lived alone. The doctor considered that the lady was suffering from dementia and was *incapable* of making a will although he would have expected her to have occasional spells of lucidity thereafter.

No further assessment was undertaken in view of the fact that the nephew and his wife offered to look after the lady who thereafter sold her house with assistance from the nephew and his wife. Around the time of selling the house a cousin of the niece visited the lady and obtained the impression that she was somewhat distressed and being discouraged from seeing her niece. In 1985 while the lady lived with her nephew and his wife a caption appeared in the newspaper

---

1 *Gibson's Executor v Anderson* 1925 SC 774.
2 *Wheelans v Wheelans* 1986 SLT 164.
3 See 25 *Stair Memorial Encyclopaedia* para 764 and authorities there cited.
4 1991 GWD 31–1885.

beside a photograph which described the niece as the wife of a man with whom in fact she merely cohabited and the lady indicated her disapproval of that situation. Later the same month as the newspaper article appeared, the lady gave her lawyer a handwritten draft of a new testamentary settlement appointing her nephew as her trustee, both him and his wife as her principal beneficiaries and entirely excluding the niece who was the previous residuary beneficiary. After moving to a residential home shortly thereafter she was visited by the lawyer and his assistant who considered her to be fully *capax* and she signed her will.

The niece raised an action of reduction of the will on the ground that it had been procured by undue influence on the nephew's part, while the testator was facile. The judge, Lord Prosser, accepted the evidence of the solicitor and his assistant together with those who had cared for the testator around the time of making the new will in that they considered her well capable of understanding what she was doing. He went as far as to say that the doctor's prediction of only lucid intervals following his assessment in 1985 had been quite wrong and was in fact countered by medical evidence that mild dementia did not interfere with judgment on matters of importance.

Lord Prosser felt that there was no particular significance in the fact that the lady took a draft settlement to the lawyer which contained formal legal terms, as it was probable that she had used her previous settlement as a model. He accepted that the lady had been influenced by the nephew and his wife in the sense that they disapproved of the niece's conduct and she may have felt that she had to choose between them, but there was no real indication of either facility or undue influence.

2.06 In another Outer House case, *Rennie v Stephen*[1], before Lord Cameron of Lochbroom, an elderly brother and sister lived together in the brother's house. He was admitted to hospital suffering from angina and incontinence. A month later he suffered a cardiac failure, a result of which was that he found it difficult to focus with one eye. He expressed a desire that his sister inherit his house and the need for a will was explained to him.

Two months later he was transferred to another hospital and on arrival a mental status questionnaire which was given to him resulted in a score consistent with severe dementia. However, his medical advisers considered him fit enough to move to a home. He refused on the ground of expense. He appeared confused and continued to be incontinent in hospital and became aggressive if unexplained demands were made of him although, if time was taken to explain matters, he appeared to accept them.

He continued to deal with his financial affairs and during this time a solicitor attended as arranged by a social worker and the will was executed, leaving his house to his sister and the residue of his estate to two other sisters.

After he had executed his will, his sister read it over to him and he indicated that he did not understand the references to a trust within the will and might make another one. His sister duly arranged for a second solicitor to attend, and

1 1991 GWD 26–1554.

this solicitor prepared and had executed a will leaving the whole estate to the sister who was originally only to receive the house. The testator's mental condition deteriorated and he died several months later.

The two other sisters challenged the second will on the grounds that their brother had lacked capacity and that the will had been obtained through facility and circumvention. They averred that the testator was physically frightened of his sister and evidence was led as to the fact that he had been intermittently incapable of recognising visitors during the week before signing the will and did not talk sensibly. His supervising physician considered him to have been *incapable* of executing a will.

His sister, the sole beneficiary, led evidence that her brother was often uncommunicative and naturally bad tempered.

Lord Cameron held that it was clear that at the relevant time the testator had been suffering from a slight yet increasing degree of dementia. He said that the fact that the testator's agreement had been sought prior to the possible move to a residential home indicated that the doctors thought he was fit to grant or withhold consent. There was also evidence that the nursing staff would not have allowed him to manage his finances if they had considered him incapable of doing so. The supervising doctor had apparently no recollection of any specific examination or of conversations with the testator and Lord Cameron felt that the mental status test taken on its own was an unreliable guide, particularly as the patient may have been confused due to the transfer of hospitals. He felt that both the test and the doctor had been contradicted by the evidence of two nurses and the hospital social worker who considered the testator to be of sound mind and the second solicitor had noticed nothing to cause him to doubt the testator's capacity. He went on to mention that there was medical evidence to suggest that neither mild dementia nor forgetfulness, confusion and aggressiveness necessarily indicated such mental impairment as to constitute incapacity.

2.07   A final case worth mentioning is *Tiarks v Paterson*[1]. In this case the niece of a testator sought reduction of a codicil and certain gifts made by the testator prior to his death in 1987 aged 82. It was alleged that a nephew exercised undue influence over the testator, who was incapable of understanding the true nature of the transactions.

The testator was a widower and heavy drinker, who was found a nursing home by the nephew near to the latter's home, although the niece, who lived in the south of England had also been looking for a suitable nursing home for him.

The testator while in the nursing home granted a power of attorney in favour of his nephew and signed a will in which both the nephew and the niece were beneficiaries together with a grand-niece. The testator gave instructions for £33,000 to be made over to each of his grand-niece and the wife of his nephew. The year before he died he executed a codicil replacing his niece's share of residue with a simple cash legacy and made other tax-free gifts to his nephew, nephew's wife and grand-niece.

1 1992 GWD 12–1328.

It transpired that the codicil had been prepared by the nephew who did not consult his uncle's doctor at the time it was instructed or signed, and it was retained by the nephew until after his uncle's death. The point was made that the principle that the court would be suspicious where a party prepared a will under which he took benefit was *not* confined to law agents[1].

However, Lord Osborne held that the suspicion of the court where a law agent prepared a will in his own favour was carried further than where another person did so, with the more general rule being that that was, at most, a suspicious circumstance. The onus of proof therefore remained on the niece. The judge found the niece to be an unreliable witness with the nephew being a 'clear and straightforward witness' who simply co-operated with his uncle.

The judge accepted that the obvious suspicion surrounding the making of the informal codicil had been explained by the testator's reluctance to incur legal fees and there was evidence that the uncle and nephew had formed a close friendship.

The conclusion of Lord Osborne was that the testator was 'a strong character who knew his own mind right to the end'.

2.08 It is apparent from these cases that:

(1) Medical evidence by doctors is not necessarily conclusive in deciding whether a person is incapable or indeed sufficiently facile to allow a successful claim later for the reduction of a will.

(2) Less medically qualified people who are seeing the testator on a regular basis or are having to explain complicated matters to him and formulate an opinion on whether they understand what they are doing have a greater weight given to their testimonies than doctors who may be only seeing the patient occasionally or on a one-off basis.

(3) Not only the testimonies but the credibility of the potential beneficiaries may play a substantial part in a final decision.

A solicitor should take all reasonable steps to protect himself and his client where there is any possibility of a suggestion that the client may be being unduly influenced. It is imperative that the solicitor interview the client alone or with a member of his staff and without the presence of any potential beneficiaries. It is also advisable that the solicitor attend the signing of the will either with members of staff or members of the medical profession to act as witnesses.

THE ESTATE BEQUEATHED BY A WILL

2.09 In the days of estate duty, before March 1975, tax was assessed on everything of which a person was 'competent to dispose' at the moment prior to his death. While this was an extremely useful phrase in deciding whether an asset

---

1 *Low v Low's Trustees* (1909) 15 SLT 330.

was to be assessed to tax or not, there were inevitably many exceptions to the general rule and different situations could arise.

It would be wrong therefore to assume that the assets on which tax is paid or on which confirmation is granted in an inventory of a deceased person's estate, make up and represent all the 'estate' of the deceased which is bequeathed in terms of his will. It would also be wrong to assume that all assets mentioned in the inventory of the testator's estate pass by virtue of the will to the beneficiaries under the will.

The question of what is being bequeathed under the will is not something which should be left to be worked out by the executors administering the estate, but something which should be considered when instructions for the will are taken initially.

The intention in the following paragraphs is to highlight a number of assets and the way in which they would be treated in relation to a general bequest of residue under a will.

Heritable and moveable property the subject of special destinations

2.10 This chapter contains a separate section on property the subject of special destinations (see paras 2.25–2.29). As a general rule, properly constituted special (survivorship) destinations have testamentary effect and would not be affected by a general clause under a will leaving the deceased's estate to a specific beneficiary. The share of the deceased's estate held under the survivorship destination, while taxable for the purposes of inheritance tax, would pass to the co-holder under the destination.

Joint bank and building society accounts

2.11 Some accounts may be held in the name of two or more people, 'jointly and the survivor'. It is clear, however, that such a narrative is not a special destination. While the bank or building society may in fact pass the full proceeds of the whole account to the survivor on evidence of death of the first to die, the deceased's share of the account does pass under the will. The proportion owned by the deceased would be derived from the amount contributed by the deceased, with the exception of an account set up for the purposes of housekeeping[1].

Gifts with reservation of benefit

2.12 The inventory of a deceased person's estate requires to list, for assessment to inheritance tax on death, gifts in which the deceased reserved a benefit. While such assets are taxed at death they may well have been legally gifted some years

---

1 *Forrest-Hamilton's Trustees v Forrest-Hamilton* 1970 SLT 338; Married Women's Property Act 1964, s 1.

before and therefore do not form part of the deceased's estate passing under the will.

Power of appointment or disposal over trust assets

2.13 Trust assets will pass in terms of the appropriate trust deed at certain times, or in the event of certain things happening as described in the trust deed. It is possible however for an individual to be given a power to dispose of trust assets to a particular person or persons, this power to be exercised in the will (or sometimes a lifetime deed) of the person given the power.

In the case of *Hyslop v Maxwell's Trustees*[1] the niece of a testator who enjoyed the liferent of his estate had been given the power to dispose of the liferented property by will or deed as she might think fit. It was held that this power had been exercised by a general settlement, although it made no reference to the power. As the power in this case was a general one, it fell under the rule.

It is also considered, although there is no authority for it, that a general settlement will exercise a *special* power, even when the power is not specifically mentioned. It should be mentioned that the law to be applied to determine whether or not the power has been validly exercised by a testamentary writing is that of the domicile of the donee, ie the person with the power at his date of death[2].

It is possible for a power of appointment in an English trust to be exercised by a general will of a Scottish domiciled person. This would not be the case where the holder of the power was English domiciled.

Another power occasionally encountered is a power of appointment whereby an appointee is charged with selecting the beneficiaries from a specified class of potential beneficiaries (see generally paras 5.59–5.61 and 6.125–6.126).

Death benefits from pension schemes etc

2.14 Death benefits under approved superannuation schemes and approved personal pensions arrangements are generally exempt from inheritance tax on settled property[3]. The main types of death benefit are a lump-sum payment, a return of contributions and a pension for the surviving spouse or dependants. Such benefits would not form part of the deceased's estate covered by his will, provided the payments are made at the discretion of the fund trustees and the deceased had no power to insist by any writing, including a will, who should receive the proceeds.

In these schemes it is often the case that the testator while alive will nominate a person or persons to whom he would wish the proceeds to go on his death, but

---

1 (1834) 12 S 413.
2 *Drurie's Trustees v Osborne* 1960 SC 444.
3 Inheritance Tax Act 1984, s 151.

provided that it is not binding on the trustees, then the proceeds will not form part of his estate for the purposes of succession or tax.

In private sector schemes, nominations are virtually always non-binding, to ensure that tax reliefs are obtained, but in the public sector, schemes constituted under statutory arrangements vary. In the Civil Service scheme it appears that the benefit can be paid to a nominee or to the member's personal representative, while in the local government scheme it always goes to the estate of the deceased member. In that case a residuary bequest would obviously include the proceeds of the death benefit.

Consideration was given to including a style of a bequest of a lump sum payable from a pension fund on the occasion of the testator's death. In the normal case, it would be wrong to describe such a clause as a bequest, because it would be expressing a wish or nomination by the testator of the person whom he would wish to benefit. This is on the assumption that the lump sum is payable at the discretion of the trustees. As already mentioned, if it was not a discretionary payment it would form part of the residue and could be bequeathed as such. It is clear that a will is not the place to deal with lump sum death benefits where the payments are discretionary.

2.15 One pension fund consulted indicated that it would ignore the will unless:

(1) the beneficiary nominated by way of a nomination card in the pension fund file had predeceased; and
(2) all the beneficiaries as listed in its rules and regulations as potential beneficiaries had predeceased.

Its views would not be affected by a specific reference in the will to a lump sum as opposed to merely general bequests of residue or the like.

Another fund took perhaps a more logical view, that if the will was dated later than the nomination, and the will contained a specific reference to the lump sum, it would look very closely at the situation to ascertain whether the will reflected the testator's final wishes on the destination of the fund. The reference in the will would not, however, be conclusive in its decision as to who should receive the lump sum.

Another fund said that while it would look at the will, it would investigate the matter fully. It might, for example, be that the nomination was to a sister and brother, but the bequest of residue was to the brother only. It would wish to know whether a relationship had broken down with the party who had been left out, or perhaps that that party no longer listed as a beneficiary had inherited funds from another source, so that he was less in need of the share of the lump sum.

2.16 It is quite evident that the will is not the place to attempt to indicate who should be the beneficiary of lump sum payments from pension funds. If someone wishes to change that beneficiary, then the pension fund trustees should be contacted with a view to changing the nomination card, or using whatever other system is adopted by the fund in question. There is strong anecdotal evidence to suggest that members forget to complete, or fail to update, nomination forms, which is why this should be considered when taking instructions for a will.

It became very clear when considering this matter that even within the same fund there may be different regulations which allow for discretionary and non-discretionary payments. In dealing with beneficiaries of these lump sums, it has become apparent that clients may not have fully understood the differences between discretionary and non-discretionary payments. Again, when taking instructions for the will, this would be the ideal time to consider the matter with a client.

If a lump sum death benefit was non-discretionary and paid to the deceased's estate, it would be included in any bequest of residue, would be taxable and would be subject to any legal rights claim along with the other moveable estate.

If the testator had the right to bequeath a periodic payment for a definite number of years in the future, then an actuarial or discounted value would have to be put on the total payments for the purposes of obtaining confirmation and paying inheritance tax, if necessary.

Some schemes, in addition to a lump sum benefit, allow a refund of contributions on death, which goes to the deceased's estate. If this is paid as of right to the deceased's estate then this sum would obviously be included in the residue of the estate bequeathed by the will.

Life assurance policies

2.17 The inventory of a person's estate may not mention certain insurance policies, for example those which have been written in trust. While their proceeds are payable because of the death of the testator, such proceeds will not pass through his estate and therefore will not be included in the bequests under the will.

The most typical example of such a policy would be one written under the Married Women's Policies of Assurance (Scotland) Act 1880 as amended by the Married Women's Policies of Assurance (Scotland) (Amendment) Act 1980.

Nominations

2.18 A nomination is a document of a testamentary nature similar to a special destination[1]. While it may be revoked, it has been held not to be revoked by a subsequent will disposing of the whole estate of the person who set up the nomination. A valid nomination comes about when a person who has money with certain kinds of bodies nominates another to receive the amount at credit on his death.

The bodies in question are limited by statute and the cash limit is also limited by the Administration of Estates (Small Payments) Act 1965, section 2. It is currently £5,000.

---

1 *Ford's Trustees v Ford* 1940 SC 426.

The main examples used to be Trustee Savings Bank deposits and National Savings Bank deposits, together with National Savings Certificates. The facilities for nominations in Trustee Savings Bank accounts were withdrawn in 1979 and for National Savings Certificates in 1981. Previous nominations are still valid and it is still possible to make valid nominations with certain friendly societies.

In so far as the testator had control over the nominated asset during his lifetime, then the proceeds must be included in the deceased's estate for tax purposes, but confirmation would not be required for such assets. Such an asset would not pass under the will, but be made over directly to the nominee.

Business interests/unquoted shares

2.19 It may be necessary to check a number of other deeds to ascertain whether a specific asset or assets can be effectively bequeathed in terms of a will. This applies in particular to business interests and unquoted shares. In making a will and bequeathing business interests or unquoted shares, it may well be a sum of money rather than the specified asset which actually passes to the beneficiary.

The terms of the partnership agreement or other agreement may well mean that while the deceased's estate for inheritance tax purposes will include an interest in the business or unquoted shares, what will end up with the beneficiary is cash, due to the fact that the agreement provides for other partners or shareholders paying out money to the deceased's estate either in a single lump sum or over a set period.

It is often the case that provision will be made for the purchase of the deceased's unquoted shareholding, possibly by means of an insurance policy on the testator's life assigned to the other company directors to make available a sum free from inheritance tax to purchase the shares.

The question arises as to whether a specific bequest of an interest in a business or unquoted shares is the equivalent of the bequest of a sum of money which the deceased's estate receives when there is a partnership agreement or other agreement which does not allow the business interest or shares to pass to the testator's intended beneficiary. This would have to be considered along with the other relevant deeds and hopefully an amicable arrangement reached, or a case made for the beneficiary to receive cash. The purpose of a will, properly drawn, should be to ensure that no such arrangements, amicable or otherwise, have to be entered into. It is essential, therefore, when considering how the testator wishes to dispose of his interest in the business or unquoted shareholding, that the other relevant deeds be considered.

It may be worth mentioning that the testator may own an asset which is used in the business, but which is not an actual asset of the business and which does not appear in the accounts. Such an asset would be liable for 50 per cent business property relief for inheritance tax purposes (see paras 4.90–4.93). There is always a special consideration here, in that such an asset could be effectively bequeathed separately from the business. Care has to be taken that the whole picture concerning business interests and assets is dealt with as one subject, to avoid any potential problems whereby the deceased's business interests end up with his partners, but an asset essential for that business ends up with another beneficiary who is not involved in the business. It is quite common to see such a business asset covered in the will by way of an offer to the other partners or directors to sell it at an open market value within a certain time following the death (see paras 4.106–4.107).

Donations *mortis causa*

2.20

'A conveyance of an immoveable or incorporeal right, or a transferance of moveables or money by delivery, so that the property is immediately transferred to the grantee, upon the condition that he shall hold for the granter so long as he lives, subject to his power of revocation, and failing such revocation, then for the grantee on the death of the granter.'

This was the definition given to *mortis causa* donation by Lord President Inglis in the case of *Morris v Riddick*[1]. The donation *mortis causa* is in effect an outright gift conditional upon the death of the donor. It follows that as soon as the donor dies, it becomes fully effective and the subject of the donation does not form part of the deceased's estate for the purpose of succession in terms of the will. In the case of *Forrest-Hamilton's Trustees v Forrest-Hamilton*[2], a woman placed her savings on deposit receipt in name of herself and her sister to be drawn by either or the survivor. The sister, who had a son and daughter (the nephew and niece of the woman), kept the deposit receipt and it was periodically uplifted and re-deposited.

The sister died. The niece's name was added to the deposit receipt and when she in turn died, the nephew's name was added. The woman had intimated to third parties that she considered the sister and her children to be her only relatives and the deposit receipt was to go to whoever survived her.

It was held (with Lord Sands dissenting and the Lord President in some doubt) that the terms of the deposit receipt taken in conjunction with the depositor's expression of intention were sufficient to instruct a donation *mortis causa* of the sum on deposit receipt in favour of the nephew.

Foreign moveable property

2.21 Provided the testator is domiciled in Scotland, Scots law will govern the devolution of his moveable property wherever situated.

Moveable property in another country may be the subject of debts or death duties which would affect its value. If, however, there was a specific bequest of such property, free of tax or other burdens, this could affect the amount of residue.

---

1 (1867) 5 M 1036 at 1041.
2 1970 SLT 338.

Foreign immoveable property

2.22   The devolution of foreign immoveable property is according to the law of the *situs* of the property. A client may well require advice from a qualified lawyer in the country where the property is situated, with the possibility of a separate will being entered into, to govern the devolution of that property.

Some countries have very specific rules about the devolution of property under their law, and give rights to, for example, spouses which cannot be superseded, even by a will effective in that country.

While foreign immoveable property may end up with the person named in a Scottish will, it is still the law of the *situs* which will apply. This is another matter which should be considered carefully at the time of taking instructions for a will[1].

Legal rights

2.23   Legal rights are the rights of a spouse, children or other issue to claim one third or one half of the net moveable estate. Legal rights have to be considered on the basis that they are mutually exclusive with the acceptance of provisions under the will in favour of the person or persons with these rights (see paras 5.56–5.58).

It is possible that the system of legal rights may be replaced in the near future[2], but it is likely that there will remain some rights to property for family members which will be incapable of defeat by a will (see paras 9.03–9.04).

General

2.24   In determining the deceased's estate (defined as meaning the assets or cash which will end up in the hands of the beneficiaries named in the will), it has to be remembered that there are burdens on the executors such as the payment of inheritance tax, debts and other expenses and that bequests may be made free of such burdens or otherwise. It should be remembered that any gifts whether chargeable when made or potentially exempt could give rise to further tax on death, even if initially made free of tax. The question of such burdens is dealt with separately (see paras 3.37–3.40 and 4.26).

SPECIAL DESTINATIONS

2.25   Purpose S2.12 consists of a legacy which purports to evacuate a special destination of heritable property, the title to which stands in the name of the testator plus another 'and the survivor'.

Section 30 of the Succession (Scotland) Act 1964 provides that a testamentary

1 On foreign property generally, see paras 2.60–2.91.
2 See Scot Law Com Report no 124 (1990).

disposition executed on or after 10 September 1964 shall not evacuate a special destination unless it contains a specific reference to the destination and a declared intention on the part of the testator to revoke it[1]. A special destination cannot be revoked by any general words of conveyance used in the will and there must be specific reference to it.

Although special destinations have testamentary effect, they are not themselves testamentary writings, so that a clause in a will revoking previous testamentary writings does not evacuate a prior special destination[2].

When considering special destinations, the assumption tends to be that they refer only to heritage. However, in the case of *Connell's Trustees v Connell's Trustees*[3] it was held that a survivorship clause was to be implied in the case of shares in English companies, as by English law the certificates would *prima facie* give the survivor a right to the whole of the shareholding. It was held, however, in *Cunningham's Trustees v Cunningham*[4] that the same presumption did not arise in the case of British Government Stock. Special destinations have been held to apply in other moveables such as bonds, stock certificates, certificates of debt issued by public companies and policies of assurance. A distinction has to be made between such assets and joint bank or building society accounts or deposit receipts which do not have testamentary effect (see para 2.11). However, the institution holding the cash will usually pay the whole amount over to the surviving holder on evidence of death. This is normal, despite the fact that it is the general law that the contributor to such joint accounts continues to own the amount contributed[5]. He can therefore bequeath his share by his will, without specific reference to the account, so that it would form part of residue if not mentioned specifically.

2.26 It follows for the avoidance of doubt that the lawyer preparing the will should ascertain from the client all assets which may be held jointly, which could be the subject of a special destination, and, if necessary, mention them all in the will specifically. Section 30 of the Succession (Scotland) Act 1964 does not refer only to the special destinations of heritage, but merely to 'a special destination (being a destination which could competently be evacuated by a testamentary disposition)'.

Even if a special destination has been properly referred to in the will, the question remains as to whether or not the testator had the power to revoke the destination in the first place. This problem has led to a fair amount of case law, in particular in connection with special destinations of heritable property.

The leading case on this subject may still be considered to be *Perrett's Trustees v Perrett*[6]. The late Mr Perrett's will contained a clause revoking all prior settlements of a testamentary nature. Mr Perrett left a house in the name of

---

1 See *Marshall v Marshall's Executor* 1987 SLT 49 and *Stirling's Trustee* 1977 SLT 229.
2 *Murray's Executors v Geekie* 1929 SC 633.
3 (1886) 13 R 1175.
4 1924 SC 588.
5 *Dennis v Aitchison* 1923 SC 819; *Connell's Trustees v Connell's Trustees*, above.
6 1909 SC 522.

wife and the survivor. The narrative clause of the disposition stated
ideration for the purchase had been paid equally by the two spouses.
so a series of bonds and assignations of heritable bonds which bore
ideration money was paid by the two spouses with destinations to
.... and the survivor, but it was admitted that Mr Perrett in fact contributed
the whole purchase price of these bonds, etc. The bonds were taken out both
before and *after* the date of the will.

The question before the court was whether the various investments mentioned were ruled by the terms of their own destinations or were carried by the
will. In the case of the heritable property, the Lord President stated that the
situation was contractual and could not have been altered other than by the joint
consent of the spouses. The deceased's share therefore passed under the survivorship destination to Mrs Perrett.

The Lord President also stated, when speaking of the title to the house that it
'bears that the consideration money had been paid equally by the two spouses,
and there is an admission in the special case that the statement is true'.

The rule, therefore, in connection with heritable property is reasonably
simply stated, in that if the purchase price is provided by both purchasers, there
is a contractual element. Therefore no evacuation is possible by one of the
purchasers unilaterally in a testamentary deed.

2.27 On the basis that if only one person contributed the whole of the purchase
price and that person could unilaterally evacuate the special destination as to his
share, then the inevitable question arises in each case as to who contributed the
purchase price and what evidence is permitted to establish the true position as to
contributions.

In the case of *Hay's Trustee v Hay's Trustees*[1] a purchaser provided the whole of
the funds for the purchase of a house, but title was taken in names of herself and
her husband 'and the survivor of them'. The narrative to the disposition stated
that the purchase price had been paid by both parties. The will of Mrs Hay
conveyed to her trustees her whole estate, 'including all means and estate held by
me at my death under special destination'. It was held that since the wife
provided the whole purchase price of the subjects, she was free to evacuate the
destination as to her one half share. Lord President Cooper said in this case that
it was agreed that the narrative in the disposition was wrong and that the whole of
the purchase price was provided by Mrs Hay.

This of course raised the question of whether extrinsic evidence could be
introduced to show that a narrative clause in a disposition was wrong. The Lord
President (Cooper) said[2]:

'. . . we have been told in the case that the narrative is false, and the question, which I have not
found too easy, is whether we have to carry this tract of law one stage further by admitting
extrinsic evidence not for the purpose of supplementing information derived from an examination of the documents, but for the purpose of contradicting that information and the
incidences which would naturally follow from it.'

1 1951 SC 329.
2 1951 SC 329 at 334.

He went on to suggest that he would welcome the opportunity of having all the decisions on survivorship destinations examined by a higher court, but did say that, with considerable hesitation, he felt that in the case under consideration the facts as found were sufficient to exclude a contractual element.

This case has tended to be mentioned by practitioners as authority for the proposition that if it could be shown that one party contributed the whole of the purchase price, then the party could evacuate a special destination irrespective of the contrary indication in the narrative clause of the disposition.

2.28   This was always a dangerous conclusion to reach, bearing in mind the Lord President's hesitation outlined above. There is now the case of *Gordon-Rogers v Thomson's Executors*[1], an Outer House case before Lord Morison. In that case, the narrative clause declared that the purchase price had been paid by the two spouses and the wife died purporting to bequeath her one-half share to a third party. There was an averment that contrary to the terms of the narrative clause the wife had contributed the whole purchase price and was therefore able to evacuate the destination of her one-half share in a will. It was argued that it was incompetent to lead extrinsic evidence to contradict the terms of the narrative clause. Lord Morison held that extrinsic evidence to contradict the terms of the narrative clause was indeed inadmissible and distinguished the case of *Hay's Trustee*, above. This decision was, of course, based on the rules of evidence rather than any specific matter relating to survivorship destinations. In the light of this case, it is perhaps more important than ever that the solicitor receiving instructions to draft the will ensures from the client that:

(1)   there are no survivorship destinations in property which the testator intends to bequeath in his will;
(2)   if there are evacuable destinations the appropriate clause should be added in the will in terms of section 30 of the Succession (Scotland) Act 1964; and
(3)   if the destination is not evacuable unilaterally that the client considers whether some action is required during his lifetime to re-organise his affairs in such a way that the property will be carried by the will.

Duty of care

2.29   The question arises as to whether there is a duty of care to third parties where a professional lawyer is employed by one person to do an act, such as prepare a will, for the benefit of another party. In Scotland, as things stand at the moment, there is no duty of care to third parties and a lawyer could not apparently be sued successfully for negligence. In the case of *Weir v J M Hodge & Son*[2] the judge, Lord

1   1988 SLT 618.
2   1990 SLT 26.

Weir, felt that he was bound by the House of Lords decision in *Robertson v Fleming*[1].

Lord Weir did comment that 'the situation has now been reached when in my view the decision in *Robertson v Fleming* is to be regarded as out of sympathy with the modern law of negligence. The question is, what can a Lord Ordinary do in such a situation?'[2]. A similar decision was reached in *MacDougall v Clydesdale Bank Trustees*[3].

The situation is to be compared with that in England where it is clearly the case that a duty of care exists between a will draftsman and the potential beneficiary. In the case of *Kecskemeti v Rubens Rabin & Co*[4], where the draftsman failed to advise the testator that the English equivalent of a survivorship destination in the title deeds meant that a clause in the will bequeathing a share of heritage was ineffective, it was held that a duty of care existed between the draftsman and the potential beneficiary which would form the basis for a claim for negligence. This followed from the leading case of *Ross v Caunters*[5].

On the face of it, it does appear that a case may have to be taken to the House of Lords to change the current law in Scotland, but it would seem that should such a case go forward, there is every chance of a neglected beneficiary being successful.

It is not for this book to discuss the merits or otherwise of special destinations and claims for negligence in relation to them, but it would seem that the client and his legal adviser must be aware of them in the context of the preparation of wills, and in particular at the earliest stage of taking instructions for a will.

2.30 One scenario where the point is extremely relevant involves divorce. It is often the case that when a man and wife separate in contemplation of divorce, they will change their wills to ensure that in the event of either of them dying before the divorce is completed, the maximum claim each would have on the other's estate is limited to what could be claimed by way of legal rights.

It would be easy to forget to deal with the question of special destinations when dealing with such wills. This could mean a half share of the property passing back to the spouse or ex-spouse, in the event of the untimely demise of a separated party to the marriage, when that party's will left the whole estate elsewhere.

On this matter, it is worth giving a word of warning on the mechanics of 'washing out' a survivorship destination in a title. If a person may evacuate a special destination and does so *inter vivos*, it has to be remembered that the other party to the survivorship destination may still hold their *pro indiviso* share of the property on that destination. This may have serious implications on the death of the survivor. A possible situation which could arise would be that a husband transfers his one half share to his wife on divorce, where that share had been held

1 (1861) 4 Macq 167.
2 1990 SLT 26 at 27.
3 1993 SCLR 832.
4 The Times, 31 December 1992.
5 [1980] Ch 297; see also *White v Jones* [1993] 3 All ER 481.

on a survivorship destination in her favour. On her death, the wife might purport to leave the whole of her estate (including the house) to children of the marriage.

If, as suggested, the husband had merely granted a disposition of his one half *pro indiviso* share to the wife, then on her death the half share which she held on survivorship destination passes back to her former husband rather than going to the children. In other words, the wife's survivorship destination has not been 'washed out' by her husband's disposition of his half share.

The correct method of transfer of the husband's one half share to the wife would have been a disposition by *both* husband and wife of the *whole* property to the wife alone.

EXECUTION OF WILLS

Formal validity

2.31 Certain minimum legal formalities are necessary if a will is to be regarded as a reliable and definitive statement of a person's testamentary wishes. Without such formalities there would be little or no protection against fraud. Unlike contracts and conveyances, for example, which are immediately effective and capable of rectification or reduction, a will is effective only on the death of its granter, after which his intentions cannot be established.

This section deals with the formalities of execution necessary to validate a formal attested will. The same formalities, of course, apply to codicils.

Methods of execution

2.32 A will can be made in one of three ways:

(1) Attested: execution before witnesses in accordance with certain statutory formalities.
(2) Holograph: in the testator's own handwriting and signed by the testator.
(3) Adopted as holograph: writing other than in the testator's own hand, but signed and adopted by the testator.

Attested wills and probativity

2.33 An attested will is probative, *ex facie* valid and, thus, proves its own authenticity.

Holograph wills and wills adopted as holograph are not probative, merely privileged, in that extrinsic evidence must be led to prove the granter's handwriting and signature. Thereafter, by virtue of confirmation, they are accorded probative status[1].

1 Succession (Scotland) Act 1964, s 2.

The law governing the execution of attested deeds has developed, since the 'authentication statutes' of the sixteenth and seventeenth centuries[1]. Relaxation of many of the former requirements deriving from these earlier statutes occurred in sections 38 and 39 of the Conveyancing (Scotland) Act 1874. The most recent modern amendment came in section 44(2) of the Conveyancing and Feudal Reform (Scotland) Act 1970, removing the need for deeds, *with the single exception of wills*, to be signed on each page.

There are three essential requirements if a will is to be probative. These are:

(1) Subscription by the testator on each page[2] or notarial execution on the testator's behalf (see paras 2.52–2.56).

(2) Attestation by two witnesses subscribing at the end of the deed, who must either see the testator sign or have the signature acknowledged by the testator.

(3) Such witnesses must be designed either in the body of the deed or in the testing clause. Alternatively, their designations may be added to their subscriptions, not necessarily in their own hand. Such designations may be added subsequent to the date of execution at any time prior to the document being registered or founded on in court[3].

Signature/subscription

2.34 The testator must subscribe his signature on each page of a will, or on the only page if there is only one[4]. The relaxation introduced by the 1970 Act in respect of other deeds, permitting signature on the last page only, does not apply to wills.

Subscription of each page is a safeguard against fraud and the need for subscription at the end of a will arises, not only directly from the old authentication statutes, but also because of the fact that the position of the testator's signature at the end indicates completeness[5]. Failure to subscribe is fatal[6].

The testator's signature should appear on the last operative page of the will, along with the witnesses' subscriptions[7] and the testing clause. If, as in *Baird's Trustees v Baird*[8], this is not done, the necessary connection between the operative provisions and the attested signature cannot be inferred.

Defective subscription may be capable of remedy under section 39 of the Conveyancing (Scotland) Act 1874[9], but a will lacking proper subscription is not probative. If the testing clause runs over from the last operative page of the will to the reverse side of the same sheet and the testator's signature is subscribed

---

1 Listed in *Halliday* I, para 3–03.
2 Conveyancing and Feudal Reform (Scotland) Act 1970, s 44(2).
3 Conveyancing Scotland Act 1874, s 38; see paras 2.36–2.38.
4 Conveyancing and Feudal Reform (Scotland) Act 1970, s 44(2).
5 25 *Stair Memorial Encyclopaedia* para 724.
6 *Foley v Costello* (1904) 6 F 365; *Taylor's Executrices v Thom* 1914 SC 79, 1913 2 SLT 337; *Robbie v Carr* 1959 SLT (Notes) 16.
7 Deeds Act 1696, c 15.
8 1955 SC 286.
9 Eg *Bisset Petitioner* 1961 SLT (Sh Ct) 19 where there was subscription on the last page only.

there, then it is likely to be held that the execution was valid[1]. A clear connection or form of words adopting the otherwise invalid will may be sufficient[2].

If a single sheet of paper is used, folded into more than one page, subscription of the last page only will be sufficient[3]. It is highly unlikely today that any solicitor would prepare a will in this form, rather in the form of individual sheets.

Equally, if a single sheet is typed on both sides so as to form two pages, subscription of the second page alone generally will be sufficient. In practice this is not recommended, if only because once registered in the Books of Council and Session it will then appear as two sheets, will look improperly attested and an executry petition will be necessary in order to obtain confirmation.

Any schedule annexed to the will, for example a list of legacies or powers in schedular form, should also be subscribed by the testator on each page or on the only page, if one.

Method and form of signature

2.35 The signature must be the testator's own act. It will be invalid if it has been guided by another person[4], but the testator's wrist can be supported[5].

The retouching of a poorly made signature by the testator does not invalidate it, but a rubber stamp of a testator's signature would be invalid as it could be added by a third party[6]. The signature need not, however, be legible.

A man or unmarried woman may sign their surname in full, preceded either by forenames in full, any recognised contraction of forenames, the initials of the forenames or any combination of these. The testator's forenames as they appear in the will should be represented in his signature. If not, such omission should be referred to in the testing clause. The converse also applies (see para 2.45).

Such old authority as exists suggests that a married woman should sign by her husband's surname, preceded by her own forenames in full, any recognised contraction of her forenames, the initials of her forenames or any combination of these. Signature by maiden surname is acceptable, although strictly wrong, and she may sign both surnames or insert the initial of her maiden surname in her signature[7]. It is unlikely that a *requirement* for a married woman to use her husband's surname would be upheld today, particularly if the married woman has never used that surname during her life. A signature prefaced by 'Mr' or 'Mrs' will not invalidate it[8].

There has been a considerable number of cases as to what constitutes a signature, most relating to holograph or improbative wills. These suggest,

---

1 *Baird's Trustees v Baird*, above at 293.
2 See eg *Russell's Executor v Duke* 1946 SLT 242; *Bogie's Executors v Bogie* 1953 SLT (Sh Ct) 332; see also paras 2.44–2.49).
3 Deeds Act 1696, c 15; *Ferguson Petitioner* 1959 SC 56.
4 *Moncrieff v Monypenny* (1710) Mor 15936; *Clark's Executors v Cameron* 1982 SLT 68.
5 *Noble v Noble* (1875) 3 R 74.
6 *Stirling Stuart v Stirling Crawfurd's Trustees* (1885) 12 R 610.
7 *Grieve's Trustees v Japp's Trustees* 1917 1 SLT 70.
8 *Ferguson Petitioner* 1959 SC 56.

amongst other things, that an incomplete signature is invalid[1]. Initials alone will not normally be sufficient unless this can be shown to be the testator's usual practice[2], but forename alone or the shortening of a name, a nickname or abbreviations of a name may be sufficient[3], as may be initials on anything but the last page[4]. It must be stressed that signature in such abbreviated forms will derogate from the probative nature of attested wills, due to the need to provide extrinsic evidence. Signature by mark is invalid[5].

The cases relating to signature by initial or mark to some extent contrast with those relating to legibility of signatures. As noted already, the testator's signature does not have to be legible[6].

Witnesses

2.36 Witnesses merely act as witnesses to the signature of the testator. They are not witnesses to, nor do they require to know, the contents of the will.

Witnesses must be aged 16 or over. Persons below that age lack the legal capacity to act as instrumentary witnesses[7].

The testator cannot act as a witness to his own signature and blind persons, persons of unsound mind and persons who are unable to write cannot act as witnesses[8].

The witnesses should be satisfied as to the testator's identity[9], but credible information as to identity, such as a simple introduction by name, is sufficient[10]. In practice, if a solicitor is supervising execution of a client's will, the client should be introduced to the members of staff acting as witnesses.

Ideally witnesses should be wholly independent and should not receive any benefit under the will.

A person receiving a benefit has been permitted as a witness[11], but a will witnessed by a legatee or beneficiary runs the risk of reduction on grounds of circumvention (see paras 2.04–2.08).

A witness may be a relative or the spouse of the testator[12]. If, as is likely in

1 In *Donald v McGregor* 1926 SLT 103, a hospital matron wrote the testatrix's wishes on a postcard and the testatrix attempted to sign, but was only able to complete 'Mary T McGr' followed by a cross. Although signed by two witnesses, the will was held to be invalid.
2 *Gardner v Lucas* (1878) 5 R (HL) 105; *Speirs v Home Speirs* (1879) 6 R 1359.
3 *Rhodes v Peterson* 1971 SC 56, 1972 SLT 98; *Draper v Thomason* 1954 SC 136; *Lowrie's Judicial Factor v Macmillan* 1972 SLT 159.
4 *Gardner v Lucas*, above.
5 *Crosbie v Wilson* (1865) 3 M 870; *Stirling Stuart v Stirling Crawfurd's Trustees* (1885) 12 R 610 at 617; *Morton v French* 1908 SC 17; and generally M C Meston and D J Cusine 'Execution of Deeds by a Mark', (1993) 38 JLSS 270.
6 *Stirling Stuart v Stirling Crawfurd's Trustees*, above.
7 Age of Legal Capacity (Scotland) Act 1991, s 9.
8 Currie, *The Confirmation of Executors in Scotland* (7th edn, 1973) p 44; *Halliday* I, para 3–12; 25 *Stair Memorial Encyclopaedia* para 723.
9 Subscription of Deeds Act 1681, c 5.
10 *Brock v Brock* 1908 SC 964.
11 *Simsons v Simsons* (1883) 10 R 1247 – brother and sister, both beneficiaries.
12 *Tenner's Trustees v Tenner's Trustees* (1879) 6 R 1111; *Brownlee v Robb* 1907 SC 1302.

many cases, the spouse is a beneficiary it is better that he or she should not be a witness.

Time of witnessing

2.37 Attestation by witnesses is of course not merely evidence of execution by the testator, it is one of the required formalities[1]. The witnesses either must see the testator sign or have the signature acknowledged by the testator as being his signature[2].

It is not necessary for both witnesses to be present together and it has been held acceptable for the testator to subscribe in the presence of one witness and acknowledge his or her signature to the other, or, alternatively, to acknowledge his signature to each witness at different times[3]. The position here may be contrasted to that under notarial execution in which the witnesses must be present to hear the deed read over to the testator and the testator give his authority to the notary to execute it on his behalf. In practice it is preferable for the signing and witnessing to occur together and to be treated as part of a single operation.

If that is not possible, then the signatures of both witnesses should be added as soon as possible. The main authority in this area is *Walker v Whitwell*[4]. In this case the testatrix dictated her will to her son and signed it. Her son and a nurse were present and the nurse subscribed it as a witness. The testator died six days later, but the son's signature was not added until after the death had occurred. The House of Lords took the view that testator's and witnesses' signatures are essential formalities forming part of a continuous process, the witnesses signing with the testator's consent which lapses on the testator's death[5].

Signature and designation

2.38 Witnesses should sign on the last operative page of the will, alongside the testator's signature. Signature by mark or initials[6] is not acceptable.

The designations of the witnesses are essential, and should be added either after their signatures by the witness or by a third party[7]. Commonly, the witnesses' designations will be added after their signatures if a docquet or short form of testing clause is used. Otherwise, their designations will be incorporated in a full form of testing clause (see paras 2.41–2.43).

---

1 Subscription of Deeds Act 1540, c 37; Subscription of Deeds Act 1681, c 5; see para 2.33.
2 1681 Act; *Cumming v Skeoch's Trustees* (1879) 6 R 693 at 697; *Lindsay v Milne's Executor* 1993 GWD 3–190.
3 *Hogg v Campbell* (1864) 2 M 848.
4 1916 SC (HL) 75.
5 See also *MacDougall v Clydesdale Bank Trustees* 1993 SCLR 832.
6 *Gibson v Walker*, June 16, 1809 FC.
7 Conveyancing (Scotland) Act 1874, s 38; see para 2.33.

Testing clause

2.39 The testing clause records the details of execution, which give a will its probative character.

If a will is subscribed by the testator on every page and witnessed at the end by two witnesses whose designations are added, then no testing clause is strictly necessary. There has never been a requirement for a will to be dated, but obviously it is desirable for the date to be recorded. This identifies the point in time of the testator's intentions. It also makes obvious the fact that the will succeeds an earlier will or wills and may even show that a will was made at a time when the testator was *incapax*[1].

The testing clause should be added at the end of the will, usually between the last operative words of the will and the testator's and witnesses' signatures. The testing clause should not be on, or run over onto, a subsequent page or separate sheet (see para 2.34).

The testing clause can be added at any time, even after the testator's death, prior to the will being registered or relied upon in proceedings in court[2]. The testing clause, as it has evolved, will generally record the place at which the will was signed, the date of signature and the names, designations and addresses of the witnesses.

It should also be used to correct or clarify, thus authenticating, any alterations in the body of the will itself. Any material alterations should be referred to in the testing clause, but the testing clause itself cannot alter the will.

Forms of testing clause

2.40 Three forms of testing clause are in use[3]. These are the full testing clause, short testing clause and docquet testing clause. The first and last are those most commonly encountered in practice.

(1) *Full testing clause*

2.41 This will record the number of pages making up the will (although this is not necessary under section 38 of the Conveyancing (Scotland) Act 1874), refer to subscription by the testator of the will and of any schedule attached to the will (for example lists of legacies or trustees' or executors' powers in schedular form), the place of execution, date of execution and the witnesses' full names, occupations and addresses. The full testing clause takes the following form:

'IN WITNESS WHEREOF these presents typewritten on this and the [number] preceding page[s] [OR together with schedule annexed hereto] are subscribed by me at [place ie town, of execution] on [date, month and year], before these witnesses B, [design: eg – Mechanical Engineer, 21 Any Street, Any Town], and [design: eg – Mrs C, Stockbroker, 25 Some Crescent, Some Town]'.

1 *Waddell v Waddell's Trustees* (1845) 7 D 605.
2 Conveyancing (Scotland) Act 1874, s 38 and see para 2.36.
3 See eg *Halliday* I, para 3–19.

It is perfectly acceptable for the date to be shown in the form '9th September 1994', as opposed to the traditional 'Ninth day of September Nineteen hundred and ninety four'. The traditional version in words is longer, less readable and more prone to error.

Providing that sufficient space is left between the words 'IN WITNESS WHEREOF' and the point at which the testator's and witnesses' signatures appear, this form of testing clause has the advantage that generally there will be space in which to record not only the above details, but also to incorporate reference to any corrections in the will.

(2) *Short form*

2.42   This will record the number of pages, refer to subscription of the will and of any schedule attached by the testator and the place and date of execution. The witnesses' designations will be appended to their signatures. This testing clause, therefore, takes the following form:

> 'IN WITNESS WHEREOF these presents typewritten on this and the [number] preceding page[s] [OR together with the schedule annexed hereto] are subscribed by me at [place] on the [date, month and year] before the undernoted witnesses whose designations are appended to their signatures'.

(3) *Docquet form*

2.43   This is an increasingly common form of testing clause, preferred by some solicitors, if only because the relevant details can be completed on the will at one time without the need for much, if any, additional typing after execution. If pre-printed in the form below, it will also assist the testator and witnesses to sign in the correct places and to add all the necessary details.

However, there are two particular drawbacks to this form of testing clause. Firstly, if insufficient space is left between the words 'executed as follows:' and 'SIGNED', it will be difficult to insert reference to any corrections which may have been made in the deed. In practice, if one makes a point of leaving sufficient space between the two parts of the docquet, as in the example below, sufficient space then may be left in which to type in the details of any such corrections. Secondly, details of place, date or witnesses may be filled in incorrectly, or illegibly.

'IN WITNESS WHEREOF these presents typewritten on this and the
[number] preceding page[s] are executed as follows:

SIGNED by me
at [place]
on the [date, month and year]
before these witnesses:

WITNESS: _____

FULL NAME: _____

ADDRESS: _____

                      _____

OCCUPATION: _____

WITNESS: _____

FULL NAME: _____

ADDRESS: _____

                      _____

OCCUPATION: _____

Corrections and alterations

2.44 Any corrections made to a will should be declared in the testing clause.
Generally these will take the form of erasures, deletions, marginal additions or
interlineations. There may also be differences between the testator's names in
the body of the will and his signature or between witnesses' names and signatures.

In the case of wills a distinction is made between the effectiveness of alterations made prior to or at the time of execution by the testator and the
effectiveness of subsequent alterations, generally holograph. In the latter
instance, the less stringent requirements afforded to holograph writings may
permit effect to be given to unauthenticated deletions, providing that the court
can be satisfied they were made by the testator, but not to unauthenticated
additions. The leading case in this area is *Pattison's Trustees v University of
Edinburgh*[1], in which reference should be made to the opinion of Lord McLaren
in relation to the position as regards subsequent alterations and additions.

Because of the difficulties which can arise in respect of unauthorised corrections or alterations – for example, it may not be clear if an alteration has been
made prior to execution or subsequently – all material alterations in a will should
be authenticated by way of reference in the testing clause.

1 (1888) 16 R 73.

With exception of references to discrepancies between witnesses' names and signatures, corrections or alterations should be inserted in the full testing clause and short testing clause after the phrase 'subscribed by me'.

In the case of the docquet testing clause, the reference can be inserted between the words 'executed as follows:' and the start of the second part of the docquet at 'SIGNED'.

Forms of correction

(1) *Names and signatures*

2.45 The testator's forenames as they appear in the will should be represented in his signature (see para 2.35). If they are not, such discrepancies should be referred to in the testing clause. Thus, if the testator's name is ABCD, but he signs the will ABD, the testing clause should contain a declaration to the effect that the testator is 'subscribing my usual signature ABD'.

Conversely, if the testator is described in the body of the will as ABD, but has signed ABCD, the testing clause should contain a declaration in the form 'whose full name is ABCD, subscribing his usual signature "ABCD"'.

The same applies to discrepancies between witnesses' names and signatures, in which case the reference should be inserted after the witness' name in the testing clause in a similar fashion.

(2) *Erasures and deletions*

2.46 In the following example, assume that the testator has changed his mind over a legacy and instead of leaving his 'gold Rotary watch' to a particular legatee, wishes instead to leave the legatee his 'solid silver hip flask'. The original words have been deleted and the replacement words typed over them. The declaration in the testing clause can take the following form:

'. . . under declaration that the words 'solid silver hip flask' occurring on the 6th line of page 2 hereof are typewritten on erasure before subscription.'

Note that if a typewritten word or words have been erased and the correction has been made over them in the testator's handwriting, the reference in the testing clause to 'typewritten' should be modified accordingly to 'handwritten by me'.

Providing that a declaration has been included in the testing clause, strictly there is probably no need for the word or words which have been added on erasure to be authenticated further, but it is sensible in practice to have such alterations initialled by the testator.

In the case of deletions, similar considerations apply. In the following example, assume that the testator wishes to delete the specific legacy of a grandfather clock to a legatee, who is already left other items in the will, and that the words deleted are 'and my grandfather clock'. The deletion, of course, will require to be either in ink or in type to be effective. A declaration in the following form can be made:

'. . . under declaration that the words "and my grandfather clock"
occurring in the 6th line of page 2 hereof have been deleted and
initialled by me before subscription.'

As with erasures, due to the declaration in the testing clause, further authentication is probably unnecessary but it is sensible to have such deletions initialled
on either side by the testator.

(3) *Additions*

2.47 Additions will be in the form of marginal additions or interlineations. In
such cases words will be added either in type or in the testator's handwriting.
With reference to Style S2, assume that the testator wishes to leave an additional
legacy in S2.10 of £3500 to his nephew John Smith and that a caret has been
inserted after the words 'I direct my Executors to pay:' with a typewritten
marginal addition of the words 'To my nephew John Smith the sum of £500'.
The declaration can take the following form:

'. . . under declaration that the words "to my nephew John Smith the
sum of £500" are inserted [OR and initialled by me] before subscription
after the words "I direct my Executors to pay:-" occurring on the 8th
line of page 3 hereof.'

The marginal addition can be initialled on either side by the testator,
although *Halliday*[1] suggests that the proper course is for the testator to sign his
forenames or initials on one side of the addition and his surname on the other.

In the case of interlineations, words will be added between the lines in the
body of the text, again in ink or in the testator's own handwriting. Assuming the
same example as above, the words 'to my nephew John Smith the sum of £500'
have been added between the words 'I direct my Executors to pay:-' and the start
of the next line '(1) To'. The declaration can take the following form:

'. . . under declaration that the words "to my nephew John Smith the
sum of £500" are interlined [OR and initialled by me] before subscription so as to read between the words "I direct my Executors to pay:-"
and "(1) To" occurring respectively in the 8th and 9th lines of page 3.'

As with other alterations, it is sensible to have marginal additions and interlineations initialled on either side by the testator.

(4) *Errors in testing clause*

2.48 If the testing clause has been completed and is found to include an error, it
can be re-typed in its correct form immediately following the end of the previous
testing clause preceded by the words 'that is to say . . .'.

Alternatively, if the error is discovered in the course of completing the testing
clause, the correct testing clause can be added from that point again prefaced by
the words 'that is to say . . .'.

---

1 I, para 3–26.

Rectification of defects

2.49   Section 39 of the Conveyancing (Scotland) Act 1874 may be used to save a will suffering from an informality of execution and, thus, improbative. It is not proposed to consider this aspect at any length, as it is beyond the immediate scope of this book, but some examples are given below[1].

It should be noted that the section can apply only if the will was subscribed by the testator and bears to be signed by two subscribing witnesses. The onus of proof rests on persons relying on the will and the application may be made by petition either to the Court of Session or to the sheriff court.

The gravity of the defect will determine whether or not section 39 is necessary and capable of saving the will. Thus, a witness's maiden name included in her signature does not require section 39[2]. It is, however, of no help if a witness has signed after the testator's death[3] or did not see the testator sign[4].

Section 39 can save a will which has not been signed by the testator on every sheet[5] or signed only on the last sheet and subscribed by witnesses who were not designed[6]. Equally, it has saved wills signed only on the second of two sheets by testator and witnesses[7].

When it is too late to add witnesses' designations under section 38, section 39 may be used to remedy the informality[8].

Testator incapable of execution

Incapax

2.50   No-one has the power to make a will for a person who lacks testamentary capacity.

Attorney

2.51   An attorney is not permitted to execute a will, even if permitted to do so by the terms of the Power of Attorney under which he is appointed.

Notarial execution

2.52   Notarial execution permits a will to be executed on behalf of a testator who is blind or unable to write for any reason, including a testator who is simply illiterate.

---

1 See generally *Currie*, pp 33–36; *Halliday* I, paras 3–41–3–45; Macdonald *An Introduction to the Scots Law of Succession* para 6–10; and para 2.34 above.
2 *Grieve's Trustees v Japp's Trustees* 1917 1 SLT 70
3 *Walker v Whitwell* 1916 SC (HL) 75.
4 *Smyth v Smyth* (1876) 3 R 573; *Forrest v Low's Trustees* 1907 SC 1240, 1909 SC (HL) 16.
5 *Bisset Petitioner* 1961 SLT (Sh Ct) 19.
6 *McLaren v Menzies* (1876) 3 R 1151.
7 *Shiell* 1936 SLT 317.
8 *Thomson's Trustees v Easson* (1878) 6 R 141.

It has been held that a blind testator can competently execute a will personally[1]. In reality this is fraught with danger and notarial execution would be advised in all such cases.

The formalities laid down in the Act must be followed exactly[2] and any defects are incapable of remedy under section 39 of the Conveyancing (Scotland) Act 1874.

Authorised officials

2.53 Notarial execution under the Conveyancing (Scotland) Act 1924 may be carried out by a solicitor, notary public, justice of the peace or Church of Scotland minister, or his assistant and successor, in his own parish. The term 'notary' is used hereafter for convenience.

Procedure

2.54 The notary must read over the entire will to the testator in the presence of two witnesses. Once this has been done, the testator in presence of the witnesses must state that he is blind or unable to write, confirm his approval of the document and authorise the notary to sign on his behalf.

The notary should then sign each page of the will and add a handwritten docquet at the end of the will in the form set down in Schedule I to the 1924 Act (or in any words 'to the like effect'), followed by his signature and designation. The two witnesses should then sign the will at the end.

Form of docquet

2.55 The statutory docquet takes the following form:
'Read over to, and signed by me for, and by authority of, the abovenamed A [without designation] who declares that he is blind [OR is unable to write], all in his presence and in the presence of the witnesses hereto subscribing.

B, Solicitor [OR notary public], Edinburgh [OR as the case may be] [OR C, Justice of the Peace for the County of _____] [OR D, Minister [OR assistant and successor to the Minister] of the Parish of _____].
E, Witness
F, Witness'

---

1 *Duff v Earl of Fife* (1823) 1 Sh App 498; *Ker v Hotchkiss* (1837) 15 S 983 and *Currie*, p 44.
2 See eg *Hynd's Trustee v Hynd's Trustees* 1955 SC (HL) 1.

An ordinary testing clause can be added, in which the date and place of signing and designations of the witnesses can be included. Alternatively, the designation of the witnesses can be added after their respective signatures and the place and date of signing added to the docquet. This latter alternative is likely to be more convenient.

Disqualification of notary or witnesses

2.56 The notary should be wholly independent and have no form of interest under the will[1], whether as an executor, trustee, legatee or beneficiary. This is true even in the case of the subsequent notarial execution of a codicil to an earlier will. In *Crawford's Trustees v Glasgow Royal Infirmary*[2] the will conferred a benefit on the notary public who subsequently carried out the notarial execution of a codicil for the testator. The codicil was held to fall as part of the original will.

If the will appoints a solicitor as an executor and/or trustee and permits the charging of remuneration by his firm as agents, the notary should not be a partner of the solicitor executor/trustee[3]. Execution by a solicitor employee of the firm is permissible[4].

If a solicitor executor/trustee is appointed and the will contains no charging provision (this being extremely unlikely in the case of a professional executor), then the above bar does not operate[5].

In order to avoid any possible pitfalls, if a partner or partners of the firm responsible for preparation of the will are appointed executor(s)/trustee(s), it is recommended that the notary should *always* be independent of the firm. If a will is prepared and charged for by a firm whose partners are not appointed executors/trustees, it would seem to be acceptable for a member of the firm to act as notary.

English docquet to a testing clause

2.57 Although formal validity from the viewpoint of private international law and the Wills Act 1963 is dealt with in paragraphs 2.73–2.75, it would be appropriate to refer here to the position of the testator who is domiciled in England (or at least whose likely alternative domicile may be in England) or who has real estate in England. It is suggested in such cases that a special docquet should be used[6]. The docquet takes the following form:

---

1 *Ferrie v Ferrie's Trustees* (1863) 1 M 29.
2 1955 SC 367.
3 *Finlay v Finlay's Trustees* 1948 SC 16; *Paterson's Executors* 1956 SLT (Sh Ct) 44.
4 *Hynd's Trustee v Hynd's Trustees* 1955 SC (HL) 1.
5 *McIldowie v Muller* 1982 SLT 154.
6 *Elder*, p 180.

'Signed by the said A as his last will in the presence of us, both being present at the same time, who, at his request, in his presence and in the presence of each other have hereunto subscribed our names as witnesses'.

If this follows an ordinary Scottish testing clause, there will be a considerable amount of duplication and an alternative is suggested below.

If the testator is in fact domiciled in England the solicitor should perhaps be asking himself whether or not he should be making a will for the testator at all (see paras 2.61, 2.72, 2.81).

However, it seems there may be some limited advantage in having a will executed also in accordance with English law either where the will is executed in England or where it is executed in Scotland but the testator owns real estate in England. In either of these cases the Wills Act 1963 is likely to ensure its validity, but the advantage of including the docquet is that it increases the number of possible grounds for validity under the Act. If the docquet is omitted, it is understood that all that would be required would be affidavit evidence as to the place of execution or as to domicile. If domicile is in doubt, then this evidence might be required anyway.

If a will in Scottish form is executed by a non-domiciled testator outside Scotland and England then the Wills Act 1963 will not help (see para 2.75).

It is understood that the additional requirements of English law over those of Scots law would be satisfied by modification of the usual form of Scottish testing clause which could read as follows:

'IN WITNESS WHEREOF these presents consisting of this and the [number] preceding page[s] are subscribed at [place] on the [date, month and year] by me the said A in presence of these witnesses B [design] and C [design] and then by the said witnesses in my presence.'

The designations of the witnesses can be added under their signatures, although it is understood that this is not actually an essential of English law.

Emergency execution

2.58 If for some reason time is pressing, for example the testator is on the point of leaving on holiday or is seriously ill and witnesses for some reason are not available and the solicitor himself is an executor appointed in the will, the will could be signed and adopted as holograph by the testator.

This, of course, in the event of the testator's death will require the will to be set up by the appropriate affidavits by two persons familiar with the testator's handwriting. If this procedure occurs, the testator should write on each page the words 'adopted as holograph' above his signature and, on the last page, preferably also add the date.

Apart from cases of serious illness or imminent death, it would normally be best to have the will re-engrossed and properly attested as soon as practicable.

Proposals for reform

2.59 Currently, the Scottish Law Commission proposals relating to execution of wills, and probativity, subscription and notarial execution in particular, can be found in its Reports on Succession[1], with draft Bill annexed, and Requirements of Writing[2].

As regards formal validity, the Commission proposes[3] that the Court of Session and sheriff courts should have power to declare to be formally valid a writing which purports to be a will, an alteration to a will or a revocation of a will, notwithstanding failure to comply with the normal requirements for formal validity. The court would require to be satisfied, via extrinsic evidence, that the testator intended the document to take effect as his will, or as an alteration to or revocation of a will.

A power vested in the courts to permit the rectification of a will prepared for a testator, when the court is satisfied via extrinsic evidence that the will does not correctly reflect the testator's instructions, is also proposed[4]. This would permit, for example, a clerical error or failure to follow the testator's instructions to be rectified.

In its 1988 Report the Commission proposed a number of changes, including the recommendation that subscription of wills should remain a requirement of validity, but that attestation by witnesses need not be essential[5].

It proposed also that notarial execution should only be permitted by practising solicitors, that a disqualifying interest should invalidate a will only in so far as it conferred a benefit on the notary, either directly or indirectly, and certain procedural changes.

The introduction of a power to make a will for a person who is incapax is not recommended by the Commission[6].

INTERNATIONAL ASPECTS AND DOMICILE

Introduction

2.60 Private international law impinges upon wills and questions of succession to a far greater degree than may at first be apparent. It is, in fact, a central feature of the law affecting wills and succession and, thus, vital that any practitioner involved in framing wills be alert to the international dimension. This is particularly so if the testator has foreign connections or owns foreign assets.

---

1 No 124 (1990).
2 No 112 (1988).
3 Report no 124, para 4–20 and clause 12 of draft Bill.
4 Report no 124, para 4–28 and clause 13.
5 Paragraphs 4–13 to 4–41 and no 124, para 4–2.
6 Report no 124, paras 4–78 to 4–80.

At the very simplest level, a Scottish estate of any size is likely to involve questions of private international law, because the testator owns assets located in another jurisdiction within the United Kingdom. For administrative purposes recognition of grants of representation as between Scotland, England and Wales and Northern Ireland happens to be regulated by statute[1]. Otherwise there is little, if any, difference between the principles to be applied to questions concerning wills and succession arising in relation to the other jurisdictions within the United Kingdom and wills and succession arising in relation to jurisdictions elsewhere.

Invariably, in framing wills a number of separate, but related, issues will be involved. The following paragraphs will consider each in turn. The first, and most important, is the question of the system of law applicable to and regulating the succession to the testator's estate. Generally that will determine the second, namely the form in which a will should be made – in other words, the system of law regulating its construction and provisions. The third issue is that of the formalities of execution required for any particular will; questions of formal validity often being regulated by the Wills Act 1963. The fourth is that of the system, or systems, of law governing the administration of the assets comprising the testator's estate; more than one system of law will apply if the testator has assets located in more than one legal jurisdiction. Finally, if a jurisdiction other than the United Kingdom is involved, it will be necessary to consider the impact of foreign taxation.

Unless the position is entirely straightforward – essentially preparation of a will in Scottish form, for a person domiciled and resident in Scotland, possessing only assets located in Scotland – some, or all, of the above issues and the applicability of other systems of law will come into play.

The applicable system of law – domicile

2.61 Under Scots law domicile will generally regulate questions of the applicable law affecting the succession to an estate, as well as the law to be applied to the making, construction, revocation and execution of testamentary writings. In other words, it is generally the case that a will should be prepared according to the rules and in a form prescribed by the law of the testator's domicile. There are two particular exceptions to this general rule. The first is the application of the *lex situs* in respect of immoveable property. The second consists of the special provisions affecting formal validity contained in the Wills Act 1963. Both of these are considered in more detail below (see paras 2.65, 2.72–2.75).

This section cannot, and is not intended to, be a treatise on domicile. For that the reader must look elsewhere[2]. However, it does seek to highlight those elements of domicile most relevant to the making of wills.

1 Administration of Estates Act 1971.
2 Eg Anton *Private International Law* (2nd edn, 1990); *Currie*, Ch 2; *Macdonald*, Ch 14; 17 *Stair Memorial Encyclopaedia* paras 23–132).

Domicile is central to questions of choice of law and generally the main connecting factor between a person and a legal system. Anton[1] describes it as importing 'a legal relationship between a person and a place governed by a single system of law'. It is nonetheless a very general and personal concept concerned with an individual's connection with the entirety of a legal system and is distinct from the concepts of nationality or habitual residence. A person can be resident in more than one country, or residence may be imputed for tax purposes, but he may only be domiciled in one.

Types of domicile

2.62   A person acquires a *domicile of origin* at birth, normally the domicile of his father and, therefore, not necessarily the country of his own birth or residence. A person retains such domicile until he acquires an alternative domicile of choice or dependence. Under Scots law a child first becomes capable of having an independent domicile at 16[2].

A domicile of origin has special significance because authorities tend to the view that it is harder to shake off than a domicile of choice. Acquisition of an alternative *domicile of choice* requires not only actual residence, but also a firm and settled intention to change one's permanent home[3]. Long residence in another country is not in itself enough to prove that a person has acquired a domicile of choice there[4]; evidence of an intention to reside permanently is necessary. 'Given adequate proof of intention to settle in a country, neither the duration nor the character of the residence are material'[5].

The *domicile of a married woman* is not necessarily, although generally will be, the same as that of her husband. After 1 January 1974 a woman no longer automatically acquired her husband's domicile on marriage by dependence[6].

Proof of domicile

2.63   Domicile is always a matter of fact and circumstance. Thus a declaration in a will as to a person's domicile (eg S1.7) is not in any sense conclusive, simply one of a number of possible factors. A person cannot establish a domicile merely by making a declaration to that effect in his will.

A person's domicile may, of course, change as time passes. Thus, if a person domiciled in Scotland moves, or plans to move, from Scotland to take up permanent residence in another country, it would be advisable for him to obtain advice in that jurisdiction in relation to his testamentary arrangements and

---

1 *Anton*, p 125.
2 Age of Legal Capacity (Scotland) Act 1991, s 7.
3 *Udny v Udny* (1869) 7 M (HL) 89; *Aikman v Aikman* (1861) 3 Macq 854.
4 *Liverpool Royal Infirmary v Ramsay* 1930 SC (HL) 83.
5 *Anton*, p 138.
6 Domicile and Matrimonial Proceedings Act 1973, ss 1(3), 4; see generally *Anton*, pp 136–7.

associated succession and taxation matters (noting that a person who gives up a United Kingdom domicile may still retain a 'deemed domicile' for inheritance tax purposes, as referred to below).

One of the difficulties under the present law is that where a person abandons a domicile of choice, his domicile of origin will immediately revive until a new domicile of choice is acquired. Thus, because a person may not yet have established a sufficiently strong intention to remain in one country for the foreseeable future, a domicile which he might have lost years before, and which has very little relevance to his affairs, revives. The Law Commissions' Report (see para 2.83) attempts to remove this difficulty.

Deemed domicile

2.64 There is a distinction between domicile as a general concept and domicile as a fiscal concept. For inheritance tax purposes domicile is given an extended meaning[1], which includes a period of three years after having left the United Kingdom and residence within the United Kingdom in 17 out of the previous 20 years of assessment.

These provisions may result in a person who is not under the general law domiciled in the United Kingdom being treated as having a United Kingdom domicile for IHT purposes. Such fiscal extension of the general law is, of course, intended as an anti-avoidance measure.

Conflict of laws

2.65 Generally speaking, in relation to matters of succession two approaches have been adopted by legal systems; one based on domicile; the other based on nationality. The two are so fundamentally different that problems arise when they encounter each other.

When faced with a potential conflict, it is necessary first to characterise the legal category into which an issue may be pigeonholed. Such 'characterisation' will determine the appropriate class of conflict of law rules to apply. If the issue is characterised as one of succession, Scots law will connect it with an appropriate legal system by reference to the deceased's last domicile.

Scots law may then determine that a foreign law applies. That system's choice of law rules, however, may not consider its own internal rules are applicable and refer the question back to Scots law or to another system of law. The device developed to resolve such difficulties is the concept of *renvoi*.

However, the general principle adopted by Scots law is to characterise from the point of view of Scots law as the *lex fori*[2] and to ignore foreign characterisation. Thus, Scots law will determine in the case of Scottish estate if a question is one of administration or of rights of succession.

---

1 Inheritance Tax Act 1984, s 267.
2 *Scottish National Orchestra Society Ltd v Thomson's Executor* 1969 SLT 325.

There is one particular exception to this approach and that is in relation to the question of whether property is moveable or immoveable. This is answered by reference to the *lex situs*; the law of the place where the property is located[1].

Thus, as a general rule, matters affecting the administration of an estate will be governed by the *lex fori*, being the place where the administration is taking place; matters of succession, including the construction of wills, by the law of the deceased's domicile (the *lex domicilii*) or, if immoveable property is involved, by the *lex situs*[2]; if the matter concerns matrimonial property, as opposed to succession, it will be governed by the *lex domicilii* at the time of marriage[3].

These general rules may be amended by legislation, as for example in the case of section 3 of the Wills Act 1963, which provides that where a law in force outside the United Kingdom falls to be applied in relation to a will, any requirement of that law whereby special formalities are to be observed by testators answering a particular description, or witnesses to the execution of a will are to possess certain qualifications, shall be treated, notwithstanding any rule of that law to the contrary, as a formal requirement only.

Section 4 of the same Act provides that the construction of a will shall not be altered by reason of any change in the testator's domicile after its execution and, as considered more fully below, sections 1 and 2 provide general rules as to the formal validity of wills.

Capacity

2.66 Testamentary capacity under Scots law is considered elsewhere in this book (see paras 2.02–2.03 and 6.87–6.96).

As a matter of private international law, the question of a testator's capacity is generally referred to the law of his domicile at the date of execution of a will[4]. In the case of immoveable property the *lex situs* may regulate the question.

Revocation

2.67 Revocation of wills generally is dealt with elsewhere in this book[5] and each Style of will (except S12) contains a direction by the testator that all prior wills and testamentary writings are revoked.

As has already been noted, questions affecting the revocation of testamentary

---

1 See *Anton*, pp 597–626; *Macdonald v Macdonald* 1932 SC (HL) 79; *Re Berchtold* [1923] 1 Ch 192.
2 *Anton*, pp 686–687; Meston *The Succession (Scotland) Act 1964* (3rd edn) pp 120–121.
3 *Anton*, pp 573–596.
4 *Anton*, p 681.
5 See paras 3.03, 6.02 and Chapter 8.

writings are generally referable to the law of the testator's domicile. This will be the domicile at the time of revocation, as opposed to the time of the testator's death.

Under private international law, questions will arise as to whether or not a will has been, or can be, expressly revoked, the testator's capacity to revoke it, the formal validity of the document revoking it and its construction. Whether or not a deed is capable of revocation is a question for the law applicable to the original deed, while the testator's capacity to revoke it is a question for the law of his domicile at the time of revocation, subject to the rules of the *lex situs* in the case of immoveable property[1].

The formal validity of a document revoking a testamentary writing, whether dealing with moveable or immoveable property, will be determined on the same principles as those affecting the validity of wills of such property[2]. It can be asked whether the document conforms to the law of any system by reference to which the revoked will would be treated as properly executed[3]. Its construction is generally thought to be governed by the same principles as those governing the will itself[4].

2.68 The rules applying to revocation should be borne in mind whenever a testator proposes to execute a Scottish will in place of an existing foreign will, even if he has acquired a domicile in Scotland. In such cases it therefore may be necessary to take foreign advice as to whether or not the foreign will is capable of revocation by the Scottish will, particularly if the former applies to foreign immoveable property.

Similar considerations will apply in the case of a new Scottish will or codicil which is intended to do any of the following: to revoke a foreign will only in part; to deal with assets worldwide *except* those located in another specific jurisdiction or other jurisdictions; to deal only with Scottish property, or property located in the United Kingdom; or to deal both with United Kingdom and certain foreign assets while standing alongside a foreign will, which deal with assets located in other jurisdictions.

In each of these examples, the standard revocation clause (eg S1.1) would require to be amended, with care and subject if necessary to foreign advice.

Where a Scottish will, or codicil, is intended to revoke the terms of a foreign will only in part, it will be necessary to draw the Scottish document in such a way as to ensure, firstly, that it effectively revokes the relevant part of the foreign will (assuming it is competent for it to do so) and, secondly, that the terms of the Scottish will are such that its operation does not extend to the assets intended to be covered by the terms of the foreign will.

1 *Sawrey-Cookson v Sawrey-Cookson's Trustees* (1905) 8 F 157 and see, generally, *Anton*, pp 694–696.
2 See paras 2.73–2.75; *Anton*, p 695.
3 Wills Act 1963, s 2(1)(c).
4 *Anton*, p 696.

The Scottish will might, therefore, be drawn in such a way as to provide by amendment of the standard revocation clause (eg S1.1) that:

'I revoke all prior wills and testamentary writings with the specific exception of my will dated _____ in so far as disposing of [eg] my immoveable property situated in [name of country].'

2.69 Alternatively, the position might be regulated by a new foreign will dealing with the succession to the relevant foreign assets only alongside a Scottish will dealing with the testator's remaining assets. Where a person is domiciled in Scotland this is likely to be a happier solution and should reduce to a minimum or entirely exclude any possibility of conflict between the terms of the two wills. It is nonetheless essential to ensure that the terms of the two wills generally are mutually compatible and, particularly, that neither should unintentionally revoke the other, whether in whole or in part.

Where the intention is to have a Scottish will dealing with assets worldwide except those located in any particular foreign jurisdiction the standard revocation clause and/or introductory narrative in the will should be suitably amended, the form of the amendment depending upon whether the foreign will pre-dates or post-dates the Scottish will.

If the foreign will pre-dates the Scottish will the standard revocation clause (eg S1.1) could be amended as follows:

'I revoke all prior wills and testamentary writings, with the specific exception of my will dated _____ regulating the succession to my estate situated in [name of country].'

If the foreign will post-dates the Scottish will the narrative of the will could be amended so as to provide immediately following the testator's name and designation:

'. . . in order to settle the succession to my estate after my death, with the specific exception of my estate situated in [name of country] provide as follows . . .'

In that case the standard revocation clause would be left unaltered as it, of course, refers only to the revocation of *prior* wills and testamentary writings.

If the testator intends to have a Scottish will dealing solely with estate in Scotland or within the United Kingdom, the following form of revocation might be used and inserted to follow the testator's name and designation: '. . . in order to settle the succession to my estate situated within Scotland [OR the United Kingdom] only, after my death provide as follows . . .'.

Here the standard revocation clause (S1.1) would require to be amended in such a way as to revoke prior wills and testamentary writings relating to estate in Scotland (or the United Kingdom). It would also be essential to consider the effect of any existing or proposed foreign will so as to ensure that its terms did not conflict with the terms of the Scottish will.

The commentary on Style S12 (see para 2.78) considers this point in the context of a will dealing with Scottish immoveable property only.

2.70 There are likely to be numerous permutations of this theme and the essential points to have in mind include the need to consider the implications of private international law either when seeking to revoke foreign wills, in whole or in part; or when foreign assets are, or require to be, dealt with under a separate foreign will; or when a Scottish will is restricted to deal only with Scottish, or United Kingdom, property. Above all, if there are to be two, or more, complementary wills dealing with assets located in different jurisdictions the draftsman must ensure that they are mutually consistent and obtain appropriate foreign advice where necessary.

The foregoing paragraphs have been concerned with express revocation. Complications are equally likely to arise as a result of rules of implied revocation, as, for example, the operation of the *conditio si testator sine liberis decesserit* in Scots law or revocation by subsequent marriage in other jurisdictions (including England and Wales).

In relation to revocation by subsequent marriage, Scots law takes the stance that domicile at the time of marriage, rather than at the time of execution of a will, will govern the effect of subsequent marriage on a will[1].

Powers of appointment

2.71 Equivalent difficulties arise in situations where a person is entitled to exercise a power of appointment, for example in respect of trust property.

A power of appointment exercised in a will is formally valid if the will is executed either in accordance with the law governing the essential validity of the power or in accordance with the internal law of the place where the property is located[2]. Furthermore, section 2(2) of the Wills Act 1963, provides that 'a will so far as it exercises a power of appointment shall not be treated as improperly executed by reason only that its execution was not in accordance with any formal requirements contained in the instrument creating the power'.

The question of the capacity of the person exercising the power of appointment is thought to be governed by his personal law, at least in the case of a general power of appointment. In the case of a special power, it is thought that this may be governed by the law of the power itself[3].

The question of whether or not a power has been effectively exercised appears to be regulated by the law applying to the appointer's will, at least in respect of a general power[4].

When it is understood that a testator may be permitted to exercise a power of appointment, for example of foreign trust property, and it is proposed to do so in

---

1 *Westerman's Executor v Schwab* (1905) 8 F 132.
2 *Anton*, p 696.
3 *Anton*, p 697.
4 *Duff's Trustees v Phillipps* 1921 SC 287.

his will, it will be desirable to obtain foreign advice as to whether or not a valid appointment can be made, the effects of such appointment and the form it should take.

The appropriate form of will

2.72 From the foregoing it will have been seen that a will generally should be prepared according to the rules and in the form prescribed by the law of the testator's domicile, except where the rules of the *lex situs* require it to be prepared, at least in relation to immoveable property, in accordance with the law of the location of immoveable property.

For the majority of testators in Scotland it is very likely that the question of domicile will be clear and that a will drawn in Scottish form will be appropriate.

At worst in many other cases the testator may simply have, or have had, an alternative domicile elsewhere within the United Kingdom. In the former case it will be necessary to consider if the testator's will should more appropriately be drawn according to the rules of England and Wales or Northern Ireland. Execution of a will by a testator who is domiciled in England (or at least whose likely alternative domicile may be in England) has already been considered in the section dealing with execution of wills (see para 2.57).

If the testator is clearly domiciled abroad, or there is reasonable doubt as to whether or not he may have a Scottish domicile, it is vital to consider if the will should be prepared elsewhere and to take appropriate foreign advice.

The following paragraphs and the flowcharts on pages 61–62 should be referred to, as to when it may be appropriate, or indeed possible, to prepare a will in Scottish attested form.

Formal validity and the Wills Act 1963

2.73 The special provisions affecting the formal validity of wills contained in the Wills Act 1963 have already been referred to. This legislation stems from the Hague Convention on the Conflicts of Laws Relating to the Form of Testamentary Dispositions of October 5, 1961.

It cannot be emphasised too strongly, however, that these statutory provisions relate solely to the *formal* validity of wills and that questions of essential validity, construction and the applicable law of succession may properly be matters for a system other than Scots law, as the preceding paragraphs have sought to demonstrate.

In terms of section 1 of the Act a will is formally valid if it is properly executed according to the law of the testator's domicile, habitual residence or nationality, *either* at the date of execution of the will *or* at the date of death. Additionally, it is validly executed if it conforms to the law of the place of execution, even if that place is none of the above.

Section 2(1)(b) further provides that so far as a will disposes of immoveable property, it is properly executed if it conforms to the requirements of the *lex situs* of the property.

In other words, the Scottish formalities of execution may be employed whenever:

(1)   the will is executed in Scotland, or
(2)   the testator qualifies by domicile, habitual residence or nationality in Scotland, or
(3)   the will deals solely with Scottish immoveable property.

For situations to which the Wills Act applies, Flowchart 1 on page 61 seeks to illustrate when it is and when it is not appropriate to execute a will in Scottish attested form.

2.74   As has already been emphasised, the provisions of the Wills Act relate solely to the formal validity of wills, and cannot be considered in isolation from other foreign considerations. It is also essential to recognise that the Act will only operate in relation to jurisdictions to which the Convention applies and at paragraph 2.75 are listed those states to which it currently applies at the date of publication of this book. In the case of any state not party to the Convention the formal validity of a will is most likely to be regulated by the internal law of that state.

Thus, in all cases, the starting point will be to establish whether or not the testator is domiciled in, habitually resident in or a national of a country or state to which the Convention and, therefore, the Wills Act, applies. Flowchart 1 deals with situations in which the Wills Act applies, Flowchart 2 with situations in which it does not.

Despite the assistance of the Wills Act, however, if a testator is domiciled abroad it is highly unlikely that a Scottish solicitor will possess the necessary expertise to be able to advise on whether or not the provisions of a will comply with the rules of succession and construction operating in another jurisdiction, or with its administrative requirements or taxation regime. Foreign advice will almost certainly be necessary.

Even when there is no doubt that a testator is domiciled in Scotland, if foreign property is owned by the testator the solicitor should consider if a will may be required in the relevant foreign country, the administrative implications of property ownership there and the impact of both United Kingdom and foreign taxation.

While in very many cases it will be found that foreign jurisdictions will recognise the application of Scots law and will accept a Scots will for administrative purposes, that however will not be the case if the *lex situs* applies to foreign immoveable property.

While Scots law will govern the devolution of a person's moveable property wherever situated, sight should not be lost of the fact that property in another jurisdiction may be the subject of liabilities or estate duty affecting its value.

There are provisions for recognition of 'international wills' which would extend the scope of formal validity, but these are not yet in force[1].

---

1 Administration of Estates Act 1982, ss 27, 28 and Sch 2 to be brought into force when the United Kingdom ratifies the International Convention on Uniform Law on the Form of an International Will.

2.75 Finally, while a will in Scottish attested form may be afforded formal validity under the Wills Act, there are still instances when it would be unsafe to have the will signed abroad.

If the testator is abroad and there is any doubt as to his domicile, habitual residence or nationality, unless the will deals solely with Scottish immoveable property, it should be executed according to the local formalities of the place of execution. If it were to turn out that the testator was neither domiciled in, habitually resident in nor a national of Scotland or the country of execution, the only ground on which its formal validity could be established under the Wills Act would be by execution in accordance with the formalities of the place of execution. In such cases the testator should be advised to take the will to a local lawyer for execution according to these formalities.

While undoubtedly involving additional costs, the reason for doing so is simply that the place of execution will be certain and identifiable and compliance with its law at date of execution, or at date of death, possible to establish.

It is definitely not the case that a Scottish attested will conforms to the law of every country.

Countries to which the Hague Convention on the Conflicts of Law relating to the Form of Testamentary Dispositions – 5 October 1961 – applies.

Ratified by:	Entered into force
Austria (subject to reservation under Article 12)	5 January 1964
Belgium	19 December 1971
Denmark	19 September 1976
Finland	23 August 1976
France (subject to reservation under Article 10)	19 November 1967
Germany	1 January 1966
Greece	2 August 1983
Japan	2 August 1964
Luxembourg (subject to reservation under Article 3)	5 February 1979
Netherlands	1 August 1982
Norway	1 January 1973
Spain	10 June 1988
Sweden	7 September 1976
Switzerland (subject to reservation under Article 10)	17 October 1971
United Kingdom (subject to reservation under Article 9 in respect of the Netherlands)	5 January 1964

Acceded to:	
Australia (subject to reservation under Article 17)	21 November 1986
Botswana (subject to reservations under Articles 1 and 8)	17 January 1969
Brunei Darussalam (formerly Brunei)	14 February 1965
Israel	10 January 1978
Ireland	2 October 1967
Poland (subject to reservation under Article 12)	2 November 1969
South Africa (subject to reservations under Articles 9, 10 and 12)	4 December 1970
Swaziland (subject to reservation under Article 9)	22 May 1967
Turkey (subject to reservations under Articles 9, 10 and 12)	22 October 1983

By extension:	
Anguilla	14 February 1965
Aruba	2 March 1986
Barbados	8 May 1965
Bermuda	14 February 1965
Belize (formerly British Honduras)	14 February 1965
Cayman Islands	14 February 1965
Dominica	14 February 1965
Falkland Islands	14 February 1965

The Gambia	14 February 1965
Gibraltar	14 February 1965
Guyana (formerly British Guiana)	9 May 1965
Hong Kong	23 August 1968
Isle of Man	14 February 1965
Montserrat	14 February 1965
New Hebrides	14 February 1965
Saint Christopher, and Nevis	14 February 1965
Saint Helena	14 February 1965
Saint Lucia	13 May 1966
Saint Vincent and the Grenadines (formerly Saint Vincent)	13 August 1966
Seychelles	14 February 1965
Turks and Caicos Islands	14 February 1965
Virgin Islands	14 February 1965

By note:

Antigua and Barbuda	14 February 1965
Bosnia and Herzegovina (formerly Yugoslavia)	5 January 1964
Croatia (formerly Yugoslavia)	5 January 1964
Fiji (subject to reservation under Article 9)	14 February 1965
Grenada	14 February 1965
Lesotho (formerly Basutoland)	14 February 1965
Macedonia (formerly Yugoslavia)	5 January 1964
Mauritius (subject to reservation under Article 10)	19 February 1966
Slovenia (formerly Yugoslavia)	5 January 1964
Tonga (subject to reservations under Articles 9 and 10)	14 February 1965

Note:
1. This list is understood to be correct as at 30 May 1994.
2. Reference should be made to the terms and extent of reservations.

Foreign rules of administration

2.76 As has already been noted, matters affecting the administration of assets comprised in an estate generally will be governed by the *lex fori* – the place where the administration is taking place.

Just as is the case in Scotland with 'foreign probates' – that is grants of representation emanating from jurisdictions other than England and Wales and Northern Ireland – the *lex situs* is likely to require the equivalent of a grant of confirmation in order to enable executors to obtain title to and administer the asset[1].

Administrative requirements and rules will vary greatly from jurisdiction to

---

1 See eg *Currie* p 25.

jurisdiction[1] and, indeed, in some jurisdictions (eg Holland) there will be no equivalent to the issue of a grant of confirmation or probate.

If assets are located abroad, consideration should be given to the question of their administration following the testator's death. The need to consider local rules of succession has already been identified. Foreign taxation also needs to be borne in mind.

Foreign taxation

2.77 For a testator domiciled in the United Kingdom the inheritance tax position will generally be clear and straightforward. As a domicile-based tax[2], its application will extend to the testator's assets located worldwide.

Foreign jurisdictions, however, may also apply tax on death to assets located abroad in forms or at rates very different to those applying in the United Kingdom[3]. This should not be ignored when framing wills for testators owning assets located abroad and specialist advice should be obtained, where appropriate.

It should be noted that the impact of foreign taxation may, of course, be relieved either as a result of double taxation agreements or by unilateral relief under the Inheritance Tax Act 1984, s 159.

Style S12 – will by testator domiciled abroad of Scottish immoveable property

2.78 Style S12, unlike the other Styles, is of significance more because of what it does not include as for what it includes and because of the potential problems likely to arise in making a will dealing only with heritable property in Scotland. It is, admittedly, not uncommon for foreigners to own heritable property here and a will in so far as dealing only with such property is accorded formal validity by the Wills Act 1963 (s 2(1)(b)), but it cannot be emphasised too strongly that S12 is a Style which should be followed only when circumstances particularly require it and certainly not without consideration of issues such as those covered in what follows.

As has already been noted, the Wills Act permits the use of a will in Scottish attested form in so far as dealing only with Scottish immoveable property, regardless of the testator's domicile, habitual residence or nationality. At this point it is also relevant to note that as a matter of general international private law, where the testator is domiciled in, habitually resident in or a national of a country to which the operation of the Wills Act does not apply (see paras 2.73–2.75), a will dealing solely with Scottish immoveable property in Scottish form and executed in Scotland will generally be effective by virtue of the operation of the

---

1 See eg John Pugh (ed) *The Administration of Foreign Estates* (1988).
2 See the Inheritance Tax Act 1984, s 6(1).
3 See *Pugh*, above.

lex situs. If executed furth of Scotland, however, it is unlikely to be so. Flowchart 2 on page 62 offers guidance in this respect.

From the administrative viewpoint, it should be noted that even where such a will has been validly executed in Scotland, for the purpose of obtaining confirmation to estate in Scotland an opinion that it is valid under the law of the country of domicile is likely to be necessary.

2.79   The *capacity* of the testator making such a will is likely to be regulated by his domicile as a matter of general law, but it would be necessary to consider if Scots law applied as the *lex situs*.

No *revocation* clause is included. The will makes no attempt to revoke the terms of a foreign will in respect of the Scottish property. Whether or not it could do so would generally be a matter for the law of the testator's domicile at the date of execution (see para 2.67).

This issue, and the question of the inter-relationship between wills made in different jurisdictions, has already been considered at paragraphs 2.68–2.70.

Style S12 appoints *executors* who will be responsible for the administration of the deceased's heritable property in Scotland. As the will relates solely to heritage in Scotland, the executors would be able to confirm only to the heritage.

Following the testator's death an opinion under the law of the country of domicile as to the executors' entitlement to administer the Scottish estate would be required, whether or not there was also a will in the country of the testator's domicile.

The question also arises as to where the executors' expenses of obtaining confirmation, paying solicitors and completion of the legatee's title to the property are to be found.

There is no provision for *informal writings*. The will, of course, is dealing only with the testator's Scottish heritable property, and, in any event, it is probable that the ability to leave informal writings would be a matter regulated by the law of the testator's domicile, which may not permit them.

The Style does not provide that the legacy of the heritable property is to be free of *government duties* in respect of the testator's death and of *delivery expenses*. Consideration would require to be given as to who would pay those taxes and expenses, as the Scottish executors have no assets under their control other than the heritable property. If the will provided that the legacy was to be free of taxes and expenses, which required to be borne by assets abroad, then it would in fact be seeking to leave a legacy of an amount equivalent to the tax and expenses payable on the Scottish property from the testator's assets situated abroad. This may not be competent, given that the point of a will in terms of the Style is to deal only with the testator's Scottish heritage and, furthermore, a stipulation that the legacy is free of tax and expenses may be wholly ineffective under the law applicable to the testator's estate.

The *subject* of the bequest is heritable property. It is possible that the testator would have a bank account in Scotland used in relation to the property and, almost certainly, it is likely there would be contents in the property. It is probable that the testator would wish such contents to be bequeathed with the house, but the executors under the will in the form of Style S12 would not be able to confirm to such moveable items. If title was required to them, then the executors appointed under the testator's foreign will, or the administrators acting on his intestacy, would require to be confirmed separately in relation to the moveable estate in Scotland.

2.80 In most cases, therefore, it is likely to be preferable for the whole Scottish estate to be left by a separate Scottish will, in which case one would have once again to consider the implications of wills prepared in more than one jurisdiction, the law applicable to the succession to the testator's estate and the formalities of execution required either under the Wills Act, which would permit such a will formal validity if executed in Scottish attested form, or otherwise in the case of a testator domiciled in, habitually resident in or a national of a non-Wills Act country.

However, a will dealing with the whole Scottish estate might be unsatisfactory for other reasons. For example, if the testator subsequently came to own substantial other assets in Scotland, this would be hazardous if the testator's initial intention was only to leave the heritable property (and, possibly, the contents and any associated bank account) to the legatee.

In relation to actual *execution* of the will, the intention would be to have the will executed in accordance with the Scottish formalities of execution. If the will was not to be signed in Scotland one would firstly have to establish if the testator was domiciled in a Wills Act country or in a non-Wills Act country. In the former case, if the will dealt only with Scottish heritable property, it could be executed according to Scottish formalities. If it dealt with other property located in Scotland and was to be executed where the testator was domiciled, habitually resident or a national, it should in that case be executed in accordance with the formalities of such place. If not, it would require to be executed in accordance with the formalities of the place of execution (see Flowchart 1).

In the case of a testator domiciled in a non-Wills Act country, if the will was not to be executed in Scotland, one would first have to establish if it was to be executed in the country in which the testator was domiciled. If so, it should be executed in accordance with the laws of such country. If not, one would next need to ask if the law of the testator's domicile recognised execution under the law of the place of execution. If it did, the execution then should be in accordance with the laws of such country. If it did not, execution should be in accordance with the laws of the country of the testator's domicile (see Flowchart 2).

In conclusion, therefore, if one were to consider using a will in the form of Style S12, there would require to be particularly strong reasons for doing so. Otherwise, as the foregoing has illustrated, numerous difficulties could be encountered. As Scots law does not require a will dealing with immoveable property in Scotland to be executed in Scottish form, it is generally likely to be the case that a foreign will governing the succession to estate located in Scotland will be preferable.

When a foreign will may be required

2.81 Quite clearly, if a person is not domiciled in Scotland it is unlikely that a Scottish will governing the succession to his estate, other perhaps than estate physically located in Scotland, should ever be prepared.

Conversely, for a person domiciled in Scotland it is very likely that a Scottish will is all that will be necessary to regulate the succession to his estate worldwide. That, however, is not an assumption which can safely be made without the benefit of foreign advice, particularly when foreign immoveable property is involved.

In the case of a Scots-domiciled testator wishing to execute a will dealing only with foreign immoveable property to which the Wills Act applies, it would be preferable in all cases for such a will to be executed in accordance with the formalities of and ideally in the form required by the *lex situs* (see Flowchart 1).

If the property is located in a non-Wills Act country, it is more likely that the *lex situs* will make execution of a foreign will governing the succession to such property a necessity (see Flowchart 2).

It is, unfortunately, not possible to give hard and fast rules as to whether foreign wills should be prepared in respect of foreign property belonging to a domiciled Scot, as this will invariably depend upon the rules of the *lex situs* particularly if a non-Wills Act country is involved. The best starting point must be to assume that a foreign will may be necessary in respect of foreign located property and, unless the solicitor drawing the will is sure of the position from his own knowledge, to obtain local advice.

It is often thought that jurisdictions in which it is common for persons domiciled in the United Kingdom to own property, particularly immoveable property, *require* a foreign will to be made – for example, Spain, France or Italy. In none of these countries does it in fact appear to be a legal requirement for a foreigner to execute a will dealing with the succession to his property there[1], but it may assist the administration of the person's estate following death if there is a will in the relevant jurisdiction dealing with property located there. There may also be local complications such as forced heirship rules, making local advice essential.

Estate planning considerations

2.82 As the preceding paragraphs have sought to highlight, legal issues of considerable complexity can arise where a testator owns assets located in more than one jurisdiction.

A proper assessment of a testator's needs, therefore, may involve several issues. His domicile, habitual residence or nationality will need to be established. The jurisdictions affecting his estate, the applicable law of succession and the form in which a will should be made need to be identified. It may also be necessary to establish if any particular jurisdiction is one which has a single law governing succession to both moveable and immoveable property or one which has a law governing succession to moveable property and another law governing succession to immoveable property. How a particular jurisdiction characterises what is

1 See, for example, *Pugh*, above.

moveable and what is immoveable and the effect of such characterisation, may also require investigation.

The following example demonstrates the sort of problems which can arise. If a testator, domiciled and habitually resident in Scotland, owns immoveable property in country A, does country A apply its own laws to the succession to such immoveable property or does it turn to Scots law to determine the succession to it? In the former case, country A may have forced heirship rules determining that a proportion of the immoveable property will pass to the testator's children. If that is not the testator's wish, at least in the first instance where the testator would wish such property to pass to a spouse, it might be necessary to establish what avoidance measures can be taken. These might consist of a sale of the property and purchase of an alternative property in another jurisdiction which does not have such forced heirship provisions, or ownership of the property through a company the shares in which would be moveable for succession purposes[1].

In essence, whenever a testator owns property abroad or has a foreign domicile, no will should be made in Scotland and no lifetime estate planning undertaken without a full investigation of the circumstances and the foreign rules of law applying. In such cases, it will be necessary to obtain advice on the law of the jurisdiction concerned, either by consulting a lawyer in the United Kingdom qualified in the relevant jurisdiction or by consulting a law firm there.

Proposals for reform
Domicile

Introduction

2.83 In 1987 the Scottish and English Law Commissions reported on 'The Law of Domicile'[2]. Late in 1991 the government announced its intention to enact the Commissions' Report. The only major point then apparently at issue was whether legislation should take effect from the commencement of a calendar year or from the commencement of a fiscal year, the latter option appearing to have been favoured by the government. It was then announced[3] by the Prime Minister, however, in a written answer to a question on proposed amendments to the rules concerning domicile, that the government had 'no immediate plans to introduce legislation on this subject'.

Nevertheless, the possibility of changes to the rules of domicile must be anticipated, perhaps along with a more detailed explanation of the government's intended approach. When, and in what form, such changes may be introduced cannot at present be predicted.

Given the fundamental nature of the changes proposed in the Commissions' Report and the possibility of future legislation, the main changes recommended and their most obvious effects are considered below.

---

1 Numerous examples of restrictions on testamentary freedom can be found in *Pugh*, above.
2 Law Com no 168 and Scot Law Com no 107.
3 See (1993) *Taxation*, 10 June, quoting Hansard, 27 May 1993, vol 223, no 188 col 600.

Both Commissions rejected introducing the concepts of nationality or habitual residence in place of domicile.

Noting that domicile is 'a relevant, but not a central connecting factor'[1] for tax legislation, the Law Commissions nonetheless considered that their recommendations should also apply in the field of taxation, believing that to do otherwise would

'be undesirable, not only because it would mean having concepts which varied with the context; but also because we are not convinced that the defects in the present law of domicile are any less significant in the taxation field than they are in other areas'[2].

This, possibly, was to avoid what were considered to be necessary reforms of the law of domicile generally being struck out because of concerns regarding taxation implications[3].

The distinction between domicile as both a general concept and a fiscal concept is worth noting when studying the Commissions' thinking as to why the present law of domicile requires reform. None of the reasons given appears to relate to the role of domicile in the context of taxation.

The main recommendations contained in the Report, and the draft Bill which accompanied it, are considered in the following sub-paragraphs. For the vast majority of persons the effect of the recommendations is that little or nothing would change.

Change of domicile

2.84 The most important recommendation, so far as adults are concerned, is the proposed change to the rules relating to the revival of domicile of origin.

Under the present law, as has already been noted, when a person's domicile of choice is relinquished his domicile of origin immediately revives until a new domicile of choice is acquired. Thus, where a domicile of choice is abandoned, but because an insufficiently strong intention to remain in one country for the foreseeable future does not exist, a domicile, which may have been lost many years before, revives.

In the draft Bill the last acquired domicile would apply until a new domicile is acquired[4]. The doctrine of revival of domicile of origin, therefore, would be abolished.

Acquisition of new domicile

2.85 There is considerable uncertainty under the existing law as to the degree of intended permanency of residence required to establish a new domicile. A 'firm and settled intention' to remain in a new country is necessary, any

---

1 'The Law of Domicile' para 9–12.
2 Ibid, para 9–14.
3 See Scot Law Com Consultative Memo, no 63 para 1–4 and Law Commission Working Paper no 88.
4 Schedule to the Bill, rule 5.

possibility of return to a country of earlier domicile, however vague, preventing such new domicile arising[1].

The Commissions' proposal is that an adult should acquire a domicile in another country if '(a) he is present there and (b) he intends to settle there for an indefinite period'[2].

'Indefinite' is considered to reflect more accurately on case law than 'permanent', while 'settle' rather than 'reside' better demonstrates the necessary degree of connection with a country, as contrasted with persons who merely propose to live there for an uncertain time and then leave.

Domicile of origin

2.86 The Commissions recommended that domicile of origin be abandoned as a special kind of domicile. Thus, a child should be domiciled in the country with which he is most closely connected[3].

Where both parents are domiciled in the same country and the child lives with either or both of them, there should be a rebuttable presumption that the child is most closely connected with that country[4]. If resident with only one parent, then the child would take the domicile of that parent[5].

At the age of 16 a person's domicile should remain the domicile he had until that time, and he acquires a domicile in another country only if it is shown that he or she is 'present there' and 'intends to settle there for an indefinite period'[6].

Proof of domicile

2.87 Proof of domicile based on a balance of probabilities should apply in all instances[7], whereas, presently, a higher standard of proof is required to establish loss of domicile of origin.

Transitional provisions

2.88 The approach favoured by the Commissions is to deem for the purposes of determining a person's domicile after the commencement of the Act, that the Act has always been in force. Consequently, the whole of a person's residential history, and that of his parents at the time of birth, potentially would have to be re-examined. It would mean, for example, that a person who had lost his domicile of origin for a domicile of choice, subsequently abandoned in favour of a peripatetic existence, would re-acquire his last domicile of choice on the commencement of the Act. This approach's advantage is that it would avoid a

---

1 Although compare *Re the Estate of Fuld (No 3)* [1968] P 675.
2 Schedule to the Bill, rule 2(2).
3 Ibid, rule 1(1).
4 Ibid, rule 1(2).
5 Ibid, rule 1(3).
6 Ibid, rule 2.
7 Ibid, rule 6.

long transitional period subject to the difficulties and artificialities of the current law.

The alternative approach, and that favoured by the government, was that adopted by the Domicile and Matrimonial Proceedings Act 1973, s 1(2) which provides:

'. . . where immediately before this section came into force a woman was married and then had her husband's domicile as a domicile of dependence, she is to be treated as retaining that domicile . . . unless it is changed by acquisition or revival of another domicile either on or after the coming into force of this section.'

In most cases, the effect of this would be that a person's domicile would not change immediately and that an old domicile would be lost only by that person taking steps necessary to lose it. This approach possesses the advantage that it does not involve the element of retrospectivity of that favoured by the Commission.

Deemed domicile

2.89   Nothing in the Commission's Report suggests any change to the special deemed domicile rules contained in the Inheritance Tax Act 1984, section 267.

Capacity and construction

2.90   The Scottish Law Commission Report on Succession (no 124) makes only two recommendations in respect of the rules of private international law[1].

The first concerns the capacity of a person to make or revoke a will, whether in relation to heritable or moveable property, in which it recommends that this be determined 'in accordance with the domestic law of the country where the person was domiciled at the time when he made or, as the case may be, revoked the will'[2].

The second concerns the construction of a document other than a will, in so far as regulating the beneficial interest in moveable property forming part of a deceased's estate, proposing that unless the document provides otherwise, it shall 'be determined in accordance with the domestic law of the country where the deceased was domiciled immediately before his death'.[3]

The Hague Convention on the Law Applicable to Succession to the Estates of Deceased Persons

2.91   The two principal effects of the Hague Convention, which was concluded on 1 August 1989, would be in respect of permitting a testator a choice of law and in respect of the law applicable to intestate estates.

---

1 Clause 32 of Bill.
2 Ibid, clause 32(1).
3 Ibid, clause 32(2).

Where a will is made, the deceased would be able expressly to choose at the time of his will the law which is to apply to it.

Where the deceased dies without having made a will, a single law would govern succession to his estate based primarily on the law of the country of his habitual residence at his death.

The Convention has not been ratified by the United Kingdom and does not apply to the formal validity of wills, testamentary capacity or issues affecting matrimonial property[1].

1 See Scot Law Com Report on Succession (no 124), Part X.

WHEN A WILL MAY BE EXECUTED IN SCOTTISH FORM

Flowchart 1 – Wills Act 1963 applying

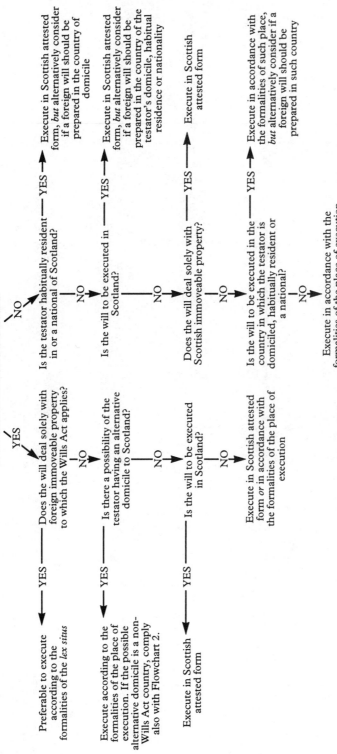

Flowchart 2 – Wills Act 1963 not applying

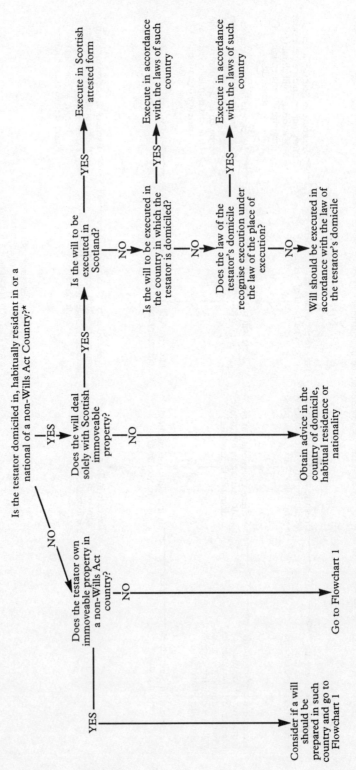

Is the testator domiciled in, habitually resident in or a national of a non-Wills Act Country?*

Does the will deal solely with Scottish immoveable property?

Is the will to be executed in Scotland?

Execute in Scottish attested form

Is the will to be executed in the country in which the testator is domiciled?

Execute in accordance with the laws of such country

Does the law of the testator's domicile recognise execution under the law of the place of execution?

Execute in accordance with the laws of such country

Will should be executed in accordance with the law of the testator's domicile

Obtain advice in the country of domicile, habitual residence or nationality

Does the testator own immoveable property in a non-Wills Act country?

Go to Flowchart 1

Consider if a will should be prepared in such country and go to Flowchart 1

*See para 2.75 for countries to which the Hague Convention on the Conflicts of Laws Relating to the Form of Testamentary Dispositions applies (ie Wills Act countries).

CHAPTER 3

COMMON CLAUSES

INTRODUCTION

3.01 This chapter considers a number of clauses covering general matters, which occur in all (or virtually all) of the Styles presented. It is thought that some provision for all of the matters covered by these clauses will be required in almost every full will that may be drafted. That is not to say that the particular clauses included in the Styles will be appropriate in absolutely every case, but some thought should be given to methods of dealing with each item mentioned.

PRELIMINARY WORDING

3.02 Each Style commences with the wording 'I, A (design) in order to settle the succession to my estate after my death provide as follows. . .'. The designation of the testator is usually achieved simply by address, although in many older styles it was common to include the testator's occupation or other position. There is no reason why this should not be done, but it is unnecessary. The key point about the designation of the testator is that its sole function is identification of the person making the will. This could only be in doubt in very rare circumstances, but if the same solicitor represents a number of members of the same family, several of whom have the same name, it may be appropriate to include some further form of identification. This should at least be done for the solicitor's internal office use, to avoid possible embarrassments on the testator's death! This matter is adressed briefly again in paragraph 9.10.

The preliminary narrative explaining the purpose of the deed being created is not strictly necessary, but it does serve the purpose of setting out succinctly exactly what will be achieved once the deed is completed and signed. This may be of positive value with some testators; and is unlikely to be detrimental in most conceivable circumstances.

REVOCATION

3.03 All the Styles of wills included in this book contain a direction by the testator that all prior wills and testamentary writings are revoked.

This clause comes first in each Style and leaves the reader in no doubt that what follows is intended to be a completely fresh start by the testator in making provision for the succession to his estate. The clause mentions prior wills *and* testamentary writings to ensure that there is no possible confusion or argument over whether any writing of a testamentary nature could somehow be distinguished and be considered to continue in force despite the direction in the new will, if the writings were not inconsistent.

The revocation clause would, however, be insufficient by itself to revoke a survivorship destination in an earlier disposition[1].

It is worth noting that in general if a testator has promised or bound himself contractually to leave his estate or a particular bequest to a particular person, a later will in contravention of this promise or contract is voidable, in so far as it is in breach of the obligation. It is therefore reducible. This does not mean that the testator cannot use the property during his lifetime. It would also be subject to a claim for legal rights on his death, possibly to the detriment of the other party to the lifetime contract[2].

Destruction

3.04 It is generally advisable for the solicitor to take the testator's instructions, in writing, to destroy previous testamentary writings in the solicitor's possession and that he suggests to the testator that he destroys any in his own possession. Where it is shown that a testator duly executed a will and had it at one time in his custody, but it is not forthcoming at his death, then the presumption will be that it was destroyed *animo revocandi* unless it is shown that destruction occurred without *animo revocandi* on the part of the testator. For example, the destruction may have been accidental, due to insanity, or done without his consent.

Testamentary writings which are not revoked may be revived[3]. In both the cases referred to an earlier will was retained in view of the lack of instructions to destroy and those earlier wills revived. This doctrine applies even when the will now revoked or destroyed contained a clause revoking the previous will.

A solicitor does not appear to have the power to destroy an earlier will without the client's express instructions. It seems strange that the testator can purport to revoke all previous testamentary writings, but due to other circumstances revive those previous testamentary writings which he had obviously not intended to revive, in view of the fact that he believed that the earlier will had been superseded. It is, however, possible to think of advantages in retaining earlier wills. If there is doubt as to the testator's capacity it might be preferable that an earlier will revives than to have an intestacy. Where a client makes relatively

---

1 Succession (Scotland) Act 1964, s 30 together with the bequest contained in S2.12 and the section on special destinations at paras 2.25–2.30.
2 *Paterson v Paterson* (1893) 20 R 484 and *McLachlan v Seton's Trustees* 1937 SC 206.
3 *Bruce's Judicial Factor v Lord Advocate* 1969 SC 296 and *Scott's Judicial Factor v Johnstone* 1971 SLT (Notes) 41.

minor amendments to a reasonably complicated will by way of a brand new will, and the new will is found to be defective, invalid or is reduced, the earlier will would revive if not destroyed. The earlier will could represent, by and large, the testator's wishes which again would be preferable to intestacy.

Subsequently born children

3.05 If a testator dies and makes no provision for children who are or who may be born subsequent to the date of his will, there is the presumption that this omission was unintentional. The settlement will be treated as revoked (the *conditio si testator sine liberis decesserit*). However, it is apparent that this *conditio* is not an absolute rule of revocation, but the possibility of it being invoked arises at the birth of a subsequent child. The *conditio* as applied in Scots law today gives the subsequently born child the *option* to apply to a court to have the will treated as revoked on the ground that there was no provision for the child in it.

The court will grant this request if satisfied that no provision is made for the later child and there is no indication that the testator intended the will to stand in spite of the birth of the child[1]. The result of a successful revocation of a will by the *conditio* could lead to an intestacy in which the surviving spouse would take his prior rights, which could allow the whole of the estate to pass to the surviving spouse depending on the values involved. A better result for the child might be achieved if he claims legal rights in his late parent's estate, letting the will remain in force. It is also a fact that the estate may well have been left to the other parent who would have been willing to benefit the child, in effect from the sum of both the estates, in due course on the second death. These matters would have to be weighed against the time, trouble and expense of litigation bearing in mind what the end result would be for the child.

To avoid a challenge the *conditio* could be expressly excluded. A simple statement that the *conditio* did not apply to a particular bequest would generally be sufficient. The *conditio* could also be excluded by implication[2].

Divorce

3.06 The divorce of a testator after making a will does not normally affect a bequest, even where the beneficiary is named as, say, 'my husband John Smith'[3]. However, if it is clearly expressed or implied in the will that the reference to 'husband' etc is not merely descriptive, but the provisions are to that individual in their capacity as such, then those provisions may lapse on divorce[4].

1 *Knox's Trustees v Knox* 1907 SC 1123.
2 On this *conditio*, see further para 6.114.
3 *Couper's Judicial Factor v Valentine* 1976 SLT 83.
4 *Pirie's Trustees v Pirie* 1962 SC 43.

It is probably fair to say that most people would not wish to continue to benefit their ex-spouses, whether during the divorce procedure or thereafter. While it is possible that this rule may change in the future, until such time as it does an appropriate amendment should be made to the will. Although many jurisdictions recognise automatic revocation of wills on a divorce or subsequent marriage, Scots law does not, at least at present (see further para 6.05).

Multiple wills

3.07   Some clients may have more than one will. If they are domiciled in this country but have heritable property abroad, they may be advised to make a will in the country where the heritable property is situated, perhaps only in respect of that property. Great care must be taken that whichever will is made later does not include a general revocation clause which may have an effect on the earlier will. If one country recognised the validity of a will made in another country, a revocation clause in the later will could have the effect of revoking the first will in its entirety.

Pension fund nominations

3.08   A testator may have nominated someone to receive a lump sum death benefit payable at the discretion of pension fund trustees. A general revocation clause in a will would not affect such a nomination which is not a testamentary writing. It is doubtful whether a specific revocation would have the desired effect and any attempt to change the nomination should be made through the pension fund trustees (see paras 2.14–2.16).

Mutual wills

3.09   Another area where revocation becomes an important issue is mutual wills. Occasionally two clients, usually husband and wife or two unmarried sisters or brothers, will ask for a mutual will. This usually means that they want to leave everything to the survivor and they will not know that the term 'mutual will' should strike fear into the heart of their solicitor. The solicitor should undoubtedly persuade them to draw up separate wills leaving everything to one another, with a destination over to a third party on the death of the survivor.

Under this arrangement, each will is in fact a separate deed in which one person bequeaths his own estate to the survivor or survivors of himself and a selected other person or persons.

Although revocation of an actual mutual will can cause a problem, there is a presumption that a mutual will is in effect two or more wills contained in one deed and therefore it is revocable[1].

However, in a mutual will where there is a bequest to the survivor of two persons, and then on the death of the last to die to a third party, this could be considered contractual and therefore not revocable before or after the death of the first to die[2].

It would, of course, be possible to overcome most of the difficulties by careful drafting. A lack of appreciation of the problems of drafting such a will could lead to very substantial problems, for example if the disposal of the estate of the second to die was conditional on the other having survived. This could mean that the estate falls into intestacy[3].

THE OFFICES OF EXECUTOR AND TRUSTEE

3.10 The Styles presented provide for the appointment either of executors or of executors and trustees.

Although governed by the same general principles of administration[4], the offices of executor and trustee are distinct.

Appointment of trustees alone is sufficient[5], while executors-nominate have all the powers of trustees, unless a will makes express provision to the contrary[6].

An executor is responsible for the collection of an estate, its realisation and distribution to the beneficiaries. A trustee is responsible for retaining an estate and its administration in accordance with continuing trust provisions.

Thus, the need for appointment of executors *or* executors and trustees is determined not by the powers available to them, but by whether or not a will contains continuing trust provisions[7].

Appointment of executors

3.11 Where the requirement is merely for the realisation and distribution of an estate, then the appointment of executors alone will be sufficient (S1.2, S2.2, S3.2, S4.2, S8.2, S11.2, S12.1).

Although in most cases it is likely that executors will have adequate administrative powers under statute and common law, it is preferable for powers to be granted in the short form[8], particularly in respect of executors acting as agents, and provisions on remuneration and resignation (see paras 3.23–3.24; 7.02).

1 *Corrance's Trustee v Glen* (1903) 5 F 777.
2 *Woods Trustee v Findlay* 1909 SLT 156; *Thomson's Trustee v Lockhart* 1930 SC 674.
3 *Baillie's Executor v Baillie* (1899) 1 F 974: *Garden's Executor v More* 1913 SC 285.
4 25 *Stair Memorial Encyclopaedia* para 1107.
5 Executors (Scotland) Act 1900, s 3.
6 Ibid, s 2.
7 See generally Wilson & Duncan *Trusts, Trustees and Executors*, pp 412–413; *Halliday* IV, para 47–77; *Macdonald*, para 13–4.
8 See Chapter 7 and S1.6, S2.24, S3.8, S4.7, S8.9, S11.9, S12.3.

No conveyance to executors is necessary, survivorship is implied and power to assume is automatic. Therefore the appointment need be nothing more than of persons as 'my executors' (S1.2, S2.2, S3.2, S4.2, S8.2, S11.2, S12.1).

However, even where an estate is simply to be realised and distributed, executors may find themselves having to retain a beneficiary's share. That will commonly arise where a will provides for a predeceasing beneficiary's share to pass to his issue, with vesting on the testator's death. In such cases it will usually be desirable to give executors power to pay or apply the income or capital of the share to or for the benefit of such beneficiary or to retain the share until the beneficiary attains legal capacity or to pay over the share to the parents or guardians of the beneficiary[1].

Such a provision of course will not be appropriate if the vesting of a beneficiary's interest is to be postponed until a later age is attained, in which case trust provisions and the appointment of trustees will be required, together with powers in the extended form[2].

Appointment of executors and trustees

3.12 Where the vesting of any beneficiary's interest is to be postponed or there are continuing trust provisions of any other description, the appointment should be of executors *and* trustees and powers will be required in the extended form[3]. Usually this will be the case when accumulation and maintenance, discretionary or liferent trusts are created by a will (although such powers are omitted in the deliberately brief Style S8).

Even if there are no continuing trust provisions in the first instance, the possibility of a continuing trust and, therefore, the need for trustees, may still arise. For example, although the initial requirement simply may be for the executry estate to be distributed to beneficiaries of full age, in the event of any beneficiary predeceasing, the testator may wish such beneficiary's issue to inherit only if they survive and attain a specified age.

As with executors, no conveyance is necessary, survivorship is implied and power to assume is automatic.

The appointment of named executors and trustees 'along with any other persons who may be appointed or assumed' (S5.2, S6.2, S7.2, S9.2 and S10.2) is so worded to ensure that any discretionary powers are granted not only to the original trustees and executors but also to any subsequently assumed[4].

Usually, the appointment will be of executors and trustees who are the same persons. It is competent, although most unusual, to appoint executors for the purpose of administering the executry estate and separate trustees responsible for the administration of any continuing trust on completion of the executry administration. Where executors and trustees are the same persons, the executors

---

1 See paras 6.45–6.51 and 6.127–6.128 for a fuller treatment of this topic.
2 See paras 6.52–6.85 and 7.03–7.27.
3 See paras 5.62–5.107 and 7.03–7.27; and S5.2, S6.2, S7.2, S9.2, S10.2.
4 See para 3.22.

cutors obtain title to the deceased's whole estate by virtue of the confirmation in their favour[1] and, generally speaking, nothing further need be done because, on completion of the executry administration, as trustees they will also have title to the trust estate through the confirmation. In the less usual case of executors and trustees being different persons, the executors will require to transfer the property to the trustees[2].

Capacity of executors and trustees

3.13 It is generally accepted that any person of normal legal capacity, whether natural (ie an individual) or juristic (ie a corporation), may be appointed an executor or trustee[3].

There was no formal disqualification of a minor or pupil as an executor and there is authority for the appointment of a minor[4]. However, there were practical difficulties[5] and it was not a practice to be recommended. In particular, it was inconvenient for minor executors to discharge their duties only through their guardians and sometimes not possible even with their guardian's approval.

As a result of the Age of Legal Capacity (Scotland) Act 1991 it will be easier for a person aged 16 or 17 to act as an executor or trustee, but persons below 16 cannot now act[6]. Whether or not a 16- or 17-year old person will be regarded by most testators as a suitable executor or trustee is another matter. However, in the case of straightforward estates, if the testator has an adolescent child, the appointment of such child as an executor should not be dismissed out of hand and there is nothing to prevent a testator appointing one or more of his children to be executors or trustees conditional upon attaining majority[7].

At one time it was not uncommon for testators to appoint the 'junior partner for the time being of Messrs . . .' whether or not in conjunction with another named partner, partners or other persons. This practice no longer seems to be common and rightly so, for although it may have been intended to ensure continuity and client loyalty, the person ultimately appointed is likely to be completely unknown to the testator, even assuming the firm itself is still in existence at the date of death. For similar reasons, it is not desirable to appoint 'the partners for the time being of Messrs . . .' or to appoint the firm itself, although the latter is possible in theory due to its separate legal *persona*.

A further disincentive to the appointment of an unnamed partner or all of the partners of a firm is that, at the time of applying for confirmation, a petition

---

1 Succession (Scotland) Act 1964, s 14(1).
2 *Wilson & Duncan*, pp 250–251.
3 McLaren *Law of Wills and Succession as Administered in Scotland* (3rd edn, 1894) II, para 1618; *Wilson & Duncan*, pp 227 ff.
4 *Hill v City of Glasgow Bank* (1879) 7 R 68.
5 See *Currie*, pp 90–91 and 120–123.
6 Age of Legal Capacity (Scotland) Act 1991, s 1(1) and s 9(f).
7 See para 3.27.

along with affidavit evidence will be needed to establish who is the specified partner or who are all the partners.

The holders of specified offices may be appointed *ex officio* as executors or trustees, either along with other persons appointed by name or alone[1] but this practice was and is relatively rare.

Bankruptcy is no bar to appointment, although insanity is.

Executors and trustees do not require to be resident in the United Kingdom but it may be inconvenient if they are not[2].

The appointment of executors and trustees may be qualified in a number of ways and such appointments are considered later (see paras 3.26–3.30).

Trustee or nominee companies

3.14   From the testator's point of view, the two most obvious advantages of corporate appointment are the guarantee of continuity and the fact of independence, especially from possible family squabbles. In addition such an appointment may suit a testator who is unsure of which individuals to appoint as executors or trustees.

S2.2 has as one of the executors a trustee company. The Style envisages that this would be the trustee company or nominee company of the firm of solicitors preparing the will. A purely administrative advantage, and potential cost benefit, in this is that company officers, normally partners in the firm, can sign all documents in connection with the winding up of the deceased's estate.

The appointment of a solicitor's trustee or nominee company has a further administrative advantage after the testator's death. Once confirmation has been obtained and exhibited, all dividends, circulars, rights issues, bonus and company communications will be sent direct to the trustee or nominee company. Where individuals are appointed, such communications normally will be sent to the first-named executor, so that unless he is a partner in the firm concerned, it will be necessary to make alternative arrangements[3].

The commonest example of corporate appointment nowadays is probably that of solicitors' trustee or nominee companies. In the past the most common example would be the appointment of a bank or a bank's trustee company. In such cases it is usual for the will to contain the appointment of the bank as executor and trustee on the bank's standard terms and conditions of appointment, including its scale of remuneration, all of which vary from bank to bank. In some cases bank's terms and conditions provide that the bank is to be trustee *sine quo non*[4]. Banks normally will insist on, and supply, the particular form of appointment to be employed.

Doubt has been expressed as to the appropriateness of subsequently assumed or appointed (as opposed to originally appointed) corporate trustees exercising

1 *Currie*, p 84; *Wilson & Duncan*, pp 239–240.
2 See para 3.20.
3 But see para 3.15.
4 See para 3.28.

discretionary powers in respect of family and personal matters[1] when such discretion is more than purely administrative in character[2].

Solicitor as executor or trustee

3.15 Where individuals are to be appointed executors or trustees and at least one of them is a solicitor, it is helpful to show the solicitor as the first-named executor or trustee in the will. The immediate practical advantage of this, following the testator's death and after confirmation has been obtained and exhibited, is that communications will be sent direct to him as first-named executor.

However, this may not always be to a testator's liking. Where it cannot be achieved at the time of the will being made, the solution after the testator's death is simply to add a crave in the oath to the inventory requesting that the solicitor be shown as the first-named executor in the confirmation.

If a solicitor is appointed executor or trustee, the will should permit him to charge fees and to resign. Both the short form and extended form of powers provide for this[3].

A testator may wish to leave a legacy to each of his executors or trustees, whether or not conditional on acceptance of office. A solicitor appointed executor or trustee should receive a small token legacy, but nothing more[4].

Number of executors of trustees

3.16 Ideally, a testator should be advised to appoint not less than two executors or trustees and also to choose persons at least one of whom is likely to outlive him. For practical reasons, it is probably not desirable to have more than four.

Conveyance to executors or trustees

3.17 Words such as 'assign', 'dispone', 'convey', 'bequeath', 'legate', 'give', 'grant', and others similar are often used. It is not necessary to use such specific words of transfer between the testator and his executors or trustees and the styles are framed accordingly.

In particular, the use of the word 'dispone' to carry heritable property to executors or trustees has not been necessary since the Titles to Land Consolidation Act 1868, section 20.

---

1 *Ommanney Petitioner* 1966 SLT (Notes) 13.
2 For more detailed information concerning corporate appointments see *Wilson & Duncan*, pp 232–235 and *Currie*, pp 84–85.
3 See paras 3.23 and 3.24.
4 See paras 6.150–6.156.

Acceptance of office

3.18 Executors and trustees cannot be compelled to accept office. A testator, therefore, should always be advised to inform executors and trustees of their proposed appointment so as to ensure in advance that they are willing to act[1].

If an executor or trustee receives a legacy conditional upon acceptance of office[2], he is not entitled to resign unless the will permits this[3].

Majority and quorum

3.19 Executors and trustees make decisions by majority, except in the rare case of an executor or trustee who is appointed *sine quo non*[4]. Each executor or trustee is, however, only liable for his own acts or omissions.

Section 3(c) of the Trusts (Scotland) Act 1921 provides that a majority of the trustees accepting office and surviving the deceased shall be a quorum, unless the will contains provisions to the contrary. A majority is the smallest number making more than half the total.

It is uncommon for a testator to appoint anything other than a majority to be the quorum, although it is competent to appoint a *sine quo non* executor and trustee[5], or to provide that a stipulated number of executors and trustees shall be a quorum.

If a testator provides that a stipulated number of executors and trustees is to be a quorum and the total falls below that number, the quorum provision ceases to be operative and the administration may continue with the lesser number[6].

A testator can direct, in the event of the executors' and trustees' number, through non-acceptance, death, incapacity or resignation, being reduced below its original, or a set, level, that they shall assume such number as is necessary to bring the total number up to the required level[7]. An appropriate form of words would be:

'. . . declaring that in the event of the number of my executors [OR Trustees] [OR Executors and Trustees] number being for any reason reduced to less than its original level [OR less than (specified number)] I direct my executors [OR Trustees] [OR Executors and Trustees] to assume immediately such additional person or persons as shall restore the number of my executors [OR Trustees] [OR Executors and Trustees] to its original level [OR to (specified number)] [OR to not less than (specified number)]'.

1 *Currie*, p 88 and pp 93–94; *Wilson & Duncan*, pp 241–247.
2 See for example S2.3.
3 See paras 3.15; 3.23; 6.149–6.155.
4 See para 3.28.
5 See para 3.28.
6 *Scott v Lunn* (1908) 15 SLT 1045.
7 *Currie*, p 87; Norrie & Scobbie *Trusts* pp 68 and 98.

Majority within United Kingdom

3.20   If it is envisaged that executors and trustees might be abroad when needed to give a decision, then it may be desirable to make an addition to the clause appointing the executors – or in the case of a full-scale trust a separate clause – stipulating that a majority of the executors and trustees who may be in the United Kingdom from time to time, even if only one, shall be a quorum.

Therefore in the case of a will containing powers in the short form, a declaration in the following form could be added to the clause in which the executors are appointed (eg S1.2): '. . . declaring that a majority of my executors who may be in the United Kingdom from time to time, even if only one, shall be a quorum.'

In the case of a will appointing executors and trustees and containing powers in the extended form, an additional clause could be inserted after the powers (eg between S5.12 and 5.13) in the following form:

'A majority of my Trustees who may be in the United Kingdom from time to time and, if there shall be only one Trustee in the United Kingdom then such Trustee alone, shall be a quorum.'

Survivorship

3.21   Appointment is joint and several and survivorship is implied, in the absence of anything to the contrary[1]. Thus, in the event of an executor or trustee dying, the ownership and administration of the estate remains with the surviving executors or trustees[2].

Assumption

3.22   In all cases where there is appointment of executors and trustees, the Styles refer to trustees who may be assumed (S5.2, S6.2, S7.2, S9.2, S10.2).

Section 3(b) of the 1921 Act gives power to sole trustees or a quorum of trustees, if there are more than two, to assume new trustees. Strictly speaking, therefore, no reference in a will is needed to the assumption of executors or trustees, but if discretionary powers are given to the original executors and trustees it should be made clear that these powers are also given to executors and trustees who are assumed[3]. As has already been noted, doubt has been cast upon the exercise of discretionary powers by corporate trustees subsequently assumed or appointed[4].

The power of assumption is discretionary and may, or may not, require to be

---

1 Trusts (Scotland) Act 1921, s 3(c).
2 *Wilson & Duncan*, pp 252–261; and *Currie*, p 77.
3 *Maclachlan's Trustees v Gingold* 1928 SLT 409; *Robbie's Judicial Factor v Macrae* (1893) 20 R 358; *Angus' Executors v Batchan's Trustees* 1949 SC 335; *Russell's Executor v Balden* 1989 SLT 177.
4 *Ommanney Petitioner* 1966 SLT (Notes) 13 and see para 3.14. On this area in general, see *Norrie & Scobbie*, pp 67–70.

exercised. There is no rule governing the number of executors or trustees to be assumed at any particular time and, usually, the power is exercised so as to maintain numbers at their original level, as a result of death, declinature, incapacity or resignation[1].

Power of assumption may be restricted or excluded by the testator. Such restriction could, for example, be by stipulating the assumption of a certain person in certain circumstances, such as on attaining the age of legal capacity or on marriage. Alternatively, the testator could stipulate a maximum or minimum number of executors or trustees, the latter normally applying as regards a quorum[2] or appoint a trustee *sine quo non*[3].

It is competent for a testator to reserve the right, whether in favour of an executor or trustee, a third party or a beneficiary, to appoint a new executor or trustee in certain stated circumstances, but such provisions are construed strictly[4].

As section 3 of the 1921 Act provides that power to assume is implied unless the contrary is expressed, a testator presumably can exclude his executors' or trustees' powers of assumption, but it is difficult to see what benefits would be achieved by so doing.

There is doubt as to whether or not an *ex officio* trustee may assume a new trustee[5].

Resignation

3.23 Executors and trustees are entitled to resign office in the absence of any provision to the contrary in a will[6], subject to the proviso that a sole trustee may not resign without having assumed a new trustee[7] or trustees or the court has appointed new trustees[8].

Resignation of a trustee who is also executor infers resignation as executor[9].

A trustee who has accepted a legacy given on condition of accepting office (S14.2) or who is appointed to the office on the footing of receiving remuneration for his services is not entitled to resign office unless so permitted in a will[10].

All the Styles, whether granting powers in the short form (S1.6, S2.24, S3.8, S4.7, S8.9, S11.9, S12.3) or the extended form (S5.12(16), S6.13(16), S7.10(16), S9.8(16), S10.11(16)), include the power to resign[11].

---

1 See Menzies, *The Law of Scotland Affecting Trustees* (2nd edn, 1913) p 60, which suggested for the avoidance of expense and delay of administration, that the number should only exceptionally be increased beyond the number originally stipulated.
2 See para 3.19.
3 See para 3.28.
4 *Welsh's Trustees v Welsh* (1871) 10 M 16.
5 *Vestry of St Silas Church v Trustees of St Silas Church* 1945 SC 110 at 121.
6 Trusts (Scotland) Act 1921, s 3(a).
7 *Kennedy Petitioner* 1983 SLT (Sh Ct) 10.
8 Trusts (Scotland) Act 1921, s 3(1).
9 Ibid, s 28.
10 See the Trusts (Scotland) Act, s 3(2); and paras 3.15, 3.18, 3.24.
11 See also *Wilson & Duncan*, pp 285–292.

Remuneration

3.24   An executor or trustee must not be *auctor in rem suam* and can derive no personal benefit at the expense of the estate. The principle applies to all actings of executors and trustees and there are recent authorities for strict interpretation of this doctrine[1].

It is entirely in order for an executor or trustee also to be a beneficiary, but he may not as an individual transact with the estate and may not purchase assets of the estate[1] unless specifically authorised to do so by the beneficiaries or by the will. The extended form of powers incorporates a provision specifically permitting this (S5.12(14), S6.13(14), S7.10(14), S9.8(14), S10.11(14); see also para 7.18).

The offices of executor and trustee are gratuitous and there is no entitlement to remuneration, other than genuine out of pocket expenses.

An executor or trustee who is employed as factor or solicitor cannot receive remuneration for his services unless authorised by the will or by all parties who have or may have an interest therein. In a situation where there are beneficiaries lacking legal capacity, or prospective beneficiaries, it would not be possible to take the agreement of all the parties, so it is essential as in the case of both the short form (S1.6, S2.24, S3.8, S4.7, S8.9, S11.9, S12.3) and extended form (S5.12(17), S6.13(17), S7.10(17), S9.8(17), S10.11(17)) of powers that executors or trustees are given power to appoint solicitors or agents from their own number and to allow them suitable remuneration[2].

Similarly, provisions applying to the running of businesses in which the trustees may be involved are included in S5.12 (5), S6.13 (5), S7.10(5), S9.8 (5), S10.11 (5)[3].

Powers

3.25   Sections 3 and 4 of the Trusts (Scotland) Act 1921 contain specific provisions relating to trustees' powers.

In the case of section 3, and subject to the provisos already considered above, such powers are implied unless the contrary is expressed in the deed.

The general powers contained in section 4 permit acts by the trustees when such acts are not at variance with the terms or purposes of the trust.

The powers of executors and trustees are considered in detail in Chapter 7.

Qualified appointments

Substitute executors or trustees

3.26   A testator may wish to provide for the appointment of a substitute executor or trustee in the event of a nominated executor or trustee having predeceased or being incapable of acting following the testator's death.

---

1   *Johnston v Macfarlane* 1985 SLT 339; *Inglis v Inglis* 1983 SLT 437; *Clark v Clark's Executors* 1989 SLT 665.
2   See para 7.22.
3   In connection with legacies to solicitors, see paras 3.15 and 6.150–6.156. See also *Norrie & Scobbie*, pp 130–6.

The simplest example of this is where a testator decides to appoint one executor, A, whom failing B, but the principle applies equally where two or more persons have been appointed. The phrase 'whom failing' is considered to cover not only A predeceasing the deceased but also A's declinature or inability to act at the time of the testator's death[1]. Therefore, the following form of words can be used:

'I appoint A, whom failing B to be my executor'.

If the testator wishes to appoint a single executor, say his wife, and only in the event of her failure other executors, the following form could be used:

'I appoint my wife A, whom failing B and C to be my executor or executors'. This relies upon the comma to work as intended, which cannot be satisfactory. If the comma was omitted, the executors appointed would be either A and C or B and C, but the wife would not in fact act alone at all. The clause also refers to both 'executor' and 'executors', which makes subsequent references in the will awkward.

It would be preferable to use a wording which puts the matter beyond doubt , such as:

'I appoint (1) A whom failing (2) B and C to be my executors'.

This possesses the advantages also of being suitable for the appointment of two or more substitute executors and accommodating subsequent references in the will to 'executors' only.

Alternatively, as in S4.2, two executors B and C, may be appointed in the first instance, with the proviso that should either fail a third, D, will act.

In the event of the testator's spouse being appointed as sole executor or as one of a number of executors, it is preferable for the spouse's appointment not to be subject to survival for a specified period (as contrasted with a spouse's interest in the estate as beneficiary). There is no advantage to be gained in doing so and postponing the spouse's entitlement to be appointed executor may merely delay the administration.

If the surviving spouse finds himself as sole executor on the testator's death, an additional, or replacement, executor or executors could be assumed promptly and prior to confirmation.

If two, or more, executors are appointed and the testator wishes to ensure a long-stop appointment in the event of both, or all, having predeceased, declining or being incapable of acting the following form is suggested: 'I appoint A and B [OR A, B and C] and both [OR all] of whom failing, D to be my executors or executor[2].

If the testator wishes to appoint as an executor or trustee one partner in a legal firm, perhaps the partner he is used to dealing with, and that partner ages with, or is older than, the testator, there is a case for the substitute appointment of a younger partner.

Conditional appointments

3.27 The executor's or trustee's appointment may be conditional, for example, on attaining the age of legal capacity, as already referred to. In such circumstances the following form is suggested:

1 *Currie*, p 85.
2 Compare S4.2.

'I appoint A, B and, in the event of his having attained the age of legal
capacity at the date of my death [OR as soon thereafter as he shall
attain the age of legal capacity] [OR if and when he shall attain the age
of legal capacity] C to be my executors.'
Other conditions, such as marriage or residence in Scotland are competent,
although in all cases no conditional nomination is given effect to unless the
condition has been fulfilled[1].

Sine quo non

3.28 Where two or more executors and trustees are appointed, it is possible to
specify that one is to be party to every act of executorship or trusteeship, or has
the right to overrule the others even if the others are in the majority when a
decision is made. This is known as appointment *sine quo non*.

In this situation the executor or trustee *sine quo non* in effect has the privilege of
vetoing the decisions and actions of the others if he accepts office. It is not
common, but may be encountered in the case of banks[2].

Although such appointments are rare, and likely to be of very limited application, the following form can be used as an addition to the clause appointing
executors and trustees:

'. . . and A who, so long as he may survive and hold the office of executor [and
Trustee] shall be a *sine quo non* of any quorum of my executors [and Trustees]. . .'.

Doubt was expressed at one time as to whether or not the appointment of an
executor or trustee *sine quo non* prejudiced the trust purposes themselves. The
correct view appears to be that the person's appointment as *sine quo non* could
only be on condition of his acceptance, the existence of the trust provisions being
presumed objects of primary importance to the testator and not subject to be
defeated by the non-acceptance of a particular person[3].

It is as well to make it clear however, that the appointment of the *sine quo non* is
conditional on his survivance and acceptance of office.

Limited appointment

3.29 Conditions limiting the period during which an executor or trustee may
act are permissible, for example a daughter while unmarried or a widow during
widowhood. Appointments of an executor or trustee *ex officio* are always limited
to the time he or she holds office[4].

Partial appointment

3.30 It is competent, although very rare, for executors or trustees to be named
to administer different portions of, or specific assets in, an estate. This could be

---

1 On conditional legacies, see paras 5.37–5.51. See also *Currie*, pp 86–7.
2 See para 3.14.
3 *Wilson & Duncan*, p 241; *Currie*, p 87; *Norrie & Scobbie*, pp 97–8; *Elder*, p 13; 24 *Stair Memorial Encyclopaedia* para 140.
4 See *Currie*, p 87.

encountered where a testator has estate in different countries and where he wished to appoint one set of executors or trustees to administer his estate, say, in the United Kingdom and another set to administer his foreign estate. In such a case, however, it would be more likely for him to have separate wills, each dealing with the appropriate portions of his estate[1]. The question of who the executors or trustees should be will probably be subsidiary to the other reasons for the decision to deal with the worldwide estate in this way.

The appointment of different bodies of executors or trustees to act in relation to different parts of the estate all within the United Kingdom appears to be possible. This would be likely to cause immense problems, particularly in respect of title and administration, and quite clearly cannot be recommended[2].

INFORMAL WRITINGS

Purposes and benefits

3.31 The validity accorded by the law to home-made codicils, lists of bequests and the like will depend on how such writings have been prepared and executed by the intending testator[3]. This risk can be largely eliminated if a will, or codicil, contains a clause permitting executors and trustees to give effect to subsequent informal writings by the testator.

At the time of drawing up a will a testator may be concerned with the broad principles of division of his estate, but not, perhaps, with some of the finer detail, particularly in respect of items such as personal effects, furniture, pictures, jewellery and other valuables. The inclusion of a clause permitting executors and trustees to give effect to subsequent informal writings is an effective, flexible and, for the testator, a convenient and inexpensive way to supplement the provisions of his will.

The use of informal writings also prevents wills from becoming cluttered up with long lists of bequests. As time passes, a testator may wish to amend such lists in any event. Informal writings can be altered or replaced easily, without needing to go to the trouble and expense of having a formal codicil prepared.

For all these reasons informal writings clauses have become a common feature of modern wills. However, they should be used with care and should not (and this should be emphasised to the testator) be regarded as an alternative to a codicil, or even a new will, if the testator's intentions were to change substantially.

Legal basis of informal writings

3.32 The legal basis by which such clauses operate is that of adoption, the principle by which improbative writings or writings lacking the necessary probative characteristics of a formal will, or codicil, are accorded validity by a

---

1 See Style S12 and paras 2.60–2.91.
2 See *Currie*, pp 88–90.
3 See paras 2.31–2.59.

properly executed deed[1]. Adoption may be express or implied, retrospective or prospective. The styles are concerned with express, prospective adoption, in other words the specific adoption of future writings – *dispensation ab ante*[2]. For the principle to operate, the adopting document, whether will or codicil, must be formally valid and clearly identify the type of informal document it seeks to validate[3].

The style clause

3.33   Most of the Styles (S1.3, S2.4, S3.3, S5.3, S6.3, S7.3, S8.3, S9.3, S10.3, S11.3) contain an informal writings clause. No excuse is made for its repetition, or for its inclusion in the types of clause which might be explained when taking instructions[4]. This is intended to highlight the effect which informal testamentary writings can have on a will, to stress their usefulness and to show that a testator has been given the opportunity to consider these implications at the drafting stage, even if the clause is left out of the will.

The clause in each of the Styles requires the informal writing to pass three tests.

Firstly, it must be a *future* writing, that is a writing of a time or date later than the will itself.

Retrospective adoption is competent. If earlier writings exist and their effect is intended to continue, amending the clause so as to save them is a solution. However, care would be needed to avoid this conflicting with the revocation of 'all prior wills and testamentary writings'. Better solutions are to have such writings prepared and signed again, or to have them re-signed and re-dated, so as to make them future writings.

Secondly, the writing must be *subscribed*. It would be essential to explain to the testator the need for this[5].

Thirdly, in the view of the executors and trustees the informal writing must be *clearly expressive of the testator's intention*. The clause, therefore, is to some extent discretionary, as the final say will rest with the executors and trustees. The onus is placed on them and difficulties can and will arise if the testator leaves informal writings that are ambiguous[6].

It is always open to a potential beneficiary under an informal writing which executors refuse to implement, to have such writing validated on application to the court, providing that it satisfies the requisite formalities enabling it to be set up.

---

1 25 *Stair Memorial Encyclopaedia* para 727.
2 *Currie*, p 55.
3 *Macdonald*, paras 6–24 and 6–25.
4 See para 9.08.
5 It is advisable in any event for future informal writings to be signed – see *Waterson's Trustee v St Giles Boys Club* 1943 SC 369.
6 *Morton's Executor, Petitioner* 1985 SLT 14; *MacRorie's Executors v McLaren* 1984 SLT 271; and *Jamieson's Executors and Fyvie* 1982 SC 1.

The clause employed in the styles will cover writings relating to estate of any description[1].

It should be noted that the general clause dealing with tax, expenses and interest must also be considered in conjunction with the informal writings clause. This is because the former clause covers *any* writing, including the type of informal writing authorised by the latter[2].

Restriction of the clause

3.34 The testator may wish to restrict the operation of the clause, for example, so as to cover only personal effects and pecuniary legacies. If so, the clause could be amended appropriately:

'I direct my executors to give effect to any future writings subscribed by me however informal the same may be *which deal with my personal effects or pecuniary legacies only* provided that in the opinion of my executors they clearly express my intentions.'

However, if the clause is to be restricted in this fashion, the classifications of 'belongings' should be considered[3].

Other uses

3.35 The use of informal writings need not be restricted to bequests of specific items or legacies of cash. They may be used in respect of any matter in the will meriting alteration, including, for example, changes to executors and trustees.

However, their use cannot be recommended in relation to more technical issues, such as adjustments to residuary shares or substantive and administrative powers or discretions.

Informal writings can also be used to record information (as can codicils), for example changes of addresses or names of executors and trustees, legatees and beneficiaries, funeral instructions and for the appointment of testamentary guardians. As noted elsewhere[4], however, a simple note placed with the will would also be sufficient, except in the case of the appointment of testamentary guardians[5].

Proposals for reform

3.36 The Scottish Law Commission's Report on Succession[6], with draft Bill annexed, proposes reforms (clause 12 of the draft Bill), which would give the Court of Session and sheriff courts power to declare as formally valid documents

1 *MacRorie's Executors v McLaren* 1984 SLT 271.
2 See para 3.37.
3 See paras 4.48–4.51.
4 See Chapter 8.
5 See paras 6.86–6.111.
6 No 124 (1990).

intended to have testamentary effect, but which have not been executed or have been imperfectly executed. The courts would require to be satisfied that the deceased intended the document to take effect as his will or as a revocation, in whole or in part, of his will. Such powers would apply to testators dying after the commencement of the Act, whatever the date of the writing.

This provision, if implemented, would not appear to prejudice either the legal basis or the effect of the informal writings clause considered here.

TAX, EXPENSES AND INTEREST

3.37 Most, but not all, of the Styles contain a general clause which directs that *any* legacy granted by any writing will be paid as soon as practicable after the death of the testator, free of government duties in respect of the death and of delivery expenses but without interest (see S1.4, S2.5, S3.4, S5.4, S6.4, S7.4, S8.4, S9.4, S10.4, S11.4).

This type of clause, while quite clear and succinct in its structure, covers several topics on which the client's instructions should be taken. The implications of not considering in detail the consequences of retaining or omitting the clause are substantial. Such a clause does not have to refer to all three aspects – government duties, delivery expenses and interest – but may refer to any combination of the three.

The clause in the Styles also refers to 'any legacy granted by any writing', which means that all such legacies in a will or codicil or any informal writing are covered by the clause. There is an obvious danger that having included the general clause in a will, the testator may decide to leave a legacy by an informal writing which, if the consequences had been fully explained to him, would have meant that the legacy would not have been given free of tax in particular. The lack of special instruction on this matter in the informal writing would mean that the general clause in the will prevails.

The same considerations apply to a codicil, although on the assumption that this is done formally by the solicitor, he should check the original will to ensure that the testator's wishes in the codicil are being implemented and that any clauses covering subsequent writings are taken into consideration.

The clause mentions that the legacies should be paid as soon as practicable and this is a protection to the executors against beneficiaries who pursue them unreasonably for early payment of a legacy. It is also a protection for the legatees against the executors unreasonably withholding payment.

The question arises as to how government duties, expenses and interest on legacies would be dealt with, if such a clause did not appear in the will.

Expenses

3.38 If a will is silent on the question of expenses where a legacy is concerned, the expenses are the liability of the legatee. If a testator in Orkney leaves antique furniture to a relative in Devon, the delivery expenses would be substantial. The consequences of the legatee having to meet this expense may be to cause the sale of the furniture in Orkney on behalf of the legatee, which may well not be what either the testator or the legatee would have wished.

If the bequest is free of expenses, the residue will bear the expenses. While this might seem fairer, that judgment depends upon the size of the residue and the proportion which the expenses bear to the residue. The obvious time to consider potential expenses is at the time that instructions are taken for drafting the will, with a decision being made on who should bear them at that time.

Interest

3.39 There is no interest payable on specific legacies of objects producing no income. A reference to interest will generally be taken to be in connection with pecuniary legacies. If no term of payment is specified, then interest runs from the date of death unless realisation was then impossible[1]. This rule applies even if the instruction is to pay 'as soon as possible after my death'[2]. It is normally the case that realisation is impossible immediately after the death and that a reasonable amount of time from which interest should run is considered to be six months after the death. If payment is directed to be made at a definite date or event, then it runs from that date or event[3]. If the rate of interest is fixed then that rules, otherwise the rate is dependent on the rate which the estate is yielding on average[4]. If the estate is non-income producing no interest will be given[5].

A higher rate of interest may be payable if the executor has delayed paying unreasonably[6].

The exclusion of interest on pecuniary legacies is often done to reduce time-consuming administration on behalf of the agents winding up the estate following the death. It is the duty of the executors to pay out the legacies as soon as practicable which must be when funds are available which are not earmarked for other purposes, such as the payment of tax. There should therefore be no loss to the legatee by such a clause excluding the payment of interest on legacies. The question of interest on pecuniary legacies is dealt with at paragraph 4.46.

Government duties

3.40 From 1894 government duties on death have had a variety of names including legacy duty, probate duty, estate duty, capital transfer tax and inheritance tax. The main aim of the reference to government duties is to exclude the payment of what is currently inheritance tax out of any legacy. It is recognised that not only have these duties had different names in the past, but the name

1 *Duff's Trustees v Scripture Readers* (1862) 24 D 552; *Waddell's Trustees v Crawford* 1926 SC 654.
2 *May's Trustees v Paul* (1900) 2 F 657.
3 *Waddell's Trustees*, above.
4 *Baird's Trustees v Duncanson* (1892) 19 R 1045; *Kearon v Thomson's Trustees* 1949 SC 287.
5 *Greig v Merchant Company of Edinburgh* 1921 SC 76.
6 *Inglis Trustees v Breen* (1891) 18 R 487.

and type of tax could well change in the future, prior to the implementation of a will which may have been prepared at any time and remain unchanged until the death of the testator.

If the will says nothing, then inheritance tax due in respect of any chargeable legacy falls on the residue of the estate[1].

On the face of it, thus, the purpose adds nothing to the situation, provided the testator wishes all the tax to be paid from residue in respect of all legacies. It is appropriate, however, to draw the testator's attention to the fact that this is the case. Should a bequest be made, perhaps of a substantial nature, the tax will come out of the residue. This may cause a disproportionate reduction in the amount of the residue as compared to what the testator intended. An obvious example of this would be where a house represented, say, three-quarters of the deceased's estate, where the whole estate is taxable. If that legacy is free of tax, the residue will bear the tax on the whole estate, which could potentially wipe the residue out.

Another difficult situation would be where the residue is left to an exempt beneficiary such as a widow, widower or charity, but there is a tax-free legacy of the house to a child and the house has substantial value in excess of the inheritance tax nil rate band limit. The legacy would not just be of the house, but of the grossed-up value of the house which when taxed would require the house to go to the legatee and an appropriate sum of money to be found by the executors to pay the tax, on the combined total of the value of the house and the tax on it[2]. This could substantially reduce the amount of residue available for the surviving spouse. The current (1994–95) effective rate of tax on the value above the nil rate band of inheritance tax is two-thirds of the amount above the limit.

It should also be remembered that grossing up may be required at a very complex level even in apparently simple wills. This applies where there are tax-free legacies to non-exempt persons, combined with another type of legacy to a non-exempt person (such as a specific legacy bearing its own tax, or a share of residue). A simple example would be a legacy free of tax to a son (perhaps of a specific asset), with the residue to be shared between a daughter and the surviving spouse. If the estate is of a sufficient size, the process of 'double grossing-up' is required[3]. The process becomes yet more complex where assets qualifying for business property relief or agricultural property relief are involved[4]. If one wishes to advise on such complex calculations, whether at the time of drafting a will or when administering an estate, reference to the specialist texts on inheritance tax will be required. Despite the enthusiasm of one (and one only) of the authors of this book, no examples are offered here!

3.41   Style S4 is an example of a will *without* the usual clause directing legacies to be paid free of tax and expenses. However, it contains a large legacy to grandchildren (S4.3) which includes a specific direction that the amount of this

---

1 Inheritance Tax Act 1984, s 211 and see *Cowie's Trustees* 1982 SLT 326.
2 Ibid, s 38(3).
3 Ibid, s 38(4),(5).
4 Ibid, s 39A.

legacy is to be paid free of tax. The possible consequences of this should be explained to the testator.

In contrast, Style S2 contains two legacies (S2.8 and S2.16) which are to bear their rateable proportion of any government duties in respect of the testator's death. This demand will reduce the value of the legacy to the legatee; and if the legatee is merely receiving a specific asset (without a cash sum or a share of residue), he may require to pay to the estate any sum necessary to meet his legacy's share of the tax due. On the wording provided, this will be a simple fraction of the total tax due on the death estate.

The freedom from government duties in the standard clause is from those payable in respect of the testator's death. This may be contrasted with a general direction that legacies are to pass 'free of tax', particularly where affected assets are liferented. If legacies left free of tax are bequeathed in liferent from the date of death, rather than outright, this may create serious practical problems. Notably, a fund will require to be retained to meet a liability which will only arise at the conclusion of the liferent – but there is no accurate way of estimating the extent of this liability. Under current rules, it would depend on the size of the estate of the liferenter and any chargeable lifetime gifts made, but of course the whole system may change between the date of the testator's death and the conclusion of the liferent. Assets liferented should bear their own share of tax due when the liferent comes to an end.

A related difficult situation which can arise concerns gifts made by the testator within seven years of his death, although the general clause does not specifically deal with such gifts. They might, however, not be considered when taking instructions for a will, as it was assumed that any tax would be payable by the transferees. Such transfers could have been chargeable transfers when made, or potentially exempt transfers which would become fully exempt if the transferor were to survive for seven years. While it is normally the transferee who takes on the responsibility of paying the additional tax due on the donor's death within seven years, occasionally a transferor will attempt to make such transfers free of tax.

If the transferor had at the time of the gift agreed to pay any tax which might become due, then in effect a debt would have been created which would crystallise on his death. This would be the responsibility of the executors. The Revenue can also look to the executors where the donee of a lifetime gift fails to pay tax on his gift.

Such additional liabilities would fall on the residue of the deceased's estate. They are certainly relevant and the position should be checked, as with all potential liabilities of the testator.

Even if no promise to pay any tax has been made at the time of making lifetime gifts, the testator may decide when a draft will is being prepared to provide for any tax that may become due. This matter is dealt with at paragraph 4.45.

This is not, however, a book primarily on tax matters. To summarise the main points of relevance in this area:

(1) It should be clearly discussed with the testator how he feels about liability to government duties on legacies, particularly where substantial specific legacies or pecuniary legacies may be under consideration; and

(2)   additional tax on chargeable lifetime transfers or potentially exempt transfers which became taxable on death are also relevant, not to the clause dealing with tax, expenses and interest, but generally when taking instructions for a will.

FUNERAL INSTRUCTIONS

3.42   It is quite common for testators to record funeral instructions in their wills. There is of course no legal requirement for a person to do so. In many cases testators may feel that their families or next of kin have adequate knowledge of their wishes. Nevertheless, a will or formal codicil is a convenient, and arguably the most appropriate, place for such instructions to be recorded.

Funeral instructions can equally readily be recorded in an informal writing[1] or note, in which case it is advisable for them to be stored with the testator's will to ensure that they are not overlooked or lost.

Some testators may wish to record specific funeral instructions in their wills. Others, having particular wishes, may not be aware that it is possible for this to be done. Many will not have considered such instructions at all.

The solicitor taking instructions should enquire if the testator has particular wishes and explain that these can be recorded in the will. This point is included in the items for discussion when taking instructions[2].

Ideally, funeral instructions should appear at a point in a will where they can be found easily and quickly, this being an example of where the use of marginal headings is particularly helpful. Usually they are inserted towards the end or, as in the Styles, as the last clause (S1.8, S2.26, S3.11, S4.10, S8.12 and S11.11).

There is a school of thought favouring the instructions being shown in capital letters, so that what is required may be seen at a glance. Many testators are unlikely to find such a practice attractive and, therefore, it is not necessarily recommended.

The form of instruction

3.43   The contents of funeral instructions are potentially as varied as testators themselves. They may range from the simplest of directions to instructions setting out in great detail the testator's wishes regarding his funeral arrangements.

Those most commonly encountered, however, are likely to include the following:

Cremation

3.44   The simplest form is that which merely directs cremation[3]: 'I wish my body to be cremated'.

---

1 See paras 3.31–3.36.
2 See para 9.08.
3 S1.8, S3.11, S4.10, S8.12 and S11.11.

Cremation and interment of ashes

3.45 'I wish my body to be cremated and my ashes interred in Stonefields Cemetery, Lair number A12.' Interment usually will take place in a cemetery or churchyard, but it is possible for ashes to be interred elsewhere, subject to the controls subsequently referred to.

Cremation and scattering of ashes

3.46 The testator simply may wish to have his ashes scattered in a garden of remembrance at a crematorium: 'I wish my body to be cremated and my ashes scattered in a Garden of Remembrance [OR in the Garden of Remembrance at the [relevant crematorium]]'.

Alternatively, if the testator wishes to have his ashes scattered in a place or spot with which he has a particular connection or towards which he feels particular affection: 'I wish my body to be cremated and my ashes scattered beside those of my dog Spotty at Powderhall Stadium, Edinburgh'.

Interment

3.47 If the testator wishes his body to be buried, the simplest form of instruction is: 'I wish my body to be interred in Berry Hill Cemetery, Lair number B12'.

If a record of the relevant information has not been kept with or in a will, experience shows that an interment will often cause problems for the executors, family or solicitor immediately after a person's death has occurred. It is not uncommon for this to be the last aspect of a funeral to be finalised. Much time and effort can be involved in tracing the relevant lair certificate, if one exists, or family lair. Thus, if a testator has purchased a lair or there is a family lair in which the testator's body or ashes are to be interred, it is sensible for the burial ground and lair number to be recorded in the will and for the certificate, if any, to be retained with it. In the case of a family lair, it is also worthwhile for the testator to establish that there actually is space for further interments.

Other examples

No service or non-religious service

3.48 The testator may not wish a religious, or any other form of, service, in which cases the following form is appropriate: 'I wish my body to be cremated and my ashes scattered in a Garden of Remembrance [OR interred in Berry Hill Cemetery, Lair number B13], but I do not wish there to be any [OR any religious] service'.

Private funeral, with no flowers and donations in lieu

3.49 If the testator wishes a private funeral service, for example without flowers but with donations in lieu thereof to a favoured charity, the following form can be used: 'I wish my funeral service to be private and that there shall be no flowers, but that donations in lieu thereof might be made to the Scottish Society for the Prevention of Cruelty to Spotty Dogs'.

Complicated or unusual instructions

3.50 If a testator's wishes or instructions are more complicated, perhaps including such things as the hymns or readings to take place at the funeral service, or directions regarding those whom the testator would wish to be present, or even not present, it may be preferable to incorporate such instructions in a separate letter, which can be placed with his will.

That certainly may be advisable where the instructions are humorous or bizarre. It is highly unlikely that such instructions would invalidate the overall effect of a will (although they might throw the testator's mental capacity into doubt), but what a testator may find amusing or merely whimsical at one point in his life may not possess the same degree of humour after his death.

Prohibitory instructions

3.51 Whether for religious or other reasons, some testators may be opposed to either cremation or interment. In such cases it is advisable to incorporate a specific instruction to that effect, for example: 'I direct that I do not wish my body to be cremated'.

Formerly, it was unlawful to cremate the remains of any person who was known to have left a written direction to the contrary. This is no longer the case[1].

Alternatively, the testator could provide: 'I direct that I do not wish my body to be interred'. In this case, however, it is more likely that the testator will wish to direct cremation, whether or not conjoined with an instruction that he does not wish to be buried.

Advance arrangements

3.52 Many funeral directors are able to offer a facility whereby a person can make advance arrangements and leave instructions for his funeral with them. These are kept by the funeral directors, who advise the customer to inform his family and solicitor accordingly.

In practice, the experience of some funeral directors suggests that such advance arrangements may not work when the time comes and that a funeral has

---

1 The Cremation Regulations 1965, SI 1965/1146.

already been organised, or has taken place, before the relevant information is found amongst the deceased's possessions.

Numerous schemes, variously titled funeral planning schemes, pre-paid funeral plans, instalment funeral plans or guaranteed pre-arranged funeral plans, are available, either through the agency of funeral directors or direct from the companies which market them.

Usually the customer purchases a 'plan', either by a lump sum or in instalments, whereby funeral costs are paid up-front.

In practice, such schemes may be prone to the same potential difficulty already identified in relation to other forms of advance arrangements.

Statutory and common law controls

3.53 There are no statutory controls governing funeral instructions per se. Cremation procedures and crematoria are governed by the Cremation Acts of 1902 and 1952, as amended, and Cremation (Scotland) Regulations 1935 (SI 1935/247) and 1965 (SI 1965/1146). Burial procedures and burial grounds are regulated by the Burial Grounds (Scotland) Act 1855, as amended. The administrative control of such matters rests with local authorities, at Islands and District Council level, under the Local Government (Scotland) Act 1973 (s 169(1)), as do council functions with regard to churchyards under the Church of Scotland (Property and Endowments) Act 1925 and Church of Scotland (Property and Endowments) Amendment Act 1933 (Local Government (Scotland) Act 1973, s 169(2))[1].

Public health considerations also may be relevant. These will normally be the responsibility of the relevant islands or district councils.

In addition to these statutory controls, the law of nuisance may also regulate what is or is not permissible[2].

The effect given to funeral instructions

3.54 Subject to the controls mentioned, in practice it is usual for a testator's instructions to be followed, so far as may be practical or costs permit. However, as it is not competent for a person's body to be disposed of by their will, in that sense it is impossible to give a binding direction. Such instructions are merely expressive of a person's wish.

A distinction is made in law, nonetheless, between instructions merely expressive of a wish, therefore not binding, and bequests involving funeral or memorial arrangements. Although a trust purpose is valid only if it confers a beneficial interest in property on another living person, the law permits an exception by recognising as valid the provision, on a customary and rational scale, for a burial place and suitable memorial to the memory of a deceased

---

1 See 14 *Stair Memorial Encyclopaedia* para 699.
2 See, for example, *Paterson v Beattie* (1845) 7 D 561.

person[1]. This has been described as a concession or indulgence shown by the law based on the 'natural and human sentiments of ordinary people who desire that there should be some memorial of themselves'[2].

What is customary or rational is a question of circumstance and degree and depends, amongst other factors, upon any other provision made for commemoration, the place selected in relation to the person commemorated, the method of commemoration and the possible extent of the cost. Thus, a direction to apply the income of a fund of £1,000 in perpetuity for the purpose of putting flowers on the grave of a deceased and her mother was held to be so extravagant that no effect could be given to it[3].

Even if the direction is in the nature of a bequest the court will not approve it if it is deemed to be contrary to public policy. For example, a bequest of the whole estate for the erection of a burial vault was considered to be so extravagant as to be contrary to public policy[4].

Enforcement of funeral bequests

3.55 The enforcement of funeral bequests, otherwise valid, is a separate issue. Should executors decline to implement them, in the absence of any beneficial interest, there is no-one with an interest to enforce them.

Disagreements can and do arise within families following a person's death and the question of whose wishes should prevail can present difficulties for the executors, family and solicitor. Responsibility is likely to rest with the executors, if only because the cost of disposal has to be borne by the estate under their control. However, few executors are likely to wish to ignore the deceased's instructions or family's wishes. There is not thought to be any Scottish authority indicating who may have the final say in the event of a dispute.

Possible solutions exist, should a testator be particularly concerned to ensure his instructions are implemented. The testator could leave a legacy to an individual or individuals, including the executors, conditional on the instructions being carried out. Alternatively, the testator could enter into a contract, for example with a firm of funeral directors, providing for his wishes to be implemented.

DONATION FOR MEDICAL PURPOSES

Anatomical examination, therapeutic use, medical education or research

3.56 A testator may wish all or parts of his or her body to be used after death, either for medical research or transplant purposes. The present statutory

---

1 *McCaig v Glasgow University* 1907 SC 231 at 244.
2 *Lindsay's Executor v Forsyth* 1940 SC 568 per at 572 per the Lord Justice Clerk (Aitchison).
3 *Lindsay's Executor v Forsyth*, above.
4 *Mackintosh's Judicial Factor v Lord Advocate* 1935 SC 406. Further examples of the attitude adopted by the courts to such bequests may be found in *McCaig v University of Glasgow*, above and *McCaig's Trustees v Kirk Session of United Free Church of Lismore* 1915 SC 426.

provisions governing such bequests are to be found in the Anatomy Act 1984, sections 4, 5 and 6, the Anatomy Regulations 1988[1], and the Human Tissues Act 1961, section 1, as amended[2].

The basic difference between these two pieces of legislation is that while the Anatomy Act controls 'anatomical examinations'[3] the Human Tissues Act controls the giving of directions for the use of any part of a body for 'therapeutic purposes' (basically transplants) or 'for the purposes of medical education or research'[4]. The distinction between 'medical education or research' and 'anatomical examinations' is that the latter can only be carried out in a department licensed under the Anatomy Act.

Broadly speaking, the rules are similar in both Acts and together produce the following results.

Procedure following death

3.57 Before death anyone may express a wish in writing, or orally during their last illness in the presence of two witnesses, that their body or any part of it be used for medical purposes[5]. If so, the person lawfully in possession of the body following the death may authorise such use, unless he has reason to believe the request had been withdrawn[6]. The person or persons 'lawfully in possession' are not defined in the Acts. In theory this might include the executors, the manager or other appropriate medical staff of the hospital where the death occurs and, possibly, the spouse or next of kin, but the better view would seem to be that it is the person in *physical* possession of the body.

Even when the deceased has not specifically authorised such use in the foregoing manner, the person 'lawfully in possession' may still direct the use of the whole or part for medical purposes if he has no reason to believe that the deceased expressed an objection or that the surviving spouse or any surviving relative objects[7].

Thus, if the deceased has requested the use of his body or organs for medical purposes, medical staff are permitted to authorise such use on their own initiative. This authority will almost always be delegated to a transplant coordinator.

Otherwise, if the deceased has not requested such use, medical staff can only proceed when they have no reason to believe the family objects and the Acts require them to make 'such reasonable enquiry as may be practicable'. In the case of organs which must be removed quickly, if a family was not readily contactable medical staff probably would be entitled to deem enquiry impracticable.

1 SI 1988/44.
2 National Health Service and Community Care Act 1990, Sch 9, para 7.
3 Anatomy Act, s 1(1).
4 Human Tissues Act 1961, s 1(1).
5 Anatomy Act 1984, s 4(1); Human Tissues Act 1961, s 1(1).
6 Anatomy Act 1984, s 4(2); Human Tissues Act 1961, s 1(1).
7 Anatomy Act 1984, s 4(3); Human Tissues Act 1961, s 1(2).

In practice, it is understood that the use of organs for transplant purposes will be declined unless the deceased's wishes are known to the hospital or he is known to have carried a donor card and the deceased's relatives have been consulted and have given their consent. Therefore, and because written wishes are unlikely to be available within the appropriate time scale, it is particularly important for a person to *inform* relatives of this wish.

Funeral arrangements

3.58 Where the whole body is used for medical purposes, a simple funeral and cremation will be carried out by the medical authorities at their expense once the anatomical examination is concluded, within a maximum permitted period of three years. Any wishes expressed by the deceased or surviving spouse or relatives must be taken into account[1].

Parts may be retained beyond the statutory period of three years providing authority has been given by the deceased, and not withdrawn, or the surviving spouse or relatives do not object[2].

Thus, testators intending to donate their bodies for medical research may wish to leave instructions regarding memorial services following death. Instructions may also be required should a testator specifically not wish parts of the body to be retained following its use.

The possibility that the bequest may not be accepted should also be borne in mind and it may therefore be desirable to incorporate funeral directions as an alternative (S2.26).

Recording instructions

Anatomical examination or medical education or research

3.59 Testators wishing to donate their bodies for the purpose of anatomical examination or medical education or research may themselves have made contact with a University Medical School's Department of Anatomy. If not, it is wise to suggest that this be done. Although the exact format may differ from department to department, a form of explanatory note or 'bequest' letter will usually be issued to the applicant and a record of the application made. Once a death has occurred, usually a telephone call to the relevant department will be all that is necessary to set matters in motion.

Applicants will be advised of the desirability of notifying their next of kin, executors or lawyers that they wish their bodies to be offered for medical research purposes and anyone wishing their body to be used for medical purposes should make that wish known, preferably in writing and ideally in their

1 Anatomy Regulations 1988, SI 1988/44, para 4(1)(e).
2 Anatomy Act 1984, s 6(3).

will or at least in a letter or note kept with it[1]. The absolute necessity, as has already been noted earlier, is however for the spouse or family to be aware of the wish.

Transplants

3.60 If donation for transplant purposes is intended, as has already been highlighted it is desirable for a person to carry a donor card. These are easily obtainable from hospitals, medical and dental practices, health centres and various public offices. Lawyers drafting wills may wish to carry a small supply and information can be obtained from BODY (British Organ Donor Society), Balsam, Cambridge CB1 6DL (telephone 01223 893636).

The standard donor card refers to the use of the kidneys, eyes, heart, liver or pancreas, for transplantation, or any part of the body for the treatment of others. Many organs must be removed as soon as possible after death and it is more than likely that insufficient time will be available in which to inspect a person's will following their death in order to see if it contains appropriate authority.

Nevertheless, it is worthwhile recording such instructions in a will, if only for the avoidance of doubt.

Form of instruction

3.61 Any form of appropriate words is acceptable. S2.26 incorporates a clause directing executors to offer the body, or any part thereof, for the purposes of spare part surgery or medical research, training or education.

It may be necessary to express whether the donation is for 'anatomical examination' or for 'the purposes of medical education or research' or both. The distinction is that the donor may be quite willing to have the body used for education or research, but quite unwilling to have it, or parts, examined and then preserved, for instance as an example of a condition.

Instructions in the following form would cover all possibilities:

'I direct my executors to offer my body, or any part thereof, to any hospital or University Faculty of Medicine, for anatomical examination, therapeutic purposes, transplantation or for the purposes of medical education or research.'

If the testator wishes any part of his or her body to be made available for transplant purposes, but is opposed to the idea of its being used for anatomical examination or medical education or research, the following form may be used:

'I direct my executors to offer any part of my body for therapeutic purposes, transplantation and the treatment of others [OR but not for anatomical examination or for the purposes of medical education or research].'

---

1 See para 3.61 and S2.26.

A request for a body to be used for 'therapeutic purposes' (transplant) may only authorise the release of certain parts under the Human Tissues Act 1961.

In the reverse case of the testator opposed to transplantation but favouring anatomical examination, medical education or research, the following form may be used:

'I direct my executors to offer my body to any hospital or University Faculty of Medicine, for the purposes of anatomical examination, medical education or research [OR but not for therapeutic purposes, transplantation or the treatment of others].'

In the intermediate case of a testator opposed to anatomical examination (or preservation), but favouring transplantation or research, the following, which emphasises the negative, may be used:

'I direct my executors to offer any part of my body for therapeutic purposes, transplantation, the treatment of others, or for the purposes of medical education or research, but not for anatomical examination or preservation.'

Finally, if testators have strong views against the use of their bodies for medical purposes, it would probably be as well for this to be recorded. Otherwise, as has been suggested, it is not impossible for others to direct such use on their own initiative.

ALTERNATIVE METHODS OF DISPOSAL

3.62 Burial and cremation are the almost universally accepted methods of disposal of a person's body. Occasionally, unusual alternatives are promoted. In recent times the opportunity of having one's ashes shot into earth orbit has been on offer. Cryogenic suspension is another possible option, at least for the well-heeled. As technology advances, who can tell what may follow? The implications of successful cryogenic suspension on the law of succession are, needless to say, beyond the scope of this book!

LIVING WILLS

3.63 The 'living will' is not of course a testamentary document or will in the conventional sense. It is an advance directive by a competent person of that person's wishes with regard to the kind of medical treatment he may wish or not wish to receive in the event of subsequent loss of capacity to decide or communicate. A living will is concerned with medical treatment and does not deal with a person's estate. Most commonly it will consist of a formal declaration requesting that life-prolonging measures be withheld in circumstances where there is no prospect of recovery. In a sense, it is a passive form of euthanasia.

There is neither space for, nor is this book concerned with, examination of the many legal, moral and medical issues involved. However, the existence of living wills, otherwise variously termed 'advance directives', 'advance declarations', 'advance health care directives', and 'treatment disposals' cannot be ignored. There appears to be an increasing public awareness of and interest in them and it is understood that over 26,000 have been distributed to date for use in the United Kingdom.

The reasons for this awareness and interest are many, but are likely to include an increased expectation of life, the ability of modern medical technology to keep people alive, increasing numbers of incurably ill and incapacitated persons, many of them elderly, and the incidence of HIV. The concept appears to have originated in the United States, where statutory recognition of living wills now exists (Patient Self-Determination Act 1990). For many years Holland has been at the forefront of developments in the field of euthanasia and, in February 1993, the Dutch parliament introduced provisions under which doctors may be protected from prosecution for carrying out the 'mercy killing' of patients, provided that strict guidelines are followed. The Canadian courts have recently indicated that living wills would be given legal recognition there.

Despite attempts over a period of more than 50 years to introduce legislation legalising euthanasia, in neither Scotland nor Britain as a whole has the legal standing of living wills been expressly clarified. To date they are not governed by statutory guidelines, nor has the question of their validity or effect come before the courts. At present it would seem that they are no more than the expression of a person's wishes, but it is now probable that the courts in England would accept the right to reject treatment in the future by way of an advance directive or living will. Although that was not the issue in point in the English case of *Airedale NHS Trust v Bland*[1], the views expressed in the judgment would seem to support that conclusion.

Considerable media attention was focused on the case of Tony Bland, a victim of the Hillsborough football stadium disaster, who had been in persistent vegetative state. A successful application was made to the High Court and House of Lords to end life-prolonging treatment for Mr Bland.

3.64 Following *Airedale NHS Trust v Bland* a Parliamentary Select Committee on medical ethics was set up, its remit extending to euthanasia and the withholding of medical treatment. A Medical Treatment (Advance Directives) Bill was presented in Parliament. Further developments in this whole area were expected.

However, the Parliamentary Select Committee[2] unanimously rejected legalising euthanasia and considered that there should be no change in the law to permit euthanasia, assisted suicide or mercy killing. While the use of living wills was commended, the Report concluded that legislation for advance directives was generally unnecessary. Only a code of practice was recommended. The Government Response in May 1994[3] to the Select Committee Report strongly supported the terms of the Report.

1 [1993] 1 All ER 821.
2 House of Lords Papers, Session 1993–94, Report of the Select Committee on Medical Ethics.
3 Government Response to the Report of the Select Committee on Medical Ethics, cm 2553.

At present the legal position of living wills, therefore, remains unchanged but the English Law Commission has issued a Consultative Paper[1] on Living Wills and its report, with draft legislation appended, is expected soon.

3.65 From the solicitor's point of view, concerns appear to have been expressed in England that a solicitor framing a living will for a client might be aiding and abetting suicide, a criminal offence under section 1 of the Suicide Act 1961. It is understood that the Crown Prosecution Service, however, indicated to the English Law Society's Mental Health Sub-Committee that it is unlikely that a solicitor instructed to draw up a living will, merely setting out an exhortation as to what should occur given certain physical or mental incapacity, commits an offence under the Act[2].

There is not considered to be any equivalent difficulty in Scotland and, historically, Scots law has tended not to interfere with medical judgment.

3.66 From the medical standpoint, the BMA's most recent statement on Advance Directives (January 1994) strongly supports the principle of an advance directive representing a patient's settled wishes regarding treatment choices when the patient may no longer be able to express a competent view. It indicates the BMA's belief as being that a patient has, through an advance directive, a legal right to decline specific treatment, including life-prolonging treatment, although it recommends that the drafting of an advance directive be done with medical advice and counselling as part of a continuing doctor/patient dialogue.

The BMA Statement also urges doctors to consider their own views and inform patients at the outset of any absolute objections they may have to the principle of an advance directive, suggesting in such cases that the doctors should offer to step aside and transfer management of the patient's care to another practitioner.

3.67 There is as yet no agreed format or model form for living wills. As an example, the form shortly to be offered by the Voluntary Euthanasia Society of Scotland[3], is reproduced (with the permission of VESS) at the end of this chapter. It includes requests, in the event of a person suffering certain specified serious medical conditions, that the person's life should not be sustained by artificial means and distressing symptoms controlled by appropriate sedative treatment, even although such treatment may be life-shortening.

The VESS form also provides for the granter to appoint a proxy who may assist in decision-making when subsequent incapacity prevents the granter from doing so personally. It should be said that the VESS form encourages the granter to lodge it with his medical records, providing copies to solicitor and family or close friends and suggests that it may be helpful for the granter to discuss the living will in advance with his doctor.

---

1 No 129.
2 The Law Society's Gazette no 26 (1991).
3 17 Hart Street, Edinburgh EH1 3RN.

In England a form primarily designed to enable AIDS sufferers to set out their wishes as to their care in the final stages of illness, but also suitable for use by anyone seeking to make their wishes clear about treatment, has been produced by the Terrence Higgins Trust in conjunction with the Centre of Medical Law and Ethics, King's College, London. This operates if a patient loses consciousness or becomes otherwise incapable of taking decisions and covers three possible health conditions; permanent physical illness, permanent mental illness and permanent unconsciousness.

Scottish solicitors already do, and are probably increasingly likely to, find themselves being consulted by clients about living wills. It must be for individual solicitors to decide whether or not they feel able to advise clients properly on the issues involved and to draft effective living wills for them. Alternatively, they might consider consulting a practitioner known to have experience in this field or an organisation such as VESS which is able to offer specialised assistance.

When consulted by a client about the preparation of a living will, in the first instance it would be desirable for the solicitor to advise the client to discuss the matter with his doctor. This will permit the client not only to address the medical issues involved, but also to establish if the doctor has personal or conscientious objections to accepting the document or making its existence known at the appropriate time or times. As the effectiveness of a living will may depend upon the declarant's capacity at the time of signing and his decision being an informed one, a note in the doctor's file that discussion has taken place may also be helpful.

If a living will is signed, the client should be advised to retain it in a safe place, preferably placing it or a copy on his medical file, and to inform his family or close friends of its existence and location and to ensure that a copy is placed on his medical file. As an additional safeguard, the client may wish to carry a note so as to alert third parties to the fact that he has signed a living will. VESS, for example, provides a plastic emergency card, similar to an organ donor card, for this purpose.

Finally, it should be emphasised to the client that, at present at least, it is not possible to say with certainty what weight would be given to the document in law, that it is most likely to be treated simply as an expression of wishes and that it can be altered or revoked by the client at any time.[1]

---

1 On this matter, the following articles may be of interest: 'Living Wills' (1989) 12 LS Gaz 21; 'The Reluctant Survivor' (1990) 140 NLJ 586 and 639; 'The Ethics of Euthanasia (1990) 35 JLSS 243; 'The Right to Die' (1991) 26 LS Gaz 20; 'Mother Knows Best' (1992) 142 NLJ 1538; 'Doctors and Death' New Scientist 20.2.93; BMA Statement on Advance Directives (January 1994); A D Ward 'Tutors to Adults : Developments' 1992 SLT (News) 325; 'A Testament of Intent' (1994) 15 LS Gaz 26.

Important: | Living Will |

Insert in Patient's Medical Records

This document should be lodged with the declarant's medical records.

A doctor having conscientious objection should immediately refer the declarant to another doctor. Living wills are accepted in the British Medical Association's ethical recommendations and by common law. The form does not ask the doctor to do anything illegal.
Duplicate copies may optionally be lodged with a solicitor and a close friend, and a further copy kept for reference.

Section A. ADVANCE MEDICAL DIRECTIVE.   *Note: This section may be legally binding.*

Section A comprises specific instructions to the health-care team in the event that I can no longer express my own wishes; it covers very serious conditions.

To the Declarant: When filling out this part of the form, you should cross out anything that does not express your true wishes, then initial any changes clearly.

Section B. LIFE VALUES STATEMENT.

This gives indications of the personal value I attach to my life under various circumstances. I ask my health care team to bear these in mind when making difficult decisions about my treatment or non-treatment, especially in situations not covered by Section A. Where I have indicated that life under such circumstances would be "Much Worse Than Death" this means that I would find the situation totally unbearable and unacceptable, and that I would prefer all life-sustaining treatment to be stopped or withdrawn rather than exist for the rest of my life in such a state.

Note: A doctor should not be liable to civil or criminal proceedings if he acts in good faith and with reasonable care in respecting the directives and values in this document.

DO NOT FILL OUT THIS FORM WITHOUT DEEP AND CAREFUL CONSIDERATION.
Complete Section A or Section B or both.

For further information and advice on living wills, you may wish to consult your doctor or one of the organisations or individuals listed below:
Age Concern England, Astral House, 1268 London Rd, London SW16 4ER;
Law Pack Publishing Ltd, 10-16 Cole Street, London SE1 4YH;
Phyllis Goodheir, 16 Woodlands Drive, Coatbridge, ML5 1LE;
The Natural Death Centre, 20 Heber Rd, London NW2;
The Terrence Higgins Trust, 52-54 Gray's Inn Rd, London WC1X 8JU;
The Voluntary Euthanasia Society, 13 Prince of Wales Terrace, London W8 5PG;
The Voluntary Euthanasia Society of Scotland, 17 Hart St, Edinburgh EH1 3RN.
Solicitors may wish to contact *The Law Society,* Law Society House, 50/52 Chancery Lane, London WC2A.
Physicians may wish to contact *The British Medical Association,* Ethics Department, BMA House, Tavistock Square, London WC1H 9JP.

SECTION A. ADVANCE MEDICAL DIRECTIVE

TO MY PHYSICIAN AND HEALTH CARE TEAM, MY FAMILY, MY SOLICITOR AND ALL OTHER PERSONS CONCERNED:
this declaration is made at a time when I am of sound mind and after careful consideration.

I UNDERSTAND THAT MY LIFE MAY BE SHORTENED BY THE SPECIFIC REFUSALS OF TREATMENT MADE IN THIS DOCUMENT.

I DECLARE that if at any time the following circumstances exist, namely:

(1) I suffer from one or more of the conditions mentioned in the *Schedule*; and

(2) I have become unable to participate effectively in decisions about my medical care; and

(3) two independent physicians (one a consultant) are of the expert, considered opinion, after full examination of my case, that I am unlikely to make a substantial recovery from illness or impairment involving severe distress or incapacity for rational existence,

THEN AND IN THOSE CIRCUMSTANCES my directions are as follows:

1. that I am not to be subjected to any medical intervention or treatment (aimed at prolonging my life) such as life support systems, artificial ventilation, antibiotics (i.e. to control infection), artificial feeding - whether enteral or parenteral (tube feeding into the stomach or into a vein), invasive surgery, dialysis (e.g. using a kidney machine), or blood transfusion;

2. that **any distressing symptoms (including any caused by lack of food or fluid) are to be fully and aggressively controlled by appropriate palliative care, ordinary nursing care, analgesic or other treatments,** even though some of these treatments may have the secondary effect of shortening my life.

HOWEVER, modes of treatment mentioned above may be applied for elimination of serious symptoms. Giving intensive care to me is to be allowed only on the condition that reliable reasons exist for the possibility that this treatment will have a better result than a merely short prolongation of life. In the event that a treatment with prospect of recovery has been started but proves to be futile, it has to be discontinued immediately.

I consent to anything proposed to be done or omitted in compliance with the directions expressed above and absolve my medical attendants from any civil liability arising out of such acts or omissions.

I offer the health-care team my heartfelt thanks for respecting my sincerely held wishes, as expressed in this directive.

I accept the risk that I may be unable to express a change of mind at a time in the future when I am incapacitated, that improving medical technology may offer increased hope, but I personally consider the risk of unwanted treatment to be a greater risk. **I wish it to be understood that I fear degradation and indignity far more than death.** I ask my medical attendants to bear this statement in mind when considering what my intentions would be in any uncertain situation.

I RESERVE THE RIGHT TO REVOKE THIS DIRECTIVE at any time, orally or in writing, but unless I do so it should be taken to represent my continuing directions. I hereby deliberately *accept the risk* that I may no longer be able to revoke my declaration if I am in a condition listed in the Schedule, in order to exclude a risk which is greater to me, namely that I should continue living in circumstances that are not acceptable to me.

<u>**S**ection A continued</u>

SCHEDULE

A Advanced disseminated malignant disease *(e.g. cancer that has spread considerably)*

B Severe immune deficiency *(e.g. Acquired Immune Deficiency Syndrome)*

C Advanced degenerative disease of the nervous system *(e.g advanced Parkinson's Disease)*

D Severe and lasting brain damage due to injury, stroke, disease or other cause

E Advanced dementia, whether Alzheimer's, multi-infarct or other, resulting in very limited awareness of the immediate environment and inability to initiate simple tasks

F Any other condition of comparable gravity

Additional instructions (if any, such as pregnancy waiver) . . . .

. . . .

. . . .

. . . .

. . . .

. . . .

. . . .

. . . .

. . . .

. . . .

. . . .

. . . .

If you would like a particular person's wishes to be taken into consideration during decisions about your medical care, please give their details here:

Name of my proxy . . . . Telephone number . . . .

Address . . . .

To my proxy: Please try to ensure that decisions are taken

                    (mark one box only)   ☐ how you believe I would have taken them

                                       ☐ using your own best judgement

The wishes of your proxy may be taken into consideration, but have no overriding force in British law - neither do the wishes of relatives. It is advisable to discuss this document with your proxy.

I have discussed this document with my doctor ☐ Mark here if Yes

Doctor's Tel. No . . . . Name of Doctor . . . .

Address . . . .

It is not obligatory to discuss your living will in advance with your doctor, but it may be helpful to do so.

SECTION B. VALUES HISTORY STATEMENT Please use this section as a guide to my values when considering the likely result of treatment.

Circle the number on the scale of one to five, that most closely indicates your feelings about each of the situations described.

	Much Worse Than Death: I Would Definitely Not Want Life-Sustaining Treatment	Somewhat Worse Than Death: I Would Probably Not Want Life-Sustaining Treatment	Neither Better Nor Worse Than Death: I'm Not Sure Whether I Want Life-Sustaining Treatment	Somewhat Better Than Death: I Would Probably Want Life-Sustaining Treatment	Much Better Than Death: I Would Definitely Want Life-Sustaining Treatment
(a) Permanently paralysed. You are unable to walk but can move around in a wheelchair. You can talk and interact with other people.	1	2	3	4	5
(b) Permanently unable to speak meaningfully. You are unable to speak to others. You can walk on your own, feed yourself and take care of daily needs such as bathing and dressing yourself.	1	2	3	4	5
(c) Permanently unable to care for yourself. You are bedridden, unable to wash, feed, or dress yourself. You are totally cared for by others.	1	2	3	4	5
(d) Permanently in pain. You are in severe bodily pain that cannot be totally controlled or completely eliminated by medications.	1	2	3	4	5
(e) Permanently mildly demented. You often cannot remember things, such as where you are, nor reason clearly. You are capable of speaking, but not capable of remembering the conversations; you are capable of washing, feeding and dressing yourself and are in no pain.	1	2	3	4	5
(f) Being in a short term coma. You have suffered brain damage and are not conscious and are not aware of your environment in any way. You cannot feel pain. You are cared for by others. These mental impairments may be reversed in about one week leaving mild forgetfulness and loss of memory as a consequence.	1	2	3	4	5

SIGNATURE OF DECLARANT to Sections A & B: . . . .

Name (print clearly) . . . . Day/Month/Year . . . .

Address. . . . .

. . . . Date of Birth* . . . .

*If you are under 18 years of age, you may still complete this document, though it may not have the same legal force.

WITNESS'S SIGNATURE: I declare that the abovenamed has signed this document in my presence. He/she has declared it to be his/her firm will, is in full capacity and fully understands the meaning of it. I believe it to be a firm and competent statement of his/her wishes. As far as I am aware, no pressure has been brought to bear on him/her to sign such a document and I believe it to be his/her own free and considered wish. So far as I am aware, I do not stand to gain from his/her death. *Note: if you live in Scotland and have difficulty in finding someone to witness the document, you may write "adopted as holograph" above your signature instead of having it witnesssed.*

Signed: . . . . Name . . . .

Address . . . .

CHAPTER 4

THE SUBJECTS OF BEQUEST

INTRODUCTION

4.01 This chapter is concerned with the subjects of legacies – the items or parts of an estate which a testator intends to go in a particular direction. Inevitably, there is sometimes an overlap with the objects of legacies – the direction in which the testator wishes the subjects to go. It is fair to say that confusion arises more often with the objects than with the subjects, but particularly in relation to specific physical items care is required to ensure that the testator expresses clearly what he wishes to bequeath. Difficulties can arise with the objects of all types of legacy, and these difficulties are explained in Chapters 5 and 6.

There are at least references to legacies in all of the Styles; however, an unrealistically wide range of individual subjects (at least for a single will) is covered in Style S2. The form of these legacies is generally absolute bequest but it is perfectly possible to restrict almost any legacy in order to give a limited interest, such as a liferent.

Problems relating to multiple beneficiaries, survivorship and destinations-over are dealt with in Chapter 5. Although such problems perhaps arise most commonly with residuary bequests, they are also of significance when dealing with specific and pecuniary legacies.

CLASSIFICATION OF LEGACIES

4.02 It is possible to classify the subjects of legacy in a number of ways. To start at the end, residue is simply what is left after all prior purposes have been implemented. Such prior purposes may be said to include not only obvious testamentary instructions to distribute part of a testator's estate other than as residue, but also the payment of debts and meeting any claims to legal rights (which claims will of course override testamentary provisions in so far as necessary).

It is possible that debts will exceed the deceased's resources in the case of an insolvent estate; or that prior testamentary purposes will exhaust an estate, in either case leaving no residue to be distributed. If legacies other than residue exceed the net amount of a deceased's estate, the process of abatement may be necessary in respect of the legacies, but that will not assist the residuary beneficiaries.

It may be a matter of deliberate policy to leave legacies other than residue in the expectation that their total will exceed the amount of estate at death, but this should not preclude making a residuary bequest. It may be that between the date of making a will and the date of death, a testator's estate increases substantially, so that residue forms a substantial part of the estate; it may also be that some or all of the prior testamentary purposes fail. Conditions attaching to legacies may not be fulfilled, leaving their subjects to fall into residue. Legacies may lapse at some time after the testator's death. The more common problem with residue is identifying exactly where it is to go and that is dealt with in Chapters 5 and 6. The absence of a residuary bequest is likely to mean that some part of the testator's estate falls into intestacy. The heirs will generally be ascertained as at the testator's death even if the intestacy only emerges at a later time[1].

The real point of including a residuary bequest is to ensure the testator's control over the disposition of his *whole* estate, subject to debts and legal (or any similar) rights. On the meaning of the estate bequeathed by a will, see paragraphs 2.09–2.24.

Given a definition of residue simply encompassing what is left after prior purposes have been implemented, there is rarely a problem with its identification. Problems with identifying *other* bequests may have effects on the extent of residue, but such problems are best dealt with in the context of these bequests. The phrase 'free residue' has been interpreted as requiring the deduction of legal rights, if claimed, as well as debts and legacies in ascertaining the amount available for distribution[2].

All of the Styles presented in this book except Style S12 contain residuary bequests. It might be suggested that if the whole estate is to pass to one beneficiary, without legacies, as in Style S1, the bequest should be of the 'whole estate'. It is, however, thought that even if there are no legacies, the purpose should still refer to 'residue', rather than 'estate' or 'whole estate', because it is possible that the testator may make some informal legacies (for which provision is indeed made in S1.4). The use of the term 'residue' will cover the whole estate if that is what is required.

4.03 Apart from residuary bequests, the main classification of legacies is a division into general legacies and specific (or special) legacies.

A general legacy, as the name implies, is one which is not of a distinct asset belonging to the testator – there is nothing to distinguish it from other assets of the same type within the estate[3]. The most common example, of course, is a sum of money, as in S2.10 (a pecuniary legacy). Other forms of general legacy are possible such as a quantity of goods or items of the same generic description.

Difficulties can arise with legacies of a specified amount of company stock, or similar. This can either be a general legacy, payable whether or not the testator possessed the stock as at the date of death; or a specific legacy, which would be subject to ademption if the testator did not own it at that date. If the words used

1 *Lord v Colvin* (1865) 3 M 1083.
2 *Sampson v Raynor* 1928 SC 899.
3 Erskine *Institute* III, 9, 11; *McLaren* I, para 1040.

incorporate a reference to 'my holding' or 'my shares in XY Ltd' or otherwise indicate that the stock in question formed part of the testator's portfolio the legacy will almost certainly be specific (although it could also be demonstrative – see para 4.05); otherwise it may be general[1]. In either event careful drafting can resolve any possible ambiguities.

4.04   A specific (or special) legacy is one of a specified item forming part of the testator's estate. It can be moveable or heritable, corporeal or incorporeal, and a wide range of such legacies can be seen in Style S2. Identification of the subject of a special legacy is obviously particularly important. The terms 'special legacy' and 'specific legacy' should be distinguished from the technical inheritance tax expression 'specific gift' found in the Inheritance Tax Act 1984, Part II, Chapter III. In inheritance tax terms, a specific gift is any gift other than a gift of residue or of a share in residue[2].

4.05   A demonstrative legacy falls somewhere between a general and a specific legacy. In such a legacy the testator indicates the source from which it is to be paid; it will usually be pecuniary but this is not necessary. The question may then be what happens should the specified source prove to be non-existent or insufficient to meet the legacy.

If the demonstrative legacy is taxative, it is akin to a specific legacy, in that it will be restricted to the specified source, or will be adeemed should that source not exist. On the other hand, if the demonstrative legacy is non-taxative, recourse may be had to residue to make up any deficiency. There is a presumption that the latter position is intended in the absence of instructions to the contrary, but the testator should always make his intentions clear[3]. When analysed, a non-taxative demonstrative legacy would seem rather pointless in most circumstances, and testators should perhaps be dissuaded from making this type of bequest.

An example of a taxative demonstrative legacy would be:

> 'To A the sum of ONE THOUSAND POUNDS to be paid from Bank of Scotland Term Deposit no. 0023467 (but only if I hold this term deposit at the date of my death, and to the extent that the proceeds of this term deposit (including interest credited and accrued to the date of my death) are sufficient to pay this legacy).'

If it were non-taxative, the wording would be as follows, after reference to the source:

> '. . . but if I do not hold this Term Deposit at the date of my death, or to the extent that the proceeds of this Term Deposit (including interest credited and accrued to the date of my death) are insufficient to pay this legacy, this sum shall be payable to the extent necessary from my general estate.'

---

1 Compare 25 *Stair Memorial Encyclopedia* para 854 with *McLaren* I, para 739. See paras 4.15–4.17 on ademption and 4.18 on *legatum rei alienae*.
2 Inheritance Tax Act 1984, s 42(1).
3 *Douglas' Executors v Scott* (1869) 7 M 504; *Chalmers v Chalmers* (1851) 14 D 57.

4.06 The classification of legacies is not merely a matter of academic interest; particularly where an estate may be insufficient to meet the legacies specified, their classification will determine the order of satisfaction. Classification will also affect matters such as abatement and ademption[1].

After payment of debts, funeral expenses and legal rights (if claimed), the order of priority for distribution of a deceased's estate commences with specific legacies. A demonstrative legacy ranks with specific legacies, at least to the extent that the specified source is available to meet the legacy; to the extent that the source is not available, any balance of a demonstrative legacy to be met from the general estate presumably ranks with general legacies, which come next in the order of priority. Finally come residuary bequests, which can only be met if there are resources available after all prior legacies and purposes have been fulfilled.

ABATEMENT

4.07 Abatement is the process of reduction which takes place where a testator's estate is insufficient to meet all bequests. The classification of bequest is important in this context, because in the absence of instructions to the contrary in the will there is a set order in which legacies abate[2].

Residuary bequests abate first; in the simplest case, legacies other than residue will exhaust the estate and then there will be no residue to distribute.

General legacies abate next. This principle enables pecuniary legacies of whatever size to be paid before any residuary bequests[3]. If, however, there is insufficient estate to meet the total of general legacies, these must be reduced and this can raise more difficult questions. If all general legacies are of the same amount, they will be reduced in equal amounts (down to the level of the total remaining estate). If general legacies are of different amounts, the rule is that they abate *proportionately*[4]. Thus if there are legacies to A of £15,000 and to B of £5,000, and total estate of only £10,000 A will receive £7,500 and B £2,500.

4.08 It is always open to the testator to regulate the order of abatement and displace the general principles. The simplest way to achieve this is probably by reference to the order in which legacies appear (which order, or any numbering does *not*, without special provision affect the rules on abatement)[5]. A claim to legal rights does not affect the rules on abatement[6].

An instruction as to the order of abatement could be provided after a list of pecuniary legacies, as follows:

'. . . declaring that if, at the date of my death, my estate should be

1 See paras 4.07–4.12 and 4.15–4.17.
2 *Currie v Currie* (1835) 13 S 290.
3 *Tennant's Trustees v Tennant* 1946 SC 420.
4 *McLaren* I, para 1067; *Erskine* III, 9, 11.
5 *McConnel v McConnel's Trustees* 1931 SN 31.
6 *Tait's Trustees v Lees* (1886) 13 R 1104.

insufficient for the payment of all of the foregoing legacies, they shall
be preferred in full in the order in which they are set out so far as my
estate shall permit[1].'

More complex situations are possible, but perhaps not to be encouraged. For
instance if there is a list of five legacies, the first three of which are to be
preferred:

'. . . declaring that if, at the date of my death, my estate shall be
insufficient for the payment of all of the foregoing legacies, legacies
(1), (2) and (3) shall be preferred in full to legacies (4) and (5); but if,
at the date of my death, my estate shall be insufficient for the payment
of legacies (1), (2) and (3), they shall abate proportionately [OR shall
be preferred in full in the order in which they are set out so far as my
estate shall permit].'

Any variation of the normal rules of abatement requires care and if there is a list
of legacies, special attention will be needed if there are subsequent alterations by
codicil.

4.09 Most Styles contain a clause declaring that legacies are to be paid free of
government duties and expenses (see eg S2.5). If there is no residuary fund to
meet such duties and expenses, they will be met out of the legacies themselves,
which may thus require abatement. Specific legacies will continue to be met in
full in preference to general legacies; and any tax on such special legacies will also
fall on general legacies. If, however, there are expenses involved (for instance in
the transfer of a specific legacy) there is an argument that the freedom from
expenses constitutes another *general* legacy which will abate proportionately
with other general legacies. This complex situation points to the need to avoid
abatement if at all possible; or alternatively to provide that very substantial
expenses attaching to a legacy should be met by the legatee.

Demonstrative legacies are treated for the purposes of abatement as if they are
special legacies to the extent that the fund from which they are to be met exists at
death; if they are to be met beyond the extent of that fund to that extent they will
abate with general legacies.

4.10 In principle, specific legacies will not abate at all; however, in practice
they may do so, for instance if debts or taxes are such that they exceed the estate
other than specific legacies. It is worth mentioning that specific legacies may be
very large, comprising (for example) a house or other heritable property. If such
debts or taxes are general burdens on the estate, again it is thought that specific
legacies will abate proportionately; if they are, however, burdens on a particular
legacy, that legacy will be reduced accordingly. For instance, if a specific legacy
is bequeathed free of delivery expenses, and there is no estate other than specific
legacies from which to meet such expenses, they will be met by each legatee in
respect of his own legacy.

In this context, the terms of the Inheritance Tax Act 1984, section 41(a),

---

1 In the example in the previous paragraph, A would receive £10,000 and B nothing, if such a provision
  were attached.

should be borne in mind. This will be relevant in a partly exempt estate, and provides that:

'Notwithstanding the terms of any disposition, none of the tax on the value transferred shall fall on any specific gift [defined as any gift other than a gift of residue or of a share in residue] if or to the extent that the transfer is exempt with respect to the gift.'

4.11 It is open to the testator to vary the normal rules of abatement, as between different *types* of legacy, either directly or indirectly. One method of achieving this (in effect) is by burdening a specific legacy with a debt which would normally be met out of residue[1]. This method is perhaps suitable with a legacy other than a pecuniary one, where the testator may wish a particular beneficiary to receive an item which may be worth a substantial proportion of the testator's estate. This wish may conflict with a desire to ensure that other beneficiaries, especially those taking residue, receive a reasonably large benefit. If a suitable debt is available to attach to such a legacy, this may be convenient.

Alternative methods of achieving the same result are to direct the executors to offer the item for sale to the beneficiary, at a price sufficient to provide for other legatees; or to make the legacy conditional on the legatee paying the appropriate amount into the estate or directly to the other legatees. In neither case can it be guaranteed that the desired legatee will in fact comply with such conditions. He may choose to forfeit the legacy. In such circumstances, the testator must decide whether his wishes as to that particular legacy are such that the desired legatee is to receive it in any event, even if it deprives other beneficiaries of much of the estate.

It is possible to provide that if the value of residue does not amount to a specific sum, special legacies should then abate (in any order desired by the testator, or proportionately), so that a minimum amount of residue becomes available. However, this is a complex method of achieving a distribution which can be obtained simply by directing a legacy of the desired minimum amount to the residuary legatee (either in preference to or ranking with other legacies). Such a legatee will then receive at least what the testator desires, and may still share in any further amount which becomes available as residue.

Preferential legacies

4.12 Another method of altering the normal rules on abatement is to declare that a particular legacy is to be preferential, either to all other legacies in the estate or to all other legacies of a particular type. The following declaration should achieve this result:

'. . . declaring that this legacy and any government duties in respect of my death and delivery expenses relating to this legacy shall be preferential to all other provisions of this will and of any other testamentary writings [OR to all other legacies in this purpose].'

1 *Greig's Trustees v Beach* (1854) 16 D 899.

As the wording indicates, one matter which might require to be considered in relation to a preferential legacy is the question of taxes and delivery expenses relating to it. In terms of the normal clause governing legacies contained in the Styles presented (see, for example, S2.4), such items are charges on residue; but in the absence of any residue, such charges will require to come from the legacies themselves. The wording used above demands in effect that legacies other than the preferential one will bear such charges in relation to it. This might be extending the preference rather further than desired by the testator and this matter should be checked.

While it is always possible that an estate will decline in size so that some general consideration as to altering the rules on abatement is required, this is likely to be uncommon in relation to most wills which contain legacies. However, the position in relation to a single very large legacy as compared to the remainder of the estate is rather different and such points should always be considered in this context in discussion with the testator.

CUMULATIVE OR SUBSTITUTIONAL LEGACIES

4.13 Questions may arise as to whether a number of legacies in favour of the same beneficiary are cumulative or substitutional. There exists quite substantial authority on this matter, but disputes will only arise where a testator has not made his intentions clear[1].

In particular, if for any reason two legacies of the same amount to the same beneficiary are included in the same deed (perhaps because one is for a special purpose or under certain conditions, while the other is free of such considerations), it should be made clear if they are to be cumulative. Otherwise, it may be assumed that the double legacy was included in error[2].

The presumption is otherwise in the case of legacies in different deeds, such as a will and a codicil[3]. However, this is a clear example of a case where the matter should be put beyond doubt in drafting. The codicil should state specifically that the new legacy is either in addition to the earlier provision, or in substitution for it. In the latter case, cancellation and substitution should be express (see Chapter 8).

In the common case of a special or pecuniary legacy being given to a beneficiary who also takes or shares in the residue, it will generally be assumed that the legacies are cumulative. Again, this should be expressed if there is any possibility of doubt.

SELECTIVE/DISCRETIONARY LEGACIES

4.14 Selective or discretionary legacies can be of two types. In the first type, the discretion available is given to executors or trustees, as to the extent and manner in which beneficiaries from within a specified class are to share. As the discretion

1 See 25 *Stair Memorial Encyclopaedia* paras 857–860; *McLaren* I, chapter XL.
2 *Elliot v Lord Stair's Trustees* (1823) 2 S 218.
3 *Stirling v Deans* (1704) Mor 11442; *Royal Infirmary of Edinburgh v Muir's Trustees* (1881) 9 R 352; *Fraser v Forbes' Trustees* (1899) 1 F 513.

affects the objects of bequest, this type of legacy is dealt with in paragraphs 5.59–5.61 and 6.125–6.126.

In the second type, the power of selection is given to the beneficiary or beneficiaries involved, to choose from a range of subjects of bequest. This type of legacy will almost invariably involve physical items and will usually affect personal belongings such as furniture or jewellery. This type of selective legacy is dealt with in paragraph 4.55 in relation to the appropriate type of item.

ADEMPTION

4.15 Ademption may be a problem which arises with special legacies. Where an item which is the subject of a special legacy no longer forms part of the testator's estate at death, that legacy is said to have adeemed. The legatee will get nothing, and in particular he will not receive the price of the subject of bequest if it has been sold[1]. This doctrine also applies to a demonstrative legacy where the source from which it is to be paid is not owned at the date of death.

Ademption will not occur where the subject of the legacy is substantially unchanged at the date of death, even if not in the exact form which existed at the date of drafting the will[2]. This point becomes particularly relevant when dealing with such items as stock and shares, including government stock. As regards stock, unless there is some form of wording to indicate that a legacy of stock is a special one (by reference to the testator's actual ownership of a particular holding of a particular stock, for instance), this will be a general legacy. It will not adeem, even if the testator does not own the relevant stock at the date of death.

As regards shares, if a holding has been reorganised or converted in some way (at least within the same company) it too will not adeem[3]. However, a legacy of shares (as distinct from stock) is not a general legacy and ademption is possible if no shares representing the original holding remain at the date of death (see para 4.102 below).

Ademption is more likely with other forms of asset even if such an asset continues to be owned indirectly. For instance, if a house owned outright at the date of drafting the will is transferred to a company (so that the testator owns shares in the company instead), ademption will occur[4].

If the legacy is of a debt due to the testator, a change in the nature of that asset will cause ademption. For instance, if there is a legacy of a particular bank account, the movement of that bank account to another branch will cause ademption[5]. The legacy of a debt due to the testator will be adeemed if the debt has been repaid by the date of death[6].

1 *Anderson v Thomson* (1877) 4 R 1101.
2 *Ballantyne's Trustees v Ballantyne's Trustees* 1941 SC 35.
3 *Macfarlane's Trustees v Macfarlane* 1910 SC 323; *Mitchell's Trustees v Fergus* (1889) 11 R 902.
4 *Ogilvie-Forbes' Trustees v Ogilvie-Forbes* 1955 SC 405.
5 *Ballantyne's Trustees v Ballantyne's Trustees* 1941 SC 35.
6 *Cobban's Executors v Cobban* 1915 SC 82.

Ademption will not occur if the asset in question has been sold, but the sale has not been completed at the date of death[1].

4.16   In drafting terms, there are a number of ways of dealing with potential ademption. With some types of asset (particularly corporeal items) it will be desirable to add an extension following a reference to a specific asset owned by the testator at the time of drafting the will:

'. . . or any other house [OR yacht] [OR car] [etc] owned by me at the
time of my death.'

With other types of asset, a more general extension may be appropriate:

. . . or any replacement therefor, as to which my executors shall be
the sole judges.'

The discretion given to the executors is necessary, because it might be difficult to decide whether one item is a replacement for another. For instance, a testator might sell a cello and 'replace' it with a violin. It would be difficult to say whether this was a replacement for the purposes of a legacy of the cello. The proper answer would of course be an amendment to the will, but in the absence of this, a discretion given to the executors should suffice for most purposes.

More care is required where the testator does, or is likely to, own more than one of the type of asset bequeathed. For instance, it may be necessary to specify in dealing with a house that it is a 'holiday house'. Again, the executors' discretion as to whether one item is a *replacement* for another should generally be sufficient and should be added where there is any real possibility of confusion in the future.

If it is known or anticipated that the subject of a particular legacy might be sold, it should be considered whether any legatee of that asset is to take the sale price. This will not occur without specific provision – a sale will generally cause ademption. It is possible to provide an alternative legacy in the form of a stated sum, or by reference to the sale price received. A suitable form of wording in such circumstances would be:

'I direct my executors to make over to A my yacht "Ariadne" or any
other yacht owned by me at the time of my death, or, in the event of
the last yacht owned by me before my death having been sold and not
replaced, the sale price of the last yacht owned by me [OR the sum of
TWENTY THOUSAND POUNDS].'

This type of wording can be adapted for any type of asset, so as to prevent complete ademption. Possibilities other than sale (such as destruction or theft) might be envisaged, in which case the following wording could be used:

'. . . or in the event of my not owning any yacht at the time of my
death, the sum of TWENTY THOUSAND POUNDS.'

Alternatively, it may be desired to provide that a legacy *will* be cancelled in the event of the testator not owning the relevant asset at the date of death. While any additional wording may only confirm what the law would achieve in any event, it

1 *McArthur's Executors v Guild* 1908 SC 743.

is helpful to put the matter beyond doubt. Suitable wording in such circumstances would be:

'. . . I direct my executors to make over to A my Mercedes car registration number K111 ABC, purchased by me in 1993, but only if I own that car (whatever its registration number) at the time of my death.'

Such a legacy will avoid any problems arising from replacement cars; and also takes account of the fact that a car may be re-registered (see paras 4.63–4.64 below).

This type of provision may cause particular difficulties where the legacy is of shares, for instance on a reorganisation or takeover, perhaps involving a share-for-share exchange. These problems are dealt with in paragraphs 4.102–4.105 and 4.120 below.

4.17 It is also possible to envisage a situation where the testator would wish ademption to take place only where an item has not been replaced in any similar form within his estate, but may envisage certain permissible replacements occurring. Once more, the proper answer would be to make changes in the will in such circumstances, as it is not really possible to cater for every eventuality. However one extension of the wording just mentioned would be:

'I direct my executors to make over to A my Mercedes car registration number K111 ABC, purchased by me in 1993, or that car if it is owned by me at the time of my death whatever its registration number, or any replacement Mercedes car owned by me at the time of my death (but not any other type of car bought by me following the sale of a Mercedes car), as to all of which my executors shall be the sole judges.'

Such a provision would have the effect of preventing ademption in the event of a particular Mercedes car not being owned or registered under the same number at the date of death, or having been replaced by another Mercedes; but ademption is confirmed in the event of another type of car having been bought as a replacement. Ademption would of course also occur where the Mercedes had been sold and no other car had been bought. While it is extremely unlikely that such provisions would be required in connection with a car, this type of wording does illustrate the possibilities available in order both to prevent and confirm ademption.

Such wording could be adapted for any other type of legacy and may be useful when dealing with particular types of investment.

LEGATUM REI ALIENAE

4.18 *Legatum rei alienae* refers to a legacy of an asset which the testator does not own. If he has merely made a mistake in attempting to bequeath something in the belief that he *did* own it, the legacy will simply fail. However, if a legatee can prove that the testator knew that he did not own the subject of the legacy, this will be interpreted as an instruction to the executors to obtain that subject. If that is not possible, such a legacy will be treated as one of the value of the subject purportedly bequeathed (if that value can be established). The onus of establishing the testator's knowledge of the situation is on the legatee and such knowledge will not be presumed[1].

In general, legacies of property that the testator does not own should not be encouraged. However, it is possible to envisage circumstances where such a legacy would be desirable. For instance, a farmer may wish his children to continue in the farming business and add the adjacent farm to that business. Of course, if the testator's estate is wealthy enough for such a purchase to be contemplated, there will be nothing to prevent an outright bequest of cash to the children, who might or might not use it to fulfil the testator's wishes. If such a testator wishes to ensure that the farm to be purchased is retained within his family, a trust or some form of conditional legacy will be required.

4.19 If a legacy such as this is contemplated, it should not be left to the legatee to prove that it was a deliberate *legatum rei alienae*. The best way to achieve the intended result is an instruction to executors to purchase the desired asset directly, as follows:

> 'I direct my executors to purchase and make over to A Meadow
> Farm, Girvan, Ayrshire, free of all debts and expenses of purchase
> and transfer.'

This would be a reference to purchase of the *dominium utile*; if any other interest, such as a tenancy or a superiority, were contemplated, this should be stated. As noted above, an outright beneficiary could be replaced by trustees who would be required to hold the asset which is to be purchased.

Particular care is required if the asset to be obtained is a valuable one. To take a ludicrous example (and ignoring questions of public policy and insanity), there could be an instruction to purchase and transfer the Mona Lisa. This could obviously not be achieved; the doctrine of *legatum rei alienae* would appear to require that the legacy would be replaced by one of an amount equal to the value of the asset. Hence it would exhaust the entire estate (in most cases at least!). This result may be acceptable to the testator, but equally he may wish to preserve some estate for residuary beneficiaries. It should also be borne in mind that the testator's estate may decline in value, and that the cost of the specified asset may increase between the date of the will and the date of death, perhaps with dramatic effect.

If these possibilities are contemplated, limitations can be imposed on the direction to purchase, for example as follows:

> 'I direct my executors to purchase and make over to A Meadow
> Farm, Girvan, Ayrshire, free of all debts and expenses of purchase
> and transfer, provided that the gross cost of Meadow Farm does not
> exceed ONE HUNDRED THOUSAND POUNDS [OR one half of the net value
> of my estate]; and if the gross cost of Meadow Farm is likely to exceed
> ONE HUNDRED THOUSAND POUNDS [OR one half of the net value of my

---

1 *Meeres* v *Dowell's Executor* 1923 SLT 184.

estate] (as to which my executors shall be the sole judges), I direct my
executors to pay [OR make over] to A the sum of ONE HUNDRED
THOUSAND POUNDS [OR one half of my net estate].'

There is no necessary correlation between the limitations imposed on the purchase price and the alternative legacy provided. If it is not going to be possible to
fulfil the testator's particular wishes, a much smaller legacy might be desirable.

SATISFACTION OF LEGACIES

4.20 The standard instruction as to the satisfaction of legacies used in the
Styles is as follows (see, for example, S2.5):
> 'Unless otherwise specified, any legacy granted by any writing shall
> be paid or made over as soon as my executors consider practicable
> after my death . . .'.

This does *not* require immediate payment[1]. As the wording used indicates, it is
possible to provide that legacies should be paid or satisfied at any time. This can
be done simply by inserting a declaration that a legacy should be satisfied, say, 12
months after the death of the testator.

Generally, executors cannot be compelled to pay legacies until at least 6
months from the date of death have expired, although there is some old authority
that the period allowed is 12 months[2].

In such circumstances provision for satisfaction of legacies within a period of
less than 6 months is probably undesirable, as it could expose the executors to
claims if the estate turned out to be insufficient to meet debts and such legacies.
If the testator insists that a legacy is satisfied before the expiry of 6 months, some
instructions should be inserted for the executors, for instance as follows:
> '. . . declaring that this legacy shall be paid 3 months after my death if
> my executors are satisfied that my estate is sufficient to meet it after
> providing for all debts and expenses.'

It has to be said that such a declaration is unlikely to provide complete protection
for the executors if the estate turns out to be insufficient. However, in a clearly
solvent estate, this will facilitate early distribution.

If, on the other hand, satisfaction is to be postponed for a long period after the
death, consideration should be given to making a declaration as to vesting. The
normal clause mentioned above will not postpone vesting[3]. It is thought that
generally any simple delayed satisfaction will be equally ineffectual to suspend
vesting. However, if there is a long postponement until satisfaction is due to take
place, it may well be advisable to add a declaration that vesting is to occur at
death, to avoid any doubts on this matter.

---

1 *Cunningham's Trustees v Duke* (1873) 11 M 543.
2 *Stair v Stair's Trustees* (1826) 2 W & S 614; *Howat's Trustees v Howat* (1869) 8 M 337; *Stewart's Trustees v Evans* (1871) 9 M 813; *Taylor and Ferguson v Glass's Trustees* 1912 SC 165; *McLaren* II, paras 2157–2168.
3 *Henderson's Trustees v Henderson* (1876) 3 R 320.

If it is intended to delay vesting until satisfaction of a legacy, consideration will require to be given to such matters as destinations-over in the event that the legacy does not vest and what is to happen to the legacy until it does so vest.

4.21   There may be questions as to the form in which legacies are to be satisfied. If one is dealing with a specific legacy of a particular asset, this will effectively determine what the legatee is to receive. It is thought that it is not open to the executors to substitute some other asset, even with the consent of the specific legatee, as this will affect the remainder of the estate. If therefore the specific legatee is to be able to choose to take something different, this must be provided for by the testator:

'I direct my executors to make over to A my antique bedside table, or if A so chooses by intimation in writing to my executors within 6 months of my death, to pay to A the sum of ONE THOUSAND POUNDS instead, in which case my antique bedside table should be dealt with as part of the residue of my estate [OR shall be dealt with as part of my articles of domestic use, as provided for in purpose (NINE) (2) below].'

It will be noted that it is of course necessary to deal with what is to happen to the asset if the legatee exercises the option to take something else instead.

If the testator wishes to leave a pecuniary legacy to a beneficiary, but to provide for the possibility of that beneficiary taking assets from the estate instead, this can create more difficulties, although it is quite a common type of provision. Both the long and short form of powers given to executors and trustees (see Chapter 7) provide that property may be transferred to beneficiaries without realisation; and also for appropriation of assets to beneficiaries. However, these powers are probably insufficient to allow a pecuniary legacy to be converted into a legacy of assets, again at least without the consent of all other beneficiaries who could be adversely affected by such a course. This possibility is, however, dealt with by a power relating to 'settlement' with beneficiaries – see further below.

4.22   Special provisions may thus be necessary if a general power is not included or is insufficient. These can take a number of forms. Most simply, a choice can be given to the affected beneficiary:

'I direct my executors to pay to A the sum of ONE THOUSAND POUNDS, or, if he so chooses by intimation in writing to my executors within 6 months of my death, to make over to A my antique bedside table, in which case the sum of ONE THOUSAND POUNDS shall be dealt with as part of the residue of my estate.'

Alternatively, a more general power of choice could be given, either to the beneficiary or to the executors:

'I direct my executors to pay to A the sum of ONE THOUSAND POUNDS, declaring that this legacy may, if he so chooses by intimation in writing to my executors within 6 months of my death [OR if my executors in their sole discretion so decide], be satisfied by the transfer to A of assets to the value of ONE THOUSAND POUNDS from my

estate, such assets to be valued as at the date of my death and chosen
by A [OR chosen by my executors].'

It should be noted that this provision can be mixed – the decision to implement
the legacy by the transfer of assets could be left to the beneficiary, but the assets
could then be chosen by the executors, or vice versa. It may be appropriate that
the valuation should be made as at the date of death, as the one fixed point in time
available, otherwise there may be unnecessary delays and complications. However, it would of course be possible for the assets to have risen in value between
the date of death and the date at which the choice is to be exercised, which may
have an undue influence on the decision. It would be possible for the valuation to
be made as at the date of intended transfer, in which case the beneficiary would
simply receive assets of the appropriate value at that date, eliminating any
advantage or disadvantage from movements in value since death.

Such choices as to the method of satisfying particular legacies are not perhaps
to be encouraged. However, a further alternative is to provide a specific power to
satisfy any legacies by the transfer of any assets to any beneficiary. Such a power
can be found in the long form of powers given to trustees under the heading
'Settlement' (see, for instance, S5.12(13) and para 7.17). This power can be
imported into any will, even where the remainder of the full trust powers are
considered unnecessary.

4.23   With regard to residuary legacies, there is less need to make any special
provision as to their satisfaction. The general duty of executors is to realise assets
before distribution; but the general power given to transfer without realisation
will provide sufficient flexibility for most situations.

However, the testator may wish to leave the discretion in the form in which
residuary legacies are to be satisfied to the beneficiaries rather than to the
executors. In this case, special provision must be made for the residuary beneficiaries to exercise such a choice:

'. . . declaring that my residuary beneficiaries may require by
instruction in writing to my executors within 6 months of my death
that my executors shall make over the free residue of my estate by
transfer to them without realisation of the assets, or any of the assets,
in my estate at the date of my death.'

It is likely that the testator will only be concerned to provide this sort of choice
for a limited number of assets within his estate, in which case a series of specific
legacies of such assets may well be more appropriate.

INSTRUCTIONS TO REALISE PARTS OF ESTATE

4.24   In general, the duty of executors appointed under a will is to realise the
testator's estate before distributing it in terms of the will. (There is an obvious
exception to this general rule about realisation in relation to legacies of specific
items.) It is thus unnecessary to include a specific direction to sell parts of the
estate in order to pay legacies.

In fact, both the basic and the full form of executors' and trustees' powers which form part of the Styles include specific permission to realise estate (see paras 7.02–7.04). This permission is not the same as a direction or instruction to the executors to sell. There is no reason why such a direction should not be included, but it will not generally be appropriate or necessary.

However, it may be that the testator specifically wishes a particular item or investment to be sold, with the proceeds to go to a particular beneficiary. There may be a number of reasons for this – for instance, the testator may know that cash rather than an asset would be particularly welcome to that beneficiary; or the testator may be reluctant to leave a direct cash legacy of any size if he fears that he may be in possession of insufficient cash assets at the date of death; or it may be that there are difficulties envisaged in transferring or transporting a particular type of asset; or the testator may simply wish a particular beneficiary to have the value of an asset which he has earmarked as the appropriate benefit for that legatee from his estate, even though that value may vary considerably between the date of the will and the date of death. In any event, there is no difficulty in framing such a legacy. An example might be:

'I direct my executors to sell my antique bedside table and to make
over the net sale proceeds after deduction of all expenses and taxes
resulting from the sale to A.'

It is important to specify whether the sale proceeds to be transferred are net or gross. Provision has also been added to cover any tax resulting from the sale as opposed to tax which may be payable as a result of the death, which would generally not form a deduction from the value of such a legacy. This issue is particularly important, as there may be an apparent conflict between this type of legacy and a general provision on expenses contained elsewhere in the will (see, for example, S2.5).

If the testator wishes the beneficiary to receive the *gross* proceeds, this should simply be stated. In such a case, any expenses will be treated in the same way as other administration expenses and tax will be borne from residue if necessary.

An instruction to sell may also be relevant in relation to the doctrine of conversion, although this is less important than in former times. An expressed direction to sell heritage will certainly convert it into moveables but only for certain limited purposes. Conversion will also occur if the exercise of a power to sell is necessary to carry out the terms of a trust[1].

It is perhaps more likely that a testator would wish to achieve conversion in the opposite direction, so as to convert moveables into heritage and prevent legal rights claims on a part of his estate. A direction to sell any particular asset will not achieve the desired result, as the cash proceeds will of course still be moveable. The answer may appear to be to couple a direction to sell or realise moveable assets with an instruction to the executors to invest the proceeds in heritage[2]. This will not achieve the desired result, as conversion in this sense does not affect claims to legal rights in the *deceased's* estate, although it would affect such rights in the estate of his beneficiaries.

---

1 *Buchanan v Angus* (1862) 4 Macq 374.
2 See *McLaren* I, paras 430–432 and 450–452 and authorities there cited; para 6.32 below.

OPTIONS TO PURCHASE ASSETS

4.25 There are various reasons why a testator might wish to provide a beneficiary with an option to purchase a particular asset, rather than to give an outright legacy of it (or indeed of some other part of the estate). Perhaps most commonly, an option will be offered to prevent too substantial a proportion of the estate going to a single beneficiary, leaving insufficient for the remainder of the testator's intended legatees. Another situation where such matters are relevant is in relation to businesses in which the testator is involved, and this is dealt with in paragraphs 4.106–4.107 below.

There are a number of decisions to be made when considering the provision of an option. Most relate to the price at which the asset is to be offered, which may either be the full market value or some discounted amount. Particularly in the latter case, a decision will be required as to when the asset is to be valued and whether the price is to be expressed by reference to a stated sum or by some kind of formula. Possibly large changes of value between the date at which the will is executed and the date of death will require to be borne in mind.

A further decision will be required as to what is to happen if the beneficiary does not exercise the option to purchase. Presumably in most cases, if the option to purchase is at a substantial discount, the testator may still wish some form of legacy to go to the person to whom the option has been offered.

It will also be necessary to clarify exactly over what property the option is to extend; and whether the price is to be affected by, for instance, debts secured over the property in question and any expenses of transfer. However, such problems are equally relevant when dealing with outright legacies.

A suitable form of wording which covers most of these points in one way or another, would be as follows:

'I direct my executors to offer to sell my interest in Meadow Farm, Girvan, Ayrshire to A, at a price of FIFTY THOUSAND POUNDS or, (if less) at a price equal to its value as independently estimated at the date of my death [OR at a price equal to fifty per cent of its value as independently estimated at the date of my death]; declaring that (1) if he accepts this offer, the expenses of transfer shall be borne by the residue of my estate; and (2) if he declines this offer, I direct my executors to make over to A the sum of TWENTY THOUSAND POUNDS [OR a one half share in the residue of my estate].'

If provision is made for the legatee to take a share in residue on declining to take up the option, it is important to make reference to this in the residuary bequest, for instance as follows:

'I direct my executors to make over the residue of my estate (or, on A declining the offer to purchase provided in purpose (TEN), one half of the residue of my estate) to B.'

LEGACIES SUBJECT TO DEBTS

4.26 Issues concerning debts affecting particular assets arise most often when dealing with heritable property. There are also particular considerations involving debts and business or agricultural property as defined for inheritance tax. These points are dealt with specifically below (see para 4.90). However, there are a number of general points in this matter which are considered here.

The basic rule is that if the subject of a legacy is burdened by a debt, the legatee takes the legacy subject to that debt, unless express provision is made in the will. While this will usually be relevant to debt secured on heritage, it can apply to other assets such as insurance policies[1].

It is also possible that household items may be, effectively, subject to debts. There can be complex issues here, as items 'bought' on hire purchase are not owned by the testator at all, while other items may have been bought with the assistance of a specific loan. This is particularly relevant to cars. It is, however, unlikely that any loan involved where the testator actually purchases an asset will be considered as a burden on that asset in the same way as applies when a loan to purchase heritage is secured by a standard security.

4.27 In order to pass on a legacy free from any debts, the intention that it should pass unencumbered must be clear from the express terms of the will – or, at the very least, there must be clear implications from the wording[2]. Certainly as regards heritage, a mere instruction to the executor to pay all debts does not discharge specific assets from any debts which may encumber them. Such a direction merely covers what the law would imply in any event. For this reason, such a direction is omitted from the Styles presented. In particular, such a direction would not control the *incidence* of debts – that is, the parts of the estate from which debts are to be met[3]. This rule has however been doubted in the case of legacies of moveables[4].

If debts do not relate to specific assets, the general rule is that they are borne by residue, presuming that residue is sufficient to meet them. Heritable debts are primarily due from heritage and moveable ones from moveables, where this is relevant[5].

However, all such general rules will yield to specific instructions in the will. There are two main possibilities – a debt affecting a particular asset may be required to be discharged from residue; or a debt otherwise chargeable on residue may be required to be discharged from a specific asset.

The first type of requirement would be achieved simply by adding the phrase 'free of debts' to the subject of the legacy. Alternatively, a declaration could be added:

---

1 *Stewart v Stewart* (1891) 19 R 310; *Brand v Scott's Trustees* (1892) 19 R 768; *Adam's Trustees v Wilson* (1899) 1 F 1042.
2 *Muir's Trustees v Muir* 1916 1 SLT 372.
3 *Gordon v Scott* (1873) 11 M 344; *Forbes's Trustees v Forbes* 1926 SLT 135.
4 *Reid's Trustees v Dawson* 1915 SC (HL) 47 at 50.
5 *McLaren* II, paras 2461–2477.

'. . . declaring that all debts affecting this legacy shall be paid from the residue of my estate.'

The second type of requirement can be met by a specific direction that a particular burden has to be discharged from the subject of the legacy[1]. Suitable wording for this type of situation would be as follows:

'I direct my executors to pay to A the sum of TEN THOUSAND POUNDS, subject to deduction from this sum of any amount which I may owe to B at the date of my death.

If the legacy in question is of a specific asset rather than a sum of money, suitable wording would be:

'I direct my executors to make over to A my interest in Meadow Farm, Girvan, Ayrshire, on condition that A pays all debts of mine outstanding at the date of my death.'

This type of provision may be desirable where the beneficiary in question is to receive a single asset which constitutes the bulk of the testator's estate, but the testator does not wish that beneficiary to be required to pay money into the estate directly. However, the testator may wish to ensure that the remainder of his estate which is going elsewhere is not further diminished by any debts which may be outstanding.

LIFETIME ADVANCES AND COLLATION

Lifetime advances

4.28 A testator may have made unequal lifetime gifts, most usually to his children, and may wish such gifts to be reflected in the eventual division of his estate in the interest of fairness between such children. If nothing is said in the will, then such advances would not be brought into account. Advances are brought into account (or collated) where a number of beneficiaries claim legal rights (collation *inter liberos*), but this rule has no direct effect on testamentary succession. However, testators may well wish a similar type of collation to occur in relation to lifetime gifts as they affect testamentary bequests.

Generally, it would not seem sensible to collate in relation to ordinary birthday or Christmas gifts and the like, so some means of defining the gifts to be collated must be found. This can be done by reference to gifts over an arbitrary value, for example £1,000; or it could be done by reference generally to gifts but excluding lesser ones defined in some other way; for instance, by requiring the testator to have obtained a receipt or have left some other form of written record.

It may be important to mention some timescale within which relevant gifts would require to have been made in order to be brought into account. While there may be relatively few advances, it is entirely possible that advances may have been made years or decades prior to the death. One solution to this would be to have the will record any gifts which have been made at the date of the will, and then require both these and future gifts to be taken into account.

1 *Fergus v Fergus* (1833) 11 S 362.

4.29 It is very important to be clear about the definition of gift, because in practical terms it can be very difficult to establish whether and to what extent a gift has taken place. This problem has been compounded because there is now no need to make a direct report of large gifts to the Inland Revenue since the introduction of potentially exempt transfers for inheritance tax[1]. Because of such problems of identifying relevant gifts, it may be helpful to give executors the final say in determining the matter.

Loans made by the testator to a beneficiary do not have to be brought into account. Such loans will be assets of the estate in any event. Rather than realise any outstanding loan made to a beneficiary, the executors could simply write it off and treat that as payment on account to that beneficiary.

There may be problems in relation to the identity of the donee. If for example a gift is made to a child of the testator who then predeceases him, that child's issue may take any testamentary bequest in place of the deceased child. The question is then whether the value of the lifetime gift to the predeceasing *child* is to be taken into account in the share passing to that child's issue. There can be no single right answer to this type of question. It is suggested that in principle the matter should be kept as simple as possible.

4.30 Advances may be taken into account in a number of ways. The simplest is to take the value of the advance as at the date of the lifetime gift. When inflation is high, this may seem unfair, and it thus may be desired to introduce some form of indexation. This can be done by reference to the retail prices index or to some arbitrary percentage figure which may be simpler to operate in practice. An example of the latter form of provision might be as follows:

> 'Considering that I have made an advance of FIVE THOUSAND POUNDS to my daughter A and that I wish to equalise the position as between my children so far as practicable, I direct my executors to pay to my son B a legacy amounting to the sum of FIVE THOUSAND POUNDS, increased by five per cent simple interest for each complete year which may have elapsed since the date of this will until the date of my death.'

If the advance has been made at some time earlier than the drafting of the will reference could be made to its date, with the 5 per cent increase running from that date rather than the date of the will.

There are a number of drafting alternatives for taking advances into account. There could be a direction to executors or trustees to take a particular sum into account in calculating an equal division of the residue. Alternatively, there could be pecuniary legacies to the beneficiaries who have not received advances, perhaps with a narrative setting out the reason for such bequests, as in the wording just mentioned.

If it is possible that further gifts may be made after the will has been drafted, it may be as well to record any gifts made to date, or alternatively merely to record

1 Inheritance Tax Act 1984, s 3A.

any imbalance between various beneficiaries at the date of the will, and then go on to provide that future advances are to be taken into account. This might be done as an addition to the residue, but it is suggested that it is preferable to treat it as a separate purpose, in an attempt to make what may be a complex situation rather more intelligible.

4.31   Purpose S4.5 is an example of a full clause directing that advances are to be taken into account. It purports to cover all advances made. It charges advances against shares due to the recipient or to his issue. It provides that executors are to decide on what is required in these calculations. Advances are taken into account at face value, with no adjustment for inflation or changes in the value of assets. If such an adjustment were required, this could be achieved by substituting for the words 'deduct such advances' the phrase 'deduct a sum amounting to the total of such advances, each such advance to be increased by the percentage change in the retail prices index between the date of the advance and the date of my death'.

S4.5 does not contain a record of any advances which may have been made. If required, this could readily be achieved by an addition at the end of the purpose, as follows:

> '. . . and I record that as at the date of this will I have made gifts to my daughter A of FIVE THOUSAND POUNDS and to my son B of THREE THOUSAND POUNDS.'

The purpose as presented does not define what advances are to be included. In practice, it leaves it for the executors to ignore trivial gifts as they think appropriate. Such a wide discretion to the executors may be considered undesirable, and can be restricted to any particular matters which may be considered open to doubt. As suggested above, an alternative is for provision to be made to ignore advances below a certain limit.

Although clauses requiring collation of lifetime advances are most likely to be relevant when dealing with residuary legatees, consideration of advances may also be required when dealing with pecuniary or specific legacies. In such cases, advances made after the date of the will are more likely to brought into account, as earlier advances can be dealt with by restricting the size of legacies to be included in the will now being drafted. In such circumstances, suitable wording would be as follows:

> 'I direct my executors to make over to A my interest in Meadow Farm, Girvan, Ayrshire, on condition that A pays to my estate the amount of any advances made by me to A after the date of this will, if such advances are recorded as such in writing by me.'

Collation and legal rights

4.32   Questions relating to the need to bring into account lifetime advances perhaps arise most often when dealing with legal rights claims. A legal rights claimant will forfeit any testamentary provision in his favour. In some respects, there is little that can or should be done about the possibility of legal rights claims when drafting a will, although specific legacies of amounts equivalent to legal rights (see paras 4.41–4.42) or directing forfeiture in such circumstances (see paras 5.56–5.58) may be contemplated.

However, a testator may consider the possibility of a legal rights claim being made by a beneficiary who may be quite happy to forfeit any testamentary provision, perhaps specifically *because* that claimant has already received substantial lifetime advances. While collation of such advances can proceed without reference to anything in a will, there are potential problems. Notably, it can be difficult to decide what particular advances require to be brought into account when collation is required. This depends on the nature of the advance and the circumstances in which it was made. For example, a commercial transaction or payment for the maintenance of a child do not require to be collated, but a gift to assist in setting up a business or in purchasing a house may require such treatment. An expression of the donor's intentions will not be conclusive in deciding this matter, but it will undoubtedly be important evidence, in a situation where the onus is on the person asserting that collation should take place to prove that a particular advance is to be brought into account. In these circumstances the donor/testator's views could be expressed in a declaration:

'I declare that I have advanced to my son A the sum of TEN THOUSAND POUNDS on 1 May 1993 to assist him in purchasing a house and that if A claims legal rights in my estate, this sum is to be collated with the amount of estate available to meet legal rights claims and deducted from the amount otherwise due to A.'

This type of declaration can be combined with other provisions on advances which could be used where testamentary provisions are also made for beneficiaries in receipt of such advances.

Given that collation will only apply in appropriate circumstances in any event, such a declaration may not be vital. However, it is also possible for the testator to assist in rebutting other evidence which might exist in favour of collation, if it is his intention that advances should not be collated[1]. This result could also be achieved by a declaration:

'I declare that I have advanced to my son A the sum of TEN THOUSAND POUNDS on 1 May 1993 to assist him in purchasing a house and if A claims legal rights in my estate, this sum is not to be collated with the amount available to meet legal rights claims but is in addition to any amount due to A on such a claim being made.'

4.33 It should be noted that collation can only arise where there is more than one claimant to the same type of legal rights[2]. Collation cannot be demanded by executors if only one child claims *legitim*, nor by a spouse where children claim legal rights, nor by children in relation to a spouse's claim, nor by any testamentary beneficiary in relation to any legal rights claim. It can thus be seen that there is a limited amount which a testator can do to ensure fairness as between

1 See *Meston* p 62.
2 *Coats' Trustees v Coats* 1914 SC 744.

different potential legal rights claimants, especially where he has made lifetime advances or where he desires a substantial part of his estate to go to other types of beneficiary entirely. The possible problems should be considered when making lifetime gifts. When drafting the will, some restorative action may still be possible, by making unequal divisions between children and providing for advances to be taken into account, as well as by making some provisions which may assist in ensuring that legal rights claims are not made.

PECUNIARY LEGACIES

4.34 Purpose S2.6 contains three pecuniary legacies. Pecuniary legacies are probably the most common type of legacy other than residuary legacies and they can cover a wide range of possibilities. Notably, they can extend from mere tokens to those only tenuously connected with the testator, up to substantial proportions of the total net estate available, perhaps going to close relatives. Pecuniary legacies may also be a vital aid to tax planning. All types of pecuniary legacies can be included within a single purpose, but if they cover a wide range of amounts and are for rather different purposes, it may be preferable at least to separate major bequests from token amounts.

The form of pecuniary legacy used in the Styles describes the amount in words only. This is deliberate, although others may prefer a combination of figures and words:

'I direct my executors to pay to A the sum of £1,000 (ONE THOUSAND POUNDS).'

While such a format may be thought confirmatory of the amount bequeathed, it does add the possibility of an inconsistency between the two forms of the stated amount. In any event, the use of figures alone is not to be encouraged, as the possibility of omitting or adding a zero should not be underestimated.

4.35 The form of pecuniary legacy used is of course in sterling. There will be nothing to prevent a legacy in a Scottish will being expressed in a foreign currency. This might be desired, for instance, where either the testator or the intended beneficiary had a close connection with another country. There are possible, and perhaps obvious, problems.

Probably the best way to provide for such a legacy is for the testator to have an account in the currency in which the desired legacy is to be expressed. Under this arrangement the legacy would be a demonstrative one, with the problems inherent in such legacies, for instance if the source does not exist at the date of death (see para 4.05 above).

If the testator does not have such a source of foreign funds available, the key point is to provide for the date at which the equivalent amount in sterling is to be computed. The date of the testator's death is perhaps the most obvious solution:

'I direct my executors to pay to A the sum of TEN THOUSAND FRENCH FRANCS, the amount in sterling required to pay this legacy to be calculated at the date of my death.'

A testator should be warned about the possibility of extreme fluctuations in exchange rates, perhaps particularly where the foreign currency is from a country outwith Europe. Such rates may fluctuate between the date of the will and the date of death, or between the date of death and the date of eventual payment.

The name of the country to which the foreign currency relates should always be included in such a legacy – for example, more than one country uses francs, and even large countries have been known to change the name of their currency from time to time.

Enthusiastic Europeans may wish to consider legacies being made in ECUs. Perhaps by the date of death it will not be necessary to provide for the calculation of an exchange rate from sterling if such a legacy is left.

4.36 The testator may wish to leave a pecuniary legacy for a specific purpose. This has been at least partially dealt with under the heading '*Legatum rei alienae*' (see para 4.18 above). However, it should be stressed that a simple legacy of money, coupled with an instruction or wish that the legatee purchases an asset (for example, a house), will not generally achieve the testator's aims. If the legacy vests in the beneficiary, the condition may be unenforceable practically; at best there would be little to prevent the legatee disposing of the desired asset shortly after purchase, if such purchase is carried out. The only effective method of enforcing the testator's desires that a beneficiary should come into possession of a certain asset is to put either the cash to purchase that asset or the asset once it has been purchased into an appropriate form of trust.

4.37 Even if a pecuniary legacy is in sterling, the legatee may of course be resident outwith the United Kingdom. As the general provision on the payment of legacies (see, for example, S2.5) requires payment to be made free of delivery expenses, such a legatee will expect payment in the country in which he is resident. While executors may simply send a sterling cheque, the beneficiary might expect some other form of transfer, such as bank draft or electronic credit. It should be borne in mind that such means of transfer can be extremely expensive. The result may be a disgruntled legatee if expenses are deducted from his legacy (and he may also have a limited argument that even quite substantial expenses should *not* be deducted); or disgruntled residuary beneficiaries if substantial expenses are indeed paid from residue.

The testator cannot solve all possible problems in this area, but he can prevent confusion. If expenses of, say, electronic transfer and perhaps deductions for currency exchange are to be borne by residue, the legacy should be specifically stated to be 'free of' such expenses. If, alternatively, such extraordinary expenses are to come of the legacy, the amount should be stated to be 'under deduction of' such expenses. Perhaps ironically, decisions on this matter are particularly vital with small legacies because of the disproportionate effect of fixed minimum charges for such services.

LEGACY OF THE INHERITANCE TAX NIL RATE BAND

4.38 If a testator wishes to take full advantage of the nil rate band for inheritance tax purposes, while leaving the bulk of his estate to his spouse, he may wish to consider leaving a legacy of specifically that amount to other beneficiaries. Style S10 contains provision for a nil rate band discretionary trust, and some of the matters relevant to a simple legacy of the nil rate band are dealt with in discussion of that Style (see paras 5.96–5.107).

The question of the amount to be included in the nil rate band legacy is a very important one. The simplest method of dealing with this would be to provide for a pecuniary legacy stating the amount of the nil rate band applicable at the time of drafting the will using the appropriate figure at that time.

However, the amount of the nil rate band has changed on numerous occasions. Provision is made by legislation for the nil rate band to increase in line with inflation, unless Parliament otherwise directs[1]. However, it has been increased by a greater amount in many years and conversely it has been frozen at £150,000 for both 1993–94 and 1994–95. A legacy of the amount of the nil rate band 'from time to time' could largely cope with such changes.

If, however, lifetime gifts have been made within seven years of the death, then those would be caught for inheritance tax purposes, so the amount to include within such a legacy has to be reduced by such gifts if actual payment of tax is to be avoided on the testator's death. Similarly, legacies other than to exempt beneficiaries (spouses, charities, etc) must be deducted. If children decide to claim their legal rights rather than renounce and hence benefit their surviving parent, then the amount of legal rights claims also has to be deducted from the amount to be put into a nil rate band trust. A further possible deduction is in relation to trusts in which the testator may have an interest in possession, which would require to be aggregated with his personal estate. Finally, the testator may have made gifts with a reservation of benefit, the value of which might require to be included with his estate, even though he no longer owns the property subject to the reservation.

Taking account of all of these items produces a legacy as follows (the wording being very similar to that used in purpose S10.5 of the nil rate band discretionary trust):

'I direct my executors to pay (or make over) to A a sum (or property to such value) as will exhaust the nil rate band of inheritance tax as set out in Schedule 1 to the Inheritance Tax 1984 or any similar statutory successor, after taking into account (1) lifetime gifts made by me which are for inheritance tax purposes aggregable with or deemed to be part of my executry estate, (2) legacies other than those exempt from inheritance tax, (3) funds in trusts which are aggregable for inheritance tax purposes with my executry estate other than those exempt from inheritance tax and (4) any claims to legitim except

---

1 Inheritance Tax Act 1984, s 8.

claims discharged without consideration after my death, as to all of
which my executors shall be the sole judges.'
A shorter form of wording could be used, for example:
'. . . the largest sum (or property to the maximum value) such that no
inheritance tax (or similar statutory successor) will be payable as a
result of my death, as to all of which my executors shall be the sole
judges.'

4.39   The reference to inheritance tax payable *as a result* of death brings in the
possibility of tax arising on transfers outwith the testator's personal estate on
death, such as lifetime gifts, trust property or gifts with reservation. However,
the merit of the longer clause narrated above is that it specifically draws attention
to the items which are likely to affect the size of the nil rate band legacy. While
the list included is not comprehensive, the possible situation may be clearer than
would be the case with a shorter form of legacy.
   There is a particular danger that such a clause may take in too much of an
estate where a substantial proportion attracts agricultural or business property
relief. This may be acceptable to the testator, but if not, an exclusion could be
added. The longer clause narrated above could be adapted by adding after the
words 'similar statutory successor':
'. . . but excluding any business property or agricultural property,
the value of which is reduced for the purposes of calculating the
amount of the transfer of value deemed to occur on my death . . .'
A similar exclusion could be added to the shorter form of clause mentioned
above. Any more general wording as to the types of relief which reduce a transfer
of value may bring unexpected and complex consequences, for instance involving the relief for the sale of quoted shares at a loss within 12 months of death[1].

4.40   Even with restrictions included, changes in inheritance tax or very large
increases in the nil rate band could have the consequence that the entire estate, or
virtually all of it, is exhausted by a nil rate band legacy. In such circumstances,
once more the obvious answer is for the testator to change his will, but it is also
possible to limit the amount of a nil rate band legacy to cope with possible
developments. This can be done either by reference to a maximum figure in
monetary terms, or alternatively by reference to a proportion of the testator's
estate at death.
   Suitable wording (to be inserted towards the end of a nil rate band legacy
before the executors are given discretion as to what the legacy includes) would be
as follows:
'. . . but declaring that the maximum amount or value to be included
in this legacy shall not exceed TWO HUNDRED AND FIFTY THOUSAND
POUNDS [OR . . . . shall not exceed one half of the value of the estate

---

1 Inheritance Tax Act 1984, s 129.

actually owned by me at the date of my death, after deducting from
that estate any debts outstanding at the date of my death.'
The reference to estate actually owned by the testator is designed to exclude trust
estate or that only brought into account because of the rules on reservation of
benefit. It should not now be necessary to provide for the deduction of tax when
valuing the testator's estate for this purpose, as the presumed intention of any
form of nil rate band legacy is that no tax should be payable on the death. This
may not always be the case, but as the intention of this declaration is merely to
limit the size of this legacy, it may make no difference if tax is in fact payable for
any reason.

If it is considered significant, the deduction of debts could be extended to
include 'any tax payable from my estate as a result of my death.'

LEGACY OF LEGAL RIGHTS

4.41 It is possible to provide for a legacy equal in amount to any potential legal
rights claim[1]. Of course, such a legacy does not add anything to what the law
allows in any event; but it does serve to focus the testator's mind on the possible
situation which may arise at his death. Such a legacy can also be used as part of a
will where the testator wishes to make provision for a potential legal rights
claimant *beyond* what could be claimed as legal rights. This might be the case
where the testator wishes to leave heritable property to a beneficiary, but to
ensure that such a legacy is not rejected in favour of what might be available by
means of a legal rights claim. Such a legacy might also be desirable where a
testator wishes to avoid the apparent conflicts which would arise if beneficiaries
would otherwise be put to making an election between testamentary provisions
and legal rights claims. In any event, if such a legacy is considered desirable for
any reason, suitable wording would be:

'I direct my executors to pay to my son A [OR to such of my children
A, B and C and any other children of mine as shall survive me equally
among them if more than one] [OR to my wife D] an amount equal
to the value of any legal rights (or any replacement therefor, as to
which my executors shall be the sole judges) which A [or my children]
[OR D] may have in my estate on my death or which A [OR my
children] would have had if he [OR they] had survived me declaring
that

(1) should A [OR any of my children] predecease me leaving issue
(including adopted issue) who shall survive me, each member of
a generation of issue of such predeceasing child shall share

---

1 *Galt's Trustees v Galt* 1945 SC 183.

equally in the part of this legacy, both original and accresced,
which would have fallen to its parent if in life and
(2)   this legacy is to bear its rateable proportion of any government
duties in respect of my death.'

Such a legacy is merely a complex pecuniary legacy, the amount being expressed
by reference to a formula so that it can be quantified at the date of death.

4.42   It is important in such a bequest in favour of children (or, indeed, in
favour of other issue) to provide for a destination-over. This is because the right
to legal rights itself is available to representatives of pre-deceasing children[1].

It is also important in such a legacy to ensure that it bears its own tax. In terms
of the normal provision in this matter included in the Styles (see, for example,
S2.5), legacies are 'free of government duties in respect of my death'. If this were
left unchanged in connection with a bequest of an amount equal to a legal rights
claim by children, it might be necessary in a taxable estate to gross up the amount
of the legacy. This would never be required in the case of an *actual* claim to
legitim[2]. If the legacy of an amount equal to legal rights does not bear its own tax,
it would in fact be of an amount greater than that available to an actual claimant.

AMOUNT OF LEGACY BY FORMULA

4.43   Apart from legacies of the nil rate band for inheritance tax purposes and
legacies based on the amount of possible legal rights claims, it is possible for the
testator to quantify a pecuniary legacy by reference to any formula he chooses.
As with all legacies of indefinite amounts, the key point is clarity as to exactly
what is being bequeathed by the testator. For instance, a testator may wish to
leave a legacy of a year's salary, perhaps to an employee but just conceivably
otherwise. The idea may be to quantify the scale of legacy which the testator has
in mind but to take account of the possibility of inflation or other circumstances
drastically altering the scale of a simple pecuniary legacy.

However, such a legacy can be fraught with difficulties. What if the beneficiary has been promoted, or has moved to a different type of job, or has left
employment entirely? Is the salary in question to be gross or net of tax and is it to
include any bonuses or overtime, whether normally worked or not? If a testator
insists on this type of legacy, the following wording may suffice:
'I direct my executors to pay to A if he is in the employment of XYZ
Limited at the time of my death a sum equivalent to the gross salary
which he received from his employment with XYZ Limited in the last
complete year of assessment for income tax purposes preceding my
death.'

By such wording, the legatee will get nothing if he has left the employ of XYZ
Limited by the date of death; conversely, he will receive a very large legacy if he

1 Succession (Scotland) Act 1964, s 11.
2 See the Inheritance Tax Act 1984, s 42(4).

has been promoted to a position which pays a high salary. In the latter case, it may be particularly important that the legacy is unknown to the beneficiary; and that the formula is based on a period ending prior to it being revealed. However, such a legacy may still end up eating into the testator's estate to a greater extent than intended. In such circumstances, a limit might be placed on the amount to be paid. This can be done by inserting the word 'maximum' before the word 'sum' in the wording suggested and inserting at the end a declaration, as follows:

> '. . . but declaring that the sum payable in terms of this legacy shall not exceed TWENTY THOUSAND POUNDS [OR one quarter of the gross value of my estate at the time of my death].'

4.44 There may be difficulties with such things as profit-related pay or share schemes, in which case executors could be given a discretion as to what items of 'salary' are to be taken into account. Because of the complications mentioned in relation to formulaic legacies, they may be rather more appropriate for very much smaller, token amounts. For instance, a legacy could be left of a sum sufficient to purchase a season of tickets at a particular theatre, or a subscription to a magazine or society. It should be noted that such legacies are still pecuniary – the formula merely defines the amount. An alternative would be to direct the executor to purchase the item referred to in the formula and make it over to the intended legatee.

PROVISIONS FOR TAX ON LIFETIME GIFTS

4.45 If a testator has made lifetime gifts which qualify as potentially exempt transfers for inheritance tax, his death within seven years of such gifts may trigger a charge to tax. Alternatively, extra tax may be payable on gifts which were chargeable when made. It is possible that the testator may have made gifts with reservation, the result being that if the reservation remains in force at the date of death, the subjects of such gifts are treated as remaining part of the deceased's estate for inheritance tax purposes.

In all such cases, the primary liability for any tax payable as a result of the death rests with the donee of the gift in question[1]. Accordingly, the testator may wish to make provision for such tax in his will. It should be noted that such provision for tax payable as a result of his death does *not* increase the size of the original gift. No grossing up of that gift, whether at lifetime or death rates is required. The legacy of tax payable constitutes a separate provision. Suitable wording for such a provision would be:

> 'Considering that I have made a gift to A on 21 October 1993, I direct my executors to pay to A a sum equivalent to the amount of any inheritance tax (or any replacement therefor, as to which my executors shall be the sole judges) chargeable on that gift as a result of my

---

1 See the Inheritance Tax Act 1984, ss 200, 201 and 204.

death, and I declare that this legacy is to bear its rateable proportion of any government duties in respect of my death.'

It will be noted that this legacy of potential tax is itself directed to bear its own tax. This will prevent the need to gross up the quantified amount of the legacy of the tax, which might otherwise arise. However, the testator may well be content to make such a legacy free of tax, in which case the normal clause on tax, expenses and interest will achieve this end (as with other pecuniary legacies).

This type of legacy has the added benefit of serving as a useful reminder of any significant lifetime gifts which may have been made by the testator.

INTEREST ON LEGACIES

4.46 The general provision on legacies included in most of the Styles (see, for example, S2.5) provides that unless otherwise specified, legacies are to be paid without interest. This is important, because without such a provision, interest runs from the date of death until payment unless realisation of the estate was impossible. Interest will run from a later date of payment if such a later date is specified in the will[1].

If no interest rate is specified, the rate payable will be the average earned by the estate over the appropriate period[2]. The difficulty and inconvenience of making calculations based on this rather vague rate are obvious. If therefore the testator desires interest to run on a legacy, it is much better to specify the rate of interest required. A suitable provision would be:

'I direct my executors to pay to A the sum of TEN THOUSAND POUNDS with simple interest at the rate of five per cent per annum from the date of my death until paid.'

If interest is to run on all pecuniary legacies, this type of provision could be inserted prior to a list of such legacies:

'I direct my executors to pay the following legacies, all with simple interest at the rate per annum of five per cent from the date of my death until paid.'

Such provision could also be included with reference to pecuniary legacies in the general purpose dealing with various matters:

'. . . declaring that all pecuniary legacies are to be paid with simple interest at the rate per annum of five per cent from the date of my death until paid.'

Including the interest provision within the general purpose on matters relating to legacies means that it would apply to any pecuniary legacy including those made by codicil or by informal writing.

Care should be taken with the rate of interest. If the rate specified is substan-

---

1 On all of this see *Duff's Trustees v Scripture Readers* (1862) 24 D 552; *Waddell's Trustees v Crawford* 1926 SC 654; *May's Trustees v Paul* (1900) 2 F 657.
2 See *Baird's Trustees v Duncanson* (1892) 19 R 1045; *Greig v Merchant Company of Edinburgh* 1921 SC 76; *Kearon v Thomson's Trustees* 1949 SC 287.

tially in excess of what the estate could earn, provision for interest may represent a practical increase in the size of those legacies affected. Of course, payment of much interest can be avoided if the executors make swift payment, but that may be difficult to achieve if there are problems in realising assets from the estate.

An alternative would be to provide for the rate of interest to be calculated by formula, such as 'the rate per annum of two per cent above the base rate of the Royal Bank of Scotland from time to time'.

4.47 The discussion of interest above applies to pecuniary legacies. The situation is rather different with other types of legacy. In general, without special provision, any income received on the subject of a special legacy will be due to the special legatee[1]. The exclusion of interest in the general purpose dealing with legacies might also serve to exclude other types of income. If income arising after death from the subject of a special legacy is to be paid to the legatee, specific provision should be made.

It is conceivable that a testator may wish interest to be payable on a legacy which does not itself produce any or much income. Such a provision can simply be added to a specific legacy as follows:

'. . . together with simple interest at the rate per annum of five per cent on the amount at which this legacy is valued at the date of my death from that date until this legacy is made over.'

SPECIFIC SUBJECTS OF LEGACIES

Furniture and personal effects

4.48 Purpose S2.9 consists of an outright legacy of a wide range of personal effects. Outright legacies of such items are much to be preferred to placing them in trust, due to the difficulties in making effective provision for different trust interests (such as liferent and fee) and because of wear and tear, replacement and the like. Its heading includes the word 'furniture', although that word does not occur within the specific items listed. Purpose S2.9(2) is a general provision, which it is hoped will be suitable for almost all testators. In fact, the items covered go far beyond furniture and contents of a house, the subjects of bequest being '. . . all my articles of personal, domestic, household, garage, garden or leisure use, ornament or consumption and my motor vehicles . . .'.

Although furniture is not specifically mentioned, it is clearly included within the items listed. Also included will be clothing (within articles of personal use), jewellery (in this case with the exception of the single item bequeathed in S2.9(1)) (within articles of personal use or ornament) and pictures (within articles of domestic use or ornament). It is important to include articles of consumption because there is authority that these are not included in a bequest

---

1 *Glasgow's Trustees v Glasgow* (1830) 9 S 87.

of 'furniture and personal effects'[1]. This may be particularly relevant to a substantial wine cellar, for instance.

Household, garage and garden items will include the kind of things found to some extent in most households such as tools, some electrical equipment and lawnmowers.

4.49 Perhaps the biggest departure from 'traditional' legacies of this type is the use of the term 'leisure use'. This is to some extent a reflection of modern living. It is envisaged that it would include (for instance) books and hi-fi equipment (both of which would probably be included in any event within some of the other items listed) and particularly sporting equipment. However, it is thought that the term may also include some very large items, such as camping equipment, diving equipment and even possibly items such as a yacht, glider, microlight or hot air balloon. It is, however, conceded that there may well be arguments over whether such large items were to be included in this general legacy and there is no real substitute for mentioning such things specifically if they are to be included (or, of course, dealing with them separately).

The items just mentioned illustrate very well the extreme breadth of the list used in S2.9(2). This in turn illustrates the need for the testator to consider exactly what he wishes to happen to what may be very valuable physical items within his estate. He may very well be content for the entire range to go to a single beneficiary (or group of beneficiaries). However, he may wish to consider making separate legacies. To take a very simple example, it may be wholly inappropriate to bequeath valuable golf clubs within such a general legacy to a beneficiary who is unlikely ever to play golf and who may simply sell them.

If very valuable items are to be included with more usual articles covered by the general legacies, specific reference should be made in the list of *types* of item otherwise included.

4.50 If separate legacies are made of certain items which would otherwise fall within the general legacy, it will be necessary to refer to such specific legacies in some way when dealing with the remainder in a general legacy. For instance, if specific items are bequeathed first, the general legacy can be of 'the *remainder* of my articles of personal, domestic . . . . [etc]' as per the general legacy.

However, a reference to the 'remainder' of the articles mentioned will not cope with legacies made outwith the will, by codicil or informal writing. These are quite likely with this type of item. Accordingly, if legacies of particular items are possible whether within the will or elsewhere, the general legacy can commence as follows:

> 'I direct my executors to make over to A, except as otherwise
> effectively bequeathed, all my articles of personal, domestic . . .
> [etc].'

This format also ensures that if a legacy of a specific item fails, for instance, by the predecease of the specific legatee, that item if within the general types

---

1 *Miller's Trustees v Miller* 1907 SC 833.

covered falls back into the terms of the general legacy, rather than into residue or intestacy.

It should be noted that a general legacy in the form given does not include any money or other financial assets, even if they are physically located with the other types of item listed[1].

4.51 It may be necessary or desirable to separate out the various articles into distinct legacies by category (quite apart from the possibility of distinct legacies of individual items, dealt with in paras 4.58–4.62). For instance, there might be occasions when it is appropriate to direct jewellery to a particular beneficiary who would not take the other types of article listed. Books might be left separately from other personal effects. The actual contents of a house and garden might be left to the beneficiary taking that house, with a separate bequest appropriate for other personal effects.

In many of such cases, it will be appropriate to give the executors some discretion as to what is to be included within a particular legacy, for example:

> 'I direct my executors to make over to A my jewellery, clothing, accessories and articles of personal ornament, declaring that my executors shall have sole discretion as to the items included in this legacy.'

In this example, the discretion given to the executors might be of particular use when considering such items as silver hairbrushes or cosmetics.

4.52 It should be noted that the legacy set out in S2.9(2) imposes no limitation on the location of the assets included. This means that items temporarily out of the testator's possession at the date of death, such as golf clubs left at the club house or jewellery stored in a bank, would be covered. This may be both acceptable and positively desirable to the testator concerned.

However, the legacy as expressed would also extend to the contents of any property other than a main residence owned by the testator. This may cause difficulties if such a property is left to a different legatee. The testator is likely to wish that legatee to receive the property bequeathed furnished.

There is no perfect, manageable solution to the possible problems envisaged here. The likelihood is that the testator would wish only items located at the other property to be included with the legacy of that property, with the entire remainder of personal effects, etc going under the main general legacy. The answer may be to insert an exclusion in the main legacy, after the words 'ornament or consumption':

> '. . . (other than any of such articles located at the time of my death at Arran Waves, Girvan, or any other holiday property owned by me at the time of my death) . . .'

A more restricted exclusion might be used:

> '. . . (other than articles of furniture [OR articles of domestic,

---

1 But compare *Speaker's Executor v Spicker* 1969 SLT (Notes) 7, where a bequest of a bureau and its contents carried a sum of money within it.

household or garden use, ornament or consumption] located at the time of my death at Arran Waves, Girvan or any other holiday property owned by me at the time of my death) . . .'

Such items excluded from the general legacy of personal effects could then be included with the legacy of the holiday property.

4.53   The testator may also wish to restrict a general legacy of personal effects to a maximum value. The items to go towards making up that value can be determined by the choice of the executors or, more usually, by the beneficiary or beneficiaries.

4.54   It may also be important to check that all significant items are actually owned by the testator (and not leased, borrowed or subject to a hire purchase contract). If any debts affecting specific items are to be paid out of residue, this should be clearly expressed (see paras 4.26–4.27). It is particularly important that if items not owned are to be purchased and made over to beneficiaries, clear instructions are given on this course of action (see para 4.18).

4.55   Purpose S2.9(1) envisages a beneficiary choosing an item of jewellery from the testator's estate. Six months from the date of death have been allowed for the beneficiary to choose. A maximum value could be put upon the item to be chosen.

   Such a choice could also be given from a large number of categories of article within an estate, for example, paintings, pieces of furniture, ornaments or books.

   Purpose S2.9(2) (the general legacy of personal effects) envisages a division between two beneficiaries. They are given an element of choice, but only if they can agree as to how the various items are to be divided. If they cannot agree, the final decision as to distribution lies with the executors, who are to ensure an 'approximately equal and fair' division. This gives sufficient flexibility to allow a practical distribution to take place.

   It is also possible to give rather more discretion to the executors. This should, however, not be complete, as a totally discretionary legacy may be open to challenge as an attempt to have someone other than the testator make his will for him. A suitably wide form of discretion would be:

   'I direct my executors to make over to such members of my family as
   they in their sole discretion may decide all my articles of personal,
   domestic, garage, garden or leisure use, ornament, or consumption
   and my motor vehicles.'

If such a wide discretion is given, there are potential problems. Notably, family members should perhaps not be included among the executors, even if provisions are inserted to prevent executors from infringing the rules against acting as *auctor in rem suam* (see, for example, S5.12(14) and paras 7.18–7.19). But even if an executor is independent, such a wide discretion may give him distinctly unwanted responsibilities. Family disputes over personal items can be notoriously bitter. It is preferable that the testator accepts the responsibility of division or passes the element of choice to beneficiaries rather than executors.

4.56   It is thus more likely that the testator will wish to give the power of choice
to his beneficiaries where more than one is involved in such a legacy. Choice is
unlikely to be appropriate for all the types of item listed in S2.9(2), but such a
selective provision may be exactly what is required when there are a number of
individuals to share, for instance, furniture. A suitable clause would be as
follows:

'I direct my executors to make over to such of my sisters A, B, and C
as shall survive me all items of furniture in my main residence at the
time of my death, to be divided by allowing each sister to choose one
item or set of items of furniture in turn, until all of the furniture has
been chosen, the order of choice to be determined by the age of the
sisters who shall survive me with the oldest to choose first, the second
oldest to choose next and so on, declaring that my executors shall in
their sole discretion determine what is included within this legacy and
what constitutes a 'set of items of furniture'.'

In this legacy, the order of choice is determined by the age of the various
beneficiaries to take, but that could as easily be left to chance. This could be
achieved by the following phrase:

'. . . the order of choice to be determined by the drawing of lots . . .'

4.57   It is possible that the testator may wish to try to ensure an equal division
by value among the beneficiaries to take, although this may not be required if
they have been allowed freedom of choice from the items bequeathed. If such
equality is to be pursued, a further declaration could be added:

'. . . declaring that my executors are to ensure approximately equal
division by value among my sisters by paying such sums in cash as are
required to any of them in addition to their share of furniture.'

This type of legacy, allowing distribution by selections to be made by beneficiaries, can be adapted to cover any of the categories of physical items which may be
owned by the testator. Examples include jewellery, paintings and other pictures,
wine, antiques and perhaps any collection of value. If a collection (formal or
informal) is involved in any such bequest (or indeed in any bequest to more than
one beneficiary), the testator should be reminded that any kind of division
between beneficiaries will involve breaking it up. He may thus prefer to leave a
collection separately to a single individual.

Specific physical items

4.58   If a testator wishes to leave specific physical items to a number of
beneficiaries, this can readily be done. Such bequests can be expressed in general
terms in a will, with perhaps an informal list made up by the testator at a later
date. Such a system has the merit of easy alteration by the testator, but there can
be difficulties in confirming the effect of informal writings. A general instruction
could take the following form:

'I direct my executors to make over to the persons indicated such
items of personal, domestic or household use, or furniture or

ornaments as I may list in a separate writing or writings to be signed and dated by me; and I direct my executors to make over to A any such items not listed and all items of garage, garden or leisure use or items of consumption and my motor vehicles, declaring that my executors may in their sole discretion determine the items included in any separate writing or writings.'

4.59 Whether legacies of separate physical items are included in a will or in separate writings, identification may be a serious problem. The testator should be reminded to add as much detail as possible, to assist the executors in this connection.

For instance, descriptions of items could be given. If jewellery or any item involving precious metal is involved, details of hallmarks, crests or other distinguishing features should be given. With antique furniture or other valuable domestic articles, a maker could be given, if this is known. Details of purchase or other method (such as inheritance) by which the testator acquired the item bequeathed might be useful. Paintings or other works of art can be differentiated by title, description, artist and date, particularly if the testator has more than one example of the artist's work. The testator could perhaps be encouraged to put (non-damaging!) stickers or labels or some other indication on certain items to confirm their identity.

The physical location of items might be thought to be of assistance, but in most cases the subjects of such legacies are capable of being moved between the date of the will and the date of death – or after the death! Care must also be taken as to whether items replaced are to be included or whether any disposal of an item will cause a legacy to be adeemed.

4.60 The general provision on all legacies included in most of the Styles (see, for example, S2.5) directs that legacies are to be made over free of delivery expenses. This should be considered carefully with legacies of single items, particularly delicate, heavy or bulky articles which may require to be transported a long distance. It may be more appropriate to make such a legacy conditional on the legatee paying for its delivery. It will be necessary to make provision for what is to happen if the legatee opts not to pay such expenses. The following wording may be appropriate:

'I direct my executors to make over to A my grandfather clock, made by James Smith and dated 1836 and situated at the date of this will in the hallway of my house at 1 Posh Avenue, but only on condition that A pays all costs of delivering the clock; and if A fails to survive or fails to agree to pay such costs within 6 months of my death, I direct my executors to make it over to B free of delivery expenses.'

The situation envisaged is that A may live far from the testator, so that delivery expenses may, like the clock, be very heavy, while B lives close at hand. An alternative would be for the clock to be sold if A fails to pay delivery costs, with the proceeds going to A.

Of course, difficulties may arise if A arranges for the clock to be uplifted and then sold instead of delivered to him! If the testator is concerned about such possibilites, he can demand that the executors make arrangements for delivery at A's expense, but there is really nothing that can be done to prevent the legatee of such a gift disposing of it as he thinks fit, if it vests indefeasibly in such a legatee.

4.61 Delivery expenses are one example of possible burdens involved in dealing with valuable physical items such as antiques or fine wine. The expenses of maintaining, securing and insuring such items may be equally significant. The testator may wish to consider additional pecuniary legacies to meet (partially or wholly) such expenses, at least for a time, if he wishes to ensure that the items are preserved within the family rather than disposed of.

It is even possible that if a distinctive, homogeneous collection of articles is involved, the testator may wish to make provision for the collection to be extended rather than merely maintained.

4.62 If valuable items are involved, inheritance tax may be an important consideration. It is worth bearing in mind the special provisions for what can loosely be termed the national heritage. The Inheritance Tax Act 1984, section 26 provides that transfers are exempt if the property transferred falls within certain categories *and* the transfer is to a body not established or conducted for profit. The relevant property includes 'a picture, print, book, manuscript, work of art or scientific collection, which in the opinion of the Treasury is of national, scientific, historic or artistic interest'[1]. Certain land, buildings and property used as a source of income for maintaining them are also included.

The exemption depends therefore not only on the identity of the legatee and the nature of the property, but also on achieving a Treasury direction to this effect. There is little that can be done specifically when drafting the will, other than ensuring that the legatee is an appropriate body. With a legacy, the matter can only be finally resolved after the testator's death and in these circumstances it may be better to consider a lifetime transfer.

Purpose S2.8 consists of a legacy of a painting which is on temporary loan to the National Gallery, London and is the subject of an undertaking in terms of the Inheritance Tax Act 1984, section 31. Such undertakings are relevant to achieving *conditional* exemption from inheritance tax, under section 30 of the Act. Once more, the type of property which can qualify includes the items mentioned above in relation to section 26 of the Act. The Treasury must designate the relevant property before it can qualify under these provisions. The difference between conditional exemption under section 30 and absolute exemption under section 26 is that the property subject to conditional exemption can remain in the ownership of individuals and families, although arrangements must be made for public access. This last requirement is being enforced more rigorously than was the case in the past.

Purpose S2.8 declares that the legacy is to bear its rateable proportion of any government duties in respect of the testator's death. That death will cause a transfer of value and the point is that the conditional exemption will not continue

---

1 Inheritance Tax Act 1984, s 26(2)(f).

unless the legatee gives fresh undertakings. It is important that executors and eventually legatees are aware of any existing conditional exemptions affecting the testator's property. However, such a legacy draws attention to the fact that with the right type of property it may be possible for items passing on the testator's death to be subject to conditional exemption for the first time, on the required action being taken by executors and legatees.

Cars, etc

4.63 'Motor vehicles' are included with the general legacy of furniture and personal effects set out in S2.9(2). This legacy will cover *any* such vehicles owned by the testator at the time of his death. It is thought that it will extend to motor-cycles, but not automatically to caravans or trailers. It will not extend to bicycles which in modern times may be extremely expensive. However, these items are likely to be included as 'articles of leisure use' in the general legacy.

The testator may wish to leave a separate legacy of motor vehicles in which case any relevant additional items may be specifically included. Suitable wording would be:

'I direct my executors to make over to A any motor vehicles, together with any caravans, trailers, or other vehicle accessories (including car maintenance tools and equipment) owned by me at the time of my death, declaring that my executors shall have sole discretion as to what is included in this legacy.'

The testator may instead wish to make an even more specific legacy of a particular car, but in such a case it is likely that problems of ademption could arise. These are dealt with in paragraphs 4.15–4.17 above.

A legacy of a particular car may be more likely when dealing with a classic or vintage model. In such a case, similar problems may arise as with any antique or work of art, including consideration of delivery expenses, storage and insurance. The testator may wish to make separate financial provision for such matters. If a testator owns more than one such car, clear identification will be required.

With a legacy of a car, it is very possible that it is not in fact owned by the testator but by his employer. In such a case it may be that the testator wishes the car to be purchased and made over to the intended beneficiary, but this should be clearly instructed (see para 4.18)[1].

4.64 The testator may be in possession of a car with a cherished or valuable number plate. The number may be significant because of its objective features, such as its age and consequent small number of letters and numbers, or because the combination makes up an apparent word or phrase, such as SUE IM or K1 LTS; or because of its personal subjective significance to the testator, perhaps because it includes his initials, with a low number; or because of a combination of these two features. In any such case, the number plate is likely to be a valuable

---

1 See also *Stark's Trustees v Stark* 1948 SC 41.

asset in its own right. It would usually be appropriate to refer to it separately in the will.

The easiest way to deal with the item is by a legacy of the car to which the number plate is attached:

'I direct my executors to make over to my son A the motor vehicle owned by me at the time of my death with the vehicle registration number ARB 1.'

This legacy should, if necessary, be excluded from any general legacy of personal effects, including motor vehicles. It is then left to the legatee to arrange a transfer to his own vehicle if he wishes. A registration number, once issued, cannot exist in limbo without the vehicle to which it is attached, although of course it can be transferred. It should, however, be noted that it is not permissible to attach a particular registration number to a vehicle older than the registration number would indicate, although the opposite is permitted.

It is possible that the testator may wish to transfer a registration number to one beneficiary, with the car to which it is attached at the date of death going elsewhere. This will, of course, be absolutely necessary if the numberplate is attached to a car not owned by the testator, which is a very common situation where the car used by the testator is in fact owned by his employer. In such a situation, special provision will require to be made for the transfer of the registration number. Suitable wording might be as follows:

'I direct my executors to make over to my son A my vehicle registration number ARB 1 either
(1) by arranging for the transfer of the number to any vehicle chosen by A, or
(2) if A so chooses, by arranging for the transfer of the number to a vehicle to be chosen and purchased by my executors at the lowest practicable price and made over to A, declaring that the expenses of transfer and (if required) purchase shall be borne by the residue of my estate.'

It would alternatively be possible simply to require the legatee to make arrangements for and bear the expense of transfer with provision for what is to happen should the legatee decline.

With a registration number which may have a family significance, the testator may require that trustees retain the number and attached vehicle until a suitably named legatee can drive! This is by no means ideal, particularly where there are no other trust purposes. The testator should be encouraged to consider other possibilities, such as transfer to the 'ideal' beneficiary's parent.

Yachts and other boats

4.65 A yacht can be a significant and expensive asset. If the testator owns one, it should at the very least be considered whether it is to be dealt with in a separate legacy, or along with other assets, whether in the residuary bequest or otherwise.

With such an expensive asset, it is particularly important to consider matters of identification and ademption. Is a legacy to extend to any replacement yacht if the one mentioned in the will is no longer owned at the date of death? How is it to be determined whether one yacht 'replaced' another? If a yacht is registered as a ship, reference to its registration number may assist in determining exactly what is intended by a particular legacy in relation to such matters.

As well as being expensive in their own right, yachts can be extremely costly to maintain. A testator may thus wish to consider, if he wishes a particular vessel to be kept within his family, including along with it a suitable pecuniary bequest.

4.66   As regards larger vessels, it is possible that a testator may own a merchant ship, or a share in one. Ships (including yachts, if they are registered) can be divided into 64 shares, which can be held separately. Almost invariably, however, merchant ships are held through the medium of a company. Care should thus be taken to distinguish between any rights as a shareholder in a company which owns a particular ship, from rights as the holder of an actual share in a ship.

One is unlikely to meet much demand for legacies of merchant vessels. However, owners of registered fishing vessels are more common, particularly in Scotland. Registration takes place under the Merchant Shipping Act 1988, section 13 and regulations made under this section.

Fishing vessels are also now capable of division into 64 shares (the number was formerly 16). Although the number of registered owners must not exceed 64 (so that a person may not be registered as owner of a fractional share of a share), up to five *joint* owners of a share may be registered and count as one person for the purposes of registration. It is not possible, however, for joint owners to deal with their interests independently of the other joint owners of their particular shares[1]. This factor should be borne in mind not only when considering the testator's rights as an owner, but also the possible eventual numbers of those taking a bequest.

While a single share out of 64 may be an unlikely bequest, ownership of a number of shares is not unusual. Owners of shares in fishing vessels may well also be in partnership with their co-owners. It may be important to check the terms of any separate agreement between such co-owners, in order to be sure of the feasibility of any testamentary intentions.

Finally, a fishing (or other) vessel, or shares in such a vessel, may be the subject of a mortgage (in this case, the technically correct term, even in Scotland). Such mortgages can be registered[2]. If the testator does have a loan secured in this way, much the same considerations apply as when dealing with a house subject to a standard security (see paras 4.78–4.80 below).

Animals

4.67   Purpose S2.10 consists of the legacy of an animal. Animals, being them-selves incapable of owning property, may not be the objects of bequests. It is meaningless, although often desired, to attempt to leave a sum of money or other

---

1 Merchant Shipping Act 1988, s 18.
2 Ibid, s 21 and Sch 3.

assets directly to an animal, however fondly the testator might regard it compared to some of his relations who would otherwise inherit.

Animals can be the subject of bequest. If they have been pets, it may well be that a testator wishes to ensure their welfare after his death. In such circumstances, the really important point should be his assessment during life of persons to whom he might wish to leave the animal, both to ascertain that person's willingness and the likelihood of the testator's wishes being fulfilled. Beyond this, it may be quite difficult to *ensure* that any animal is properly cared for after its owner's death.

Some attempt has been made to this end in purpose S2.10. The legacy is of the testator's existing dog at the time of the will, or any dog which may have replaced it (or, indeed, have been obtained in addition to Spotty). It is accompanied by a legacy of £1,000, 'provided [the legatee] accepts responsibility for its welfare for the remainder of its natural life'. It has to be confessed that this provision is less than water-tight, although it will usually serve the intended purpose of giving peace of mind to the testator.

The situation envisaged is that the executors will obtain the legatee's agreement to accepting responsibility for the animal before making payment of the legacy. The legacy is thus in effect conditional on the responsibility being accepted.

4.68 There are, however, real practical problems. If the acceptance of responsibility is indeed a condition, it is merely a suspensive one until responsibility is accepted. At that point, the dog and the legacy will vest indefeasibly in the legatee. Put brutally, having picked up the cheque and Spotty, there is nothing to stop the legatee calling in at the vet to arrange for a lethal injection for one while on his way to the bank with the other. Of course, this is not likely in most cases but testators may wish to put things on a somewhat more certain footing.

Can more be done? The condition could be made in a sense resolutive, by demanding that the legatee signs an undertaking obliging him to return the legacy in the event of the animal not being properly cared for, the judgment on this matter to be made by the executors. Again, the practical problems are obvious. The same would apply to a legacy which only vests on the death of the animal and if, in the opinion of the executors, the animal has been properly cared for during its life. Quite apart from the difficulties created for executors by such provisions, the prospect for the new owner of receiving a substantial sum on the animal's death may, in some cases, hasten that event.

It is thought that some kind of trust arrangement can achieve the desired end, again with the person to look after the animal receiving financial provision in addition to the animal itself. A liferent for the life of the animal, with the capital going *elsewhere* on the creature's death would positively encourage the liferenter to keep his charge in good health. The trustees could be given discretion to ascertain the welfare of the animal, before making payments of income, to ensure that the animal's life was not being unduly prolonged in abject misery.

Equally, a full discretionary trust, again relying on the discretion of the trustees (perhaps carefully briefed in a letter from the testator) to ascertain the welfare of the animal might be considered.

However, it is likely that a full trust for this purpose would be considered excessive, although such a trust might also be of use in connection with other testamentary intentions. This may be one case where an annuity is the most appropriate arrangement. Such an annuity could be paid to the person to look after the animal during its life, with the obvious incentive of maintained payments should Spotty prosper[1]. There is even some authority indicating that such an arrangement would be enforceable[2].

4.69 Some testators prefer, as they see it, to be accompanied into the happy hunting ground by their pets and wish to leave specific instructions as to their demise. If the testator wishes to ensure this result, a legacy could be left to an individual along with the animals, conditional on that individual arranging a swift (and presumably painless) end. Given the British public's attitude to animals, it is hard to conceive of a bequest *more* contrary to public policy, but this is thought to be in the moral rather than the technical sense of this term. Such a legacy would thus be possible, if perhaps not to be encouraged.

4.70 Other animals may of course form the subjects of bequest. It is worth a reminder that some, such as racehorses or pedigree cattle, can be extremely valuable. The latter are likely to be part of an agricultural business, but may be bequeathed separately. There is, however, a wide range of possibilities for racehorses.

The testator may conceivably operate racehorses within a business. However, they are often owned for the purposes of pleasure. A testator may only have a share in a horse; his involvement may be through a partnership or company. It is important to ascertain the exact position if the testator intends to leave a specific legacy of his interest. A general legacy might take the following form:

'I direct my executors to make over to A all of my interests in any horses at the time of my death, including interests held through the medium of a syndicate, partnership, company or otherwise.'

This bequest might be restricted to racehorses, if the testator has other equine interests. There may be a fine dividing line between, for instance, a horse kept for hunting which takes part in point-to-points and a horse whose main involvement with humans is in national hunt racing.

Finally, it should be borne in mind that the expense of upkeep of a racehorse can be extremely heavy. Very few make any kind of profit. In such circumstances the testator may wish to accompany the legacy of a horse with a fund for its upkeep. A destination-over may be appropriate, mentioning the possibility of the legatee declining to accept the bequest of a horse, so that it can be effectively disposed of by the executors.

---

1 For details of annuities, see paras 4.129–4.135, but it should be noted that it may be extremely difficult to meet the legacy by a purchased annuity based on the life of an animal.
2 See *Robson's Judicial Factor v Wilson* 1922 SLT 640; *Flockhart's Trustees v Bourlet* 1934 SN 23; and the entertaining article by Norrie 'Trusts for Animals' 1988 JLSS 386, which deals in some detail with the possibilities in this area.

Land and buildings

4.71 Any land or buildings owned by the testator are likely to be among the most valuable items within his estate. As such, it is important that a decision is made as to whether land or buildings are to form the subject of specific legacies or are merely to be dealt with as part of the residue.

If land or buildings are to be left in specific legacies, the extent of the testator's interest should be established. He might be the owner of the *dominium utile* or merely a tenant. He might have the superiority without the *dominium utile*. He might be only the proprietor of a *pro indiviso* share. Some of these possibilities are dealt with in the succeeding paragraphs in relation to specific legacies. However, as a general point, it might be considered appropriate that any legacy should be of the testator's 'interest' in any particular piece of land, without further definition. This would simply cover whatever rights the testator may have at the time of his death.

Probably, a more exact specification is desirable. For instance, if the testator owns and wishes to bequeath only the superiority in a particular piece of land, this should be expressed as follows:

'I direct my executors to make over to A my interest as a superior in Grange Lane, Edinburgh [together with any feu duty outstanding at the date of, or accruing after, my death].'

The question of whether any legacy is to be subject to debts affecting the property is also dealt with below, but the existence or otherwise of such debts will require to be checked. It should also be ascertained whether any heritable property owned by the testator is subject to a special destination, which it may be possible and desirable to evacuate in the will (see purpose S2.12 and paras 2.25–2.30 above).

Particularly where separate legacies of different pieces of land (and especially different flats within a single block) are involved, it is important to check the description of the subjects left in each bequest. It is not by any means necessary to include a full conveyancing description (by reference or otherwise) in such legacies but at least a short conveyancing description should be used. If a fuller specification would assist in removing any possible doubts, this should be utilised.

4.72 The testator may wish to leave *all* land and buildings owned by him at the date of his death to a single specified legatee. This could be worded as follows:

'I direct my executors to make over to A all interests (including interests as tenant) in any land or buildings owned by me at the time of my death, free of all expenses of transfer, heritable debts and securities and other capital burdens affecting such interests at the time of my death.'

Aspects of this clause are discussed further in relation to the legacy of a house (see para 4.76). The phrase 'land and buildings' is preferable to 'heritable property' as the former is both more comprehensible to testators and more likely to be what a particular testator intends. 'Heritable property' would also include, for instance, the creditor's rights in heritable debts.

It is thought appropriate to mention the expenses of transfer; these might be encompassed in the freedom from delivery expenses included in the general clause on legacies found in most of the Styles (see, for example, S2.5), but arguably the expenses of transfer of heritable property should be distinguished from delivery expenses, the latter being more appropriate to physical items.

4.73 A testator may wish to leave a single holding of heritable property owned by him to be divided among a number of beneficiaries. This can be done by leaving the property so that it ends up in the common ownership of the intended group of beneficiaries. This type of legacy does not differ from any other where multiple beneficiaries are involved (see paras 5.02 ff).

However, the testator may wish to divide up a single holding in his ownership into separate physical areas. This might be done, for instance, with a block of flats, or with an area of land contiguous to pieces already owned by intended beneficiaries. Such a legacy is more difficult to express properly, but the following form of words might be used:

'I direct my executors to make over as to approximately one half by area to A and as to approximately the other half by area to B the piece of land known as Summer Fields, Brodick, Isle of Arran, free of all expenses of transfer, heritable debts and securities and other capital burdens affecting the land at the time of my death, declaring that my executors are to implement this legacy by disponing two separate areas of land as nearly equal in size as possible, but my executors shall have sole discretion as to the exact areas to be disponed to each legatee.'

A division between a number of beneficiaries could also be directed by reference to approximate values of different areas as the date of death.

4.74 As buildings adhere to the land on which they are built, it is not possible to leave separate legacies of land on the one hand and buildings included on the same on the other. If that is the testator's desire, it is probably best that he considers imposing a condition that a lease be granted to the person to whom he wishes to leave the building.

Such a condition may also be desirable for other reasons – for instance, a testator may wish to leave effective use of a piece of land to one beneficiary (perhaps of a younger generation than himself), but to leave ownership and an income to another.

A condition to *offer* property to be let before its conveyance to an intended beneficiary is perfectly acceptable and the intended tenant need not be a beneficiary in his own right. Indeed, a condition requiring that an offer of let be made does not necessarily imply anything other than seeking an arm's-length tenant[1]. Suitable wording to achieve this type of aim might be as follows:

'I direct my executors to make over to A the farm and lands of Grassy Mains, Dunkeld, Perthshire, including the farm house and other

---

1 *Gore-Browne Henderson's Trustees v Grenfell* 1968 SLT 237.

farm buildings, free of all expenses of transfer, heritable debts and securities and other capital burdens affecting the farm at the time of my death, but on condition that before conveying the farm to A my executors shall offer to B an agricultural tenancy of the farm (including the farm house and other farm buildings) for 5 years at full market rent and on other normal terms and conditions for an agricultural tenancy (as to all of which my executors shall be the sole judges) [OR but on condition that A shall satisfy my executors before they convey the farm to him that he has offered to B an agricultural tenancy (including the farm house and other farm buildings) for 25 years at one half of full market rent but otherwise on normal terms and conditions for an agricultural tenancy (as to all of which my executors shall be the sole judges)].'

One point which should be watched with legacies of land and buildings is the effect of including a destination-over. This would have the somewhat surprising effect of creating a substitution rather than a conditional institution, which should be avoided (see para 5.27).

Leases

4.75 If the testator has the landlord's interest in a lease, there is nothing special about a legacy of the tenanted land. The land bequeathed will simply pass subject to the terms of the lease. The testator may wish to make specific provision for the legatee to receive outstanding rents or amounts arising after the date of death.

There are more complications where the testator owns the tenant's interest under a lease. The position is (and was, even prior to the Succession (Scotland) Act 1964) that if a lease specifically prohibits assignations or bequests, a testator may not make a valid legacy of his interest. (An express prohibition on assignation will not, however, prevent an executor acting under the Succession (Scotland) Act 1964, section 16 to transfer the tenant's interest to any one person actually entitled to succeed to the deceased's intestate estate[1].)

Where there is an implied prohibition on assignation, the Succession (Scotland) Act 1964, section 29 provides as follows:

'A bequest by a tenant of his interest under a tenancy or lease to any one of the persons who, if the tenant had died intestate, would be or would in any circumstances have been entitled to succeed to his intestate estate by virtue of this Act shall not be treated as invalid by reason only that there is among the conditions of the tenancy or lease an implied condition prohibiting assignation.'

It should be noted that the potential legatee in such circumstances is any person who *could* be entitled to succeed on intestacy in terms of the 1964 Act. This gives a very wide range of possibilities. For agricultural holdings and crofts, the range of potential legatees is extended to include the testator's son-in-law or daughter-

---

1 See also *MacLean v MacLean* 1988 SLT 626.

in-law[1]. Where there is no prohibition on assignation, express or implied, an interest under a lease may be bequeathed to any person.

The succession to certain types of tenants' interests is controlled by statute and a purported legacy cannot alter the statutory succession rules[2]. The wording required for the legacy of a tenancy is very simple:

'I direct my executors to make over to A my interest in the tenancy of 6 Glebe Street, Inverness, free of all expenses of transfer.'

A fuller form, bequeathing the legacy of a farm tenancy, can be found at S2.14. Further comments on the legacy of a tenancy with reference to this Style purpose can be found in paragraphs 4.85–4.86 below.

House

4.76   The intention of the legacy at S2.11 is to bequeath a house, or share of a house, free of all burdens to a legatee. This can be used in any situation where a testator wishes to leave a house specifically to one beneficiary. It can equally be applied to any other piece of heritable property.

The need to make such a bequest often arises where two unrelated persons combine to purchase a home, whether or not they are in a relationship. They are likely to wish the person resident with them to receive the whole house, possibly along with the contents. They may also wish the remainder of their estates to go to other beneficiaries, often members of their respective families. Indeed, they may simply be happy to have rules on intestacy apply to assets other than their share in the house. In such a case, a simple legacy of the interest in the house, coupled with the residuary bequest to appropriate members of the family, will suffice.

In order to cover the situation where the parties may have moved separately without altering their wills, the subject of the legacy could be restricted as follows:

'. . .. my interest in any house occupied together by me and [the legatee of the house] as our normal residence at the time of my death. . .'

There may be problems in deciding what constitutes a person's normal residence, but discretion could be given to the executors to resolve this matter.

It was not thought necessary in purpose S2.11 to use the word 'dwellinghouse' as the extension to cover a house 'occupied as my normal residence' makes the intended subject clear. However, consideration may be given in certain cases to making some addition to cover garden ground, other buildings within the property, outhouses and the like, if there is felt likely to be any doubt that the house is being bequeathed along with the normal items which would accompany it. The word 'pertinents' could be used, but might be thought too technical. 'House and grounds' could also be considered, but this may be thought somewhat clumsy. Inserting the phrase 'together with its pertinents' after 'house'

---

1 See the Agricultural Holdings (Scotland) Act 1991, s 11; Crofters (Scotland) Act 1993, s 10.
2 See, for example, the Housing (Scotland) Act 1988, s 31.

may well be the most economical (if technical) method of covering all items to be
included if this is considered in any way necessary.

It may be desired to specify a particular house – for example, 'my interest in
the house known as "Treetops", 16 Don Street, Aberdeen'. This can be followed
by the alternative of 'or any house occupied as my normal residence at the time of
my death', in order to avoid the possibility of ademption if the house has been
changed by the time of death.

4.77 It should be noted that the legacy is of the testator's 'interest' in the
house. A very common situation may be two equal shares, but such a legacy will
cover any interest from the smallest fractional share to total ownership. Arguably, it would also cover the testator's interest if he was a tenant, but that should
be specified if it is in fact the case. If the testator is a co-owner who desires the end
result to be the legatee receiving complete ownership of the house, then the wide
meaning of 'interest' is desirable. However, particularly if the house is owned in
unusual *pro indiviso* shares, the exact position should be confirmed, possibly
with the exact fractional share being specified.

The restriction of the legacy to the testator's 'normal residence' should
prevent any difficulty should the testator own other heritable property in his own
right, such as a holiday cottage.

If the testator owns the whole house the words 'my interest in' can be omitted
from both places where they occur in purpose S2.11, but nothing is lost by
leaving these words in.

4.78 The legacy at S2.11 is to be free of all heritable securities and other capital
burdens. This provision is necessary if a testator wishes the legatee to receive the
house unencumbered by building society loans and the like. These would
require to be paid from other assets in the testator's estate. Without such a
provision, the house would pass subject to such heritable debts and could not be
conveyed to the legatee until he had repaid such debts to the executor or directly
to the lender, or made other arrangements to assume responsibility for them[1].

It should be noted that the freedom is from capital burdens – there is thus no
question of the legatee being relieved of such expenses as local authority rates
(where relevant) or council tax. The legacy will be free of inheritance tax under
the general provision contained in most of the Styles that legacies are to be paid
'free of government duties' (see S2.5). However, a bequest of a house is perhaps
one of the most likely items of estate which a testator would wish to see bearing
its own share of inheritance tax, rather than have the burden fall on residue.

Of course, the testator may wish the house or share in it to go to the legatee
subject to any heritable debts. In such a case, the words 'heritable debts and
securities and other capital burdens affecting my interest in the house at the time
of my death' should be omitted from the legacy. The legatee will require to repay
or assume the debt in return for receiving the testator's share in the house. In

1 *Brand v Scott's Trustees* (1892) 19 R 768.

effect, this might be described as a bequest of the testator's reversionary interest in the property.

4.79 Particular problems can arise with endowment assurance policies issued in connection with a loan to purchase a house, and often assigned to the lender (although less often than in the past)[1]. These problems only arise where a policy is assigned to the lender in security for the loan; they do not thus in general affect mortgage protection policies or any other form of life assurance or indeed endowment assurance itself where the policy is not assigned. In such cases, the legacy can be framed so as to be free of heritable debts, or subject to them, as preferred. The existence of the proceeds of an insurance policy in the executors' hands (or paid directly to the lender) will not affect the legatee whose bequest depends purely on the wording of the legacy. He will either receive the house after the heritable debt has been repaid, or require to make arrangements for its repayment; the fate of the insurance proceeds is of no concern to him.

4.80 The situation is different where an endowment policy has been assigned. In that case, the debt due to the lender is apportioned rateably between the value of the house and the value of the policy[2]. This produces the following possibilities:

(1)   If the words 'free of all . . . heritable debts and securities' etc are included, the legatee will receive the house, unencumbered, and the executors will receive and be entitled to retain, usually for the benefit of residue, the balance of the insurance proceeds unused on repaying the loan. This is thought to be the most likely consequence desired by the testator in such circumstances.

(2)   If the words 'heritable debts and securities' etc are omitted, the legatee's bequest will be subject to the heritable debt attributable to the house. It should be noted that the debt concerned will not be the whole amount due to the lender, but only the proportion attributable to the value of the house as compared to the value of the policy.

(3)   The testator may wish the legatee to receive only the value of the house under deduction of the *whole* debt due to the lender, and thus ensure that the whole value of the endowment policy goes in effect to his executors for use elsewhere. The wording of the legacy will require adaptation by omitting the words 'heritable debts and securities and other capital burdens affecting my interest in the house at the time of my death' and inserting the following:
'. . . but subject to the whole amount of any debt or other capital
burden affecting my interest in the house at the time of my death,
whether the debt or other capital burden is secured wholly or partly
by my interest in the house or otherwise.'
This does require the debt to 'affect' the interest in the house and there will

---

1 On the problems these create in the law of succession, see G L Gretton 'Endowment mortgages and the law of succession' 1987 JLSS 303; *Graham v Graham* (1898) 5 SLT 319.
2 See the article by G L Gretton referred to above.

usually be a security over it. If the debt for which the legatee is to become responsible is on the face of it wholly unconnected to the house (for instance, by being wholly secured by a life policy), further variation will be required, as follows:

> '. . . but subject to repaying the whole debt outstanding at the time of my death secured by my assignation of any endowment assurance policies on my life.'

(4) The final possibility is that the testator wishes the legatee to receive not only the unencumbered house but also any free balance from any endowment policies assigned by him in security of the debt. This will require an addition to the original legacy, as follows:

> '. . . together with my reversionary interest in the proceeds of any endowment assurance policies on my life assigned by me in connection with my ownership of the house.'

This would cover not only a policy assigned when the house was purchased, but any additional ones assigned later. However, extreme care requires to be exercised with bequests of this kind and they should probably only be used where the policies are actually assigned. If a legacy was made of a house 'free of all . . ... heritable debts and securities' etc, together with a legacy of the proceeds of insurance policies which were *not* assigned (but perhaps, as is common, only deposited), the result would be that the legatee would receive both the house unencumbered, and the insurance proceeds, whereas the executors would require to meet the heritable debt from resources other than the policies issued in connection with it. The following form of words would avoid this consequence, where policies are not assigned:

> '. . . together with my interest in the proceeds of any endowment assurance policies on my life issued in connection with my ownership of the house after deduction from these proceeds of the whole amount of any debt or other capital burden secured by my interest in the house.'

It should be stressed that the most likely clause required by a testator is the standard one by which the legacy passes unencumbered. The variations are included to give an idea of the possibilities open and emphasise the need to be clear as to the testator's exact desires. They also point to some of the dangers of drafting such a bequest without considering the *exact* consequences of the wording used, in what is a very common situation.

4.81 It may be that the testator has more than one house at the time of his death. Purpose S2.11 covers any house occupied as his main residence at the time of death. This could be thought to carry more than one property but the clear implication of the clause is towards a single house.

If a single legacy is to carry more than one property, purpose S2.11 could be adapted as follows:

> 'I direct my executors to make over to A my interest in all dwelling houses owned by me at the time of my death, free of all expenses of transfer, heritable debts and securities, and other capital burdens affecting my interests in such houses at the time of my death.'

This legacy would cover holiday homes, as well as any domestic property kept for letting (subject, of course, to the terms of any leases in force at the date of death).

If the testator wishes to leave separate legacies of different houses, it will be necessary to describe each one distinctly. This can be done by using postal addresses, but that may cause problems if replacement property is acquired. It may be appropriate to describe one house as a holiday home, with provision made for replacement holiday property. Similarly, a property could be described as a 'house owned for the purpose of commercial letting', again with provision for replacement. These two possible categories, together with a house occupied as a residence, will be sufficient for the needs of almost all testators. If any real doubts are anticipated, discretion could be given to executors as to which property is intended to be included in any particular legacy.

Farm (in hand)

4.82 Purpose S2.13 contains a legacy of a farm *owned* by the testator. In principle, this is no different from any other type of legacy. If it is desired to cover the possibility of the testator changing farms without changing his will, an alternative could be inserted as follows:

'. . . or my heritable interest in any farm owned by me at the time of my death.'

This covers the possibility of the testator disposing of a whole farm, and purchasing a share in another. The word 'heritable' is included to make it clear that the item bequeathed is the physical asset of the farm – this distinguishes it from the testator's *business* of farming (including goodwill, cash, debtors, etc) which he may or may not wish to leave elsewhere (for instance, the farm may go to a child and the business interests to a spouse). In purpose S2.13 the testator leaves certain moveable business assets, listed in the legacy, along with the farm.

Of course, if the testator owns only a share in the farm from the outset, the legacy should be of his 'interest' or 'share' in the appropriate farm.

There may be good reasons for describing the farm somewhat more fully, for instance by a conveyancing description by reference: 'the farm and lands of Hilly Mains, Gorebridge more particularly described in, disponed by and delineated in red on the plan attached to Disposition by Q in favour of S dated 1st and recorded in the Division of the General Register of Sasines for the County of Midlothian on 7th, both days in March, 1980.'

The need for a somewhat fuller description is particularly necessary where parts of farms have been added or sold off; it is common for farming units to amalgamate, and perhaps use only one of the names previously used. This is a more likely problem with rural property than an urban dwellinghouse. It is also possible that a testator may wish to make separate legacies of more than one farm owned by him.

4.83 The next problem to consider is related to the previous one, in that a testator may wish to bequeath individual fields or parts of farms to different beneficiaries (for instance, where they own adjoining property). In this case, description of the subject of the legacy is particularly vital. It is suggested that the best way to achieve certainty is by reference to an approximate area and, especially, reference to a plan. There is no reason why a plan should not be attached to or kept with the will – whether or not it forms part of the testamentary writing, it will provide a welcome guide both for executors and beneficiaries. A suitable form of words to take the matter beyond doubt would be as follows:

'. . . the field known as Cherrytrees extending to six and one-quarter acres or thereby, hatched in black on the plan attached, being the southernmost field in the farm and lands of Grassy Mains . . .'

4.84 The legacy as framed includes the farmhouse. It may be that the testator wishes to exclude this from his bequest (as where he wishes his spouse to have the farmhouse, and his son to have the farmland, perhaps to be worked in conjunction with a farm already owned by the son). Once more, description is vital, particularly if as is likely the farmhouse is not yet on a separate title. Is a kitchen garden included with the farmhouse? Are any outhouses to go with the farmhouse, or do they all go with the working farm buildings? A full conveyancing description will probably be necessary in the end, and if doubts are likely to arise (and the testator is willing) a basis for this could be laid in the will. A plan would be particularly useful in this case. A simple form of exclusion for a farmhouse would be as follows:

'The farm and lands of Grassy Mains, Girvan, Ayrshire, under exception of the farmhouse, garage, kitchen and ornamental garden and garden shed, but including all other farm buildings . . .'

It might be prudent to warn the testator of some of the potential difficulties in separating a farmhouse from the farm to which it is attached, for instance, problems on sale, or in obtaining planning consent for a use unconnected with farming. There may also be difficulties with burdens in the title of the farm.

It may also be necessary to consider the availability of agricultural and business property relief for inheritance tax purposes. This is mentioned further in paragraphs 4.90–4.93 below.

The list of moveable items included can of course be varied – the attempt is to include all items of a farming nature. Particular care is required when a farmhouse and other items such as furniture or personal belongings are left to different legatees. There may need to be a clear direction for items where dubiety might arise – for instance, is a Range Rover used mainly for farming purposes, or is it mainly a leisure vehicle that *can* be used on the farm?

It should be noted that the legacy includes 'my rights in all premiums, subsidies and quotas' and that all moveable items are qualified by the phrase 'all insofar as belonging to me'. This avoids any question of whether any or all of such incorporeal rights are separable from an area of farming land, a point which may be open to some debate. Certainly, specific investigation will be required where a farmer wishes to leave any rights to quota, premium or subsidy separately from his farming enterprise. Such legacies should probably be discouraged.

However, potato quota and the relatively new premiums relating to sheep, suckler cows and beef cattle attach to producers rather than land and should thus be capable of testamentary bequest. Separation from a particular holding may, however, be very unwise and severely devalue the land. The relationship between milk quota and land is much closer, although this quota may attach to a landlord's or a tenant's interest in a particular holding. Those interested in the nature of milk quota and particularly its separability from land should consider the case of *Faulks* v *Faulks*[1].

The phrasing used in relation to this type of asset in S2.13 is sufficiently flexible to cope with the introduction of further, similar farming assets (or, depending on one's point of view, restrictions) in future.

Farm (tenancy)

4.85   The tenant's interest under a lease vests in his executors in terms of the Succession (Scotland) Act 1964, section 14. Thus the direction in purpose S2.14 to the executors to make over the tenant's interest in a farm is as valid as any other legacy[2]. The bequest is of the 'interest in the tenancy of' the appropriate farm. It may be simpler, and preferable, to refer to a legacy of the 'lease'. The latter follows the wording of the Agricultural Holdings (Scotland) Act 1991, section 11 and the former the wording of the Succession (Scotland) Act 1964, section 16.

If a legacy is to be effectual, it must be of the whole of the tenant's interest. There is thus no need to specify or attempt to exclude any buildings or the like. In addition, the legacy must be to a single individual[3]. The range of farming items that can be included (which may extend to items such as timber, as well as more obvious moveable farming equipment) might depend at least in part on the terms of the lease. To avoid any complications, all of the items listed as included in purpose S2.14 are qualified by a restriction that they are only bequeathed 'insofar as belonging to' the testator. The comments on subsidies, quotas and premiums in paragraph 4.84 are also relevant to farm tenancies.

4.86   There are limitations on the ability of a testator to bequeath any interest as an agricultural tenant. The case of *Kennedy* v *Johnstone*[4] confirms that if the lease specifically excludes assignees, the tenant has no power effectively to bequeath his interest. This will eliminate most formal agricultural leases from being included as legacies, although it may still be possible to bequeath a lease based on a verbal agreement, informal writings or where there is no explicit exclusion. In addition, it is worth bearing in mind that even if a lease does exclude assignees, the landlord may validate the bequest by accepting the legatee as tenant[5].

Even if assignees are not excluded, the range of eligible legatees is limited by section 11 of the Agricultural Holdings (Scotland) Act 1991, to the testator's

---

1 [1992] 15 EG 82.
2 See also the Succession (Scotland) Act 1964, s 16(8).
3 *Kennedy* v *Johnstone* 1956 SC 39.
4 1956 SC 39.
5 *Kennedy* v *Johnstone*, above; *Cormack* v *McIldowie's Executors* 1975 SLT 214; *Reid's Trustees* v *Macpherson* 1975 SLT 101.

'son-in-law or daughter-in-law or any one of the persons who would be, or would in any circumstances have been, entitled to succeed to the estate on intestacy by virtue of the Succession (Scotland) Act 1964'. If, as will presumably (and usually) be the case, the intention is to maintain the existence of the tenancy for as long as possible, the class of eligible legatees is further narrowed to 'near-relatives' in terms of the Agricultural Holdings (Scotland) Act 1991, section 25 and Schedule 2, Part III. This class includes only the surviving spouse and children (including adopted children) of the tenant.

Furthermore, the effective legacy of an agricultural tenancy depends on intimation of the bequest to the landlord within 21 days of the death of the tenant[1]. This vital provision is strictly enforced. It is thus suggested that the legatee be informed of the bequest on the will being made, if the testator agrees. In addition, the need to intimate should be prominently noted on the will itself to promote swift action on the testator's death[2].

Right of occupancy

4.87 A right of occupancy is akin to a liferent and occurs where a beneficiary is given the right to occupy heritable property, but is free of the ordinary burdens of occupancy[3]. The right of occupancy may therefore be relevant when dealing with a dwellinghouse or, occasionally, other heritable property. Whereas a liferenter will have to meet insurance, feu-duty, ordinary repairs and (formerly) rates a person occupying under a right of occupancy will have such items paid for him. This will generally require that a fund be retained by trustees to meet such outgoings[4]. The circumstances where such a right may be appropriate are extremely limited; it should perhaps not be encouraged and no style is given here[5].

Croft

4.88 A legacy of a croft is shown at S2.15. Such a legacy is governed by very similar considerations as apply to a normal agricultural lease. In order to be effective, the legacy must be in favour of the son-in-law or daughter-in-law of the testator or any one of the persons who would be, or would in any circumstances have been, entitled to succeed to the estate on intestacy[6].

If the testator wishes to leave his rights to a croft elsewhere, it will be necessary to obtain the approval of the Crofters Commission before such a legacy can take effect.

---

1 See the Agricultural Holdings (Scotland) Act 1991, s 12.
2 On all of this, see Gill *The Law of Agricultural Holdings in Scotland* (1982) paras 470 ff; *Meston* pp 95 and 109 ff; note also *Coats v Logan* 1985 SLT 221.
3 Dobie *Manual of the Law of Liferent and Fee in Scotland* (1941) p 226.
4 *Clark v Clark* (1871) 9 M 435.
5 *Elder* p 75; *Encyclopaedia of Scottish Legal Styles*, volume 9, p 269.
6 Crofters (Scotland) Act 1993, s 10.

The period after death within which a legatee must give effective notice to the landlord is 2 months, rather than 21 days.

The statutory rules on croft legacies apply to the croft tenancy only. A crofter may wish to make separate provisions covering any other agricultural tenancies he may have, land or houses *owned* personally, or other personal assets.

Timeshares

4.89   Purpose S2.22 consists of the legacy of a timeshare. It is extremely widely drawn, consisting of 'my whole interest of whatever kind in the timeshare at . . .'. This would cover any changes made by the testator, or otherwise occurring in his rights in the particular timeshare. Examples might include the purchase of additional weeks or any kind of swap.

It may be necessary to consider the nature of a testator's rights in any particular timeshare. Although occasionally in the United Kingdom timeshares are established on the basis of co-ownership of heritable property (perhaps by means of *pro indiviso* shares in Scotland), more commonly the arrangement takes the form of a club. In the latter situation, the testator's rights will be a moveable asset.

The testator will be bound by the club rules. It would often be a good idea to see these rules (or any other documentary evidence of the manner in which the timeshare is constituted) at the time of drafting a will including a specific legacy of a timeshare. It is understood that in a club arrangement, transfer of ownership will usually be by a simple deed of transfer, with the formal certificate of ownership then being docqueted with details of the new owner. The timeshare's rules may contain specific provisions for transfer on death, which may influence the form of the legacy.

Another possible structure is a company limited by guarantee, where the testator may have, in effect, a shareholding to bequeath. The wide terms of S2.22 should extend to such a format.

Any form of timeshare ownership may be joint, and in such cases it often includes a survivorship destination which may or may not be capable of evacuation (on this matter generally, see paras 2.25–2.29 above).

It is possible to have an interest in a foreign timeshare by means of membership of a United Kingdom club, in which case there should be no difficulties with a legacy and registration of the legatee as new owner of the asset.

However, if the scheme for a foreign timeshare is set up abroad, the testator's rights may be heritable. Certainly if that is the case, and perhaps even if not, it may be necessary and will usually be desirable to obtain advice from a local lawyer. Particularly where the timeshare right is heritable, it will usually be appropriate to prepare a will in accordance with the law of the place where the timeshare property is located.

It may be that the testator wishes to leave timeshare interests (which may cover a number of weeks) to more than one beneficiary. A joint bequest may be suitable; however, the testator may wish to leave specified periods to different beneficiaries. In such a case, it would be essential to check the rules in order to ascertain the correct procedure (if such is available) to split the testator's interest.

Business and agricultural property

4.90 The inheritance tax reliefs for business and agricultural property are now among the most crucial available, especially since the maximum rate of relief is now 100 per cent[1].

It is worth being reminded of the appropriate definitions. Relevant business property is defined as follows[2]:

'(a)   property consisting of a business or interest in a business;

(b)   shares in or securities of a company which are unquoted and which (either by themselves or together with other such shares or securities owned by the transferor) gave the transferor control of the company immediately before the transfer;

(bb)   unquoted shares in a company which do not fall within paragraph (b) above and which immediately before the transfer satisfied the condition specified in subsection (1A) below [this subsection demands voting control of more than 25% of the shares in the company];

(c)   unquoted shares in a company which do not fall within paragraph (b) or paragraph (bb) above;

(cc)   shares in or securities of a company which are quoted and which (either by themselves or together with other such shares or securities owned by the transferor) gave the transferor control of the company immediately before the transfer;

(d)   any land or building, machinery or plant which, immediately before the transfer, was used wholly or mainly for the purposes of a business carried on by a company of which the transferor then had control or by a partnership of which he then was a partner; and

(e)   any land or building, machinery or plant which, immediately before the transfer, was used wholly or mainly for the purposes of a business carried on by the transferor and was settled property in which he was then beneficially entitled to an interest in possession.'

Subject to meeting other conditions and restricted by a range of exclusions, categories (a), (b) and (bb) qualify for 100 per cent relief, while the remaining categories qualify for 50 per cent relief[3].

Agricultural property is defined as[4]:

'. . . agricultural land or pasture and includes woodland and any building used in connection with the intensive rearing of livestock or fish if the woodland or building is occupied with agricultural land or pasture and the occupation is ancillary to that of the agricultural land or pasture; and also includes such cottages, farm buildings and farmhouses, together with the land occupied with them, as are of a character appropriate to the property.'

4.91 It should be remembered that only the agricultural value of agricultural property qualifies for relief. This value is defined as[5]:

1 See the Inheritance Tax Act 1984, ss 103–114 and 115–124B.
2 Ibid, s 105(1).
3 Ibid, s 104.
4 Ibid, s 115(2).
5 Ibid, s 115(3).

'. . . the value which would be the value of the property if the property were subject to a perpetual covenant prohibiting its use otherwise than as agricultural property.'

Agricultural property relief is available at 100 per cent if the interest of the transferor in the property immediately before the transfer carries the right to vacant possession or the right to obtain it within 12 months; or the land has been tenanted since before 10 March 1981 (with certain other conditions applying in this last case). Otherwise agricultural property relief is available at 50 per cent[1].

The existence of these reliefs may be of great significance when drafting wills, but of course the possibility of substantial changes should be borne in mind. The reliefs can have a significant effect when defining what is to be included in a legacy of the nil rate band for inheritance tax[2].

4.92 One important general consideration is the identity of the legatees who are to receive such property. Usually, it will be inappropriate for an exempt beneficiary (such as a spouse) to receive property qualifying for 100 per cent relief, as this would in effect mean that the relief is wasted. The same applies to a lesser extent in relation to property qualifying for 50 per cent relief. This consideration is particularly important when an estate is to be divided between a spouse and children. The new levels of relief make this a particularly vital consideration.

Another possible matter to be considered is the position of a legatee *after* receipt of a legacy of such property. To take a simple example, it will make an enormous difference if a legatee receives just over 25 per cent of the shares in a private trading company, rather than exactly this amount or less.

If a property owned by the testator is used in a company of which the testator has control, it might be asked whether the intended legatee of that property is also to be given a controlling interest in the company, so as to maintain the right to relief.

4.93 A further vital issue concerns debts. The value of property which qualifies for relief is its value after deduction of liabilities. This has rather different effects as between business and agricultural property. The position for business property is governed by the Inheritance Tax Act 1984, section 110(b), which provides that:

'. . . the net value of a business is the value of the assets used in the business (including goodwill) reduced by the aggregate amount of any liabilities incurred for the purposes of the business.'

It is, therefore, the *purpose* of the loan which is relevant.

For agricultural property, the general rule for inheritance tax applies. This is set out in the Inheritance Tax Act 1984, section 162(4): 'A liability which is an incumbrance on any property shall, so far as possible, be taken to reduce the value of that property'.

This means that a loan *secured* over a farm will reduce the amount qualifying for agricultural relief. If the loan is otherwise secured (for instance, over a house, although it is appreciated that this may be impractical), the full value of agricultural

1 Inheritance Tax Act 1984, s 116(2).
2 See paras 4.38–4.40 above.

property will qualify for relief. If a debt is unsecured, it is understood that as a matter of practice, the Capital Taxes Office will treat the debt as reducing the values of agricultural and other property proportionately.

These rules may require consideration in deciding who is to receive property qualifying for relief and the value of legacies of such property as compared to other legacies.

It is obviously essential for those drafting wills to be aware of the availability of such reliefs. Most cases can be tackled without difficulty and it is not intended to cover the detailed tax rules which may be relevant in a minority of situations in this publication.

Trees and woodlands

4.94   There is a specific inheritance tax relief available in connection with woodlands, which may also qualify to some extent for business or agricultural property relief. Details can be found in the Inheritance Tax Act 1984, sections 125–130. The basic relief involves a *deferral* (rather than exemption) of tax on the value of trees until their disposal by any transferee.

There is nothing particularly vital in this relief as regards the drafting of wills, but the situation may be of great relevance to the legatee in due course. It is also possible that the testator is already in the position of deferring tax on trees which he received on an earlier transfer of value. Among other factors, the existence of this relief might persuade some testators to attempt to leave trees separately from the land on which they are growing.

As with other plants and crops (subject to a limited exception for agricultural crops), such a separation is not strictly possible in terms of property law. The trees adhere to the land and will be carried with any legacy of it.

However, it is possible effectively to solve this problem, at least to a limited extent. A legacy of the land can be made conditional on the legatee of the land allowing the intended legatee of the trees to enter, cut and take the growing timber. Such a legacy might take the following form:

'I direct my executors to make over to A the woodlands known as Hillcrest Pines, Perth, but only if A enters into a contract to the satisfaction of my executors to allow B without payment to enter into the woodland and cut and remove the trees growing there [to a maximum value of TWENTY THOUSAND POUNDS as estimated by an independent valuer at the time of cutting], but subject to B bearing the costs of such cutting and removal and also the costs of restoration and re-planting trees to such reasonable extent as A may require (and as to which my executors shall be the sole judges).'

An alternative would be for the testator to direct his executors to enter into the appropriate contract prior to making over the land to the beneficiary taking it.

In either case, the person intended to take the trees does not acquire a right of property in them, but merely a contractual right. However, this right is itself capable of being transferred or bequeathed.

Sporting and fishing rights

4.95 Salmon fishings, being a separate heritable estate in Scotland, can undoubtably be the subject of a distinct legacy. A testator's right may be as owner or tenant. He may be a *pro indiviso* proprietor, with rights either as a common owner of the entire fishings, or to a limited amount of time on the relevant beat. But in any event, his right can be bequeathed quite separately from the land from and over which the right to fish is exercised. A suitable form of legacy might be:

'I direct my executors to make over to A my rights in the salmon fishings on the River Elgin known as the Upper Beat and Junction Pool [OR my rights of whatever kind in any salmon fishings at the date of my death].'

There may be disadvantages in separately bequeathing salmon fishings distinct from other rights over adjacent land. Care should be taken if such land includes accommodation or areas required for the practical exploitation of the fishings, such as boathouses, stores and the like.

Other sporting rights are not separate from the land or water over which they are exercised. They will be transmitted with legacies of rights over the land and water unless otherwise specified. Such rights over the land or water may be in the form of full ownership or tenancy.

Effective separation can be achieved by making provision for a beneficiary to acquire a contractual right (usually in the form of a lease) to the sporting rights under consideration. This can be done either by a direction to the executors or by imposing a condition on a legacy, such that the intended legatee of the sporting rights receives an appropriate lease from the owner of the appropriate land[1].

If the testator only has rights under a sporting lease, its terms may be crucial in ascertaining whether an effective bequest can be made.

Businesses

4.96 Purpose S2.18 consists of a very widely expressed legacy of a business. Just in case any aspect of this legacy is regarded as open to doubt, the executors are given discretion as to what is included and are empowered to demand discharges and indemnities from the legatee. The business in question is that of a sole trader, which in many ways may be more difficult to define than other formats in which a business may be carried on. If it is possible that the business may change its format into a partnership or company, a wider form of wording may be appropriate[2]:

'I direct my executors to make over to A my whole interest of whatever kind in the business presently carried on by me under the name Intercontinental Garden Gnomes at 2 Acacia Avenue, Musselburgh

---

1 See para 4.94 above on similar arrangements to separate rights to trees from the land on which they are growing.
2 But see paras 4.94–4.105.

(including my interest as a partner or shareholder if the business is carried on by a partnership or company at the time of my death), together with (if the business is then carried on by me as a sole trader) the whole property . . . [etc].'

4.97   There are a number of matters which may require to be considered in any legacy of a sole trader's business. Perhaps most importantly, it will usually be necessary to consider whether any business premises are included in the legacy. If they are included, the rights under which business premises are held may require to be dealt with specifically. If business premises are not included, consideration may be required as to what effect this will have on, say, goodwill, particularly if the business premises are left to another legatee, who may even conceivably compete with the legatee to whom the business itself is left.

Particular care should be taken with regard to business bank accounts and other financial assets. Sole traders are apt to mix up personal matters with business affairs. If the business is to be left separately from personal assets, this will require to be carefully sorted out. In many ways, leaving such matters to the discretion of the executors represents rather too easy a way out – apart from for the executors! The opportunity might usefully be taken at the time of drafting the will to clarify exactly what the business comprises.

The legacy in S2.18 is of 'my business presently carried on under the name Intercontinental Garden Gnomes' at a specified address. This format will allow the legacy not to be adeemed should the business change its name or its address. As the reference is simply to the business being carried on, it will not matter if the testator has effectively retired, leaving the running of the business to others while retaining ownership.

More difficulties will be created if the testator were to enter into a different type of business entirely, particularly if the new business was in addition to, but separate from, the old.

If such a legacy is intended to include *any* business carried on by the testator, the purpose should commence:

'I direct my executors to make over to A any business carried on by me at the time of my death, declaring that my business is presently carried on under the name . . .'

The legacy includes the doubtless unwelcome bequest of the liabilities of the business. That provision, coupled with the requirement to indemnify the executors, should be sufficient to ensure that the legatee will only take over the assets if he is willing to take on the liabilities. The executors may demand that all debts are discharged or indemnities are given within a specified timescale. This may be important, to ensure that the completion of the administration is not unduly delayed. If desired, provision for the type of indemnities to be given could be included directly in the will.

4.98   The testator may specifically wish to leave not the business as a going concern, but various assets making it up, perhaps to separate legatees. This type of legacy may be required or desirable where intended legatees are in business on their own account and may be able to take advantage of the testator's stock, clients, work in progress or premises. There is no reason why separate legacies cannot be left of such items, for instance as follows:

'I direct my executors to make over to A the plant, machinery, work in progress and stocks used in my business presently carried on under the name Intercontinental Garden Gnomes at 2 Acacia Avenue, Musselburgh; and I direct my executors to make over to my wife B the remainder of the assets used in my business, including any interest in any premises, contracts, book-debts, bank or other accounts and goodwill, subject to any liabilities in the business, declaring that my executors shall be the sole judges as to what is included in each part of this legacy and subject to such discharges and indemnities as my executors may require.'

It should be noted that despite the business being broken up as a result of this request, the transfer on the testator's death should still qualify for business property relief for inheritance tax purposes, if the business was in operation immediately before the death. This is because the deemed transfer of value for inheritance tax takes place immediately *before* the death; and the fate of the business afterwards is of no significance.

One point to bear in mind particularly with such a bequest is the question of goodwill. This may be an asset of considerable value which may largely disappear if a business is broken up. (Again, this would take place only after the legacy has been implemented following the death, so the value of goodwill would be included in the testator's estate. It would at present usually qualify for 100 per cent business property relief.) However, a more fundamental point may be whether a legacy of goodwill, without any other aspect of the business, can be effectively made. Goodwill is a notoriously intangible asset; if it is of value, care should be taken that an effective disposal which preserves that value is made by the will.

Partnership interests

4.99 Purpose S2.17 consists of a legacy of a partnership interest, although its terms are general enough to cover the testator's interest in a business if it is carried on by him as a sole trader or, probably, if it has been incorporated. However, the latter case in particular should be dealt with by a codicil or fresh will. The same will generally apply if the testator has retired from the partnership business. The situation envisaged in S2.17 is that the testator remains a partner in the firm between making the will and the date of his death.

Partnerships can change their members very frequently. There might also be changes of name or amalgamation with other firms. However, the phrasing used in S2.17 ('my whole interest of whatever kind in the firm of Stevens Festival Souvenirs as it is presently constituted or as it may be constituted at the time of my death') is wide enough to cope with most such changes. If desired, the possibility of incorporation can also be included (see the wording suggested in para 4.96 above).

4.100 Of course, this legacy of a partnership interest is not the equivalent of appointing the legatee as a partner. Such an appointment may or may not be possible in terms of the constitution of the partnership concerned. Permission for such appointment would be unusual in most commercial partnerships, although such provisions are not unknown in family partnerships. If this possibility was permitted, the legacy might take the following form:

'I direct my executors to make over to my youngest son A my whole interest of whatever kind in the firm of Crosby, Stills and Nash, as it is presently constituted or as it may be constituted at the time of my death and I nominate A as a partner in the firm in terms of the power conferred on me by Clause (TENTH) of the Minute of Agreement entered into by me, Alasdair Crosby, Fforbes Stills and Cameron Nash, dated 10 January 1986, subject to all debts and liabilities incurred by me as a partner outstanding at the time of my death.'

With any such bequest (and perhaps where any legacy of a partnership interest is involved), it would be useful to examine the partnership deed. There may be special provisions as to what is to happen on the death of a partner, notably on valuation of the partnership assets. There may also be provisions covering the timescale within which a deceased partner's share is to be paid out to his beneficiaries, which may be very relevant when drafting the will.

4.101 Another possibility is that the testator may wish to leave not his full interests in any partnership, but merely any balance in his capital account. This may be with or without a revaluation of partnership assets.

The position may be that a sudden demand for withdrawal of one partner's full capital might effectively destroy the business. This could, of course, be the effect of any large, unexpected withdrawal of partnership assets. For this reason, the testator might make a legacy of any partnership interest conditional on the legatee leaving the capital on loan to the partnership, perhaps at a preferential or even nil rate of interest.

Another alternative would be to provide that the surviving partners can pay out the beneficiary over a structured timescale, with or without interest. Such provision might take the following form:

'I direct my executors to make over to A my whole interest of whatever kind in the firm of Stevens Festival Souvenirs as it is presently constituted or as it may be constituted at the time of my death, but declaring that the surviving partners may at their option satisfy this legacy by payment of ten equal annual instalments of the amount of my partnership interest as valued at the time of my death without interest [OR with simple interest commencing to run after the first payment has been made at two per cent above the base rate of the Royal Bank of Scotland from time to time on the outstanding balance each year], the first payment to be made one year after the date of my death.'

The phrase 'my whole interest of whatever kind' is wide enough to include profits between the last accounting date and the date of death – in effect, accrued income. In the event that only capital interests are to be included in a partnership legacy, the phrase should be:

' . . . my whole capital interest of whatever kind, but excluding any current profits due to me but unpaid at the time of my death . . .'

Private company shares and shares in general

4.102 Purpose S2.16 contains a legacy of shares in a private company. There are some features particularly relevant to a private company, dealt with below, but many considerations are common to holdings in both public and private companies.

The most important is probably the question of what is to happen if the shares bequeathed are no longer owned by the testator at the date of death. As noted in paragraph 4.15 above, the legacy will not generally adeem if shares are simply converted into different shares, or classes of share, or stock in the same company, or there is a reorganisation such that a holding is converted into a different number of shares in that company[1].

There are other possibilities. The company concerned may change its name. The company may be taken over with the result that shareholders obtain shares in the acquiring company as a replacement for their original holding. Such conversions might well be considered to cause ademption unless special provisions are made. The following wording, as used in S2.16, is thought to cover these possibilities:

' . . . or such other shares or stock as may represent the same at the time of my death as a result of any amalgamation, takeover or reorganisation of this Company, as to which my executors shall be the sole judges . . .'

While it is considered that this wording would include a mere change of name, it could be argued that such a change does not occur as a result of 'amalgamation, takeover or reorganisation'. This would be particularly relevant with a public company, where it would be unusual to include the company registration number as has been done in S2.16. The inclusion of the number puts identification of the company beyond doubt. If the possible renaming of the company was felt to be a matter requiring consideration, the word 'renaming' should simply be added to the list of possible changes.

A legacy of shares may be only part of the testator's holding. In such a case, the number of shares included in the legacy should simply be stated, but it becomes all the more important to provide for possible changes in the company and for the executors to have the discretion as to how the specified number may be represented following such changes.

4.103 It is possible that the testator may simply sell shares and replace them with shares in a different company or companies. This is particularly likely where a holding is merely an investment as will generally be the case with holdings in a public, quoted company. If such a sale and replacement takes

---

1 *Macfarlane's Trustees v Macfarlane* 1910 SC 325.

place, ademption will generally occur. This will usually be acceptable if the testator really desires a beneficiary to receive only shares in a specified company. If that is not the intention, a new provision by will or codicil bequeathing the replacement shares is the best solution. It would, however, be possible to insert a general provision in an attempt to avoid ademption:

> '. . . or any shares or stock acquired as a replacement for these shares (including shares bought as replacements therefor before or after the sale of these shares, as to which my executors shall be the sole judges).'

Such a wide provision might involve the executors in unreasonable research as to the origins of any particular holding at death. At the very least, if such a wide provision is to be used, the testator should be requested to maintain careful records of which particular holdings were acquired as replacements for holdings previously held.

Another possibility to avoid complete ademption is to provide for the beneficiary to receive a sum of money if the particular holding, or any holding representing it, is not owned at the date of death. This could be done as follows:

> '. . . or in the event of my not owning any such shares or stock at the time of my death, I direct my executors to pay to A the sum of TEN THOUSAND POUNDS [OR the sum of FIVE POUNDS in respect of each share owned by me at the date of this will].'

4.104   A further problem which might arise is in relation to dividends on the particular holding bequeathed. The general clause dealing with legacies included in most of the Styles (see, for example, S2.5) excludes the payment of interest. While interest is not exactly the same as a dividend on a particular holding, it might be thought (probably incorrectly) that this clause would also operate to prevent a beneficiary receiving any dividends on shares specifically bequeathed and received during the executry. The possibility of exclusion can be avoided by adding the following words to a legacy of shares and stock:

> '. . . together with any dividends or interest received on such shares or stock after my death . . .'

It is thought that such a provision would cover only receipts deriving directly from the holding in question or any replacement. It would not give a general right to interest on the legacy if, for instance, no income were received during the period of executry administration.

There are undoubtedly possible problems with legacies of shareholdings, but with private company shares these are likely to be on a relatively manageable scale. Furthermore, a testator is much more likely than would generally be the case in relation to holdings in quoted companies to have understandable and possibly irresistible reasons to pass on such shares in a family will.

4.105   Just as with rights in partnerships, it may be appropriate to consider the company's constitution in its memorandum and articles when drafting a will including legacies of shareholdings. In particular, the possible effect of rights of pre-emption should be considered; and articles may make specific provision for what is to happen on the death of a member.

If rights of pre-emption do exist, such that the testator's intended legatee may be barred from receiving the shares, it might be important to add some form of alternative legacy, for instance as follows:

'. . . or if the transfer of these shares or stock to A should be prevented by right of pre-emption or otherwise, I direct my executors to pay to A a cash sum equal to the higher of (1) a fair market value at the date of my death of such shares or stock which cannot be transferred and (2) any price received by my executors for such shares or stock, as to all of which my executors shall be the sole judges . . .'

A testator may prefer to insert the lower of the two values referred to in such a provision.

Apart from dividends or interest, it may be necessary to consider other rights which a testator may have in relation to a company. These could include rights to a balance of salary as a director, or other benefits received or due in that capacity or as an employee. Very commonly, there might also be a balance due on a loan account to the company. While such items should usually be dealt with by separate legacies or as part of residue, they could be included in a specific legacy of all interests in the company as follows:

'I direct my executors to make over to A my whole rights and interests of whatever kind as director and shareholder in Spotty Dogs Dinners Ltd (company number 1001002) including all shares and stock of whatever classes in that company or such other shares or stock as may represent the same at the time of my death as a result of any amalgamation, takeover or reorganisation of that company, as to which my executors shall be the sole judges.'

There might also be a company pension scheme, although any benefits due from such a scheme would be held by separate pension fund trustees and not by the company. However, as a death benefit from a pension scheme might be extremely valuable, dealing with private company shares should always act as a reminder that this aspect should be dealt with, whether in the will, or, more usually and perhaps essentially, by lifetime nomination (see para 2.14).

Options to purchase

4.106 The testator may wish to leave purposes which may be called 'legacies', but which are perhaps more accurately described as 'options to purchase'. The beneficiary of such provision, unlike other legatees, is not receiving something for nothing. He has the right to purchase an asset for a sum of money which is basically the open market value at the date of death, taking into consideration the type of asset which is involved. This means that the residue of the testator's estate will not be denuded by such a legacy, as the subject will be replaced by a sum of money which will go to the residuary legatees.

This type of option can be used with any asset in the testator's estate, but is perhaps most likely with business assets. One appropriate situation might be where the testator owns property used in a business. This could take the following form where the property concerned is the premises where the business is carried on:

> 'I direct my executors to offer to sell any interest I have in the property at 175 Albany Street, Edinburgh to Biggar Services Limited (Company Number: SC999999) of 175 Albany Street, Edinburgh at its market value on a willing buyer, willing seller basis as at the date of my death but such option will be exercisable within six months of my death and the purchase price must be paid within one year of my death otherwise this provision will fail.'

Such a building may be a valuable item in the testator's estate and while he would not wish to cause his fellow directors a problem by the building falling into the hands of an unsympathetic relative, neither would he wish the asset to leave his estate without consideration being paid.

The legacy therefore gives the company an option to purchase the building on a willing buyer, willing seller basis with a reference to the market value at the testator's death. There is a time limit put on for both the acceptance of the option and the payment of the purchase price. Such time limits are of course purely arbitrary and have to take into consideration, at the time instructions for the will are taken, what is a reasonable time for the company to raise the funds for the purchase while ensuring that there is not undue delay in payment of residue to the ultimate beneficiaries.

The building, which is owned by the testator, would not be subject to the memorandum or articles of association of the company and it is therefore considered appropriate that the option be in favour of the company and not the individual directors.

4.107 Another situation where such an option may be appropriate involves shares in a private company. The following wording relates to shares in the same company as was mentioned in the immediately preceding paragraph:

> 'I direct my executors to offer to sell all (but not some only) of any shares I own in Biggar Services Limited (Company Number: SC999999) of 175 Albany Street, Edinburgh to A at market value as at the date of death on a willing buyer, willing seller basis but such option will be exercisable within six months of my death and the purchase price must be paid within one year of my death otherwise this provision will fail.'

There will inevitably be restrictions on the transfer of shares and the memorandum and articles of association would have to be checked. It would seem only sensible to give the option to purchase the shares to someone, presumably a co-director or co-directors of the testator, who would be acceptable as owners of the shares, and to whom the shares could be legally transferred.

The terms and conditions of the legacy are similar to those in connection with the property mentioned in the preceding paragraph.

Such arrangements are sometimes financed by directors taking out life assurance on their own lives and, during life, assigning the policies to the people who will be given the option to purchase the shares. Such an arrangement gives the assignees a tax free lump sum which can be used to purchase the building or the shares[1].

Finally, it would have to be borne in mind that if the option were exercised this would in effect be a sale, so that instalment option for inheritance tax would no longer be available.

Intellectual property

4.108 Rights to most forms of intellectual property are generally capable of transfer on death, and hence may be the subject of testamentary bequest. Some such rights are, however, subject to specific statutory rules, which may assist in determining the appropriate form of legacy.

Perhaps the most commonly encountered form of intellectual property is copyright. Those owning copyrights may transfer them by testamentary disposition[2]. A suitable form of legacy, carrying all of an author's works would be as follows:

> 'I direct my executors to make over to A the copyrights of my published and unpublished works [together with the benefit of all publication contracts entered into by me].'

It would be usual to leave the benefit of any contractual rights already obtained from copyrights to the same person receiving the copyrights themselves, but theoretically at least these might be treated as separate items of property to be left to different beneficiaries.

It would also be possible to leave a legacy of the copyright in a single work, or series of works, as follows:

> 'I direct my executors to make over to A the copyrights of my books "Spotty the Dog" and "Spotty the Dog Barks Again", together with the copyrights of any other books or stories (published or unpublished) featuring Spotty the Dog (as to which my executors shall be the sole judges), together with the benefits of all publication contracts entered into by me in connection with stories featuring Spotty the Dog.'

If a copyright is shared, the right is held as common property and each owner may make a separate legacy of his share.

4.109 It is possible to include in a will an appointment of literary executors. This is in many ways an administrative appointment, which may be important especially in relation to unpublished and unfinished works. However, it should be made clear where any profits deriving from unpublished works are to go, if not to those appointed as literary executors. It may be appropriate to treat such profits as part of another legacy, or as adding to residue, or as forming part of a trust fund set up elsewhere in the will. Appropriate wording for one such form of appointment and legacy would be:

---

1 See para 2.19.
2 See the Copyright, Designs and Patents Act 1988, s 90(1).

'I appoint my Trustees A and B to act as my literary executors and to take possession of my papers and manuscripts, to enter into contracts for the publication of completed but unpublished works as at the date of my death and in relation to incomplete works to enter into contracts with authors and publishers for their completion, all as they in their absolute discretion shall think fit; and I direct my literary executors to make over to the Trust Fund established in terms of purpose (SEVEN) all profits from and copyrights in such unpublished and incomplete works.'

4.110 It may be particularly important that copyrights are specifically dealt with in a will, because of the terms of the Copyright, Designs and Patents Act 1988, section 93. This provides that where there is a bequest, whether specific or general, of either an original document or other material item recording or embodying a literary, dramatic, musical or artistic work which was unpublished at the date of the testator's death, the copyright is *also* carried by the bequest unless the testator displays a contrary testamentary intention. This extends also to material items containing a sound recording or film. The point is that a general legacy of physical items, such as that of personal effects exemplified in S2.9(2) will carry not only the physical property in any unpublished manuscripts and the like, but also the copyright in such works, unless the testator makes specific provision in his will.

The terms of the Copyright, Designs and Patents Act 1988, section 90(2) are also of significance. Any transmission of copyright (including that by testamentary disposition) may be partial. This means that only some of the rights attached to copyright can be bequeathed, or that the right can be restricted to a period less than the 50 years which would normally apply after the death of the testator.

4.111 The Copyright, Designs and Patents Act 1988 introduced certain 'moral rights' in relation to works subject to copyright. These are a right to be identified as the author or other creator of a work, the right to prevent derogatory treatment of a work and the right to prevent false attributions[1]. These rights endure after death, for the same term as copyright in relation to the first two and for 20 years after death in relation to the third. The right to prevent false attribution vests in executors. The other two rights may be specifically bequeathed, but if they are not so bequeathed they pass along with the copyright in the relevant work. As the rights include the possibility of seeking civil remedies, including damages, they could be valuable. A suitable form of legacy covering such rights would be:

'I direct my executors to make over to A my rights conferred by the Copyright, Designs and Patents Act 1988, sections 77 and 80 (or any statutory replacement or extension for these rights, as to which my executors shall be the sole judges) in relation to all my published and unpublished works.'

1 See the Copyright, Designs and Patents Act 1988, ss 77, 80 and 84.

4.112   Rights in performances, which are distinct from copyright, may also be bequeathed by testamentary disposition[1].

Rights in designs, whether registered or unregistered, can also be the subject of bequest[2]. A suitable form of legacy would be:

'I direct my executors to make over to A the rights in my design of a sprocket flange [registered under No A123456].'

As registered designs have to be renewed every five years it may be necessary or desirable to leave a suitable pecuniary legacy, to cover the renewal fees, particularly if the design is not yet producing any income for its owner.

Patents are a further form of intellectual property which can be transferred on death[3]. A suitable form of legacy might be:

'I direct my executors to make over to A all patent rights owned by me at the date of my death [OR my patent No B23456 in the "Spotty" sprocket flange].'

Again, renewal fees may be required for a patent and the testator may wish to leave a suitable legacy or a trust fund for this purpose.

4.113   Trade marks are a further form of intellectual property that might just conceivably form the subject of a legacy. However, it is far more likely that they would form part of the assets of a business, incorporated or otherwise, and pass with a bequest of that business or a legacy of company shares.

Contractual rights

4.114   A testator may have various rights under a variety of types of contracts. Some at least of these rights may be capable of being bequeathed. This will not apply to rights under, for instance, contracts of employment which involve too great an element of *delectus personae*. Matters relating to leases (which are simply a form of contract) have been dealt with above (see para 4.75).

It is possible that the testator's rights under any contract may expire between the date of making the will and the date of death. For this reason, it is as well to qualify a legacy of contractual rights with the phrase 'if any'.

It is obviously the case that only contractual rights with the prospect of lasting for a reasonable length of time are likely to be the subject of a bequest, although provision can be made for what may be rights under a series of similar contracts.

It may be desirable to check the contract documentation at the time of drafting the will, not least to ensure that the contractual rights in question are capable of forming the subject of a legacy.

Perhaps the best example of a contractual right which might be the subject of a legacy is an option. A suitable form of legacy (which could readily be adapted for a number of different types of contractual right) would be as follows:

'I direct my executors to make over to A my rights under the option to

---

1 Copyright, Designs and Patents Act 1988, s 192.
2 Ibid, s 222(1).
3 Patents Act 1977, s 31.

sell ground at Middle Farm, Dalkeith, Midlothian, granted to me in terms of missives between myself and John Smith, 1 Walker Avenue, Edinburgh, dated 4 and 6 January 1994 (or any replacement therefor, as to which my executors shall be the sole judges).'

Rights of action

4.115 A right of action is a form of incorporeal property which is perhaps unlikely to form the subject of a legacy. By their very nature, rights of action tend to be unpredictable and it is unlikely that any testator would wish to make a legacy based on a vague possibility of obtaining such a right prior to his death. There may, however, be longstanding claims, for instance under insurance policies.

It is also possible to envisage a situation where a testator is in possession of such a right and anticipates his death in the near future. Indeed, it is possible that a right of action may be connected with his impending demise, for instance deriving from an accident. This type of situation lies behind certain provisions of the Damages (Scotland) Act 1976, as amended by the Damages (Scotland) Act 1993. Section 2 of the 1976 Act provides for a deceased's executor to bring or continue an action for personal injuries. Any sums recovered belong to the estate; but it is perfectly possible for a testator to bequeath the right to receive such sums to the beneficiary of his choice.

Quite apart from any rights arising out of a claim for personal injuries, a testator may have rights against another person arising out of contract, delict, or from some other reason. As regards contract, any right of action would be included in a bequest of the contractual rights themselves, but it is possible that an action may already have arisen at the time of drafting the will. It is possible that the contract itself has been avoided.

Pursuit of an action may be possible in some cases by a beneficiary or more typically the executors taking the place of the deceased.

In any event, the following form of words might be suitable as a legacy of this type:

'I direct my executors either (1) to make over to A my rights of action against B if A can effectively pursue such rights or (2) otherwise to pursue such rights and to make over to A any sums received in respect thereof.'

Rights in trusts and estates

4.116 A testator may have a vested right in a trust or estate, perhaps most commonly a vested fee in a liferent trust. It is essential to the nature of a vested right that its holder may dispose of it and this can be done by will. The exact form of legacy will of course depend on the nature of the trust right involved. A suitable general form of words would be:

'I direct my executors to make over to A my rights in the trust of B,

established in terms of B's will dated 6 January 1983 and recorded in
the Books of Council and Session on 10 April 1994.'
While a vested right in a trust is clearly an asset which may be effectively
bequeathed, more doubts may arise about a contingent right or a mere *spes
successionis*. However, it is thought that such rights can be the subjects of
legacies, although of course such legacies will be ineffectual if the testator fails to
acquire any vested right under the trust in question. For such a legacy, the words
'my rights' in the wording quoted above should be substituted by 'any rights I
may have at the date of my death'[1].

Debts

4.117 A debt due to the testator is an asset of his estate, which may be
bequeathed like any other. If the right to receive the sum due is to be left to a
third party, the form of legacy should be as follows:
> 'I direct my executors to make over to A my right to repayment of any
> balance outstanding of the sum of TEN THOUSAND POUNDS, loaned by
> me to B, as evidenced by Minute of Agreement between myself and B
> dated 5 October 1993, together with any interest outstanding.'

If the loan has been repaid by the date of death, this type of legacy will be
adeemed[2]. Difficulties may be caused if the loan has in effect not been repaid, but
been replaced by a different loan at the date of death. The executors can be given
discretion to decide whether the legacy has been adeemed, but fresh provision,
or provision anticipating the replacement of one debt with another, would be
preferable.

A legacy to a third party of debts due to a testator is unlikely to be commonly
encountered. It is much more likely that a testator would wish to write off a loan
made during his lifetime. This is in effect a legacy of the amount of the loan.

There is an example of such a legacy in purpose S2.20. Technically this could
be described as a legacy of the creditor's right in the loan to the debtor, so that
the loan itself is extinguished by confusion.

If the date of the loan is known, this should be included in the legacy, as an aid
to identification and clarification. It may also be appropriate to examine the
terms of the loan agreement or other documentation to check on exactly what is
being discharged by such a legacy. If the loan is secured, it will be appropriate to
direct the executors to discharge the security. It is as well to discharge any arrears
of interest, although these are probably included in such a legacy in any event[3]. It
would be possible to restrict the legacy to a proportion of any balance outstanding. Care would be needed in such a case in relation to any interest which might
be written off; this too might be proportionate.

---

1 On legacies of trust interests, see *McLaren* II, paras 1560–1562.
2 See *Cobban's Executors v Cobban* 1915 SC 82 and paras 4.15–4.17 above.
3 See *Cunninghame* (1871) 10 M 49.

4.118   An alternative to a bequest of any balance outstanding would be a direction to executors to write off the balance of any loan. A further alternative would simply be a cancellation by the testator of any outstanding debt due[1].

A further possibility is that the testator may wish to extend the terms of the loan, which of course gives a rather more limited benefit to the debtor[2]. This can be coupled with the legacy of the creditor's right in the loan to a third party, but this right might simply form part of residue. An extension of the terms of the loan could take the following form:

> 'Considering that I have made a loan of FIVE THOUSAND POUNDS to A repayable on demand in terms of the receipt signed by A on 1 February 1994, I direct my executors to extend the terms of the loan made to A, so that it is only repayable five years after the date of my death, with no interest being due at or before that time.'

Accounts

4.119   It is possible for a testator to leave the contents of a particular bank or building society account to a beneficiary. Such an account is merely a form of contractual right, in the form of a debt due to the account holder. Of course, the extent of such a legacy may well vary, depending on the testator's operations on the account in question[3]. This may be exactly what the testator intends, in that he can effectively alter what a particular beneficiary is to receive without any need to alter his will. Indeed, such a legacy within the direct control of a testator might be a useful suggestion for those testators obsessed with waging family war by means of will and codicil.

It is particularly important that provision is made in the legacy of an account for a possible replacement of the designated account by another. As noted in paragraph 4.15 above, there is specific authority that ademption will occur where a bequeathed account is moved to another branch of the same bank[4]. It is not certain that ademption would occur if there was a move from one type of account to another with the same branch of the same organisation, but with terms of accounts changing so rapidly, the risk should not be taken.

It may well be appropriate to include interest in the legacy of an account. An appropriate form of wording would be:

> 'I direct my executors to make over to A the sum at credit of my account numbered 727083 with the Pitreavie Building Society, George Street, Edinburgh (or any replacement account with the Pitreavie Building Society, as to which my executors shall be the sole judges), together with interest accrued at the date of my death and arising after my death.'

---

1 See *Elder* p 49, form 57.
2 *Alexander v Lowson's Trustees* (1890) 17 R 571.
3 *Gellatly's Trustees v Royal Infirmary of Edinburgh* (1905) 13 SLT 38.
4 *Ballantyne's Trustees v Ballantyne's Trustees* 1941 SC 35.

Shares in public companies and unit trusts

4.120　Most of the comments about private company shares made in relation to purpose S2.16 in paragraphs 4.102–4.105 above are also relevant to shares in public companies, including especially quoted shares.

It would be unusual to include the company number in a legacy of quoted shares. Without such an inclusion, it would then be appropriate to add the word 'renaming' to the list of possible changes in the company in which the shares bequeathed are held, in order to prevent such changes causing ademption.

It is much more likely that replacement of an actual holding, whether by reorganisation, takeover or simple reinvestment will take place when dealing with quoted shares. Such shares are more liable to be held purely as an investment than is the case with shares in private companies.

It is probably the case that some of the difficulties identified in paragraphs 4.102–4.105 in connection with legacies of holdings of shares militate against encouraging such specific legacies, at least of shareholdings in large public companies held essentially as investments. In addition, demergers or other reorganisations might not only make identification difficult but radically alter the value of any particular legacy. A testator should at least be warned of the possible difficulties. There are seldom insurmountable reasons demanding that public company shares be left in a specific legacy to a particular individual.

Many of the same considerations apply to unit trusts. While unit trust holdings are not traded between individual investors (but rather between investor and manager), they may form the subject of a specific legacy. The legatee can be registered as the new holder of the testator's holdings. It should be made clear that the legacy includes any units (whether certificated or not) which have accumulated with the testator's ordinal holding, as such accumulations are a common method effectively of paying income on unit trusts investments.

Personal equity plans

4.121　A testator may wish to leave his holding in a personal equity plan as a legacy. There is no reason in principle why he should not do so. A personal equity plan, while consisting of shares or unit trusts, has some of the characteristics of a bank or other account. There are, however, possible problems.

It is probably easiest if the testator wishes his beneficiary simply to receive the *proceeds* of a plan. In such a case, a suitable wording would be:

'I direct my executors to pay to A the proceeds of my personal equity plan number A123456 with Standard Life.'

A number of points should be considered. It is probably desirable to add 'together with any dividends or interest received in respect of this plan after my death', to avoid any conflict between the specific legatee and those entitled to income from the estate.

Possible ademption should also be considered. If the plan number were to change, perhaps by consolidation with other plans, this may cause difficulties. However, the number is also of assistance in identification if the testator owns more than one plan with the same organisation. The words 'or any replacement for this plan, as to which my executors shall be the sole judges' could be added. This would also cover the situation where the plan has been transferred to another provider.

If the testator holds only one plan, or all plans are going to the same beneficiary, it may well be better to omit specific references and simply bequeath 'the proceeds of all personal equity plans owned by me at the time of my death.'

4.122 If the testator wishes to leave the contents of different plans to different people, extreme care may be required. As noted above, different plans with the same provider may be consolidated and be dealt with under the same reference number. If the testator intends to go on adding to a plan, or taking out further plans in future years, his holdings in this medium may grow considerably. It should be checked whether he is content for such a legacy of personal equity plan proceeds to increase accordingly. Equally, the testator may realise personal equity plans before his death, in which case he may wish to provide an alternative pecuniary legacy[1].

If a testator wishes to leave the actual shares held in a personal equity plan, this may be difficult, impractical or even impossible. In certain cases the rules of a plan may prevent transfer. For these reasons, an alternative should always be provided as follows:

> 'I direct my executors to make over to A the holdings of shares, other investments and cash balance in my personal equity plan number A123456 with Standard Life, or, in the event that such transfer is impossible or impractical in whole or in part, as to which my executors shall be the sole judges, I direct my executors to pay the proceeds of this plan (to the extent that it is not transferred) to A, together with (in either case) any dividends or interest received in respect of this plan after my death.'

It should be noted that the tax exemption for personal equity plans ceases on death.

Stock (including government stock)

4.123 A testator can make a legacy of a particular holding of stock, whether gilts or otherwise. As the stock may be replaced or change its form between the date of drafting the will and the date of death, many of the same considerations apply as is the case for legacies of shareholdings (see purpose S2.16 and paras 4.102–4.105).

However, a legacy of loan stock, or at least government stock, is a general legacy, which apparently will not adeem even if the testator does not own the particular holding at death, unless there are clear indications in the will that the legacy is only of the testator's particular holding owned at the time of drafting[2].

---

1 For an example of such a legacy which can be adapted for this context, see para 4.16.
2 See 25 *Stair Memorial Encyclopaedia* para 854; and para 4.15 above.

Given that most stock produces a fixed or quantifiable rate of interest, consideration should be given to whether a legacy of stock is to include interest running from the date of death. The general provision on legacies included in the Styles (see, for example, S2.5) excludes interest on legacies unless specific provision is made. Such provision may well be appropriate with legacies of stock. (Some care is required in the administration of the estate in these circumstances, as both the testator's death and, usually, the transfer by executors to the legatee are potentially chargeable events for the purposes of the accrued income scheme for income tax.) The following form of wording might be appropriate for a legacy of stock:

'I direct my executors to make over to A my holding of £20,000 11% Treasury Stock 1999 (or any replacement Government Stock as to which my executors shall be the sole judges), but only if I hold £20,000 nominal of some form of Government Stock at the date of my death, together with interest running on the stock from the date of my death until made over.'

National savings

4.124 To the extent that government stock constitutes a national savings asset[1], it has been dealt with above (see para 4.123). However, there are a range of National Savings products which may, or in some cases may not, be the subject of specific legacies.

Premium bonds may not be transferred. They may be held and take part in the draw for up to 12 months after the end of the month of death. It would thus be possible, although perhaps unlikely, for a testator to direct that any prizes won after death should be paid to a particular beneficiary.

National Savings Ordinary Investment bank accounts are no different from other savings accounts (see para 4.119). Therefore any balance at credit on such accounts can be left as a specific legacy.

National Savings Certificates can be the subject of a legacy. Any certificates bequeathed can be held in addition to the maximum imposed on the holding of any individual for any particular issue. However, if certificates inherited take an individual above the maximum, he can no longer utilise any amount of his limit unused prior to the inheritance.

The Department of National Savings issues a range of bonds, including the Income Bond, the Capital Bond, the FIRST Option Bond and the Pensioners' Bond. All such bonds are capable of transfer and can therefore be the subjects of legacies. As with National Savings Certificates, any amount inherited can be in addition to the normal individual maximum imposed. However, there are possible problems in that the recipient of the FIRST Option Bond must be 16 or over at the time of transfer; and the recipient of a Pensioners' Bond must be 65 or

---

1 Ie when held on the National Savings Stock Register.

over at the time of transfer. As the testator would not be able to know the age of intended legatees at the time of his death, and in any event destinations-over may take bequests to other than his original intended legatee, it may be as well to make provision for what is to happen should it turn out not to be possible to transfer the bonds themselves. Suitable wording might be as follows:

'I direct my executors to make over to A, whom failing to B, any Pensioners' Bonds held by me at the time of my death, declaring that if it should not be possible for any reason to transfer these bonds, I direct my executors to pay to A, whom failing to B, the proceeds of their realisation, together with any income payable after the date of my death.'

Life insurance policies and bonds

4.125 A testator may wish to leave the proceeds of a particular life insurance policy on his own life in a specific legacy. There is no particular problem about this. Such a legacy could take the following form:

'I direct my executors to make over to A the whole proceeds received from Scottish Amicable life insurance policy number A2/1278.'

If the testator does wish to make such a bequest, particularly if the proceeds are likely to be substantial, he should be encouraged to consider making a lifetime gift of the policy either into trust or directly to the intended beneficiary. This is generally easy to achieve (policy documents often contain the appropriate forms) and would take the policy proceeds outwith the testator's estate for inheritance tax purposes. Such a gift would be a potentially exempt transfer.

A testator may also have rights in policies on the life of another person. Such policies are simply assets of the testator's estate. They will not mature on the death of the testator and indeed may run for many years afterwards without any proceeds being paid. Such policies may be a form of pure investment. There may be regular premiums to be paid, for which the testator may wish to make provision in his will. Suitable wording for a legacy of this kind of policy right would be as follows:

'I direct my executors to make over to A my interest in Equitable Life policy number VM111223 on the life of Mrs Morag Jones, together with the sum of ONE THOUSAND POUNDS to assist A in paying the remaining premiums on this policy.'

There are a large number of types of single premium insurance policy, which generally go under the name of bonds, but which may well mature on the testator's death. These are essentially investment vehicles and any amount payable on death will more usually represent a return on this investment rather than the genuine proceeds of life cover. In any event, such bonds can be the subject of legacies; again, identification by the number of the bond would be useful, although the testator may wish to make provision for one particular bond to be replaced by another for the same or a similar amount, perhaps allowing discretion to the executors as to identifying a replacement.

Lloyd's interest

4.126 A Lloyd's underwriting interest constitutes an asset which can be bequeathed. An example of such a legacy can be found at S2.19. The bequest does not make the legatee a name at Lloyd's, but merely gives the legatee the benefit of the Lloyd's assets. While the legacy could alternatively have been of specific shares or cash, a legacy of Lloyd's assets is commonly given because of the 100 per cent business relief for inheritance tax purposes which is generally available for these assets. Lloyd's funds are an area of complexity and the style given here is a fairly simple legacy. More specific arrangements may be needed in appropriate cases.

Lloyd's assets include the Lloyd's deposit (traditionally stock exchange investments but often now a bank guarantee secured over other assets), special and personal reserve funds (usually stock exchange investments and cash), stop loss policy and estate protection plan insurance arrangements, the undistributed profits for the open years of account (of which there will be at least three at any time), and income and gains on the deposit and reserves. The style legacy attempts to cover all of these various assets. If a bank guarantee is held as part of the deposit then consideration should be given as to whether to include the property taken as security by the bank for this guarantee. Such property will usually attract inheritance tax relief and it has been included in the Style. The size and identity of the various assets involved should be considered in each case.

The Lloyd's interest will be subject to losses of any of the open years and to any other expenses relating to the interest. The legacy includes liability for income tax and capital gains tax in respect of underwriting profits or deposit and reserve income and capital gains. These tax liabilities are liabilities of the executors, but are put with this legacy so as to keep all of the Lloyd's related profits and losses together.

4.127 The legacy has also been made subject to the appropriate proportion of inheritance tax. The point of a legacy of Lloyd's funds is generally to obtain inheritance tax business property relief and such a legacy should not generally be in favour of a surviving spouse. Usually not all of the Lloyd's funds will be granted business property relief. It may be possible to provide that the legacy of the Lloyd's funds is not of the whole of the Lloyd's funds but only of the part of these which attracts business relief. The subject of the bequest will thus attract the whole of the business relief. This is a particularly difficult area and reference should be made to more specialised texts[1].

Because of the complexities of the subject matter, the executors' decision as to what is to be included has been made conclusive.

---

1 See Oerton (1990) Capital Taxes and Estate Planning Quarterly 81; *Butterworths Wills Probate and Administration Service* Form 1A.14.3.

Bets

4.128 It is not perhaps very likely that the potential proceeds of any betting transactions will be at the forefront of the testator's mind when drafting a will. However, if one of the reasons for the will being drafted is anticipation of an early death, a testator may have in his possession potentially valuable items subject to fortune. An increasingly important example may be a ticket in the national lottery. A more traditional example might be a wager on a horse race (it being entirely usual for serious gamblers to bet on major races up to years in advance of their taking place). Entry into pools competitions may be made (by standing order) for quite a long period in advance. It is possible that Elvis Presley may be found alive, aliens may land on Earth, or the Scottish football team may win the World Cup. There seems no reason in principle why a testator should not bequeath any potential proceeds from his skill as a forecaster.

However, there may be serious practical problems as, traditionally, gambling debts have never been enforceable by law. This will not create difficulties where no name is attached to the crucial evidence, such as a betting slip or lottery ticket. The pools companies may also pay to the legatee or executors of a deceased entrant. In any event, suitable wording for such a legacy might be:

'I direct my executors to make over to A any betting slips or other evidence of wagers [OR lottery tickets], together with my right to collect any resultant winnings.'

ANNUITIES

4.129 It may be that provision of an annuity forms a suitable legacy in certain cases, perhaps for an employee or even a spouse. In many ways, this is similar to providing a liferent, but the amount of income to be received by the annuitant will be fixed (although provision can be made for its increase). If the annuity is actually to be provided out of estate assets, in effect continuing trusts will be required; provision can thus be made for its purchase, but this has certain problems.

An annuity may be a legacy which the testator specifically wishes to rank above others for the purposes of abatement if necessary (see paras 4.07–4.11).

Purpose S2.21 contains direction to pay an annuity. As a continuing trust may be created, an annuity may be more suitable in wills where there are already trust purposes. Purpose S2.21 involves a single individual, but there is no reason why there should not be more than annuitant, or indeed an annuity can be provided to a class of beneficiaries. In the case of multiple annuitants, the legacy should commence:

'I direct my executors to pay to A and B an annuity of . . .'
This would imply equal shares and survivorship. If it is desired to exclude survivorship, other than in a class gift, the word 'equally' should be inserted, or the annuity should be made payable to 'each of' the various beneficiaries. In general, the rules on multiple beneficiaries would apply to the legacy of an annuity in the same way as to any other bequest (see paras 5.02–5.14).

The annuity in purpose S2.21 goes on to provide for payment of the desired annual sum. If it is envisaged that the annuity may last for a number of years, consideration could be given to increasing it by some such wording as follows:

'. . . an annuity of TWO THOUSAND POUNDS to be increased by 2% compound each year following my death. . .'

This is not particularly recommended, as the effects of compound interest can be devastating over a number of years.

Provision can also be made to increase the stated sum in the period between the date of the *will* and the date of death of the testator to cope with inflation; but regular review of the will is a better solution to this type of problem.

The annuity is declared to be subject to income tax. This would be implied in any event, but draws attention to the fact that the payers of the annuity must deduct basic rate tax on making each payment[1]. If a direction is given to make payments 'free of tax' or 'free of income tax', this can cause great confusion as to the amount to be paid[2]. This is not recommended.

If a testator insists on specifying the amount the annuitant is actually to receive, after the deduction of tax, appropriate wording might be:

'. . . such sum as after deduction of income tax at the basic rate shall amount to TWO THOUSAND POUNDS. . .'

4.130   An annuity will generally start to run from the date of death but it can be directed that it should commence from a later date (say three months after the testator's death). The executors can instead be given discretion as to when the annuity is to commence.

The date of commencement should be distinguished from the intervals at which the annuity is to be paid. This can be stated by the testator, for example, '. . . payment by equal or quarterly instalments in arrears. . .'. However, it is suggested that in this instance the executors are given flexibility to vary the dates of payment. This facilitates tying payment of the annuity to the payment dates of government or other stock, which may be the most convenient way for it to be financed.

If the intervals of payment are stated, it is possible to add provision for interest at a stated rate in the event of late payment by the trustees of each instalment. The payment of interest, although not its rate, would be implied in any event.

4.131   Strictly, there is no need to make specific provision as to the funding of the annuity. However if such provision is not made, the executors have the difficulty of deciding what to retain to meet the payments and this will affect the distribution of the rest of the estate. While this is more acceptable in cases where there are other continuing trust purposes, it is by no means ideal.

Provision can be made for paying the annuity either by creating a separate fund or by permitting purchase of an annuity from a commercial provider, as has been done in S2.21(1) and (2). The latter has the merit of certainty and enables the administration of the estate to be completed, but may be more expensive and

---

1 Income and Corporation Taxes Act 1988, ss 348, 349.
2 *Wordie's Trustees v Wordie* 1922 SC 28; *Richmond's Trustees v Richmond* 1935 SC 585.

reduce the amount left for residuary beneficiaries. It is also possible that the annuitant may defeat the testator's wishes (see further below). The former would delay administration and indeed itself cause further administration, but is perhaps more likely to meet the testator's wishes.

Purpose S2.21 gives the executors (trustees for this purpose) discretion as to the amount of funds to be retained. A third alternative may be added as follows:

'. . . (3) by arranging for one or more of the residuary beneficiaries under this will to take over liability for payment of the annuity.'

Such an arrangement would be very simple from the point of view of administration. In practical terms, the residuary beneficiary would grant a bond of annuity direct to the annuitant and the executors would be discharged.

4.132 Questions then arise as to what is to happen if the income produced is insufficient or excessive (one of which is likely except perhaps where government stock is used). Purpose S2.21 provides for recourse to capital in the event of insufficiency, but only the capital of the separate fund. It can instead be provided that recourse should *not* be had to capital but that the annuitant should merely receive the income available, with the right to claim surplus income from other years. Without specific provision, recourse may be had to the capital of the whole estate if income is insufficient to meet the annuity[1]. If the income of the fund is surplus to the amount required to pay the annuity, purpose S2.21 provides for its accumulation with the capital of the fund for the period permitted by law[2]. This is useful to provide for years where the income may be *insufficient*. The accumulated income would be subject to the higher rate of income tax applicable to discretionary trusts[3].

An alternative is to provide for immediate distribution of any surplus as follows:

'. . . declaring that any surplus income may be distributed at any time as part of the residue of my estate. . .'

Making provision for surplus income is particularly important where vesting of the residue is postponed. If it is to be distributed in these circumstances, it should be made particularly clear to whom it is to go; this could be to '. . .such residuary beneficiaries as are alive when the surplus income arises. . .'. It should be remembered that any surplus income distributed in this way will be taxable on the residuary beneficiaries.

4.133 Purpose S2.21 also gives the trustees power to commute the annuity by payment of a capital sum to the annuitant, subject to his written consent. This may be useful to bring burdensome administration to an end, although again the interests of the annuitant and residuary legatees require to be balanced. Commutation will not involve inheritance tax consequences in respect of the capital paid

---

1 *Colqhoun's Trustees v Colqhoun* 1922 SC 32.
2 See the Trusts (Scotland) Act 1961, s 5(2)(b).
3 Income and Corporation Taxes Act 1988, s 686.

to the annuitant[1]. However, the balance released for residuary beneficiaries may be treated as a transfer of value by the annuitant[2].

It has been suggested that the commutation merely fulfils a bequest already charged at the testator's death and a comparison can be made to the provisions as to the redemption of an English surviving spouse's life interest[3]. It might also be argued that any deemed transfer of value does not attract inheritance tax as it was not intended to confer gratuitous benefit[4]. Neither of these arguments is conclusive and the possibility of a transfer of value should not be ignored. Exemptions, including the annual exemption, may reduce this transfer and any balance remaining should be potentially exempt for the annuitant.

If an annuity is financed by retention by the trustees provision is required to deal with the fund on the termination of the annuity. This is dealt with in purpose S2.21 simply by passing the fund (together with any income accumulated beyond the permitted period or any balance on commutation of the annuity) to the residuary beneficiaries. This amount will vest along with the remainder of residue, even if it is indeterminate at the date of death and the remainder of residue vests at that date.

It can be specifically provided that vesting is postponed until the date of distribution. It can also be provided that the separate fund, or any part of it, passes to separate beneficiaries entirely on the termination of the annuity.

The death of the annuitant will involve aggregation of the annuity fund with his own estate for inheritance tax purposes, as the annuitant will have an interest in possession in the fund. This may bring an inheritance tax charge for the trustees[5].

4.134 It will be seen that retention of a fund to pay an annuity involves complications and possible expense. It may thus seem eminently sensible to allow for its provision by purchase from a commercial provider of annuities. It should be noted that there is no implied power of purchase, so express provision should be made[6].

The difficulty with providing for the purchase of an annuity is that without careful drafting, it is open to the annuitant to claim the purchase price of the annuity instead. This would defeat the testator's intentions and is an example of repugnancy (see paras 5.54–5.55 below). Such a consequence can only be avoided if there is a continuing trust, and the annuity is purchased in the names of the trustees with payments to the annuitant for his alimentary use[7]. Strictly speaking, the payments may not require to be for 'alimentary use', but this is mentioned in many of the authorities in this area. Such wording has the added merit of protecting the annuity from the debts of the annuitant. It does not

---

1 Inheritance Tax Act 1984, s 53(2).
2 Ibid, s 52(1).
3 Ibid, s 17(c).
4 Ibid, s 10.
5 Ibid, ss 49, 50 and 201.
6 *Graham's Trustees v Graham's Trustees* (1898) 1 F 357.
7 *Brown's Trustees v Thom* 1916 SC 32; *Dempster's Trustees v Dempster* 1921 SC 322; *Arnold's Trustees v Graham* 1927 SC 353.

however defeat the necessary continuing nature of the trust if payments are made directly to the annuitant, which would in effect remove the administrative burdens otherwise created by the continuing trusts[1].

There is no doubt that provision for purchase of an annuity will remove many of the difficulties inherent in a bequest of this nature. Normally, purchased annuities have an income tax advantage, in that part of the payments received by the annuitant will be a return of capital. However, this specifically does not apply to 'any annuity purchased in pursuance of any direction in a will'[2].

It may thus be preferable to give an outright legacy; the legatee can then purchase an annuity should he so wish and obtain the income tax advantages. The same would of course apply on commutation of an annuity. In either case no guarantee could be given that the legatee would act accordingly. It is thought that a condition attached to such a legacy would either involve repugnancy, or would in any event still fall foul of the Income and Corporation Taxes Act 1988, section 657(2)(c). It may be that a bequest to a third party, on condition that the third party provides an annuity for the intended annuity beneficiary, would succeed in retaining the income tax advantages of a purchased annuity, but such an arrangement is likely to be unduly complex for the vast majority of cases.

4.135 Finally, the following shorter form of annuity may also be considered as a possibility:

'I direct my executors to pay to A an annuity of TWO THOUSAND POUNDS during his life payable subject to income tax, declaring that my executors may provide for payment:

(1) by setting aside part of my estate as a separate fund;

(2) by purchasing a suitable annuity;

(3) by arranging for one or more of the residuary beneficiaries to take over liability for payment; or

(4) by commuting it for a capital sum with the consent in writing of the annuitant;

and in relation to paragraphs (1) and (2), the annuitant shall have no further claim on the residue of my estate, and in relation to paragraphs (3) and (4), the annuitant shall have no further claim on my executors.'

Most of the points made in the text above apply to this provision.

TRUSTS FOR SPECIAL OR GENERAL LEGACIES

4.136 As the need for or desirability of putting assets in trusts more often derives from the nature of the beneficiary (the object of bequest) rather than its subject, trusts are dealt with in detail in the next two chapters. Many of the trust provisions in the styles relate to residue or parts of residue, but it is perfectly

---

1 *Branford's Trustees v Powell* 1924 SC 439.
2 Income and Corporation Taxes Act 1988, s 657(2)(c).

possible and desirable on occasions to put specific assets or pecuniary legacies into trusts.

Examples can be found in S6.5, which contains a liferent of a house to the testator's mother (see paras 5.81–5.82); and in S10.5, which includes a nil rate band discretionary trust (see paras 5.94–5.107).

One very important matter is the need to define clearly the funds or property held in trust. The phrase generally used is something like 'the Discretionary Fund' or 'the Trust Fund', both of which would generally be accepted as capable of including specific assets as well as cash. If there were felt to be any doubts about this, particularly where the assets to be held in trust are exclusively specific items rather than cash, the phrase used could be 'the Trust assets' or 'the Discretionary property'. The point about defining the trust fund becomes particularly relevant when considering an accumulation and maintenance trust for a limited fund or, conceivably, for specific assets. This might be relevant for a large pecuniary legacy, such as that of £100,000 to grandchildren in S4.3. The main style of accumulation and maintenance trust presented (Style S7) is for the whole residue of the testator's estate. It is a general provision affecting '. . . any part of the residue of my estate held for a beneficiary under the age of 25 years which is referred to as "the Trust Fund" . . .'. (see purpose S7.7).

4.137 If a limited part of the testator's estate is to be held on an accumulation and maintenance trust for beneficiaries aged under 25 there are two possible ways of achieving this. The first is to include a general purpose, along the following lines:

'I direct my Trustees to hold any part of my estate which falls to a beneficiary who has not attained the age of 25 years in accordance with purpose (SEVEN) [OR as appropriate].'

This would mean that the accumulation and maintenance trust provisions simply extended to any part of the testator's estate.

In the accumulation and maintenance trust purpose itself, the phrase 'the residue of' would simply be deleted wherever it occurred and minor alterations would be required to purpose S7.7(4) if the beneficiaries were not issue of the testator. As the accumulation and maintenance trust provisions would then extend to any assets in the estate, suitable specific or general legacies could then be included for appropriate beneficiaries.

However, this method has the severe drawback that if small or token legacies (whether pecuniary or specific) ended up falling to beneficiaries under 25 (perhaps because of a destination-over or even the operation of the *conditio si institutus sine liberis decesserit*), such items would require to be held in an unwieldy trust structure.

Accordingly, a better course is simply to provide for an accumulation and maintenance trust to apply to each relevant legacy, as follows:

'I direct my executors to pay to such of A, B and C as shall survive me equally among them if more than one the sum of ONE HUNDRED THOUSAND POUNDS declaring that if any part of this legacy falls to a beneficiary who has not attained the age of 25, my Trustees shall hold the same as a separate fund in accordance with purpose (SEVEN) [or as appropriate].'

The accumulation and maintenance trust provisions could then direct the trustees to hold for eligible accumulation and maintenance trust purposes any part of any legacy granted in any affected clauses, which was being held for a beneficiary under the age of 25 years. A younger age could of course be selected. The provisions in S7.7 would again require slight modification if the beneficiaries were not issue of the testator. This formulation could cope with different sets of beneficiaries taking under separate clauses of the will.

However, the very brief form of accumulation and maintenance trust in S8.8 might be much more appropriate for a legacy other than residue which is to be held on accumulation and maintenance trusts. The reference in the legacies affected could then be to a clause setting out these shorter terms.

Assets or pecuniary legacies can also be held on liferent or discretionary trusts. Styles S5, S6, S9 and S10 can readily be adapted so that the trusts provisions apply to a more limited part of the estate, rather than the whole of or shares in residue, as in the versions presented.

As trust purposes will generally contain references to 'my Trustees', it is important when putting specific assets into trust to ensure that executors (or, indeed, other persons) are also appointed as trustees.

CHAPTER 5

THE OBJECTS OF
BEQUEST – GENERAL

INTRODUCTION

5.01 This chapter is concerned with the objects of bequest – the intended recipients of the testator's estate or items from it. Problems can arise in a general context, for example where there is more than one possible recipient of a legacy, or in a specific context, for example where the intended beneficiaries are subject to physical, mental or legal disability, or are children from a relationship other than the testator's current one. Such problems can arise whether dealing with general, specific or residuary legacies, and whatever their subject.

MULTIPLE BENEFICIARIES

5.02 The simplest form of will is where the testator has a single beneficiary and is prepared for his estate to fall into intestacy should that beneficiary fail to survive him. That would be quite an unusual will; more commonly, the testator will wish to benefit a range of legatees and will consider how his estate is to be divided. Most of the Styles provide for some form of division of the estate. At its simplest, the division will consist of one or more specific legacies with the residue going to a single individual, but problems can arise if a legacy or the residue is to be shared or the intended beneficiary does not survive the testator. The latter problem is dealt with below (see paras 5.15–5.19); the former is addressed here.

One solution with multiple beneficiaries is simply to deal with each legatee separately, making specific provision for what is to happen in the event of that legatee predeceasing. No such provision will be necessary if the testator is content for failed specific legacies to fall into residue and for failed residuary legacies to fall into intestacy. These consequences may not be desirable; but if there are a large number of beneficiaries a will with repeated provisions for a legatee predeceasing may appear unduly repetitive and unwieldy. However, such a scheme has the merits of clarity and may be particularly suitable where one is dealing with a testator without children or other close relatives, wishing to pass his estate on to a limited number of beneficiaries.

To give an example of the operative provisions of such a will (and assuming that purposes (ONE) to (FIVE) have been taken from Style S2):

'(SIX) I direct my executors to pay

(a)   To my friend A the sum of FIVE THOUSAND POUNDS; and

(b) To my friend B whom failing his son C the sum of TEN THOUSAND POUNDS.

(SEVEN) I direct my executors to make over

(a) One half of the residue of my estate to my friend D ; and

(b) One half of the residue of my estate to my friend E whom failing my friend F.'

This will could be completed by using purposes S2.24–2.26. In such a will it is important to note that if A were to predecease, the legacy of £5,000 would fall into residue; and if D were to predecease the half share of residue bequeathed to him would fall into intestacy. Specifically it would *not* pass to E.

It would of course be possible (and perhaps likely) in the event of one beneficiary failing to survive the testator that he would wish another of his existing beneficiaries to take the legacy bequeathed to the person who has failed to survive. Such provision would fit readily into the type of will just referred to, but in the event of a beneficiary being potentially entitled to more than one legacy, it should be made clear that the bequests are cumulative.

Although it is possible in effect to provide for multiple beneficiaries by separating out their interests, it may be more convenient to give a single legacy (particularly of residue) to a number of persons. It is then that questions relating to accretion may arise.

ACCRETION AND CLASS GIFTS

5.03 The basic rule where a legacy is given to more than one person is that if one or more of the legatees fail to survive the testator, the share due to that legatee will accresce to the others[1]. Such a legacy could take this form:

'I direct my executors to pay to A, B and C the sum of SIX THOUSAND POUNDS.'

If all three legatees survive, each would take £2,000; if two survive, each would take £3,000; if one survives, he will take the whole £6,000.

This general rule on accretion is easily displaced however. All that is required is the use of what have been termed 'words of severance' attached to the legacy. Examples of such words of severance are 'equally', 'equally among them', 'in equal shares' and 'share and share alike'. If such words of severance are used, accretion will not operate in the event of one or more beneficiaries predeceasing; each is simply entitled to his own share[2].

To exclude accretion in the clause just referred to, it would simply be necessary to frame it as follows:

'I direct my executors to pay to A, B and C equally among them the sum of SIX THOUSAND POUNDS.'

In this case, if one or two of the legatees predecease, £2,000 or £4,000 will fall

1 Stair *Institutions* III, 8, 27; *Andrew's Executors v Andrew's Trustees* 1925 SC 844.
2 *Paxton's Trustees v Cowie* (1886) 13 R 1191; *White's Trustee* 1957 SC 322; *Fraser's Trustee v Fraser* 1980 SLT 211; *Young's Trustees v Young* 1927 SC (HL) 6.

into residue; this may be perfectly acceptable but if a testator wishes to avoid this consequence he should provide for a destination-over in the case of each share. He would probably be better to provide for separate legacies if that was his wish.

Accretion can also be effectively and elegantly excluded in the case of legacies of equal size by use of the phrase 'each of', as for example:

'I direct my executors to pay to each of A, B and C the sum of TWO THOUSAND POUNDS.'

If the legacy in a format excluding accretion is itself of residue or a share of residue, the predecease of one legatee will put his share into intestacy. This is likely to be a much more damaging consequence than in the case of a specific legacy. If shares of residue are given to beneficiaries who do not form a class (see para 5.04), it is important to consider destinations-over if accretion is to be excluded.

The use of the words of severance, particularly 'equally' might be thought to make the position very clear for the testator and others reading the will, but the danger of excluding accretion cannot be ignored. However, it is possible to preserve accretion even using such words by restricting the legacy to the survivors of the intended legatees, as for example:

'I direct my executors to pay to such of A, B and C as shall survive me equally among them the sum of SIX THOUSAND POUNDS.'

5.04 Using words of severance provides an exception to the normal rule that accretion will operate on a legacy to more than one person. There is however an exception to that exception in the form of class gifts. Notwithstanding words of severance, accretion *will* operate on a legacy to a class[1]. This is fortunate in that with gifts to a class of beneficiaries it will usually meet with the testator's expectations that the share of a beneficiary predeceasing will go to others in that class. It may be, however, that children of that deceased beneficiary should stand in their parent's place, but this can also be dealt with in a class gift (see further below and paras 5.26–5.27).

Probably the most common form of class gift is one to 'my children'[2]. This may be extended to 'issue'[3]. More unusual classes are possible[4].

It is important to note that if the beneficiaries who form a class are merely listed by name and not by reference to the class of which they form part, this does not constitute a class gift as such[5]. Thus, a legacy 'to A, B, C and D equally among them' will not involve accretion even if all four legatees are in fact children of the testator. If, in fact, it is desired to avoid accretion, one possibility is that any class designation affecting the multiple beneficiaries is *deliberately* omitted.

However, reference to a class is certainly helpful for clarity. It may be that the

1 *Muir's Trustees v Muir* (1889) 16 R 154; *Roberts' Trustees v Roberts* (1903) 5 F 541.
2 See, for example, *Mair's Trustees v Mair* 1936 SC 731.
3 But see *Boyd's Trustee v Shaw* 1958 SC 115 at 121 per LP Clyde.
4 Eg nieces and nephews – see *Clow's Trustees v Bethune* 1935 SC 754; executors or trustees – see *Elder* p 40, form 45.
5 *Graham's Trustees v Graham* (1899) 2 F 232.

testator wishes to make a legacy to what is undoubtedly a class of beneficiaries, but specifically to avoid accretion. This can be achieved by making separate legacies listing the beneficiaries; alternatively if the phrase 'each of' is inserted before the class designation, it is thought that this will avoid accretion, unless words of survivorship are also used[1].

Accretion is probably desirable in most family wills where the legatees are children or remoter issue. Apart from the question of destinations-over (see paras 5.26–5.27) the form used in the Styles is 'to such of my children A, B and C and any other children of mine as shall survive me equally among them if more than one . . .'.

This is clearly a class gift, the class being such children as survive the testator. The use of the words 'equally' will not prevent accretion operating in the event of one or more children predeceasing, although of course the provisions as to destinations-over may then come into effect (see further below). If it is specifically desired to exclude accretion, then a suggested wording (deliberately omitting words of survivorship) is as follows:

'. . . in equal shares to each of my children A, B and C and any other children of mine . . .'

DIVISION AMONG BENEFICIARIES

5.05 If a legacy is simply given to a number of beneficiaries, the presumption is that equal shares are intended, whether or not the word 'equally' is used. This was indicated above; the wording 'to A, B and C the sum of SIX THOUSAND POUNDS' would carry £2,000 to each beneficiary if they all survived.

It is, however, possible that the testator wishes a legacy to pass in *unequal* shares. This is inappropriate for a pecuniary gift, where separate legacies should be used, but it may be desirable with some item of physical property, especially heritage. A suitable form of wording would be:

'I direct my executors to make over my interest in the house Arran View, Girvan, free of all expenses of transfer, heritable debts and securities and other capital burdens affecting my interest in the house at the time of my death as to a ONE HALF SHARE to A whom failing to B, as to a ONE QUARTER SHARE to C whom failing to his children equally among them if more than one and as to a ONE QUARTER SHARE to D whom failing to his wife E.'

This is obviously a provision of some complexity. As the legacy stands there is provision to deal separately with each legatee's share in the event of any of them predeceasing, but there is no provision dealing with the situation if *all* potential beneficiaries of a particular share were to predecease (for example, if both A and B were to predecease). Notably there will be no accretion in these circumstances and shares undisposed of will fall into residue or intestacy. It is also worth noting

---

1 See *Elder* p 40, forms 38 and 39, and p 44, note 23.

that as the subject of the legacy is heritable, there is a presumption that the destinations-over create substitution, not conditional institution. This is dealt with further in paragraphs 5.26–5.27. The effect of this could be that if a primary beneficiary, having survived the testator, failed to dispose of the subject of bequest (whether by lifetime or testamentary disposition), the subject would pass on that beneficiary's death in terms of this will rather than according to the intestacy of the beneficiary.

5.06 It is perhaps more likely that the testator would wish shares to accresce to the others sharing in the particular legacy; and indeed this might be preferable to providing destinations-over for each share in such a legacy. In either event, a declaration would be required to provide for accretion. Care would be required as to intended size of share in the event of a primary beneficiary predeceasing. Simplifying the previous legacy somewhat, the following wording might be suitable:

> 'I direct my executors to make over my interest in the house Arran View, Girvan, free of all expenses of transfer, heritable debts and securities and other capital burdens affecting my interest in the house at the time of my death as to a ONE HALF SHARE to A, as to a ONE QUARTER SHARE to B and as to a ONE QUARTER SHARE to C, declaring that if any of A, B or C predecease me the survivor or the survivors of them shall take the share or shares (original and accresced) of those predeceasing equally among them if more than one survive me.'

With such a bequest, if A were to predecease, B and C would take one half each; if B or C were to predecease, A would take five-eighths and the remaining survivor three-eighths; and if only one beneficiary were to survive, he or she would take the whole legacy.

5.07 More complex alternatives can readily be imagined, if perhaps not encouraged! For instance, in this example it might be desired that A should retain his 'comparative advantage', such that he would always have a share twice as large as any other beneficiary. If that were the case, he would have to take a two-thirds share of the share of B or C should one of them predecease.

The situation is further complicated if there *are* destinations-over for particular shares, as in the first alternative in paragraph 5.05. Again, it is likely that the testator would wish shares to accresce to the other sharers in the legacy in the event of the failure of the destinations-over and it must be made clear in what proportions such accretion is to take place.

If the situation *is* complex, it is suggested that the best way to approach it is to separate out the shares in the legacy to as great an extent as possible, in effect creating separate legacies of *pro indiviso* shares. If accretion among the sharers is intended on the failure of preceding purposes, such a separation might mean that some repetition of instructions is required, but that is a small price to pay for clarity. An example of such a separation would be:

> 'I direct my executors to make over my interest in the house Arran View, Girvan, free of all expenses of transfer, heritable debts and

securities and other capital burdens affecting my interest in the house at the time of my death in the following proportions:-

(1) ONE HALF SHARE to A, whom failing to X whom failing to B and C;

(2) ONE QUARTER SHARE to B, whom failing to his children equally among them, whom failing to A and C;

(3) ONE QUARTER SHARE to C, whom failing to his wife Y, whom failing to A and B.'

It will be noted that words of severance, such as 'equally between them' are *not* used in the ultimate destination-over for each share which takes it to the other sharers of the legacy. This would mean that accretion would operate if it became necessary, to take the whole legacy to a single survivor of A, B and C.

It will be seen that clear instructions are required; the likelihood is that the testator will not have considered the possible predecease of some of his legatees to the extent required if shared legacies are considered desirable in the first place.

Common sense is also needed when dealing with such situations. It may be thought to be apocryphal, but wills actually exist which purport to distribute a one-third share of residue to each of A, B and C. . . and D!

As noted at the beginning of this section, a legacy to a number of beneficiaries will generally imply equal shares. However, particular problems are likely to arise where different families, or branches of families are involved. This raises the thorny topic of *per capita* or *per stirpes* division.

Per capita and per stirpes division

5.08 Those who have read the various Styles may have noted the absence of the time-honoured phrases '*per stirpes*' and '*per capita*'. This is a deliberate omission, as the authors wish to avoid Latin phrases and other relative obscurities wherever possible. However, it is admitted that replacing the expressions with English equivalents was one of the most difficult tasks encountered; and it is appreciated that those drafting wills may wish to retain the older form of wording, particularly when dealing with destinations-over. This is dealt with, and alternatives are provided, below.

While questions are most likely to arise in providing for generations beyond the primary beneficiaries, doubts about division are possible in immediate bequests. If one encounters a legacy 'to the children of A and the children of B', and A has one child while B has three, the intention may be either that A's child should take one half with B's children sharing the other half; or that A should take one quarter, with B's children each taking one quarter.

The general rule is that unless the will clearly provides or indicates otherwise, or the context otherwise requires, division among beneficiaries is *per capita*[1]. Thus, in the example given above it is likely that the second possibility will

---

1 *Hay Cunningham's Trustees v Blackwell* 1909 SC 219; *Campbell's Trustees v Welsh* 1952 SC 343; but cf *Bailey's Trustees v Bailey* 1954 SLT 282; *Boyd's Trustee v Shaw* 1958 SC 115.

prevail, ie that A's child and each of B's children would all take one quarter of the legacy[1].

This result arises because the class of beneficiaries consists of the children of A and the children of B. There is no element of representation involved and there is nothing in the wording or context to indicate that there are intended to be two separate classes of beneficiary, each to take one half of the legacy. This illustrates the need to be absolutely clear as to the intended division; if different families or branches of a family are to take on a *per stirpes* basis, it is crucial to identify which beneficiary is the head of a particular stirps[2].

The mere addition of the words '*per stirpes*' to a bequest to a number of people will not automatically achieve division other than on a *per capita* basis unless the will makes it clear where the stirpital division is to start. If the legacy mentioned above was 'to the children of A and the children of B *per stirpes*', the division would still be one quarter to each of the four children if they all survived. True stirpital division would only arise if there was representation on the predecease of any of the children of A or B.

5.09 If a testator's intention is to achieve stirpital division at the level of immediate beneficiaries, the most effective method is to divide the legacy directly into the appropriate shares. Thus, in the above example, this could be done by leaving 'one half to the children of A and one half to the children of B', giving one half to A's single child and the other half to be divided equally among B's three children (ie one sixth each). The consequences for accretion should be noted, however; if A's single child were to predecease, his one-half share would not accresce to B's children although accretion *would* operate within the class gift to B's children.

5.10 Doubts about the shares to go to different beneficiaries are most likely to arise where there are destinations-over and representation by the issue of pre-deceasing beneficiaries, particularly in family wills. When dealing with different branches of a single family, doubts about the intended division can arise in two different ways. There may be different numbers of children at the same level of relationship to the deceased (eg one child of the deceased has two children while another has four, both children having predeceased the deceased). Alternatively, there may be survivors among the deceased's issue who stand at different relationships to the deceased (eg both children and grandchildren survive, the latter with or without their own parents surviving).

The following form of words is used in a number of the Styles (see, for example, S3.6):

> '. . . declaring that should any of my children predecease me leaving issue (including adopted issue) who shall survive me, each member of a generation of issue of such predeceasing child shall share equally in

---

1 *Bogie's Trustees v Christie* (1882) 9 R 453; *Cobban's Executors v Cobban* 1915 SC 82.
2 *Thomson v Cumberland* November 16, 1814, FC; *Haldane's Trustees v Murphy* (1881) 9 R 269.

the part of my estate, both original and accresced, which would have
    fallen to its parent if in life.'

It is thought that this wording achieves a genuine stirpital division. If any of the
children predecease the testator leaving issue, those issue will take whatever the
deceased child would have taken. At *any* level, a generation of children will only
take what their parent would have taken; and this applies whether or not an
entire generation has died out. Some of the possible eventualities which might
arise can be illustrated diagrammatically:

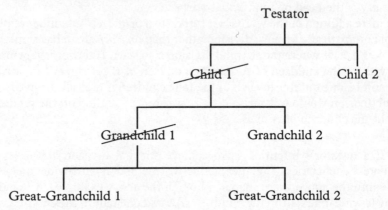

Figure 1

Child 1 has predeceased; child 2 will take one half of the bequest. The other half
will go to the issue of child 1. If both grandchild 1 and grandchild 2 had survived,
they would each have taken one quarter of the bequest. Grandchild 2 takes its
one quarter share. As grandchild 1 has not survived, its children share equally in
its one-quarter share taking one eighth each.

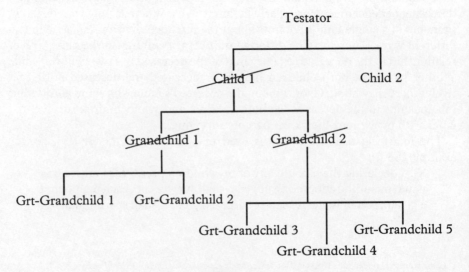

Figure 2

In figure 2, child 2 will take one half of the bequest. The other half will again go to the issue of child 1, but this time there are five great-grandchildren who must share in this half. Each member of this generation is to share equally only in the part which would have fallen to its parent; thus great-grandchild 1 and great-grandchild 2 each take one-eighth share; while great-grandchild 3, great-grandchild 4 and great-grandchild 5 each take one-twelfth share.

5.11 Obviously, the wording offered is untested in the courts; however the commonly-used phrase '*per stirpes*' has (perhaps surprisingly) received little direct judicial consideration. Authority on various types of wording that have been used tends to be confused, contradictory and dependant on the particular circumstances of bequest. In this situation, it is hoped that those drafting wills might consider the version presented in the Styles as acceptable in the common situation where stirpital division is intended. It has the merit that using the phrase 'generation of issue' may be more readily understood by testators than the Latin phrase it replaces[1].

5.12 It may, however, be that those drafting wills will prefer to retain the use of a phrase with which they, if not their clients, are wholly familiar. In these circumstances, and adapting the appropriate legacy from the Styles, the following wording can be used:

'. . . declaring that should any of my children predecease me leaving issue (including adopted issue) who shall survive me, the issue shall take *per stirpes* the part of my estate both original and accresced, which would have fallen to such predeceasing child if in life.'

This provides stirpital division with each child of the testator at the head of its own stirps.

It is also worth mentioning the following commonly-used wording, which was judicially considered in *Boyd's Trustee v Shaw*[2]:

'. . . declaring that if either of [the primary beneficiaries] should predecease me, the share of the predeceaser shall pass to his issue equally amongst them if more than one.'

Despite the normal rules directing that a gift to a plurality of persons inplies a *per capita* division, it was held that the issue were intended to take *per stirpes*. The issue consisted of three children and four grandchildren (in families of one and three) whose parents had predeceased the testator. This result was reached because the issue were in different degrees of propinquity to the deceased and were conditionally instituted to a common ancestor. However, it should be noted that this wording will not achive stirpital division where surviving issue are in the same relationship to the testator, even if from families of very different sizes; division would then be *per capita*. Such a result will of course suit certain testators, but could not be guaranteed to arise. It depends on the level of

---

1 The authors are particularly grateful to Professor Michael Meston of the University of Aberdeen, who commented favourably on the wording offered as achieving stirpital division.
2 1958 SC 115.

generations which survive the testator and thus involves a considerable degree of speculation.

Another alternative is simply to avoid consideration of issue of the testator beyond grandchildren (which will cover most cases). The following wording could be used:

'. . . declaring that should any of my children predecease me leaving children who shall survive me, the children of such predeceasing child shall share equally in the part of my estate, both original and accresced, which would have fallen to its parent if in life.'

This has the merit of being in a reasonably explicable format. If remoter issue do come into consideration, it may be that the *conditio si institutus sine liberis decesserit* (see paras 6.118–6.119 below) will come into effect to allow them a share of the legacy, although this would not include any share previously accrescing.

5.13 In all cases, it is thought that the wording used in the majority of the Styles and quoted above will achieve a true stirpital division. In addition, descendants will not share in the estate while their own ancestors with a closer relationship to the deceased survive (eg grandchildren will not take where their own parent survives, although if that parent is deceased they can share along with *other* children of the deceased).

There have been attempts to argue that as the expression 'issue' includes all descendants, without further instructions grandchildren should share with their own parents if descendants of both degrees survive. However, a direction that division was to be *per stirpes* was considered sufficient to exclude this possibility[1]. The wording used throughout the Styles here would also have this effect.

It may, however, be that the testator specifically wishes to include all issue within a particular bequest, whatever their degree of relationship and whether the parent of any generation of issue survives to take. The term 'issue' does generally include all descendants[2]. This would be an unusual bequest and it is thought that very specific wording should be used. The following might be suitable:

'To my issue, specifically declaring that each of my issue of whatever degree shall share equally, notwithstanding the survival of its parent.'

Such a bequest could of course be preceded by a division among, say, children, such that there was an initial sharing among different branches of a family. However, it should be stressed that such a complex and unusual scheme is unlikely to be suitable in all but the rarest of circumstances.

5.14 It is possible, if not perhaps particularly likely, that the testator would wish to achieve a genuine *per capita* division, perhaps across different generations but more especially where the nearest surviving descendants are all in the same relationship to himself. Thus, where child A has two children and

1 *Mellis's Trustees v Ritchie* 1909 SC 626.
2 *Turner's Trustees v Turner* (1887) 24 R 619.

child B has four children (all six thus being grandchildren of the testator), the testator may wish all of his grandchildren to benefit equally if they are to benefit at all. If the legacy is *directly* to the grandchildren, there is thought to be no difficulty as the presumption of *per capita* division will apply to such a class gift.

If the grandchildren are only to benefit in the event of their own parent predeceasing the testator, there is some authority to the effect that *per stirpes* division will be implied where survivors are in different degrees of propinquity to the deceased[1]. In any event, if *per capita* division is indeed desired, the matter should be put beyond doubt. If *per capita* division across different generations is intended, suitable wording would be as follows:

'. . . declaring that should any of my children predecease me leaving issue (including adopted issue) who shall survive me, such issue shall share equally in the part or parts of my estate (both original and accressed) which would have fallen to such predeceasing child if in life, declaring that such shares will be equal notwithstanding the fact that such issue may be of different degress of propinquity to me.'

This version would mean that all grandchildren would benefit equally. In the more remote possibility that there were predeceasing grandchildren, *their* issue would also take an equal share along with surviving grandchildren.

If *per capita* division is only to arise where the survivors are all of the same degree of relationship to the testator, it is thought that the following wording would achieve this:

'. . . declaring that should any of my children predecease me leaving issue (including adopted issue) who shall survive me, such issue shall share equally in the part or parts of my estate (both original and accressed) which would have fallen to such predeceasing child if in life, declaring that such shares shall be equal if all such surviving issue are of the same degree of propinquity to me, but that otherwise each member of a generation of issue shall share equally in the part of my estate, (both original and accressed) which would have fallen to its parent if in life.'

The complexity of such provisions and the remote possibility of their ever being fully applied points to the undesirability of using them in most cases. However, they may be useful for certain testators. They also illustrate the need to consider the possible means of division of estate, particularly with testators who already have a large number of descendants of different generations, perhaps with certain branches of generations having already died out at the time of drafting the will. This point is dealt with further at paragraphs 6.115–6.116.

SURVIVORSHIP

5.15   Beneficiaries designated in a will can take only if they survive the testator. Most of the Styles make some provision for what is to happen if particular

---

1 *Boyd's Trustee v Shaw* 1958 SC 115, discussed in para 5.12; see also *Laing's Trustees v Sanson* (1879) 7 R 244.

beneficiaries do not survive. One form of survivorship occurs where a legacy is to a number of beneficiaries, as 'to A, B and C and the survivors or survivor of them'. The effects of such a clause are discussed above (see paras 5.03–5.04), but basically this implies accretion of the share or shares of beneficiaries who predecease to the survivors. In this case, survivorship affects only the amount of the legacy taken by each beneficiary.

Survivorship is perhaps more significant where the fact of a beneficiary's survival excludes another beneficiary entirely, unless, in certain circumstances, that beneficiary is a substitute rather than a conditional institute – see paragraphs 5.26–5.27. This involves consideration of legacies involving destinations-over. The simplest form of such a legacy is 'to A whom failing to B' (see, for example, S2.6(3)), which form of words is probably appropriate in a simple legacy or in the appointment of executors. If A does not survive the testator, B will take the legacy in question.

A full version of a survivorship destination, on the other hand, is in the form '. . . if A does not survive me for 30 days . . .' (see, for example, S3.6). This is appropriate where the destination-over is somewhat more detailed, so as to be best expressed in a separate purpose. In effect, the need for the beneficiary to survive the testator for 30 days imposes a suspensive condition on the legacy.

The period used in all of the Styles is 30 days. While there is no particular significance attached to this length of period, it is long enough to account for a second death arising from a common calamity in most cases; and short enough to prevent uncertainty and undue delay in the administration of the estate. The latter consideration may suggest that a shorter period is more desirable, with seven days being not uncommonly seen. Such expressions as 'one calendar month' are also seen, but may be considered as less definite than a specified number of days.

Perhaps the situation most commonly envisaged where a condition as to survivorship for a period is included is the common calamity, where the testator and the beneficiary are both fatally injured but the beneficiary survives the testator for some days. The testator may well prefer to direct the disposition of his legacy in the event of the beneficiary's death, rather than have it form part of the beneficiary's estate (testate or intestate).

Such a survivorship provision should not be included entirely as a matter of course. The testator may be quite happy to have his bequest pass to the primary beneficiary even if this is for a very short period. Equally, a longer period than 30 days may be desired, perhaps if the testator is particularly concerned to avoid 'bunching' his assets with those of the primary beneficiary. This might be for tax reasons (see para 5.19 below). Much depends on the balance the testator wishes to strike between the primary beneficiary and those who would take should he fail to survive the designated period.

Commorientes

5.16 There are in fact a number of reasons why survivorship should be addressed in wills. Failure to do so may bring the presumptions in section 31 of the Succession (Scotland) Act 1964 into play in the event of a common calamity.

The basic rule is that where two persons have died in circumstances indicating that they have died simultaneously or rendering it uncertain which, if either of them, survived the other, then for all purposes affecting succession to property, it shall be presumed that the younger survived the elder[1]. This could be relevant in the situations envisaged in many of the Styles, particularly where provision is made for a spouse with children taking should the spouse not survive (see, for example, S3.6). If the testator and his children are killed in a common calamity, it is presumed that the children survived the parent (subject to the exception noted below if the testator makes further provision).

The presumption can be relevant in situations where unrelated parties are involved. Thus in S1.5, the residue is to pass to D whom failing to E. If the testator, D and E are all killed in circumstances where the order of their deaths is uncertain, D's or E's estate will only benefit should one of them be younger than the testator. If only one of them is younger, only that one's estate will benefit; if both are younger the estate of the youngest will take.

5.17   It should be remembered that the presumption as to the younger surviving the elder only comes into play where the order of deaths is uncertain; if that order can be proved, then the statutory rules have no relevance. In addition, there are two statutory exceptions to the presumption of the younger surviving the elder.

Firstly, where the two persons of whose deaths the order is uncertain are husband and wife, there is a presumption that neither survived the other[2]. This is intended to prevent the situation which would arise if the normal presumption applied, particularly in the case of childless couples. If the normal presumption applied in the case of a common calamity, the estate of the elder spouse would pass to the younger; if that younger died intestate, the combined estates would pass to that younger spouse's relatives alone. Because of the presumption that neither survived the other, both estates will be wound up as if the other spouse had not survived. This will either be in terms of the spouses' respective wills, or under the rules on intestacy.

This presumption draws attention to the need for precision in drafting wills to cope with survivorship destinations. In particular, when dealing with husband and wife, it is insufficient to make provision for a destination-over in the event of one spouse 'predeceasing'. A presumption that neither spouse survived the other does not indicate which spouse is to be presumed to have predeceased[3]. This wording may not prevent intestacy in the event of a common calamity. For destinations-over in the Styles involving spouses the conditions for the spouse to take involves survival for the 30 days after the testator's death. This avoids the need for proof of predecease before the alternative provisions can take effect.

---

1 Succession (Scotland) Act 1964, s 31(1)(b).
2 Ibid, s 31(1)(a).
3 *Ross's Judicial Factor v Martin* 1955 SC (HL) 56.

Style S11 deals particularly with the case of a spouse who has no children at the time the will is drafted. Imposing the condition as to survivorship is particularly important in such a case, because without it the estates of both spouses may end up in the family of only one of them. Indeed, that Style goes on to make provision for the return of part of the combined estates to the other spouse's family even where the second spouse to die has benefitted from the other estate.

5.18 Where the order of deaths is uncertain, the second exception to this statutory presumption of the younger surviving the elder is found in section 31(2) of the Succession (Scotland) Act 1964. It is rather complex; if the elder person has left a testamentary disposition containing a provision, however expressed, in favour of the younger if he survives the elder, and failing the younger in favour of a third person, *and* the younger person has died intestate, then it shall be presumed for the purposes of that provision that the elder survived the younger.

This rule is quite likely to be relevant in the event of a common calamity affecting parent and child. A legacy may be in the form '. . . to my son A, whom failing to his children equally among them if more than one . . .'. If the testator and A are killed in an accident and the order of their deaths cannot be determined, normally A would be presumed to have survived the testator. However, if A was intestate, the testator is assumed to have survived A, so that the legacy goes to A's children. Of course, this might be the result of A's intestacy in any event, but if A had been married, prior rights might have carried the amount of the legacy to his spouse. It should be noted that this presumption only applies for the purposes of the legacy and the testator's will; for all other purposes of succession, A will be assumed to have survived the testator. It should also be noted that intestacy to any extent is sufficient to bring section 31(2) into effect[1].

Inheritance tax and survivorship

5.19 Another important reason for including a provision as to survivorship in a will relates to inheritance tax. If a legacy is simply to an individual, who dies shortly after the testator, inheritance tax could be due on the death of each. Quick succession relief[2] could provide some measure of redress, but this will never be complete and may not be available for some reason. It only applies at all if tax has been paid on the first death.

If, however, a will contains a condition as to the survivorship of a beneficiary for a specified period not exceeding six months, inheritance tax is only charged on the death of the original testator. This applies whether the beneficiary survives the specified period to take the legacy or dies within it, so that the legacy passes to those taking under the destination-over. Without this specific rule[3], tax could be charged on the termination of the survivorship period or on the

---

1 See *Meston* p 25.
2 Relief for successive charges – see the Inheritance Tax Act 1984, s 141.
3 Contained in the Inheritance Tax Act 1984, s 92.

beneficiary's earlier death[1]. It is to prevent this possible double charge to inheritance tax that survivorship periods in wills must not exceed six months.

RENUNCIATION

5.20 A purpose dealing with what happens if a beneficiary renounces his rights under the will has been included in each of the more complex Styles: S5.11, S6.12, S7.9, S9.7 and S10.10. The basic effect of this purpose is to produce the same effect as if the beneficiary renouncing had predeceased. If the renunciation occurs without directions in the will as to its effects the beneficiary renouncing will not be treated as having predeceased which increases the chances of the legacy renounced falling into residue or intestacy.

The effect of such a purpose depends on the terms of the purpose containing the benefit which is renounced, if the latter purpose contains a destination-over that will come into effect. Indeed, it is really only purposes containing destinations-over which justify the inclusion of a specific renunciation purpose. If the Purpose containing the benefit which is renounced did not contain a destination-over, the effect of renunciation is that a legacy other than residue will fall into residue and a residuary legacy will fall into intestacy.

If a renouncing residuary beneficiary is survived by a child, then the residue clause will usually pass the benefits to the children of the renouncer (see for example S10.7). The key point in dealing with such matters is to ensure that there is a clear and definite beneficiary on failure or renunciation, since otherwise intestacy will result. It is of course possible that intestacy will produce the intended result on renunciation, but this would perhaps be unduly optimistic and no accurate forecast could be made.

5.21 The renunciation purpose as it appears in the Styles applies to any benefit under the will, whether of residue or otherwise. It would be possible to restrict the purpose so that it only applied to a particular legacy. In this case, the purpose would begin: 'In the event of any benefit conferred by purpose (THREE) [OR as appropriate] being renounced in whole or in part. . .'.

If the purpose the benefit of which is being renounced contains no destination-over then the renunciation of benefit purpose as it appears in the Styles cannot bring in, for example, the legatee's child, since had the original legatee predeceased, then the subject of the bequest would have fallen into residue. The purpose as framed therefore cannot alter the class of possible beneficiaries; it can merely alter the order of beneficiaries who are already included within the will.

There are circumstances (although they are likely to be rare) where it might be desirable to have a different destination-over following a renunciation than applied to the original benefit renounced. For example, the testator may be quite happy that a friend should benefit, either directly or (if the friend considers it preferable, perhaps for tax reasons) through the medium of his family.

---

1 Because property held subject to a contingency would have ceased to be so – see the Inheritance Tax Act 1984, s 43(2)(a).

However, if the friend were to predecease the testator, the testator might wish to direct his legacy to a different beneficiary, particulary if the original beneficiary's family is not known personally to the testator. In such circumstances, the original legacy might be in the form:

> '(FOUR) I direct my executors to pay to A whom failing to B the sum of TWENTY THOUSAND POUNDS.'

The renunciation of benefit purpose could then read:

> 'In the event of any benefit conferred by purpose (FOUR) being renounced in whole or in part, the benefit of such part or parts thereof shall pass to the children of A equally among them if more than one, declaring that should any of the children of A predecease the date of renunciation leaving issue (including adopted issue) who shall survive that date, each member of a generation of issue of such predeceasing child shall share equally in the part of my estate, both original and accresced, which would have fallen to its parent if in life.'

5.22   The renunciation or disclaimer of the benefit may be of the whole or a part of an interest. Where there may be problems in England in relation to partial disclaimers, the Inland Revenue has accepted that in Scotland this is possible[1]. The renunciation of benefit provision as framed in the Styles makes this clear in any event.

Where the renunciation is carried out by a person who was not an original beneficiary at the time of the testator's death, but came in as a result of the death of an original beneficiary, the reference to predeceasing the testator rather than predeceasing the time of vesting of the benefit then being renounced could have peculiar effects. It would be possible for the reference at the end of the purpose to be altered from 'predecease me' to 'predecease the time or times of vesting'. The possibility of such a default beneficiary renouncing a benefit (or more likely being old enough to renounce such a benefit) is probably remote and so can usually be ignored.

5.23   There will be circumstances when the purpose covering renunciation of benefit is not appropriate. In smaller estates, a surviving spouse may be better off in relation to benefits from his spouse's estate by claiming prior and legal rights than by taking the residue under the will subject to the children's legal rights claim (see paras 6.31 and 9.18). It may be possible for the surviving spouse to create intestacy by renouncing the provisions in his favour under the will and then to claim legal rights. This would not be possible if the renunciation of benefit provision is included, since the renunciation would merely mean that the children will become entitled to the whole estate; there would be no intestacy.

In the case of estates where there is doubt as to the value of benefits which might be renounced, then the purpose should probably not be included. Since some of the advantages of including such a purpose relate to taxation (see para 5.24), then in smaller estates there would generally be a nil or limited benefit in

---

1 See Inland Revenue Statement of Practice E18.

including such a provision. It is also fairly pointless where a will contains no destinations-over.

The purpose dealing with renunciation of benefit may perhaps be most needed where there is a liferent with postponed vesting of the fee (see Style S5). This is because without special provision, renunciation of a liferent would not generally accelerate vesting of the fee[1]. The result of omitting to deal with renunciation can be the creation of what has been termed a 'shadow liferent', where payment of income is due to residuary or intestate beneficiaries until the actual death of the liferenter[2].

In fact, in S5.7 as presented, the provisions as to capital are brought into effect directly by a renunciation, but the importance of the point can be emphasised by a separate provision.

A general renunciation purpose may also be needed in *any* case where there is a destination-over to beneficiaries who would not take from residue, or on intestacy in the case of a residuary bequest. It may also make matters easier if a deed of variation is inappropriate because of the limited size of the estate.

In the case of a two-year discretionary trust (see Style S9), there may seem little point in including the provision, since the trustees themselves will determine the beneficiaries. It would, however, apply to the destination which is directed in the event of the trustees failing to appoint within the two-year period (S9.7).

5.24 There are possible tax advantages in including a renunciation of benefit purpose. It may form an alternative to a deed of variation for inheritance tax purposes; and it may also have income tax advantages.

If a beneficiary wishes to pass on benefits given to him under a will, then he could simply gift property to a new beneficiary, or he could enter into a deed of family arrangement or deed of variation. Such deeds have always been possible in appropriate circumstances but are now generally only seen in relation to the specific inheritance tax relief for deeds of variation[3] and, to a lesser extent, the similar relief for capital gains tax[4]. In 1989 the government announced that it intended to withdraw the relief for deeds of variation but the implementation of this was postponed and at time of writing appears to have been abandoned. The attack was not on renunciations or disclaimers, which were not seen as objectionable to the same extent. The draft legislation which appeared in the Finance Bill of that year did not restrict the inheritance tax advantages deriving from a renunciation. Basically, the renunciation is not itself a transfer of value and inheritance tax is charged as if the renounced benefit had never been conferred[5].

The renunciation of benefit provision as framed in the Styles is intended to

1 See *Middleton's Trustees v Middleton* 1955 SC 51, where it was held that a renunciation was not equivalent to the 'expiry' of the liferent, at which latter event only vesting of the fee was to take place in terms of the trust deed.
2 The possible complications were explored in an article by G L Gretton 'Vesting, equitable compensation and the mysteries of the shadow liferent' 1988 SLT (News) 149.
3 Inheritance Tax Act 1984, s 142.
4 Taxation of Chargeable Gains Act 1992, s 62(6)–(10).
5 Inheritance Tax Act 1984, s 17(a) and 142(1).

allow a beneficiary to renounce a benefit in whole or in part with the result that the renounced benefit would pass to a beneficiary whom the testator would wish to benefit; this may not of course be a person whom the original *beneficiary* would wish to benefit! There is no definitive solution to the determination of who the alternative beneficiary should be and in particular circumstances the testator may wish or be willing to vary this with a renunciation in mind. This may particularly be the case where the testator has discussed his intentions with his intended beneficiaries. It is possible to structure the provision so as to take renounced benefits to alternative beneficiaries in a tax efficient manner. There is however a limit to the detail which can reasonably be included and the situation at the time of any possible renunciation cannot be predicted with certainty.

Within these limitations, the provision as framed in the Styles is a substitute for a deed of variation. It is of course still possible to enter into a deed of variation under which the original beneficiary accepts, but then assigns the original benefit to a new beneficiary entirely. However, should the tax advantages of deeds of variation suddenly be abolished, a provision dealing with renunciation of benefit provides a further degree of flexibility.

It is worth noting that a disclaimer of an interest in settled property may be made at any time without inheritance tax effects. The two-year time limit which applies to other variations does not apply here[1]. However, a disclaimer of any property will only be possible as a matter of general law if the beneficiary has not taken *any* benefit from the property at the time of his renunciation.

5.25 If a beneficiary decides to pass all or part of the benefit to his minor child (still defined for this purpose as a child under the age of 18) then even if the gift is outright, the parent-child settlement provision for income tax will apply[2]. This applies to benefits passed on by deed of variation as well as to outright gifts. The effect is that the income from the property gifted belonging to the minor child will be aggregated with the renouncing parent's income and the child's personal income tax allowance and benefit of lower rate bands will not be available.

It is thought that a renunciation does not trigger these particular anti-avoidance provisions for income tax. This is not clear from the legislation, but appears to be accepted by the Inland Revenue[3]. If the income tax anti-avoidance provisions do not apply, then the child's personal allowance and lower rate bands are available against the income from the renounced benefit.

At one time there was a stamp duty advantage in proceeding by way of renunciation rather than by variation, but there is now no difference[4].

---

1 Inheritance Tax Act 1984, s 93.
2 Income Corporation Taxes Act 1988, s 663.
3 See *Practical Tax Planning* (Longmans), paras G3-0141, G3-0210; Capital Taxes News and Reports, November 1989, p 7 and February 1990, p 40; Laidlow *Tax Planning for Post-death Variations* (1993) para 9–29.
4 See the Finance Act 1985, s 84(1) and the Stamp Duty (Exempt Instruments) Regulations 1987, SI 1987/516, Schedule, category M.

DESTINATIONS-OVER

5.26 Destinations-over have already been mentioned in relation to survivorship (see paras 5.15–5.19); they also raise questions relating to vesting (see paras 5.28–5.36). Destinations-over take two forms in the Styles – the simple 'To A whom failing to B' (see, for example, S2.10(13)); and the full provision referring to the eventuality of the primary beneficiary predeceasing (see, for example, S3.6). The condition as to survivorship may be extended to demand for survivorship for a specified period following the death of the testator.

It is also possible to provide for multiple destinations-over, as in the form 'To A whom failing to his wife B whom failing to C'. This may be particularly suitable where the testator's prime intention is to benefit a particular family primarily at the level of one generation, but thereafter at the level of succeeding generations. In these circumstances, a combination of the two forms of destination-over used in the Styles may be appropriate, as follows:

> 'To A whom failing to his wife B, declaring that should both of A and B predecease me leaving issue (including adopted issue) who shall survive me, each member of a generation of issue shall take the share, original and accresced, of this legacy which would have fallen to its parent if in life.'

Utilising the shorter form to cope with possible multiple destinations-over, it may make matters clearer to add a form of emphasis, as in 'To A whom failing to B whom both failing to C'. It is not thought that such emphasis adds anything substantive to the intention expressed, but it does make the testator's intentions clearer.

The use of the phrases 'To A and B' or 'To A or B' are to be discouraged where destinations-over are required. The latter has been construed as being to the same effect as 'To A whom failing to B'[1]; but the wording causes unnecessary confusion. The former suggests joint rights in the subject of bequest, although in limited circumstances a destination-over may be implied. It may be equally important to *exclude* the possibility of a destination-over being implied, particularly where a joint legacy is to go to different generations of the same family[2].

A destination-over dictates what is to happen if a primary beneficiary fails to survive, but there can be complications. In the simple form 'To A whom failing to B', A is the institute and B is either the conditional institute or the substitute. In the former case, once the legacy has vested in A, B has no possibility of inheriting. The destination-over ceases to have effect. In the latter case, where B is the substitute, B can inherit on the institute's (A's) death if B survives A, unless A has disposed of his rights in the property either by lifetime disposition or by will. However, mere possession of corporeal moveable property by the institute will be sufficient to defeat a substitution[3]. As a substitution includes a

---

1 *Bowman v Bowman* (1899) 1 F (HL) 69.
2 On all of this see *Cobban's Executors v Cobban* 1915 SC 82; *Black's Trustees v Nixon* 1931 SC 590 and *Clow's Trustees v Bethune* 1935 SC 754.
3 *Robertson v Hay-Boyd* 1928 SC (HL) 8.

conditional institution, B as a substitute would also take the legacy should A fail to acquire a vested right.

5.27 There are strong presumptions operating in this area. The testator is assumed to have intended conditional institution where moveable property is involved[1]. Substitution is presumed where the subject of bequest is heritage[2]. Where the subject of bequest is mixed, conditional institution is presumed[3].

As with all presumptions, these can be overcome by the wording of the will. However, the phrase 'whom failing' is neutral[4]. It seems likely that the majority of testators in most situations would wish conditional institution to apply. Indeed, it would probably come as a surprise to testators (and perhaps to some advisers) that a testator's will could continue to govern the disposition of a bequest in certain circumstances, even after the death of both the testator and the later death of a primary beneficiary. It is thus fortunate that the presumptions usually operate in favour of conditional institution. As such a presumption applies to mixed bequests of heritage and moveables, it is perhaps likely to apply in the case of most residuary gifts.

The most likely situation in which specific wording would be required to overcome a presumption is where a specific legacy of heritage is involved[5]. An effective way of dealing with this problem would be to adopt the longer form of destination-over used in the Styles, as follows:

'To A, declaring that should A predecease me [OR predecease the date of vesting], this legacy shall pass to B.'

Any reference to the institute's death as the contingency upon which the destination-over is to operate will suggest conditional institution rather than substitution.

In the more unlikely event where the destination-over importing substitution is required for a legacy of moveables or a mixed estate, it is thought that the following would be effective:

'To A and on A's death either before this legacy has vested in him or after it has so vested but in the event that A has failed to dispose of it, to B.'

The complexity of such a clause points to the need for careful consideration before using it. It may well be preferable for the testator to put the subject of bequest into trust for both of A and B, should he wish to control the situation following his own death to such an extent. A liferent or a discretionary trust may be equally effective to this end. Creating an effective substitution rather than a conditional institution in a destination-over is only possible should the institute not act to defeat the destination-over during his lifetime, while a trust would put the testator in full control as to the ultimate destination of the bequest. This point is illustrated by the fact that a destination-over in the form of a substitution

---

1 *Crumpton's Judicial Factor v Barnardo's Homes* 1917 SC 713.
2 *Watson v Geffen* (1884) 11 R 444.
3 *McLay v Chalmers* (1903) 11 SLT 223; *Bruce's Trustees v Hamilton* (1858) 20 D 473.
4 *Watson v Geffen* (1884) 11 R 444.
5 *Simpson's Trustees v Simpson* (1889) 17 R 248.

cannot have the effect by itself of suspending vesting. It does not render the institute's right conditional, but merely directs what is to happen in certain circumstances on the institute's death. A conditional institution can have the direct effect of suspending vesting until the date of payment (although of course that may itself coincide with the date of the testator's death)[1].

VESTING

5.28 Vesting is a subject that causes a great deal of concern among those drafting both complex and simple wills. A huge number of court cases, particularly from the nineteenth century, have revolved round questions asking if or when a particular legacy has vested in a particular beneficiary. In general, however, such disputes will only arise in relation to wills where the position is left unclear. In most cases, problems can be avoided by careful drafting and reliance on a number of presumptions operating in this area. It is, however, necessary to consider some of the technical rules in this area.

Vesting occurs when a legatee acquires a right of property in the subject of the legacy. In relation to wills, this can only occur (at the earliest) on the death of the testator. Until that time, the potential beneficiary merely has a hope of inheriting – a *spes successionis* – as it is always open to the testator to alter his instructions until the date of his death. In one sense, vesting of legacies is always postponed, for the period between the date of the will and the date of death; conditions attaching to legacies (including a condition, explicit or implicit, as to the survival of the legatee) must be fulfilled at that time at the earliest. (For instance, a destination-over in the form of a conditional institution can only come into effect by ascertaining the situation on the death of the testator.)

However, questions in relation to vesting usually arise in connection with a period *after* the testator's death. There are really only two possibilities – vesting will either occur immediately on the testator's death, or it will be delayed until some later event, often the termination of a liferent or the occurrence of a set of circumstances set out in the will or trust provisions within it.

5.29 A number of basic preliminary points arise here. Vesting should be distinguished from payment or physical transfer of a fund or assets to a beneficiary. The vesting of a right to a legacy is almost certain to occur before a beneficiary obtains possession of it – to take the most simple example, payment of a legacy vesting on death is likely to be delayed until confirmation is obtained and other administrative procedures are carried out. Payment of a legacy to a beneficiary lacking full capacity can be delayed by the testator's instructions, even if that legacy has vested. But it is not possible to delay payment of a legacy to a beneficiary of full capacity *unless* there are intervening trust purposes (such as a liferent) or unless vesting is postponed[2].

---

1 On these complex matters, see Gretton & Reid *Conveyancing* Chapter 24 and further references there.
2 See *Miller's Trustees v Miller* (1890) 18 R 301; see paras 5.54 and 5.55.

There is no *necessary* connection between vesting and payment, although they may occur simultaneously or virtually so. Indeed, the testator may direct that vesting is to occur only on the date of payment, which can be useful when dealing with discretionary or accumulation and maintenance trusts, from which payments may be made at a number of different times – see Style S10, especially S10.8(4), (7).

A legacy can thus vest in a beneficiary without any prospect of immediate payment. Perhaps the best example of this is a vested fee where the fiar has to await the termination of a liferent before payment can be made – and it would be possible to delay payment further beyond that termination, should the beneficiary lack legal capacity at that later time (see Style S6, and on the last point S6.11). The important thing is that the interposition of a liferent interest does not prevent the fiar acquiring a vested right. It does not matter if the liferent is created by means of full trust provisions, or is simply a burden on the assets bequeathed (as in Style S6) – the fiar can still acquire an immediate vested right[1]. One key point is that such a vested right forms part of the *beneficiary's* estate immediately on the testator's death; on the beneficiary's death before the date of payment, his right will be distributed as part of the beneficiary's estate, not in terms of the testator's will.

Postponed vesting means that no beneficiary has a definite interest in the subject of the bequest. To obtain such an interest, a beneficiary must await fulfilment of the conditions set out in the will or the trust. This will entail survival until a specified event occurs, such as the attainment of a stated age or the termination of liferent (see Style S5). If vesting is postponed beyond the testator's death, it cannot be known as a certainty who the beneficiary or beneficiaries will be, as it cannot be known who will survive to take the bequest when vesting *does* occur. Thus no interest in a legacy where vesting is postponed will form part of any potential beneficiary's estate until vesting actually occurs.

The distinction between immediate and postponed vesting is most clearly seen in liferents, where it is equally possible for vesting in the fiars to occur on the testator's death (as in Style S6) or on the termination of the liferent (as in Style S5). However, vesting is also postponed where a discretionary trust is established, whether an accumulation and maintenance trust (see, for example, Style S7) or otherwise (see, for example, Styles S8 and S9). In such a case, vesting is generally postponed until a decision is made to give the discretionary beneficiaries a benefit, whether by the discretion of the trustees, in terms of the testator's instructions at the end of a discretionary period, or under a 'longstop' provision.

5.30 If vesting does not take place on the testator's death the other main possibility for the date of vesting is the time of distribution. However, as noted above, *payment* may be further suspended beyond the date of vesting. Thus the earliest possible date for vesting is date of death and the latest possible is the date

1 *Carleton v Thomson* (1867) 5 M (HL) 151.

of payment; and in the absence of any express instructions from the testator, vesting will take place either at the date of death or the date of payment[1].

As with other matters in wills the prime role of interpretation as to vesting is to ascertain the testator's intentions[2]. Normally, an expressed declaration as to the date of vesting will settle any doubts and this technique is adopted in certain of the Styles (see eg S7.7(4)). However, even an expressed declaration as to vesting is not conclusive, if the stated date cannot be reconciled with the terms of the legacy or the will in general[3].

Declarations as to vesting can be used in cases where there may be doubt as to what is intended, but it is probably true that more reliance is placed on presumptions in this area than in many others. There are perhaps two presumptions especially that lead to specific instructions being omitted in many cases. The first is a presumption in favour of early vesting, that is generally vesting on the testator's death[4].

In addition, many wills, especially simple ones, contain no possible contingency which would provide a date later than the testator's death at which time vesting could possibly take place.

The second important presumption in cases of doubt is that it is presumed that the testator's will should be construed so as to avoid intestacy[5]. The application of such a presumption might result in immediate or postponed vesting. This presumption is however only likely to come into consideration after the testator's death, in a situation which was not in contemplation at the time when he drafted the will. This emphasises the importance of avoiding the problem by providing clear instructions where the distribution of an estate, or part thereof, is to be delayed to a time after death.

As noted above, mere postponement of payment will not of itself postpone vesting, and nor will the interposition of a liferent or other form of trust necessarily have this effect. In assessing whether vesting is postponed, a distinction is drawn between a condition directing payment on an event certain to happen (eg the arrival of a certain date or the death of a person) and an event uncertain to happen (eg the attainment by a person of a specified age, or one person's survival of another). The former type of contingency will not of itself delay vesting[6], while the latter will do so[7].

Given the general presumption in favour of early vesting, it is perhaps most essential that specific provision is made should it be desired to postpone vesting. In the context of a liferent, this is seen in S5.7. It is also likely that early vesting will be what is desired by most testators, even if payment is postponed for some reason, as where a liferent is interposed.

---

1 *Marshall v King* (1888) 16 R 40.
2 *Carleton v Thomson* (1867) 5 M (HL) 151; *Bowman v Bowman* (1899) 1 F (HL) 69.
3 *Carruthers v Carruthers* 1949 SC 530.
4 *Carleton v Thomson* (1867) 5 M (HL) 151; *Taylor v Gilbert's Trustees* (1878) 5 R (HL) 217; *Webster's Trustees v Neil* (1900) 2 F 695.
5 See eg *Gillies' Trustees v Hodge* (1900) 3 F 238; Henderson *The Principles of Vesting in the Law of Succession* (2nd edn, 1938) pp 19–20.
6 *Mowbray's Trustees v Mowbray's Executor* 1931 SC 595.
7 *MacIntosh v Wood* (1872) 10 M 933; see also para 5.38 below.

5.31 There are a number of reasons why postponed vesting should only be considered as an option with some care. As it is not possible to know the identity of the beneficiaries until vesting occurs, it will not be possible for all the beneficiaries of any trust created with postponed vesting simply to agree to wind up or vary the terms of the trust. This is only possible where interests are vested[1]. It would be possible for the liferenter to assign his liferent to expected fiars or renounce his interest (assuming in either case that it was not an alimentary liferent). In the latter case, a clause dealing with the consequences of renunciation might be desirable (see paras 5.20–5.25). But outright payment of the trust fund simply by agreement would not be possible, imposing at the very least extra administrative burdens. Thus, postponing vesting can cause a reduction in flexibility, although the provisions in the Styles presented with this book should preserve this to a great extent.

The time of vesting will have an effect on the valuation of a beneficiary's estate. If vesting is immediate, then the beneficiary or his executors will become entitled to funds in due course (apart from the possibilities of the loss by poor investment of trust funds or advances of capital). Such an interest will thus generally have a value. This value will come into calculations of legal rights in the beneficiary's estate, on his death. Such an interest can also be used as a security for a loan to a beneficiary. This is not possible if vesting is postponed. Finally, vesting may affect the tax consequences, particularly as the rules obtaining at the date of death may well differ from those at the time at which the will was written. In fact, at present there are few differences in tax terms between an immediate and a postponed interest. For inheritance tax purposes, the right of a fiar of a trust, whether vested or not, is a reversionary interest. This is excluded property and is generally outwith the charge to inheritance tax[2]. For estate duty purposes, that was not the case and a charge could arise on the actuarial value of the reversionary interest at the time of the beneficiary's death. Where vesting was postponed, the value was in effect nil, because the beneficiary by predeceasing the date of vesting could not take a benefit of any value.

For capital gains tax, the disposal of most reversionary interests will not give rise to a chargeable gain[3]. Although differences are now few, tax considerations may again become significant in future.

5.32 In addition to immediate vesting on death and postponed vesting there is a hybrid version, vesting subject to defeasance. This can only occur where a legacy is given subject to a resolutive condition (see paras 5.37–5.48). Vesting will occur, but will be defeated if the event specified in the condition takes place. In general, a resolutive condition depends on factors other than those personal to the legatee. Personal factors include the legatee's survival or attainment of a specified age; extraneous factors include (most commonly where vesting subject to defeasance is involved) the birth of issue to someone other than the legatee.

---

1 See *Wilson & Duncan* p 138; *Gray v Gray's Trustees* (1877) 4 R 378 at 383.
2 Inheritance Tax Act 1984, s 48.
3 Taxation of Chargeable Gains Act 1992, s 76.

If vesting subject to defeasance occurs, it is not possible at the date of the testator's death (or other date of vesting) to know exactly how the estate will be wound up. The legacy will have vested for the time being, but if the defeasance event occurs, the legacy will be carried away as if it had never vested[1]. On the other hand, if the defeasance event does *not* occur, vesting is treated as having taken place at the original date; and if the defeasance event has not taken place before any dates specified in the will (for example, the termination of a liferent), vesting in the original beneficiary will at that time become complete and indefeasible. It can be seen that vesting subject to defeasance has some characteristics of both immediate and postponed vesting.

Vesting subject to defeasance is a relatively recent concept, emerging fully only after the House of Lords decision in the case *Taylor v Gilbert's Trustees*[2]. However the doctrine is applicable only in a limited number of circumstances emerging from decided cases and it seems that it will not readily be extended beyond these circumstances. This is despite the fact that on the face of it, the doctrine would seem to be useful in a number of situations apparently dependent on resolutive conditions.

5.33 The three recognised types of vesting subject to defeasance are as follows:

(1) A legacy to A in liferent and to A's issue in fee, whom failing to B in fee. On the testator's death B would take a vested right in fee if A had no issue at that time. If A has issue at the date of testator's death, B will never take any right in the fee. If A produces issue during the course of the liferent, B's right in the fee will be defeated – and as the fee will in either case have vested in A's issue, B will not obtain a right in fee even if A's issue fail to survive the end of the liferent[3]. If, however, A has never had any issue by the end of the liferent, B will take an indefeasible right at that time.

A variation on this possibility is a condition that A's issue shall take the fee only if they survive the termination of the liferent, or indeed attain a specified age (perhaps *after* surviving the period of liferent). In such cases there will be vesting of the fee subject to defeasance in B, but the defeasance event will be the *survival* of issue of A until the termination of the liferent or their survival until the specified age. In such cases, defeasance of B's right will not occur on the mere birth of issue[4].

(2) A legacy to A in fee, with a direction to *hold* for A in liferent and his issue in fee. This is a somewhat more amorphous category. If at the testator's death, A has no issue, the fee will vest in A; defeasance will occur if issue are born to A *and* such issue survive the termination of the liferent. If such issue do not survive, the fee will form part of A's estate. It is vital that in this case there is an absolute gift of fee to A in the first instance; the effect of the

---

1 See *Henderson* pp 4–5.
2 (1878) 5 R (HL) 217. This subject is dealt with very fully in 25 *Stair Memorial Encyclopaedia* paras 928–952; and *Henderson* Chapter VI.
3 *Steel's Trustees v Steel* (1888) 16 R 204.
4 *Taylor v Gilbert's Trustees* (1878) 5 R (HL) 217; *Gregory's Trustees v Alison* (1889) 16 R (HL) 10; *Munro's Trustees v Monson* 1962 SC 414.

liferent must be no more than an additional burden or trust purpose in the event of issue surviving. If A's total rights amount to a liferent alone (whether this is explicit or implicit), the doctrine of vesting subject to defeasance will not apply[1].

(3) A legacy to A in liferent and to B in fee, whom failing to B's issue in fee. This is perhaps more common. On the testator's death, B will take a vested right in the fee; the defeasance event is B's death before the termination of the liferent leaving issue who survive him. On that event, the issue will take a vested right in the fee, although there is an argument (and the words of the will may demand) that vesting in the issue will be suspended until the termination of the liferent. It should be noted that a destination-over is normally sufficient to suspend vesting, but that this is not the case if it is in favour of children or issue, who may or not be in existence at the time of payment[2].

5.34 The situations mentioned in the previous paragraph represent the 'classic' types of vesting subject to defeasance, where the defeasance event involves the birth of issue. They illustrate that there are a number of conditions which must apply before the doctrine of vesting subject to defeasance comes into play. The need for the gift to the legatee in whom defeasible vesting is to occur to be absolute has already been mentioned.

It is also essential that the party in whom defeasible vesting is to occur is clearly ascertained at the time of the testator's death. To adapt the first type of situation mentioned in the previous para, if a bequest is to A in liferent and to A's issue in fee, whom failing to the survivors of A's brothers in fee, vesting subject to defeasance will not occur in A's brothers at the testator's death. There is a personal condition involved, in that the survivors of A's brothers cannot be ascertained until the termination of the liferent, so vesting is suspended until that time.

On the other hand, where there is a class of beneficiaries in whom vesting subject to defeasance can take place, this will not be precluded by the fact that the members of that class will not be finally ascertained at the date of the testator's death[3].

Vesting subject to defeasance is also excluded if there is more than one type of contingency on which defeasance will occur. This can best be seen if there is more than one destination-over. Continuing the adaptation of the first type of situation mentioned above, a legacy may be 'to A in liferent and to his issue in fee, whom failing to B, whom failing to C' (assuming that C is a named individual, rather than B's children or issue). In order for B to take in that case

---

1 See, for examples, *Lindsay's Trustees v Lindsay* (1880) 8 R 281; *Tweeddale's Trustees v Tweeddale* (1905) 8 F 264; *Donaldson's Trustees v Donaldson* 1916 SC (HL) 55; *Livingstone's Trustees v Livingstone* 1939 SC (HL) 17; *Nicol's Trustees v Farquhar* 1918 SC 358; *Scott's Trustees v De-Moyse Bucknall's Trustees* 1978 SC 62.

2 *Allan's Trustees v Allan* 1918 SC 164; *Gibson's Trustees v Gibson* 1925 SC 477; *Wylie's Trustees v Wylie* (1902) 8 F 617.

3 *Corbet's Trustees v Elliott's Trustees* (1906) 8 F 610; *Steel's Trustees v Steel* (1888) 16 R 204.

not only must A have no issue, but B must survive the termination of the liferent (as must C, if he is to take on B's failure).

This is an example of a double contingency; another would occur where the words of the will clearly require survival of the termination of the liferent. The double contingency rule has caused much confusion, through a series of cases. A true double contingency (more than one type of event causing defeasance) can be distinguished from cases where defeasance can occur on a number of different occasions, such as the birth of issue at different times. Defeasance may also occur on one of a number of *alternative* contingencies and this also will not prevent defeasible vesting[1].

5.35 Vesting subject to defeasance almost invariably involves a liferent. In the Styles presented in this book, Style S6 involves immediate vesting and Style S5 involves postponed vesting. In order to create vesting subject to defeasance in Style S5, an ultimate destination-over to a named individual could be included in purpose S5.7. Such a beneficiary would take the fee subject to defeasance in the event of children of the testator or any of their issue surviving the termination of the liferent.

It is thought that vesting subject to defeasance will generally not be desirable. If that is the case, it will simply be necessary to impose a personal condition on any ultimate destinations-over which are desired. This can readily be done by requiring survivorship of the ultimate beneficiary at the time of failure of any more immediate beneficiaries so that postponed vesting will remain in place.

5.36 As noted, vesting subject to defeasance is generally thought to be limited to the classes of case mentioned, with any extension of its application thought to be severely restricted. There have been various judicial and academic comments hostile to its extension[2].

However, something very similar to the doctrine has been applied in a number of cases other than those involving the emergence of issue. These have included recovery from mental illness[3]; a condition dependent on a legatee remaining unmarried[4]; and a condition depending on survival of certain categories of relative[5].

Extension is, however, thought to be difficult, and probably the onus of establishing that vesting subject to defeasance has occurred lies on the party asserting this. There is a very practical problem here – if vesting subject to defeasance occurs, what exactly can the beneficiary in whom a legacy has vested defeasibly *do* with his legacy? If the defeasance event occurs, can the 'new' beneficiary always recover from the beneficiary in whom the legacy was previously

---

1 On this complex topic, see *Lees' Trustees v Lees* 1927 SC 886; *G's Trustees v G* 1937 SC 141; *Moss's Trustees v Moss's Trustees* 1958 SC 101; *Coulson's Trustees v Coulson's Trustees* 1911 SC 81; 25 *Stair Memorial Encyclopaedia* paras 936–938.
2 See 25 *Stair Memorial Encyclopaedia* para 941.
3 *Yule's Trustees v Deans* 1919 SC 590; *McCall's Trustees v McCall* 1957 SLT (Notes) 16.
4 *Smith's Trustees v Smith* (1883) 10 R 1144.
5 *Craig's Trustees v Don's Trustees* 1957 SLT (Notes) 3.

(defeasibly) vested? If the beneficiary in whom defeasible vesting has occurred can simply dispose of his rights in the legacy, then on the occurrence of the defeasance event the subject of the legacy may simply not be available to fulfil the testator's intention. On the other hand, if the vested beneficiary's rights are subject to severe restrictions, these rights may not in fact amount to very much[1].

Because of these problems, vesting subject to defeasance may only be of real relevance where a liferent is involved. However, it is clear that there are a number of situations where such a doctrine might be useful; and there are certainly a number of situations where a testator wishes to impose conditions on some or all of his legacies. His ability to do so, and the means by which this can be achieved often require to be addressed when drafting wills.

CONDITIONAL LEGACIES

5.37   In general, a testator may attach such conditions to legacies as he wishes. As has been said when considering a particularly difficult condition:

'This may not be a happy position for the legatee but a testator may do what he wishes with his own and, if he chooses to qualify his bounty with troublesome conditions, the legatee, if he takes it at all, must take the bad with the good[2].'

However, the exact effects of imposing conditions can vary depending on their nature and there are a number of different categories of conditions.

Even before establishing what are the effects of a particular condition, it is necessary to establish whether a condition has been created at all. Where the apparent condition is as to survivorship, with a destination-over attached, it might create a substitution rather than a conditional institution (see para 5.27). The effect of this is not to impose a condition on the primary beneficiary (the institute), but rather to direct what is to happen *after* the termination of the institute's enjoyment of the property. However, substitutions are relatively rare and it will certainly not be the intention to create a substitution in other than exceptional circumstances.

As noted above (para 5.29), there is a distinction between the vesting of legacies and their payment. This distinction is also important in considering conditions which may be attached to legacies. If a condition (for instance a condition as to survivorship) merely relates to payment, that will not prevent vesting; and if a beneficiary were to die before receipt of the legacy it will nevertheless form part of that beneficiary's estate. In such a legacy it is only the payment which is conditional rather than the legacy itself[3].

5.38   An important aspect to consider in dealing with conditional legacies is the distinction between events which are certain to happen and those which are not (often referred to as a distinction between *dies certus* and *dies incertus*). If a legacy

1 This problem is analysed extensively in 25 *Stair Memorial Encyclopaedia* paras 946–951.
2 *Veitch's Executor v Veitch* 1947 SLT 17 at 19 per Lord Sorn.
3 *Alves' Trustees v Grant* (1874) 1 R 969.

is given which is to take effect on a day which is certain to happen, it is in truth unconditional (at least in relation to that apparent condition). Further conditions may of course be imposed on the same legacy, but making a legacy dependent on a certain event is merely to delay payment. Examples of events certain to happen are the termination of a liferent, the death of any particular person (at least in the current state of medical knowledge) and (less commonly) the arrival of a particular specified date.

Conditions referring to events which are uncertain to happen are 'true' conditions, as the legacies on which such conditions are imposed will take effect only if the conditions are fulfilled. Examples of such conditions are the beneficiary's survival until a specified age, or the beneficiary's survival of another person or a specified event. The marriage or remarriage of a particular person would also fall within this category, as would conditions requiring a person to carry out or refrain from some course of action. Legacies can refer to events both certain and uncertain, the point being that only if a legacy is conditional on an event uncertain to happen is it truly dependent on that condition being fulfilled before it can take effect. This is so even if payment of the legacy may be postponed until a later (but still certain) event occurs[1].

There is a further distinction between casual and potestative conditions. The former are not within the power of the beneficiary to control and indeed may relate to matters wholly extraneous to the beneficiary's experience or existence. The latter usually impose a duty on the beneficiary to perform (or refrain from performing) some act – the whole point of the condition is to meet some wish of the testator. It is the latter type which may more commonly be thought of as 'conditional legacies', although casual conditions are in fact much more common in practice.

A final distinction can be drawn between suspensive and resolutive conditions, both of which depend on events uncertain to happen. The expressions more commonly used in England, and occasionally in Scotland, are conditions precedent and conditions subsequent, respectively. A suspensive condition operates to suspend vesting until the condition is fulfilled. A resolutive condition will not prevent vesting, but the legacy will fail if the event detailed in the condition occurs later. The latter type of condition is not particularly common, as in essence it involves vesting subject to defeasance, which, it seems, can only apply in restricted circumstances (see paras 5.32–5.36 above). In either case, the condition may in fact be fulfilled at the date of the testator's death or other date of vesting; with a suspensive condition that will be the end of the matter, but a legacy subject to a resolutive condition could still be defeated in future.

The wording used by the testator will determine the nature of the condition. However, in cases where it is not otherwise clear, it has been stated that conditions personal to the legatee will suspend vesting, while conditions extraneous to the legatee tend to be resolutive[2]. A distinction has also been suggested

1 *MacIntosh v Wood* (1872) 10 M 933.
2 See *Henderson* pp 4–5.

that where the fulfilment of a condition gives something to the legatee, it is suspensive; and where fulfilment takes something away, it will be resolutive.

5.39 If a testator wishes to impose a condition on any legacy, it is important to consider whether it is to be suspensive or resolutive. If it is to be suspensive, provision must be made for what is to happen until it is fulfilled; if resolutive, provision must be made for what is to happen if the condition ceases to be fulfilled.

It is possible for a condition to be suspensive at first and if the suspensive condition is then fulfilled for it then to be resolutive. This is only possible if the condition relates to a continuing state of affairs, as opposed to the occurrence of a single event. However, the problem which arises with all resolutive conditions will then be particularly acute – once a condition has been fulfilled such that a legacy has vested in a beneficiary, it is extremely difficult to make provision to deprive that beneficiary of the legacy should the condition cease to be fulfilled. This can be done in relation to a right in fee during the existence of a liferent, but is much more difficult with outright legacies. It is probably accurate to say that the only effective of method of maintaining adherence to a continuing condition is to put the subject of legacy into some form of trust, with the condition or conditions attached as provisions of that trust.

5.40 A number of types of legacy are in fact conditional without appearing to be so and the wording of a will may impose conditions without this being immediately obvious. Such types of legacy are dealt with, for the most part, elsewhere in the text.

Most obviously, all legacies are in a sense conditional, in that they depend on the legatee surviving until the will becomes operative, that is at the date of the testator's death at the earliest.

However, a condition is also imposed, in effect, in the legacies involving multiple beneficiaries or where survivorship clauses or destinations-over are used. That condition is the survival of one or more beneficiaries as compared to other beneficiaries (not the testator). The position in relation to this condition may be assessed at the date of testator's death, but may equally well be assessed at some later date, where vesting is postponed (see para 5.15).

Indeed, the nature of a condition may help to determine whether or not vesting *is* postponed. To take an example, a destination-over attached to a right of fee will generally postpone vesting until the termination of the relevant liferent[1].

Similarly, a condition as to survivorship will generally postpone vesting until the date of payment. However, if a legacy is to a number of beneficiaries 'and the survivor of them', it may vest in the last beneficiary to survive even before the date of payment arrives. This is not a common construction and will require an

---

1 Unless the destination-over is in favour of children or issue; see *Middleton's Trustees v Middleton* 1955 SC 51; *Bowman v Bowman* (1899) 1 F (HL) 69; *Wylie's Trustees v Bruce* 1919 SC 211; *Allan's Trustees v Allan* 1918 SC 164.

indication that vesting in the last survivor is to occur immediately he attains that status[1].

A condition as to survivorship for a specified period after the testator's death (30 days, for example) will also act to postpone vesting until that period has elapsed. This provision is included in most of the Styles presented.

5.41 Conditions as to survivorship for a period beyond the testator's death, whether stated directly or implied by a destination-over or survivorship clause, are probably the most common type of condition imposed in wills. A similar type of condition is that a legatee attains a specified age. This may of course be combined with a condition that the legatee survives another beneficiary or another event, such as the termination of a liferent. It is always better, when dealing with references to a specified age, to refer to that age directly; references to the age of majority were commonly used in the past. This age has altered over time; it is currently 18, although for most purposes the age of legal capacity (16, following the Age of Legal Capacity (Scotland) Act 1991) is now more significant (see paras 6.46–6.51, 6.87–6.96).

A condition as to a legatee surviving until a specified age is an obvious example of a personal condition. If it is truly a condition attached to the legacy, it will thus operate to suspend vesting until the beneficiary attains the stated age.

However, it is also entirely possible that references to attainment of a specified age operate only to postpone *payment* until the beneficiary attains the age stated; should the beneficiary predecease the date of payment the legacy would form part of his estate. This is entirely a matter of interpreting the will in question.

If it is not made absolutely clear, there are a number of rules deriving from decided cases to assist in determining whether vesting or mere payment is postponed. These include considerations deriving from the exact form of the gift (especially where the condition is attached), whether there is a destination-over and what is to happen until the specified age is attained, notably in relation to interest and advances of capital[2].

In the Styles, it is intended that the matter is put beyond doubt. Most contain a purpose dealing with 'Beneficiaries lacking capacity', under that side heading. A beneficiary below the age of 16 (at least in Scotland) lacks legal capacity. This purpose is dealt with elsewhere (see paras 6.127–6.128); but for present purposes it is clear that such a clause relates *only* to payment and does not prevent legacies vesting in beneficiaries prior to their attaining the age of 16, or other age of legal capacity. Otherwise, declarations as to the date of vesting (as, for example, in S5.7) will control the situation.

It is easier to impose enforceable conditions if the will creates a trust in any event. A condition as to age is likely to be added to a clause dealing with survivorship. Appropriate wording would be (following a legacy to A):

'. . . but only if the said A attains the age of 21 . . .' or

---

1 See *Henderson* pp 84–99.
2 See *Alves' Trustees v Grant* (1874) 1 R 969; *Graham's Trustees v Graham* (1899) 2 F 232; *Ralston v Ralston* (1842) 4 D 1496; *Wilson's Trustees v Quick* (1878) 5 R 697; and *Henderson* Chapter III.

'. . . only in the event of the said A attaining the age of 21 . . .'

5.42   There are a number of subsidiary matters to be dealt with if a condition as to attaining a specified age is to be included. The most important (as with any condition) is to provide for what is to happen if the condition is not fulfilled, unless the testator is content simply for it to pass into residue (or if a legacy of residue is involved, into intestacy). A destination-over can be added, as follows:

'. . . declaring that should A fail to survive me or fail to attain the age
of 21, this legacy shall pass to B . . .'

Such a destination-over is helpful in emphasising that vesting, as opposed to mere payment, is postponed until the specified age is attained. More complex issues can arise where destinations-over to issue of the original legatee are involved. Notably, if they *also* require to attain the specified age before obtaining a vested right, this should be stated. It will not happen automatically and on the failure of the primary beneficiary, the legacy will vest immediately in the conditional institute[1]. However, if such a provision is used it may postpone vesting for an undesirable length of time.

Equally, it is probably best to insert a provision (for the avoidance of doubt) should the condition as to attaining a specified age *not* apply to beneficiaries, including issue or children, taking under a destination-over. This could read as follows:

'. . . declaring that should A fail to survive me or fail to attain the age
of 21, this legacy shall pass to his children equally among them if
more than one, irrespective of their ages at the date of my death or the
death of their parent.'

There is no reason why a condition as to attaining a specified age should not be attached to a gift to a class of legatees, such that each only takes if and when he attains the specified age. However, this is perhaps more likely to be construed as involving a direction as to the time of payment alone, rather than the time of vesting[2]. If postponement of vesting is to be until each member of the class attains a specified age, then suitable simple wording would be:

'. . . to such of my children as attain the age of 25 . . .'

Alternatively (or additionally), a destination-over can refer to the members of the class respectively failing to attain the specified age[3]. It is also possible to provide for a legacy to vest in a class of beneficiaries only when the youngest attains a specified age. As this would create a complex and somewhat uncertain situation it is not to be recommended. However, if it is essential, it should be clearly expressed, perhaps as follows:

'. . . declaring that vesting shall be postponed until the youngest of
the said children attains the age of 21 or dies before attaining that
age. . .'

It should be noted that this type of provision especially may postpone vesting for

1 *Cattanach's Trustees v Cattanach* (1901) 4 F 205.
2 *Waters' Trustees v Waters* (1884) 12 R 253; *Henderson* pp 39–41.
3 *Buchanan's Trustees v Buchanan* (1877) 4 R 754.

a very long time; in almost all circumstances an accumulation and maintenance trust is likely to be preferable, presuming that the age restrictions referable to such a trust do not cause problems.

5.43 Another vital subsidiary issue with any condition which is perhaps most clearly focussed when it relates to attaining a specified age is what is to happen until the condition is satisfied. Depending on the nature of the condition, this may involve quite a substantial period of time. Of course, it also arises in the case of a simple clause demanding survival for 30 days after the testator's death.

A fundamental principle is of significance here – only if vesting is suspended can a suspensive condition attached to a legacy be truly effective. A beneficiary of full age (now 16 in Scotland), not otherwise suffering from incapacity can demand payment if a legacy has vested, notwithstanding instructions to the contrary in a will. If there are no apparent trust purposes, this might suggest immediate vesting; but if vesting is clearly postponed until fulfilment of a condition as (as suggested above), a trust is in effect created.

If this is done without providing full trust purposes (perhaps even without the formal appointment of trustees), the executors will have difficulty in knowing what to do until the condition is satisfied. If the only condition involves surviving the testator for a limited period, no practical problem will arise. No beneficiary can demand payment of a legacy before six months from the date has elapsed.

If the period possibly involved is longer, it is suggested that provisions for a full trust should be included. The exact type would depend on the condition concerned, but survival to a specified age of 25 or less might indicate an accumulation and maintenance trust. A liferent (for a period of less than the beneficiary's life) might be equally suitable if the testator is content for the beneficiary to have an interest in any income which arises. However, such a liferent provision may have adverse inheritance tax consequences.

If no formal trust is created (and this may be considered unnecessary if the condition is attached to a relatively small legacy), the effect of a condition suspending vesting would seem to be to create a trust in any event. Until the condition is fulfilled, it is likely that any income would require to be accumulated (for the permitted period – see para 5.69). This could create tax difficulties. The additional rate of tax (which combined with the basic rate is now known as 'the rate applicable to trusts') would apply for income tax purposes. For inheritance tax purposes there would be a settlement without an interest in possession. Quite apart from tax considerations the lack of formal trust powers may lead to difficulties with investment, particularly important if a substantial fund is involved. For this reason, if a conditional legacy is included in a will, at the very least the short form of trust powers should also be included.

5.44 The need for full trust purposes is even more evident where one is dealing with a resolutive condition. The problem here is that if a full vested right is given to a beneficiary, it is impossible practically to deprive that beneficiary of the legacy if a continuing condition ceases to be satisfied. There is an exception to this in the case of vesting subject to defeasance (see paras 5.32–5.36 above), but the categories of bequest to which this doctrine applies are limited. These categories usually relate to the birth of issue; but the concept also appeared to have been applied to a condition that a widow should not remarry[1]. This was significant, in that the legacy was of furniture, in which the widow took a right of fee. The same decision in relation to a legacy of residue in fee was reached in *Beaton's Judicial Factor v Beaton*[2]. However, in neither case was the problem addressed as to what would actually happen if the widow were to dispose of her legacy and then remarry – but it would have been incompatible with a full right of fee should she not have been able to do so.

The same problem is likely to arise in connection with any condition requiring a beneficiary to maintain any continuing state or course of action over a period of time. A condition preventing remarriage may be the most likely; but there are other possibilities, which lack any judicial backing to allow them to be treated as involving vesting subject to defeasance.

An example of such a condition might be a requirement to reside in a particular house or a particular country (see para 5.46). With such conditions, it would be possible to convert the resolutive condition into a suspensive one, by imposing a time limit during which the condition should be fulfilled (with vesting on the expiry of the stated period). Alternatively, full trust provisions should be included.

5.45 It is worth considering certain conditions which can validly be imposed and which will lead to forfeiture of a legacy if not fulfilled.

Legacies conditional on the marriage of a beneficiary are unlikely to be as common as they once were. Such a condition would be perfectly valid, however, unlike some other conditions in connection with marriage (see para 5.49). Such a condition is thought to be analogous to a condition as to attaining a specified age[3]. It should thus be made clear whether such a condition relates to vesting or mere payment of a legacy.

A legacy can also be made conditional on the marriage of a third party[4].

Similar considerations apply to a legacy conditional on a child being born to a legatee. This of course is a separate matter from any possible legacy to the child itself.

5.46 Conditions as to residence have already been mentioned. These are likely to be enforceable, allowing that there may be difficulties in defining the quality of residence required. A requirement to 'occupy' a particular house has been held valid[5]. However, there may be less difficulty in interpreting such terms in Scotland than has been evident in English authorities[6]. There may also be particular difficulties if the condition is resolutive, should the required degree of

---

1 *Smith's Trustees v Smith* (1883) 10 R 1144.
2 1950 SLT (Notes) 63.
3 See *Henderson* pp 42 ff.
4 *MacIntosh v Wood* (1872) 10 M 933.
5 *Veitch's Executor v Veitch* 1947 SLT 17.
6 *Wemyss v Wemyss' Trustees* 1921 SC 30 and compare with *Sifton v Sifton* [1938] AC 656.

residence cease after the legacy has vested[1]. The same considerations apply to a condition that a beneficiary should *not* reside in a particular place or with a particular person. Such conditions have been held valid, although they are possibly subject to attack as contrary to public policy, especially the prevention of residence where a spouse or a relative is involved[2].

Residence may also be required in a country rather than at a particular address. Once more, such a condition is thought to be enforceable, but the quality of residence may be particularly difficult to define, especially if no time limit for such residence is imposed. In this context, see particularly *Sifton v Sifton*[3] and *Re Gape's Will Trusts*[4], where use of the word 'permanent' was held to clarify the concept of residence required. In these circumstances, it may be desirable to define the condition in terms for which there is a reasonable amount of established authority, such as 'residence for tax purposes' or 'domicile' in the desired country. The latter, but not the former, expression could be used where the country in question is Scotland. However, if it is at all likely that the quality of residence will be challenged in establishing whether the condition has been or continues to be fulfilled, it may be desirable to add provision for a decision to be made by the executors, for example:

'. . . to A, but only if she is resident in Scotland at the date of my death, as to which my executors shall be the sole judges . . .'

It may also be desirable to include a definite period of time during which any condition as to residence requires to be fulfilled. This has assisted in preventing such conditions being treated as void for uncertainty in England[5].

5.47 The Styles presented include (at S2.6(2)) a legacy conditional on the beneficiary being in the testator's employment at the date of death. While this is thought to be valid and enforceable, a doubt is thrown up by the case of *Simpson v Roberts*[6]. The condition in that case extended to a requirement that the legatee continued in the employment of the testator's husband after her death. The husband dismissed the legatee, but it was held that the legatee was entitled to the legacy in any event – the legatee had been willing to remain in employment.

This is perhaps an example of the principle that potestative conditions will be treated as fulfilled if the legatee has done all in his power to fulfil them[7]. A similar result was reached when the condition was that the legatee should be 'looking after' the testator at the date of death, but the legatee was herself ill at that time[8].

Purpose S2.3 contains a legacy to an executor, on condition that he accepts office. This is entirely acceptable and may in any event be a condition implied by law.

---

1 See *Re Coxen, MacCallum v Coxen* [1948] Ch 747.
2 See paras 5.49–5.51; *Reid v Coats* 5 March 1813, FC; *Grant's Trustees v Grant* (1898) 25 R 929; *Fraser v Rose* (1849) 11 D 1466.
3 [1938] AC 656.
4 [1952] Ch 743.
5 See, for example, *Walcot v Botfield* (1854) Kay 534.
6 1931 SC 259.
7 See *Henderson* pp 344–345; *Pirie v Pirie* (1873) 11 M 941.
8 *Cumming's Trustees, Petitioners* 1960 SLT (Notes) 96.

A condition can be imposed as to the taking of a particular name[1].

5.48 If the testator wishes to impose conditions on a legacy, it should be considered whether they are to apply only to the original legatee or to any person taking in his place. Particularly where a destination-over is involved, it is unlikely that a condition will carry over to the conditional institute, except perhaps where the condition itself relates to survivorship. Indeed, the destination-over may only come into effect on a particular condition not being fulfilled.

In these circumstances, it is essential to ascertain whether any particular condition is to effect *all* potential beneficiaries. If so, the condition must be attached separately to the legacy to each beneficiary; or alternatively (and more elegantly), it should be narrated in a form of a declaration:

'. . . declaring that no beneficiary shall take under this purpose unless. . .'

In either event, it may be important to provide for what is to happen in the event of no potential beneficiary fulfilling the condition – an ultimate unconditional destination-over either to a named beneficiary or to residue would usually be appropriate.

Ineffective conditions

5.49 A distinction must be drawn between an ineffective *legacy*, which will fall in its entirety and an ineffective *condition*, which will fly off allowing the legacy to go to the specified beneficiary unconditionally. In England, if certain conditions are unlawful, the whole legacy falls but this result is less likely in Scotland where ineffective conditions will generally be disregarded[2].

A condition may be ineffective because it is impossible, uncertain, illegal or against public policy. In England, a resolutive condition (condition subsequent) is more likely to be void for uncertainty than a suspensive one (condition precedent), but there is no such distinction in Scotland. The fact that a condition may be described as capricious does not in itself make it objectionable unless it falls within one of the other prohibited categories[3].

Many questions in this area relate to conditions in connection with marriage (or similar states). A condition that a beneficiary should never marry is ineffective[4]. Other directions in this area may be void from uncertainty, particularly where a direction is to marry, or refrain from marrying into a particular race or religion; the former may also be void under the Race Relations Act 1976[5].

However, a condition that a beneficiary should receive a legacy only if he

1 *Hunter v Weston* (1882) 9 R 492; *Munro's Trustees v Spencer* 1912 SC 933.
2 See *McLaren* II, para 1094.
3 *Balfour's Trustees v Johnston* 1936 SC 137 and compare *McLaren* II, para 1095.
4 *Ommanney v Douglas* (1796) 3 Pat 448; *Aird's Executors v Aird* 1949 SC 154; *Young v Johnston and Wright* (1880) 7 R 760.
5 See 25 *Stair Memorial Encyclopaedia* para 866.

marries a certain person or refrains from doing so is valid[1]. It is also entirely permissible to provide for an interest (such as a liferent) to continue for so long as a beneficiary remains married, or indeed unmarried[2].

A condition demanding that a couple be reconciled is valid[3]. But a condition demanding that a couple divorce or separate will not be effective[4]. Similarly, a condition demanding that a widow have 'no association whatever with another man' has been held invalid, although on the basis that it was void from uncertainty[5].

A condition demanding that a beneficiary should not reside with her parents has been held void[6]. Similarly, a requirement that a daughter should not live with her mother has been held to be ineffectual[7].

5.50 Conditions as to a beneficiary's own religion can be void for uncertainty. However they can be expressed with sufficient clarity, as was the case in *Blathwayt v Baron Crawley*[8].

Conditions as to residence in a particular place can cause difficulty, as the quality of required residence may be difficult to establish[9]. However, this is perhaps less likely in Scotland, where a requirement as to residence in a particular place does seem likely to be effectual[10].

Conditions which turn out to be impossible to fulfil are ineffective[11].

5.51 In contrast to cases where ineffective conditions allow a legacy to go to a beneficiary unencumbered, ineffective legacies fall in their entirety. Such legacies tend to be defeated because they are considered to be contrary to public policy. There is a reasonably large body of case law establishing that effect will not be given to excessive schemes designed to perpetuate the memory of the testator or similar purposes[12]. It is thought that reasonable provision for tombstones and the like should cause no problems and even more extensive and expensive schemes may be permitted if there is some element of public benefit[13]. If a modest memorial is desired this can certainly be included in the will.

---

1 *Forbes v Forbes* (1882) 9 R 675; *Henderson* p 343.
2 *Kidd v Kidd's Trustees* (1863) 2 M 227; *Smith's Trustees v Smith* (1883) 10 R 1144; *Sturrock v Ranken's Trustees* (1875) 2 R 850.
3 *Barker v Watson's Trustees* 1919 SC 109.
4 *Wilkinson v Wilkinson* (1871) LR 12 Eq 604.
5 *Beaton's Judicial Factor v Beaton* 1950 SLT (Notes) 63.
6 *Grant's Trustees v Grant* (1898) 25 R 929.
7 *Fraser v Rose* (1849) 11 D 1466; but compare *Balfour's Trustees v Johnston* 1936 SC 137; *Reid v Coates* 5 March 1813 FC.
8 [1976] AC 397.
9 See for example *Re Field's Will Trusts* [1950] Ch 520.
10 See *Wemyss v Wemyss' Trustees* 1921 SC 30 and para 5.46.
11 See *Dunbar v Scott's Trustees* (1872) 10 M 982, where the condition involved the purchase of a commission in the army; and *Milne v Smith* 1982 SLT 129, where there was a direction as to combining businesses when this was simply not possible because of their structure.
12 *McCaig v Glasgow University* 1907 SC 231; *McCaig's Trustees v Kirk-Session of the United Free Church of Lismore* 1915 SC 426; *Aitken's Trustees v Aitken* 1927 SC 374; *MacKintosh's Judicial Factor v Lord Advocate* 1935 SC 406; *Lindsay's Executor v Forsyth* 1940 SC 568; *Sutherland's Trustees v Verschoyle* 1968 SLT 43.
13 *Aitken's Trustees* 1927 SC 374; *Campbell Smith's Trustees v Scott* 1944 SLT 198.

Although the reported cases have concentrated on provisions for memorials and the like, it is thought that public policy grounds could be advanced to strike down other provisions with no perceived public or private benefit. Public policy grounds can certainly be invoked to strike at conditions in order to render the legacies affected unconditional. It is conceivable that public policy might also be invoked in an attempt to defeat legacies given for what might be considered illegal or immoral purposes, although this is perhaps rather more difficult to envisage in modern times than in the past[1].

PRECATORY LEGACIES

5.52 Conditional legacies must be distinguished from precatory legacies. Conditional legacies *require* someone to do something, or some state of affairs to be fulfilled, before they can take effect, or impose conditions the failure of which causes benefits to be withdrawn. Precatory legacies, on the other hand, merely express the testator's *wish* that some course of action be carried out. An appropriate form for such a legacy would be as follows:

'I direct my executors to pay to A the sum of TEN THOUSAND POUNDS and express the wish (but without imposing any obligation) that A should pay this sum within 2 years of my death to B.'

Alternatively, the wishes could be expressed in a separate note or letter to the recipient of the legacy. This might be suitable for dealing with personal belongings or furniture, where the testator might not wish to clutter the will with detailed instructions and may be content to rely on the designated person, who may of course be an executor or trustee. Of course, it must be accepted that the wishes might not be carried out. That is in the nature of such a legacy. A form for such a legacy of furniture, with reference to a separate note, is as follows:

'I direct my executors to make over to A the furniture owned by me in any house occupied by me at the date of my death and express the wish (but without imposing any obligation) that A should, within two years of my death, distribute the furniture in accordance with any note or letter of my wishes in relation to those items declaring that my executors shall be the sole judges as to what constitutes 'furniture'.'

Such a legacy may be a useful and practical method of dealing with such items, although the same object can be achieved by giving executors a measure of discretion directly, without actually leaving the items to any other individual. (See further on such assets paras 4.48–4.57.)

However, as part of the wording above indicates, there is a further reason for putting a legacy in this format. This derives from the terms of the Inheritance Tax Act 1984, section 143, which is as follows:

'Where a testator expresses a wish that property bequeathed by his will shall be transferred by the legatee to other persons, and the legatee transfers any of the property in accordance with

1 See, for examples, *Johnston v McKenzie's Executors* (1835) 14 S 106; *Young v Johnston and Wright* (1880) 7 R 760; but compare *Troussier v Matthew* 1922 SLT 670.

that wish within the period of two years after the death of the testator, this Act shall have effect as if the property transferred had been bequeathed by the will to the transferee.'

This provision occurs in the same part of the Inheritance Tax Act as that dealing with variations of the deceased's estate. There are obvious parallels; indeed, it provides what might be seen as an opportunity to provide for what is in essence a variation within the confines of the will. This impression is confirmed by the terms of the Inheritance Tax Act 1984, section 17(b), which directs that a transfer to which section 143 applies is not a transfer of value.

The Budget proposal and draft legislation in 1989 which threatened to restrict severely the possibilities attached to variations and the like applied to section 143 transfers. These proposals were withdrawn with a threat to return with more specific, targeted measure, but this has not yet appeared. It must be at least possible that something akin to section 143 would survive, even if the tax advantages of other types of variation were to be restricted.

5.53 A precatory legacy might be used as an alternative to a discretionary trust, perhaps involving an amount equal to the nil rate band for inheritance tax purposes. The idea would be to leave such a legacy to a spouse, but express the wish that the spouse should pass it on to children (or indeed any non-exempt beneficiaries). Such a wish would and could not be binding, so that if the spouse decided that the retention of the legacy was required, this could be done; however, if the legacy were passed on, this would be treated as a transfer by the deceased. The same result would be achieved by a deed of variation, but such a legacy would obviate the need for such additional procedure. The main difference from a discretionary trust (apart again from the absence of administrative requirements and machinery) would be that the sole discretion would be in the hands of the spouse, without the possibility of independent trustees assessing the situation. This might be regarded as a positive advantage by many testators. It should be noted that there are no capital gains tax privileges attached to implementation of a precatory bequest.

Further and more ambitious possibilities exist if the testator wishes to benefit a charity. In such a case, the wish expressed could be for a legacy to be passed on by an individual to a charity, either named or within the discretion of the legatee. Such a legacy could run as follows:

'I direct my executors to pay to A the sum of FIFTY THOUSAND POUNDS and express the wish (but without imposing any obligation) that A should pay this sum within two years of my death to such a charity or charities as A in his sole discretion may decide.'

If the nil rate band has been used elsewhere and A is a non-exempt beneficiary, this legacy will be taxable; however, if A goes on to fulfil the testator's wishes, section 143 of the Inheritance Tax Act 1984 will apply, so that the ultimate transfer is treated as an exempt charitable legacy made by the deceased.

However, it is also possible for A to take advantage of the gift aid scheme set out in the Finance Act 1990, section 25, as amended. Any single gift to a charity in excess of £250 will be treated as made after deduction of basic rate tax, in the same manner as a covenanted payment to charity. The result of such treatment is that the donor (the legatee in this case) gets income tax relief at his highest rate on the deemed gross amount of the payment, presuming that he has sufficient taxed income to cover it. It does not matter that the actual funds derive not from that person's income, but simply from fulfilling the wishes of a deceased person and utilising resources from the estate. The effect of this scheme on the legatee's income tax position could be dramatic; it brings benefits to both the legatee and the charity, and of course fulfils the testator's wishes.

As with all tax planning devices, this must be subject to a warning as to possible Inland Revenue attack, whether by changes in the legislation or through the courts. However, if a testator truly wishes to benefit a charity and is prepared to risk that his legatee may not fulfil his wishes, such a scheme is certainly worth considering.

In any event, precatory legacies in general may be worth considering for less ambitious tax planning reasons, or because such legacies directly meet the testator's non-tax needs, as mentioned above.

REPUGNANCY

5.54 Conditions may be ineffective because they fall foul of the law relating to repugnancy. This becomes relevant where a will contains provisions that are mutually inconsistent. The normal result will be that the beneficiary takes the legacy unaffected by the conditions, as long as a full right of fee is given by the legacy. The principle is that a testator cannot give something outright, but then attempt to attach conditions inconsistent with full ownership. This is another reason why a trust is required should the testator really wish to ensure that his wishes continue to be met after his death.

There are a number of established classes of repugnant legacies. Most importantly, a direction to trustees to *retain* property (perhaps until a beneficiary attains a specified age) is inconsistent with that beneficiary being given an absolute and unqualified vested right. As long as the beneficiary has full legal capacity[1], he can demand payment unless there remain trust purposes to be fulfilled. Mere directions to trustees to manage property for the owner are insufficient to prevent the owner vindicating his rights[2].

It would doubtless come as a shock to many testators to learn that a beneficiary could claim immediate payment of even a substantial legacy on his 16th birthday. In these circumstances, the only effective method to ensure that payment is delayed until a later age is to suspend vesting until that later time[3].

This would usually be best achieved by an accumulation and maintenance

1 Now attained at the age of 16, following the Age of Legal Capacity (Scotland) Act 1991.
2 *Miller's Trustees v Miller* (1890) 18 R 301; *Yuill's Trustees v Thomson* (1902) 4 F 815; *Greenlees's Trustees v Greenlees* (1894) 22 R 136; *Hargrave's Trustees v Schofield* (1900) 3 F 14; *Smith's Trustee v Michael* 1972 SLT 89.
3 *White's Trustees v White* (1896) 24 R 386; *Walker v Buchanan* (1905) 8 F 201.

trust, *provided* that the desired age is 25 or less. For relatively small legacies or shares of residue, the short form provided in Style S8 may be particularly suitable.

However, it is recognised that many testators may not wish to see even limited trust provisions attached to an otherwise simple will. If they still wish to delay beyond a potential beneficiary's 16th birthday it is possible to make the legacy subject to a suspensive condition that the beneficiary attains the specified age. This is by no means ideal. As noted in paragraph 5.43 above, a trust will in effect have been created, but probably without entirely suitable trust provisions. In effect the legacy will be in limbo until the desired age is attained.

It may also be possible to delay payment by attaching trust purposes to *other* legacies, such as to require retention of the subject of bequests under consideration until these other trust purposes have been fulfilled[1].

Alternatively, the testator may simply prefer to insert a legally ineffective provision that payment of the legacy should not take place until the beneficiary attains the desired age. It is perhaps unlikely that most 16-year-olds will be sufficiently legally informed to be aware of their rights in such a matter. Such a course may expose executors to some risk in retaining property after a beneficiary has attained full legal capacity. It is thought that at the very least testators should be advised of the position in these circumstances[2].

5.55 It should be considered whether *in fact* the testator wishes to give a full unqualified right to the beneficiary. It may be that a liferent is suitable, which can of course be enlarged to a right of fee at a later date. This is again a form of postponed vesting; and restriction to a liferent has been recognised as a clear case where the doctrine of repugnancy will not apply[3].

A further recognised class of repugnant bequest involves an apparently outright legacy declared to be for alimentary use[4]. Alimentary liferents are effectual (even if, perhaps, not to be recommended), but an attempt to render a bequest of fee alimentary will fail.

As noted above (para 4.134), a legacy coupled with a direction to utilise it to purchase an annuity is repugnant, unless a continuing trust is set up. This is because if the annuity is simply conveyed to the beneficiary, he could convert it back into capital[5].

The same applies to a direction to purchase other property for a beneficiary, if the beneficiary would simply have the right to dispose of the property[6].

1 *MacCulloch v Macculloch's Trustees* (1903) 6 F (HL) 3; *Graham's Trustees v Graham* (1899) 2 F 232.
2 On this matter generally, see Barr & Edwards 'Age of legal capacity: further pitfalls (1)' 1992 SLT (News) 77.
3 See for example *Miller Richard's Trustees v Miller Richard* (1903) 5 F 909; *Chambers' Trustees v Smiths* (1878) 5R (HL) 151 and compare *Graham v Graham's Trustees* 1927 SC 388.
4 *Wilkie's Trustees v Wight's Trustees* (1893) 21 R 199; *Henderson* pp 324 ff.
5 *Kennedy's Trustees v Warren* (1901) 3 F 1087; *Dempster's Trustees v Dempster* 1921 SC 332.
6 See *Henderson* pp 329–332.

FORFEITURE

5.56 The term 'forfeiture' is used in a number of senses in relation to wills and succession. Firstly, it refers to the principles under which an 'unworthy heir', especially one responsible for a particular death, is disqualified from benefit in a particular estate. As a testator is unlikely to anticipate any potential beneficiary being affected by these rules, it is not something which can really be addressed when drafting a will[1].

Secondly, forfeiture refers to the consequences of a beneficiary failing to satisfy a resolutive condition. This matter has been dealt with above (see paras 5.37–5.48); the key point which must be dealt with is what is to happen should a beneficiary forfeit a legacy in these circumstances.

Thirdly, provision can be made for forfeiture of a benefit in specific circumstances. Most commonly, this can be done in relation to any beneficiary who challenges the provisions of the will in any way. This might be useful where there are any provisions which the testator might regard as in any way contentious or likely to cause dispute between beneficiaries. Suitable wording would be as follows:

'In the event of any beneficiary challenging the provisions of this will, such beneficiary will forfeit any benefit conferred by this will and the benefit shall pass to the beneficiary or beneficiaries who would have been entitled and on the terms and conditions which would have applied had the beneficiary so challenging predeceased me.'

There are limits to the effect of such a provision, as the jurisdiction of the courts cannot be entirely excluded. But such a clause is not necessarily against public policy, particularly if there is a valid reason for wishing to exclude potential challenges to the will.

Such provision might equally well be attached to a specific purpose, perhaps particularly where physical items such as furniture are being divided among a group of beneficiaries or certain matters are left to the discretion of executors. Suitable wording in these circumstances might be:

'. . . declaring that should any beneficiary under this purpose challenge the decision of my executors, such beneficiary will forfeit his share in the benefit conferred by this purpose.'

Finally, and most importantly, forfeiture arises when a beneficiary claims legal rights. If legal rights are claimed, it is not generally possible to take benefits under a will dealing with the same estate. This rule has existed for many years and is now given statutory effect by the Succession (Scotland) Act 1964, section 13. Every testamentary disposition by which provision is made in favour of the spouse or of any issue of the testator takes effect as if it contained a declaration that the provision so made is in full and final settlement of legal rights. Given the implied forfeiture now provided by the statute, it is probably unnecessary to include a specific forfeiture clause where the claiming of legal rights is the only

---

1 On this matter see 25 *Stair Memorial Encyclopaedia* paras 668 ff.

possible challenge envisaged. However, there is nothing to stop such a clause being included and it may help to clarify exactly what is to happen on legal rights being claimed.

5.57 Problems can arise, notably as to the effect of forfeiture on other beneficiaries, especially issue of the person forfeiting should they also be beneficiaries under the will. Generally the answer to this depends on the terms of the will. If the provisions in favour of the issue are separate, independent benefits, forfeiture by the parent will not involve forfeiture by the issue. But if the benefits are inter-dependent, forfeiture by the issue will occur on the claim to legal rights by the original beneficiary[1].

If there is not an express forfeiture clause, but only one inferred by the operation of the Succession (Scotland) Act 1964, section 13, it seems unlikely that forfeiture will occur for any beneficiary other than the one actually claiming legal rights[2].

If the forfeiture is of liferent provisions and vesting is postponed, the forfeiture may not accelerate it. This may demand accumulation which may not be desirable[3]. In these circumstances, specific provision for forfeiture may be desired. Suitable clauses can be found in S5.7 and S6.12; the cautious may wish to add the alternative 'or forfeiture' to the other events treated as bringing the fee provisions into effect, but it may well be safe to rely on a forfeiture being treated in exactly the same way as a renunciation.

5.58 Incidentally, the operation of a forfeiture clause brings the principle of equitable compensation into play. This is a complex doctrine, once thought to be abolished by section 13 of the Succession (Scotland) Act 1964. This was found not to be the case in *Munro's Trustees v Munro*[4]. The doctrine involves the amount which would have gone to the legal rights' claimant going to compensate those who have been prejudiced by the claim[5].

If the effect of a forfeiture by a legal rights' claimant does not involve forfeiture by that claimant's issue, this may in fact encourage such claims, as the claimant's family will benefit in any event. As noted above, non-forfeiture by a claimant's issue is likely to be more common than otherwise and will be the case

---

1 See *Dixon v Fisher* (1833) 6 W & S 431; *Campbell's Trustees v Campbell* (1889) 16 R 1007; *Hurll's Trustees v Hurll* 1964 SC 12; *Ballantyne's Trustees v Ballantyne's Trustees* 1952 SC 458; *Munro's Trustees v Munro* 1971 SC 280; *McCartney's Trustees v McCartney* 1951 SC 504; *Seafield's Trustees* 1975 SLT 31. The case of *Ballantyne's Trustees* had a recent sequel in *Ballantyne's Trustees v Ballantyne* 1993 SLT 1237. The original case had held that the effect of a forfeiture clause was to involve forfeiture of the provisions in favour of a particular son's issue when that son claimed legal rights and thus forfeited the provisions in his own favour. The question in the new case was whether the son's issue must also be held to have forfeited their rights in a share in the estate arising on the termination of a liferent in favour of a daughter; it was held that the effect of the forfeiture applied only to the son's original share. While he would have forfeited any rights in the daughter's liferented share, the conditional institution of that share in favour of his issue constituted a separate gift.
2 Compare *Nicholson's Trustees v Nicholson* 1960 SC 186.
3 *Muirhead v Muirhead* (1890) 17 R (HL) 45.
4 1971 SC 280.
5 See G L Gretton 'Vesting, Equitable Compensation and the Mysteries of the Shadow Liferent' 1988 SLT (News) 149.

with all wills relying on section 13 of the 1964 Act. In such circumstances, a specific forfeiture clause covering issue of potential claimants or perhaps other beneficiaries under a destination-over, as well as such claimants themselves, would be desirable. Suitable wording (which can be restricted to the potential claimants or adapted for other beneficiaries if that is what is required) is as follows:

> '. . . declaring that should any beneficiary claim legal rights (or any replacement therefor, as to which my executors shall be the sole judges) in my estate, such beneficiary will forfeit any benefit conferred by this will on himself or herself [and any benefit conferred on his or her issue shall also be forfeited] and such benefit shall pass as if such beneficiary [and his or her issue] had predeceased me.'

The rule in section 13 of the 1964 Act only takes effect 'unless the disposition contains an express provision to the contrary'. It is thus clearly envisaged that a testator may wish to make provision for legal rights to be claimed in addition to benefits conferred by a will, although the circumstances where this might be desired are likely to be rare. It would generally be easier to make further provision for the potential legal rights' claimant in the will. However, a provision preventing forfeiture may occasionally be desirable where the provisions in favour of the potential legal rights claimant include items which the testator is particularly keen for the beneficiary to have (particularly perhaps to ensure that such items pass down the family line). Again, such provision may be desired where the only testamentary provision for a potential legal rights' claimant is of heritable property, in which a legal rights' claimant would not share on a claim being made. In any event, given the terms of the Succession (Scotland) Act 1964, section 13, the wording should be particularly clear. The following would be suitable:

> 'It is expressly provided that no benefit conferred by this will shall be forfeited in the event of any beneficiary claiming legal rights in my estate (or any replacement therefor, as to which my executors shall be the sole judges).'

If only a restricted prevention of forfeiture was required, the reference to 'any beneficiary' could be replaced by reference to named individuals (perhaps extending to their issue, if destinations-over were involved). It would be possible to include in such a provision an attempt to restrict the rights of a beneficiary taking both under the will and under a legal rights' claim, in order to prevent an excessive amount of the total estate going to such a claimant. Such a provision would be extremely complex. In such circumstances, it would seem much better to reconsider the scheme of the will, to ensure that any potential legal rights' claimant would in fact benefit to a greater extent by accepting his testamentary provision.

POWERS OF APPOINTMENT AND
DISCRETIONARY LEGACIES

5.59 A power of appointment is a power given by the testator to his executors, trustees or some other person or persons to divide his estate or part thereof as the donee of the power decides. Of course, this may be achieved by the use of a discretionary trust (see paras 5.68–5.72, 5.87–5.107) and such a trust may be the best way to achieve the desired end. However, there is no strict need to interpose a trust in order to provide appropriate discretion. While full discretionary trusts are included among the Styles presented, it may be preferable to have a simple discretionary legacy.

Powers of appointment or discretionary legacies may be general, providing an unlimited choice to the donee; or, more usually, special, restricting the donee to a specified class of beneficiaries[1]. In fact, a general power of appointment is close to full rights of ownership and a very broad power may be void as an attempt to delegate the power of making a will to someone other than the testator. It is essential that the class is sufficiently defined[2].

A special power of appointment is much more common and effective. In essence, it is simply a legacy to a class, but accompanied by directions, for instance, that the legacy is to be divided in such proportions and under such conditions as the holder of the power may direct. The holder of the power may not go beyond the class in exercising it[3]. The way in which the power can be exercised can be restricted by the testator in any manner he chooses. An example of such a power would be:

'I direct my executors to pay to such of my brothers and sisters A, B and C as survive me the sum of TEN THOUSAND POUNDS, to be divided in such proportions (which may include zero or the whole) as my executors in their sole discretion shall decide, and failing such division within six months of my death in equal shares.'

This legacy will vest in equal shares at the date of the testator's death, subject to total or partial defeasance as and when the power is exercise[4].

This would also be the result even if no provision was made for division on the failure of appointment[5].

However, vesting *could* be postponed where a power of appointment or discretionary legacy is used, but this would depend on the normal factors leading to postponed vesting (see paras 5.28–5.36 above).

It is permissible for the holder of the power to exclude members of the designated class entirely[6]. However, specific provision has been made in the wording given above for total exclusion if required, so that there are no doubts about this matter.

The testator may impose conditions as to how the holder of a power of appointment is to exercise this power. These conditions must be fulfilled if the power is to be validly exercised[7].

1 The word 'class' is used here in a non-technical sense and may refer to any group of beneficiaries.
2 *Bannerman's Trustees v Bannerman* 1915 SC 398 and paras 6.125–6.126.
3 *Mowbray's Trustees v Mowbray* 1929 SC 254.
4 *Henderson* pp 232 ff; *Watson v Marjoribanks* (1837) 15 S 586; *Johnston v Johnston* (1868) 7 M 109.
5 *Hill's Trustee v Thomson* (1874) 2 R 68; *Weir v Young* (1898) 5 SLT 233.
6 See the Powers of Appointment Act 1874.
7 See, for example, *Campbell's Trustees v Campbell* (1903) 5 F 366.

5.60   A testator may wish to leave a discretion to pay to none of the designated class of beneficiaries, in which case a destination-over should be included and the sum mentioned should be stated to be a maximum, as follows:

> 'I direct my executors to pay to such of the children of my brother A as survive me a total sum not exceeding ONE THOUSAND POUNDS in such proportions (which may include zero or the whole) as they in their sole discretion shall decide, declaring that if my executors exercise the discretion so as not to pay any share of this legacy to the children of my brother A, any unused share shall pass to B.'

Equally, the testator may wish to ensure that each member of the designated class receives a minimum share of the legacy. This can be achieved by wording such as this:

> 'I direct my executor to pay to such of my brothers and sisters as survive me a total of ONE THOUSAND POUNDS, in such proportions as they in their sole discretion shall decide, but subject to each such brother or sister receiving a minimum of TWO HUNDRED POUNDS.'

Again, a declaration could be added for any amount in excess of the total minimum payments to the brothers and sisters who survive, which the executors decide not to utilise, to be paid elsewhere.

An alternative to this type of provision would be for separate legacies of £200 to be made for each surviving brother and sister, with an additional, separate legacy providing a further sum to be paid at the discretion of the executors.

Such legacies are readily adaptable for any group of beneficiaries.

5.61   If the testator is the holder of a power of appointment, this may be exercised by means of his own will, if that is permitted by the terms of the power in his favour. The power may be exercised without direct reference to its existence[1].

This, however, is undesirable; if the testator is the holder of a power of appointment which has not been exercised at the time of drafting the will, consideration should be given to exercising it, either immediately or by including suitable provisions in the will. Research will be required into the terms of the power held. This might arise particularly when the holder of the power of appointment was a liferenter. Some such wording as follows would be suitable:

> 'Considering that in terms of purpose (TENTH) of the will of A dated 4 January 1970 and recorded in the Books of Council and Session on 1 May 1993 the Trust Fund liferented by me was to be divided among the sons of B in such shares as I thought fit, I appoint that this Trust Fund shall be made over as to ONE THIRD to C and TWO THIRDS to D.'

It would be unusual for any other type of power of appointment not to be exercised during life, in the event that the potential beneficiaries were of full legal capacity when the power came into existence. The absence of full trust provisions makes early exercise of such powers of appointment generally extremely desirable, otherwise the funds in question appear to be held in limbo.

1 *Burns' Trustees v Burns' Trustees* 1935 SC 905.

TRUSTS – GENERAL

5.62 It is perhaps inevitable that more complex estates will require the use of trusts, particularly if the testator demands that his wishes control his property to any significant extent beyond his death. This is particularly the case where beneficiaries include children, whether of the testator or otherwise. There will then be the added necessity of keeping what may be very substantial funds out of the hands of beneficiaries who perhaps lack the maturity to maintain such wealth. This is a matter likely to be of great concern to most testators, even if considered less important by such potential minor beneficiaries!

Many of the considerations applicable to trust provisions for children are also applicable to adult beneficiaries. Trusts for children are dealt with specifically in the next chapter. These include a bare trust.

Where it is wanted to keep control of funds out of the hands of adults it is however not possible to use the bare trust for minors since a *capax* adult is able to demand payment by trustees who hold funds vested in that adult where there are no other trust purposes to fulfil. Funds may be retained on a bare trust for an *incapax* beneficiary[1], but in these cases it should be considered whether a curator or judicial factor (despite their disadvantages) should not be appointed to the *incapax*.

In the case of a *capax* beneficiary full trust purposes must be set out if trustees are to control funds beyond age 16.

An accumulation and maintenance trust can be used for adult beneficiaries while they remain under 25 but that is likely to be only a short term answer. There are therefore really just two possible kinds of trust appropriate for adult beneficiaries: the liferent trust and the discretionary trust.

Liferent trusts

5.63 The liferent trust was certainly the more common trust in the past and allows a specified beneficiary the right to the income of the fund while the capital passes to beneficiaries determined by the testator (although it can be subject to a power of appointment granted to the liferenter). The administration of the capital is controlled by trustees chosen by the testator. A testator can provide an income for a beneficiary but give control to trustees. This separation may be important in relation to a business or family company where the liferenter is not thought suitable to control the property but nevertheless should have an income from it.

Probably more important is the fact that generally the liferenter will not be able to dissipate the family wealth by selling or spending it and instead it is preserved for the following generations. Similarly, the liferenter will not be able to leave the trust property by will to whoever he wishes. The capital passes to the beneficiaries determined by the testator.

---

1 Mackenzie Stuart *The Law of Trusts* (1932) p 354.

This control may be subject to considerable limitation (1) if the liferenter is given a power of appointment over the capital either to whoever he wishes or within a specified class, and (2) if the trustees are given power to advance capital to the liferenter. The Styles presented here do not grant powers of appointment to the liferenter since they are conceived as family wills where the testator intends his children ultimately to benefit equally, so that a power of appointment is not appropriate. If distinction between the children was desired by the testator, then that could be provided in the testator's will and not left to the liferenter's decision.

The Styles do, however, allow for the trustees to appoint capital (S5.8) to the liferenter and the problems of this are considered later (see paras 5.78–5.79).

Alimentary liferent

5.64　A liferent may be made alimentary, that is one where the liferenter has no power to deal with the liferent once accepted by assigning it or burdening it. Nor can it be claimed by creditors. Alimentary liferents have fallen into disfavour largely because of their great inflexibility: if a rearrangement of a trust is desired then a petition to the court is necessary. An alimentary liferent can, however, be coupled with a power to the trustees to advance capital so that flexibility can be allowed for. A liferent can easily be made alimentary by the simple addition of the word 'alimentary' or it could be done in rather fuller fashion. In Style S5, purpose (SIX) could be replaced by the following terms:

'I direct my Trustees to hold the residue of my estate for my said wife for her alimentary liferent use only and the same shall not be capable of anticipation or subject to her debts or deeds or liable to the diligence of her creditors.'

A 30-day survivorship clause as in S5.6 could be provided.

Unless there is particular concern as to a beneficiary, it is thought preferable not to make a liferent alimentary.

Liferent trusts – tax considerations

Inheritance tax

5.65　At one time tax considerations were a major factor in the decision to create testamentary liferent trusts. Where one spouse left his estate to the other in liferent then while there was a charge to estate duty on the first death there was no further charge on the second death. This is no longer possible under inheritance tax, where relief is given on the first death and not on the second death irrespective of any testamentary provisions. The estate duty surviving spouse relief continues to be available for liferent trusts set up by a predeceasing spouse, who died before the introduction of capital transfer tax on death in 1975[1]. For inheritance tax purposes a liferent may be considered neutral.

---

1 Inheritance Tax Act 1984, Sch 6, para 2.

The value of the liferented fund is treated as belonging to the liferenter[1]. The effect of this is that on the termination of the liferent, the liferenter is treated as disposing of the fund; this disposal will be aggregated with disposals from the testator's own estate. The termination may take place during the liferenter's lifetime, in which case it will be treated as a potentially exempt transfer. If it takes place on the liferenter's death, the liferented fund will be aggregated with the personal estate passing on death. In either case, the trustees will be primarily liable for any inheritance tax due on the termination[2], if necessary, as a proportionate share of the total amount due on the death of the liferenter.

Any disposal of a liferent interest will be treated as if it was a termination[3]. The rules will apply to proportionate disposals or terminations of the liferent.

Because a liferenter is only entitled to income, but for inheritance tax purposes is treated as owning the underlying capital, this may have an unfortunate effect on any inheritance tax due on the liferenter's own estate. Unless the transfer from testator to liferenter is exempt (for example where the liferenter is the testator's spouse), there may be a danger of relatively rapid successive charges to inheritance tax where testator and liferenter are of similar ages. While this will not be of immediate concern to the testator, such considerations may be of relevance where the testator is attempting to look at the overall tax liabilities for his family, over a period of time. It should be noted that there is no inheritance tax charge where a liferenter's interest is enlarged into a right of fee, as, for example, occurs in the full accumulation and maintenance trust, S7.7[4].

Income tax

5.66 The trustees are liable for basic rate income tax and subject to their revenue expenses the trust income represents the amount of the beneficiary's income. Generally the existence of a liferent trust is neutral as compared with the beneficiary owning funds outright. The changes in advance corporation tax on dividends in the Finance Act 1993 necessitated special provision to ensure that their treatment was the same in Scotland as in England[5]. This change in effect means that the net income of the trust will be treated as accruing directly to the beneficiary. A further change made was to the effect that revenue expenses must be set against dividend income before being set against other types of income[6].

Capital gains tax

5.67 Liferent trusts are now favourably treated for capital gains tax purposes. They are entitled to an annual exempt amount of half that available to

---

1 Inheritance Tax Act 1984, s 49(1).
2 Ibid, s 201.
3 Ibid, s 51.
4 Ibid, s 53(2).
5 Finance Act 1993, s 118.
6 Ibid, s 79(3).

individuals[1]. This amount is subject to sub-division between trusts set up by the same settlor. In 1994/95 the full trust annual exempt amount therefore amounted to £2,900. This is irrespective of the number of beneficiaries of the trust.

The rate of tax is the basic rate of income tax[2]. In 1994/95 this was 25 per cent. It should, however, be noted that if there is a liferent fund within a trust subject to the rate applicable to trusts, such as an accumulation and maintenance trust or a discretionary trust, then the whole trust including the liferent fund will bear tax on capital gains at this higher rate. In 1994/95 this was 35 per cent. The lower 25 per cent rate will apply only where the whole trust is a liferent trust. A liferent trust could be used as a capital gains tax saving device if it was thought that the beneficiary himself was likely to incur a higher rate of tax on his own gains. There was a proposal to assimilate the treatment of capital gains in trusts with the treatment currently applying to an individual[3] but this now appears to have been abandoned[4].

No hold over relief is available on capital gains arising to the trustees on the transfer of funds to beneficiaries, unless the assets in question qualify for holdover relief as business assets[5]. If, of course, funds vest in a beneficiary on the death of the liferenter then there will be an uplift of cost values to the date of death values and no gain will arise on this uplift[6]. This treatment will apply by concession on the death of any person with an interest in possession in settled property, whether or not that interest is a liferent for the whole of that person's life[7].

Discretionary trusts

5.68 The other type of trust suitable for adults is the discretionary trust, where no fixed interests are generally given and instead the trustees have a discretion over the distribution of income and capital. It affords the possibility of creating a long-term situation of limbo where trustees can hold property and distribute funds, constrained only by the requirements on distribution of income after the expiry of an accumulation period and also by tax considerations. Quite apart from specific considerations relating to children (see para 6.61), a testator may wish to leave the division of his estate to be decided only after his death when the extent and nature of his assets and liabilities can be determined, when the requirements of the individual members of his family can be looked at in real and not in abstract terms, and when the possibility of tax mitigation can be considered in the light of the rules at that time. He may wish to leave funds in a form of limbo unallocated to any of his family. This may have important consequences as to who within a family has control of a company or business and on the

---

1 Taxation of Chargeable Gains Act 1992, Sch 1, para 2.
2 Ibid, s 4.
3 Inland Revenue Consultative Document on Resident Trusts, March 1991.
4 See [1993] STI 516.
5 See the Taxation of Chargeable Gains Act 1992, s 165.
6 Ibid, s 73.
7 Extra Statutory Concession D 43.

valuation of such property. Leaving property in this state may result in an overall reduction of tax.

It may not be possible to use a liferent trust because of the restrictions on creation of liferents. It may not be possible to use an accumulation and maintenance trust which qualifies for inheritance tax reliefs because it is difficult to accommodate more than one generation, due to the 25-year limits, or because the testator wants to benefit beneficiaries over age 25. These are some of the cases where a discretionary trust may be considered. It is worth mentioning that there will usually be considerable discretions available to the trustees of an accumulation and maintenance trust including the payment of income and the advance of capital. It is also possible to have an accumulation and maintenance trust under which the trustees have power to select which beneficiaries of a class shall be included at all (see paras 6.53–6.58 and 6.65–6.85).

However, the term 'discretionary trust' is generally taken to mean a trust which is none of a bare trust, a liferent trust, an accumulation and maintenance trust or one of the other special trusts which exist for inheritance tax purposes, for example trusts for disabled people or newspaper trusts[1] and it will be so used here.

5.69 There are some constraints on a discretionary trust. The restrictions on accumulation of income mean that after a certain period the income must be distributed although the allocation need not be fixed or rigid. The accumulation periods which might be available are 21 years from the date of the testator's death, or the minority of any person living or *in utero* at the time of the testator's death, or the minority of any person who would if over age 21 be entitled to the income directed to be accumulated[2].

Where a trust is fully discretionary it cannot be said that a minor beneficiary would be entitled to any particular share of the income had he been aged over 21, and so the third of these periods is not available. Since the point of a discretionary trust is often to delay a decision for longer than is possible by other methods the second period will not usually be appropriate because beneficiaries may already be over 21. The usual period therefore will be 21 years from the testator's death (but see below).

It is not actually necessary for there to be accumulation of income for there to be a discretionary trust. The trustees can be directed to distribute the income each year and still retain a discretion over capital.

The style of discretionary trust presented here in Style S9 is a two-year discretionary trust, which can readily be extended for an indefinite period – see paragraph 5.93.

It actually directs distribution of income during this two-year period and not accumulation. This is done so that a full accumulation period can be provided after the end of the two-year period. The commencement of the permitted

---

1 Which are listed in the Inheritance Tax Act 1984, s 58(1).
2 See the Trusts (Scotland) Act 1961, s 5, as extended by the Law Reform (Miscellaneous Provisions) (Scotland) Act 1966, s 6; *Wilson & Duncan* pp 107 ff.

accumulation period can by this method be delayed until the trust actually becomes discretionary in relation to income, by inserting an intervening interest during which accumulation may not take place[1].

The trustees must thus distribute income during the intervening period until final determinations are made. The trustees will determine the appropriate accumulation period in their deed of appointment resolving matters in relation to the trust fund, which seems acceptable[2]. This period may certainly be 21 years from the testator's death, or the minority of any person who would, if over 21, be entitled to the income directed to be accumulated. More arguably, the accumulation period could also be 21 years from the date of the deed of appointment, but this may not, in fact, be permitted[3]. The point is that as with other aspects of the resolution of the testator's estate, the effective accumulation period can be finally established as part of the discretion available to the trustees.

This style of discretionary trust is distinguished by the two-year period running from the date of the testator's death. Within that period, it is possible to act within the trust so as to distribute or set up other arrangements and for inheritance tax purposes the end result will be treated as if done by the deceased[4]. During this period the trustees have a wide discretion as to the disposition or resettlement of the funds and if they fail to do this then the Style provides for a fixed determination.

Only inheritance tax reasons are relevant in restricting the discretionary period to two years. This could be extended for a considerably longer time if the consequences of the discretionary trust for inheritance tax purposes are acceptable. Since there is no general limit to the duration of a trust in Scotland, the time limit could be dispensed with entirely (see further para 5.93).

Discretionary trusts – tax considerations

Inheritance tax

5.70 A discretionary trust is subject to a separate regime for inheritance tax purposes[5]. Full consideration of the inheritance tax rules on discretionary trusts is outwith the scope of this book. Briefly, there will be the ordinary charge on the transfer of value taking place on the testator's death. Thereafter there will be a periodic charge every ten years and a proportionate charge on distributions during the first ten years and between ten-year anniversaries, based on the number of quarters of a year which have elapsed since the trust commenced or since the last periodic charge. The rate of tax on a periodic charge is 30 per cent of the lifetime rates of inheritance tax. Since the lifetime rate is one half of the death rate which is now a flat 40 per cent, the maximum rate of tax will be 30 per cent of one half of 40 per cent, or only 6 per cent every ten years.

---

1 *Carey's Trustees v Rose* 1957 SC 252; *Wilson & Duncan* p 108.
2 See *Re Cattell* [1914] 1 Ch 177.
3 See *Norrie & Scobbie* p 88.
4 Inheritance Tax Act 1984, s 144.
5 Ibid, ss 58–69.

Although the detailed rules are still very complicated it can be seen that the rate of tax is not heavy and the discretionary trust may therefore be an option worth considering. It must, however, be combined with the warning that discretionary trusts have not always been so lightly treated and may not continue to be so in future. The potential long life of discretionary trusts, without a perpetuity period in Scotland, makes possible changes in the tax rules a matter to be kept in mind.

Income tax

5.71 Where income is being held at the discretion of trustees, or is to be accumulated, that income is liable to both basic and additional rates of income tax, the combination of which is now known as the rate applicable to trusts[1]. At 1994/95 rates this amounted to 25 per cent plus 10 per cent – 35 per cent in total. For dividend income, the rate would be 20 per cent tax credit plus 15 per cent, still bringing out 35 per cent in total. The trustees must meet the additional tax due on all of such income although there is an allowance for the administrative expenses attributable to revenue. Where the trustees distribute income to a beneficiary the income is paid with a tax credit representing the basic and additional rates of income tax at the time at which the income is actually distributed. Thus, a distribution of £65 in 1994/95 will be received by a beneficiary with an associated tax credit of £35 even if the income arose in an earlier year when the tax paid was higher. If the same trust contains income subject to a liferent, that income will suffer only basic rate tax.

The 35 per cent rate of tax is now one which cannot be paid by individuals, who can only pay tax at nil, 20 per cent, 25 per cent or 40 per cent. As a result the beneficiary will suffer additional tax to take him up to 40 per cent or will be able to recover tax to bring him down to the nil, 20 per cent or 25 per cent rates which his own total income attracts. Where a beneficiary is entitled to a repayment because his tax rate is lower than the trust rate of tax, there is no short cut to the repayment: the trustees must pay the tax and the beneficiary must reclaim it. If income is being distributed at the discretion of trustees on a regular basis, the trust structure will create an additional administrative hurdle. There was a proposal that the income tax position of discretionary and accumulation trusts might change to provide for a basic rate band at half of the personal rate and thereafter higher rate tax[2] but the government has announced that this is not to be implemented[3].

Capital gains tax

5.72 A discretionary trust will attract its own annual capital gains tax annual exemption at one half of the personal amount[4]. In 1994/95 the amount for trusts was £2,900. This relief is available irrespective of the number of beneficiaries of

1 Income and Corporation Taxes Act 1988, s 686 as amended.
2 Inland Revenue Consultative Document on Resident Trusts, March 1991.
3 See Inland Revenue Press Release [1993] STI 516.
4 Taxation of Chargeable Gains Act 1992, Sch 1, para 2.

the trust. The full personal annual exemption will be available if the beneficiary of a trust is mentally disabled or in receipt of attendance allowance[1].

The rate of capital gains tax now follows the rate of income tax and so was 35 per cent in 1993/94 and 1994/95[2]. However, in contrast to the income tax position when there are different parts of the trust attracting different income tax rates (see para 5.71), there is no equivalent for capital gains tax purposes. The higher 35 per cent rate applies to the whole trust even if part of the trust is held as a liferented fund. The higher rate applies to a trust where there is any part of the trust subject to additional rate tax at any time during the year of assessment, whether before or after the disposal.

Holdover relief from capital gains tax is available for transfers of property into or out of discretionary trusts[3].

TRUSTS – SPECIFIC STYLES

5.73 The following paragraphs deal with the majority of the specific trust provisions occurring in the Styles presented. The main exceptions are the Styles including accumulation and maintenance provisions. This is because such provisions necessarily relate to beneficiaries under the age of 25 (and usually younger),who will most commonly be the children or remoter descendants of the testator. Such trusts are dealt with in the succeeding chapter, on specific objects of bequest.

The trust provisions mentioned can of course be adapted for use in situations other than those dealt with directly in the Styles. The same is true to a more limited extent with the accumulation and maintenance trust provisions covered in the following chapter.

Notably, virtually all of the trust Styles presented deal with provisions for direct family – spouse, children (with destinations-over for remoter descendants) and grandchildren. There is little in the Styles which is necessarily exclusive to provisions for direct family. The Styles can be used to provide, for instance, liferents for persons other than the testator's spouse. Indeed, a liferent of a house for the testator's mother is shown at S6.5. Any form of trust for children or remoter descendants can be used in relation to persons other than the testator. The adaptations required to convert the family trust Styles to provisions of more general application are usually both minimal and obvious; but care should be taken that references such as 'my children' (referring to children of the testator) should be suitably adapted throughout the Style, not merely where such an expression first occurs.

1 Taxation of Chargeable Gains Act 1992, Sch 1 para 1.
2 Ibid, s 5.
3 See ibid, s 260.

Style S5 – liferent of residue to spouse whom failing children with vesting postponed

5.74 Style S5 provides for a liferent to the testator's spouse. Some of the reasons for considering such a trust have been discussed (see para 5.63). The trustees are given a wide degree of flexibility in dealing with the trust, especially in relation to distributions of capital. Vesting of the capital is postponed until the actual time of distribution. A bare trust for young children and others lacking capacity is included but a full accumulation and maintenance trust for children at the end of the liferent could be provided.

Purpose (FIVE) – personal effects to wife

5.75 Purpose (FIVE) leaves the testator's personal effects to his wife. The terms are as in Style 2 (S2.6(2); see paras 4.48–4.57).

The point of this provision is that these items are not generally suitable subjects for a liferent: consumable stores will be consumed, ordinary furniture will wear out and motor vehicles will deteriorate. The position may of course be different for items of family or economic value.

Purpose (SIX) – liferent to wife

5.76 Purpose (SIX) grants a liferent to the surviving spouse. The word 'liferent' has been used rather than a more traditional formula, such as 'paying her the free income for all the days of her life'. This has been done since the Style envisages that the liferent may not last for the liferenter's lifetime, as it may cease before then by advance of capital or by renunciation.

The entitlement to the liferent provides that the wife must survive for a 30-day survivorship period. The survivorship provision can have odd effects in certain situations.

If the husband testator dies followed, say, a week later by the wife then in terms of this Style she will not have been entitled to the liferent for the week. The destination of the trust funds will be determined by the husband's will. The inheritance tax charge will depend on the husband's estate alone.

If there had been no survivorship period then the wife would (perhaps notionally) have been entitled to the liferent for the week. On her death the husband's will would still determine the destination of the trust funds but the inheritance tax charge would depend on the wife's estate alone. That may or may not be advantageous to the family as a whole depending on the sizes of their respective estates, the tax situation at the time, and whether the residuary beneficiaries under each of their wills are the same.

If the beneficiaries of their estates are different then the wife's beneficiaries will not want her to have had a short liferent, while it would be in the interests of the husband's residuary beneficiaries to show that she had been entitled to it. The wife's beneficiaries could resolve the matter since they, with her executors, could decline to accept a liferent since the widow would not have had the opportunity within the time available to decide whether to accept or renounce the liferent. As a result of these considerations a survivorship clause has been included but the situation would be more flexible if it were not included. Unlike the situation with outright entitlement where the existence or otherwise of the survivorship provision will alter the destination of the funds, the provision where there is a liferent trust does not alter the destination of the funds. Its use can prevent an acceptance or renunciation of the liferent based on pure tax saving-considerations.

The liferent could be made alimentary (see para 5.64).

Purpose (SEVEN) – termination of liferent

5.77 Purpose (SEVEN) deals with what happens on the termination of the liferent. There are three situations envisaged when the liferent would terminate.

Firstly, the liferent might fail by the liferenter predeceasing the testator: in that event no liferent ever exists. Secondly, the liferent might terminate by the death of the liferenter or by the trustees exercising their powers to advance capital under purpose (EIGHT). Thirdly, the liferent might be renounced by the liferenter after it has been enjoyed.

In any of these events the funds pass to the testator's children or remoter issue in similar terms to those set out in the basic style of will shown in Style S3 (S3.6). However, the children or issue are ascertained not at the time of the testator's death but at the time when the liferent terminates. Thus, a child who survived his father (the testator) but predeceased his mother, survived by issue would have been entitled to benefit under Style S3 but would not benefit under this purpose. Instead, his issue would receive his share.

The Style envisages that termination or renunciation may occur not only all at once, but in parts and over a period. The liferenter might take the view that she had ample funds for her own needs and decide to renounce, say, half of her liferent. The half share of the funds would then vest in the testator's children then alive or the issue of any predeceasing children. The remaining half of the trust funds would continue in trust until the liferenter's death. At that time the surviving children and issue of predeceasing children might be different from those who received one half of the trust fund when the renunciation took place. The capital beneficiaries may therefore vary during the lifetime of the trust. This is really only a consequence of postponed vesting.

There is express mention that vesting is postponed until the date or dates of failure, termination or renunciation of the liferent. Vesting may thus occur on an unlimited number of occasions in respect of parts of the trust fund.

This Style provides that at the end for any reason of the liferent the capital passes to the specified beneficiaries. If beneficiaries are under age 16 then the trustees have the powers in the usual provision for beneficaries lacking capacity (S5.10). There is no reason why a full accumulation and maintenance trust should not be added. This could be done in the same way as in Style S7. A second declaration would be added to the termination of liferent purpose (S5.7) in the form it appears at S7.6. The full accumulation and maintenance trust purpose at S7.7 would be inserted. The exclusion of apportionment paragraph in that style (S7.7 (10)) could be deleted because there is already a general exclusion of apportionment provision in Style S5 (S5.9). It is suggested that the accumulation and maintenance trust purpose be inserted between S5.9 and S5.10 so that the two purposes dealing with children are together and so that the purposes dealing with the liferent are together.

Purpose (EIGHT) – distributions from capital

5.78   Purpose (EIGHT) provides for a great degree of flexibility within the trust. It empowers the trustees to make distributions of capital to any beneficiary or prospective beneficiary. Since vesting is postponed it cannot be known for certain that the testator's children will in fact be beneficiaries, because they may predecease the liferenter. As a result they can only be described as prospective beneficiaries, that is beneficiaries who will become entitled unless a certain event (their own death before the liferenter) occurs. The liferenter is the only actual beneficiary.

5.79   Proviso (1) requires that the liferenter's consent be taken when advances are made to the children or issue. This is for the practical reason that the testator has seen the liferenter as the principal beneficiary and it seems unfair to reduce her liferent without her agreement.

Such a requirement for consent might prove to be inconvenient for tax purposes. If the prospective beneficiaries were her children and they were minor then the parent-child settlement provisions for income tax purposes would strike[1]. This would mean that the children's income would be aggregated with the liferenter's income. Had there been no requirement for consent then the liferenter would not have been seen as a settlor in relation to the funds passing to the children. Where a distribution is made to children, those children may wish to allow the liferenter to continue to have the benefit of the distributed funds. If the liferenter has consented to the distribution then this is likely to be a gift with reservation of benefit for inheritance tax purposes. If there is no consent requirement it will be more difficult to show that the liferenter has reserved anything because she took no part in the arrangements and herself made no disposal by way of gift[2].

The trustees can distribute capital to the liferenter. This is a power of very great consequence. If this power were exercised in full then the children would not benefit from the trust at all. They might have discharged their legal rights in consideration for receiving a larger share of the trust capital at the death of the liferenter. The liferenter might leave her estate to third parties rather than to the children and if the children were not her children then they would not even have a claim to legal rights on the liferenter's estate.

It would be possible to minimise the problem by having the power to advance capital to the liferenter restricted to some proportion of the total capital. This could be done by adding a further proviso, which might be in the following terms:

---

1 Income and Corporation Taxes Act 1988, s 663.
2 Finance Act 1986, s 102.

'(4) the value of any distribution to my wife when added to the value (as at the date or dates of distribution) of any previous distributions to her shall not exceed one half of the sum of (a) the value of those previous distributions, (b) the value of the part remaining in trust for my wife's liferent immediately prior to such distribution and (c) the value (as at the date or dates of distribution) of any distributions to any prospective beneficiaries.'

This limits distributions to the surviving spouse to one half of the trust fund. The basis of calculation varies since distributions are taken into account at their value at the time they were made while the trust fund is valued at the time a distribution is in prospect. Distributions to both the spouse and to children have to be added back to make the calculation.

It is considered that a prospective beneficiary is one who would be entitled to a share of the capital if the liferent terminated at that time. It would not include, say, a grandchild of the testator whose parent was alive. The grandchild's parent would be the prospective beneficiary and the grandchild, while having some form of contingent right in the event of his parent predeceasing the liferenter, would not be the immediately prospective beneficiary and would not be within the class of prospective beneficiaries to whom an advance could be made.

It would be feasible for possible remoter beneficiaries to be included as proper persons to whom distributions could be made. If that were done it would then be possible to distribute funds to grandchildren and thus to leave out children entirely. The testator might not have intended that result (at least without the children's consent), and the children themselves might have discharged their legal rights in the expectation of inheriting a greater share of the trust funds. A provision requiring the consent of closer prospective beneficiaries could be incorporated but would increase the complexities of the Style.

In terms of this Style it would also be possible for other arrangements to be made by which such persons could benefit. For example, a child of the testator could assign his prospective right to share in the trust capital to his own child who would then become the prospective beneficiary and an advance could then be made to that grandchild. There might be income tax difficulties on this approach in relation to the parent-child settlement provisions[1].

The class has been limited here since it seems to achieve the testator's and beneficiaries' reasonable expectations better and because it is less complicated.

5.80 Proviso (2) is a hotchpot clause and requires advances to any prospective beneficiary to be brought back into account, so as to ensure equality between the various beneficiaries. Clearly there is an advantage (apart from to the profligate) in receiving funds sooner by way of advance, rather than waiting until the liferenter's death. It would no doubt theoretically be possible to calculate actuarially the advantage but a very broad brush has been taken here. An advance is to be taken into account at its value at the time of the advance, with no

---

1 Income and Corporation Taxes Act 1988, s 663.

allowance for changes in capital values and no interest charge. This has been done in the interests of simplicity. Very often advances made to children will be made to all of the children together so that the problem may not arise.

Since the capital beneficiaries may change over time it would be possible for an advance to be made to a child of the testator who then predeceases the liferenter. It seems only right that that child's issue should be charged with the amount of the advance to that child. That is the reason for the reference in this proviso to the share to which a prospective beneficiary to whom an advance is made 'is or would have been' entitled. It refers to the share to which he would have been entitled had he not died before the final vesting or alternatively had he not assigned his interest to someone else.

Proviso (3) provides that any distributions are to vest on payment. Purpose (SEVEN) already provides for vesting to be postponed in relation to funds passing to children or remoter issue. This proviso makes the same position clear for distributions and in particular in relation to the liferenter who is not mentioned in purpose (SEVEN).

The Style includes provisions relating to beneficiaries lacking capacity, so that the trustees can deal flexibly with funds falling to children either because they are under-age when the liferent fails because of their surviving parent's predecease, or where the liferent terminates on their surviving parent's death, or where an advance of capital is made to them.

Style S6 – liferent of house to mother, liferent of half residue to spouse whom failing children, half residue to children, with vesting on death

5.81 Style S6 envisages a fairly large estate where the testator owns a house occupied by his mother and where he can afford to split his estate between his wife and children. Obviously, the exact terms are capable of adaptation to a considerable number of analogous circumstances.

Purpose (FIVE) – liferent for mother

5.82 Purpose (FIVE)leaves a liferent of the house occupied by his mother to her. It envisages the sale and replacement of the present house by another house. It would exclude a house where the testator and his mother were living together. The practical situation relating to, for example, granny flats and whether the testator could be said to occupy the same property would have to be considered.

The liferent fund consists of such a house or the proceeds of sale of such a house sold after the testator's death. Thus, if the testator's mother was unable to live on her own, then the house could be sold and she would be entitled to the income from the sale proceeds. If this were not desired, then the liferenter could be given the liferent use of such a house on a more limited basis. This could be done by deleting the words 'or the property representing such house following a sale after my death' and adding at the end of this purpose:

'. . .so long as she requires such house for her own personal occupation as to which my trustees shall be the sole judges.'

The trustees have been given the final decision on this because it might be that the liferenter became incapable of giving her consent to giving up the house.

It would have to be considered whether any furniture should be included in the liferent, but see paragraph 5.75.

This liferent has no 30-day survivorship period included. It is envisaged that the testator's mother is in occupation at the date of his death and so is likely to accept the liferent.

Purpose (SIX) – personal effects to wife

5.83 Purpose (SIX) leaves the testator's personal effects to his wife for the same reasons as this was done in S5.5 (see para 5.75).

Purpose (SEVEN) – liferent of half residue to wife

5.84 Purpose (SEVEN) leaves the liferent of half the residue to the testator's wife and is otherwise in the same terms as S5.6 (see para 5.76).

Purpose (EIGHT) – half residue to children

5.85 Purpose (EIGHT) leaves the remaining half of residue to the children or issue of the testator and is in the same terms as S3.6

Purpose (NINE) – termination of liferents

5.86 Purpose (NINE) provides that the liferented funds are to pass to the children or issue on the same terms as for the share of residue. The provision relates to both liferented funds, that of the house for the testator's mother and that of the residue for the widow. The provisions for children are the same as in purpose (EIGHT), but the matter has been treated separately in the interests of clarity and also because of problems over the definition of residue. Had the liferented funds been stated to form part of the children's half of residue, it might have been suggested that the liferented funds should be taken into account in calculating the residue, which would lead to a circular argument.

Vesting on this Style is on death, *a morte testatoris*. Thus the beneficiaries who will receive the capital of the liferented funds are known at the date of the testator's death. If, therefore, a child survived his father and took a share of the half of residue under purpose (EIGHT), but then died before his mother and grandmother, that child would remain a beneficiary of the capital of the liferented funds. When the liferented funds were set free, that child's executors would receive the child's share and the destination of that share would depend on the child's will or intestacy.

This Style contains no equivalent of the purpose dealing with distributions from capital found in S5.8. The situation here is rather different with immediate vesting. On failure, termination or renunciation of either of the liferents the funds set free pass to the children or issue since their existing right of fee then becomes unencumbered. There is no real need for a power to advance to them here. It would be possible to include a power to advance capital to the liferenter but that would mean that there was not full vesting in the children at the date of the testator's death.

Style S9 – two-year discretionary trust

5.87 Some of the reasons for considering a discretionary trust have been mentioned before[1]. The Style presented is a two-year discretionary trust, that is one where the trustees are given a two-year period within which to decide on which beneficiaries within the class are to benefit. The format is governed to some extent by the inheritance tax legislation.

Purpose (FIVE) – residue

5.88 The trustees are directed to hold the residue for such of a class of beneficiaries as they may determine. The class consists of the testator's wife, his issue, the spouses of issue, and family trusts. The reference to trusts would include a trust where one of the beneficiaries under the first three categories was a beneficiary to some extent of that trust: that beneficiary need not be the only beneficiary of that trust. The class should be sufficiently wide to ensure that there will be beneficiaries alive especially if the duration of this form of trust is to be extended beyond two years (see para 5.93). The class could also include charities[2].

There is no minimum share which any beneficiary mentioned must receive. The trustees could decide to appoint the whole funds to one or more of the beneficiaries in the class.

The trustees exercise their discretion by a minute which need not be a formally executed deed.

The trustees may exercise their power at any time or times. They may carry out the appointment in stages at different times. They may appoint before the administration of the executry is complete. The Capital Taxes Office at one time was known to object to appointments where the trustees had not superseded the executors by the administration of the executry having been completed. In England at least it is suggested that the power could be exercised before probate (confirmation) was obtained and this is significant in relation to the payment of inheritance tax prior to the obtaining of confirmation[3]. It is not believed that in Scotland trustees or executors could appoint prior to confirmation.

5.89 Declaration (1) provides that the trustees may impose conditions and provisions on their decisions and indicates some of the possibilities. They may create fixed legacies, various trust interests, powers of appointment or may continue the trust as a discretionary trust.

---

1 See paras 5.68–5.69.
2 For some problems where it is desired to include charities, but they have not been included, see [1990] Capital Taxes and Estate Planning Quarterly 25.
3 See generally Oerton [1993] Trusts and Estates 44.

Declaration (2) gives the trustees power to renounce their discretion which they would not otherwise have power to do. In this event the destination-over in declaration (5) comes in. This provision is included to increase the flexibility given to the trustees in case it might prove to be of use in some future unforeseen event.

Declaration (3) gives the trustees discretion over the income of the trust for the two-year period and to the extent that they have not appointed or renounced, their discretion over capital. The inheritance tax provisions require that no person is entitled to an interest in possession during this two-year period until the determination is made[1] and so it is not possible to provide a fixed right to income to any particular beneficiaries. The trustees are directed to distribute the income during this period and do not have a power to accumulate it. This has been done so that a full period of accumulation can be provided for when the trustees exercise their discretion. It postpones the start of an accumulation period from the date of death to the date of the trustees' determination. During the two-year period the trustees will have to decide on income distributions in advance of the time when they are required to decide on capital distributions. It would be quite competent as an alternative to provide for accumulation from the date of death if this was desired (see also paras 5.68–5.69).

5.90 Declaration (4) is designed to avoid problems for the trustees if they should decide to set up a continuing trust under this purpose. If they appoint funds outright then the classes of beneficiaries set out at the beginning of the purpose are likely to be sufficient. If, however, they establish a trust then persons within those classes will be the main beneficiaries, but in the event of failure of all of those main beneficiaries during the currency of the trust there will need to be an ultimate destination somewhere. If, for example, the trustees decided to establish an accumulation and maintenance trust for the testator's children and the children all died before vesting without leaving issue, without marrying and without there being other family trusts, and the testator's spouse had also died (which may not be as unlikely as the list might suggest), then the discretionary residue would have to fall back into the testator's intestacy. The testator's children would have survived him so they would be his intestate heirs. By the time in question they would also have died so that their wills or intestacies would determine the destination of the discretionary residue. Their intestate beneficiaries would include spouses and relations on both paternal and maternal sides of the family so that the testator's spouse's family would be included. The testator's children's wills could include any beneficiaries. Some of these possible beneficiaries are likely not to be acceptable to the testator.

5.91 Declaration (4) provides that the class may be widened to include remoter members of the testator's family and to allow the trustees to provide for an ultimate destination-over to them. This provision does not come in on failure of all of the beneficiaries within the main class set out at the start of S9.5. It is

1 Inheritance Tax Act 1984, s 144.

available on the failure of all of the testator's issue before all of the discretionary residue has vested. There might therefore still be some beneficiaries within the original class in existence (the testator's spouse, spouses of issue, trusts) but the trustees might not wish to benefit them although they still could do so.

Two options for the extended class are given. Defining the extended class by reference to the testator's grandparents means that the class includes the issue of the testator's grandparents. It would thus include the testator's parents, his brothers and sisters and their issue, the testator's uncles and aunts and their issue, and spouses and trusts connected with them.

The second option is of defining the class by reference to the testator's children's grandparents. This will include relations in both the testator's family and in the family of the testator's children's mother. The choice on these or any other additional class will depend on the circumstances in each case.

The extension of the class in this way does not mean that persons within this extended class *will* benefit. It merely means that the trustees may exercise the powers and discretions given to them for the benefit of an extended class of beneficiary in the event of the failure of more closely connected beneficiaries.

It would be possible to allow the trustees the same or greater flexibility by simply defining the initial class of beneficiaries by reference to the issue of the testator's grandparents, but it is thought that many testators would be reluctant to include as possible beneficiaries persons whom they did not wish to benefit at all. Drafting the extension of the class in the way of S9.5(4) may be more acceptable to the testator since it operates only if the testator's issue are no longer alive. As examples of what might happen using this provision, the trustees might appoint in the following ways:

(1)   They might appoint an accumulation and maintenance trust to the testator's children equally, failing them to their issue, failing them to the surviving children or their issue, whom all failing to the testator's nephews and nieces.

(2)   They might alternatively appoint a liferent to the spouse with capital to the children with vesting postponed, whom failing to the children's issue and the survivors and their issue, whom all failing to the testator's aunt, whom failing to the testator's great-nephews and nieces.

5.92   These destinations-over may seem to provide for very remote eventualities and in many cases that will be so. However, they are available to the trustees in the light of the circumstances at the time and need not be decided on in any detail by the testator. When the testator's family is relatively small and the trustees do wish to establish a trust the possibility of failure of all members is not that unreal and failure to have a provision in the form of S9.5(4) could result in inappropriate beneficiaries becoming entitled. Without the extension of this form, attempts by the trustees and surviving beneficiaries within the class to rearrange matters so as to include remoter beneficiaries are likely to prove to be in fraud of the trustees' power of appointment[1].

---

1 *Colquhoun's Trustees v Marchioness of Lorne's Trustees* 1990 SLT 34.

Declaration (5) is the destination-over in the event of the trustees having failed to exercise in full their discretion over capital or in the event of the trustees having renounced their powers under declaration (2). If there was no destination-over then the undetermined parts of the residue would fall into intestacy.

Longer duration trusts

5.93 As mentioned before (see paras 5.68–5.69) it is only inheritance tax reasons which suggest a two-year period and there is no reason why a discretionary trust should not continue indefinitely. This Style could quite readily be adapted to this form of trust.

The two-year period could be extended for a fixed period of, for example, 60 years. This would require the substitution of the number 60 in three places: at the end of the initial part just before declaration (1); in declaration (3), first line; and in declaration (5). It might be desired to add a power to accumulate income during a much longer period, but not more than 21 years.

Alternatively, no time limit at all could be provided but this requires a more substantial alteration. In the initial part the direction should be to hold 'the residue of my estate and the income therefrom' and the words 'within 2 years of my death' should be deleted. There should be a new declaration (3):

'Subject to any determination or determinations which may be made my trustees may accumulate the income of the residue and add the same to capital during the period of 21 years from the date of my death or may, and after the period of 21 years from my death shall, apply the whole of the income of the residue without any apportionment being made to or for behoof of any one or more of the beneficiaries in such shares or proportions and in such manner as they may determine.'

Declaration (5) is then only required because of the existence of the power of renunciation of the trustees powers. This declaration would then have to be altered to read:

'. . .in the event of my Trustees having renounced the power to make a determination taking effect in relation to the whole or any part of the residue they shall on and from the date of such renunciation hold the whole or such part of the residue absolutely for. . .'

Nil rate band discretionary trust

5.94 A further variety of the discretionary trust would be to set up part of the estate as a discretionary trust but leave the residue to the surviving spouse. This might have both taxation and family advantages. These possibilities are discussed in relation to Style S10 – see paragraphs 5.96–5.107.

As an alternative to deciding on any of these variations of a two-year discretionary trust at the time of drafting the will it would of course be possible to use the two-year discretionary trust Style and leave it to the trustees to decide within the two-year period to set up such a longer term trust.

Letter of wishes

5.95 Style S9 grants very wide and unrestricted powers to the trustees to decide on who should benefit from the discretionary trust. Many trustees, and not just professional ones, will prefer to have some indication as to whom the testator had in mind to benefit. There will be the competing interests of the surviving spouse and of the children and remoter generations. There may be future contingencies which the testator has not considered. Particular concern will be as to whether children or grandchildren are to be treated equally or are to be differently, perhaps on the grounds of owning particular family assets and thus requiring more or less funds to support them, or of having done better or worse in life financially or socially, or of having special medical or other needs. The testator may thus wish to provide a letter indicating his desires.

The letter of wishes by the testator should be drafted so that it is clear that only wishes and not directions are being given: it is essential that the testator does not impose a particular division by letter when his will gives a discretion. It must always be clear that the wishes do not amount to a direction to the trustees[1]. An express declaration that the wishes are not to bind the trustees should be included. The circumstances of each possible letter of wishes differ so much that it is not possible to suggest a standard style.

Style S10 – nil rate band and discretionary trust will

5.96 The comments here follow from those made on Style S9. This Style sets up a discretionary trust for a limited part of a testator's estate for a specific purpose relating to possible inheritance tax savings.

Reasons for considering a nil rate band trust

5.97 There are many cases where a husband and wife each have funds but the survivor will require at least the bulk of them to live comfortably after the death of the first of them. In such cases most of the first spouse's estate will need to be left by will to the survivor. It is then not possible in practice for the first spouse to leave substantial funds by will to their children or grandchildren because these funds are required by the survivor.

Where the surviving spouse inherits estate from the predeceasing spouse there will be no inheritance tax charge on that death because there is no tax on property passing between spouses. On the death of the survivor the total joint estates will be subject to tax.

If it were possible to pass some funds to the children or grandchildren on the

---

1 25 *Stair Memorial Encyclopaedia* para 823.

first death then it would be possible to use the first spouse's nil rate band as well as the surviving spouse's nil rate band. The benefit of the first spouse's nil rate band is completely lost by leaving the whole estate to the surviving spouse.

The nil rate band discretionary trust is one solution to this problem. The idea is that the first spouse to die leaves the amount of the nil rate band to his trustees and executors to hold for a number of beneficiaries, in such proportions and by such methods as the trustees may decide. The class of beneficiaries would usually include the surviving spouse, children and grandchildren but others could be included as wanted. The surviving spouse would not be a truster and so there is no question of a reservation of benefit for inheritance tax purposes. The trustees could pay out at least the bulk of the trust income to the surviving spouse so the income position would be similar to the position if the surviving spouse had inherited all of the predeceasing spouse's estate. On the death of the surviving spouse the trust would not be added to the surviving spouse's estate for the purpose of calculation of tax. By this means it is possible to obtain the benefit of two nil rate bands (one on the death of each spouse) and for the surviving spouse to have the effective use of the funds in the discretionary trust.

The discretionary trust could also be used to make payments of income or capital to the children or grandchildren. It could in addition be used instead of a deed of variation (the tax advantages of which were threatened in 1989) to rearrange the provisions of the will shortly after the first death. Generally such a trust increases flexibility in dealing with the estates of two spouses particularly, although the principles mentioned would apply to any combination of testator and a single beneficiary.

Amount to be included in trust

5.98 As with a legacy, in a simple case the amount to be put into such a trust is the amount of the nil rate band at the time of drafting the will. However, it is usually preferable to produce a formula to cope with the possibility of the nil rate band changing, and the various factors which could affect the amount of the band left available to be put into trust. This has been discussed when considering an outright legacy of the nil rate band (see paras 4.38–4.40). The fund specified in S10.5 is based on an appropriate formula.

It is not necessary to put the full amount of the nil rate band into such a trust. Some smaller fixed figure could readily be substituted and a proportionate benefit obtained. The fund should however be reasonably substantial so that the expenses of administering the trust do not become disproportionate.

Comparison with nil rate band legacy

5.99 It is sometimes suggested in appropriate cases that an outright legacy should be left to the testator's children of the amount of the nil rate band that exists from time to time, so as to take maximum advantage of the inheritance tax reliefs. While a testator may fix the amount of a legacy to children with a view to making use of this, he may not review matters often and the amount may fall far below what would be possible for tax purposes. It is of course possible to draft a legacy tied to the amount of the nil rate band from time to time, in the manner just mentioned. This, however, is subject to difficulties in relation to lifetime gifts, legacies, legal rights, etc as discussed in paragraphs 4.38–4.40. A description of funds or property in the form of purpose S10.5 would cover these objections.

There is, however, another serious objection to leaving property outright to children in such terms. During the life of capital transfer tax and inheritance tax there have been a number of very substantial increases in the amount of the nil rate band, well in excess of the inflation rate. The complete abolition of the tax has been mentioned in various pre-Budget rumours. If these rumours were ever to be fulfilled, then the whole estate might be exempt and the surviving spouse would receive nothing, although there could be a legal rights claim. The introduction of 100 per cent business and agricultural reliefs compounds these problems. It would, of course, be possible to fence the amount included in such a legacy to the children with some limitation to a proportion of the total estate, or a maximum absolute amount, as mentioned when dealing with an outright legacy (see paras 4.38–4.40).

One alternative to cover this situation would be to include the surviving spouse within a discretionary class in the terms included in this Style. In this case, if the tax has been abolished then the trustees retain a discretion to distribute whatever seemed appropriate in the circumstances without the embarrassment or difficulties of attempting to persuade children to give funds back to the surviving parent. This Style may therefore be preferable to a fixed nil rate band legacy to the testator's children.

Nil rate band trust-taxation considerations

(1) *Inheritance tax*

5.100   The amount to be put into the nil rate band trust is designed to be within the nil rate band so that no inheritance tax is payable on the death leading to the creation of the trust.

As noted in paragraph 5.70, discretionary trusts are subject to a ten-yearly charge to tax. Because of the amount in this trust, it is likely that no tax would actually be payable every ten years. If tax was payable it would be charged only if there was an amount in the trust in excess of the nil rate band in force at the time of the potential charge. The maximum rate of tax is currently 6 per cent. It is quite possible that such trusts could attract significantly higher taxation in the future. It is possible (if unlikely) that such a trust could mean that the family was worse off in relation to inheritance tax, but the flexibility included in the trust provisions will assist in coping with changes in the tax rules.

Discretionary trusts are also liable to a proportionate charge based where property leaves the discretionary trust regime. However, for a nil rate band discretionary trust, the rate chargeable on any capital distributions within the first ten years should be zero[1].

---

1 Inheritance Tax Act 1984, s 68.

A nil rate band discretionary trust is only likely to be appropriate where the residue is left outright to the surviving spouse. If the residue is left in trust to beneficiaries other than the surviving spouse this will affect the calculation of the rate of inheritance tax for periodic charges. Any liferented residue will be brought into account in the computations and will increase the liability[1]. It is thought that a liferent of the residue to the surviving spouse would not be treated as starting a trust relevant for these purposes until the spouse's liferent terminates[2] so that this kind of trust would not affect the inheritance tax calculations on the nil rate band discretionary fund.

(2) *Income tax*

5.101 Discretionary trusts are subject to the basic and additional rates of income tax, now known in total as the rate applicable to trusts and set at 35 per cent for 1993–94 and 1994–95. The income tax treatment of discretionary trusts is dealt with in paragraph 5.71.

(3) *Capital gains tax*

5.102 As noted and explained in para 5.72, a discretionary trust pays capital gains tax at 35 per cent on gains over the annual exempt amount, set at half the amount for an individual. This annual relief is in addition to the beneficiaries' own annual reliefs.

Nil rate band trust – practical considerations

5.103 A nil rate band trust will require some additional administration and expense. Proper trust accounts will have to be kept. Separate trust tax returns will have to be made.

It is envisaged that the trust funds will largely consist of cash or stock exchange investments which produce an income for distribution. It is not generally appropriate to hold a house occupied by the surviving spouse since it is likely that the spouse will be treated as having a liferent of the house which defeats the object of the exercise.

The practical problems can be substantial but it should be possible to run the trust in a fairly straightforward and flexible way. These factors should be set against the expected inheritance tax saving which amounts at current rates to 40 per cent of the £150,000 nil rate band or £60,000.

Purpose (FIVE) – discretionary fund

5.104 Purpose (FIVE) only operates if the surviving spouse survives for 30 days. If the surviving spouse does not so survive then no discretionary fund is set up and the estate will pass according to Purpose (SIX) which leaves the residue to

---

1 Inheritance Tax Act 1984, s 66(4)(b).
2 See ibid, s 80.

the children equally. The main object of this Style is to achieve an inheritance tax advantage rather than to achieve flexibility.

It would, of course, be possible to provide that the nil rate band trust was to operate whether or not the surviving spouse survived if flexibility was wanted. In that case the references in S10.5 to '. . . within two years of my wife's death . . .' should be changed to read '. . . within two years of my or my wife's death, whichever is the later . . .' at the end of the initial part of the purpose and in S10.5(3) and (4).

The purpose defines the funds falling into the trust so that only funds not causing an inheritance tax liability will be included. The amount available might well be reduced by a number of factors, which are discussed in paragraphs 4.38–4.40.

If the funds passing to the trust exceed the nil rate band for any reason then it would be possible for the trustees to appoint the excess to the surviving spouse within the two-year period and so avoid inheritance tax[1].

The inheritance tax due in the first instance would have to be paid prior to confirmation unless it could be postponed because of tax being referable to business or agricultural property or land.

Property passing to the trust is such as will exhaust the nil rate band for inheritance tax purposes. The value of property for real purposes could therefore be greater than the amount of the nil rate band, but reduced by, for example, business property relief to the amount of the nil rate band. It would be up to the trustees to determine the exact property put into the trust. If, however, there is specific property where business property relief is available, then it will be preferable to say expressly whether or not this is to be included in the property put into the discretionary fund. This is an area where there can be difficulties. A gift of cash to be raised from business or agricultural property is not itself to be given business or agricultural property relief[2]. The reference to this property might be in the following terms:

'. . . and I declare that so far as possible the subject of this bequest
      shall be satisfied by my interest in the partnership of A and B and Co.'

This might be added after the reference to claims to legitim at (4) and immediately prior to the provision making the trustees judges of all of the problems in this area.

The trust itself is similar to the two-year discretionary trust in Style S9, to which reference is made (see paras 5.87–5.95). However, in distinction to that Style, the trustees' decisions here must be made not within two years of the testator's death but within two years of the death of the later of the testator and the testator's spouse. There is no particular necessity for the trust to be limited to two years from the spouse's death but that ties in with the two-year variation period in relation to the surviving spouse's death and it seems preferable to include some limit given the intention of the Style.

---

1 Inheritance Tax Act 1984, s 144.
2 Ibid, s 39A(6). On the whole question of business and agricultural reliefs in the area of nil rate band trusts, see Oerton [1990] Capital Taxes and Estate Planning Quarterly 77.

Purpose (SIX) – residue to wife

5.105   The residue is left to the testator's spouse.

Purpose (SEVEN) – residue to children

5.106   In the event of the spouse not surviving for 30 days the residue passes to the children. The residue here will include the amount of the nil rate band trust since this also only operates in the event of the spouse surviving for more than the 30-day period.

The text for the accumulation and maintenance trust is as in Style S7.7 (see paras 6.65–6.80).

Letter of wishes

5.107   A letter of wishes may be desirable so that the trustees can demonstrate to, for example, children or grandchildren why the surviving spouse should receive the major income benefit from the trusts (see para 5.95).

CHAPTER 6

THE OBJECTS OF
BEQUEST – SPECIFIC

INTRODUCTION

6.01 The purpose of this chapter is to address issues arising from the nature of specific potential beneficiaries. Most testators wish to benefit their families and hence most wills are essentially family settlements. Even where testators have no descendants, the tendency is a desire to pass estate on to other relatives, such as siblings or nephews or nieces. However, it is, of course, entirely possible for a testator who has no close relatives to pass his estate on to completely unrelated beneficiaries. This is the position envisaged in Styles S1 and S2.

One particularly important issue to address when dealing with the specific objects of bequest is whether there is a need for a destination-over in the event of a primary beneficiary failing to take for whatever reason (see paras 5.26–5.27). In legacies to family members, destinations-over will usually involve bringing in issue or other family members and this will be sufficient to cope with most situations; the position may actually be easier with legacies to unrelated individuals. But in all cases, certainly with other than minor specific bequests, consideration should certainly be given to the testator's wishes should the primary beneficiaries fail to take.

For many testators, the starting point when consideration is given to making a will for the first time is marriage, the event itself often being the stimulus for a first will. The Styles concentrate mainly on the preparation of wills for married persons. Only Styles S1, S2 (and to a limited extent S11) contemplate the testator without immediate family and dependants. In practice, many of the Styles, or parts thereof, can very readily be adapted for use in cases of testators without either spouse or children. Chapter 9 contains consideration of a number of practical scenarios involving both married and unmarried testators. It would, however, be useful to summarise the main issues concerning marriage, cohabitation, separation and divorce.

MARRIAGE AND REVOCATION

6.02 It should be noted particularly that a will is not revoked by subsequent marriage. Equally, it should be noted that a will is not revoked by subsequent separation or divorce. On each of these occasions, therefore, a person should review his testamentary arrangements.

COHABITATION

6.03   Scottish succession law gives no rights to cohabitants, whether of different sexes or otherwise. Such parties should therefore give particular consideration to their testamentary arrangements, especially if heritable property is involved.

The following comments apply to cohabitants of opposite sexes, although many points are relevant to same-sex relationships.

A period of cohabitation may be relatively short, for example prior to the parties' subsequent marriage. On the other hand it may be considerably longer or, in the case of parties who do not intend to marry, permanent.

Style S11 (see paras 6.25–6.27 below), a short form of will by husband in favour of wife where there are no children at present and whom failing both spouses' siblings, can very readily be adapted to such situations. S11.2, S11.5 and S11.6 would require to have the references to 'wife' removed, although it would be sensible in S11.5 to retain the *commorientes* provision, requiring the beneficiary to survive the testator by 30 days. This would ensure that in the event of common calamity the parties' estates would remain separate. This might have important inheritance tax implications[1]. The will could also make similar provisions to those in S11.7, which are intended to ensure that in the event of one party having inherited the other's estate, each party's estate will revert on the second death to their respective families.

In the case of long-term cohabitants, who may already have children or at least contemplate having children at a later date, S11.6 could be adapted by deletion of the word 'wife' and insertion of the cohabitant's name instead. S11.7 could be amended similarly to cover the situation where the testator is not survived by the other party or children or other issue.

There is probably no entirely suitable descriptive term for a cohabitant and therefore no substitute for actually using the other party's name in a will. If a term is considered necessary perhaps consideration could be given to adopting that fine Scottish expression 'bidey-in'. This might be thought to describe the depths of the appropriate relationship particularly well and has the merit of covering either sex in a heterosexual or homosexual relationship. Unfortunately, litigation or legislation would probably be necessary to define the term with sufficient exactitude. This suggestion to commence using such a term can be taken as seriously as any reader wishes.

It is possible that a testator may wish provisions in favour of a cohabitant to be conditional on the relationship continuing until the date of death. There is no real difference here as compared to a married couple except that the formal end of a marriage is much easier to ascertain. The proper answer in such circumstances is that the termination of a relationship should be marked, among other things, with a change in both wills; but the cautious may wish to add a condition to a bequest to a cohabitant, as follows:

---

1 See the Inheritance Tax Act 1984, s 92 and para 5.19.

'. . . provided that I am living together with A at the time of my
death, as to which my executors shall be the sole judges. . .'
As 'living together' is a somewhat nebulous concept, the discretion to the
executors to make a decision is probably essential. But care will then be needed
to ensure that the executors appointed know the testator's living arrangements
sufficiently well to come to a decision. All in all, such a condition attached to a
bequest may cause long-term problems, but some testators may insist on this
type of provision. Such testators should most certainly be advised of the desirability of changing their wills on the termination of their relationships.

Just as with married persons or persons intending to marry, the taking of title
to heritable property automatically in name of both parties with a survivorship
destination is not good practice. Generally, it would be better if the title is taken
without a survivorship destination, so that succession to heritable property is
regulated by wills in appropriate terms.

BEFORE MARRIAGE

6.04 If parties who marry have already made wills in each other's favour, then,
because a will is not revoked by subsequent marriage, there is no need for them
to make fresh wills following, or in contemplation of, marriage. In particular,
provision in favour of a fiancé(e) is not conditional upon a marriage taking place
unless this is specifically provided for in the will[1].

Perhaps the only problem of which to be aware is the possible change of name
on subsequent marriage, but this should not cause difficulties of identification in
other than exceptional circumstances – for instance, if there were other members
of the same family as the new spouse with the same name, such that confusion
might be caused as to exactly who the testator wished to benefit.

If one or both parties, for particular reasons, wished to make wills in contemplation of, and conditional upon, marriage, then, for example, with reference to
Style S11, a declaration could be inserted between S11.1 and S11.2 as a separate
clause in the following terms:
'I declare that this will [OR the provisions of this will in favour of A]
shall take effect only in the event of my intended marriage to A] [OR
him] [OR her] being duly solemnized.'
The parties may also wish to make alternative provision in the event of the
marriage *not* being duly solemnized, such as taking the estate or the legacy
concerned back to members of their own family or other individuals. It would
perhaps be must unusual to encounter a will being made in such terms today, but
the above provision is offered as a possibility for such circumstances.

It should be mentioned that these comments apply to parties domiciled in
Scotland. The position under English law is very different and great care should
be exercised in the case of a party who may be domiciled in that, or indeed any

1 *Ormiston's Executor v Laws* 1966 SLT 110.

other, jurisdiction. English law requires very specific and direct reference to the forthcoming marriage if an existing will is *not* to be revoked by the marriage taking place.

SEPARATION AND DIVORCE

6.05   When parties to a marriage separate, and take legal advice, the terms of their existing wills, if any, should be reviewed and new wills made if appropriate. It should be noted that the Scottish Law Commission Report on Succession[1] recommends that divorce should result in the automatic revocation of testamentary provisions in favour of a former spouse, to the effect that the former spouse will be assumed to have failed to survive the testator. It would generally be the case that the testator would wish to cut out his spouse at this time, but it should be noted that the spouse's legal rights will continue to be exercisable against the testator's estate until a divorce takes place, or until such rights are specifically discharged in a formal separation agreement. It is usually the case in the event of a formal separation agreement being prepared that each party will discharge all rights in the other party's estate. This should certainly be the advice given and an action for professional negligence may lie if such advice is not offered.

The problem here is that the practical breakdown of marriage may take place long before any formal arrangements are made. In most cases (with any luck), the unhappy event is likely to be long after testamentary provisions in favour of the spouse have been made. At the time when a practical breakdown occurs, it may be hoped that a reconciliation will eventually take place and in such circumstances a testator may be reluctant to alter provisions made in favour of the spouse. In such circumstances, a bequest conditional on the spouses living together at the time of death as was mentioned above in the context of parties unmarried but living together might be contemplated; but the real answer is to keep testamentary arrangements under close review until matters are resolved one way or the other.

When separation occurs, one of the problems often encountered is the existence of a survivorship destination in the title to the parties' heritable property. In the event of one party dying before a formal separation agreement can be completed, the survivorship destination will carry the predeceasing party's interest to the surviving party. This is a particular example of the problems which can arise from the use of such destinations.

It is also worth noting here that when final property arrangements are made between separating parties, whose title to heritable property is in joint names with a survivorship destination, the proper course is for *both* parties to convey their interests to the party who is to keep the property. It is not sufficient for the party giving up property rights merely to convey his share, as he will then retain the survivorship rights in the other party's share[2].

---

1 Scot Law Com no 124 (1990) para 4–39.
2 On the unhappy consequences of such an arrangement, see, eg, *Gretton & Reid* pp 412–413 and para 2.33 above.

USE OF TERMS

Wife/husband and similar expressions

6.06 In the Styles presented, the method of identifying a spouse who is to be a beneficiary or executor is 'my wife [OR husband] A residing with me. . .'. The same phrase would be used where an intended beneficiary was the wife of another party: 'B's wife [OR husband] residing with him [OR her] . . .'.

A number of points arise from this. Firstly, by naming the spouse the testator makes it clear that the bequest *can* only be in favour of that named individual; specifically it cannot go to benefit a different wife if the testator has remarried by the time of death. The same applies if the reference is to the named wife of a third party as a beneficiary under the will.

Secondly, if the person named is no longer the wife or husband of the other party at the time of death or payment, it is a question of circumstances as to whether that person takes from the provisions in his or her favour. If a legacy is not made a part of general provisions for family, such that use of the term 'wife' or 'husband' is merely an aid to identification, the named beneficiary may take even if divorced or separated from the other spouse by the relevant date[1]. On the other hand, the use of the word 'wife' or 'husband' may import a condition, such that the party named requires actually to be in the relationship to the deceased before he or she can benefit[2]. While the latter construction may appear the more natural and the words 'residing with me' add to the likelihood of it being adopted, it should not be relied upon, given the authorities mentioned above. It is imperative that a will is altered immediately if the named individual no longer occupies the position of spouse to the relevant party.

6.07 Similar issues arise where a couple are not actually married, but the term 'wife' or 'husband' is used in the will. If the term is accompanied by a name it is thought that it will make no difference to the bequest if the couple have never actually married by the time that the will comes into operation, but merely cohabit at that date. The true position for a *third party* beneficiary may of course not even be known to the testator and the existence of the marriage would have to be expressed as a clear condition to prevent the legacy taking effect, in the event that someone referred to as the wife or husband of a named party was not in fact married to that party. This is certainly the case if the named party and his or her purported spouse are still living together at the relevant time. If they have separated, having never been married, it is much more likely that a bequest in favour of someone designed as a party's spouse could be defeated.

If it does become vital because of a condition in a will to establish that a couple

---

1 *Henderson's Judicial Factor v Henderson* 1930 SLT 743; *Couper's Judicial Factor v Valentine* 1976 SLT 83.
2 *Pirie's Trustees v Pirie* 1962 SC 43.

were in fact married, the possibility of establishing a marriage by cohabitation and repute should be borne in mind in appropriate circumstances[1].

6.08 Thirdly, if the true desire of the testator is to make provision for the 'wife' or 'husband' of an individual (whether of the testator, or more probably of a third party), without concern as to the particular identity of that spouse, the best course is probably not to name the beneficiary. In these circumstances the legacy would go to the person occupying the position of spouse at the relevant time – and that person might be different from the one who was the relevant spouse at the time the will was drafted[2]. Establishing the testator's true intentions may require some delicate questioning, but the key point is to establish whether the intention is to benefit an actual individual, or merely anyone occupying the particular marital relationship in question.

Fourthly, consideration should be given to the extension of the designation to include the words 'residing with me [OR him] [OR her]'. It may be that in fact spouses reside physically in separate locations in cases where there is no question of legal separation or the practical break-up of the marriage. In such circumstances, it may be particularly important to specify the other spouse's address, to make it clear that the legacy is to go to that spouse *despite* the fact that the couple physically live apart.

6.09 A related issue is whether the phrase 'living with me' or 'living with [another beneficiary]' is merely a designation assisting in the identification of the intended beneficiary or whether it imposes any type of condition. If the latter is implied, the fact that the spouses have separated without divorcing at the time of payment may defeat the legacy; however, it is thought that the former is much more likely, so that the phrase referring to a person residing with another person will be treated merely as an aid to identification.

Accordingly, in certain circumstances it may be appropriate or necessary to convert the phrase into a true condition, such that the legacy is only payable *if* the spouses are living together as husband and wife at the relevant time. This is unlikely to be the normal requirement, but may be entirely appropriate where the spouses have already had periods of separation prior to the drafting of the will. The testator is merely making provision for a situation which may arise again in future. There is no doubt that a condition as to a couple 'living together' is valid – unlike its converse![3].

While imposing a condition such as this may well be appropriate when dealing with marriages other than the testator's it perhaps emphasises the need for fresh provisions should the testator's own marriage be the one that suffers a break-up. It is thought that any attempt to impose conditional bequests dependent on the state of the testator's own marriage could well lead to marital disputes continuing even beyond the death of one party to the marriage.

---

1 See for a recent example (presumably involving intestacy) *Kamperman v MacIver* 1994 GWD 5–278.
2 *Towse's Trustee v Towse* 1924 SLT 465; *Burns' Trustees v Burns* 1961 SC 17.
3 See 25 *Stair Memorial Encyclopaedia* para 875; *Barker v Watson's Trustees* 1919 SC 109.

The use of the term 'unmarried' as a description attached to potential beneficiaries implies only those who have never been married, as opposed to those who are simply not married at the relevant time, for instance because they are widowed or divorced[1].

Blood relationships

6.10   Most wills include provisions in favour of relations. Apart from questions relating to adoption (see paras 6.39–6.40 below), the relationship referred to in any case will be a blood relationship. This makes it important to be clear whether any reference to a purported relationship goes beyond blood ties – for instance, does a gift to 'nephews' include people who have always been regarded as such by the testator, and who have referred to him as 'uncle'? If it is a general class gift to all of the testator's nephews, it will not include non-blood relatives unless specific provision is made (or, conceivably, evidence is led after the testator's death as to the inclusion of such persons in the term used, as it was used and understood by the testator).

Similar considerations can arise with any relationship. It is suggested that if the testator does have intended beneficiaries in such a category, they should be dealt with separately from any blood relatives of the same purported type. This may involve some delicate questioning of the testator in appropriate circumstances, but all that the adviser can do is confirm that the normal interpretation of such terms will involve a blood relationship.

In general, if a legacy is left to a relative of the testator, there will be no requirement for the beneficiary to prove conclusively that he is in fact in the appropriate relationship to the testator. For instance, if a legacy is left to the testator's nieces (daughters of his brother), without them being identified other than as his nieces, it will not generally be expected that these nieces prove that their father was, in fact, the testator's brother. Such proof might be available if required, particularly in modern times, by such methods as DNA testing. In the unlikely event that the testator insists that a blood relationship is proved in any circumstance, such as to confirm what appears to be the position without such proof, it will be necessary for specific provision to be included for this in the will. Such a requirement may perhaps cause extreme difficulties after the death and should not be encouraged unless the testator has a special reason for wishing to establish that purported relatives unquestionably fall within the requisite category. However, if such provision was required, it could run as follows:

'. . . on condition that [such beneficiaries] prove to the satisfaction of
my executors that they are [say] the blood issue of A. . .'

It would be necessary to use some such term as 'blood', because without further provision 'issue' would normally include adopted issue. It is of course possible that the testator would wish to include adopted issue but exclude purported natural issue who were not in fact related by blood, in which case specific provision should be made to include adopted issue as an additional category.

---

1 *Soutar's Trustees v Spence* 1937 SLT 207.

Child/children

6.11   A key issue with the use of the terms 'child' or 'children' is whether adopted or illegitimate offspring are included in such terms. As such issues affect children other than those of the testator, but more importantly are also of concern in dealing with relationships other than parent/child, they are dealt with in general terms below (see paras 6.37–6.40).

A child conceived but not yet born will be included in any provision for children, at least where this interpretation is to the benefit of that child[1]. This interpretation also applies to references to other relationships, where appropriate.

The terms 'child' and 'children' generally refer only to sons and daughters of the parent or parents to which reference is made, unless there is some indication that remoter descendants are to be included[2]. Accordingly, if remoter descendants *are* to be included, whether as immediate beneficiaries or in consequence of a destination-over, this should be made clear. If the intention is to pass benefits on to further generations on the failure of a child or children, the use of the term 'issue' is likely to be appropriate. If remoter descendants are to be included whether or not more immediate descendants are also included, it is best to include specific reference to the various classes of descendant for whom provision is being made, with or without listing those to benefit by name (see paras 5.02–5.15).

Issue/descendants

6.12   In contrast to 'children', 'issue' includes all descendants – it is not, unless something appears to limit it to immediate children, restricted to the next succeeding generation of the person immediately referred to (whether such a person is a testator or some third party)[3].

If the term 'issue' is used, questions may arise as to the division of a legacy among those making up the relevant class. Whilst stirpital division is probably implied[4], this matter should always be put beyond doubt. The problems arising in this area are addressed at paragraphs 5.08–5.14 above.

It might be thought that the term 'issue' is in itself unduly technical and perhaps old fashioned. It has, however, the merit of a large amount of judicial authority on its use and meaning, and of being well understood by those drafting wills. However, if it is considered desirable to use another term, 'descendants' will generally serve the same function. Indeed the use of this term, probably more comprehensible to most testator clients, might be more in keeping with some of the aims of the Styles presented. The authors have refrained from

---

1 *Elliot v Joicey* 1935 SC (HL) 57.
2 *Mair's Trustees v Mair* 1936 SC 731; *Yale's Trustees* 1981 SLT 250.
3 *Stewart's Trustees v Whitelaw* 1926 SC 701; *Bailey's Trustees v Bailey* 1954 SLT 282; *Boyd's Trustee v Shaw* 1958 SC 115.
4 *Turner's Trustees v Turner* (1897) 24 R 619.

adopting such a robust approach to this particular question, having already eliminated the time honoured phrase '*per stirpes*' from the wording used in this area! There is, however, English authority on the use of the term 'descendants'[1]. The use of the term 'descendants' might also shorten the wording required in some cases, and those using the Styles presented may prefer to adopt it.

Should it be desired to adopt this wording, it can be inserted into the purpose dealing with destinations-over (see, for example, S3.6) by substituting the word 'descendants' for the word 'issue' in each place where it occurs. This substitution can also be made elsewhere in the Styles as necessary.

Brothers/sisters and related expressions

6.13 The terms 'brothers' and 'sisters' will generally include relations of the whole or the half blood. Accordingly, if it is desired only to include full brothers and sisters, this should be expressed clearly. This can probably best be achieved by naming the intended beneficiaries specifically; alternatively, if it is essential to use a class designation, it is thought that the use of the term 'full' in conjunction with the intended class will have the desired effect.

The term 'siblings' can be used where a single expression is required to cover the degree of relationship required in respect of both sexes.

The term 'collateral' is sometimes used informally in the same sense, but this is more correctly a wider expression. It simply implies descent from a common ancestor, but it does not necessarily imply that all persons covered necessarily share the same parent or parents.

Nephews/nieces

6.14 The terms 'nephews' and 'nieces' include nephews and nieces of the half blood as well as those of the full blood[2]. If that is not what is desired, once more this should be clearly expressed (see para 6.13 above).

Cousins

6.15 The term 'cousins' may be dangerous, as individuals vary in their intended meaning when using the word. Occasionally, it is used by some to stretch far beyond any blood tie, but this is a recipe for disaster for usage in a will. If it is intended to benefit such people (or indeed if there is any doubt at all about the relationship), the intended beneficiaries should be named specifically. It might be desirable to add some further designations such as 'sometimes referred to as my cousin'.

If the term 'cousins' is used, it generally means first cousins, also known as full cousins or cousins-german – that is, the children of an individual's aunt or

---

1 *Re Flower* (1890) 62 LT 210.
2 *Clow's Trustees v Bethune* 1935 SC 754.

uncle[1]. Accordingly, if other classes of cousin are to be included, these should be specifically mentioned. Again, perhaps specification by name is the most desirable course of action, given possible confusion over the range of terms used in this area.

For the avoidance of doubt, the technical meaning of certain expressions might be useful:

(1)   A person's second cousin is the child of the first cousin of that person's parent.

(2)   A person's third cousin is the child of the second cousin of that person's parent.

(3)   A person's first cousin once removed is a child of that person's first cousin, or the first cousin of that person's parent.

Unfortunately, a person falling within category (3) is sometimes referred to as a second cousin. This has led to understandable confusion and evidence may be necessary as to the testator's meaning in using a term such as 'second cousin'[2].

Accordingly, if it is not possible or desirable to specify the intended beneficiaries by name, the best course is to set out the chain of relationships connecting them to the testator (or other person whose 'cousins' are to be included).

Family

6.16   A legacy to a person's 'family' should be avoided. The term lacks precision, even if the testator is clear about who is meant. Further specification should always be sought and once more listing of relatives included by name or at the very least by class of relationship should be used.

If the term 'family' *is* used, it will generally be taken as meaning only children[3]. However, there may be further restrictions on the meaning, or extensions in appropriate circumstances. For instance, a bequest of a house to 'my dear family' was restricted to those four children (out of six children of the testator in total) who were living in the house with the testator at the relevant time[4].

Relations/relatives

6.17   The terms 'relations' and 'relatives' should be avoided, at least without further specification. If such terms are used, it is essential to define the class intended to benefit more accurately, by specifying the degree of relationships to which the benefit is to stretch – for example, cousins, nephews and nieces, brothers and sisters; it should also be made clear if the class is to include those in

---

1 *Copland's Executors v Milne* 1908 SC 426.
2 *Drylie's Factor v Robertson* (1882) 9 R 1178.
3 *Low's Trustees v Whitworth* (1892) 19 R 431; *Greig's Trustees v Simpson* 1918 SC 321.
4 *McGinn's Executrix v McGinn* 1994 SLT 2.

a closer relationship to the person specified than the type of relative indicated. These difficulties indicate the undesirability of using the terms[1].

If they *are* used, there is some old authority that the terms indicate those who would be entitled to succeed on the intestate succession of the person specified[2].

If it is desired to make provision for a particular class of relatives who are more distantly related to the person concerned than cousins, it would probably be best to specify the chain of relationships involved.

Dependants

6.18 The term 'dependants' should be avoided. A legacy to dependants will fail, as the term is so imprecise as to make the beneficiaries uncertain[3].

Next of kin and similar expressions

6.19 The phrase 'next of kin' requires some care and should perhaps be avoided. When applied to a beneficiary, it is usually taken to mean those persons who would inherit if the deceased were to have died intestate. As regards those domiciled in Scotland, this would mean considering the classes of relative listed in the Succession (Scotland) Act 1964, section 2(1), in the order in which they are there listed. However, the term probably implies the omission of representatives of relatives who have predeceased – in other words, if there are survivors of a class of relative and other members of that class have predeceased leaving issue, only the surviving members of the class itself would qualify as next of kin[4].

Any general interpretation as to the meaning of the phrase may be defeated by other terms in the will and the context in which terminology is used[5].

The expression 'next of kin' may have a much narrower meaning when used in the context of the appointment of executors[6].

Given the various possible meanings of the phrase and resultant possible confusion, the term 'statutory successors' has been suggested as preferable where some such expression is required[7].

6.20 Some such phrase may be particularly necessary where the subject of bequest is something that the testator is determined to preserve in his family at the closest possible level to himself. This will be especially vital where the

---

1 See *Cunninghame v Cunninghame's Trustees* 1961 SLT 32.
2 See *Johnston's Trustees v Johnston* (1891) 18R 823; *Scott v Scott* (1885) 2 Macq 281.
3 See *Robertson's Judicial Factor v Robertson* 1968 SLT 32.
4 See *Gregory's Trustees v Alison* (1889) 16 R (HL) 10; *Young's Trustees v Jones* (1880) 8 R 242.
5 See *Nelson's Trustees v Nelson's Curator Bonis* 1979 SLT 98 where the deceased had a daughter who was held to be excluded from the term 'next of kin' *as used by the testator*, the residue of the estate going to his siblings and their representatives. See also *Borthwick's Trustees v Borthwick* 1915 SC 227; *Honeyman's Trustee v Andrew's Trustees* 1918 2 SLT 12.
6 See 25 *Stair Memorial Encyclopaedia* para 879.
7 See, for example, *Halliday* IV, para 47–36(4).

ultimate possible destination of residue is to other than intended family bene-ficiaries.

There are a number of possible problems with this type of bequest. Firstly, it may be exactly the type of legacy which is unsuitable to be shared among a number of beneficiaries; yet particularly at the more remote levels, a testator may well end up having a number of relatives of equal propinquity. This problem can be solved by directing the bequest to the oldest (or indeed youngest) member of the class of relatives surviving at the date of death (or other date of distribution).

Secondly, especially with this type of legacy, it may be considered desirable to exclude the testator's spouse from possible beneficiaries, as such a person is not a blood relative of the testator's own family. It is possible that a spouse would not in any event be considered as falling within the class 'next of kin' as so described, but the matter should be put beyond doubt. There may also be grounds for attempting to exclude other beneficiaries who would take on intestacy, perhaps on the ground that they are older than the testator and the subject of bequest should only descend by generations. Given the need to deal with representation in intestacy and the tracing of propinquity of relatives through ancestors, this may be difficult to achieve satisfactorily.

A possible form of words to take a legacy to a single member of the nearest class of 'next of kin' (but specifically excluding a spouse) is as follows:

> 'To the oldest member of the class of statutory successors who shall
> survive me, this class being composed of those who would inherit my
> estate were I to die intestate, but expressly excluding from this class
> any spouse of mine.'

This should cater for most eventualities. If the legacy is simply to be shared between all the nearest surviving relatives, along with representatives of those predeceasing, the words 'the oldest member of' should be deleted.

6.21   The main problem with trying to increase the class of *excluded* successors is that representation applies in intestate succession. Exclusion of an older successor might also be taken to exclude his issue. A bare exclusion of 'ancestors', for instance, might have the result of excluding such ancestors' issue, perhaps leaving no potential beneficiaries. However, the testator may specifically wish to exclude his own parents or grandparents from whom the subject of bequest may in any event have derived, perhaps by lifetime gift. If it is considered important to exclude the possibility of the bequest passing back up the family line to any extent and thus to keep it out of the hands of older generations, the following wording may be suitable:

> '. . . but expressly excluding from this class:
> (1)   any spouse of mine;
> (2)   any member who is older than me at the date of my death, but
>   not the issue of any such excluded member (so that any such
>   excluded member shall be assumed to have predeceased me).'

The expression 'next of kin' could be used in relation to a person other than a testator, perhaps in a destination-over on a failure of a named legatee. The possibility of that legatee's intestate succession being governed by a different legal system (which might give a different meaning to the expression 'next of kin') should be borne in mind (see paras 6.22–6.23 below).

Heirs and similar expressions

6.22 Most of what has been said about the term 'next of kin' applies also to 'heirs'. The two terms are not interchangeable, as 'heirs' may be thought to include a wider class of potential beneficiaries[1]. However, it will generally be taken to mean those who would inherit on intestacy, rather than under a will[2]. The expression 'heirs' may again be useful when it is important to keep an asset in a particular family.

There is a presumption that a legacy to 'heirs' involves ascertaining the heirs as at the date of the testator's death, or at the date of vesting where this is postponed[3].

A legacy may be in favour of the testator's heirs or the heirs of a legatee, perhaps as a destination-over in the event of that legatee predeceasing. In the latter case, the heirs will be ascertained at the date of death of the legatee, or the date of vesting where this is later[4].

If the expression is used, the question of when heirs are to be ascertained should be put beyond doubt. If the legacy is to the testator's own heirs, the appropriate date will usually be his death, and the position can be covered as follows:

'. . . to my heirs as ascertained at the date of my death.'

If vesting is postponed, the date of vesting can be substituted for the date of the testator's death. Both of these instructions would be in keeping with the presumptions which would apply anyway. It is possible that the testator would wish his heirs, if they are to benefit, to be ascertained as at the date of his death even where vesting is postponed, and in such a case it is essential to include a direction to this effect.

There are more potential difficulties if the legacy is to another person's heirs, particularly if this is a direct bequest rather than as a result of the destination-over. Heirs can be ascertained in relation to any person only after that person's death. It would thus be necessary to await the death of a named person before the identity of the beneficiaries could be ascertained, with vesting necessarily postponed until that date[5]. For this reason alone, such a direct legacy to a person's heirs is perhaps not to be recommended.

6.23 Heirs will generally be ascertained according to the law of succession applicable to the relevant person. This should be borne in mind; in other jurisdictions, there may be different heirs for different classes of property, as was

---

1 *Gregory's Trustees v Alison* (1889) 16 R (HL) 10.
2 *Haldane's Trustees v Sharp* (1890) 17 R 385; *Macmillan, Petitioner* 1987 SLT (Sh Ct) 50.
3 *Gregory's Trustees v Alison* (1889) 16 R (HL) 10; *Young's Trustees v Young* (1901) 3 F 616; *G's Trustees v G* 1937 SC 141; *MacDonald's Trustees v MacDonald* 1974 SLT 87; *Henderson* p 228; Meston 'Bequests to "heirs"' 1974 SLT (News) 109.
4 *Wylie's Trustees v Bruce* 1919 SC 211; *Barr's Trustees v Inland Revenue* 1943 SC 157; *MacMillan, Petitioner* 1987 SLT (Sh Ct) 50.
5 *Gollan's Trustees v Booth* (1901) 3 F 1035.

the case in Scotland before 1964, when it was necessary to apply the expression 'heirs' differently according to whether the subject of bequest was heritable or moveable.

It would be possible to define heirs by reference to the law of Scotland, by some such wording as follows:

'. . . to the persons who would have inherited A's moveable estate
were he to have died intestate, domiciled in Scotland.'

It is of course necessary to specify moveable estate, as intestate succession to heritable estate is governed by the law applicable where the heritage is located.

It is probably fair to say that legacies to the testator's own 'heirs', 'next of kin' or 'statutory successors' should only be required in very limited circumstances. The expressions might be more useful in relation to a named legatee, where the testator wishes to ensure that the legatee's family benefits rather than the bequest going to residue on the failure of the named legatee. Such expressions would also be relevant in a case where the testator has specific legacies to family members but the residue goes outwith the family. Here again, the testator may wish to ensure that the specific legacies end up with his own heirs (however distant) and use of such a term may assist in achieving this objective.

Executors/personal representatives

6.24 A testator may wish to provide for a legacy or a destination-over to follow the remainder of another person's estate, whether that person is a beneficiary or otherwise. A provision referring to, say, the person's issue may not have this effect as the person concerned may have made a will directing his estate elsewhere. As noted, a reference to 'heirs' or 'next of kin' would generally be taken as referring to intestate beneficiaries or some of them. Accordingly, expressions such as the person's 'executors' or 'personal representatives' might be used.

Unfortunately, such terms have no very clear meaning in Scots law[1]. In particular, there is some authority that such terms should be taken as referring to those benefitting on the *intestacy* of the person named, rather than to testamentary legatees. In these circumstances, if a legacy is in fact to go to the beneficiaries of an individual whether testate or intestate, it is best to avoid such words. The matter could be put beyond doubt by some such wording as follows:

'To A, whom failing to those taking the residue of A's estate under
any testamentary disposition, or to the extent that the residue is not
disposed of by testamentary disposition under the rules of intestacy.'

It is essential that the persons concerned should be restricted to those taking the residue of the named person's estate; the situation might become impossible in the event that the person named had made a will including a large number of legacies. Of course, even with this restriction, such a provision might have the effect of splitting a legacy among a large number of residuary or intestate beneficiaries. In these circumstances, it is generally better in almost all cases that

---

1 See *Henderson* pp 170 ff.

a testator attempts to regulate the disposal of legacies directly under his own will, rather than place reliance on the rules of succession applicable on some other person's death.

PROVISIONS FOR FAMILY: WITHOUT CHILDREN

6.25 The existence or prospect of children acts as one of the most common and important means of stimulating a testator to instruct the drafting of a will. Arguably, however, it is even more important where a testator has a spouse or other long-term relationship, but no children as yet.

This is because the order of succession on intestacy in the Succession (Scotland) Act 1964, section 2 brings in a spouse only if the deceased has no surviving parents or siblings; of course, no provision whatsoever is made for partners from long-term relationships other than marriage. The rules of intestate succession, particularly as regards the provision made for parents of an intestate individual seem unlikely to meet with the wishes of many people in this situation. It seems extremely likely that the prime desire of testator with a spouse but no children would be to provide for that spouse, with provision made for children if they are in existence by the time the will comes into effect. Distribution other than to the parents of the testator is perhaps likely to be desirable in the event of the spouse not surviving and no children being in existence at that time. This forms the basic premise behind Style S11.

Style S11 – will by husband in favour of wife where no children at present and whom failing to both spouses' siblings

6.26 Style S11 is intended to cover the situation of a married couple where there are no children at present and where it is intended that the spouses' estates revert to each of their families.

There is no presumption of survivorship as between husband and wife[1], so that if both husband and wife die at the same instant neither will be presumed to have survived the other. Their respective estates will pass to their own families as heirs on intestacy.

Where there is a survivorship clause, on a bequest to the surviving spouse the effect is to extend the presumption of non-survivorship for the length of the period so that the testator's will determines the destination, even if the surviving spouse should survive for a short time after the testator's death. The testator may in those circumstances wish to alter the beneficiaries from those who would take on intestacy. That is what has been done in this Style by including the testator's parents. The possibility of a common calamity is perhaps somewhat greater with childless parents than in most other circumstances.

Style S11 goes further by making provision for the testator being the survivor

---

1 Succession (Scotland) Act 1964, s 31.

of the spouses by surviving for longer than the survivorship period and so inheriting the predeceasing spouse's estate. In this event the joint estates of the spouses are then divided equally between the families of both spouses.

The scheme of the will should work well and fairly as between the two families provided the surviving spouse leaves his will unchanged. It is of course quite possible that the surviving spouse might make another will leaving his estate to whoever he wishes. There is no restriction on the surviving spouse doing this. The effect here is not to produce mutual wills and there is no intention of doing so. If the testators are concerned about this then they should consider liferent trusts for each other (see paras 5.63–5.67, 5.74–5.86).

This Style is identical to Style S3 except for an additional purpose (SEVEN).

Purpose (SEVEN) – failure

6.27 The purpose applies where the testator is not survived by his wife or children. The reference to 'so surviving' is a reference to the fact that there is a survivorship period on the bequest to the wife in purpose (FIVE).

The estate is to pass one half to the testator's surviving brothers and sisters and one half to the wife's surviving brothers and sisters where the testator has inherited the wife's estate. He would have done this (assuming that she left a will in similar terms) by surviving her for 30 days. The executors are made judges of the question of whether the testator did inherit the residue of his wife's estate. One can imagine this as an area where there could be argument. The provision would operate where the predeceasing wife had left legacies to third parties and the residue to the husband testator, but it would not operate if the predeceasing wife left only, say, one half of the residue to her husband.

The wording of the first part of purpose (SEVEN) could be altered to cater for this, for instance by providing that its terms would come into effect where the testator has inherited any *part* of the residue of his wife's estate – or indeed any part of her estate at all.

Where the testator did not inherit his predeceasing wife's estate then the residue passes only to the testator's own surviving brothers and sisters.

The declaration at the end of the purpose brings in the issue of predeceasing brothers and sisters on the same basis as purpose (SIX). It has been included separately since it applies to both eventualities under this purpose.

Defining when a person has no children/issue

6.28 Purpose S11.6 deliberately envisages that the testator may have children after the date of the will, who may survive him or predecease leaving issue themselves. Purpose S11.7 only comes into effect where there are no children or issue surviving at the date of death – they may never have come into existence, or have been born and predeceased by the time of the testator's death, with the same consequences in either case. The situation envisaged is that the testator has no children at the time when the will is drafted and, probably, has never had children at any time.

More difficult questions can arise, notably where certain consequences are to follow from a person (whether the testator, a relation or an unrelated party) dying without children or issue. This can have at least two meanings – either the person must *never* have had children or issue for the consequences to follow, or no children or issue must be in existence at the appropriate time (which may be the date of the testator's death or a later date of vesting). It is clear that for the purposes of vesting, the phrase 'without issue' is accorded the former meaning; the same applies rather less conclusively to the phrase 'failing issue'[1].

As such phrases are capable of more than one interpretation, it is preferable to direct that desired consequences come into effect if the named person dies 'without *leaving* issue'. This ensures that it is simply the existence of issue at the date of the appropriate death which will be taken into account, rather than the fact that issue may have existed at an earlier date[2].

PROVISIONS FOR FAMILY: WITH CHILDREN

6.29 Perhaps the most common situation encountered in this area is where instructions are given for the drafting of a will when both spouse and children exist. Provision is to be made for both of them, either together or for children only in the event of the failure of the spouse. In fact, the basic provisions of the majority of the Styles presented follow this format. This kind of division is dealt with further in paragraph 6.112 below.

There is a great deal which can be said concerning provisions for children. In most of the Styles presented, provision is made for the testator's own children, but of course provision can equally well be made for the children of other individuals, whether relations of the testator or not. Much of what follows on children applies whether one is dealing with those of the testator or of someone else. However, it is first necessary to consider the situation where both spouse and children exist, but the testator wishes to provide for the spouse alone (should that spouse survive).

Provision for spouse to the exclusion of children

6.30 Styles S3, S7, S8 and S11 provide for substantially the whole of the testator's estate to pass to his spouse if she survives him, whether or not children also survive. Styles S4, S9 and S10 provide for substantial amounts to be passed to the spouse. It is envisaged that provision for one's spouse will be a primary aim of most testators coupled with an expectation that the estate will eventually pass to children on the death of the surviving spouse. The liferent provisions in Styles S5 and S6 or a discretionary trust based on Style S9 can be used to ensure that most or all of an estate does eventually reach the children. In what has been said above and in what follows, reference is made to the testator's spouse;

1 *Carleton v Thomson* (1867) 5 M (HL) 151; *Henderson* pp 207–215.
2 *Halliday v McCallum* (1867) 8 M 112.

however, the same considerations will apply where the testator has children with a partner other than in marriage.

It may be the testator's desire to ensure that the whole of the estate reaches the spouse in all circumstances. This may be the case where the children have grown up and have been independently successful; or where relationships have deteriorated between parent and children. While the first wills mentioned above will achieve this result if they are implemented, there is always the possibility that the children will claim legal rights in the moveable estate of the testator, or any statutory replacement for such rights. There is a limit to what can be done in this situation, but certain possibilities do exist, particularly for modest estates.

6.31   It is sometimes suggested that if a testator's estate does not exceed the limits for prior rights, and he wishes his spouse to take the whole estate, the best course is not to make a will.

Prior rights, of course, apply only on intestacy. Their level was increased with effect from 26 November 1993 to: a right in a dwellinghouse to a maximum value of £110,000; in furniture and plenishings to a maximum value of £20,000; and in financial provision to a maximum value of £30,000 (where issue of the deceased survive). The effect of these increases is that quite a substantial estate can now pass under prior rights.

However, if a will is not made there may be problems with the appointment of executors and other administrative matters. In addition, the estate may have grown substantially since the matter was considered. For these and other reasons, positive encouragement *not* to make a will is generally considered undesirable.

Accordingly, if a testator considers it possible that he may wish his estate to pass under prior rights it is still preferable to make a will in favour of the spouse. It is then still possible for the surviving spouse to renounce the rights under the will, if by creating total or partial intestacy such a spouse would take more under prior rights than under the will[1]. However if such a set of circumstances is envisaged and potentially desirable, it is *essential* that a destination-over does not come into effect on the surviving spouse's renunciation.

This is seen, for example, in S3.6; the provision in favour of children only comes into effect if the spouse fails to survive, not if she does survive and then renounces her rights. It goes without saying that in such circumstances a clause such as that contained in, for example, S5.11 should not be included (see para 5.20), this clause directing that a party renouncing should be treated as if he had pre-deceased. (This matter is mentioned again in Chapter 9, at para 9.18.)

There are more limited possibilities of preserving a spouse's position where the potential estate is in excess of the prior rights limits. It is possible to obtain a lifetime discharge of legal rights; but this may not be readily given in the circumstances where it is feared that such rights might be claimed to deprive a spouse of part of any testamentary provision. Alternatively, children may be too young to give an effective discharge.

---

1 See *Kerr, Petitioner* 1968 SLT (Sh.Ct) 61.

6.32   The only truly effective method for a testator to avoid the possibility of legal rights being claimed is to divest himself of his estate. This can be done by means of a lifetime trust, which can include a liferent or discretionary power in favour of the truster[1]. It is essential that the trust is effectively created, which requires the delivery (actual or constructive) of the assets to the trustees. If this is achieved to a sufficient extent in relation to the testator's estate, he will simply have no significant property left in personal ownership to be subject to legal rights' claims. The trust created can preserve effective control and use of the property in the truster's hands until his death. This strategy does have a degree of risk, but has been approved as effective in various cases. Lifetime trusts can also be used effectively for specific assets, especially insurance policies.

Outright gifts will achieve the same result, but by definition will deprive the testator of any element of control[2]. Such gifts may be more open to attack as sham transactions, perhaps surprisingly to a greater extent than if trusts are involved[3]. There may be problems in providing sufficient evidence that the gift in question has actually taken place.

It is sometimes suggested that legal rights can be avoided by investment of the whole estate in heritable property. This is frankly impractical and any rights replacing legal rights in future may well extend beyond a right in moveables.

The doctrine of conversion should be remembered in this context. Notably, a direction in a will to sell heritage will not act to convert it to moveable estate from which legal rights can be claimed. However, conversion will apply if missives for sale have been concluded prior to a death.

Conversely, and with possibilities as an extreme plan to avoid legal rights' claims, missives concluded for the purchase of heritage prior to death would convert moveables into heritage[4].

Description of children

6.33   In legacies in favour of children in the Styles presented, the mode of description adopted is 'such of my children A, B and C and any other children of mine as shall survive me, equally among them if more than one. . . .'. This could also be used when another party's children are described, as follows: '. . . such of A's children B, C and D and any other children of his as shall survive me, equally among them if more than one. . .'. It should be noted that the provision for survivorship refers to the life of the testator, not the parent of the children in such a case.

In such clauses, provision can then be made for a destination-over in favour of the issue of children who fail to survive the testator.

As noted in paragraph 5.04 above, this constitutes a class gift and the benefit of

---

1 *Collie v Pirie's Trustees* (1851) 13 D 506; *Buchanan v Buchanan* (1876) 3 R 556; *Scott v Scott* 1930 SC 903; *Campbell v Campbell's Trustees* 1967 SLT 30.
2 *Hutton's Trustees v Hutton's Trustees* 1916 SC 860.
3 *Buchanan v Buchanan* (1876) 3 R 556.
4 On these points, see 25 *Stair Memorial Encyclopaedia* para 816.

the specified legacy will accrue to the survivors of the class if some die without leaving issue. The same result would be achieved if the children were not specifically named. This mode of description could be adopted for any class gift, including especially any other class of relations. While the following comments are directed at provisions dealing with children, they are equally applicable to legacies in favour of any class of beneficiaries.

6.34 It is generally thought preferable to include the names of children in existence at the date of drafting the will, for ease of reference and to focus the testator's attention on who his intended beneficiaries are to be. It is admitted that if the testator has other, unnamed children at the date of drafting the will such wording might cause problems. However, the reference to 'any other children' should make it clear that any such other children are intended to be included. It is perhaps unlikely (but not entirely inconceivable) that a testator may have forgotten the names of all of his children; but this is much more likely when dealing with children of an individual other than the testator. This form of reference should also exclude the possibility of the *conditio si testator sine liberis decesserit* coming into operation (see para 6.114 below).

6.35 Conversely, and very importantly, it may be desired to exclude certain children from benefit, perhaps because they have already received lifetime gifts or because the testator has fallen out with some of his offspring. Another example would be where it is desirable to exclude certain children from the class of residuary beneficiaries, because of specific legacies in their favour. Such exclusion could arguably be achieved by simply omitting the words 'and any other children of mine'. However, there is really no viable alternative in such circumstances to excluding by name those children whom the testator does not wish to benefit. It is only by such specific exclusion that the testator's intentions are clearly expressed, although disgruntled offspring may still wish to contest matters after the death. The appropriate wording would be:

'. . . to such of my children A, B and C, but specifically excluding D, as shall survive me equally among them if more than one. . .'

A desire to exclude certain children in existence at the date of the will may be accompanied by a wish still to benefit possible future children. While an exclusion can still be accompanied by the phrase 'and any other children of mine', this might be thought to create a conflict with the exclusion. Because of this, such wording should only be used where there is perhaps a genuine danger of some children being forgotten by the testator, which is more likely when dealing with the children of a third party.

If there is merely a desire to include possible future children this should be done by adding the phrase 'and any other children of mine born or adopted by me after the date of execution of this will' after the wording suggested above.

While adopted children are generally put in the same position as natural children (see paras 6.39–6.42), there seems to be no convenient single phrase to cater for both possibilities in such wording.

There may be a desire to exclude certain children not by name but by reference to some state or condition fulfilled or unfulfilled at the date of death or other relevant time. In such cases, the exclusion should follow the phrase 'and any other children of mine equally among them if more than one'.

Possible examples of such exclusions include children who have attained, or who have not attained, a certain age; children who have or have not married; and children residing at a certain address or in a certain country at the date of death or other relevant time[1].

If the excluded children can be identified by a fairly definite state, such as a specified age or whether they have married or not, such a provision causes few difficulties – the condition should simply be added to the exclusion. But a condition as to residence, for instance, can require the addition of a discretion granted to the executors as to whether the exclusion should apply. Suitable wording would be as follows:

'To such of my children A, B and C and any other children of mine as shall survive me equally among them if more than one, but specifically excluding any children who no longer reside with me at the date of my death (as to which my executors shall be the sole judges). . .'

Such discretion to the executors will be even more necessary where any exclusion is to be based on more nebulous factors such as, for instance, the financial success of the children. Indeed, in such circumstances a full discretionary trust may well be more appropriate (see paras 5.68–5.72, 5.87–5.107 above).

6.36   If certain children are to be excluded for any reason, it is vital to consider the terms of any destination-over, and whether the issue of excluded children are also to be excluded.

It is thought that in the Styles presented, the destinations-over in favour of the issue of beneficiaries are not independent provisions. The effect of this is that the exclusion of some beneficiaries will also exclude their issue (compare the position on forfeiture – see para 5.56 above). If this is the intention, it should however be put beyond doubt by adding at the end of the destination-over in the appropriate clause '. . . but specifically excluding the issue of any excluded child'.

If the opposite situation is to apply and the issue of excluded children are *not* to be excluded, a declaration should be added to this effect:

'. . . but specifically declaring that the issue of any excluded children shall not be excluded in the event of such children predeceasing.'

There are further possibilities. One is that a condition directing exclusion is to apply as much to the issue of any children as to the children themselves. In these circumstances, the exclusion should be attached to the end of the purpose, as, for example:

'. . . but specifically declaring that any child or issue of mine who survives me and has attained the age of 30 at the date of my death shall be excluded from benefit under this purpose.'

A final possibility is that the exclusion of a child of issue is to be equated with its predecease, so that the issue of those excluded will benefit immediately. This can

---

1 *McGinn's Executrix v McGinn* 1994 SLT 2.

be achieved simply by declaring that the excluded children or issue are to be treated as if they had predeceased, at the appropriate point in the purpose. An example would be:

'. . . to such of my children A, B and C (but specifically excluding D as if for this purpose D had predeceased me), as shall survive me equally among them if more than one. . .'

If making the exclusion equivalent to predeceasing is to apply to an exclusion applying to all issue, the wording could be as follows:

'. . . but specifically declaring that any child or issue of mine who survives me and has attained the age of 30 at the date of my death shall be assumed for this purpose to have predeceased me.'

Illegitimate children

6.37 In respect of deeds executed on or after 25 November 1968, it was provided that in deciding who were to be beneficiaries through any relationship, the persons concerned were to be treated as related even if the relationship was illegitimate[1]. This provision was in sharp contrast to the common law, under which all expressions such as 'children' or 'issue' were presumed to refer to legitimate relationships only. An illegitimate relation was treated as an 'utter stranger'[2]. The common law principle can still be of great relevance in construing old deeds[3].

The principle established in the 1968 legislation has now been subsumed in the more general reform (which replaces the earlier reforming legislation) contained in the Law Reform (Parent and Child) (Scotland) Act 1986, section 1(1):

'The fact that a person's parents are not or have not been married to one another shall be left out of account in establishing the legal relationship between the person and any other person; and accordingly any such relationship shall have the effect as if the parents were or had been married to one another.'

This fundamental principle is applied to deeds[4]. The effect of the reforms in 1968 and 1986 is that illegitimate relationships are treated in exactly the same way as legitimate ones, not only for the purposes of testate and intestate succession but in relation to matters such as the two *conditios* (see paras 6.114 and 6.118–6.119) and the principles of accretion (see para 5.03).

It should be noted that the effect of the abolition of the status of illegitimacy applies to all relationships, not merely that between parent and child. Hence construction of such terms as 'grandchildren', 'brother', 'sister' and 'cousin' will ignore the question of whether any person's parents are or ever have been married. Although the remarks in this paragraph are couched in terms of the relationship between parent and child, the principles mentioned are of very general application.

1 See the Law Reform (Miscellaneous Provisions) (Scotland) Act 1968, s 5.
2 *Clarke v Carfin Coal Company* (1891) 19 R (HL) 63.
3 See for a recent, if complex, example *Wright's Trustees v Callender* 1993 SLT 556.
4 Law Reform (Parent and Child) (Scotland) Act 1986, s 1(2).

One very important restriction on the fundamental principle in relation to wills is that it only applies unless a contrary intention is expressed by the testator[1]. This contrary intention may be expressed in any manner.

It has been suggested that a contrary intention can simply be expressed by use of the term 'lawful' attached to the term of relationship under consideration, as for instance 'lawful issue'[2]. It certainly seems likely that a reference to 'legitimate' or 'illegitimate' will continue to have effect as an expression of contrary intention permitted by section 1(4). However, one of the fundamental principles behind the reforms mentioned has been to remove any stigma from the status of illegitimacy. Particularly as time goes on, those children who may still be loosely termed illegitimate should come to be regarded as just as 'lawful' as any other offspring. 'Legitimate' and 'illegitimate' may be considered equally or more pejorative in due course.

6.38 In these circumstances, if a testator does desire to exclude illegitimate children, some such wording as follows may be more appropriate:

'To the children of A, but expressly excluding any children whose parents were not married to each other either at the time of conception or birth of such children and who did not marry each other thereafter.'

The reason for providing the alternatives of conception and birth is to cope with the situation where a child is conceived in wedlock, but its father dies or its parents divorce before the child is born. The use of the final word 'thereafter' refers to the possibility of the parents marrying either after conception but before birth, or alternatively after birth. The reference to the parents being married 'to each other' is presumably necessary, as a testator concerned about such matters would be even more appalled should the child in question have been conceived or born while the parents were in marital relationships other than with each other.

It is conceivable that a testator who wishes to exclude a child whose parents were not married at the time of its birth is in fact more concerned with their marital state at the time of conception. Such a testator may still wish to exclude children who only achieve legitimacy by virtue of their parents marrying even before the child's birth or after the birth has taken place. However, the principle of legitimation by subsequent marriage has a long pedigree and may be acceptable to testators concerned about such matters.

If, however, such an extreme view of moral rectitude is to be catered for in a will, then reference to the birth or subsequent marriage (or both) should be deleted from the provision suggested above.

Any such attempt to exclude illegitimate children does not provide a watertight solution to all possible problems about which a testator may be concerned. Notably, there can be little guarantee that *any* married couple are in fact both the biological parents of any 'child'. The principle that it is a wise

---

1 See the Law Reform (Parent and Child) (Scotland) Act 1986, s 1(4)(c).
2 See, for example, *Meston* p 94; and see *Sharp's Trustees v Sharp* 1894 2 SLT 124.

person who knows his own father is particularly relevant when considering succession.

It is unlikely to be acceptable or indeed practical to demand more than that a child's apparent parents are married. A condition could be imposed as to providing proof of the biological relationship between child and parents, such proof to be to the satisfaction of the executors. Advances in medical science have made relatively conclusive proof as to such matters more available than was the case in the past.

However, different advances, particularly in fertility treatment, have also made possible biological relationships much more complex. In such circumstances, it will generally be preferable to rely on an apparent relationship of parent and child rather than investigating the matter too thoroughly, unless very specific instructions on this question are received from the testator.

Adopted children

6.39   The general policy of the law in relation to adopted children is to treat adopted persons as if they were the natural children of the adopters (and not of anyone else, including especially the biological parents of the children in question). For the purposes of succession, 'adopted persons' means persons adopted in pursuance of an adoption order under the Adoption Acts, or whose adoption is otherwise recognised in Scotland[1].

In relation to the construction of wills, the general policy is given statutory effect by the Succession (Scotland) Act 1964, section 23(1), which provides:

'for all purposes relating to –
(a)   the succession to a deceased person (whether testate or intestate), and
(b)   the disposal of property by a virtue of any *inter vivos* deed, an adopted person shall be treated as the child of the adopter and not as the child of any other person.'

This provision appeared to be reinforced by section 23(2), of the same Act, although there was undoubtedly some confusion caused by the interaction between the two subsections. It is worth quoting section 23(2) in full:

'In any deed whereby property is conveyed or under which a succession arises, being a deed executed after the making of an adoption order, unless the contrary intention appears, any reference (whether expressed or implied) –
(a)   to the child or children of the adopter shall be construed as, or as including, a reference to the adopted person;
(b)   to the child or children of the adopted person's natural parents or either of them shall be construed as not being, or as not including, a reference to the adopted person; and
(c)   to a person related to the adopted person in any particular degree shall be construed as a reference to the person who would be related to him in that degree if he were the child of the adopter and were not the child of any other person;
provided that for the purposes of this subsection a deed containing a provision taking effect on the death of any person shall be deemed to be executed on the date of death of that person.'

1 See the Succession (Scotland) Act 1964, s 23(5); Adoption (Scotland) Act 1978, s 38.

The relationship between these two subsections was thought to cause difficulty, notably on whether section 23(2) in any way constricted or restrained section 23(1)[1]. Any difficulty on this matter has now been resolved by the case of *Salvesen's Trustees, Petitioners*[2], which directs that the general rule in section 23(1) is to prevail. It was held that section 23(2) was intended to deal with the particular situation where a deed had been executed (or because of the proviso, left unaltered) where the testator (or other maker of a deed) knew both of the provisions of the Act and of the existence of an adoption order. The question is whether in such a situation the maker of the deed intends to benefit adopted persons where reference is made to any relationship. The effect of section 23(2) is that a contrary intention *must* be expressed in the deed if such references are *not* to have that result[3].

6.40 As well as dealing with the relationship between adopted children and their parents, the 1964 Act also deals specifically with relationships with other children (natural or adopted) of the adopting parents. Where the adopting parents are spouses who have *both* adopted a person, other children of those spouses will be treated as that person's brothers or sisters of the whole blood; in other cases, other children of those parents will be treated as brothers and sisters of the half blood. In relation to the drafting of wills, this generally makes little difference, as references to relationships will usually include those of both the whole and the half blood. Thus references to 'brothers and sisters' will usually include siblings by adoption in terms of the 1964 Act.

It can be seen that the statutory provisions in favour of adopted children go far beyond regulating their relationship with their adopting and their natural parents. In brief, the general position is that any reference to any relationship will not distinguish between cases where that relationship arises biologically or through adoption – but adopted persons will only benefit from references to their relationships arising by adoption, with their natural relationships treated as terminated.

Adopted persons can also benefit from the *conditio si testator sine liberis decesserit* (see para 6.114), and the rules on accretion, where relevant; for instance, in a bequest in favour of a class of relatives which might include adopted children (see paras 5.03–5.04 above).

If the relative seniority of members of a class is of importance, adopted persons are treated as if born on the date of their adoption; where two or more members of a class are adopted on the same day, they rank among themselves in accordance with their respective times of birth[4]. This may be of relevance in the construction of wills, for instance where some provision is made for, or condition is triggered by, some event involving the oldest or youngest child of a particular person.

1 See, eg, A J McDonald (1965) 10 JLSS 95; 14 JLSS 204.
2 1993 SLT 1327.
3 See *Salvesen's Trustees, Petitioners* 1993 SLT 1327 at 1332 per the Lord President (Hope).
4 Succession (Scotland) Act 1964, s 24(1A), as added by the Children Act 1975, Sch 2, para 5.

6.41   One problem arising from the Succession (Scotland) Act 1964, section 23(2) remains unresolved by the case of *Salvesen's Trustees, Petitioners* – if it is in fact a problem. That is whether a reference to 'issue' (as opposed to 'child' or 'children') displays a 'contrary intention' for the purposes of this statutory provision. 'Issue' might be thought to imply a biological relationship and hence adopted persons other than children of the immediate party would be excluded. This problem attracted a range of opposing views, notably in a series of articles in the Journal of the Law Society of Scotland. This discussion followed a suggestion in a note attached to a style will, which directed that in any destination-over to the issue of a beneficiary, the term issue should be accompanied by the phrase 'including adopted issue'[1].

With uncharacteristic timidity, the Styles presented in this book include the phrase 'including adopted issue' when dealing with destinations-over in favour of issue[2]. It is thought to be at the very least strongly arguable that these words may be unnecessary, adopted issue beyond the level of children being included by virtue of section 23(1) and (2). This view is reinforced, although not confirmed, by *Salvesen's Trustees, Petitioners*. The 'issue' who were in dispute in that particular case included adopted children of the truster's son (ie, adopted grandchildren). The trust deed did not make specific provision for adopted issue. No objection to the adopted grandchildren was taken on the ground that the word 'issue' expressed a contrary purpose for the purposes of section 23(2). Unfortunately, however, the point does not appear to have been specifically addressed. It may thus be considered safer to continue making reference to adopted issue beyond the level of children[3].

6.42   One thing that is undoubtedly clear is that adopted persons can be specifically excluded from benefitting from provisions in favour of children, issue or other relatives under a will. In terms of section 23(2), a 'contrary intention' to the presumed intention of including adopted relationships will then appear.

In the unlikely event that this is required by a testator, it can be achieved by attaching the phrase 'but excluding adopted children/issue/etc' to specific provisions. The word 'natural' or 'biological' could instead be attached to the class of relative mentioned, the first word being perhaps specifically suggested by section 23(2). Alternatively, a general exclusion can be attached as a declaration:

    'It is declared that reference to any form of relationship with the
    testator or with any other person in this will shall be construed as
    excluding any relationship deriving from adoption.'

This, of course, will not restore natural children of the testator or any other persons who have been adopted to a position of being included as children of their biological parents. In the event that this is desired, it is suggested that it

---

1   See 1979 JLSS (Workshop) lxxxv; 1980 JLLS (Workshop) 159, 165, 162; 1981 JLSS (Workshop) 182, 192, 206; *Meston* p 92.
2   See, for example, S3.6.
3   The Scot Law Com Report on Succession, no 124 (1990) para 91 recommends legislation to put this matter beyond doubt.

should be done specifically, ideally by referring to the biological child by name and certainly by referring to the 'natural' or 'biological' child of the appropriate person.

Certain items are excluded from the general rules on adopted persons. Notably, where the terms of any deed provide that any property or interest in property is to devolve along with a title, honour or dignity, nothing in the statutory rules mentioned dealing with adopted persons is to prevent that devolution[1].

Provisions for children generally

6.43 Before considering appropriate methods of making provision for children it is worth looking at whether children are or might be beneficiaries in various circumstances.

Children may be primary beneficiaries mentioned in the will. Alternatively, children may be named to take as default beneficiaries in the event of a primary beneficiary predeceasing the testator. An example would be the very common situation where a parent leaves his whole estate to his spouse whom failing to his children. The likelihood of the default provisions actually operating is quite high. Where, however, the primary beneficiary is of a younger generation than the testator the likelihood of the default provision in favour of children operating may be less.

In these cases the children are actually mentioned in the will but it is quite possible for children who are not mentioned in the will to become beneficiaries. One common example of this would be where the *conditio si institutus sine liberis decesserit* (see paras 6.118–6.119) applies, where the only beneficiaries mentioned in the will would be children or nephews and nieces. The issue of those beneficiaries might take in their place.

Another situation would be where all of the testamentary bequests failed because all of the beneficiaries predeceased. In that case the will survives to appoint executors and to give them administrative powers but the beneficiaries of the estate will be determined by the law on intestacy and there may be child beneficiaries involved. The exact beneficiaries can never be known in these circumstances because they will change over time.

There are cases where it is not possible for a child to inherit in any circumstances (for example, an outright bequest to a charity with alternative charities provided for) but these are likely to be few in number. It would, of course, be possible for provisions regarding beneficiaries lacking capacity to be incorporated in every will; but the practical solution must be to consider the likelihood of minor beneficiaries being involved in the testator's wishes as expressed along with the consequences of not including special provisions, and to include provisions or not as a result of that consideration.

When it has been decided that children are to be beneficiaries, or that they

---

1 Succession (Scotland) Act 1964, s 23(3).

may be beneficiaries on the failure of prior beneficiaries, or if there are circumstances in which children may benefit even although they may not be mentioned in the will, it is necessary (1) to decide whether to make provisions for them; and if so then (2) to decide the age at which they will become entitled to benefit. These two questions are intimately linked with each other.

Where no specific provisions are made for children

6.44 Where children are beneficiaries and the will makes no specific provisions for payment to them, then the subject of the bequest will vest in the child on the death of the testator: there will be vesting *a morte testatoris*. The problem is that the executors are faced with making payment to someone who is not capable of giving them a proper receipt and who may not have guardians.

The whole area of legal capacity of children was recast by the Age of Legal Capacity (Scotland) Act 1991 which came into effect on 25 September 1991. Although the age of majority remains at 18, a person attains full legal capacity at age 16. This is subject to the possibility that prejudicial transactions entered into by 16- or 17-year-olds may be reduced before the person becomes 21[1].

As a result of this change, where there are no provisions regarding children, the beneficiary will be entitled to demand payment from the executors at age 16. Acceptance of funds does not seem likely to cause substantial prejudice to the beneficiary and it is thought that executors could be required to denude in the beneficiary's favour. This whole area is discussed in greater detail in various articles[2].

Where a beneficiary is under 16, then the beneficiary generally has no legal capacity and his guardian acts on his behalf, as a tutor did under the previous law[3]. It therefore seems that regard must be had to the earlier law in determining how far executors are safe to distribute funds to beneficiaries under 16.

6.45 It seems that executors holding a fund which is vested in a beneficiary under 16 are at least bound to pay the income of the fund, or so much as is necessary for the child's maintenance or education. Where there are no provisions as to the administration of the fund, as there would not be in the circumstances under discussion, it seems that the executors may properly pay the child's share to his guardian provided the circumstances of the guardian are such as to leave no doubt as to the guardian's responsibilities. If there is doubt as to this then the executors should require caution[4]. Caution is unknown in practice in these circumstances and the practical answer is usually for the executors to retain the funds themselves until age 16.

1 Age of Legal Capacity (Scotland) Act 1991, ss 1 and 3.
2 See Barr and Edwards 'Age of legal capacity: further pitfalls' 1992 SLT (News) 77; Nichols 'Can they or can't they? Children and the Age of Legal Capacity (Scotland) Act 1991' 1991 SLT (News) 395; Norrie 'The Age of Legal Capacity (Scotland) Act 1991' 1991 JLSS 434.
3 Age of Legal Capacity (Scotland) Act 1991, s 5(l); see paras 6.98–6.100.
4 *Menzies* pp 503, 505; *McLaren* II, para 2519.

Under the previous law, while a discharge granted by or on behalf of a minor or pupil might be valid, it was nevertheless still possibly reducible within the *quadriennium utile*[1]. Following the 1991 Act, 16- or 17-year-olds may grant their own discharges subject to the rather unlikely possibility of them being set aside as prejudicial transactions.

In relation to persons under 16 their guardians could sign a discharge and the beneficiary would not generally be able to have the discharge set aside. This is because the relevant procedure only applies to transactions by 16- and 17-year-olds, and in addition the ability to reduce a transaction on the ground of minority and lesion within the *quadriennium utile* has been abolished (Age of Legal Capacity (Scotland) Act 1991, section 1(5)). The situation where no provision has been made for children is not thus very satisfactory.

Without any provisions governing bequests in favour of children, the taxation consequences are similar to those where there is a bare trust for minors (see paras 6.48–6.51).

Bare trusts – payment at 16

6.46 The situation where no provision for children is made is one example of vesting *a morte testatoris* with payment being postponed in some circumstances until age 16. Some of the difficulties of this situation can be overcome by making testamentary provisions allowing much wider powers to the executors. Such provisions appear under the side heading 'Beneficiaries lacking capacity' in most of the Styles (S3.7, S4.6, S5.10, S6.11, S7.8, S8.5, S9.9, S10.8 and S11.8). The terms of this purpose are dealt with further below (see paras 6.127–6.128). This provision follows from a recognition that while it is not possible to postpone payment to a beneficiary beyond age 16 where there are no conditions attached to the bequest, it is still possible to allow greater certainty and flexibility to the executors before then. Where a major beneficiary is given a vested unqualified and indefeasible right of fee, the beneficiary is entitled to payment despite any contrary directions by the testator[2].

It is still possible for a will executed before 1970 to refer to retention of funds until a beneficiary's majority and that will mean age 21[3]. A reference in a will executed before the Age of Legal Capacity (Scotland) Act 1991 came into force to 'retention until majority' will mean age 18. In neither case can the executors now insist on retaining any legacy beyond the age of 16. For wills executed now, it is, however, quite competent for the testator to give directions to administer a beneficiary's funds while that beneficiary remains under 16.

Under the provisions included in the Styles mentioned above, the executors may retain the capital and the income of the bequest until the child becomes 16,

1 *Wilson & Duncan* p 378.
2 *Miller's Trustees v Miller* (1890) 18 R 301; *MacKenzie Stuart* p 353.
3 Age of Majority (Scotland) Act 1969, s 1.

or may pay out all or part of the capital or income to the child for his benefit, or may pay out the capital or income to the child's guardian or the person having custody of the child. There is no question of a requirement for caution and there can be no reduction or setting aside. This establishes what is in effect a bare trust for beneficiaries under the age of 16.

6.47 It should be noted that it is the executors and not the child or child's guardian who have control as to what is to happen. A child's parent, therefore, cannot insist on payment and the executors are relieved of unfortunate legal consequences whether they decide to pay out or to retain funds. It is thought that these provisions should give the executors the necessary flexibility to deal with property falling to children.

These provisions establish a situation where the property vests in and belongs to the minor beneficiary but the executors are given administrative powers to deal with the property on the beneficiary's behalf until the beneficiary attains age 16. If the beneficiary should die before age 16 then the property forms part of his executry estate, and his will or the rules of intestacy in relation to him will determine who will then receive those funds. The testator cannot decide on substitute beneficiaries once the property has vested in the original minor beneficiary. If the testator wishes to decide on substitute beneficiaries in this event he must instead postpone vesting and create a trust which has a greater life of its own than a bare trust. He can then add destinations-over.

Tax considerations

6.48 The tax consequences of the minor beneficiaries' provisions establishing a bare trust and the position where there are no such provisions are the same. The provisions are drafted so that they apply in relation to a beneficiary lacking capacity. This could be by reason of age but it could also be by mental incapacity of an adult beneficiary[1]. Children will be the usual beneficiaries involved and that is why the provisions are often referred to here as minor beneficiaries' provisions.

(1) *Inheritance tax*

6.49 Since the property belongs to the child beneficially it will be subject to a charge to tax in the event of the death of the child. This is in effect the same as for a liferent trust (see para 5.65), but differs from an accumulation and maintenance trust or a discretionary trust where a charge to tax arising on the death itself would be avoided (see paras 5.70 and 6.56). In many cases the size of the inheritance tax threshold (£150,000) makes these considerations irrelevant.

(2) *Income tax*

6.50 While funds are retained by the executors during the administration of the executry the usual provisions regarding estates in the course of administration

1 See paras 6.127–6.128.

will apply[1]. Thereafter, the beneficiary is entitled to the income as it arises, whether it is physically paid to him or not. It forms part of his income for income tax purposes. If the child is a higher rate tax payer then additional tax may be due and will be payable by the child's guardian. A request could be made to the executors to help meet the liability but at least where there are minor beneficiaries' provisions it is not thought that the executors could be forced to comply.

The more usual situation would be that the child would be able to use executry income (and later, trust income) against its personal reliefs and so recover any overpayment of income tax. The parent-child settlement provisions for income tax[2], which demand aggregation of the income of children deriving from property which itself was a gift by the parent with the income of the parent, do not apply where the donor parent is deceased. The repayment claim would be made by the child's guardian who would actually receive the repayment.

Since, in most cases, children will not be already using their personal income tax reliefs, using provisions establishing a bare trust may be a very effective way to proceed for income tax purposes.

(3) *Capital gains tax*

6.51   Since the subject of the bequest actually belongs to the child it is the child's property for capital gains tax purposes[3]. If there is a disposal it is the capital gains tax position of the child which must be regarded for such matters as the annual exempt amounts, losses and tax rates. Again the provisions for minor beneficiaries in the Styles will generally work to the beneficiary's advantage. Where the executors hold funds for a number of minor beneficiaries it will be possible to use all of the beneficiaries' personal annual capital gains tax exempt amounts: this may be compared with the position for a liferent trust[4] and an accumulation and maintenance trust[5].

This is the capital gains tax position when the executry is completed. Until then the executors still have the executry annual exempt amount, being the full personal amount for the year of death and for the two full tax years thereafter[6] and the rate of tax is the basic rate[7].

Payment after 16 – trusts for children

6.52   Where the provisions on beneficiaries lacking capacity are used or no specific provision is made, this involves immediate vesting and payment being made at age 16. Where the testator thinks that 16 is too young an age for

---

1 See the Income and Corporation Taxes Act 1988, s 696.
2 Income and Corporation Taxes Act 1988, s 663.
3 See the Taxation of Chargeable Gains Act 1992, s 60.
4 One half of the annual capital gains tax annual exempt amount, and tax charged at the basic rate of income tax – see para 5.67.
5 One half of the annual capital gains tax annual exempt amount and tax charged at the rate applicable to trusts (the combination of basic and additional rate tax) – see para 6.58.
6 Taxation of Chargeable Gains Act 1992, s 3(7).
7 Ibid, s 4(1).

beneficiaries to receive funds and wishes to delay matters, then it is necessary to postpone vesting of the bequest for children until some later age and to create some form of trust. Postponing vesting will mean that the child is not entitled to demand payment at age 16, because there are other trust provisions to be satisfied. These other trust provisions fall into three main categories:

(1) accumulation and maintenance trusts;
(2) liferent trusts; and
(3) discretionary trusts.

These categories overlap and one may turn into another in whole or in part, but it is convenient to consider them separately. As an accumulation and maintenance trust is designed specifically for beneficiaries below a certain age – specific objects of bequest – this type of trust is considered in detail in the following paragraphs; the other types of trust may be used equally well for adults and are dealt with to a large extent in Chapter 5.

Accumulation and maintenance trusts

6.53 To some extent the accumulation and maintenance trust is a creation of statute, but something on the same lines has been in use for a long time. Basically the trustees accumulate the income of a fund until the beneficiaries are thought to be of a suitable age to be able to cope with the funds (usually 21 or 25), at which time the trustees distribute the funds to them.

The income is generally retained in the trustees' hands and does not belong to the beneficiaries.

The testator determines in the will who is to benefit in the event of the death of a beneficiary prior to the vesting date. This is in contrast to the bare trust situation where it is the beneficiary's succession which determines this (see para 6.47). This difference applies for all kinds of trusts with postponed vesting. The beneficiaries in each case may well be the same (under the trust in the will or on the beneficiary's own succession), but, for example, provision for a minor beneficiary's wife might not be made in a trust with postponed vesting, when provision would exist on the beneficiary's intestacy or by virtue of legal rights. The beneficiary may of course provide for anyone to inherit in terms of his own will.

The trustees' power to accumulate income is restricted by law to one of a number of periods. The periods relevant to wills are 21 years from the testator's death, or the minority or respective minorities of persons living or *in utero* at the testator's death, or where accumulation is to start at some time later than the testator's death (as, for example, following an intervening liferent), the minority or respective minorities of persons who would (if over age 21) be entitled to the income directed to be accumulated[1].

As a result, it is usual to limit accumulation until the beneficiaries respectively become 21. Thereafter, until the capital vests (usually at 25) the beneficiary is

---

1 See *Wilson & Duncan* pp 107 ff.

entitled to a proportionate share of the trust income. During the time when a beneficiary is between the ages of 21 and 25 the trust is therefore not actually an accumulation and maintenance trust at all in respect of that beneficiary, but a liferent trust. Prior to this time, the trustees have wide powers to distribute income to the beneficiaries for their maintenance. They would also usually have powers to distribute capital to the beneficiaries at any time.

While vesting of the capital is usually at age 25, there is no reason in law why it must occur then. It could occur earlier or later. The usual limitation on the duration of such trusts is that there cannot be a liferent in favour of a beneficiary who was not born at the date of the testator's death (see para 6.60).

6.54 There are limits to what can constitute an accumulation and maintenance trust for inheritance tax purposes[1]. For these purposes, the beneficiaries must be children of a common grandparent or the children of predeceasing children of a common grandparent, or alternatively the trust must be limited to a life as an accumulation and maintenance trust for a maximum of 25 years. Only beneficiaries under the age of 25 can benefit while it remains an accumulation and maintenance trust. If it is possible for a beneficiary over the age of 25 to benefit (except on the failure of other beneficiaries), then the trust will not qualify as an accumulation and maintenance trust for inheritance tax purposes from the outset. No interest in possession (liferent) must subsist in the trust or part of it while it remains an accumulation and maintenance trust.

The advantages of being an accumulation and maintenance trust for inheritance tax purposes are that there is no periodic charge to inheritance tax every ten years, and there is no charge to inheritance tax on the distribution of funds from the trust (see in contrast para 5.70 above). These are significant advantages, although the rise in inheritance tax thresholds has meant that they are of limited relevance for small estates.

While it is not *necessary* for an accumulation and maintenance trust in a will to qualify as an accumulation and maintenance trust for inheritance tax purposes, it is generally sensible to ensure that it does so qualify. Only trusts which do qualify will be considered here.

(1) *Tax considerations generally*

6.55 When considering the tax consequences of an accumulation and maintenance trust, this will be done in relation to the full form of accumulation and maintenance trust which appears in Style S7 (S7.7). This provides for accumulation of income until each child respectively becomes 21, for each child to be entitled to an equal share of income between ages 21 and 25, and for payment of an equal share of capital at 25. The trustees have power to pay out income and capital from a beneficiary's prospective share. (The specific provisions of this Style are considered in more detail in paras 6.65–6.80).

---

1 Inheritance Tax Act 1984, s 71.

(2) *Inheritance tax*

6.56 As mentioned above, inheritance tax has been the governing factor in the detail of accumulation and maintenance trusts. Qualifying as an accumulation and maintenance trust for inheritance tax purposes has meant that such a trust is taken out of the discretionary trust regime (see para 5.70).

Where a beneficiary under 21, who is prospectively entitled to a share of capital at 25 and on whose behalf income is being accumulated, dies, then provided that the trust is held for other beneficiaries who are themselves within the approved class of beneficiaries for an accumulation and maintenance trust (broadly by them being aged under 25), there will be no charge to inheritance tax on the trust funds and they will not be aggregated with that beneficiary's personal estate. If the funds were held on a bare trust under the provisions for beneficiaries lacking capacity, where the whole funds actually belong to the beneficiary, then the whole funds would be liable to inheritance tax on the beneficiary's death. If the funds were held for the liferent of a beneficiary (either from the beginning of the trust or under an accumulation and maintenance trust after the beneficiary has become 21), then the trust funds are treated as belonging to the beneficiary and are liable to inheritance tax on his death[1]. The treatment of trust funds on the death of a potential beneficiary under an accumulation and maintenance trust is thus similar to a fully discretionary trust – that is, the death will not generally have any effect on the trust funds directly.

Although the rise in inheritance tax thresholds has reduced the importance of inheritance tax considerations when considering possible use of accumulation and maintenance trusts, it is suggested that they should still be borne in mind. What was a small estate at the time of drafting a will may turn out to be a substantial estate on death. In addition, tax thresholds have not always been so relatively high. They may not remain so for ever.

(3) *Income tax*

6.57 Where income is being accumulated for a beneficiary (or the trustees merely have a power to accumulate) then the trust is liable to both basic and additional rates of income tax, the total now being known as the rate applicable to trusts[2]. Because of the administrative difficulties in trustees receiving and paying income subject to a 35 per cent charge, the trustees may wish at some point to convert the trust to a liferent trust to avoid the rate applicable to trusts. Provision is made for this possibility in S7.7(8).

When a beneficiary becomes 21, then under the Style he becomes entitled to a share of the income. The trust ceases to be one to which the rate applicable to trusts applies, to the extent of his share. Thereafter, the trustees will pay the higher rate only on the proportion of the trust income which they are

---

1 Inheritance Tax Act 1984, s 52.
2 See the Income and Corporation Taxes Act 1988, s 686; and para 5.71, where the income tax treatment of accumulation and discretionary trusts is described.

accumulating (or have power to accumulate) for beneficiaries under 21. The trust is then a mixture of an accumulation and maintenance and a liferent trust for income tax purposes. The trust income is split into the appropriate proportions.

(3) *Capital gains tax*

6.58 As a trust the accumulation and maintenance trust will attract its own annual capital gains tax annual exempt amount at one half of the personal rate[1]. Most of the considerations are similar to those affecting other discretionary trusts (see para 5.72). In contrast to the income tax position, when there are different parts of the trust chargeable at different income tax rates[2], there is no equivalent for capital gains tax purposes. The 35 per cent rate applicable to trusts applies to the whole trust even if part of the trust is held as a liferented fund. This will usually come to be the case in accumulation and maintenance trusts when a beneficiary becomes 21, as he will have a liferent of a share of the trust until vesting takes place at age 25. Thus, when a trust has beneficiaries aged both under 21 and over 21 but under 25, the rate of capital gains tax will be 35 per cent for the whole trust. This problem could be circumvented by the trustees appointing liferents to all of the beneficiaries under 21 in the year of assessment prior to a disposal. In this way the whole trust could become a liferent trust and so the basic rate of income tax only would apply to capital gains (see para 5.67). The Style of accumulation and maintenance trust presented provides for this (S7.7(8)).

It should also be noted that capital gains tax holdover relief is available where assets pass directly out of an accumulation and maintenance trust, but this does not apply where a beneficiary has an intermediate liferent[3].

Liferent trusts

6.59 As an alternative to an accumulation and maintenance trust for children it is possible to grant them a liferent. They would be beneficially entitled to trust income but while they were under 16, the provisions for beneficiaries lacking capacity (see paras 6.46 and 6.127–6.128) would operate to allow the trustees to retain the income on the child's behalf or to pay the income to the beneficiary or to his guardians. A liferent for children is not otherwise different from a liferent for adults (see para 5.63). In England, a liferent for a minor will usually trigger statutory accumulation until age 18, but this is not the case in Scotland.

The advantage of a liferent trust over an accumulation and maintenance trust or a discretionary trust is generally in its simplicity. In tax terms, there are none of the problems associated with the rate applicable to trusts; generally it is a much simpler form of trust. The advantage over a bare trust is that it enables

---

1 Taxation of Chargeable Gains Act 1984, Sch 1, para 2.
2 See para 6.57 above.
3 Taxation of Chargeable Gains Act 1992, s 260 (2)(d).

payment of the capital to be postponed beyond age 16 until it is thought suitable for the beneficiary to receive funds.

6.60 There are restrictions on the creation of liferents, in that it is not possible to create a liferent in favour of a person who was not born at the operative date of the deed (which means here the date of the testator's death)[1]. Where the testator is a parent of the beneficiary, then by definition the child must have been born or at least be *in utero* at the date of the parent's death. There is no problem in a testator granting a liferent to someone other than his own child who is not born at the date of signing the will, provided that the beneficiary has been born or is *in utero* at the date of the testator's death.

Where a testator wishes to benefit a class of beneficiaries which is not closed then a simple liferent will generally not be suitable, because it is not possible to provide for additions to the class born after the date of the testator's death. It would be necessary to make use of an alternative to a liferent for the full length of a person's life. This might be a prospective entitlement to capital on the beneficiary attaining some specified age, for example 25, 40 or 60, coupled with a right to the income of that fund prior to vesting. In the event of the beneficiary not attaining the specified age, then alternative destinations-over should be provided. It is such alternative destinations-over which constitute the reason for postponing vesting of the capital. They also explain why the right to income does not fall foul of the restriction on creation of liferents[2]. Doubts have been expressed as to how far such provisions do actually circumvent the restrictions[3]. If too improbable an age is specified, for example 110, then the result seems inconsistent with the aims of those restrictions. It might be that an intended liferenter could claim the fee. It is, however, the case that in *Shiell's Trustees*[4] the time of division was the death of the last survivor of four children who or whose issue were to take the income before the time for division. The issue of pre-deceasing children were held not to be entitled to the capital before the death of the survivor of the children.

If under a liferent the fee is destined for persons unborn at the time the deed comes into effect (usually the date of the testator's death), there may be problems with the creation of a fiduciary fee[5]. This means that the liferenter also holds the fee on a temporary basis, in trust for those who will take on his death, until the fiars are finally ascertained.

This is a complex area of law and in general the best advice would be to avoid attempting to create any kind of liferent interest where the beneficiaries of either income or capital are unlikely to be ascertained at the date of the testator's death.

The tax consequences of liferent trusts for children are largely the same as for

1 See the Law Reform (Miscellaneous Provisions) (Scotland) Act 1968, s 18; *Wilson & Duncan* p 90; 13 *Stair Memorial Encyclopaedia* para 1632.
2 *Shiell's Trustees v Shiell's Trustees* (1906) 8 F 848.
3 *Wilson & Duncan* pp 91–93, *Dobie* pp 261–263.
4 (1906) 8 F 848.
5 See *Newlands v Newlands' Creditors* (1794) Mor 4289; Trusts (Scotland) Act 1921, s 8(1); *Wilson & Duncan* pp 62–70; 24 *Stair Memorial Encyclopaedia* para 32.

liferent trusts for adults (see paras 5.65–5.67 above). However, the ability to utilise the child's personal allowances for income tax may be particularly useful.

Discretionary trusts

6.61 A fully discretionary trust allows trustees discretion as to who of a class should benefit, to what extent, when, and on what conditions. This can be useful when the testator cannot decide who should benefit. A discretionary trust may be of particular value when dealing with children. Children may be very young or unborn at the time of making the will and the testator may want to leave the selection of suitable beneficiaries until the candidates are older. Alternatively, a testator may wish to keep funds out of the hands of children for a period.

Most of what has been said in paras 5.68–5.72 and 5.87–5.107 about discretionary trusts for adults is of equal application to such trusts for children. This includes tax considerations. Again the ability to utilise the personal tax allowances of minor children may be particularly relevant. This is because discretionary trusts will suffer tax at the rate applicable to trusts (35 per cent) on *receipt* of income; this amount will also be available for repayment on distribution to beneficiaries with unused tax allowances.

Summary of provisions for children

6.62 The practical and tax consequences of the various possible provisions which may be made for children are summarised in the table on page 290.

It is, however, clear that many tax rules will prove to be only temporary and are very much more likely to change than the rules of the substantive law of wills and trusts. The Inland Revenue Consultative Document on the income tax and capital gains tax treatment of United Kingdom Resident Trusts published in March 1991, to which reference has already been made, may have provided some pointers for the future, although it is now known that the central proposals will not be implemented. This document also provides a useful summary of the present position.

PROVISIONS FOR CHILDREN: SPECIFIC STYLES

Styles S7, S7A and S8 – accumulation and maintenance trusts

6.63 These Styles are of particular relevance when one is dealing with children (or at least beneficiaries under the age of 25). These may be children of the testator or otherwise.

Style S7 provides for a full and flexible accumulation and maintenance trust. The start of the Style is similar to Style S3. The whole estate is left to the surviving spouse as in S3.5, with the children only taking on the failure of the spouse. It is the provisions which come into effect on that failure which are relevant in relation to beneficiaries under 25.

PROVISIONS FOR CHILDREN – SUMMARY OF TRUST AND TAXATION CONSEQUENCES

Provisions	Vesting	Payment	Inheritance tax on death of beneficiary	Income tax		Capital gains tax		
				Trustees	Beneficiary	Annual relief	Rate	Holdover on transfer to beneficiary
No provisions	On death	To child's guardians if appropriate, otherwise 16	Yes	None	Beneficiary's rate	Beneficiary's relief	Beneficiary's rate	No transfer
Bare trust for minors	On death	16	Yes	None	Beneficiary's rate	Beneficiary's relief	Beneficiary's rate	No transfer
Accumulation and maintenance trust	Postponed	Flexible but usually 25 (21 at most on short form)	No if subsequent beneficiaries within class	Rate applicable to trusts 35%	Beneficiary's rate if income distributed, otherwise no effect	½ personal relief	Rate applicable to trusts 35%	Yes, (unless beneficiary has liferent before vesting)
Liferent trust	Postponed	Flexible but restrictions on creation of liferents	Yes	Basic 25%	Beneficiary's rate	½ personal relief	Basic rate 25% (unless part of trust is A & M or discretionary)	No
Discretionary trust	Postponed	Flexible	No	Rate applicable to trusts 35%	Beneficiary's rate if income distributed, otherwise no effect	½ personal relief	Rate applicable to trusts 35%	Yes

NOTE: The tax position is for 1994/5

Purpose S7.6 – residue to children on failure of spouse

6.64   Purpose (SIX) of Style S7 provides for the testator's children to take on failure of the spouse and incorporates the same terms as for the basic will in Style S3. It provides for the issue of predeceasing children to take in their parent's place and for the survivors of the children to take where a predeceasing child leaves no issue.

It differs from Style S3 in declaration (2) which directs the trustees to hold any part of the residue falling to a beneficiary who has not attained age 25 in accordance with purpose (SEVEN), which provides for an accumulation and maintenance trust.

While it would be possible to provide for the accumulation and maintenance trust in purpose (SIX), it has been drafted separately in this Style. This is because at the time of the death it is statistically likely that the testator's own children will in fact be aged over 25, so a direct bequest to them seems preferable. If the bequest is direct to an accumulation and maintenance trust the trustees would be holding as bare trustees for the beneficiaries over 25 (since in terms of the accumulation and maintenance trust vesting occurs at age 25). The trustees would then simply convey the appropriate share to those beneficiaries. However, this Style is drawn as a direct bequest to children or issue coupled with a direction to hold funds for younger beneficiaries on an accumulation and maintenance trust.

The Style provides that only a share of residue falling to a beneficiary under 25 is to be held on an accumulation and maintenance trust. This would not cover a mere legacy to a beneficiary under 25 for which the provisions for beneficiaries lacking capacity in purpose (EIGHT) would be relevant. However, it is perfectly possible to provide an accumulation and maintenance trust for a specific or pecuniary legacy – see paragraphs 4.136–4.137.

The Style is intended to benefit the testator's own children. This class of beneficiary cannot increase because the testator cannot have more children after his death (apart from a child *in utero* who would be included in any event).

If, however, the beneficiaries are not the testator's children but the children of a third party then the class could increase after the testator's death. Such beneficiaries might for example be the testator's grandchildren. This Style is not suitable for that circumstance and different provisions would be required. An alternative Style (S7A) for a potentially increasing class of beneficiaries is discussed at paragraphs 6.81–6.84.

The main Style would be suitable for children other than those of the testator if it were acceptable for the class of beneficiaries to close at the date of the testator's death. The Style could then be adapted by altering the beneficiaries in S7.6.

Purpose 7.7 – accumulation and maintenance trust for beneficiaries under 25

6.65   Purpose (SEVEN) starts as a direction to the trustees to hold any part of the residue falling to a beneficiary under 25 for the trust purposes then set out. This direction relates only to the residue and not to any lesser interest. Any funds falling under this purpose are defined as 'the Trust Fund'. This expression is used only in purpose (SEVEN) and not elsewhere in the Style. In the purpose dealing with trustees' powers, for example, the reference is to 'the estate'. The latter expression is wider and is intended to cover any property held by the executors. The expression 'the Trust Fund' has been specially defined for ease of reference in purpose (SEVEN).

The trust fund may have just one beneficiary and limited assets or it may encompass a number of resididuary beneficiaries and the whole residue of a testator's substantial estate. This will depend to some extent on the ages of the beneficiaries at the testator's death. The funds are held prospectively for the individual beneficiaries, but there are destinations-over to other beneficiaries in the event of failure.

The individual trust purposes will be considered in turn.

(1) *For beneficiaries contingently*

6.66   This section provides that the funds are held contingently for the beneficiaries on their attaining a vested interest. Vesting is in general to occur on payment of the beneficiary's share at 25, as provided by paragraph (4). The beneficiaries referred to are children or issue. This follows from the destination in purpose (SIX) to the children or issue of predeceasing children. Funds may therefore be being held for beneficiaries of more than one generation.

(2) *Accumulation*

6.67   The trustees are directed to accumulate income until beneficiaries respectively become 21. This is a reference to the accumulation period for the duration of the minority or respective minorities of any person or persons who under the terms of the will would if of full age be entitled to the income directed to be accumulated[1]. This is distinct from the accumulation period for the minority of beneficiaries in life or *in utero* at the death of the testator. That period could be used for the most common cases but the Style allows for the possibility of issue of whatever degree of the testator's children to be beneficiaries (paragraph (5)). It is possible that some of these issue might be born after the testator's death. The other possibility for accumulation is for a period of 21 years from the testator's death. That period does not fit well with an accumulation and maintenance trust requiring beneficiaries to benefit outright or to receive an interest in possession by age 25. That period can be used, and depending on the children's ages accumulation could be carried out, up to their 25th birthdays. Use of a 21-year period would have to be coupled with provisions terminating accumulation as each beneficiary became 25 if the accumulation period had not expired by then. As a result, the first period mentioned is the most practical one for this kind of trust and is used in this Style.

---

1 Trusts (Scotland) Act 1961, s 5(2)(d).

Minority for the purposes of accumulation periods still means age 21 and not age 18[1], nor age 16.

It appears to be accepted that a trust can still qualify as an accumulation and maintenance trust if the accumulation period has expired[2].

(3) *Income*

6.68 This paragraph provides that the trustees are to pay out the income of a beneficiary's prospective share between ages 21 and 25. This interest, although lasting only for four years, does amount to a liferent[3] and to an interest in possession for inheritance tax purposes. Each beneficiary receives only the income of their own prospective share which will be a proportion that is fixed at a given time, although the proportion could increase in the event of another of the beneficiaries dying without issue. The proportion of one of the testator's children could not decrease under this Style, because the testator cannot have any more children. The number of principal beneficiaries cannot increase.

The requirements of an accumulation and maintenance trust for inheritance tax purposes in relation to vesting of interests in the fund require only that the beneficiary either becomes absolutely entitled or becomes entitled to an interest in possession by age 25. When a beneficiary becomes entitled to a fixed right to the income or an interest in possession then the trust ceases to be an accumulation and maintenance trust to that extent. There is therefore no reason under this Style why vesting in the capital need be at age 25.

The limitation to this age is provided by the limitation on the creation of liferents for a beneficiary's lifetime to beneficiaries who are in life or *in utero* at the date of the testator's death. Thus, it is possible to create a liferent for the lifetime of the testator's own children or for remoter issue who were born or *in utero* at his death. An attempt to create a liferent in relation to subsequently-born beneficiaries would result in such beneficiaries being entitled to claim the capital outright from the trustees[4]. All that can be done for subsequently-born beneficiaries is to give them a prospective right to capital on attaining a certain age, together with the right to income until the vesting date, and provide for destinations-over in the event of failure to attain that age. That is what has been done in this Style. Having only one set of provisions rather than alternative ones depending on whether a beneficiary was born before or after the testator's death is much simpler and for this reason it will generally be preferable to limit the provisions in this way. It is possible to give the trustees powers to postpone vesting to the maximum extent possible (see para 6.79).

(4) *Capital*

6.69 The trustees are to pay out the capital and accumulated income to beneficiaries on their respectively attaining age 25. Vesting is to occur

---

1 *Wilson & Duncan* p 108.
2 Chapman *Inheritance Tax* (8th edn) para 25-10-4.
3 *Dobie* p 1.
4 Law Reform Miscellaneous Provisions (Scotland) Act 1968, s 18.

then except for advances of income or capital under paragraph (7) where vesting is on payment.

(5) *Failure of beneficiaries*

6.70 Where a beneficiary does not survive to take a vested interest at age 25 then that beneficiary's issue who survive and attain age 25 will take in that beneficiary's place and on the same conditions, that is subject to the same accumulation and maintenance trust. Where a beneficiary predeceases the vesting time without leaving surviving issue the share then passes to beneficiaries who would have been beneficiaries if the predeceasing beneficiary had never existed. It is necessary to look at these two provisions in some detail.

Firstly, where a beneficiary dies leaving issue it is quite possible and likely that those issue will have been born after the testator's death. As a result the accumulation period running for the minority of a person in life at the date of the testator's death is not appropriate (see para 6.67).

Such a beneficiary cannot receive a liferent for his lifetime (see para 6.68). To qualify as an accumulation and maintenance trust the Inheritance Tax Act 1984, section 71 requires that either not more than 25 years have elapsed since the commencement of the trust, or all the persons who are or have been beneficiaries are or were either grandchildren of a common grandparent or children of such grandchildren who predeceased.

According to this Style, since issue means children and remoter issue of whatever degree, it is possible for grandchildren of a child of the testator to benefit but that grandchild will not be within the permitted class. If that eventuality is reached the trust will not qualify as an accumulation and maintenance trust. It is thought that it does not, however, prevent the trust qualifying until the eventuality occurs. An inheritance tax charge would therefore occur on the death of the last qualifying beneficiary and thereafter there would be a discretionary trust. One solution to this problem would be to exclude all such remote beneficiaries but in this Style it has been chosen not to do this on the basis that this is what is assumed a testator would want if it were possible for the full implications to be explained sufficiently lucidly. Another solution to this problem on present tax rules would be for the trustees to exercise their power under paragraph (8) to create an interest in possession within three months of the death of the last qualifying beneficiary in favour of the then prospective beneficiaries. This would avoid the discretionary trust regime[1].

The Capital Taxes Office may be taking the view that a reference to issue rather than to children in the class of beneficiaries of an accumulation and maintenance trust means that the grandchildren of a common grandparent condition cannot be satisfied, so that only the 25-year condition is possible. The view taken here is that so long as the grandchildren of a common grandparent condition is in fact satisfied then the trust will be an accumulation and maintenance trust under that head and will not be limited to the 25-year period. The point is not, however, settled.

---

1 Inheritance Tax Act 1984, s 65(4).

6.71   Secondly, where the beneficiary dies without issue, the share of the trust fund set free passes to the beneficiaries who would have been entitled if the predeceasing child or issue had never existed. This is drafted so that the survivors of all of the testator's children and the issue of predeceasing ones will share in the fund set free. The reference is not restricted to the remaining beneficiaries prospectively entitled to the accumulation and maintenance trust funds. It is intended to include: (1) beneficiaries who were old enough at the date of the testator's death by being over 25 then to have been entitled to take directly under purpose (SIX); (2) those who were under 25 at the date of the testator's death but who have subsequently become 25 and have become vested in a share of the accumulation and maintenance trust fund before the death of one of the younger accumulation and maintenance trust beneficiaries; (3) those remaining beneficiaries over age 21 but under 25 who are then entitled to an interest in possession; and (4) those remaining beneficiaries of the accumulation and maintenance trust under 21.

Where the predeceasing beneficiary is under 21, then in relation to substitute beneficiaries within category (4), there will be no liability to inheritance tax on the beneficiary's death because the accumulation and maintenance trust will continue with different beneficiaries. Substitute beneficiaries in category (3) are still under 25 and so there would be no inheritance tax liability there on them becoming entitled to an interest in possession in a larger share. Where the substitute beneficiaries are in categories (1) or (2), there will be a charge to inheritance tax on the death of a predeceasing beneficiary since the funds would cease being subject to an accumulation and maintenance trust; but this would not stop the trust from qualifying from the start. There are special rates of tax in this event[1].

This charge could be avoided if the default beneficiaries were restricted to those within the qualifying class of accumulation and maintenance trust beneficiaries who are under 25. There might, however, be no such beneficiaries and it seems unfair to the older beneficiaries to exclude them from benefit in what are probably fairly remote circumstances, when the inheritance tax charge may be insignificant. It is also in the interests of simplicity to have one set of default provisions applicable to predeceasing beneficiaries who may be either over or under 21.

Where the predeceasing beneficiary is over 21 then he will have an interest in possession in a share of the fund and his death will cause an inheritance tax charge (see paras 6.55–6.58).

It does not matter who the substitute beneficiaries may be, since the inheritance tax consequences will generally be the same. Fairness suggests that all of the original residuary beneficiaries should be included.

---

1 Inheritance Tax Act 1984, s 71(5).

(6)   *Prohibition of accumulation*

6.72   The rules on disposal of prohibited accumulations are not straightforward. While accumulation seems possible under most circumstances envisaged under this Style, it is always possible that the law or circumstances may change sufficiently to prohibit accumulation. In the interests of certainty, therefore, express provision has been made for what is to happen. The income is to be paid to the beneficiaries then, and from time to time, prospectively entitled to the capital and in the same proportions in which they are so entitled. The beneficiaries would thereafter have a liferent or interest in possession in their share of the funds.

(7)   *Application of income or capital*

6.73   While accumulation of income is directed the trustees may nevertheless distribute income to beneficiaries. For inheritance tax purposes the application of income is limited to applications for 'the maintenance, education or benefit' of a beneficiary[1].

In practical terms this does not seem to impose much of a restriction, since 'benefit' is accorded a wide meaning. There does not seem to be much authority in Scotland on how wide it really is, nor how wide it is for inheritance tax purposes. The phrase 'maintenance, education and benefit' is used in the English Trustee Act 1925 and there is some authority on that:

'The word "benefit" used in the statutory power is a word of wide meaning, unlike "advancement" which contemplates some definite purpose for preferring the beneficiary in life. The inclusion of the word "benefit" does not, however, absolve the trustees from the duty to decide whether the payment in the particular manner which they contemplate is for the benefit of the beneficiary. If the power of advancement is exercised for the benefit of the beneficiary, its exercise will not be made improper by the fact that other people may benefit incidentally as a result. Great care is, however, required to ensure that in the exercise of such a power the person really benefitting from the exercise will be primarily the object of the power, and the power must not be exercised so as to procure a benefit to the trustees[2].'

In England such a power enables the trustees to resettle funds for the beneficiary in certain circumstances but it is not believed that this would be permitted in Scotland.

6.74   The power to advance income relates to the time when income is being accumulated prior to a beneficiary becoming 21, after which the beneficiary is entitled to the income anyway.

While vesting of the capital is postponed until age 25 the trustees can advance any part of the capital of the share of a beneficiary at any time before or after that beneficiary attains 21. For inheritance tax purposes the application of capital need not be for maintenance, education or benefit, but in the interests of simplicity the same restrictions have been included for both. If the advance of capital to a beneficiary was made as part of a general rearrangement of family interests, as part of which it was intended that the beneficiary to whom funds

---

1 Inheritance Tax Act 1984, s 71(1).
2 *Butterworths' Encyclopaedia of Forms and Precedents* (4th edn), volume 20, p 370.

were advanced was to transfer these funds to someone else, then the trustees
would have to be very careful as to their own position. If there was thought to be
a problem then paragraph (7) could be split up into separate powers for income
and capital as follows:

'(7) My Trustees may apply for the maintenance, education or benefit
of any beneficiary of a share of the Trust Fund the income thereof
including accumulated income in whole or in part and any such
applications shall vest on payment.

(7A) My Trustees may advance outright to any beneficiary of a share
of the Trust Fund the capital thereof in whole or in part for any
purpose my trustees may decide.'

Alternatively it might be possible to use paragraph (9) to achieve the same end.

6.75   According to the Style, the application must be of income or of capital of
the particular beneficiary's own prospective share and not from another beneficiary's prospective share. This has been done in the interest of equality
between the various beneficiaries.

Where income or capital is distributed unequally between beneficiaries, the
trustees will have to keep separate accounts of the funds for the various beneficiaries, so as to be able to show that what each beneficiary receives is an equal
share overall.

It is, however, possible for trustees to be given a discretion as to the application of income while being directed to distribute the capital equally. It may be
that one beneficiary has greater needs than the others at one particular time and
another beneficiary at some other time. One beneficiary may be better able to
utilise income tax reliefs at a particular time. Overall the truster may be happy to
see income applied unequally since this may reflect what he would have done
himself had he been alive. If this were wanted, the Style mentioned above
separating income and capital could be altered so that the revised paragraph 7A
read:

'(7A) My Trustees may apply for the maintenance, education or
benefit of any beneficiary of a share of the Trust Fund who is not then
entitled to an interest in the income the income in whole or in part of
the Trust Fund to which any beneficiary is not then entitled as a result
of paragraphs (3), (6), (8) or (9) hereof.'

6.76   It is also possible for the trustees to be given a discretion as to which of a
class of beneficiaries will be entitled to receive the capital and for the trust still to
remain an accumulation and maintenance trust for inheritance tax purposes.
Style S7 is an equal entitlement trust and makes provision for beneficiaries over
and under 25. If it was desired to provide an accumulation and maintenance trust
that was fully discretionary as to capital, it would not be possible to include
beneficiaries who were over 25 at the time of the testator's death. They cannot be
beneficiaries of an accumulation and maintenance trust and the trustees' discretion
would have to be exercised prior to a beneficiary becoming 25. When the testator
is considering his will he cannot know which of his children will be over or under

25 at the time of his death. It would be possible to provide for a discretionary accumulation and maintenance trust as to capital in relation to those beneficiaries who did happen to be under 25, but since the discretion would not extend to older beneficiaries there seems little point in doing this. Fully discretionary accumulation and maintenance trusts are practical for lifetime trusts because the truster knows the identity and ages of the beneficiaries, but they do not seem practical in the context of a will and can be very dangerous unless diarised records of children's ages are kept.

There is, however, a way round this where the testator wants to leave a discretion over capital to his executors. That is to use a two-year discretionary trust provided for in Style S8. The residue could be left to the spouse whom failing to a two-year discretionary trust. The trustees then have a two-year period within which to decide to distribute funds outright or to set up some other kind of trust. The trustees could appoint funds out on a discretionary accumulation and maintenance trust knowing the beneficiaries who were then alive and their ages (see paras 5.87–5.92).

(8)   *Advance of income or capital entitlements*

6.77   The trustees can advance the ordinary times when a beneficiary would become entitled to income (age 21) or capital (age 25). By advancing the income entitlement age, the trustees are empowered to create an interest in income in whole or in part in any beneficiary prior to the ordinary time when that right would occur at 21. This power gives the trustees an alternative to an outright appointment of capital provided by paragraph (7).

Where the power was exercised in favour of a young beneficiary the trustees could make use of the provisions for beneficiaries lacking capacity in Purpose (EIGHT). A beneficiary between ages 16 and 21 would be entitled to demand payment of his share of the income.

There are a number of possible reasons why the trustees might want to advance an income entitlement. It might be important for the beneficiary to be entitled to his own income so as to be able to satisfy a lender as to the beneficiary's income and thus his ability to repay a loan.

Many of the other reasons are tax ones. Where a beneficiary is entitled to a share of the income then that part would not be subject to the rate applicable to trusts for income tax (see para 5.71). The administrative cost of paying this higher tax rate and then the beneficiary reclaiming it in whole or in part can therefore be avoided.

If the trust ceases to be a qualifying accumulation and maintenance trust for inheritance tax purposes because beneficiaries have become too remote, as for example grandchildren of a predeceasing child who was one of the principal beneficiaries, then the trustees could create interests in income and have a liferent trust rather than a discretionary trust for inheritance tax purposes. If the trustees knew that they were likely to realise a substantial capital gain in the near future they could convert the whole trust into a liferent trust so as to have the capital gain taxed at basic rate and not at the rate applicable to trusts (see paras 6.55–6.58).

At one time a tax planning device known as the 'General Franco' scheme worked to bring about the avoidance of a capital transfer tax charge by giving a beneficiary a right to income and a contingent right to capital. Other such opportunities may present themselves in future.

6.78 As an alternative to the advance of an income entitlement, the trustees can advance the date of a capital entitlement. This can be similar to a simple advance of capital under paragraph (7). However, the trustees could also appoint prospectively rather than immediately. Rather than distributing capital there and then, the trustees could, for example, appoint that all the beneficiaries would become entitled to capital at age 21. They need not wait until each beneficiary approached age 21 before they appointed, when the matter might be overlooked. A current example of the use of this power would be to enable capital gains tax holdover relief to be obtained. This is possible from transfers from an accumulation and maintenance trust but not from a liferent trust[1]. A general advance of the vesting age in a trust would enable holdover relief to be obtained.

An appointment could be revocable so that the trustees could change their minds. If not previously revoked, an appointment would become irrevocable when it became operative.

(9) *New trust purposes*

6.79 The inheritance tax requirements impose considerable constraints on the drafting of an accumulation and maintenance trust. Once a beneficiary has a liferent in a trust then the trust is no longer an accumulation and maintenance trust to that extent and so the restrictions do not apply. With a liferent trust there are no restrictions on qualifying beneficiaries, and so it is possible for the trustees to be given wide discretions to create new trust purposes covering both income and capital. This is what paragraph (9) does.

Paragraph (9) is very wide and allows the trustees to create entirely new trust purposes. The beneficiaries of these new trusts may include the beneficiary then entitled to the income together with his issue and his and their spouses. With the beneficiary's consent, any other beneficiaries may be included. Within the class consisting of the beneficiary, his issue and his and their spouses the trustees can act without the beneficiary's consent. This has been done principally for tax reasons. It might enable provisions not to be caught by the parent-child settlement provisions for income tax because the beneficiary had taken no part in the appointment.

It might be possible to postpone a capital gains tax liability by postponing the vesting date to some higher age, since the beneficiary would not have been party to this. Holdover is not now generally available from a liferent trust, so this power may be an alternative to an appointment at 21 under paragraph (8).

The new trusts which could be set up are very wide and include discretionary powers or powers of appointment to the trustees or others such as liferenters of

---

1 Taxation of Chargeable Gains Act 1992, s 260.

funds. Regard would have to be had to the usual restrictions on creation of liferents and on accumulation of income.

(10) *No apportionments*

6.80 A beneficiary of this trust may be entitled to a share of income because he is between 21 and 25 (paragraph (3)), or because accumulation has been prohibited (paragraph (6)), or because the trustees have appointed a right to income to him (paragraph (8)).

In these circumstances, apportionment of income would be required. The Style excludes the requirement to apportion for the reasons explained at paragraph 7.28.

Style S7A – alternative style to include future-born beneficiaries

6.81 The main accumulation and maintenance trust Style (S7) deals with the case where the class of beneficiaries is fixed at the testator's death. This may well not be the case, as for example where the beneficiaries consist of a class of the testator's grandchildren or nephews and nieces. In these cases additional members of the class could well be born after the testator's death. Allowing for such possibilities makes the drafting very much more difficult and the length of the alternative style indicates some of the difficulties.

The alternative Style (S7A) runs on exactly the same lines as Style S7 with a modified purpose (SIX). This provides that the residue is to be held for such of the grandchildren who are born before the youngest grandchild in life attains 25. Grandchildren born after the testator's death will therefore be included. The class will close when the youngest grandchild in life becomes 25 and no further grandchildren will be included. There is no reason in principle why the class could not remain open indefinitely, but as a practical matter it is important not to have to leave funds in suspense and there might of course never be any further grandchildren. The likelihood is that there will be no further beneficiaries born more than 25 years after the youngest member of the class is born.

Declaration (1) brings in the issue of grandchildren who predecease the testator. Grandchildren who survive the testator but do not survive until vesting but leave issue are dealt with under the terms of the accumulation and maintenance trust contained in the following purpose. Declaration (1) therefore refers to issue surviving the testator rather than issue surviving the date of vesting.

Declaration (2) provides that grandchildren or issue representing predeceasing grandchildren who are already aged 25 or over at the date of the testator's death will be entitled to an equal share outright.

Declaration (3) provides that where any of the grandchildren or issue representing predeceasing grandchildren are under 25 at the date of the testator's death, their funds are to be held for those beneficiaries, together with any grandchildren who may be born after the testator's death in accordance with the accumulation and maintenance trust purposes provided in purpose (SEVEN), but with various modifications.

These modifications are necessary to provide for a scheme of equal division, given that the class may increase through the birth of additional beneficiaries. In the standard Style of accumulation and maintenance trust for children the class cannot be increased because the testator cannot have any more children. In that case the prospective share of each beneficiary is fixed from the start, although it can be subject to alteration subsequently on the death of a beneficiary. In this alternative Style the prospective share is subject to reduction in the event of a new beneficiary being born.

6.82 Purpose S7A.6(3), clause (a) provides that the share of any of the prospective beneficiaries is calculated by reference to the number of grandchildren under 25 in life at any time and including in the calculation the issue of any predeceasing grandchildren. The share of any particular beneficiary is fixed definitively when capital vests in a beneficiary. But for this provision it might be possible to argue that a beneficiary should repay part of his entitlement which he had received at age 25 in the event of an additional beneficiary being born thereafter. Definitive fixing of the share also happens should the whole of that prospective beneficiary's share be appointed outright to him, or be appointed on separate trust purposes under paragraph (9) of the accumulation and maintenance trust.

This clause refers to taking into account beneficiaries whose age does not exceed 25. That this particular wording is required is a peculiar result of a new rule on the attainment of age by any person. A person now attains an age at the beginning of a relevant anniversary of the date of his birth[1]. As a result, twins will attain an age at the same instant, not (as previously) one after the other according to the precise time of day at which they were born. As a result, the calculation of an equal share for each of twins must be defined carefully. If the share of a twin is to be defined as an equal share as between the beneficiary becoming 25 and the other beneficiaries under 25, then the other twin is left out of account in the calculation with the result that the twins will receive a larger than appropriate fraction of the fund available. As an example, if there were five beneficiaries of whom two were twins, in the last mentioned scheme each twin would be entitled to $1/(1 + 3) = 1/4$, so that the twins together would receive a half and the remaining three beneficiaries would be left with the other half. It is for this reason that the alternative style refers to beneficiaries whose age does not exceed 25 for the purposes of the calculation of the prospective share of each beneficiary and in consequence the share to which each beneficiary actually becomes entitled.

6.83 Clause (b) attempts to cope with partial advances of capital or appointments on different trust purposes since there could be a wide variety of arrangements. The alternative Style leaves it to the trustees to decide what is fair in the circumstances.

---

1 Age of Legal Capacity (Scotland) Act 1991, s 6.

6.84 Clause (c) ensures that all funds will vest in a beneficiary under 25 by providing that if funds slip through the net of previous provisions, the youngest in life becomes entitled to what is left. This prevents any possible argument that there could in any circumstances be funds undisposed of, such as by the trustees exercising a discretion under clause (b) in an odd way, which could give rise to an argument that the trust was not an accumulation and maintenance one for inheritance tax purposes.

This alternative Style then uses the same provisions for the accumulation and maintenance trust as appear in the main Style S7. Purpose (SIX) of the alternative style has had to be made considerably more complicated, but the circumstances with which it deals are also considerably more complex than is the case with the basic accumulation and maintenance trust. It would have been possible to deal with some of the matters in this Purpose within the terms of the accumulation and maintenance trust purpose (SEVEN), but it was desired to keep the accumulation and maintenance trust Style the same for both versions in the interests of simplicity.

Where the alternative Style is used then the beneficiaries will not be the testator's own children; they will be grandchildren, nephews and nieces, or unrelated beneficiaries. The testator will not be able to appoint guardians to these beneficiaries. Purpose S7.13 should therefore be deleted.

Style S8 – short form of accumulation and maintenance trust

6.85 It is appreciated that the Styles of accumulation and maintenance trust discussed may seem long and somewhat daunting to testators. With this in mind, there is also offered a shorter, simpler style which may be of use in many but not all circumstances – Style S8. This shorter form is also designed to meet the requirements of an accumulation and maintenance trust for inheritance tax purposes (see paras 6.53–6.58).

Having discussed the longer version at some length it is appropriate merely to mention the differences between that and this shorter Style.

The shorter form cannnot have as late a vesting age as 25 because of the restrictions on accumulation of income (see para 6.67), and therefore 18 or 21 will be the usual ages for the shorter Style.

The shorter Style provides that vesting and termination of the power to accumulate income occur at the same time. The result is that there is no period when a beneficiary has an entitlement to income as opposed to being a person in whose favour the trustees can exercise a discretion to pay income. This simplifies the trust somewhat. There is no reference in the short form to the disposal of prohibited accumulations of income (see para 6.72), but this is probably an unlikely event.

Income or capital can be distributed by the trustees in whole or in part at any time under both forms.

The full Style allows the trustees to advance the entitlements to income (para 6.77), but the short form does not. The full form allows the trustees to advance the date at which capital will vest while the short form does not. Since the short form provides for an accumulation and maintenance trust throughout its duration, while the full one operates as a liferent trust for beneficiaries between ages 21 and 25, there is no similar capital gains tax problem on vesting (see para 6.77). No resettlement is possible as it is in the fuller trust (see para 6.79).

The longer form requires an exclusion of apportionment provision (see paras 6.80 and 7.28), but as there are no income entitlements under the short form this provision is not required.

The shorter form cannot cope with grandchildren or other primary residuary beneficiaries who are born after the testator's death. This is no different from the full form of accumulation and maintenance trust in S7.6 but both of these are different from S7A.6 which does allow for later-born beneficiaries.

The short form is made possible principally (1) because fewer provisions are required where there is no income entitlement provided for beneficiaries which in turn is made possible by the lower vesting age, and (2) by accepting a certain loss of flexibility. In many circumstances it may be found preferable to use the fuller form.

The shorter form may be added as a purpose following the residue purpose as shown in Style S8. This is the only difference from Style S3. The provisions on beneficiaries lacking capacity are still required because their objective is different. Income or capital distributions under the powers of an accumulation and maintenance trust would still be subject to these provisions. They will apply also to legacies, whereas the accumulation and maintenance trust will not, as drafted in the Styles, apply to such legacies but only to residue or a share of residue.

The shorter form of accumulation and maintenance trust could also be included in the other Styles as a replacement for the longer form shown in purpose S7.7 This might be appropriate where a full version of trustees' powers was wanted, but only for the shorter period possible with the short form of trust.

PROVISIONS FOR CHILDREN: GUARDIANSHIP AND TESTAMENTARY APPOINTMENT OF GUARDIANS

6.86 While the following paragraphs are concerned with testamentary appointment of guardians, it is first necessary to explain in a bit of detail the significant changes to the law, including that affecting guardianship, introduced by the Age of Legal Capacity (Scotland) Act 1991, which came into effect on 25 September 1991. This provision is mentioned elsewhere in the text.

It is also worthy of note that the Scottish Law Commission's Report on Family Law[1], with draft Bill annexed, makes recommendations which, if introduced, would have a significant impact not only on the position of children and their guardians, but on Scots family law generally.

The following paragraphs will summarise the principal changes introduced by

---

1 Scot Law Com no 135 (1992).

the 1991 Act in relation to the legal capacity of children; they will then consider guardianship in the wake of the Act; then they will briefly refer to the role, powers and duties of guardians; and finally they will examine how testamentary guardians may be appointed in various sets of circumstances. With exception of the last, this can be no more than a summary of the salient features of the law as it presently stands. For detailed analysis the reader will need to look elsewhere[1].

Age of Legal Capacity (Scotland) Act 1991

6.87 Prior to the 1991 Act, children under the age of 18 fell into two categories; pupils (girls under 12 and boys under 14) who were represented by their tutors; and minors (girls between the ages of 12 and 18 and boys between the ages of 14 and 18), who were represented by their curators.

Following the 1991 Act children were re-classified into two new groups, persons under the age of 16 and persons between the ages of 16 and 18. Curatory was abolished[2] and pupillarity was extended until age 16, although the term 'pupil' disappeared. The terms 'tutor' and 'tutory' became 'guardian' and 'guardianship' respectively[3]. Guardians were given the powers and duties previously applying to tutors[3] and their rights of guardianship are defined as 'parental rights'[4].

The right to guardianship now exists automatically only for:

(1)   A child's parents, if married at the time of its conception or subsequently[5];
(2)   A child's mother, if unmarried[5].

Otherwise the right to guardianship can arise in one of only two ways:

(3)   Guardians appointed by the court under section 3 of the Law Reform (Parent and Child) (Scotland) Act 1986[6]; or
(4)   Testamentary guardians appointed by a parent under section 4 of the Law Reform (Parent and Child) (Scotland) Act 1986[6].

Legal capacity: persons under 16

6.88 Persons under the age of 16 have no legal capacity to enter into any transaction[7], other than 'of a kind commonly entered into by persons of [their] age and circumstances [and] on terms which are not unreasonable'[8]. 'Transaction' means 'a transaction having legal effect', as defined in section 9. An unreasonable transaction is void[9]. Therefore, any legal transaction or undertaking, except

---

1 For example Wilkinson & Norrie *The Law Relating to Parent and Child in Scotland* (1993).
2 Age of Legal Capacity (Scotland) Act 1991, s 5(3).
3 Ibid, s 5(1).
4 Law Reform (Parent and Child) (Scotland) Act 1986, s 8, as amended by the 1991 Act, s 9.
5 Ibid, s 2(1).
6 See the 1991 Act, s 5(2).
7 Ibid, s 1(1).
8 Ibid, s 2(1)(a),(b).
9 Ibid, s 2(5).

one within the narrow exception under section 2(1) or the three special exceptions referred to below, has to be carried out on behalf of a person under 16 by his guardian.

No specific provision is made in the Act for the reduction of bad bargains made by the child's guardian, which, of course, differs from the former position of minors under the *quadriennium utile*[1].

Special exceptions

6.89   In addition to the narrow exception under section 2 of the 1991 Act, there are three special exceptions, affecting:

(1)   *Testamentary capacity*[2]:

'A person of or over the age of 12 years shall have testamentary capacity, including legal capacity to exercise by testamentary writing any power of appointment[3].'

(2)   *Consent to adoption*[4].

Under the previous law[5], an adoption order, or an order freeing a child for adoption, normally required the minor child's consent. Now a child aged 12 or over has legal capacity to consent to the making of an adoption order over him or freeing him for adoption.

(3)   *Consent to medical treatment*[6].

Persons under 16 can consent to 'any surgical, medical or dental procedure or treatment where, in the opinion of a qualified medical practitioner attending' them, they are 'capable of understanding the nature and possible consequences of the procedure or treatment'. The sole test is a child's capacity, in the opinion of one doctor, to understand the nature and possible consequences of the procedure or treatment. The Act, however, is silent as to a child's capacity to refuse treatment, the parent's right to consent on behalf of a child, the position in the event of a disagreement between child and parent and confidentiality[7].

LEGAL CAPACITY: PERSONS AGED 16 AND 17

6.90   Sixteen and 17-year-olds have full legal capacity to enter into any transaction[8], subject only to their being permitted to have certain prejudicial transactions, as defined in section 3 of the 1991 Act, set aside.

---

1 The previous rules relating to the reduction of transactions on grounds of minority and lesion having been abolished: 1991 Act, s 1(5).
2 1991 Act, s 2(2).
3 See para 2.02.
4 1991 Act, s 2(3).
5 Adoption (Scotland) Act 1978, ss 12 and 18.
6 1991 Act, s 2(4).
7 See Norrie 'The Age of Legal Capacity (Scotland) Act 1991' (1991) 36 JLSS 434.
8 1991 Act, s 1(1)(b).

Prejudicial transactions

6.91 'Prejudicial transaction' is defined as a transaction which 'an adult, exercising reasonable prudence, would not have entered into in the circumstances of the applicant at the time of entering into the transaction [and] has caused or is likely to cause substantial prejudice to the applicant'[1]. This remedy applies to transactions entered into while the applicant was aged 16 or 17 and must be raised before the date of the applicant's 21st birthday[2]. This may be contrasted with the previous law under which a minor could apply to the court within the *quadriennium utile* – four years from attaining the age of 18 – to have a transaction entered into with his curator's consent if he had one or on his own if not, reduced on grounds of minority and lesion. As has already been noted, reduction on such grounds was specifically abolished by section 1(5).

The exercise of testamentary capacity and power of appointment, consent to adoption and consent to surgical, medical or dental procedure or treatment cannot subsequently be challenged as 'prejudicial transactions'[3].

Ratification of proposed transactions

6.92 A transaction liable to be set aside as a 'prejudicial transaction' may be ratified before it is entered into by way of joint summary application by both parties to the proposed transaction to the sheriff court[4], from which there is no appeal[5]. A transaction so ratified cannot later be challenged by the child[6]. The court is not permitted to ratify the transaction if it appears to the court that an adult, exercising reasonable prudence and in the circumstances of the young person, would not enter into the transaction[7]. A young person may ratify a transaction after he has reached the age of 18 and, if he does so in the knowledge that it could be set aside by an application to the court, this bars any such application[8]

Miscellaneous provisions

Domicile

6.93 A person first becomes capable of having an independent domicile at 16[9] (see para 2.62).

1 1991 Act, s 3(2).
2 Ibid, s 3(1) and (4).
3 Ibid, s 3(3)(a), (b), (c) and (e).
4 Ibid, s 4(1).
5 Ibid, s 4(3).
6 Ibid, s 3(3)(j).
7 Ibid, s 4(2).
8 Ibid, s 3(3)(h).
9 Ibid, s 7.

Witnessing

6.94 Persons may only act as instrumentary witnesses if over the age of 16[1] (see paras 2.36–2.38).

Majority

6.95 The age of majority is still 18, but specific provisions are made for most purposes.

Potential difficulties

6.96 A number of the concepts introduced by the 1991 Act are indistinct and, thus, open to judicial interpretation or subsequent legislation. This is particularly so, in the case of children under 16, of transactions falling under the general exception of section 2 and consents to medical treatment; and in the case of children aged 16 and 17, of prejudicial transactions[2].

Guardianship following the 1991 Act

6.97 Before the 1991 Act, the term 'guardian' was used to denote a person, usually a parent, who looked after a child's financial and other interests, such guardianship lasting until the age of 18. The guardian of a pupil was a tutor, the guardian of a minor a curator. Legally, only those offices were recognised.

Guardianship is now defined as one of the 'parental rights' listed in section 8 of the Law Reform (Parent and Child) (Scotland) Act 1986, as amended, and whether or not exercised by a parent. These rights include 'guardianship, custody or access, as the case may require, and any right or authority relating to the welfare or upbringing of a child conferred on a parent by any rule of law'[3].

As has already been noted, the right to guardianship exists automatically only for a child's parents, if married at the time of conception or subsequently, or a child's mother if its parents are unmarried.

Where parents are married to each other, both are the child's guardians, either being able to act without the other[4].

The right to guardianship, of course, extends to adopted as well as to natural children[5].

The right of guardianship can be obtained by someone who does not have the right automatically, including a father who does not have parental rights, in one of only two other ways: (1) application to the court under section 3 of the 1986 Act; or (2) appointment by a parent in a testamentary deed under section 4 of the 1986 Act, as amended.

Consequently, tutors-legitim and tutors-dative cannot now be appointed to

---

1 1991 Act, s 9.
2 See *Wilkinson & Norrie* pp 354–356.
3 Law Reform (Parent and Child) (Scotland) Act 1986, s 8, as amended by the Age of Legal Capacity (Scotland) Act 1991.
4 Law Reform (Parent and Child) (Scotland) Act 1986, s 2(4).
5 See *Wilkinson & Norrie* p 521.

children and testators can no longer appoint special tutors to administer property bequeathed to a child. Section 5(4) of the 1991 Act abolishes the office of factor *loco tutoris*, with the result that the court would now simply appoint a judicial factor. Curators *ad litem* and curators *bonis* remain, but neither can be appointed solely by reason of age[1].

Parental rights and powers continue to be vested in local authorities and voluntary organisations under the Social Work (Scotland) Act 1968[2], in circumstances where a child has no parents or guardian, or they are unfit or incapable of having care of a child in terms of the Act, or a child has been abandoned.

Guardianship and custody

6.98   Guardianship can be distinguished from custody, although more often than not the two will go hand in hand.

A guardian's powers and duties are effectively confined to management of the child's estate, unless the guardian also has custody of the child. Custody of the child vests in the custodian the control and care of the child's person and upbringing.

Both parents of a child have equal rights of custody in the absence of a court order to the contrary[3]. An award of custody does not automatically affect guardianship. Thus, if one parent is awarded custody on divorce or separation, both parents may continue to be entitled to guardianship of the child[4]. Disputes between the parents, as guardians, on any matter affecting the child's welfare can be resolved on application to the court under section 3 of the 1986 Act.

The role, powers and duties of guardians

6.99   Guardians are placed in the position formerly occupied by tutors, the principal difference being that their authority extends until a child reaches 16, and guardianship 'is now to be understood . . . in the sense of tutory at common law'[5]. More often than not a child's guardian or guardians will be its parent or parents and the terms 'guardian' and 'parent' are here used interchangeably. The powers and duties summarised below, however, are essentially those applying with reference to the law as it stood in relation to tutors.

A parent's guardianship confers a right to manage a child's property and, on a child's behalf, to contract, litigate and, generally, act in any matter where a child is incapable of acting on his own behalf. The parent as guardian is a child's legal representative or administrator in law. At the same time he or she has a duty to

---

1 1991 Act, s 5(3).
2 Social Work (Scotland) Act 1968, s 16, as substituted and extended by the Children Act 1975, ss 74 and 75.
3 Guardianship Act 1973, s 10(1), as repealed and replaced by the Law Reform (Parent and Child) (Scotland) Act 1986, s 2(1).
4 Clive *The Law of Husband and Wife in Scotland* (3rd edn, 1992) p 516.
5 *Wilkinson & Norrie* p 358.

protect the child, administer the child's estate fairly and to represent the child to its advantage in any legal transaction[1].

A guardian acts on behalf of a child in all matters concerning the administration of the child's property or estate, may grant receipts and discharges, and possesses the power to contract on the child's behalf. Formerly, this was based on the notion that a pupil had no legal personality, which permitted a tutor to act without the child's consent and in spite of the child's opposition.

At common law tutors had a duty to preserve[2] a child's estate and not attempt to improve it, since any such attempt would necessarily involve an element of risk[3]. This made it necessary for tutors to seek special authority from the court in any circumstances where their actings might be at variance with such duty[4]. Later, tutors were deemed to be trustees under the Trusts (Scotland) Acts 1921 and 1961[5] and, accordingly, in addition to their common law powers, guardians have the statutory powers of administration and investment afforded to trustees, are bound to recover debts owing to a child by raising actions and doing diligence as necessary, and, on a child's attaining 16 (as formerly, in the case of tutory, on minority), to account for all intromissions with the child's estate, making good any losses resulting from their administration.

The fact that the 1991 Act makes no specific provision to protect a child from a guardian's mismanagement or bad bargains has already been noted[6]. The possibility, however, that a child might have a remedy against his guardian on the ground of breach of trust as a trustee, has been mooted[7].

6.100   In addition to their powers of administration and contract, guardians have power to litigate. For example, where a child has been injured by another's negligence, the guardian can sue for damages on the child's behalf.

The guardian's power to act generally in all matters on a child's behalf would have included consenting for him to medical treatment. As has already been noted, the position has been substantially altered in this respect by the 1991 Act, s 2(4)[8].

A guardian also has a right to a child's custody, unless there has been an award of custody excluding the guardian. Although custody is not defined precisely in Scots law, it is taken to be the right of a person to have a child living with him, including control of the child's place of residence[9], education and upbringing[10]. It has always been open for these rights to be challenged, as, for example, a person's control of a child being regarded as injurious to the child[11] and persons claiming an interest may apply to the court[12].

1 *Wilkinson & Norrie* p 363.
2 See, eg, *Linton v Commissioners of Inland Revenue* 1928 SC 209 at 213.
3 *Stair* I, 6, 3; Erskine *Institutes* I, 7, 16.
4 See, eg, *Cunningham's Trustees* 1949 SC 275.
5 Trusts (Scotland) Act 1921, s 2.
6 See paras 6.45 and 6.48.
7 See Norrie (1991) 36 JLSS 434.
8 See para 6.89.
9 See *Pagan v Pagan* (1883) 10 R 1072.
10 See *Zamorski v Zamorska* 1960 SLT (Notes) 26.
11 See eg *Beattie v Beattie* (1883) 11 R 85.
12 Law Reform (Parent and Child) (Scotland) Act 1986, s 3.

Access is the right to have reasonable contact with a child, effectively a modification of the rights of the person having actual custody.

In addition to guardianship, custody and access the definition of parental rights in the 1986 Act includes 'any right or authority relating to the welfare or upbringing of a child conferred on a parent by *any rule of law*'. These non-statutory rights will include such things as control of education and religious upbringing, discipline, choice of name, and choice of nationality[1].

The rights and powers of the guardian are wide and the extension to age 16 of what formerly applied to girls under 12 and boys under 14 may be seen as removing some of the 'rights' children formerly possessed during minority. Despite the changes introduced by the 1991 Act, the law continues to place rather more emphasis on the rights of guardians than on the rights of children in their care.

Capacity of guardians

6.101 A guardian requires to possess legal capacity, although it is not clear from the terms of the 1991 Act if a person aged 16 or 17 can competently act as a guardian. However, section 1(3)(g) permits a person under 16 to be appointed as guardian to any child of his and to exercise parental rights in relation to any child of his own, and *Wilkinson & Norrie* submit (at p 382) that the age limit on a person being appointed guardian other than to his own child is 16.

Formerly, nomination of a person below the age of majority was not null, but only became effective when the nominee reached majority[2]. Presumably it must also now be competent to nominate as a guardian a person under 16 or, alternatively, to nominate a person as guardian conditional upon attaining the age of 16.

The court's role

6.102 Any person claiming an interest in respect of an order for parental rights may make an application to the court under section 3 of the 1986 Act. The court may make such order as it thinks fit in the circumstances and in any proceedings will regard the welfare of the child as the paramount consideration and will not make an order unless it is satisfied that to do so will be in the best interests of the child[3].

Thus, it seems that, in the case of a testamentary appointment, the court could overrule a parent's appointment if, in all the circumstances, this was deemed to be appropriate.

---

1 See Scot Law Com Report no 135 (1992) p 7.
2 10 *Stair Memorial Encyclopaedia* para 1063.
3 1986 Act, s 3(2).

Appointment of guardian by parents on death

6.103   Section 4 of the Law Reform (Parent and Child) (Scotland) Act 1986 was amended by Schedule 1 to the 1991 Act to read as follows:

'The parent of a child may appoint any person to be guardian of the child after his death, but any such appointment shall be of no effect unless the appointment is in writing and signed by the parent; and the parent at the time of his death was guardian of the child or would have been such guardian if he had survived until after the birth of the child.'

There is, therefore, a double test. Firstly, the appointment must be in writing and signed. Secondly, the parent must be, or would have been but for his death, the child's guardian. In the case of married parents, the surviving parent usually will continue as sole guardian, although the predeceasing parent can appoint a guardian to act jointly with the survivor.

When the parents are unmarried, only the mother can appoint a testamentary guardian. A parent who does not have parental rights, and therefore is not the child's guardian, cannot appoint a testamentary guardian. Thus, if a father does not have parental rights, for example because he has never had them or has been deprived of them by process of law, he cannot appoint a guardian.

If parents are separated or divorced, either's ability to appoint a testamentary guardian will depend upon whether or not he or she has parental rights over the child. Adoptive parents are able to appoint testamentary guardians to their adopted children. If a father does not have parental rights, for example because he was not married to the child's mother, it would be open to him to apply to the court for parental rights following her death. In that way he might become sole guardian of the child or, if the mother had appointed a testamentary guardian, joint guardian with her appointee.

Section 4 of the 1986 Act does not permit a testamentary guardian to make a similar appointment in the event of his or her own death.

A will is a convenient, and arguably the best, place to record the appointment of a guardian. If parents do not wish to incorporate the appointment in their wills, they can of course do so by separate letter or subsequent codicil (see para 3.31 and Chapter 8). The Act's requirement is simply that the appointment be 'in writing and signed by the parent'.

There is old authority to the effect that a legacy given to a guardian appointed by will is forfeited if the nominee does not accept office[1]. In these circumstances the following could be added to any legacy to a guardian, if the testator wishes to avoid such forfeiture occurring:

'. . ..whether or not A accepts office as guardian of my children.'

The possible appointment of testamentary guardians is an issue of such importance that it should be included in any aide-memoire for taking instructions (see Chapter 9).

---

1 *Scrimzeour v Wedderburn* (1675) Mor 6357.

Obtaining consent

6.104 Before appointing guardians, parents should be advised to ensure that the intended guardians would be willing to act. If a guardian is not asked whether he is willing to act, he is perfectly entitled to decline[1]. This possibility should be the real incentive for the parent to discuss matters with the intended guardian first. After all, guardianship is a weighty responsibility.

Commonly, parents will wish to appoint a married couple as guardians. Both, or the survivor, can accept office. If both accept and one subsequently dies, the survivor will continue as guardian. If two or more are appointed, any one or more can accept, unless the deceased has indicated to the contrary[2].

How to appoint guardians in a will

6.105 It is relatively unlikely that one parent will wish to appoint a guardian to act jointly with the surviving parent. Equally, it is unlikely that such appointee would wish to act, or feel comfortable in acting, along with the surviving parent. This, however, is perfectly competent under Scots law, and the result can be produced unintentionally by careless drafting.

(1) *Appointment of same guardian(s) by both parents*

6.106 Commonly, both parents are likely to wish to appoint the same person or persons as guardian or guardians. If so, the following forms would be suitable.

If the wills of both parents contain a *commorientes* clause (see paras 5.15–5.18):

'In the event of my [husband/wife] so failing to survive me, I appoint A [OR and B] to be guardian [OR guardians] to my children'[3].

If the parents' wills do not contain a *commorientes* clause:

'In the event of my said [husband/wife] failing to survive me [OR predeceasing me], I appoint A [OR and B] to be guardian [OR guardians] to my children.'

Were one parent to survive (in the case of a *commorientes* clause by the specified period), the appointment in the predeceasing parent's will would be ineffective, while the appointment in the surviving parent's will would be effective on his or her subsequent death.

If both parents were to die simultaneously (or within the period specified in the *commorientes* clause) there would be a valid appointment flowing from both wills.

(2) *Appointment of different guardian(s) by each parent*

6.107 In the circumstances described in the preceding paragraph, if parents each had appointed a different guardian or guardians and both died simultaneously

---

1 Erskine *Principles* I, 7, 16; *Stair* I, 6, 11.
2 *Young v Watson* (1740) Mor 16346; *Drummore v Somervil* (1742) Mor 14703.
3 See S3.10, S4.9, S5.15, S6,16, S7.13, S8.11, S10.14.

(or within the period specified in the *commorientes* clause) the result would be the appointment of joint guardians.

If parents each wish to appoint a different person or persons as guardian or guardians, it should be established if it is their intention that such a person or persons should act along with the surviving parent, in which case sub-paragraph (3) below would be appropriate, or if such guardian or guardians should act only in the event of the death of the other parent, in which case sub-paragraph (4) below is appropriate.

(3) *Appointment of guardian(s) to act jointly with surviving parent*

6.108   If a parent wishes to appoint a guardian or guardians to act jointly with the surviving parent, the following form would be suitable:
'I appoint A [OR and B] to be guardian [OR guardians] to my children, along with my [husband/wife].'
This would also enable such guardian or guardians, on the event of the surviving parent's death, to act jointly with the surviving parent's nominee or nominees, if any.

(4) *Appointment of guardian(s) to act only after death of other parent*

6.109   A parent who is content for the other parent to have sole parental rights and responsibilities after his or her death, still may wish to ensure the appointment of his or her own nominee or nominees on the event of the other parent's subsequent death. Provision for the appointment of a guardian or guardians to take effect only after the surviving parent's death is perfectly competent[1]. In such cases, the following form of words would be suitable:
'In the event of my said [husband/wife] and I both having died before any of our children has attained the age of legal capacity, I appoint A [OR and B] to be guardian [OR guardians] to such child or children until they respectively attain the age of legal capacity, along with anyone similarly appointed by my said [husband/wife].'
This clause would accommodate not only the appointment of the same guardian or guardians by both parents, but also the appointment of a different person or persons by each parent. If different persons were appointed, following the surviving parent's death the result would be joint guardianship involving the nominees of both parents.

(5) *Appointment of guardian(s) by single parent having parental rights*

6.110   In the cases of unmarried mothers, widows or widowers the position is simple and the following form of words would be suitable:
'I appoint A [OR and B] to be guardian (OR guardians] to my children.'

---

1 *Lockhart v Ellis* (1682) Mor 16301.

Proposals for reform

6.111   The principal recommendations in respect of guardianship within the Scottish Law Commission's Report on Family Law[1] acknowledge that existing family law emphasises parental rights rather than parental responsibilities. It concludes that there should be a statutory statement of parental responsibilities, including the responsibility to safeguard and promote a child's health, development and welfare, to provide direction and guidance in a manner appropriate to the child's stage of development (in both cases until the age of 18), to maintain personal relations and direct contact with the child on a regular basis, if not living with the child (in both cases until the age of 16) and to act as the child's legal representative, administering in the interests of the child any property belonging to the child (clause 1).

The Report also recommends that it should be made clear that parents have parental rights, parallel to their responsibilities, in order to enable them to fulfil these responsibilities (clause 2(1) and (4)).

Specific recommendations include the following:

(1)   Existing parental rights of guardianship, custody and access should be replaced by new rights expressed in such a way as to reflect the policy that both parents, even after separation, normally should have a continuing parental role to play in relation to the upbringing of a child.

(2)   In the absence of any court order to the contrary, both parents should have parental responsibilities and rights, whether or not they are or have been married to each other (clause 3(1)). This would remove the existing discrimination against unmarried fathers and their children.

(3)   It should continue to be the position that where two or more persons have any parental right, each may exercise that right without the consent of the other(s), unless any deed or decree provides to the contrary (clause 2(2)).

(4)   Any person taking a major decision relating to a child in the exercise of any parental responsibility or right should, whenever practical, establish the child's views and give them due consideration, having regard to the child's age and maturity, there being a presumption that a child of the age of 12 or more would have sufficient maturity to express a reasonable view (clause 6).

(5)   For the avoidance of doubt, it should be made clear that a child may apply for an order relating to parental responsibilities or rights, guardianship or the administration of its property (clause 11(3)).

(6)   A guardian should have the same responsibilities in relation to a child as a parent has and to enable the guardian to fulfil these responsibilities a guardian should have the same parental rights as a parent (clause 7(5)).

(7)   The guardian of a child should be able to appoint another individual to take his place as the child's guardian in the event of his death (clause 7(2)).

(8)   If two or more persons are appointed as guardians any one or more should

1   Scot Law Com no 135 (1992).

be able to accept office, even if both or all do not accept, unless the appointment expressly provides otherwise (clause 7(4)).

(9)   The parent or guardian acting as a child's legal representative in relation to a child's property should no longer be regarded as a trustee for the purposes of the Trusts (Scotland) Act 1921, Schedule 2 and the right of legal representation in relation to a child should carry with it the right to do any act in relation to the child's property which the child is legally incapable of doing but could have done if of full age and capacity (clause 10(3)(b)).

(10)   A parent or guardian, who as legal representative has administered or dealt with a child's property, should continue to be liable to account to the child on ceasing to be the child's legal representative for his intromissions with the property. In accounting, the parent or guardian should not be liable in respect of any of the child's funds used in the proper discharge of the parent's or guardian's responsibility to promote the child's welfare. In such administration the parent or guardian should be required to act in the way a reasonable or prudent person would act on his own behalf (clause 10).

PROVISIONS FOR BOTH SPOUSE AND CHILDREN

6.112   The majority of the Styles presented envisage either a division between spouse and children; or provision for spouse along with a destination-over in favour of children. As the specific Styles form the basis for more general discussion of the objects of bequest, they are dealt with elsewhere.

Style S4 envisages a division of residue between spouse and children, while Style S3 provides for the whole residue to go to the spouse with a destination-over in favour of children. The latter could readily be adapted to provide for the residue to be split into fractional shares, or alternatively by providing for a legacy in favour of either spouse or children, with the residue to go to the other.

A particular factor in the decision to make a division between spouse and children in larger estates is the desire to utilise the inheritance tax rules to maximum advantage, if this is feasible. Basically, in a situation where both spouse and children exist, this involves leaving the amount of the nil rate band for inheritance tax to children, with only the amount above that threshold passing to the spouse. This prevents only a single nil rate band being available on the eventual deaths of both parents, on the assumption that the whole estate will pass to the children on the death of the second spouse. The bequest to children can be direct, but can also be in trust, with that decision depending to a great extent on their age (see paras 6.43–6.62). If there is a fear of insufficient estate being left to provide for a spouse, that spouse can be included among the beneficiaries of a discretionary trust, which can be used to utilise the nil rate band available to the testator (see paras 5.96–5.107).

If the testator does wish to split the estate between spouse and children, the first decision is really the proportions which each are to take. Much would depend on the age of the parties, with the likely preference being in favour of full provision for the spouse when children are young.

Linked to the question of amounts is the manner in which division is to be achieved – by specified legacies (perhaps including legacies of specific assets), or by splitting the residue into appropriate fractions, or by a combination of both. Again, there is nothing of significance in such a split being desired among members of an immediate family. They are, in this respect, no different from other legatees.

Finally, it will require to be decided whether any legacies require to be bound up with trust provisions. Again, this will be linked with the questions relating to amount and the age of the parties. For example, the amount to be given to a spouse may best be achieved by the use of a liferent, while the amount to go to children may be best included within an accumulation and maintenance trust.

Often, these decisions will be clear and the end result will only be a simple will. If the testator does require a more complex division as between spouse and children this can usually be achieved without difficulty. A combination of legacies and a fractional division of residue, perhaps involving trusts where appropriate, will achieve the desired result.

PROVISIONS FOR CHILDREN TO THE EXCLUSION OF SPOUSE

6.113 As most of the Styles presented here envisage the existence of a full family, including spouse and children, provisions for children are generally only included along with provisions for a spouse, or brought into effect on the failure of a spouse. However, it is entirely possible that a testator who has, or who has had, a spouse may wish only to benefit his children (at least from residue). This may be because a spouse has predeceased, or because spouses have divorced or separated, or even because the testator considers that sufficient provision has already been made for the spouse, either from that spouse's own resources or because of lifetime provisions made by the testator. It is also possible that the testator may never have had a spouse but has had children for whom he wishes to make provision in his will.

In any such situation, all of the Styles presented which provide for both spouse and children can readily be adapted to provide for children alone. This will of course happen automatically on the death of the spouse prior to that of the testator. If the testator wishes to omit any reference to a spouse from the outset, any specific purpose referring to a spouse (for example, S3.5, S7.5, S8.5, S10.6, S11.5) should be omitted; and in any purpose which currently contains a destination-over for children (for example, S3.6, S7.6, S8.6, S10.7, S11.6), the words 'If my said wife [or husband] does not survive me for 30 days, but in such event only . . .' should be omitted. Such alterations will make it clear that the whole estate is to go directly to the children of the testator.

To an even greater extent than applies when attempts are made to exclude children from benefit when providing for the testator's spouse alone, it may be extremely difficult to exclude the spouse when attempting to provide exclusively for children. This is because of the ability of the spouse to claim legal rights, particularly as it seems likely that some such right for a spouse is likely to continue or even be strengthened under any potential replacement for the legal rights system.

There is a limit to what can be done to avoid legal rights of the spouse. In particular, the strategy which exists in smaller estates to avoid children claiming legal rights by creating complete or partial intestacy (see paras 6.30–6.32) will not be effective in avoiding a spouse's legal rights, because children have no equivalent of prior rights on intestacy.

In such circumstances, if it is considered vital to attempt to exclude any such claims by a spouse, consideration must be given to the other strategies suggested in paragraphs 6.30–6.32. In particular, consideration could be given to the use of effective trusts created during life, rather than relying on testamentary instructions[1].

CONDITIO SI TESTATOR SINE LIBERIS DECESSERIT

6.114 The provisions for children in the Styles presented direct that the legacy is to go to named children 'and any other children of mine'. This wording prevents the operation of the *conditio si testator sine liberis decesserit*.

This may be vital, in that the effect of the *conditio* being successfully invoked is that the will is revoked, with intestacy the usual result. This *conditio* comes into operation where a testator has made a will containing no provision for his children who may be born after the will has been made. The idea behind the rule is that a testator must be presumed to have intended to provide for such children; and if he has failed to do so, any such child can invoke the *conditio* to revoke the will. Only a child in this category can invoke the *conditio*, which does not apply where other heirs on intestacy may be involved[2].

It should be particularly noted that the effect of the *conditio* being invoked is not to bring after-born children into the same position as those born before the making of the will, but is simply to revoke the entire will.

The presumption leading to revocation might be thought to apply most strongly where the testator dies shortly after the birth of the child or children attempting to invoke it, but a long gap will not necessarily prevent revocation taking place[3].

The *conditio* does, however, involve merely a presumption, not an absolute rule. The presumption can be rebutted, but this will generally require very clear evidence that it should not apply[4].

Given that the presumption can be rebutted, one very clear way for the

---

1 See, in addition to the authorities mentioned in paras 6.30–6.32, *Rowley v Rowley* 1917 1 SLT 16.
2 *Stevenson's Trustees v Stevenson* 1932 SC 657.
3 *Milligan's Judical Factor v Milligan* 1910 SC 58.
4 See, for example, *Stuart-Gordon v Stuart-Gordon* (1899) 1 F 1005.

testator to do this would be to make specific provision in his will. This could most obviously be done by making a fresh will excluding specifically children whom the testator desires not to take, but it would also be possible to achieve the exclusion of the *conditio* in anticipation.

This could be done by adding the phrase 'notwithstanding the birth or adoption of any further children' in substitution for 'and any other children of mine', where the latter phrase currently occurs in the Styles presented.

Perhaps more comprehensively, a declaration could be included as a separate purpose:

> 'I declare that this will is not be revoked by any claim made as a result
> of the birth or adoption of any child to or by me after the will has been
> executed.'

It should be noted that the Scot Law Com Report on Succession[1] recommends the abolition of this *conditio*.

PROVISION FOR MORE REMOTE DESCENDANTS

6.115 Although the more likely scenario is that a testator would wish to provide for his own children, it is quite common to wish to pass on estate to the next generation or even beyond. This could be done in isolation, or in combination with provisions for children. Style S4 is an example of this, with a legacy to grandchildren (S4.3) and provision for half the residue to go to children (S4.4).

Of course, the form of destination-over to issue presented in most of the Styles would mean that the estate or the part dealt with goes to descendants at the nearest surviving level in each branch of the family; but such a destination-over will only come into effect if closer generations have died out. It may be envisaged that the testator wishes to provide directly for more remote descendants than his children.

There are a number of possible reasons for this, but the primary one is likely to be that at the time of drafting the will the testator's own children have been sufficiently independently successful so as not to require, in the testator's estimation at least, any benefit from his estate. Linked to this reason may be tax considerations – it may be desired to avoid a possible double charge to inheritance tax on a transfer to children followed relatively quickly by further transfers to succeeding generations.

Alternatively, it may be that the testator has fallen out with his children, but specifically does not wish to cut remoter issue out of benefitting from his estate. In this last case particularly, it may well be that the remoter issue are still young. In such a case, trust provisions are really essential, because the testator will be certain to wish to prevent the parents of those more remote descendants obtaining control of the estate bequeathed.

In any case where direct provision is being made for descendants beyond the level of children, a number of problems arise. These chiefly relate to ascertaining exactly who are to be included in the class of beneficiaries to take and when that class is to be defined. Such considerations also arise when one is dealing with

---

1 No 124 (1990) para 4–49.

issue of a person other than the testator. As the importance of such matters is not confined to legacies involving children or more remote descendants, they are dealt with further below (see paras 6.120–6.121). In addition, particular points relating to the Style of accumulation and maintenance trust required for a class which may not be closed at the date of the testator's death are dealt with above (see paras 6.81–6.84).

6.116 One vital point with any bequest beyond the level of children is the *proportion* in which beneficiaries are to take. For example, if a legacy is to grandchildren, are they to take in equal shares for each grandchild (whenever that number is to be ascertained), or are the shares in the estate still to depend on the number of children? Furthermore, if destinations-over to issue beyond grandchildren are involved, how is a division at the level beyond grandchildren to be made? These are really questions as to whether division is to be made *per capita* or *per stirpes*, which is dealt with at paragraphs 5.08–5.14. There is really nothing particular about arriving at this decision where destinations-over involve a level more remote than the grandchildren, where the grandchildren are to be primary beneficiaries, but the division as between the grandchildren themselves may require special consideration.

There are really two alternatives. If all grandchildren are to take equally, the wording should simply follow that used when dealing with children:

> '. . . to such of my grandchildren A, B and C and any other grand-children of mine as shall survive me equally among them if more than one. . .'

There is no need to name the grandchildren, although this may be helpful for identification purposes. This clause takes no account of grandchildren born after the testator's death, a problem which is addressed further below. With such a clause, a destination-over to issue of grandchildren can follow, in virtually the same form as is used for children. If, however, the primary division is to be based on the number of *children* possessed by the testator, the wording can become rather more complex. The problem is to ensure that if grandchildren predecease without leaving issue, accretion applies firstly within families of the same parent and then within the entire class of grandchildren. It is thought that the appropriate result can most readily be achieved by making an initial division based on the testator's own children, and then including specific declarations. The following wording is offered, without particular enthusiasm, for a situation where the testator has three children:

> 'I direct my executors to make over the residue of my estate as to a one third share to such of the children of A as shall survive me, equally among them if more than one; as to a one third share to such of the children of B as shall survive me equally among them if more than one; and as to a one third share to such of the children of C as shall survive me equally among them if more than one, declaring that:
>
> (1)   Should any of the children of A, B or C predecease me leaving issue (including adopted issue) who shall survive me, each member of a generation of issue shall share equally in the part of

my estate, both original and accresced which would have fallen to its parent if in life;

(2) Should any of the children of A, B or C predecease me without leaving issue, the surviving issue (including adopted issue) of my child who was the ancestor of the predeceasing child shall share in the part of my estate which would have fallen to such predeceasing child in the same proportions in which such issue shall share in the remainder of my estate;

(3) Should any of the children of A, B or C predecease me and no issue of my child who was the ancestor of the predeceasing child survive, the surviving issue (including adopted issue) of my other children shall share in the part of my estate which would have fallen to such predeceasing children in the same proportion in which such issue shall share in the remainder of my estate.'

It is possible that this long and complex clause merely instructs what the law would to a large extent imply in any event, at least to the extent of declaration (2). The basic provision involves legacies to three classes of beneficiary (the children of A, B and C respectively). Accretion within each class would apply in any event. However, declarations (1) and (3) are more important, directing destinations-over which would not be automatically imported (for instance by the *conditio si institutus sine liberis decesserit*). Most importantly, these declarations prevent intestacy in the event of complete failure of one class of beneficiaries, and provide guidance on what is to happen where a sub-branch of a family dies out.

A clause of this type may be useful in any situation where division is required between a number of beneficiaries, but on failure of any of these beneficiaries or their issue, the bequest is to go to the survivors among the other primary beneficiaries and *their* issue. The exact wording in any such case would require care to cope with the various possible eventualities.

6.117 A particular problem which can arise especially with legacies to issue more remote than children is whether those born after the testator's death are to be included. This can be a very real problem. It is dealt with in the context of the accumulation and maintenance trust for grandchildren in the comments on Style S7A above (see paras 6.81–6.84) and in paragraph 6.123 below.

CONDITIO SI INSTITUTUS SINE LIBERIS DECESSERIT

6.118 In the Styles presented, where provision is made for the testator's children or remoter issue, provision is also made for a destination-over in the event of any of the primary beneficiaries failing to survive (see, for example, S3.6). This destination-over takes the form of representation by issue of the primary beneficiaries on a *per stirpes* basis (see paras 5.08–5.14).

The *conditio si institutus sine liberis decesserit* is in many ways equivalent to a common law rule achieving the same result.

The *conditio si institutus* is an equitable doctrine. It applies where a testator has left any form of legacy to particular types of legatee. The doctrine directs that the children or other issue of any such legatee should take in the event of the legatee failing to survive, in preference to any other conditional institute named in the will, any residuary legatee or any intestate beneficiary[1].

The classes of legatee affected by the doctrine are very limited. It affects the testator's children and remoter descendants; and his nephews and nieces if the testator stood *in loco parentis* to such beneficiaries[2]. However, the latter condition is generally felt to be meaningless. The testator has put himself in such a position by making provision for nephews and nieces in the first place, and no evidence of lifetime interest in the nephews and nieces is required[3]. Indeed, evidence will be required to rebut the presumption that the doctrine applies to nephews and nieces[4]. The doctrine will not be extended to relationships beyond those mentioned, for instance to siblings, however close the practical relationship with the testator[5].

The doctrine now extends to illegitimate and adopted children, and illegitimate and adopted children of those within the relevant classes of legatee (see paras 6.37–6.43). It does not extend to step-children, unless these have been adopted[6].

The premise behind the *conditio si institutus sine liberis decesserit* is a presumption that the testator *would* have made provision for those instituted by its application, if he had considered the matter. Like all such presumptions, it can be rebutted. This is of relevance in drafting wills, because of course one of the main sources of evidence of the testator's intentions on such a matter will be the will when it comes into effect.

6.119 It is important to note that the mere existence of a survivorship clause or a destination-over in favour of persons other than those who would take under the *conditio si institutus* does not exclude its operation[7]. The same applies to the fact that the testator may have known of the death of the descendant or nephew or niece, but did not alter the terms of his will.

In these circumstances, express exclusion of the issue of the relevant legatees is the most effective way of excluding the *conditio si institutus*. This can be achieved by inserting, after the primary bequest, the following words:

> '. . . but expressly excluding any issue of my children in the event of any of my children predeceasing me, declaring that should all of my children predecease me, this legacy shall pass to A.'

This wording can be adapted to cover any class of descendant affected, or

---

1 *Bogie's Trustee v Christie* (1882) 9 R 453; *Hall v Hall* (1891) 18 R 690; *Waddell's Trustees v Waddell* (1896) 24 R 189; *McDougal's Trustee v Heinemann* 1918 SC (HL) 6; *Knox's Executor v Knox* 1941 SC 532; *Devlin's Trustees v Breen* 1945 SC (HL) 27; *Miller's Trustees v Miller* 1958 SC 125.
2 *Hall v Hall* (1891) above.
3 *Bogie's Trustees v Christie* (1882) above.
4 *Knox's Executor v Knox* 1941 above.
5 *Hall v Hall*, above.
6 *Sinclair's Trustees v Sinclair* 1942 SC 362.
7 *Devlin's Trustees v Breen* above; *McGregor's Trustees v Gray* 1969 SLT 355.

nephews or nieces. The scheme envisaged by such wording is that if some children survive the testator, the whole legacy will accresce to the survivors; if all predecease, provision is made for an ultimate destination-over. If such a legacy is not, however, to accresce to the survivors of the class, the final declaration should read:

> '. . .declaring that should any of my children predecease me, the
> share or shares of such predeceasing child or children shall pass to A.'

It *may* be sufficient to exclude the *conditio si institutus* if the will makes some other form of provision for the issue of the relevant legatees, but this should not be relied upon[1].

Other inconclusive factors relevant to the exclusion of the *conditio si institutus* would be the fact that legatees were called by name rather than by a class designation, especially if provision is made for the issue of some beneficiaries but not of others. But again, if it is truly essential to exclude the *conditio si institutus* there is no real substitute for doing so directly.

There may be good reasons for doing this, particularly where nephews and nieces are involved, or perhaps where substantial lifetime provisions have already been made for those who would take under the *conditio si institutus*. The matter should certainly be considered when taking instructions.

It should be noted that if the relevant legatee is dead at the time when the will is drafted, the *conditio si institutus* will generally not take effect[2].

If the *conditio si institutus does* apply, there are complicated issues as to whether those benefitting under it take only the share which would have been taken by their predeceasing parent, or accresced shares in addition[3].

PROVISIONS FOR RELATIVES OTHER
THAN DESCENDANTS

6.120 Although provisions for spouse and children are perhaps the most commonly encountered, a testator may wish to leave all or part of his estate to other classes of relative, either directly or by means of a destination-over on the failure of primary beneficiaries. To some extent, this possibility has already been mentioned in relation to Style S11. However, that Style envisages a spouse being in existence, with a destination-over to brothers and sisters coming into effect only on the failure of the spouse. Legacies to other relatives may be required to meet the primary intentions of certain testators.

Usually the most important point for such a testator will be to avoid the

1 See *McNab v Brown's Trustees* 1926 SC 387; *Paterson v Paterson* 1935 SC (HL) 7; *Douglas's Executors* (1969) 7 M 504.
2 See *Low's Trustees v Whitworth* (1892) 19 R 431; *Travers' Trustees v Macintyre* 1934 SC 520; *Miller's Trustees v Miller* 1958 SC 125.
3 On this matter, see, for example, *Macdonald* p 116 and authorities there cited; and *Henderson* pp 368–370.

consequences of intestacy, notably the rule whereby on the failure of children, siblings and parents will share in the intestate estate[1].

Most testators will generally not wish to pass estate on to members of a generation older than themselves, although special provision may be required for persons to some extent dependent on the testator. A testator may also be quite happy to pass estate back to parents when such estate has been derived from them, particularly where the testator has reason to believe that he is likely to predecease older relatives and has no suitable younger relatives who may be able to benefit. An example of this kind of situation can be found in S6.5, which envisages the liferent of a house for the testator's mother. The consequences of such a provision for inheritance tax should be borne in mind, as the house in that case would be aggregated with the mother's personal estate on her eventual death.

There is nothing particularly special about legacies to relatives other than descendants. If provision is required for older relatives, it is perhaps more appropriate to include specific legacies without destinations-over rather than residuary bequests. The reason for this is that on the failure of such older relatives, legacies will fall into residue rather than intestacy.

It is particularly important in bequests to older relatives to specify the relationship. A mother or father by adoption will be included where those terms are used and this will also be the case where the word 'parent' is employed. The testator's natural parents will be excluded in such circumstances. Further ancestors will also be traced through the adoptive parents[2]. However, more care is required where, for instance, only one parent has adopted the testator and it is intended to benefit the other 'parent'. In such a case, reference by name is really essential.

Equal care should be taken with step-relationships, where long-standing practical arrangements may not reflect the legal position. Clarification of who was intended to be the beneficiary can cause much trouble and distress after the death. Once more it is best to include specification by name. This can perhaps be accompanied by an explanation (such as 'to A, husband of my mother B and commonly referred to as my father'). It is appreciated that obtaining such delicate information may be somewhat difficult. If, however, the testator gives some indication that all may not be as it appears on the surface, it is really essential to clarify the position.

6.121   For a testator without spouse or descendants, the most likely beneficiaries are his siblings, if any. A suitable form of words would be:

'I direct my executors to make over the residue of my estate to such of my brothers and sisters A, B and C and any other brothers and sisters of mine as shall survive me equally among them if more than one, declaring that should any of my brothers or sisters predecease me leaving issue (including adopted issue) who shall survive me, each

---

1 Succession (Scotland) Act 1964, s 2(1)(b).
2 See the Succession (Scotland) Act 1964, s 23(1)(a); and paras 6.39–6.42 above.

member of a generation of issue of such predeceasing brother or sister
shall share equally in the part of my estate, both original and accresced, which would have fallen to its parent if in life.'

This is simply an adapted version of the form of legacy used for children in the
Styles. Provision for the possibility of brothers and sisters coming into existence
in future should perhaps only be included while this remains biologically possible. However, the possibility of future half-brothers and half-sisters should be
borne in mind, as should the possibility of the testator's parents adopting new
brothers and sisters for the testator in future. These, however, may be circumstances in which the testator would specifically wish to restrict provision for
siblings to those actually in existence at the date of drafting the will.

It may also be specifically desired to exclude nephews and nieces from benefit
where, for instance, the testator has not had much contact with such relatives. In
such a case, a different destination-over is important, because otherwise the
rules of intestacy may operate to take the share of predeceasing siblings to their
children if such siblings should predecease the testator. The form of legacy set
out above is a class gift and in the absence of any destination-over accretion will
operate to take the whole legacy to surviving siblings. Once more, if that is not
the desired outcome, specific provision should be made to prevent accretion (see
paras 5.03–5.14).

It is likely that a bequest to any other class of relatives (as opposed to named
individual relatives, who would for these purposes simply be treated in the same
way as any other named individuals) will also constitute a class gift. Examples
will include 'nephews and nieces' and 'cousins'. Just as with direct legacies to
grandchildren, great care is needed to specify the proportion in which the estate
is to be divided, whether destinations-over are to operate and the effect of such
destinations-over on proportionate division. All that has been said in paragraphs
6.115–6.117 above applies equally to legacies to other classes of relative. It is
perhaps true to say that a *per capita* division may be the more likely intention
with more distant relatives than would be the case with direct descendants.

It is also the case that legacies to classes of relatives may involve difficulties in
ascertaining exactly which beneficiaries are to take from among possible
members of that class. While such problems can arise with bequests to any
multiplicity of beneficiaries, they are particularly acute and common where
relatives are involved. Some of these problems are addressed in the succeeding
paragraphs.

ASCERTAINING BENEFICIARIES FROM WITHIN
A CLASS

6.122   There are a number of possible problems which become particularly
acute when legacy is left to a class of issue beyond children, whether directly or
by means of a destination-over, and whether issue of the testator or otherwise.
However, similar problems can also arise with any legacy to a class.

Where a legacy is left to children, with a declaration that the issue of pre-deceasing children shall take their parent's share of the estate, a question which might arise is whether the issue of children already dead at the date of making the will would take. The general answer to this question is in the affirmative, despite the apparent futurity implied in the phrase '*should* any of my children predecease me leaving issue'[1]. The rights of such issue do not extend to a right to invoke the *conditio si institutus sine liberis decesserit*, however.

The testator will probably know whether any of his own children are already dead at the time of drafting the will. The normal phrasing used in provisions for children (see, for example, S3.6) in the Styles presented envisages actually naming the children who will take. With this type of wording, therefore, the position should be addressed directly when drafting the will. If issue of children already dead at the time of drafting the will are to take, the simplest form of wording would probably be to omit specific references to named children and references to any other children of the testator, so that the primary legacy would read: '. . . to such of my children as shall survive me equally among them if more than one'. The fact that the declaration as to any of the children predeceasing contains words of futurity will not then prevent the issue of a child already deceased at the date of the will taking on the death of testator.

If it is considered necessary to deal with this situation more specifically (and this may be more desirable on the grounds of clarity and reliability), the following form of words would be suitable:

'I direct my executors to make over the residue of my estate to the survivors of my issue as follows: one equal share to my son A, one equal share to my daughter B, one equal share to be divided among the children of my deceased daughter C and (if necessary) one equal share to each other child of mine, declaring that should any of my issue predecease me leaving issue (including adopted issue) who shall survive me, each member of a generation of issue of such predeceasing issue shall share equally in the part of my estate, both original and accresced, which would have fallen to its parent if in life.'

This rather complex clause is a class gift, to the testator's children and the children of his daughter C. These children of C form a sub-class. The wording would mean that if any issue predecease without leaving issue of their own, accretion would take place within the appropriate class or sub-class. The reference to an 'equal share' rather than a specific fraction prevents the need to specify an exact number of shares. This also allows provision to be made for any future children that the testator may have.

This type of clause can readily be adapted to cater for issue other than those of the testator; or for other types of class gift.

6.123   Where there is a legacy to a class of beneficiaries other than the testator's own children, one vital problem is defining when that class is to close. The

---

1 *Wardlaw's Trustees v Lennox's Executors* 1940 SC 286; compare *Stuart's Trustees v Walker* (1905) 12 SLT 801.

number of the testator's own children will be finalised at (or conceivably(!) shortly after) the date of the testator's death. While that number may contract before any later date of vesting, it cannot increase.

But many other classes of beneficiaries can increase in size after the testator's death. Perhaps most obviously, this can apply to the testator's issue at a more remote level than children, but it can also apply to the children of third parties. It can apply to other types of class of beneficiary – for instance, it is possible that in some cases a class consisting of the testator's siblings will increase in size after the testator's death, perhaps as a result of a parent's second marriage or because the siblings cover a large range of ages.

The problem is dealt with to some extent in the case of an accumulation and maintenance trust for grandchildren in Style S7A and paragraphs 6.81–6.84. It is, however, a general problem with legacies to a class and requires some further comment.

The general rule is that unless otherwise specified the class of beneficiaries to take closes at the time when the legacy is to be paid, if the entire legacy is to be paid at one time[1]. This time may be (most usually) the testator's death but it can be later where vesting or payment is postponed. Where vesting or payment is not postponed, the law generally favours the class to benefit being finally ascertained at the earliest possible date. Like all rules of construction, this can be displaced by clear instructions to the contrary.

Various possibilities occur. It may be that the testator intends to restrict the class to those alive at the date of drafting the will – if that is the (somewhat unlikely) intention, it is easy to express, as those to benefit are known at the date of drafting and can be referred to by name or by reference to, say, a number of children. As this would be an unusual way of restricting a class it should be made very clear, perhaps as follows:

'To A, B and C, [being] the children of D as at the date of this will and expressly excluding any other children of D.'

Conversely, and more commonly, the testator will wish children or issue which come into existence after his death to benefit. This is virtually impossible to achieve if distribution of the whole estate is to take effect on the testator's death. The presumption that children coming into existence at a later date are to be excluded is strong in such a case[2]. This is because it would otherwise be necessary to hold the estate, or part of it, to await the possibility of further beneficiaries coming into existence. There might be no effective time limit on the period in which that possibility could be fulfilled.

The situation can be dealt with if there is a specific legacy to a class of beneficiaries, with distribution of the residue being delayed until sometime after the death of the testator; for instance, on the termination of a liferent or other trust interest. But even here, a limit must be imposed beyond which new beneficiaries coming into existence will not take. This can most readily be stated

---

1 *Wood v Wood* (1861) 23 D 338; *Henderson* pp 189 ff.
2 See, for example, *Stopford Blair's Executors v Heron Maxwell's Trustees* (1872) 10 M 760.

to be the same date as the final distribution of the estate held in trust. Otherwise the problem of uncertainty will remain unresolved.

For example, the following Purpose might be added to Style S5:

'I direct my executors to pay to each of the children of A, born or adopted before the date of my death, or after my death but before the termination of the liferent aftermentioned, the sum of ONE THOUSAND POUNDS, such sums to vest at the later of the date of my death and the date of birth or adoption of any such child, declaring that any such sums vesting after the date of my death shall be payable from the residue of my estate liferented by my wife.'

The complexity of this provision would be increased by a destination-over in favour of issue of A; or provision for accretion in the event of the predecease of any such child without issue. As framed, the issue of any children who have predeceased the testator would not take. It should be borne in mind that any payments from the liferented residue to new beneficiaries will constitute a deemed partial termination of the liferent for inheritance tax purposes, entirely outwith the control of both the liferenter and the trustees. The liferenter's annual exemption may be available to offset this, but notice of its availability must be given by the liferenter to the trustees[1].

6.124 If vesting or even mere payment of the subject of a legacy is postponed until some date after the death of the testator, it is easier to provide for further members of a class coming into existence after that death. Indeed, the presumption implied by law in this situation is that members of a class coming into existence after the death of the testator but before the date of distribution will be intended to benefit.

This applies even if the rights to the legacy in question have vested in the members of the class in existence at the testator's death. If other beneficiaries come into existence, the shares of those who already have a vested right will simply diminish[2].

If vesting is in fact postponed until some date after the testator's death (for instance until the termination of a liferent), beneficiaries born after the death of the testator will be included in any event. The main difference from the position where mere payment is postponed is that if beneficiaries have survived the testator but predeceased the date of vesting, their estates will not benefit.

If a legacy to a class is payable only as and when members of that class attain majority (or presumably some other specified age or date), the class will close when the eldest member of the class attains the appropriate age[3]. This presumption too can be varied; for instance, to provide for the class to close when the *youngest* beneficiary in life at the testator's death attains the appropriate age, as in Style S7A (see para 6.81). The point is that some provision should be made for a

---

1 Inheritance Tax Act 1984, ss 52 and 57.
2 See *Carleton v Thomson* (1867) 5 M (HL) 151; *Murray's Trustee v Murray* 1919 SC 552; *Hickling's Trustees v Garland's Trustees* (1898) 1 F (HL) 7.
3 *Buchanan's Trustees v Buchanan* (1877) 4 R 754; *Scott's Trustees v Scott* 1909 SC 773; *Howden's Trustees v MacPherson* 1911 2 SLT 308.

date at which the class is to close, otherwise it is conceivable that the estate could never be finally wound up.

If a legacy is held in a discretionary trust, it is again likely that beneficiaries added to a class after the testator's death will be entitled to benefit[1]. Once more, however, provision should be made within the terms of the trust for the date at which the class is to close.

Selection by trustees or executors – discretionary provisions

6.125   It is possible for provision to be made for a class of beneficiaries who may or not be relations but to leave the selection among this class and the proportions in which the legacy is to be paid to the discretion of trustees or executors[2]. This aspect has been dealt with to some extent in paragraphs 5.59–5.61, in relation to powers of appointment and discretionary legacies. Discretionary power given to trustees or executors may derive from the establishment of an actual discretionary trust or may arise under a simple legacy or a power of appointment.

S9.5 provides for a two-year discretionary trust (which can readily be extended to last for a longer period). The class to benefit under this provision consists of spouse, issue, spouses of issue and any trust established for such persons. However, such a discretionary trust can be established for, or to include, any type of beneficiaries; for instance, brothers and sisters, their issue and spouses, or the issue of any named person with or without their spouses. The class can also consist of a group of individuals without any relationship between them; or a group of institutions such as charities; or any combination of the above. The point is that as long as the class is sufficiently defined, the actual people from within the class to benefit can be left to the trustees[3]. In such circumstances, a letter from the testator indicating his wishes on the matter would be useful, but is not essential.

The testator cannot pass a complete discretion to trustees or executors as to who is to benefit from any part of his estate[4]. If such a complete discretion is the true desire of the testator an outright bequest should be made to individuals, who may be the same persons as his trustees, accompanied by a letter of request indicating his wishes (see para 5.52–5.53).

More usually, the discretion will be restricted to a particular class of beneficiaries. In all cases, the testator must be certain to define the class who may benefit with sufficient clarity. There is a danger that too great a discretion may render the legacy void from uncertainty[5].

There is also a danger that the testator attempts to allow his trustees to make a will for him by omitting any proper definition of the class to benefit[6]. But if there

---

1 *Potter's Trustees v Allan* 1918 SC 173.
2 The word 'class' is used here in a non-technical sense and may refer to any group of beneficiaries.
3 *Crighton v Grierson* (1828) 3 W & S 329; *Reid's Trustees v Cattanach's Trustees* 1929 SC 727.
4 *Bannerman's Trustees v Bannerman* 1915 SC 398.
5 *Anderson v Smoke* (1898) 25 R 493; *Sutherland's Trustees v Sutherland's Trustee* (1893) 20 R 925; *Salvesen's Trustees v Wye* 1954 SC 440.
6 See, for example, *Grimond v Grimond's Trustees* (1905) 7 F (HL) 90; *Blair v Duncan* (1901) 4 F (HL) 1.

is a class, even a large one, of potential beneficiaries defined, the fact that the trustees are left to select among them as to who should benefit at all and in what proportions will not render the legacy void. An instruction to benefit those members of the class considered 'most deserving' will not defeat the legacy[1]. In general, it is thought that in modern times more discretion will be permitted than would have been the case in the past[2].

Uncertainty as to who is to benefit arises most often where bequests are made for charitable or similar purposes, rather than to a class of relatives or other individuals. Charitable bequests are largely dealt with below (see paras 6.141–6.147).

6.126   If a class of individuals is sufficiently defined when drafting the will, the discretion left to executors or trustees can vary. For instance, the discretion can be limited to deciding *when* shares in the legacy are to go to beneficiaries, not the extent to which they are to share at the end of the day. This is broadly the policy adopted in the accumulation and maintenance trust (Style S7), where those benefitting are to take an equal share, but the trustees have some discretion over how they are to receive it (see paras 6.63–6.85).

The style of discretionary trust presented in Style S9 allows absolute discretion to the trustees, as to the shares in which beneficiaries are to take or whether they are to take at all. This is probably appropriate where a very wide class of beneficiaries is involved, but some restriction may be desired where the discretionary class is more restricted.

For instance, where the beneficiaries are the cousins of the testator or the children of a third party, the testator may desire to insure that a minimum amount or proportionate share goes to each beneficiary. This type of restriction can be achieved by adding a separate declaration, but care is required. For instance, if the testator desires each discretionary beneficiary from a trust to receive a minimum of £10,000, it should be made clear when this is to vest. This might be when each beneficiary attains the age of 18. It should be made clear what is to happen if a beneficiary predeceases the date of vesting of the minimum entitlement; and in particular whether any destination-over applies or whether the trustees' discretion revives in such circumstances.

Although trustees' discretion can be fettered in terms of the will, this can lead to very complex provisions. In such circumstances, it is probably better for specific bequests to be made of amounts or shares over which the trustees' discretion is not to extend. Alternatively, if the testator is less certain of his intentions, full discretion can be left to the trustees but a letter indicating preferences can be left to assist the trustees in their selection of the extent to which individual discretionary beneficiaries are to take.

---

1 *Mitchell's Trustees v Fraser* 1915 SC 350.
2 See 25 *Stair Memorial Encyclopaedia* para 823.

PROVISIONS FOR BENEFICIARIES LACKING CAPACITY

6.127   A provision dealing with beneficiaries lacking capacity appears in most of the Styles (see, for example, S3.7, S4.6, S5.10, S6.11, S7.8, S8.8, S9.6, S10.9). As mentioned above (see paras 6.43–6.45) the provisions noted here give the executors wide flexibility in their dealings with children, among others.

The provisions refer to any part of the testator's estate, which will thus cover not only residue but also legacies. The reference is to a beneficiary who has not attained full legal capacity. Previous versions of this type of provision generally referred to a beneficiary who had not attained the age of 18, but a change was necessary as a result of the passing of the Age of Legal Capacity (Scotland) Act 1991. A person now attains full legal capacity in Scotland at age 16 so a reference to age 18 is not now appropriate (see paras 6.44–6.47).

It would be possible simply to refer to children who had not attained the age of 16. However, Scotland seems somewhat unusual in adopting age 16 as the age of full capacity. For instance, English law retains age 18 for these purposes and thus Scottish executors will quite often be faced by non-Scottish beneficiaries of 16 or 17 who do not have full legal capacity. The problem existed even prior to the passing of the 1991 Act in relation to jurisdictions which retained an age of full legal capacity greater than 18, but such jurisdictions were not so frequently encountered. This provision is a useful means of dealing with such beneficiaries.

If an age greater than 16 is in fact specified in such a clause, then there will simply be a continuation of the bare trust which will be deemed to have existed since the testator's death. There may be no real practical difference from the situation which applied before the beneficiary attained age 16. Many 16-year-old beneficiaries will not in fact know or be advised as to their rights. While there are many cases where standard wordings in deeds cannot in law receive effect according to their terms (for example, many irritancy provisions), it seems misleading (to testators as well as to beneficiaries) to include an age over 16. The executors might be at some risk of a claim by beneficiary over 16 if losses were suffered before payment.

6.128   It should be noted that the reference to full legal capacity is wider in its coverage than just children. It could also apply to an adult *incapax* beneficiary. If such a beneficiary had a curator appointed, then the executors would be bound to pay to the curator; but if there was no curator appointed then the executors could use the protection afforded by this purpose.

This Purpose is often referred to as a 'minor beneficiaries' purpose. This is slightly misleading not only because the beneficiary may be an adult *incapax* beneficiary, but also because although a 16-year-old has full legal capacity, he remains a minor since he has not by then attained majority. The phrase 'minor beneficiaries' does have the benefit of perhaps being slightly more comprehensible to a lay person than the side heading used, 'Beneficiaries lacking capacity', but it seems likely that little explanation would be required for that heading.

On the arrangement set out in the Styles under this provision alone, vesting will be on the testator's death. As there are no other reasons to prevent payment, a beneficiary who is 16 or over and not *incapax* will be entitled to demand payment from the executors. They cannot resist such a demand (see paras 6.46–6.47).

The executors are given power to pay or apply funds for the beneficiary's benefit. They could thus spend funds on aliment for the beneficiary or his education. They could pay funds into a bank or building society account held by the beneficiary, or could invest funds themselves in the beneficiary's name. The exact manner in which such acts are carried out is for the executors to decide.

The executors could retain funds until the beneficiary becomes 16, or perhaps otherwise attains or regains capacity. Although funds falling under this purpose have vested in the beneficiary, the executors can make use of the powers of investment and management granted to them elsewhere in most of the Styles.

Alternatively, in terms of the purpose, the executors could pay over funds to the beneficiary's guardian or custodian. Where the beneficiaries are the testator's own children, then beneficiaries will have lost at least one of their guardians. If the testator is the surviving parent, then minor children will have no formal guardians unless one has been appointed by the parents or by the court. The persons having the custody of the child are included as proper recipients on the beneficiary's behalf.

The receipt of the guardian or custodian is to be a sufficient discharge to the executors.

In the case of an adult *incapax* there might well be no guardian or custodian but the executors could properly expend funds on such a beneficiary's behalf. It is not intended that the purpose permits payment to someone other than a curator with *de facto* physical custody of an adult *incapax*, such as the manager of a nursing home or hospital.

DISABLED AND *INCAPAX* BENEFICIARIES

6.129   The purpose dealing with 'Beneficiaries lacking capacity' contained in most of the Styles directs that if any part of the deceased's estate is held for a beneficiary 'who lacks full legal capacity', the trustees have power to make over any part of the income or capital for the benefit of the beneficiary. The capital is of course to be paid over when full legal capacity is attained. This can be a useful clause in dealing with beneficiaries who have become *incapax* and where the testator has not made other provision for recognising their incapacity. This clause means that the asset may be held to the beneficiary in question and that either income or capital can be made over as and when required at discretion of the trustees. This could preclude the necessity of setting up a curatory if the beneficiary had no other substantial assets.

Generally speaking, provision is made for disabled beneficiaries by way of a trust. The advantages of a trust are obvious, in that the trustees can look after the assets and there is no involvement on the beneficiary's part in the administration of the assets. He is merely in receipt of benefits.

It is quite likely that there will already be a suitable trust in existence for a disabled or *incapax* beneficiary at the time when a will is drafted. If that is the case, then any legacy for such a beneficiary should simply be left to that trust, although this may complicate the tax position of such a trust. However, care should be taken as there may be more than one trust for an *incapax* beneficiary in existence at any one time. If there is any possible doubt, the exact details should be ascertained and specified in the will, for example as follows:

'I direct my executors to pay to the trust established for the benefit of A by his father B by Deed of Trust dated 4th and registered in the books of Council and Session on 8th January 1992, the sum of TEN THOUSAND POUNDS.'

6.130 Alternatively, it may be necessary or preferable to establish an appropriate trust in the will itself. It will be important to consider what type of trust should be set up, particularly in view of the fact that there may be substantial state benefits being paid to the beneficiary which could be lost depending on the type of trust created.

Very often, it would not make sense to set up a liferent trust, as the liferenter would have a *right* to the income which would then be taken into consideration in assessing benefits.

Following the replacement of supplementary benefit by income support, the situation of claimants who are also beneficiaries under a discretionary trust has improved. The rules now state that only income or capital actually made over to the beneficiary by the trustees will be taken into account in ascertaining the benefit due. There is no attempt to imply some form of 'notional' income or capital entitlement which would reduce the social security benefits. The Department of Social Security does not apparently make any distinction between payments from trust income and those from trust capital paid to the beneficiary – it is their character in the hands of the recipient which is relevant. However, it would be important in ascertaining their effect how regularly payments of capital were made.

It seems clear that a one-off payment may be made out of trust income in any tax year to a beneficiary in a discretionary trust. The beneficiary for income tax purposes will be treated as having received income, but for income support purposes will be treated as having received capital. If regular payments are made and the Department of Social Security treated these as income, then obviously the social security benefits received by the beneficiary would reduce pound for pound, although some regular payments will be ignored. These may include provision of groceries, bedclothes, bus passes, and payment of telephone accounts and other household expenses.

It is essential that some thought goes into the establishment and administration of this type of trust to ensure that social security benefits are not lost.

6.131 As a discretionary trust is likely to be appropriate, this can be framed in terms similar to those found at S9.5. These would obviously omit the two-year limitation (see para 5.93 for the alterations necessary to extend the period of discretion). While other possible beneficiaries can be included, it might seem tempting to arrange that only the intended *incapax* beneficiary and any trust established for his benefit were listed as the discretionary beneficiaries. However, if the *incapax* beneficiary then dies and the trust established still contains assets, these will fall into the *testator's* intestacy unless the trustees have available a wider class of beneficiaries to whom final distribution can be made.

This may be one occasion where it is appropriate to include the testator's statutory successors in the class of discretionary beneficiaries, so that the trust can be wound up after the death of the *incapax*. By definition, it is possible that the *incapax* will die intestate and the testator may well prefer to deal further with his legacy in his own will, rather than to rely on the *incapax's* intestate succession. Of course, the discretionary nature of the trust means that the trustees can select from what may be a large number of statutory successors, whereas if the testator's intestacy applied, distribution would be restricted to what the law required in the proportions in which statutory successors must take. Furthermore, other beneficiaries could be included among the discretionary class so as to take the trust fund outwith the testator's intestate succession entirely. Such an extention of the class would commonly include charitable beneficiaries, perhaps working in the same field of disability suffered by the 'primary' discretionary beneficiary.

If the discretionary trust does have a wider class of potential beneficiaries, it is obviously important that a letter of wishes is left to the trustees indicating the testator's primary intentions. However, such a letter will not fetter the discretionary nature of the trust. If the testator insists that the *incapax* beneficiary *must* benefit, the discretionary class should be restricted as indicated at the beginning of this section.

6.132 If it is considered desirable to set up a trust for an *incapax* in a will, it might be asked whether it is not appropriate to set one up which qualifies as a trust for a disabled person, under the Inheritance Tax Act 1984, section 89. That section applies to certain property transferred into settlement after 9 March 1981 and held on trusts:

'(a) under which, during the life of disabled person, no interest in the settled property subsists, and
 (b) which secure that not less than half of the settled property which is applied during his life is applied for his benefit.'

As the terms of such a trust must give no interest in possession (to the disabled person or anyone else), it will necessarily be a discretionary trust in any event.

Difficulties might arise in complying with the second leg; but it is thought that these can be overcome fairly readily. Obviously, the disabled person would require to be included among the class of discretionary beneficiaries. A separate declaration should then be included, as follows:

  '. . . declaring that not less than one half of the Discretionary Fund
  which is applied during the lifetime of A must be applied for the
  benefit of A. . .'

It should be noted that such a declaration affects only capital, not income. This is thought to be permissible[1]. If there are doubts about this, the words 'or income therefrom' can be inserted into the declaration mentioned above. This may be considered desirable by the testator in any event.

It should be noted that in order to benefit from a full capital gains tax annual exemption (the same as that available to individuals), the disabled person must be *entitled* to at least half of the income from the trust property, or no such income may be applied for the benefit of any *other* person[2].

It should also be noted that it is only one half of the fund (or income, if the additional words are inserted), *which is applied in any way* which must be applied for the benefit of the disabled person. In other words, the trustees retain a discretion as to whether the income is to be applied at all. The retention of this discretion is important if state benefits are not to be jeopardised. Of course the income can then be utilised for other beneficiaries within the discretionary class, with capital being available should the disabled beneficiary require it.

6.133   The effect of qualifying under these rules is that for inheritance tax purposes, the disabled person is treated as beneficially entitled to an interest in possession in the settled property[3]. This has a number of consequences, not all of them wholly beneficial. However, the normal discretionary trust regime will not apply, which eliminates 10-year charges or charges on distribution of capital to the disabled person. Transfers to and from the disabled person's own estate will not incur inheritance tax charges. Lifetime transfers (perhaps by other relatives) into such a trust will qualify as potentially exempt transfers. But on the death of the disabled person, the trust fund must be aggregated with his personal estate, as is the case with any trust in which an interest in possession subsists. Similarly, transfers of capital to *other* beneficiaries will be treated as potentially exempt transfers made by the disabled beneficiary.

A disabled person is defined for the purposes of the inheritance tax rules in section 89(4) of the Inheritance Tax Act 1984. A person qualifies if he was, when the property was transferred into settlement:

(a)   incapable, by reason of mental disorder within the meaning of the Mental Health Act 1983, of administering his property;
(b)   in receipt of an attendance allowance; or
(c)   in receipt of disability living allowance under section 71 of the Social Security Contributions and Benefits Act 1992 by virtue of entitlement to the care component at the highest or middle rate.

It should be noted that qualification depends on the condition of the disabled person at the time when the property is settled. Later recovery will not prejudice the status of the trust. However, as a trust set up by a will does not come into effect until the testator's death at the earliest, it may be that the disabled person's condition has changed between the date of drafting the will and the time when

1 See McCutcheon *Inheritance Tax* (3rd edn, 1988) pp 617–618.
2 Taxation of Chargeable Gains Act 1992, Sch 1, para 1(1)(b).
3 Inheritance Tax Act 1984, s 89(2).

the trust comes into effect. It should also be noted that the qualification is not restricted to *mentally*-disabled persons.

This last point illustrates that it might be unwise to rely on meeting conditions for a disabled trust for inheritance tax at the time when death occurs. The advantages of such a trust are limited in any event and must be balanced against possible disadvantages. It is thought that other factors, principally the benefits of pure discretion, will be more relevant when dealing with provisions for a disabled person. It may be possible to bring such provisions within the inheritance tax conditions without too much trouble, but this should rarely be a priority when considering drafting in these particular circumstances.

PROVISIONS FOR OTHER INDIVIDUALS

6.134   If the testator is making provision for individuals unconnected other than by friendship or limited acquaintance, there are a number of matters which require to be considered. This is also the case if the acquaintance runs somewhat deeper, as with effective cohabitants who remain unmarried, particularly if there are no children for whom provision requires to be made.

It may thus be necessary to provide for a cohabitant of the testator, who may be of the same or opposite sex. This possibility has been dealt with to some extent above (see para 6.03). However, one question which is particularly important with a major legacy to a cohabitant (but which is also apposite in relation to any large legacy to an unrelated individual), is what should be done about destinations-over in the event of the primary beneficiary failing to take for any reason.

Where provision is made for relatives, this can generally be done by providing for a class; if no member of the class of relevant relatives survives, the testator will generally be happy for the legacy to go to *other* relatives, perhaps most commonly issue of those nominated in the first place. This is less likely to be the desired course with unrelated individuals who might be chosen as legatees by the testator solely on the basis of their individual personal qualities or attractions to the testator. If the primary beneficiary is an unrelated individual, it may be that a destination-over should be in favour of the primary beneficiary's family or other beneficiaries who might take the primary beneficiary's estate. However, it might equally well be that the testator would prefer completely different individuals or institutional beneficiaries, such as charities, to take in such circumstances. The testator's own family may well be low down any list of priorities. The point is that when a testator leaves a major legacy (residuary or otherwise) to a non-related individual, he may even have it as a main intention to prevent his estate reaching his own family. If that is the case, it is important that destinations-over are provided. If it is really crucial that the testator's own family does not take, it is of course essential to prevent intestacy. This can be done by providing an ultimate destination-over to a charity or other institutional beneficiary.

It may equally be the case that a testator is determined that a legacy to an individual should (in the event of that individual not taking) be disposed of according to that primary beneficiary's own succession, whether testate or intestate. In such a case, some such destination-over in favour of beneficiaries described in paragraphs 6.19–6.24 above will be appropriate.

A major legacy to an unrelated individual may simply be in recognition of the testator's personal relationship with that individual. If the primary beneficary does not take in these circumstances, the testator may be quite happy for the legacy to revert to his own family. However, if the testator has no issue (which is quite likely in circumstances where this type of provision is made), it may still be important to avoid intestacy, perhaps to prevent the estate going (in part) to parents. In these circumstances, it should be clarified exactly what relative the testator wishes to benefit in the event of his primary beneficiary failing to take.

If legacies are left to a range of individuals, consideration will require to be given to questions relating to accretion and survivorship, as with any case where multiple beneficiaries are involved (see paras 5.02–5.14).

PROVISIONS FOR EMPLOYEES

6.135 If a testator is considering making provisions for employees, there are one or two important matters which must be borne in mind. In the first place, is provision to be made for all employees (or perhaps all employees of a particular type, such as domestic servants), employed at a particular time, perhaps the time of the testator's death? In such a case, the provision would simply be for 'all of my employees' or 'all of my domestic servants'. However, there may be problems with identifying who is to take if such legacies are used. There has been some judicial consideration of this matter. 'Servants' may be construed more widely than might be anticipated, perhaps including employees in any capacity[1]. However, 'domestic servants' has been limited to indoor servants and thus might exclude, for example, a gardener or chauffeur[2]. The term 'dependants' should be avoided in this context, as it could refer to members of the testator's family; it has been held in particular circumstances to lead to a legacy being void for uncertainty (see para 6.18).

In these circumstances, it is suggested that more definition is required than a simple generic term such as 'employees' or 'servants'. Examples might include 'to each of my domestic servants (including any chauffeur or gardener) who reside in my property and who are employed by me at the date of my death'; or 'to each of the employees of my engineering business at the date of my death'. Perhaps better still, the employment positions the holders of which are to benefit should be specified in all cases – 'butler', 'housekeeper', or 'mechanics, apprentices and clerks'. Best of all, the employees could be specified by name, but this will not always be possible where the testator wishes to leave legacies to the holders of particular positions regardless of who occupies the positions at the relevant time.

---

1 *Stirling Maxwell's Executors v Grant* (1886) 13 R 1854.
2 *McIntyre v Fairrie's Trustees* (1863) 2 M 96.

6.136 However, with any legacy in favour of employees, the main question is whether the legacy is conditional on the employee being in employment at the time when the legacy is to take effect. The legacies in S2.6(2) and S2.6(3) illustrate this point. The legacy in S2.6(2) only takes effect if the housekeeper is in employment at the date of death; in contrast, that in S2.6(3) is to a gardener and friend who will take whether or not he remains in the position of gardener until the testator's death. This is clear from three factors – the contrast with S2.6(2), the additional designation of the legatee as a 'friend' of the testator and the destination-over in favour of the legatee's son. However, the matter might be in more doubt if such a legacy stood in isolation. The easiest way to avoid such doubts might be to omit the additional designation provided by reference to the employment of the legatee; alternatively a declaration could be added, as follows:

'. . . whether or not he is in my employment at the date of my death.'

More difficulties may exist if it is essential that the legacy *is* conditional on the legatee being in the testator's employment at the relevant time. The case of *Simpson v Roberts*[1] involved a legacy to a housekeeper 'providing she is in my employment at the time of my death; or in that of my husband should he survive me'. The husband did survive his wife; the housekeeper was in his employment until dismissal on his second marriage, although she would have been willing to continue in employment if asked. It was held that the housekeeper was entitled to her bequest, as she had done all in her power to fulfil the condition, but had been prevented by the act of another. It is thought that the situation would be different if the dismissal had been carried out by the testator, or the housekeeper had resigned of her own accord. If it is desired to put the matter beyond any doubts caused by the case, the following form of wording (which also takes account of the possibility of notice) may be adopted:

'. . . provided that she has not left my employment or been dismissed
or given or received notice at the time of my death.'

If a condition is attached in any form as to the employment continuing at the relevant time, there may also be a desire to provide leeway should the employment have terminated through supervening circumstances, perhaps beyond the control of the legatee. Some such wording as follows may be suitable:

'. . . provided that she is in my employment at the time of my death,
unless the termination of her employment has occurred because of
her retirement or circumstances (other than her dismissal) beyond
her control (as to which my executors shall be the sole judges).'

It can be seen that fairly complex provisions can be attached to such legacies, but in most cases a simple clause will be sufficient. Confusion is unlikely in practice and lengthy conditions may have a tendency to increase rather than resolve difficulties. However, if a substantial sum or share of the estate is involved, precise instructions as to the legatee fulfilling any condition will be desirable.

---

1 1931 SC 259.

6.137 It is possible to create a trust for employees that benefits from favourable treatment for inheritance tax[1]. A transfer of shares in a company, including a transfer on death, will be an exempt transfer if the following conditions are met:

(1) The terms of the transferee trust must fall within section 86(1). This means that the property must be held and applied only for the benefit of:
   (a) persons of a class defined by reference to employment in a particular trade or profession, or employment by, or office with, a body carrying on a trade, profession or undertaking; or
   (b) persons of a class defined by reference to marriage or relationship to, or dependence on, persons of a class defined in para (a).
   Where the persons are defined by reference to employment by or office with a particular body, the class of persons to benefit must comprise all or most of the persons employed by or holding office with the company concerned, or the trusts must be those of an approved profit sharing scheme.
(2) The trustees of such a trust must at the time of the transfer or within one year thereafter:
   (a) hold more than one half of the ordinary shares in the company; and
   (b) have a majority of votes on all questions affecting the company as a whole.
(3) The trust must not permit the trust property to be applied at any time for the benefit of:
   (a) a person who is a participator in the company[2];
   (b) a person who is a participator in any *other* close company that has made a disposition whereby property became comprised in the same settlement, which but for the Inheritance Tax Act 1984, section 13 would have been a transfer of value;
   (c) a person who either after the transfer in question or in the ten years before it, has been a participator in either the company in question or in any such company as is mentioned in (b);
   (d) Any person connected with the persons mentioned in (a), (b) or (c).

It should be noted that the power to make payments which are the income of any person for income tax purposes is *not* included as a permission to apply trust property for the benefit of persons prohibited in terms of paras (a) to (d) above[3]. Such persons must thus only be excluded from capital entitlement.

6.138 If a trust qualifies as an employee trust, quite apart from the exemption for transfers *to the trust*, it will also qualify for certain other privileges. Notably, it will be exempt from the ten-year charge on discretionary trusts; and any exit charges and transfers from the trust will only arise in limited circumstances and at a reduced rate. If there are interests in possession in less than five per cent of

---

1 See the Inheritance Tax Act 1984, ss 28 and 86..
2 Participator being defined widely by reference to the Income and Corporation Taxes Act 1988, Part X, Chapter I, but see also the Inheritance Tax Act 1984, ss 13(5) and 28(5).
3 See the Inheritance Tax Act, s 28(6).

the property in the employee trust, charges on the termination or transfer of such interests will be avoided[1].

It can be seen that the terms of such a trust require to be quite complex in order to incorporate the statutory provisions mentioned. A full discretionary trust would be appropriate, but this would require to incorporate the exclusions from capital benefit mentioned above. As is the case with a charitable trust, the best course would be to set up the trust during the testator's lifetime, obtaining the necessary Inland Revenue approval. The bequest of shares to such an approved trust will then qualify for the exemption mentioned.

Such a trust may conceivably be of interest for non-tax reasons. Notably, if the testator is the effective owner of a suitable company and does not wish his family to take it over, he may very well be happy to see effective control in the hands of employees. If that is the intention, the tax exemption available should not be ignored.

PROVISIONS FOR HOLDERS OF OFFICES

6.139 It is possible that legacies (especially small ones) may be left to individuals in particular positions – ministers of particular churches are probably the most common example, but similar provision can be made for doctors, teachers or other holders of established posts or offices. In all such cases, just as with employees, it should be established whether the legacy is to a particular individual or to any holder of the post in question. In the former case, it is best to refer to the individual by name, perhaps adding to the designation that he is 'currently' the holder of the particular post. In the latter case, it is best to omit the name of any current holder of the post, but to refer to the occupant 'at the time of my death [OR other time of payment]'.

PROVISIONS FOR BUSINESS ASSOCIATES

6.140 Many of the considerations applicable to provisions for employees apply also to provisions for business associates, such as partners or co-directors of a company. It should be considered whether those to benefit are any individuals occupying the relevant positions at the time of the testator's death or other relevant time. This is perhaps unlikely, but is not impossible, perhaps particularly with token legacies. Having established the answer to this question, it is also necessary to ascertain whether intended beneficiaries are to take only if they occupy the appropriate position at the relevant time. Exactly the same kind of provisions can be inserted as were mentioned in paragraphs 6.135–6.136 in relation to employees. However, if such legacies are conditional on the beneficiary occupying the appropriate position, it is perhaps less likely that any reason for not

---

1 Inheritance Tax Act 1984, ss 58(1)(b), 72 and 86(4)(b).

occupying the position will excuse the legatee so that he takes in any event. A possible exception to this is the case of ill-health.

Finally, it may be appropriate or even necessary to consider matters other than the testator's wishes when drafting provisions in favour of business associates. This will not be the case with simple token or pecuniary legacies; however, it may well be that the most likely bequest to such associates are of assets or shares in the business, in which both the testator and legatee may be involved. In such cases, it will be necessary to consider the constitution of the business – perhaps the memorandum and articles of a company or a partnership agreement. The point is that there may be restrictions on the transfer of partnership assets or company shares, although usually transfer to other directors or partners will specifically be permitted. However, there may be provisions as to values to be attributed, or the proportions in which business assets must be offered to associates. It would be unfortunate to create a conflict between the provisions of a will and what is permitted by the business constitution and this should usually be avoided by comparing the two at the time of drafting the will. These aspects are dealt with in paragraphs 4.99–4.105.

PROVISIONS FOR CHARITY

6.141   A number of legacies to charities are shown at purpose S2.7. Whether or not a body is a charity is not a matter of great consequence as far as the law relating to legacies is concerned in Scotland. It is quite competent to leave legacies to non-charitable bodies, for example political interest groups (see para 6.147 below). What is essential is that the legatee is designed sufficiently accurately so that there can be no doubt as to which body is intended – and that the correct body is in fact specified. This is particularly the case if there are alternative Scottish and United Kingdom institutions, as it will be hard to displace a clearly designated body even if another was intended by the testator[1].

The main point of ascertaining whether a body is or is not a charity relates to the inheritance tax treatment. If the body is a charity, then the charity exemption will apply[2]. If it is intended to obtain the relief, then the testator should be sure that the intended beneficiary is indeed a charity. Confirmation of the position can be an important function for those drafting wills and may prevent disputes later.

6.142   A body which is not approved by the Inland Revenue as a charity cannot call itself a charity[3]. If no published documentation can be found for any particular charity (and perhaps in any event), reference may be made to the public index of Scottish charities maintained by the Inland Revenue. The index

---

1 *Nasmyth's Trustees v NSPCC* 1914 SC (HL) 76; compare *Wilson's Executors v Scottish Society for the Conversion of Israel* (1869) 8 M 233.
2 Inheritance Tax Act 1984, s 23.
3 Law Reform (Miscellaneous Provisions) (Scotland) Act 1990, s 2.

includes the name and contact address of all charities with whom the Inland Revenue has had contact since 1 January 1970 and enquiries can be made in person or in writing[1].

The Inland Revenue is prepared to answer telephone enquiries[2] and confirmation of any information contained in the index can be supplied in writing. The Inland Revenue can also supply lists of charities by the postcodes of the contact address on the index, or by common words in the names of charities. While the latter type of list may be useful where a testator has a wish to benefit charities of a particular type, it is by no means infallible. To take an example, charities concerned with the welfare of dogs may only have the word 'animal' in their name.

The index may also be a useful way to confirm the exact name of a charity. Very often charities operating in the same area or field of work may have very similar names, and thus exact designation is essential. Disputes between competing potential charitable beneficiaries are likely to result in the dissipation of the intended benefit in the course of resolving the matter, by court action if necessary.

For this reason, declaration (a) of the Style purpose S2.7 provides that if the charity has been wrongly designed, then the executors are to make over the legacy to a charity with similar purposes. The decision is up to the executors and possible alternative beneficiaries will have to accept their view on the matter.

Similarly, if the charity has changed its name or amalgamated with another charity, then the executors are to give effect to the charitable intention of the testator as nearly as may be. The executors are given the sole power to resolve problems over definition of the beneficiary. Such provisions will generally prevent the need for any *cy pres* scheme to meet the testator's intention.

6.143 Declaration (b) of purpose S2.7 provides that the receipt of an authorised official of any body is to be a sufficient discharge to the executors. Without this, there could be doubt as to the person from whom the executor should properly seek a discharge. Some charities might operate on the basis of signature by all of their trustees or council members, but this seems an unnecessarily demanding requirement. The clause refers to an officer of any body rather than any charity in case it turns out that the body in question is not charitable.

It is quite possible for the testator to indicate that he wishes a charity to use the legacy for a specific purpose. Thus, paragraph S2.7(3) gives a legacy to a medical faculty for research into AIDS.

A very common wish is to have money given to a United Kingdom charity spent in Scotland. Care should be taken if the restriction is, or may be likely to be, impracticable or even impossible of fulfilment. If it proves impossible to comply with the restriction, then the testator should consider what should happen in that event. Either the legacy could fail, or alternatively the testator could provide

---

1 The appropriate address is now: Financial Intermediaries and Claims Office (Scotland), Trinity Park House, South Trinity Road, EDINBURGH EH5 3SD.
2 On 0131 551 8127.

that it should be used for as similar a purpose as possible, or alternatively for the general purposes of the charity concerned.

It is possible for the testator to leave the selection from among existing charities to his executors or trustees. Such a legacy could take the following form:

'I direct my executors to pay the sum of ONE THOUSAND POUNDS to
such charities as they in their sole discretion may decide.'

Such a wide discretion is unlikely to meet the wishes of most testators; a limitation can be imposed on the choice available by specifying a locality from which the executors must select or a particular area or charitable activity, for example 'medical charities', 'religious charities', or 'educational charities'. It is, however, essential that any further definition of the charitable activity should merely qualify the word 'charity' as opposed to forming a possibly non-charitable alternative.

6.144   The clauses in purpose S2.7 provide for legacies to specific pre-existing charities. It is possible for the testator to have greater control over the destination of funds. This can be done by the testator setting up a new charity in his will with specific or general purposes, or he could direct the executors to convey the funds to a charitable trust set up by him during his lifetime.

It is possible for a testator to set up a new charity by the terms of his will. This, however, is not generally recommended. When a lifetime charitable trust is being established, it is usually essential to have the Inland Revenue approve a draft deed of trust as being charitable before any funds are committed to it. This is not possible in the case of a will because it is not a draft trust deed and it is not necessarily definitive. While the Inland Revenue (at the address mentioned in para 6.142) will look at a draft will, it can only give a limited response. A will is still a private document. What may be acceptable as being charitable for tax purposes at the date of drafting a will may turn out not to be acceptable as at the date of death. This may be because of changes in the law, but Inland Revenue practice may also change.

Some of the problems of attempting to be too specific are demonstrated by the case of *Russell's Executors v Inland Revenue*[1], where the House of Lords, reversing the Court of Session, ultimately held to be charitable a direction in a will that the residue of an estate should be left 'to the Town Council of North Berwick for use in connection with the Sports Centre in North Berwick or some similar purpose in connection with sport'. The Town Council of North Berwick was no longer in existence at the date of the testator's death, but that was only an administrative shortcoming. The main question was whether the reference to 'some similar purpose in connection with sport' took the bequest outwith the ambit of what was charitable. The wording was directly specified in the will, albeit the charity was to be operated by trustees separate from the executors. That was what really caused the problem. It is suggested, therefore, that a better alternative would be that trustees are given directions to set up a charitable trust

1 1992 SLT 438, reported as *Guild v IRC* 1992 STC 162.

with particular purposes which must receive charitable status. A possible direction might be in the following form:

> 'I direct my executors to establish a charitable trust to provide for the education of the public in Scotland in the philosophy and science of cosmology in such a way that the trust receives charitable status for tax purposes, all according to arrangements to be made by my executors.'

Even if wording in these terms is not charitable for tax considerations, the establishment of the trust in a form approved by the Inland Revenue for charitable purposes will be treated as a variation of the will and charitable relief for inheritance tax purposes will be back-dated to the date of death[1]. If a trust is not charitable between the date of death and the date of a variation creating a charitable trust, then capital gains realised in that period will be taxable. It should be possible for the income tax relief for income payable to charity to be obtained on the income during that period. This income tax treatment represents a recent change by the Inland Revenue[2]. However, the purposes should still be framed as far as possible with the intention of achieving charitable status as from the date of death.

6.145   An alternative to a direction to executors to set up a trust with purposes which can be approved by the Inland Revenue before being finalised, is to set up a general charitable trust. It is settled law that effect will be given to a general charitable intention[3]. But words other than, or in addition to, the term 'charitable' should generally be avoided[4]. While the word 'charitable' will not create uncertainty sufficient to make a legacy void, the same does not apply to other terms which may be considered similar, such as 'public', 'benevolent', or 'religious'[5].

Although general charitable intention is sufficient to create a valid bequest, there must usually be some mechanism to carry it into effect, such as the appointment of executors or trustees[6]. The general charitable trust can be set up in the will, which can also record the testator's wishes as to how he would like the executors as trustees (or separately appointed trustees) to exercise their powers. These wishes will not bind the trustees, but given that the testator will select the individuals concerned, this procedure may be sufficient. A direction could take the following form:

> 'I direct my executors to hold the residue of my estate for such purposes as are charitable both in law and for the purposes of the Income Tax Acts and to apply the income and capital thereof as they

1 See the Inheritance Tax Act 1984, s 142.
2 See Statement of Practice SP 4/93.
3 See, for example, *Dick's Trustees* 1907 SC 953; *Blair v Duncan* (1901) 4 F (HL) 1; *Hay's Trustees v Baillie* 1908 SC 1224; *Wink's Executors v Tallent* 1947 SC 1470; *Ballingall's Judicial Factor v Hamilton* 1973 SLT 236; *Cumming's Executors v Cumming* 1967 SLT 68.
4 See, for example, *Blair v Duncan* (1901) 4 F (HL) 1; *Campbell's Trustees v Campbell* 1921 SC (HL) 82; *Mackintyre v Grimond's Trustees* 1905 SC (HL) 90; *Reid's Trustees v Cattanach's Trustees* 1929 SC 727.
5 See, for example, *Robbie's Judicial Factor v Macrae* (1893) 20 R 358.
6 *Angus' Executrix v Batchan's Trustees* 1949 SC 335.

in their sole discretion may determine, but I record my wishes, without binding my executors, that they should apply so far as charitable the income and capital for the benefit of the inhabitants of East Lothian [OR the teaching of medieval Scottish music] [OR the support of blind children] [OR the benefit of orphaned children in East Africa] [OR the study of the means of reducing environmental pollution particularly in the Forth Valley and Estuary].'

6.146 While it is not essential that the expression of wishes itself should be charitable, the way that these wishes have been incorporated means that the trustees can give effect to them only if they are charitable. Wishes are merely expressions of desire, and not directions, although care must be taken to ensure that what appears as a wish is not in law a direction[1]. However, it is preferable if the wishes expressed are likely to be charitable. There is no point in a testator executing a will believing that some pet project would be charitable if there is no real likelihood that the trustees can implement this.

Where a testator sets up a general charitable trust, it is important that he does indicate his wishes in some way so that the trustees have some idea as to what he intended. If these wishes are not indicated, then the trustees' own views and ideas will govern the trust.

The testator's wishes could be set out in the will or they could be set out in a separate letter which itself did not form part of the will. If the wishes are lengthy or complicated, or likely to change, then a separate letter may be more appropriate. If the expression of wishes is contained in a separate letter, then the precise wording is not so important; but it must always be clear that the wishes are again just that and do not bind or direct the executors. Because of the variety of circumstances, it is not possible to offer a useful style. Arguably, wishes should be kept out of the will as a matter of principle, on the basis that a will should cover only directions rather than general intentions or wishes of the testator.

A final, relatively practical alternative, although one which is not enforceable, will be for the testator to communicate verbally his wishes to his executors, but the problems with that course of action are obvious.

A further general alternative is for the testator to set up a charitable trust in his lifetime which will receive charitable status and to which he could bequeath funds under his will. The relatively recent accounting and other requirements for charities may make this course unattractive, unless substantial funds are to be gifted to the charitable trust during the testator's life[2]. The terms under which such a trust might be established are outwith the scope of this book.

1 25 *Stair Memorial Encyclopaedia* para 823.
2 See, for example, the Charities Accounts (Scotland) Regulations 1992, SI 1992/2165.

PROVISIONS FOR OTHER INSTITUTIONS AND LEGAL PERSONS

6.147 Legacies can be left to persons other than individuals, trusts and charities. For instance, although it is perhaps unlikely, there is nothing to stop a testator leaving a legacy to a company. In such a case, many of the same considerations apply as are involved when dealing with charities. Thus, it is essential to identify the company by its proper name and address, particularly if there is any possibility of confusion with similarly-named entities. The company's unique registration number may be useful in such circumstances. Provision should also be made for a receipt to be given by an authorised official.

Legacies to a partnership (as opposed to individual partners) are perhaps even more unlikely, but are not impossible. They are not to be encouraged, but if the testator insists, it is important to specify in what proportions the partners are to benefit.

A more likely type of institutional legacy would be in favour of a club or society which does not qualify for charitable status. Again, provision should be made for obtaining a receipt from a suitable official.

Although charitable bequests are perhaps the most common examples of legacies qualifying for exemption from inheritance tax, it is worth mentioning that a range of other bodies also qualify for this treatment. Once more provision should be made for obtaining a receipt from an authorised official.

Exemption is available for legacies to political parties[1]. It should be noted that parties qualify under this section based on their performance at the general election prior to the transfer of value in question. This will usually be the transfer of value occurring on the testator's death and hence exemption could not be guaranteed at the time of drafting the will. The qualification is that two members of the party were elected to the House of Commons, or one member was so elected and at least 150,000 votes were cast for the party.

A list of bodies which qualify as exempt transferees of any property are listed in the Inheritance Tax Act 1984, Schedule 3 (and see also s 25). These include most museums, galleries and libraries, the National Trust and certain similar specified bodies, local authorities and universities. Of course, many such bodies also qualify as charitable.

Exemption is available for transfers of land to housing associations[2].

Exemption is also available for transfers to bodies not established for profit of certain property of outstanding scenic, historic, scientific, architectural, aesthetic or artistic interest, along with funds for the upkeep of such property[3]. However, exemption depends on a Treasury direction, which may be subject to conditions. Charitable status may well be important for the body in question (usually a trust). While such property could be left to an appropriate (discretionary) trust by will, it would usually be better to carry out such transfers during

1 Inheritance Tax Act 1984, s 24.
2 Ibid, s 24A.
3 Ibid, s 26.

the testator's lifetime, as details are likely to be subject to negotiation. If the appropriate body is set up during the testator's lifetime, further appropriate property can be left to this body by will, with Treasury direction sought at the time of transfer.

Much the same applies to maintenance funds for historic buildings, specific provision for which is made by the Inheritance Tax Act 1984, section 27 and Schedule 4.

If exemption is being sought in this type of field, the situation is undoubtedly usually better addressed during the testator's lifetime. There is a most useful booklet dealing with the available reliefs obtainable from the Inland Revenue. This is IR67 'Capital taxation and national heritage.'

PROVISIONS FOR ANIMALS

6.148   It is not possible for animals to be the objects of bequest. If a testator wishes to make provision for animals generally, the appropriate route is through a charitable legacy. Alternatively (and not uncommonly), a testator may wish to make provision for individual animals, usually pets. This can be done with appropriate conditions or trusts attached to a bequest of the animal to a suitable person who would be required to care for it (see paras 4.67–4.70 above).

PROVISIONS FOR EXECUTORS AND TRUSTEES

6.149   Purpose S2.3 contains a legacy to an executor on condition that he accepts office as such. This is a perfectly acceptable form of condition; indeed it is implied that a legacy to an executor or trustee is conditional on the position being accepted[1]. However, it is better that such a condition is imposed directly. The rule that a legacy to an executor or trustee is presumed to be conditional on taking up office can be displaced by evidence that it was in fact given for personal reasons, although this may prove difficult[2]. The conditional nature of legacies in favour of executors may even be relevant where the legacies are not contained in the same part of the will as that in which the appointment is made.

In these circumstances, if a legacy to an executor is *not* conditional on office being taking up, this should be made clear. The following wording will be suitable:

'I direct my executors to pay to A whether or not he should accept
office as executor the sum of ONE THOUSAND POUNDS.'

It is, of course, common in the Styles presented for executors to be appointed from among the testator's own family, who are then appointed residuary beneficiaries. It is not thought that a refusal to accept office in these circumstances

---

1 See *Mellis's Trustees v Legge's Executor* (1898) 25 R 954. On appointment of executors and trustees, see paras 3.10–3.30, especially 3.23.
2 See *Henderson v Stuart* (1825) 4 S 306.

would prejudice their rights as beneficiaries, but there could be a small risk of such a challenge. If this is thought at all likely, it might be desirable to confirm that such a beneficiary is to receive his legacy, whether or not office is accepted.

A similar issue arises in connection with the power to resign. An appointed executor who has received a legacy conditional on taking up office is not entitled to resign unless otherwise provided in the will[1]. It may be thus appropriate to allow such an executor to resign, if the testator wishes. Such a power is included in the full form of trust powers in the Styles presented (see, for example, S5.12(16)). If such powers are not included, a short declaration can be added to the appointment or the legacy:

> '. . . declaring that A may resign office not withstanding any benefit hereunder.'

A testator may provide legacies for all executors or trustees acting under his will; that is, without naming each executor or trustee specifically. Such a bequest should usually be restricted to executors or trustees *appointed* by the testator (whether under the will containing the bequest or otherwise). If it is extended to executors or trustees who might be assumed after the testator's death, this might be unlimited[2].

While it is not directly related to provisions made specifically by the testator for executors or trustees, it is also important to consider whether such executors or trustees might have a potential conflict of interest between their role as such and their position as individuals. If that is at all likely, a clause authorising such conflict should be included, to prevent the doctrine of *auctor in rem suam* operating (see, for example, S5.12(14) and paras 7.18–7.19 below).

If provision is made for executors of someone other than the testator (usually in a destination-over), this might be considered as in fact constituting a legacy to that individual's heirs, whether testate or intestate. This matter is dealt with at paragraph 6.24.

PROVISIONS FOR THE TESTATOR'S SOLICITOR

6.150 The following paragraphs are concerned with the propriety and the potential risks of professional misconduct of solicitors benefitting personally from clients' wills. (For other implications in this field, see paras 3.15 and 3.24.)

Whether the testator is a relative, friend or grateful client and whether the legacy is to be in the form of cash, a specific item or a share of residue, solicitors should be alert to the professional risks of preparing, or being responsible for the preparation of, wills and codicils which benefit them.

At the time of publication, the matter, perhaps surprisingly, is not regulated by any specific professional practice rule. Instead, and apart from obvious ethical considerations, there have been a series of decisions in point by the Scottish Solicitors' Discipline Tribunal.

---

1 Trusts (Scotland) Act 1921, s 3(2).
2 See *Elder* p 44, note 28.

Professionally, it is a cardinal rule that solicitors should put their clients' interests before their own. This general principle is now legislated for in rules 1 and 2 of the Code of Conduct (Scotland) Rules 1992, which state that solicitors must be independent, should not compromise their professional standards in order to promote their own interests and should not be influenced by the fact that a particular course of action would be to their benefit[1].

For some considerable time the acceptable practice was to proceed on the basis that if anything other than a nominal benefit was to be conferred on a solicitor by a will or codicil, he should advise the testator to consult another solicitor. *Professional Ethics and Practice for Scottish Solicitors*[2] states that:

'There is no reason why a client should not leave money in his will to a solicitor, who may well have given much help and friendship exceeding the bounds of professional duty over the years, but if a client wants to do this by anything more substantial than a token legacy, you *must* send him to another solicitor for independent advice[3].'

In practice, and as considered below, the difficulty for solicitors lies in judging the extent to which such legacies may be regarded as 'token'.

Professional misconduct

6.151 In recent years, a number of cases involving solicitors' benefits under wills have been considered by the Scottish Solicitors' Discipline Tribunal[4]. Resulting from the earlier cases, what currently must be treated as the definitive position was set out in (1989) 34 JLSS 389[5].

This reminded the profession of the general rule that a solicitor must not accept instructions to prepare a will, or cause a will to be made, in which he, his family or his partners benefit in a *material* way. Two specific exceptions were recognised.

The first exception is that a solicitor may ordinarily make a will for his spouse, his parents or children, or 'perhaps' his collaterals, on the understanding that any potential beneficiary is not materially disadvantaged. An example was given, namely that it would be permissible for a solicitor to make a will for his widowed mother dividing the whole residue between himself and his brother who was the only other member of the family; but the making of such a will would not be acceptable if the solicitor also had a surviving sister who was not to benefit. Consequently, where the solicitor is to receive a greater benefit than other members of the same class of beneficiaries, it would seem to be unsafe for the

---

1 See generally A Phillips *Professional Ethics for Scottish Solicitors* (1990, Butterworths).
2 R M Webster and Janice H Webster (The Law Society of Scotland, 2nd edn) p 13.
3 Reference there was made to (1983) 28 JLSS 276; *Re A Solicitor* [1974] 3 All ER 853; and *Ross v Gosselin's Executors* 1926 SC 325, in which it was not considered enough merely to tell the client of the position.
4 See, for example, (1983) 28 JLSS 276, 320 and 406; (1989) 34 JLSS 388; (1991) 36 JLSS 82; and (1994) 39 JLSS 149. Previous articles on the same topic appeared in 1975 SLT (News) 57 and (1982) 27 JLSS 319.
5 As confirmed by the Annual Report of the Scottish Solicitors' Discipline Tribunal for the year to 31 October 1990.

solicitor to prepare the will and instead the solicitor should insist that the testator consults another solicitor.

The second exception concerns the amount of the legacy. It was stated that there could be no objection to a solicitor preparing a will which contains a specific bequest of a small item of limited value in the testator's estate or a relatively small pecuniary legacy. Not infrequently this occurs where the solicitor is one of the executors and a small legacy is given to each executor, conditional upon accepting office (see para 6.149). In principle this exception appears clear enough. In practice it is probably less so and must hinge on the value of the legacy and whether or not it can be regarded as a mere 'token'.

It was considered, further, that it could never be acceptable for a solicitor to prepare a will for a non-relative leaving a share of the residue to the solicitor.

Apart from the two exceptions referred to above, the rule otherwise was regarded as absolute. In other words, the solicitor must send the testator to another solicitor for independent advice or, alternatively, withdraw entirely from acting for the client.

The essential element of these statements was considered to be that the solicitor should neither take instructions for nor make such a will, either personally or within his firm, and if *per incuriam* such a will was made up without the solicitor's knowledge, it would be his or her duty to renounce the bequest at the earliest possible date.

Token legacies

6.152   On the basis of the second exception referred to above, it would seem to be permissible for a solicitor to prepare a will containing a legacy of a small item of limited value or a token sum in favour of the solicitor. Indeed, in the reports of the two most recent cases[1] the existence of the exception was recognised by the Tribunal. In the first of these cases the statement in *Webster* was acknowledged as setting out the acceptable practice. Nevertheless, solicitors remain faced with the difficulty of determining the acceptable limit of a token legacy.

In the case referred to in (1991) 36 JLSS 82, a solicitor had prepared wills for a husband and wife and an unrelated client each containing legacies in his favour of £1,000 and for a further client containing a legacy in his favour for £250 as one of a number of executors. The solicitor had known the husband and wife for over 20 years and the aggregate of their estates was in the region of £80,000. The estate of the third client was around £60,000 when the will was made. The estate of the fourth client is not recorded in the published reports, but it is interesting to note that the solicitor was to receive the legacy along with the other executors receiving equal amounts.

The tribunal found in *each* instance that the legacies were in themselves substantial, both in amount and in proportion to the respective estates, and went

---

1 (1991) 36 JLSS 82 and (1994) 39 JLSS 149 and Report of the Scottish Solicitors Discipline Tribunal, above, pp 4–5.

beyond what ordinarily would be regarded as token amounts. In all four instances the solicitor was found guilty of professional misconduct.

In its decision the view was taken that 'it would be wholly inappropriate for the Tribunal to set down what figure or what proportion of a testator's estate would constitute the upper limit of a token legacy'. This would seem to leave the solicitor in a quandary. On the basis of this decision, it might not be unreasonable to assume that an amount of less than £250 is likely to be an acceptable level of token legacy. However, there does in fact appear to be a double test requiring the legacy to be acceptable not only 'in amount' but also 'in proportion' to the value of the testator's estate. In theory, therefore, the amount could be greater in the case of a large estate or smaller in the case of a more modest estate. The size of the legacy in relation to the eventual value of the testator's estate on death might also be relevant.

6.153   It might then be asked what options, therefore, are open to the solicitor?

Token legacies are likely to arise in three situations. Firstly, the testator may be the solicitor's spouse or a close member of family. The first of the above exceptions normally should cover such circumstances.

Secondly, the legacy may be made to all of the testator's executors. If the solicitor executor is to receive no more than any other executor *and* the legacy is of a token amount, that is unlikely to be exceptionable. However, if the legacy is to be more substantial, the solicitor may not be able to rely in safety on the fact that he is merely one of several executors each receiving an equal amount, and it would be preferable to decline it or, at least, reduce it to nominal level.

Thirdly, there is every other case. While a token legacy continues to be professionally acceptable, it is probably unsafe to assume that it can be anything other than a truly token amount. £100 to £150 possibly should be regarded as the maximum. Even then, while in the eyes of most people it may be acceptable 'in amount', it might still be unacceptable 'in proportion' to the value of the estate in question. If a larger amount is involved, undoubtedly the safest courses are to decline the proposed legacy, refuse to incorporate it in the will, or reduce it to a nominal level. Should the testator be insistent – and it is doubtful that many testators will be offended if it is explained to them that their solicitor runs the risk of acting unprofessionally by accepting the client's instructions – he should be advised to seek independent advice. If a cash legacy or bequest of a specific item is involved, only the question of the legacy to the solicitor need be referred elsewhere. The solicitor can complete the testator's will and leave the legacy in his favour to be incorporated in a codicil, independently prepared. However, if a residuary bequest of any amount is involved the testator must be referred to an independent solicitor to have the whole will prepared.

An alternative, of course, would be for the testator to execute a subsequent informal writing incorporating the legacy in favour of the solicitor. On the face of it, that would seem to be a wholly acceptable solution, providing it could be demonstrated that no pressure had been exerted on the testator to do so. However, once the testator's death occurred, could that be proven or disproven? On balance, therefore, and unless the legacy is of a small amount, the better view would be to recommend independent advice.

Possible reform

6.154   It is worth noting the views of the Council of the Law Society of Scotland as reported in the Journal of the Law Society of Scotland[1]. There it was stated that:

'. . . the Council of the Society decided on 31st May (1991) that apart from family wills there ought to be a total prohibition against a solicitor preparing a will containing a legacy in his favour or in favour of his family or other connected persons. The Council agreed that in the case of existing wills drawn prior to this decision being intimated, if the solicitor declines to accept the legacy, or arranges for a new will to be prepared, the preparation of the previous will ought not to be treated as professional misconduct.'

At most, this may be regarded as a statement of principle. It certainly lacks the force of a practice rule and is unlikely to have persuasive effect in the event of alleged misconduct. However, it possibly signals the direction in which, eventually, this issue will go. The subject is understood to be under review by the Law Society of Scotland.

Conclusions

6.155   It is suggested that the present position can be summarised as follows:

(1)   Solicitors should not accept instructions to prepare wills, or cause wills to be made, in which they, their families or their partners benefit in a material way.
(2)   It is never acceptable for solicitors to prepare wills for non-relatives leaving to themselves or their partners a share of residue.
(3)   It is acceptable for solicitors to prepare wills containing small token legacies in their favour or in favour of their partners, but on balance these are better avoided.
(4)   Solicitors may make wills for their spouses, parents or children, and perhaps collaterals, on the understanding that any potential beneficiary is not materially disadvantaged.
(5)   Apart from cases falling within (3) and (4), solicitors otherwise must refer the testator to another solicitor for independent advice or, alternatively, withdraw entirely from acting for the client. It is not acceptable to refer the matter to another partner, associate or assistant in the same firm. The referral must be to an unconnected individual or firm.

Validity of the will

6.156   The question of the validity of a will in which a solicitor has been found to breach professional rules is an entirely separate matter. Even if misconduct has occurred, the validity of the will is likely to remain unaffected, unless it can be challenged on other grounds as a matter of general law[2].

---

1 (1991) 36 JLSS 251.
2 See, for example, *Read v Cattanach* 1990 GWD 31–1839.

CHAPTER 7

TRUSTEES' POWERS AND OTHER TRUST CLAUSES

INTRODUCTION

7.01 Giving powers to executors is one of the most important reasons for considering making a will. Where executors merely realise and distribute executry funds, then there may be no difficulties and the executors can cope entirely satisfactorily with the powers granted by statute or at common law. Where funds are being held for a period and especially where funds are held for minor beneficiaries, then wider powers and fewer restrictions are generally thought advisable. Families are generally not pleased to be told that an otherwise advantageous step cannot be taken because it is outwith the executors' powers.

Most of the law in this area derives from consideration of the position of trustees generally rather than executors specifically. The powers contained in any particular will govern what is open to trustees, who must fall back on statute and common law powers for acts not expressly authorised[1].

SHORT FORM OF TRUST POWERS

7.02 The powers granted in the Styles in the short form (see S1.6, S2.24, S3.8, S4.7, S8.9, S11.9) are very wide. The executors are given the fullest powers to do various acts as if they were absolute beneficial owners. Lord President Cooper stigmatised this as 'an odd clause'[2], but this is now the usual form. The Court of Session is now prepared to consider variations to incorporate such powers and accepts that in appropriate circumstances, the provisions of the Trustee Investments Act 1961 can be a barrier to the sound investment of available funds[3].

Granting such apparently unlimited powers to trustees does not give them unlimited discretion to do entirely as they please. They must always act within their duties as trustees within the general trust purposes[4]. These short powers are intended to free the trustees from any administrative impediment to their carrying out the trust purposes in whatever way they think best.

The references to retention, realisation and management of the testator's

---

1 See generally *Wilson & Duncan* Chapter 21.
2 *Moss's Trustees v King* 1952 SC 523 at 527.
3 *University of Glasgow, Petitioners* 1991 SLT 604.
4 *Moss's Trustees v King* 1952 SC 523; *Norrie & Scobbie* pp 36–37, 114–117.

estate are generally self-explanatory. Investment is discussed subsequently (see para 7.05) as is appropriation (see para 7.15). The reference to the transfer of property without realisation is intended to assist in situations when there may be a tax advantage in transferring assets to beneficiaries as compared to a sale by the executor[1]. The executors are given express power to resign office (see para 7.21) and to appoint an agent from their own number, allowing normal charges (see para 7.22).

EXTENDED FORM OF TRUST POWERS

7.03 A full set of trust powers is included in the longer trust Styles (see S5.10. S6.11, S7.8, S9.8, S10.11). The introductory part of this Purpose is very similar to the abbreviated powers clause in the shorter forms of will. The short form also covers resignation of trustees and appointment of agents which are separately covered in this fuller style. This form adds the power to do whatever the trustees may consider necessary or expedient for the administration of the trust.

Arguably, adding specific powers adds little to the generality of the introductory part or of the short version of powers, but there are two main points in the long enumeration of powers.

Firstly, in a trust many of the powers listed are more likely to be useful. It is therefore preferable for them to be mentioned specifically so that there can be no argument that the trustees do not possess them. Persons dealing with the trust often seem more reassured by seeing specific authorisation for a transaction than by being asked to rely on general powers.

Secondly, general powers would not cover a number of acts unless specifically included. These include the provisions allowing the trustees to act in situations where a trustee would otherwise be barred from acting as being *auctor in rem suam*, such as the power to be paid for running a trust business (para 7.08); provisions dealing with conflicts of interest generally (paras 7.18–7.19); permission to participate in discretion (para 7.20); and remuneration of agents (para 7.22). Provisions allowing for agents are specifically included separately in the short form of powers. Powers dealing with the following matters also require specific authorisation:- nominees (para 7.11); delegation (para 7.12); resignation (para 7.21); foreign situations (paras 7.23–7.26); and renunciation of powers (para 7.27).

(1) Retention etc

7.04 Retention, sale and purchase of the estate are already mentioned in the preamble to this Purpose. Sale and purchase are generally covered by statutory

---

1 See *IRC v Matthew's Executors* 1984 SLT 414; Scobbie & Reid 'Testamentary Trustees and the Tax Man' (1985) JLSS 62.

provisions but it might be considered rather odd if these basic powers were not actually mentioned here.

The trustees have a statutory power to grant leases of any duration. The wording here is to cover not only the grant of leases, but also the taking of the tenancy of a lease of any property. Hiring relates to moveables which the trustees might wish to acquire or dispose of in this way.

(2) Investment

7.05 The terms of this power are intended to enable the trustees to use the trust funds to purchase almost any kind of asset they might think appropriate. Irrespective of the powers given to trustees they must still consider the interests of beneficiaries[1]. Their responsibilities may be greater depending on the type of trust asset involved[2].

Deposits are mentioned separately since strictly these are not investments. It may be that the trustees wish to retain part of the trust funds in cash, either through aversion to what are usually regarded as more profitable forms of investment, or through an investment outlook that is decidedly bearish.

Investments in the ordinary meaning are assets which produce an income[3], so express mention of assets which do not produce income is necessary. This could include insurance policies, stocks producing only capital growth but no income, furniture, stamps, wine and other corporeal moveables. The reference to bearer securities is to obviate the prohibition in section 15 of the Trusts (Scotland) Act 1921.

There is no geographical limitation on where the estate may be invested. Some older styles referring to investment in any part of the world might be thought to be unduly restrictive in view of the likelihood of industrial activity in space. It would be very unfortunate to be deprived of the opportunity to invest in the first colony on Mars – after all, trusts can have a very long lifespan.

(3) Insurance policies

7.06 Although insurance policies are specifically mentioned in the investment power (2), a separate power is included because there may be policies which would not ordinarily be thought of as investments. These might include personal accident or term policies which might be taken out to cover inheritance tax liabilities, although this is perhaps more common in *inter vivos* trusts.

The power would also cover buildings, contents and other non-life policies, which the trustees may have a positive duty to effect[4]. There is reference to

---

1 *Martin v City of Edinburgh District Council* 1988 SLT 329.
2 *Bartlett v Barclays Trust Company (No 1)* [1980] Ch 515 – trustees owning a majority shareholding in private company.
3 *Wilson & Duncan* p 340.
4 *Mackenzie Stuart* p 212; *Menzies* p 182.

insurance on a first loss or other basis. This may reassure trustees as to how they can deal with what is a difficult area.

(4) Management of heritage

7.07 By section 2(1) of the Trusts (Scotland) Act 1921, trustees are given powers to deal with heritage, including powers to lease, feu, excamb, abate rents and settle heritably-secured debts. The power in the Style is somewhat wider and includes express references to buildings, timber and minerals. This clause empowers the various operations which may be required: the allocation of the profits or expenses of such operations is governed by power (11) (see para 7.14).

(5) Businesses

7.08 This power involves a substantial extension of the trustees' statutory powers in this area. Ordinarily trustees have no power to carry on a business. They would be empowered to carry it on only so long as was necessary to avoid realisation at a preventable loss[1].

This power is intended to allow the trustees to carry on or to set up a business and to do it in whatever way makes business sense. The trustees may themselves manage the business and be paid for their services. Alternatively, they may entrust its management to someone else, as they may think fit. They need not exercise very close or detailed supervision and are entitled to be indemnified for any losses arising.

The level of supervision required may vary with the size of an interest in a business (see para 7.05). Notwithstanding this, the trustees must still take care as to how in general terms the arrangements are set up and are to continue, in the same way that an immunity clause will not protect trustees against gross negligence or bad faith (see para 7.29).

There is specific reference to carrying on a business through any companies, although the other powers probably give sufficient authority for what might be required. Power to continue a testator's business has been held to include power to form a company to carry on the business. It was seen as a mere change of form with the benefit of limited liability[2].

This power is also wide enough to cater for the possible flotation of a company and necessary actions leading to this, as well as amalgamations, reconstructions and the like. It may, however, be considered desirable to mention such matters specifically[3].

1 *McLaren* II, para 2180.
2 *MacKechnie's Trustees v Macadam* 1912 SC 1059.
3 See *Halliday* IV, para 47–82(16).

(6) Borrowing

7.09 There is a statutory power to borrow on heritable or moveable security under the Trusts (Scotland) Act 1921, section 4(1)(d), in addition to a common law power to borrow without security. It was thought preferable to include this power expressly to avoid any possible doubts as to its existence otherwise[1].

The provision includes power to *lend* with or without security, the latter of which would not ordinarily be possible.

The provision also includes power to grant or continue a guarantee or indemnity for the benefit of a beneficiary. Trustees would properly be wary of exercising this power, but there might be circumstances in which they were prepared to assist a beneficiary in this way.

(7) Occupation by beneficiaries

7.10 The power which the trustees possess 'to invest' means to purchase an investment which produces some profit or interest. The purchase of a house for a beneficiary's occupation without return or at a low rent has been held not to be an investment[2]. There is now a statutory power to acquire with trust funds 'any interest in residential accommodation (whether in Scotland or elsewhere) reasonably required to enable trustees to provide a suitable residence for occupation by any of the beneficiaries'[3]. The power in the Style goes further than that, by not restricting the property to a dwellinghouse – it can be any kind of property. In particular, it envisages an interest-free loan to a person who is entitled to the income of the fund or to a person to whom the trustees could within their discretion pay income. It does not empower free use of trust property by persons who are not immediate actual or immediate prospective beneficiaries.

The ability to lend funds interest free could be useful where a beneficiary wishes to buy a house. The trustees could lend funds to the beneficiary for this purpose. This would leave the capital in the trust but the benefit of the funds would be obtained directly by the beneficiary.

There is no point in charging interest on a loan to a beneficiary entitled to the income. The result would be that he would pay interest to the trustees who would suffer income tax on it. That (taxed) income would then form part of the beneficiary's income for tax purposes. The position might be different if there were a number of beneficiaries or where the beneficiary would get tax relief on the interest.

In terms of the power, no security is required although the trustees could of course ask for it.

---

1 *Wilson & Duncan* p 326.
2 *Moss's Trustees v King* 1952 SC 523.
3 Trusts (Scotland) Act 1921, s 4(1)(ee).

(8) Nominees

7.11 Ordinarily, trustees are required to keep the trust estate under their own control, so that investments and accounts should be registered in their own names and not in the names of agents or nominees for them. In practice, this can prove inconvenient. This power is intended to authorise, for example, trust investments being held in the name of a nominee, a trust bank account being held in the name of the trust solicitors, and third parties to have custody of trust investment certificates. Some authorisation of delegation appeared inevitable in relation to Stock Exchange investments under the now abandoned TAURUS system. However, reduced Stock Exchange settlement times with rolling settlement means that it will be very difficult to circulate stock transfers round a number of trustees in the time available. The proposed CREST system of settlement will necessarily involve delegation.

(9) Delegation of investment management

7.12 Following on from power (8), the trustees are ordinarily not empowered to delegate any of their functions, thus an express power to delegate their investment management function has been included. This power can only be granted revocably and is limited to dealing with investments and deposits. In practice it would be used to allow stockbrokers or other investment managers to manage a portfolio on a fully discretionary basis.

(10) Additions

7.13 This apparently peculiar provision suggesting that the trustees may accept pennies from heaven means that the trustees can accept property to which they may become entitled after the testator's death. Clearly in their capacity as executors they would be entitled to any further property subsequently found to belong to the deceased. This paragraph is to cover situations where property falls to the trustees in terms of some other trust deed or will.

The only readily credible possibility is a situation where a testator has taken out an insurance policy on his own life held by trustees for his children, with the intention that the policy monies would be used to meet inheritance tax on his death. If the policy trust is simply held for the children absolutely, whether or not they are minor, it will not be proper for the policy trustees to pay the inheritance tax liability on the testator's death in respect of testamentary trust property then held on a normal accumulation and maintenance trust. This is because it cannot be known until the children attain age 25 whether they will in fact benefit. All that might be done is perhaps for the policy trustees to lend the policy proceeds to the testamentary trustees to enable the latter to meet the tax.

If, however, the policy trust provided that the beneficiaries included a trust under which the testator's children were prospective beneficiaries, then the policy trustees could convey the policy proceeds outright to the testamentary trust and the testamentary trustees could accept it.

(11) Allocation between capital and income

7.14 The wording here gives the trustees power to determine what is income and what is capital. It does not affect the principal trust provisions setting out who is entitled to income or capital, but merely allows the trustees themselves, for example, to decide on the proportion of expenses or of the proceeds of some company share rearrangement which should be charged or credited to income or capital, so as to be able to avoid or settle possible disputes between different beneficiaries. Without this provision it might be necessary to attempt to find an answer under the general law[1].

Although this power is thought to be administrative only, so that it would not affect the existence or otherwise of an interest in possession, the breadth of its terms could conceivably be considered by some to have an effect on such interests. This effect could be thought to negate what would otherwise be an interest in possession for tax purposes, for instance in a liferent trust; or alternatively to prevent one coming into existence, for instance in an accumulation and maintenance trust. While these fears may be groundless, particularly in the light of the decision in *Robertson's Trustees* v *IRC*[2], those of a nervous disposition may prefer to include a declaration at the beginning of the powers purpose, that the powers listed are '. . . without prejudice to the foregoing provisions . . .'.

Where mineral extraction or timber operations are being carried out or are anticipated, the testator's instructions should be sought at the drafting stage, since the result implied by law may be quite different from what he had in mind. The rule may be different where minerals are used for estate or personal purposes as opposed to commercial purposes, and where mines have previously been worked as opposed to new workings[3]. The rules relating to timber and to stock dividends and share distributions by companies are other areas where the law may provide consequences that are unanticipated.

This power may be particularly useful in relation to that relatively recent but increasingly common phenomenon of investment, enhanced scrip dividends. These may cause difficulties not only in connection with the general law, particularly as to those entitled as between income and capital in liferent trusts, but such problems may also extend into their tax treatment. The Inland Revenue has now issued Statement of Practice SP 4/94, setting out its interpretation of the tax consequences which follow from the treatment of enhanced scrip dividends as income, capital or requiring division between the two. The Inland Revenue has stated that it will not generally interfere with trustees' decisions as to the appropriate treatment in any case, as long as that treatment can be justified in

1 See generally *Dobie* pp 86 ff.
2 1987 SLT 534, reported as *Miller* v *IRC* [1987] STC 108.
3 *Dobie* pp 88 ff.

law. The power given to trustees by power (11) will be of enormous assistance should justification for particular treatment in one direction or the other be required.

(12) Appropriation

7.15   This power allows the trustees to appropriate funds to represent the share of a particular beneficiary. The trustees could set aside particular assets as earmarked for a beneficiary and thereafter that beneficiary's interest in the trust would subsist in those assets. That interest would be tied to those assets whatever value they subsequently had, either in themselves or in relation to the other assets in the trust. As an administrative power this does not entitle the trustees to ignore the principal trust provisions; they must appropriate assets equivalent in value to the value of the beneficiary's interest.

The trustees can set aside particular assets to represent only a part of a beneficiary's interest, so that thereafter a beneficiary's prospective share would be represented by (1) the appropriated assets or whatever might subsequently replace them, and (2) a reduced proportionate share in the remaining assets in the trust, the proportion depending on the relative values of the appropriated asset and of the beneficiary's share at the time that the appropriation was made.

The power refers to shares 'prospective or otherwise'. The trustees can appropriate in relation to present or future beneficiaries. In an accumulation and maintenance trust the prospective share refers to the situation where the trust is, in relation to any beneficiary, still an accumulation and maintenance trust, that is one where the beneficiary is not entitled to the income. 'Otherwise' refers to the situation where a beneficiary is entitled to the income, which would be the case if he was over 21 or if a right to income had been appointed to him. In this situation his right to capital would still be prospective, but his right to income would be actual and vested.

The trustees are given power to determine the valuation at which property is to be appropriated. This is to give the trustees the final say in valuing assets such as private company shares or heritage which may not be easy to value.

7.16   The situations where this power might be useful are quite diverse. The trustees might decide to lend cash to a beneficiary, perhaps to help him to buy a house, and the trustees might feel that since a simple loan was not ordinarily as appropriate an investment as, say, equities, then they should hive off the amount of the loan. The effect would be that the value of the loan would crystallise part of the beneficiary's share, while the remaining assets in the trust continued to be invested in assets with some growth prospects.

The trustees might want to buy a house themselves for a beneficiary's occupation. They might want to treat this as an ordinary trust investment, although as an investment this would require specific authorisation as mentioned in power (7). The value of the occupation to the beneficiary is an income element. The trustees need not under the inheritance tax rules pay out income of the trust equally to the beneficiaries while it remains an accumulation and maintenance trust (that is before beneficiaries become actually entitled to the income). It may be done unequally, so that they could allow one beneficiary under 21 to occupy the house and still accumulate the balance of the trust income in which he would also share.

If the beneficiary is entitled to the income (by being over 21 or having a right to income appointed to him) he will be entitled only to the income element appropriate to his share. The trustees themselves might apportion the value of this benefit in relation to the other trust income, in order to determine the share to which each beneficiary was entitled. It might, however, be preferable for the trustees to appropriate the house to that beneficiary's share. The beneficiary would then occupy it and on attaining age 25 would become entitled to the property itself. In addition he might be entitled to a reduced proportionate share of the remainder of the trust.

Another use for the power might be where one beneficiary was non-resident and wanted his share invested in high-yielding government securities on which the income can be paid free of income tax to non-residents. More generally, one beneficiary might want to receive income while another, with an already high income, might prefer less income and want funds invested for capital growth.

Using the power to appropriate is likely to be seen as fair because it separates out various beneficiaries' interests to reflect their own needs.

(13) Settlement

7.17   This power is intended to allow the trustees power to transfer whatever assets they please in satisfaction of a beneficiary's share. This ability is not available without express or implied direction[1]. Whereas the power to appropriate is used during the currency of the trust, the power of settlement is used on the distribution of funds to beneficiaries on the vesting of capital in them. The trustees are given power to make the decisions and the beneficiaries have no formal say. Trustees would still need to take care with the exercise of this power; for example, in allocating minority shareholdings in a company, the exercise might give a beneficiary a majority shareholding[2].

The reference to the trustees being able to compel acceptance was originally included so as to avoid *ad valorem* stamp duty which would otherwise have been due on a transfer of property in settlement of a pecuniary legacy. Following the Stamp Duty (Exempt Instruments) Regulations 1987 (SI 1987/516), there is now no stamp duty on this event if the appropriate stamp clause is included in the deed of transfer, but the provision has been retained so as to emphasise the trustees' powers.

This power should not be exercised without due consideration. A decision to allocate a particular asset before antecedent purposes have been carried out may be regarded as revocable[3].

---

1 *Duncan's Trustees* 1951 SC 557.
2 *Lloyds Bank v Duker* [1987] 1 WLR 1324.
3 *IRC v Matthew's Executors* 1984 SLT 414.

(14) Conflict of interest

7.18   A trustee or executor may not enter into transactions where his personal interest conflicts with his fiduciary duties – he would thereby be acting as *auctor in rem suam*. There may be cases where a trustee would want to transact in some way with himself. This is particularly so where family members are trustees and there is some family property or partnership interest in which both the trust and the trustee have separate pre-existing interests. It would also cover situations where a professional trustee wants to charge for his services. This is covered separately under power (17), but the generality of this paragraph would probably be sufficient. A similar problem arises if a trustee is to manage the trust business and be paid for his services. This is also covered under power (5).

It is a fundamental rule that the fiduciary relationship between executors and trustees on the one hand and beneficiaries on the other should prevent the former from entering into any transaction or otherwise acting so that personal interests benefit at the expense of duties to the beneficiary[1]. Breach of the duty not to act as *auctor in rem suam* can lead to an obligation to account for any property or profit obtained by the executor or trustee. A constructive trust will be created. There is also the possibility of liability in damages to the beneficiary for any loss which he may have suffered.

Thus, where executors dative transferred a tenancy to one of their own number in part-satisfaction of that executor's entitlement as beneficiary and that executor subsequently made a profit by entering a compromise with a landlord, the executor had to account for any gain made. It made no difference to the strict application of the doctrine that the executor was the only qualified recipient of the tenancy[2]. The Scottish Law Commission has recommended that an executor should be empowered to transfer a tenancy to himself at an agreed value[3].

The most common form of transaction which might be struck at would involve a trustee wishing to buy trust property[4]. This might extend to relatives of the trustee, or companies or other bodies in which he had an interest. Contracts of loan or employment contracts are other likely eventualies which might be affected.

The rule can strike at transactions carried out through a third party acting for an executor[5]. Normally if a situation of conflict arose, the proper course would be for the trustee to resign[6].

Apart from the liability on the trustee in breach mentioned above, the consequence of an act which falls foul of the limitation is not to render it void but merely reducible, so that no subsequent title can be regarded as safe[6].

To enable transactions to take place safely, express or clearly implied powers are necessary[7]. Power to trustees to sell any part of the trust estate, including power to

---

1 See 24 *Stair Memorial Encyclopaedia* paras 170 ff.
2 *Inglis v Inglis* 1983 SLT 437.
3 Scot Law Com Consultative Memorandum no 71, September 1986, p 124.
4 *Johnston v Macfarlane* 1987 SLT 593.
5 *Clark v Clark's Executors* 1989 SLT 665.
6 *Wilson & Duncan* p 366.
7 *McLaren* II, para 2236; *Mackenzie Stuart* p 184; *Norrie & Scobbie* p 133.

sell to any of the beneficiaries, is not sufficient to permit a sale to a *trustee* who is also a beneficiary[1].

The recent case of *Sarris v Clark*[2] confirmed that implied authorisation was possible. In that case, the testator had entered into partnership with his wife and granted a lease to that partnership, circumstances which were almost bound to produce conflict with her appointment as executor. The doctrine of *auctor in rem suam* did not necessarily apply in these circumstances, but specific authorisation is preferable and more likely to avoid litigation such as has dominated the family's affairs following the death of Mr Clark.

Consent would also be a defence to an action against a person alleged to have acted as *auctor in rem suam*[3]. Again, this would depend on taking action after the death when the situation could have been covered in the will.

7.19   Power (14) is intended to allow the trustees to transact, notwithstanding any conflict of interest, with themselves as individuals and whether or not they are connected with any trust, partnership or company. It would, for example, empower the purchase by the trust of property belonging to a trustee or the sale to a trustee of trust property. Although the power is expressed very widely, the general fiduciary duties on trustees would still require them to act in the interests of beneficiaries, for instance by paying or obtaining a fair price on such a purchase or sale. If the testator is aware at the time at which the will is being drafted of some potential future conflict (perhaps because he is already in partnership with his proposed executor or trustee, who is likely to wish to purchase trust property in the form of partnership assets), there may be a case for referring to this possibility specifically. This would emphasise the express authorisation being granted to a trustee in such circumstances to act as *auctor in rem suam*. This could be done by inserting the following wording in paragraph (14) between 'by this deed' and 'notwithstanding':

> '. . .(including in particular any transactions or acts in relation to any partnership in which I and A may be partners at the time of my death). . .'

Similar specific authorisation could be given, for instance, if it was known that a trustee might have a particular wish to buy a house or other property belonging to the testator. While the general authorisation given to the trustees by power (14) as worded would be sufficient to cater for such eventualities, such specific mention of the eventuality might be of assistance in disputes arising after the death.

Equally, the testator might wish to exclude certain transactions from the general permission given by this provision, which is very wide. This could be done by inserting an exclusion at the end of the power, for example as follows:

> '. . . but expressly excluding any power to lend money or other assets to any trustee.'

---

1 *Johnston v MacFarlane* 1987 SLT 593.
2 1993 SCLR 927 (a development from the same situation which led to *Clark v Clark's Executors* 1989 SLT 665).
3 24 *Stair Memorial Encyclopaedia* para 17.

In terms of the basic form of power (14), the trustees or trustee with whom there is or may be a conflict must not be the only trustees or trustee. There must be at least one other trustee independent of the conflict for the protection to apply. In certain circumstances, it might be desirable to remove this restriction on the protection and make it absolute, but this should only be on clear instructions.

(15) Participation in discretion

7.20   This follows on from power (14) and allows the trustees to participate in a decision by the trustees to advance income or capital, in the exercise of a discretion available to trustees, to themselves as individuals where they are also beneficiaries. The trustees making such a decision are required to include at least one trustee who is not benefitting, so that there is some degree of practical restraint. The trustees in exercising their discretion must of course still act within the terms of the trust although the court will not readily interfere with the exercise of the trustees' discretion[1].

(16) Resignation

7.21   Ordinarily a trustee may resign office. This is included as one of the statutory powers available to trustees unless the contrary is expressed in the deed[2]. This does not cover a trustee who is appointed as a trustee on the footing that he will be paid for acting as trustee or trust agent. A trustee resigning in this case would continue to be liable as if he were a trustee. Nor does it cover a situation where the trustee is given a legacy conditional on his accepting office[3].

The terms of this power are intended to enable trustees in such situations to resign. It may well be worth checking with the testator whether trustees are to be given this option, particularly where they may be recipients of a fairly substantial token legacy in return for acting.

(17) Agents

7.22   There is a statutory power to appoint agents and to pay them suitable remuneration[4]. Ordinarily, trustees exercise their office gratuitously and cannot charge for their services except for necessary outlays. The rule applies whether the trustees would otherwise seek payment for their services as trustees in a professional capacity, or as advisers to the trust[5]. This power enables the trustees to appoint one of their own number as an agent for the trust and to pay him for his services. This would otherwise fall foul of the restriction on a trustee acting as

---

1 *Wilson & Duncan* p 335.
2 Trusts (Scotland) Act 1921, s 3(a).
3 Ibid, s 3(2).
4 Ibid, s 4(1)(f).
5 See *Fegan v Thomson* (1855) 17 D 1146; *Aitken v Hunter* (1871) 9 M 756; *Wilson & Duncan* pp 367, 400.

auctor in rem suam discussed in paragraphs 7.18–7.19. Power (17) is really a specific example of the general rules on conflict. A power to charge is not a legacy to the executor or trustee such as to restrict his ability to resign unless specifically authorised[1].

(18)   Non-resident trustees

7.23 In general, without specific authorisation in a trust deed it is not permitted for a Scottish trust to be exported by the trustees themselves.

Usually the consent of the court will be required to the proposed export of a trust where there are no provisions in the deed itself. The facts of each individual case are of great significance and the court will require some foreign connections with the jurisdiction concerned. In many cases this will mean that exporting is not possible. There are signs in recent years that the court is being slightly more liberal in this matter[2].

If there is no power, then United Kingdom trustees who resign in favour of foreign trustees may be personally responsible to the beneficiary[3]. It may be possible to avoid such problems by the trustees taking indemnities from suitable parties. It is of course preferable for express provision to be made for exporting the trust in any case where that might be a possibility.

It is appreciated that many testators may not be keen on this type of provision and there is no necessity for it to be included. It is likely only to be a real possibility in a substantial trust, or one where there are known foreign connections. The difficulty with this approach is that circumstances may change rapidly after the trust has been set up or between the date of drafting the will and the testator's death. Beneficiaries may move abroad or assets may appreciate very substantially.

On the other hand, even with substantial assets it may not be worth exporting a trust with a view to capital gains tax saving or deferment; for example, a business may be being carried on through a branch or agency in the United Kingdom, which will render gains on United Kingdom property liable to tax[4]. Very often the export of a trust will trigger a capital gains tax charge[5]. As with most of these powers they should be considered carefully in each case.

There are several aspects involved in exporting a trust, including having foreign trustees (power (18)), carrying on the administration abroad (power (19)) and the possibility of changing the proper law of the trust (see paras 7.25–7.26).

Trustees of a Scottish trust may live outside Scotland. Non-residence in the United Kingdom (not Scotland) is a ground on which a trustee may be removed from office by the court[6]. With modern communications, this may seem somewhat outdated. It has been suggested that it is not advisable to appoint any

---

1 See *Collie* 1933 SLT 46.
2 Jones & Macintosh *Revenue Law in Scotland* (1986) pp 94–96.
3 Menzies *The Law of Scotland Affecting Trustees* p 57.
4 Taxation of Chargeable Gains Act 1992, s 10(1).
5 Ibid, s 80.
6 Trusts (Scotland) Act 1921, s 23.

foreign trustees unless a majority of all trustees are resident in Scotland, but there is no suggestion that this is invalid. There are cases where the court has appointed foreign trustees[1].

This power enables the appointment of non-resident trustees and this will prevent their removal under the provisions in the 1921 Act.

This power also permits trustees to resign office following their assumption of non-resident trustees. Resignation alone is already mentioned in power (16) but this goes rather further and allows non-resident trustees to act alone and United Kingdom resident trustees to resign in safety.

(19) Administration abroad

7.24 The second aspect of exporting a trust is having the administration carried on outside the United Kingdom. This is independent of the residence of the trustees themselves. It is quite possible for the administration to be carried on in a jurisdiction where there are no trustees.

It is also possible for trustees who are physically in the United Kingdom to be treated as non-resident for tax purposes. Thus, for capital gains tax purposes a professional trustee will be treated as being non-resident where the property was settled by a non-resident[2].

This power authorises the administration to be carried on outside the United Kingdom. The trustees would still have to be sure that the trust would be recognised by the law of the place where the administration was being carried on. Civil-law states will generally not recognise trusts at all and the consequences could be most peculiar. The 1984 Hague Convention on the law applicable to trusts and their recognition will help where states have incorporated this into their domestic law. The United Kingdom has done this by the Recognition of Trusts Act 1987 which came into force on 1 August 1987.

Change of proper law

7.25 There is a third possible aspect of exporting a trust which involves changing the law which regulates the trust. It is perhaps more appropriate in relation to *inter vivos* trusts. It has not been thought appropriate to show such a power directly in the Style but a power in the following terms could be included:

> 'To change the proper law of this trust by deed or deeds and therein to make such consequential variations or additions to this trust as my Trustees may consider expedient, but no such deed shall be valid if or to the extent that it would result in any of the provisions hereof or of any appointment hereunder not being enforceable or exercisable or being revoked or revocable.'

This wording gives the trustees power to change the proper law of the trust from its existing Scots law.

---

1 *Mackenzie Stuart* p 303.
2 Taxation of Chargeable Gains Act 1992, s 69(2).

Reference to the proper law of a trust is perhaps increasingly used as a means to determine matters to do with a trust in relation to international aspects. The truster's freedom to choose the proper law is becoming more generally recognised, particularly with the coming into force of the Recognition of Trusts Act 1987. By articles 6 and 8 of the Schedule to the Act, the law chosen by the truster will govern the validity of the trust, its construction, its effects and the administration of the trust.

The use of the term 'proper law' is not one which is used in the Act, but it has an international as well as a local currency. It is included here on the basis that this is a power which could be used only after the most careful consideration.

The idea that trustees may be able to alter the proper law during the currency of the trust may be seen as a development of the increasing freedom of the truster to select the proper law. It is very different from the previous powers dealing with exporting a trust which allow non-resident trustees to be appointed and to have the administration carried on abroad. In those cases the trust remains a Scottish one subject to the jurisdiction of the Scottish court and subject to interpretation under the rules of Scots law. There may of course be considerable practical difficulties in enforcing matters through the Scottish courts where the trustees and the administration are abroad. Even so, in principle Scots law still determines most matters to do with the trust.

The idea may not be one which is likely to be viewed enthusiastically by a Scottish court but it seems that the type of clause set out above might receive effect. There could be considerable difficulties where a Scottish court decided that the change was not possible, while the courts of the purported new proper law decided to the contrary. It would therefore no doubt be prudent to take the consents of beneficiaries where possible. In England it appears that this power will receive effect.

7.26 The circumstances when this power might be of use are very much more limited than the previous export powers. The power could be used where beneficiaries move permanently abroad and it seemed more convenient to transfer the trustees, the administration and the proper law to the country of residence. The powers could also be used to keep the trust much further out of the clutches of the United Kingdom tax or other authorities.

The complications inherent in having the law governing the trust altered to some other law could be immense. Provisions in this power which have been drawn up with regard to Scots law would have to receive a meaning having regard to the provisions of some other law. Accumulation periods, perpetuities and the nature of a beneficiary's interest are only a few of the areas where results could be quite unexpected under another system. Extensive advice on any proposed new proper law would be essential. The trustees have been given powers to make necessary adjustments so that matters fit more closely than they would otherwise do.

It has been suggested that the existence of this kind of power could mean that, for example, what would otherwise be an accumulation and maintenance trust could not be treated as such, because it would always be possible for the trustees to change the proper law of the trust in such a way that persons precluded from being beneficiaries of an accumulation and maintenance trust could benefit. The proviso to the power suggested above is intended to meet this objection by providing that a deed varying the terms must be only for consequential variations and must not alter the trust provisions.

(20) Renunciation of powers

7.27 This somewhat odd provision was originally introduced as a defence against Capital Taxes Office attacks on trust deeds made on the basis that widely-framed administrative or investment powers could subvert the principal trust provisions of liferent or accumulation and maintenance trusts, so as to deprive them of their status as such. At one time the argument ran that wide powers to the trustees to apply trust monies (which might come from revenue rather than capital) in taking out insurance policies could deprive a liferenter of income; thus that part of the trust was not a liferent trust, but was a discretionary trust for capital transfer tax (as it then was) purposes. Similar wide powers, it was argued, might conceivably mean that it was possible for persons over the age of 25 to benefit from what was intended to be an accumulation and maintenance trust. These attacks ignored the fact that trustees were still bound by the principal trust provisions and the Revenue argument has now had to be abandoned. This followed the distinction established and confirmed by the courts between administrative and dispositive powers. Administrative powers will not usually override dispositive powers[1].

All the provisions included in the purpose setting out the long form of powers are intended to be administrative powers, so on present arrangements there should be no problem.

It is, however, the case that trustees cannot bind their successors or limit the future exercise of their powers[2] and so in the face of such arguments the only way out was: (1) a variation of the trust to limit the powers with the consent of all the beneficiaries of the trust if ascertained vested major and *capax*; or (2) a full variation by a petition to the court under the Trusts (Scotland) Act 1961.

In the interests of flexibility this provision has been included to enable the trustees to limit powers if any should in the future turn out to be offensive for some tax reason or possibly for some family reason.

APPORTIONMENT

7.28 A beneficiary may be entitled to a right to trust income by virtue of provisions in a number of the Styles. This is the case where a beneficiary has a liferent for life as in Styles S5 and S6, or where a beneficary has a right to income where there has been an accumulation and maintenance trust for children, when

1 *Robertson's Trustees v IRC* 1987 SLT 534.
2 *Menzies* p 164.

they will often become entitled to a share of the income between the ages of 21 and 25 as in Style S7.

In these cases the Apportionment Act 1870 together with the common law require that income be apportioned on purchase or sale of investments and at the start and termination of liferent interests[1]. Apportionments at the start of a liferent usually mean that no income is due to the beneficiary for some time after the beginning of the period, and that there will be a balance of apportioned income due to the deceased beneficiary's executors after his death. Apportionment on purchase and sale is usally neutral overall, as between income due to capital and income due by capital. A very great deal of administrative work is necessary to carry out the calculations. Generally, the application of apportionment means little overall change in income entitlements, although it will alter the timing of payment in what appears to most people to be a peculiar way. It is therefore a requirement which is best avoided, and so the relevant Styles provide that the need to apportion income is excluded on any occasion.

A form of apportionment is still required for income tax purposes on the purchase or sale of certain fixed interest securities under the accrued income provisions[2].

If apportionment requires to be done on the occasion of a beneficiary becoming 21 and then entitled to income, then that beneficiary will not become entitled to income until income begins to arise in respect of the period after he becomes 21. Income actually received after he becomes 21 but apportioned to the earlier period will strictly suffer the rate applicable to trusts for income tax[3] and will cause the trust capital gains tax rate to remain at 35 per cent[4]. This is a further reason to exclude the requirement to apportion income.

In the liferent trusts there are separate purposes (S5.9 and S6.10). In the accumulation and maintenance trusts it is done by a paragraph included in the main trust purpose (S7.7(10) and S10.8(10)). There is no real significance in this difference of treatment.

IMMUNITIES

7.29   The form of immunity clause used in the Styles (see S5.13, S6.14, S7.11, S9.9, S10.12) is a formulation of some longevity and is substantially that shown in *Elder*[5]. It does not relieve trustees from the consequences of any act they may do – trustees must act in their office with proper diligence. The clause will not relieve the trustees from the consequences of a positive breach of trust but it may reduce the standard of care otherwise required of a trustee[6].

1 *Dobie* pp 132 ff.
2 See the Income and Corporation Taxes Act 1988, ss 710–728.
3 35 per cent in 1994–95.
4 [1990] Trusts and Estates 5; M D Wood [1992] Capital Tax Planning 119.
5 Form 216(a) at p 174.
6 *McLaren* II, para 2275 and Supplement p 283; *Mackenzie Stuart* pp 377–380; *Wilson & Duncan* pp 390–391; *Elder* p 175.

Parts of the clause reflect the position at common law or under statute and thus serve only to bring the matter to mind. There is ordinarily implied in a trust deed a provision that a trustee will be liable for his own acts and intromissions and that he will not he liable for omissions[1]. Trustees will not be liable to beneficiaries for defaults of agents who have been properly appointed and who are acting within the scope of their legal authority[2]. Depreciation in the value of an investment would not render trustees liable if the investment had been properly made or retained.

It should perhaps be said that some testators are understandably reluctant to include such a wide immunities purpose as, on the face of it, it appears to give executors and trustees *carte blanche* to carry out administration in a totally inefficient and negligent manner, without penalty. This is, of course, not entirely the case, but given the extent of statutory and common law immunities available in any event, it might be acceptable to omit a clause of this nature. Certainly, the matter may require to be considered carefully with certain testators, who may require reassurance; the clause should perhaps not be automatically included in every case.

1 Trusts (Scotland) Act 1921, s 3(d).
2 *Wilson & Duncan* p 391; *Mackenzie Stuart* p 376.

CHAPTER 8

CODICILS

INTRODUCTION

8.01 Formal attested codicils are a convenient means of making minor alterations to existing wills, including the appointment of additional or replacement
executors and the addition or amendment of legacies. A codicil is to be read
together with the will which it modifies[1]. As will be seen, however, some
alterations do not require a formal codicil and for these a simple informal writing
may be sufficient.

Codicils are equally competent for alterations of a more substantial nature,
such as changing the division of residue, but in such cases should be used with
care. The terms of the will and any intervening codicil(s) to be amended must be
studied thoroughly and appropriate adjustments made. As will be seen, preparation of a new will may be preferable.

THE STYLES

8.02 Two Styles of codicil are offered (S13, S14), both referring to Style S2.
There is an obvious stylistic difference between the two. Style S13 revokes
certain provisions of the will and sets down amending and additional provisions
in their place. Style S14 instead inserts a substitute wording into the will itself.
Neither method is preferred to the other, although the second is more likely to be
appropriate where a single clause or complete clauses in a will are to be replaced.
It is also the best method of altering the terms or conditions of original legacies,
since an attempt simply to *add* a condition to an original legacy may fail, because
of the doctrine of repugnancy (see paras 5.54–5.55). This would also be the case
where a major change was being made, such as substituting a full right for one of
liferent.

The Styles highlight the principal types of alteration for which codicils are
well suited, some of which are considered in more detail below. In this chapter
the terms 'executor' and 'executors' may also be read as 'trustee' and 'trustees'
respectively.

The following alterations by codicil are alterations incorporated in the Styles:

---

1 *Kilgour v Kilgour* (1845) 7 D 451.

(1) Change in the testator's address – S13.0 (preamble).
(2) Revocation of the appointment of an executor or executors – S13.1 and S14.0 (preamble).
(3) Appointment of replacement executor or executors – S13.1 and S14.1.
(4) Legacy to executor conditional upon acceptance of office – S14.2.
(5) Substitutional legacy – S12.2.
(6) New legacy – S13.4 and S13.5.
(7) Note recording death of legatee under will – S13.2(2).

WHEN A CODICIL IS UNNECESSARY

8.03 It is not necessary to prepare a codicil merely to record changes in the names (for example, following marriage) or addresses of executors, legatees and beneficiaries, nor to record their deaths. If a codicil is being prepared for other reasons, such things can be included as a matter of record. Otherwise, a separate note placed with the will is quite sufficient and more than is often provided by testators.

Funeral instructions can be added, or amended, by codicil, as can provisions relating to the appointment of testamentary guardians. Both, however, can be dealt with separately.

If the will contains provision for subsequent informal writings, a formal codicil may not be necessary provided that the proposed alteration is within the scope of such clause (see paras 3.31–3.36).

A codicil, of course, can be used to introduce provision for subsequent informal writings, if this has not been included already in the will.

CHANGE OF EXECUTORS

8.04 If the testator wishes to change his executors, while in many cases it will be possible for this to be achieved under an informal writing, it will generally be preferable to do so in a formal codicil.

The terms in which the original executors were appointed in the will (S13.1) should be considered. For example, is there a substitute or conditional appointment in the will and, if so, is that to be continued by the codicil? Alternatively, is a substitute or conditional appointment to be introduced by the codicil?

Are any of the original executors also solicitors, and, if so, does the will allow them to charge professional remuneration and to resign? Alternatively, are any of the new executors to be introduced by the codicil also solicitors? If so, and the will does not allow them to charge or to resign, appropriate provisions should be included in the codicil.

Are all or any of the original executors left a legacy conditional on accepting office (S14.2) or appointed on the basis of receiving remuneration? If so, does the will permit them, respectively, to resign or to charge? If not, appropriate provisions should be made in the codicil. (On all of the above, see paras 3.10–3.30.)

Are any executors who are also solicitors left legacies in the will or are to be left legacies in the codicil? If so, consider if this is permitted or advisable (see paras 6.150–6.156).

As in Style S2 (S2.2 and S2.3) and codicil Style S14 (S14.1 and S14.2) if the appointment of executors is contained in one clause and a legacy to them conditional on acceptance of office in another clause, is the wording of the legacy in the will made to them by name or simply to 'my executors'? The latter will result in legacies payable to all of the deceased's executors, including those appointed in a subsequent codicil.

It is also important to ensure that the change correctly reflects the form of appointment of executors and/or trustees contained in the will. If the will appoints persons as executors *and* trustees (it is perfectly competent, although unusual, to appoint executors and separate persons as trustees – see para 3.12), a codicil revoking the appointment of any such person should do so in both capacities. Equally, the codicil should appoint the new executors and/or trustees in the same capacities.

ALTERATIONS TO LEGACIES

8.05 The most common alteration to legacies in a codicil are likely to be:

(1) revocation of existing legacies (S13.3);
(2) substitutional legacies (S13.2(1), S13.3);
(3) additional legacies to existing legatees (S13.4);
(4) new legacies to new legatees (S13.5 and S14.2).

If legacies are being altered, the conditions, if any, applying to them in the original will should be considered and it should be established if similar conditions are to be applied to those introduced by the codicil. For example, if the will states that legacies are to be paid free of government duties and expenses, but, where appropriate, without interest (S1.4, S2.5, S3.4, S5.4, S6.4, S7.4, S8.4, S9.4, S10.4, S11.4), is this to apply to the altered legacies? In this context, particular reference should be made to the terms of the tax, expenses and interest clause (S2.5).

If the legacies to be introduced by the codicil are increasing or replacing legacies in the will or are bequeathing additional items to legatees, the wording of the codicil should make it clear if they are cumulative or substitutional[1].

---

1 S13.2 and S13.3 and see para 4.13; *Halliday* IV, para 47–84.

CHANGES AFFECTING THE SUBJECT OF A LEGACY

8.06 Since the time of execution of the testator's will, changes may have occurred which affect the subject of a legacy.

For example, the will may have included specific or demonstrative legacies, such as particular shareholdings or sums in bank accounts, which have since changed following a company reorganisation or transfer to another bank or account. It will be desirable when preparing the codicil to establish if such legacies are still to be operative and make the necessary amendments (see paras 4.15, 4.102 and 4.117–4.118).

Similarly, if the testator's will bequeaths a specific item or items it will be desirable to confirm that such items still belong to the testator or if the bequest is to be adjusted in any way. For example, if the will bequeaths certain pictures by a particular artist to a legatee, and the testator has since increased his collection of that artist's pictures, the testator may wish to add the additional pictures to the bequest. Alternatively, if the will bequeaths 'all my pictures by (named artist)' does the testator wish the legatee to have the additional pictures as well?

If the testator no longer owns the subject of a particular legacy, although such a legacy will adeem, this fact can be recorded. If the item has been given, say, to the intended legatee, it would be worth recording this too. Quite apart from making the testator's intentions entirely clear, such information is helpful, if only to save the executors on the testator's death having to search for an item which no longer belonged to him. The information may also be relevant for inheritance tax purposes.

CHANGES AFFECTING THE TESTATOR AND/OR BENEFICIARIES

8.07 Since the date of execution of the testator's will the circumstances of the testator and/or beneficiaries may have changed in ways affecting the provisions originally made in the will.

Conditio si testator sine liberis decesserit

If the testator has had a further child or children since making the will, the *conditio si testator sine liberis decesserit* could lay the will open to reduction at the instance of any subsequently-born child who did not benefit from it. The wording of the will in relation to provision for the testator's children, therefore, should be studied and the testator's intentions recorded (see para 6.114).

Conditio si institutus sine liberis decesserit

Similar considerations apply in relation to a beneficiary under the will who has since died. In such circumstances the *conditio si institutus sine liberis decesserit* may apply to carry such predeceasing legatee's legacy to his issue. The effect of this *conditio* in the particular circumstances should be confirmed, the testator's wishes established and the codicil framed appropriately (see paras 6.118–6.119).

REVOCATION AND EXECUTION

8.08 The rules of revocation apply equally to codicils as they do to wills (see paras 3.03–3.09).

It is not strictly necessary, therefore, to state in a codicil that 'except in so far as amended by this codicil I confirm the terms of my said will in all respects' or similar words to that effect[1].

The execution requirements for codicils are the same as those applying to wills (see paras 2.31–2.59).

INTERVENING INFORMAL WRITINGS

8.09 If the testator's will permits the executors to give effect to informal writings, it should be established if any such writings have been prepared since execution of the will. Such information will be relevant not only to their effect on the will itself, but also to the terms of the proposed codicil.

Reference should be made to the terms of the informal writings clause in the Styles (S1.3, S2.4, S3.3, S5.3, S6.3, S7.3, S8.3, S9.3, S10.3, S11.3; and see paragraphs 3.31–3.36).

CODICIL OR NEW WILL?

8.10 It really is not desirable for a testator to have a whole string of codicils. Quite apart from the fact that interpretation of the testator's testamentary intentions will become that much more difficult to follow, the greater the number of codicils the greater the opportunity for error.

Obviously, in practice it may be difficult to draw a line as to when a testator should be advised that it would be more appropriate for a new will to be prepared rather than a codicil.

The particular circumstances will dictate this. Where the will is simple and the codicil or codicils merely add additional legacies, then there is probably more leeway than there would be in cases where the will is relatively complicated and the alterations to be incorporated in the codicil are themselves complicated. However, if an arbitrary line is to be drawn, then it is suggested that *two* codicils should be treated as an acceptable limit.

---

1 See and compare *Halliday* IV, para 47–87.

Where a legacy is to be revoked, or a share of residue redirected away from a beneficiary, the testator may prefer that the original recipient should not know this. If so, a fresh will will be necessary, unless the original provisions are contained in an intervening codicil which can be replaced in its entirety and destroyed.

An excessive number of codicils may be treated as affecting the date of a testator's testamentary expression, which may be relevant in certain circumstances, particularly in relation to changes in the law[1].

The question of expense may be in the minds of the solicitor and client, perhaps leading to the conclusion that a codicil is to be preferred to a will. Depending of course on the terms of the will and the proposed alterations or additions, it may very well take as long or longer to prepare a codicil than it would to prepare a fresh will, thus costing the client as much or more. With the assistance of styles and word processing it may be simpler, and no more costly to the client, to prepare a new will.

CAPACITY

8.11 When there is doubt as to the testator's testamentary capacity, it may be preferable to execute a codicil rather than a new will. If a new will was made then the whole will might be set aside. If only a codicil was made then only the codicil might be set aside leaving the earlier will intact[2].

---

1 See 25 *Stair Memorial Encyclopaedia* para 887.
2 *Horsburgh v Thomson's Trustees* 1912 1 SLT 73.

CHAPTER 9

TAKING INSTRUCTIONS AND PROBLEM SOLVING

INTRODUCTION

9.01 The intentions behind this chapter are to consider some of the matters which should be addressed whenever instructions are taken for drawing up a will and to give possible solutions for a range of problem situations which might be encountered. In connection with the latter aim especially, this involves some repetition of points that have been mentioned already when dealing with particular aspects of the Styles or alternative clauses. This is deliberate, in that the commentary on the Styles deals with sections of wills somewhat in isolation, while this chapter attempts to draw together planning points which may arise in dealing with whole wills for clients in a variety of circumstances.

TAKING INSTRUCTIONS

9.02 It might be considered possible and desirable to draw up an all-encompassing type of questionnaire with which practitioners should arm themselves in preparation for taking instructions for a will. While such an aid could be helpful in an executry, to ensure that all the right questions are asked, it would seem less appropriate for wills.

Instructions may be about to be taken from a current client, coming merely to tinker with or update an existing will. It may be a current client who has experienced what he considers to be a substantial change in circumstances, such as having married, divorced, had a child, bought a house or received an inheritance.

The client could be new to the firm or be making a will for the first time, whether at a young age or having intended to get round to doing so for a number of years.

A questionnaire or aide-memoire would only be of limited assistance, perhaps to newly-qualified practitioners. They already have access to such materials from their studies in the Diploma in Legal Practice. What may be of more assistance is some consideration of the structure of an interview with a client who has ostensibly come to make a will, an analysis of what the client wants to achieve, and ways in which instructions may be implemented, if possible, with the minimum amount of original drafting.

The last point mentioned is not intended to suggest that what is being advocated is the 'pigeon-holing' of a client into a particular style of will, which may not be what that client wants. It is undoubtedly the case that some practitioners encourage, if not persuade, their clients to opt for a simple, standard type of will, which may be accepted with some reluctance. They may indicate to their client, for example, that 'trusts are expensive to run' and should therefore be avoided entirely. Such an attitude may ignore the fact that a trust in the will would be the ideal way to implement the client's wishes. Perhaps it could be set up and run with the minimum of administration to keep costs down.

One of the reasons for the initial advice to avoid trusts may of course be a perceived lack of expertise on the part of the practitioner involved. It is fair to say that with the reduction in the numbers of trusts over recent years, there has been a resultant reduction in the numbers of practitioners who maintain an interest in the subject. There are, unfortunately, also a number who consider that it is sufficient to leave a legacy to a beneficiary 'in trust' without feeling that there is any need to elaborate with further clauses and powers.

It goes without saying that if a practitioner is to have a face-to-face meeting with a client with a view to taking instructions for a new will, he should make the most of it. That is not to say he should try to sell additional legal services with the terrier-like zeal of a double-glazing salesman, but he should be aware of possible further business and take the time and opportunity to ensure that the client feels he is being properly cared for.

The modern-day client is of a somewhat more itinerant breed than his predecessors, with an eye for a competitive quote. Loyalty to a solicitor may be less than total. It seems inevitable that solicitors will have to be even more committed than ever in the future to ensure that clients are not only properly cared for, and advised, but feel that they have received the sort of attention which ensures their return to the same practitioner in the future.

Claims on estate

9.03 It has always been essential when taking instructions for a will to be able to inform the client (1) what would happen if he did not make a will and (2) even if a will is made, who may claim what. The first question is obviously relevant where the will is being made for the first time, but the second question is relevant even where there is a will in place. The answers to both questions may be subject to change in the future, as the Scottish Law Commission has made a number of recommendations on the reform of this area of law (see para 9.07).

Prior rights

9.04 In the event of an intestacy on a death after 26 November 1993 where there is a surviving spouse and issue the spouse has a right to prior rights as follows:

(1) An interest in a dwellinghouse up to the value of £110,000 or cash to that value where the interest exceeds £110,000[1].
(2) Furniture and plenishings to a value of £20,000[2].
(3) A cash sum of £30,000 if there are issue or £50,000 if no issue[3].

Legal rights

9.05 The legal right of the spouse is to one third or one half of the net moveable estate, depending upon whether there are issue. Similarly, the issue have a right to one third or one half of the net moveable estate, depending upon whether there is a surviving spouse. It may be important to a testator to attempt to defeat the legal rights of spouse or children (see paras 6.30–6.32, 6.113; 9.09).

Intestate succession

9.06 The remaining one third or one half of the net moveable estate and any additional heritable property not required to meet the prior rights, ie the free estate or 'dead's part' passes in accordance with the rules of intestate succession[4].

The spouse comes rather low down the list of intestate beneficiaries who inherit the free estate and it is often at this stage that spouses with no children will be quite aghast that part of their estate could pass not to their surviving spouse, but to their own brothers and sisters in preference to their surviving spouse if a will is not made. This point is mentioned again later in paragraph 9.16.

It is also worth remembering that there is representation in legal rights but not, of course, in prior rights.

Proposals for reform

9.07 There are a number of recommendations for reform which are contained in the Scottish Law Commission Report on Succession[5].

This Report contains a large number of recommendations in connection with a number of matters relevant to succession. Some of the main recommendations which deal with the share of the estate passing to the surviving spouse and issue, are as follows, with references being to the Report paragraphs and clauses of the attached draft Bill[6]:

1 Succession (Scotland) Act 1964, s 8(1), as amended by the Prior Rights of Surviving Spouse (Scotland) Order 1993, SI 1993/2690.
2 Ibid, s 8(3) as amended.
3 Ibid, s 9 as amended.
4 See the Succession (Scotland) Act 1964, s 2(1).
5 Scot Law Com no 124, (1990).
6 It is worth noting that the figures mentioned in the Report and draft Bill were suggested prior to the last change to prior right limits for deaths after 26 November 1993.

(1) Where a person dies intestate survived by a spouse but no issue the spouse should inherit the whole intestate estate[1].

(2) Where a person dies intestate survived by issue but not by a spouse, the issue should (as under the existing rules) inherit the whole intestate estate[2].

(3) Where a person dies intestate survived by a spouse and issue, the spouse should have a right to £100,000 or the whole intestate estate if less. Any excess over £100,000 should be divided equally, half to the spouse and half to the issue and the Secretary of State should be given powers to alter the figure of £100,000 by statutory instrument[3].

(4) Where a person dies either testate or intestate, the surviving spouse should continue, as of right, to be entitled to a fixed legal share of the deceased's spouse's estate, as should the issue of the deceased[4].

(5) In relation to the legal shares of spouse and issue there should be no distinction between heritable and moveable property[5].

(6) A surviving spouse's legal share should be 30 per cent of the first £200,000 of the net estate and 10 per cent of any excess over £200,000.

Where there is no surviving spouse the issue's legal share should be 30 per cent of the first £200,000 of the net estate and 10 per cent of any excess over £200,000.

Where there is a surviving spouse the issue's legal share should be 15 per cent of the first £200,000 of the net estate and 5 per cent of any excess over £200,000.

However, the estate subject to the issue's legal share should not include the first £100,000 of any net estate to which the surviving spouse succeeds[6].

These recommendations are no more than that at the moment. There is no sign that progress is being made in implementing them. All these recommendations are of interest to the legal profession and there may have to be a review of wills in the event of their implementation at some point in the future. Any detailed discussion of such implications with the client might be counter-productive, as it would serve to confuse the issue when explaining the law of intestate succession as it exists at the time of taking instructions for and drafting the will.

Format of interview

9.08 The format of an interview in taking instructions for a will often follows the layout of the deed, starting with the appointment of executors and finishing with funeral instructions. This is not in fact a particularly logical way of approaching such an interview and a suggested list of points for discussion, which could be put in the form of an aide-memoire, would be as follows:

---

1 Para 2–3; clause 1(2).
2 Para 2–4; clauses 1 and 2.
3 Para 2–7; clause 1.
4 Paras 3–1 to 3–12; clause 5.
5 Paras 3–15 and 3–16; clauses 5 and 7.
6 Otherwise than by virtue of a claim for legal share; paras 3–18 to 3–29; clauses 5(3) and 7.

(1) designation, testamentary capacity and domicile of client (see paras 9.10–9.11);

(2) the estate which is to be bequeathed by the will (see para 9.12);

(3) the beneficiaries who will take the estate bequeathed by the will whether as legatees or residuary beneficiaries (see para 9.13);

(4) solving the problem and choosing the Style of will (see paras 9.14–9.26);

(5) executors (see para 9.27);

(6) guardianship, funeral instructions and living wills (see paras 6.98–6.111, 3.42–3.67);

(7) explanation of some standard clauses (see para 9.28), for example, those dealing with revocation, informal writings, tax, expenses and interest and trust powers and charging;

(8) date for review of will (see para 9.29).

The earlier chapters of this book contain a great deal of detail on most aspects of the above points for discussion. It may be worth highlighting a few important points in each category and developing the concept of problem-solving.

A client attends a meeting with instructions for his will often with an idea as to who is to benefit. There is no reason, however, why the practitioner should not mould the interview in such a way as will best allow him to advise the client, and also with a view to solving the 'type of will' problem as quickly as possible. It may in fact be worthwhile giving the client the bare bones of how you expect the interview to go, and even tell the client in advance why it would be useful to deal with the matter in this particular way.

Exclusion of spouse or issue

9.09 A testator, for whatever reason, may desire that a spouse or issue take as little as possible from his estate on death. This matter is also dealt with in paragraphs 6.30–6.32 and 6.113. While a will may be drawn up excluding either category as beneficiaries it is not possible to exclude their claims for legal rights. It is thus appropriate to consider this problem briefly, before looking at other difficulties where a completed will provides the effective solution.

While a divorce may be contemplated, some time may have to elapse before it is completed, which would relieve the spouse of any legal right to the testator's estate. The testator may therefore wish to have suggestions made at the time of drafting a new will as to how such claims could be avoided.

In view of the fact that legal rights are to moveable estate one suggestion is to convert moveable assets into heritable property. This might be somewhat inconvenient for the testator, not to mention financially unattractive if no rent or only poor rents can be obtained from the properties.

Another suggestion is to make gifts during the testator's lifetime to third parties. Again, it could be inconvenient to reduce substantially the estate of the testator where that estate is needed to maintain him in the way to which he has become accustomed. These gifts, however, would not be added back for legal rights calculations provided they were not made to those beneficiaries now making the claim.

Perhaps the best way to cover the situation would be for the lifetime transfer of at least the moveable estate into an *inter vivos* liferent trust with the income payable to the testator and the capital passing either to a named beneficiary or to a beneficiary named in the will.

The trust estate would be settled property on the deceased's death and would not form part of the deceased's moveable estate for the purposes of legal rights.

Designation of testator

9.10 The designation of the testator will take the form of his full name and address, possibly with the addition of occupation after the name (see para 3.02).

The detail in this description of a testator may depend upon whether there is a genuine possibility of confusion in the event of the death. A father and son may have exactly the same names, including middle names, and address. If neither has left any estate to the other it might be necessary to look at the assets bequeathed to determine which will is for which person. The use of the words 'senior' and 'junior' could be useful in this situation to differentiate between the two.

This is perhaps a slightly contrived and unlikely scenario, but what does often arise is that the testator is either known by another name, or has had a number of addresses which may be mentioned in other deeds or certificates which have not been changed by the date of death.

If the testator is known by a particular name, for example George (known as 'Doddy') then this should be how he is designed in the will to ensure there is no possibility of confusion where people have only ever known him as 'Doddy'. Some people will actually open accounts with the bank or purchase shares in the name by which they are known rather than their given name, and in the event of the death of that person the description or designation in the will must tie up exactly with the confirmation to the estate. The confirmation is the executor's authority to complete title and it would certainly pre-empt problems with different descriptions of the testator in other deeds or certificates if the will dealt with any alternatives in how the testator is known.

The same considerations apply in respect of the testator's address. It is mentioned elsewhere in this book that it is advisable to check other deeds which govern the deceased's assets when taking instructions for a will[1]. These other deeds may have an earlier or different address for the testator and it may be useful to mention this in addition to the current address in the will by saying 'formerly of. . .'.

While a person may be known by a different forename to different sections of the community, occasionally someone wishes to change either their surname or full name and wishes to formalise the change so that other documents such as passport may also be changed. In Scotland the normal method of dealing with

---

1 See for example paras 4.99–4.107.

this is by making a statutory declaration before a notary public. Such a declaration should obviously be registered in the Books of Council and Session and extracts or copies will undoubtedly be intimated to many relevant parties such as bank managers to enable names on cheque books to be amended. At the very least a copy of the statutory declaration should be placed with the will. A client when making such a declaration will probably not wish to enter into the expense of changing every deed which bears their previous name. It would probably be quite unusual to leave a document such as a will in the previous name where a statutory declaration has been entered into but there would seem to be no reason why a will could not be implemented, providing the declaration was available at the death and was submitted with the will and any other relevant deeds when confirmation is subsequently obtained following the death.

There is a procedure for a change of established name to be recorded by the Registrar[1].

Testamentary capacity and domicile

9.11   There are separate sections in this book dealing with both testamentary capacity (see paras 2.02–2.08) and domicile (see paras 2.61–2.65). The practitioner must obviously satisfy himself that the testator has testamentary capacity before taking instructions. It also makes a considerable difference whether a client is domiciled in Scotland and is purporting to bequeath his estate wherever situated, or is domiciled abroad and is seeking to make a will only in respect of, say, Scottish heritable property. In the great majority of cases these matters will become clear very quickly and with any luck there will be no need to dwell on them when taking instructions.

The estate which is to be bequeathed by the will

9.12   The section on this subject at paras 2.09–2.24 will draw to the practitioner's attention the fact that there are a number of ways to achieve testamentary effect without making a formal will. It is essential therefore to know what the client is *able* to bequeath and what he *wishes* to bequeath. It may be necessary to take other steps to ensure that what the client wishes to bequeath is in fact covered by the will.

By explaining to the client the need for considering each asset and how it is held, the solicitor may therefore elicit the extent of the estate. This opens up for consideration other matters such as inheritance tax planning.

Clients may often be reluctant to discuss the full value of their estate when giving instructions for a will and this can be a useful way in which to open up discussion on that particular point.

One of the most simple tax-planning ploys today is to give away assets and survive for seven years. If the testator, as a result of discussions when giving instructions to draft a will, intimates that he has decided, on your advice, to give

1 See the Registration of Births, Deaths and Marriages Act 1965, s 43.

away immediately substantial assets or insurance policies to cover future tax, this could obviously affect the way the will is drafted and what assets are included in the estate bequeathed. It could mean that a simpler will than first envisaged would be appropriate for this client.

It has to be remembered that the burden of inheritance tax in the event of a death within seven years becomes relevant not only for the gift but also for the effect on the remaining estate bequeathed by the will. It means that fairly accurate calculations of potential inheritance tax should be done to ensure that the client has the full picture.

The beneficiaries

9.13   Chapters 5 and 6 deal with beneficiaries in considerable detail.

It should go without saying that beneficiaries should be clearly described and identified by name and address in the will, and perhaps relationship to the deceased, if any.

The age of the beneficiary is obviously very relevant and should be ascertained. Another main point is to find out who is to benefit in the event of a beneficiary predeceasing the testator and the age of the beneficiaries who would take in his place.

There is automatic representation where a descendant of the testator predeceases and leaves issue, or the testator is an uncle or aunt of a predeceasing beneficiary who leaves issue[1]. This version of representation would have to be specifically excluded if the testator did not wish it to apply. By the same token, if the testator wished, say, a cousin's child to take if the cousin predeceased, an appropriate reference would require to be inserted.

The client needs to know in what circumstances a specific or pecuniary legacy would fall into residue or a share of residue into intestacy if no appropriate provisions were made, and when representation would take those bequests to the next generation. For this purpose, the adviser must also be aware of the current law as it applies to adopted and illegitimate beneficiaries and other forms of marriage such as habit and repute (see Chapter 6).

PROBLEM SOLVING

Introduction

9.14   It is to be hoped that we are a long way away from punching into a computer a number of facts about a client such as 'divorced with two children under the age of 12' and having the computer at the press of a button produce a suggested format for a will. Having said that, there are a number of situations which arise where clients have similar personal circumstances and whose

---

1 The *conditio si institutus sine liberis decesserit* – see paras 6.118–6.119.

situation would be covered by a particular type or style of will. The following paragraphs aim to cover a number of those common situations and provide the sort of advice which could be given to clients, with a suggestion as to the type of will which could be used.

Domicile and foreign heritable property

9.15 The Commissary Office in Edinburgh deals with any application for confirmation to property in Scotland where that person has died domiciled abroad. It deals with around 120 cases of foreign domicile per annum, and if this is anything to go by there are obviously not large numbers of people dying domiciled abroad with any substantial assets in Scotland. What a practitioner is more likely to come across, however, is the domiciled Scot who owns heritable property abroad.

In view of the fact that the *lex situs* applies to the foreign property, as already mentioned elsewhere in paragraph 2.65, it may be necessary to consider a will in that foreign country for the devolution of the heritable property. There is always a danger in having more than one will in different countries in case one inadvertently affects the other. Another possibility is that the testator considers setting up a company in the foreign country where the heritable property is situated and making the heritable property an asset of the company.

The testator would thereafter own shares in the company which would be considered moveable and thus preclude the necessity of having a will in the foreign country. The shares could be left to the person who was to be the beneficiary of the heritable property. Such an arrangement would have to be considered in the light of the law of the country in which the heritable property was situated.

Spouse/no children

9.16 It has already been mentioned earlier in this chapter (para 9.09) that if an intestate's estate exceeds the prior rights limits the surviving spouse would receive in addition to those prior rights, where there are no children, one half of the net moveable estate. The other half of the net moveable estate along with any excess heritable property not needed to meet the prior right to an interest in a house could, for example, go to the deceased's brothers and sisters before the spouse.

This is not usually desired and a simple will leaving everything to the surviving spouse is sufficient to preclude this happening. The only person to have any legal right to the testator's estate would be the surviving spouse who would receive the whole estate under the will anyway.

The will would also say who would be the next in line to benefit from the estate should the surviving spouse predecease or die co-temporaneously with the testator (see Style S11).

Children/no spouse

9.17 It will be important to a testator whose spouse has died, or where there has been a divorce, to consider the ages of the children when a will is made. The testator may wish to ensure that the children do not benefit before attaining an age in excess of 16, and in those circumstances a trust of some sort would have to be interposed. This would normally be an accumulation and maintenance trust, giving each child an equal share as and when it attained a certain age, with the possibility of receiving income from its share of capital prior to vesting in that capital. This type of arrangement allows children to learn how to deal with the income prior to obtaining control of the capital. A simple accumulation and maintenance trust need not be much longer nor more detailed than a clause for beneficiaries lacking capacity (see Style S8 for a shortened version and Style S7 for a longer version).

Where the testator's estate is a fairly large one, an interesting suggestion might be to divide the testator's estate by the number of children plus one and to set aside the additional share of the estate on a discretionary trust with all the children as potential beneficiaries. This would allow the testator to inform the trustees of that particular trust that they should use the income and capital from this trust to benefit any of the children who for whatever reason needed assistance in the years following the testator's death. This might be due to the fact that they had failed in business, made a bad investment or lost their money for any reason.

There would be no additional inheritance tax implications for this discretionary trust once it was up and running, provided it did not exceed the nil rate band at any given time. It could give peace of mind to certain clients who found themselves in this particular situation, where the children who were the principal beneficiaries were young, and there was no spouse.

Spouse/children (1)

9.18 There is a somewhat unusual situation which arises where the estate of the testator does not exceed the prior rights limits. The testator may have left his whole estate to his spouse, and for the sake of argument, the estate might consist of a house worth £100,000, contents worth £15,000 and cash and investments worth £30,000. These amounts are all within the prior rights limits, but there are of course no prior rights due to the fact that there is a will.

If there is a child and the child claims legal rights on its late parent's estate then the moveable estate will consist of the contents and cash less any debts etc and this will form the net moveable estate on which the child has a claim of one-third which from these figures will be seen as a reasonably substantial sum.

If, however, the testator had died intestate the whole of the estate would have gone to the surviving spouse and there would have been no moveable estate on which the child could make a claim. This is somewhat unusual, in that had there been no will, the law suggests that it is equitable that the surviving spouse should receive the whole of the deceased's estate. If the testator had made a will in which he says that the spouse is to receive the whole of his estate, the law gives a fairly substantial proportion of the moveable estate to the child, should it claim.

It may be possible for the surviving spouse to create an intestacy by giving up all rights in respect of the will and thereby achieving the desired result[1]. The wording of the will would have to be thoroughly checked, for example if a renunciation clause is included (see S5.11), a simple renunciation of her interest by the spouse would not achieve the desired result.

It may be that the testator, when the whole situation was explained to him would decide that in all the circumstances it was best not to have a will and allow the rules of intestate succession to apply. This would mean that the testator would not be able to choose the executors who he wished to act, nor to put in legacies.

There is, however, nothing to stop a will being drawn up purely to appoint executors and (perhaps) to leave legacies, with the residue undisposed of. The rules of intestate succession would therefore apply to the residue. In general, it is preferable if a will is made.

This may be an unusual situation, but it does highlight the understanding that is required of the intestate position in order to advise a client fully on making a will, particularly where the testator's estate is made up of suitable items which are in value close to the prior rights limits[2].

Spouse/children (2)

9.19   Where a testator's estate is in excess of the prior rights limits but is not what would be considered a particularly substantial estate, probably the most frequently-used type of will is one which leaves everything to the surviving spouse, whom failing the children.

In these circumstances one of the main considerations is whether a bequest to the children should be made on the first death.

In the circumstances outlined, it is likely that the surviving spouse would need assets not only already in her personal ownership, but also inherited from the first to die, to allow the survivor to maintain herself in the way to which she had become accustomed. Having said that, it is always worth looking forward to the potential value of the joint estates in the event of the death of the survivor, bearing in mind that with this type of will there is a 'lost' nil rate band for inheritance tax on the first death. The first £150,000 of the deceased's estate might be considered to have escaped tax twice, once in terms of the surviving spouse exemption, and once by being within the band of estate which is charged at nil per cent. If it is possible to make a legacy to the children on the first death, then it is obviously advisable for inheritance tax reasons, but it should not be done without consideration of the requirements of the surviving spouse.

In view of the children's legal rights, the possibility of including a legacy

1 *Kerr, Petitioner* 1968 SLT (Sh Ct) 61.
2 On this situation, see Style S3 which is a Style without a renunciation clause, so that the surviving spouse could create an intestacy if she survives and disclaims her interests; and see paras 6.30–6.32.

roughly equivalent to the legal rights claim could be considered (see paras 4.41–4.42).

It has been mentioned elsewhere in this book, in particular in paragraphs 2.25–2.30, that irrespective of what is mentioned in the will, a special destination will almost always take the deceased's half share of a house to the surviving spouse. If the heritable property was not held on a survivorship destination, then the testator could have bequeathed his half share of the house to the children who could continue to allow their surviving parent to reside there, but who would nevertheless own half the house. This would reduce the potential value of the survivor's estate for the purposes of inheritance tax. Such a scheme has to be looked at with some caution, in view of the fact that the children could force a sale if they so wished. A proportion of principal private residence relief for capital gains tax would also be lost. It is worth bearing in mind that even if there is a survivorship destination which would preclude the bequest in a will taking effect, it would still be possible to enter into a deed of variation which would be acceptable to the Capital Taxes Office, redirecting the half share of the house to the children.

Spouse/children (3)

9.20 A testator may have a reasonably substantial estate and his spouse may also have estate of her own, which would mean that if one came to own the total amount there could be fairly considerable inheritance tax payable on the second death.

However, it may be that it would substantially reduce the standard of living of the surviving spouse were a substantial bequest to be made in the will of the first to die.

It may well be that practitioners merely assume that in all the circumstances, it is best to take that inheritance tax charge on the second death and give the whole of the estate from the first to die to the survivor. If possible, a nil rate band legacy could be given to the children (see paras 4.38–4.40), but the spouse would lose the income from that share of the estate.

Another possibility is for a nil rate band bequest to be made into a discretionary trust where both the surviving spouse and children are beneficiaries. The trustees and executors will be aware of the situation that the income from the discretionary trust is required by the surviving spouse. While it should not be dealt with in such a way as to make it look as though the surviving spouse is receiving the income as of right, the object has been achieved of ensuring that the surviving spouse has the income and capital, if necessary, from the whole of her own and the inherited estate.

Provided the value of the assets in the discretionary trust does not exceed the nil rate band for inheritance tax purposes at any given time, then there will be no implications for that tax. On the death of the survivor, the discretionary trust may be wound up and, in effect, a nil rate band will be available for the trust assets, bearing in mind the other nil rate band available on the surviving spouse's own estate (see Style S10 and paras 5.96–5.107).

Spouse/children (4)

9.21 This paragraph deals with a similar problem to that mentioned in the previous paragraph. A testator may be, on the face of it, fairly wealthy on paper, but on investigation it becomes apparent that the greater part of the wealth is tied up in the value of a half share of a dwellinghouse. This problem has a potential solution, namely transferring the deceased's half share of a dwellinghouse into a nil rate band discretionary trust, but then allowing the surviving spouse to continue to live in the property. This leaves open the likelihood of the Inland Revenue claiming that the surviving spouse has an interest in possession in the trust, with the result that in the event of her death, very little would have been achieved. The trust assets treated as subject to an interest in possession would be aggregated with her own estate for the purposes of calculating tax.

It may be possible for the half share of the house to be transferred to a discretionary trust as a legacy in the will of the first to die. Then the surviving spouse can 'purchase' the house from the trustees. It may be possible to do this without any cash changing hands, if a security is created over the property, so that in the event of the death of the wife the house would appear in her estate as an asset, but an appropriate debt would also appear as due to the trustees.

If cash did change hands, it could be invested and the trustees could use capital and income at their discretion, principally to maintain the spouse.

Close consideration would obviously have to be given to this scheme to ensure that it did not fall foul of the inheritance tax legislation at the time of implementation.

Spouse/children (5)

9.22 A very common set of circumstances today with so many marriages ending in divorce is the situation where two people marry for a second time, but each with children from their first marriage.

In this situation each spouse, were he or she not to make a will, would be ensuring that his or her surviving spouse had the prior rights to an interest in a house, contents and a cash sum, plus a legal right to one third of the net moveable estate. The natural children of the deceased would have a right to one third of the net moveable estate, plus the free estate, being the remaining third of the moveable estate plus any excess heritage not required to meet the prior rights.

If, on the other hand, the will was made leaving everything to the natural children, then the new spouse could only claim his or her one-third share of the net moveable estate as a legal right.

The options available can cause a dilemma and the matter is often dealt with by giving one half of the testator's estate to the surviving spouse and one half to the natural children. This might, however, not be totally satisfactory, where for example there is a half share of a house involved. Who on the death of the first to die should receive the house? There is no simple answer.

Another possibility is for the husband and wife to make identical wills, whereby each makes a will leaving everything to the other, and on the death of the survivor an equitable split is directed between the two sets of natural children. This calls for a great deal of trust in one another, due to the fact that there is nothing to stop the survivor inheriting everything and changing the will in favour of his or her natural children alone.

Another possibility is for each to leave his or her estate in trust for the survivor. The survivor would have the use of the house and income from all the assets of the deceased's estate. On the death of the survivor, the trust capital will have been preserved by the trustees and can be made over to the truster's natural children with the natural children of the survivor taking their own parent's free estate. Neither the surviving spouse nor the children can encroach on capital unless the trustees agree. A liferent trust is the obvious type, but a discretionary trust could achieve the same ends.

While this is not an ideal solution for everyone and it may depend upon the value of the testator's estate, it is one way of ensuring that the client's wishes are met. It gives the client peace of mind to know that while the surviving spouse will be provided for, his natural children will ultimately benefit.

Families – general

9.23 A client might well want to make a will covering every possible eventuality for the next 30 years. Any attempt at implementing a complicated will to comply with the client's wishes in this respect may well be counter-productive. It is much better to consider making a will for the circumstances pertaining at the date of drafting, with a view to covering only, say, five years or a period until something significant may happen, such as beneficiaries attaining a certain age or a business being sold.

Business owners (1)

9.24 Wealthy people, who have either large business interests, or who have done a great deal of giving during their lifetime, are sometimes attracted to the possibility of a two-year discretionary trust. This allows consideration to be given to who should benefit from a list of beneficiaries given in the will. Decisions can be made at a more leisurely pace than that which is required if any specific bequests are made in the will, and the views of all interested parties can be taken with the final decisions being made by the trustees. The choice of trustees in this situation is obviously crucial.

This has proved to be particularly useful where someone has died owning substantial business interests. The trustees should obviously be given the power to carry on the business or company concerned.

Business owners – (2)

9.25 Company directors and business owners with young families may be attracted to the type of will where specific legacies are given, with the residue being left in liferent to the spouse and in fee to the children, perhaps on an accumulation and maintenance trust.

The executors and trustees are selected carefully and the powers to the trustees are also formulated in such a way to ensure that in the event of the death of the testator the business or company could be continued by the trustees until such time as it is either sold or the children are old enough to make a decision for themselves as to whether they are going to go into the business. The surviving spouse may or may not be involved in the business but the liferent ensures that the income from the interest in the business or company maintains the spouse and the children.

An accumulation and maintenance trust covers the possibility of the spouses dying in a common calamity, and the same powers are available to the trustees to continue the business or company.

This type of will is, if anything, likely to gain in popularity due to the fact that with 100 per cent business and agricultural property relief being available for inheritance tax, there is less urgency for business owners to consider tax-planning schemes. Such schemes usually envisage giving business assets away with a view to reducing potential inheritance tax. The current opposition parties have given some indication that the business and agricultural property exemptions would probably continue if they came to power, but of course the position cannot be predicted with any certainty.

Mutual will

9.26   One may be approached by clients who say they want a mutual will, but analysing what the testators want may allow the solicitor to offer a solution, which fits the testators' requirements and does not necessitate drafting a mutual will (see para 3.09 where some of the problems of mutual wills are discussed).

The testators normally wish to ensure that their estates pass to one another and that their combined estates pass on to a third party on the death of the survivor.

This may be achieved by two simple wills implementing these wishes. If there is genuine concern that the survivor could change his will after inheriting the estate of the first to die, they could leave each other a liferent of their estates with the fee to the third party. The income would be paid to the survivor and the trustees would have power to advance capital.

This suggests itself as a better solution than a real mutual will with all its potential problems. It is worth noting a comment by Elder at page vii of his book on wills where he says: 'No apology is offered for the omission of Mutual Wills; they should be avoided wherever possible'.

Executors/trustees

9.27   This book contains a very full section on executors and trustees (see paras 3.10–3.30). The only point to be added is that in considering this chapter, it will be apparent that there are situations which arise where executors and trustees need to be 'horses for courses'. It is rather pointless to set up a complicated will in which one envisages the possibility of a business or company being run by the trustees for a lengthy period if those trustees do not have the expertise to run the business.

It is also the case that there is no point in setting up a trust such as the discretionary trust for widow and children mentioned above in order to make use of the deceased's nil rate band, if it is not made known to the executors and trustees that the main, if not sole, income beneficiary of that trust is to be the spouse while she is alive.

Explanation of some standard clauses

9.28 Clients today are much more likely to read the whole of their wills and demand some explanation of clauses which may to the adviser appear to be standard. Again, this book deals very fully with items such as revocation, informal writings, tax, expenses and interest and powers and charging (see, in particular, Chapter 3). The practitioner should be able to deal with the client's questions not only at the time of taking instructions for the will, but possibly at the time of a second meeting when the client returns to the office to have the principal signed and witnessed. Having read the will, clients are perhaps more likely to raise questions as to why there is, for instance, a power to appropriate assets to beneficiaries, or about accumulations. The details supplied in Chapters 5, 6 and 7 about the various trusts and trust powers should assist in providing any explanations necessary.

Date for review of will

9.29 This is a difficult but important point. It has already been mentioned that very good advice to a client is that he should review his will on a regular basis. It has also been offered as good advice that if personal circumstances change, he should review his will at that point. In addition, one should not try to make a will at any given time for every eventuality. People have a tendency to make a will and forget about it, perhaps because to consider it means to consider their impending demise.

As computers become more sophisticated and more readily used in lawyers' offices, it is more than likely that there will be a review procedure implemented automatically. Bells should start sounding when a client's will has remained unconsidered for a certain length of time in the will safe, without being extracted for updating. There is no reason why, perhaps every five or ten years, a letter should not be sent to all clients to advise them of the length of time since their will was made. It could possibly even remind them of the main contents of the will, and ask if the testator felt that there was any need to consider updating, even if only in relation to addresses and the like.

Practitioners should find this a useful way of reminding clients of their existence. It might lead to some advertising of other services which are on offer.

CONCLUSION/VARIATIONS

9.30 Different forms and formats of interviews work for different people. If there is one general message, it is that the interview is of paramount importance, not just in relation to the formal business of taking instructions for a will, but in generally maintaining a particular client as a loyal (and productive) client of the firm.

A final point to consider is that for the best part of 20 years, those drafting wills have tended to do so knowing that if there was a problem, or a change of mind by the family or other beneficiaries, a deed of variation could be prepared to resolve matters. In 1989, the then Chancellor caused a scare by suggesting the withdrawal of the beneficial tax treatment available to such deeds. While such a threat was eventually withdrawn, that episode should serve as a warning not to take anything for granted in this field.

A combination of simplicity and maximum flexibility is essential. It is hoped that the Styles presented in this book, together with the detailed alternatives and commentary set out in the preceding chapters, will assist in achieving this end.

APPENDIX OF STYLES

STYLE 1   Short form of will by testator with no dependants excluding legacies

STYLE 2   Short form of will by testator with no dependants including legacies

STYLE 3   Short form of will by husband in favour of wife whom failing children with vesting on death

STYLE 4   Short form of will by husband with legacy to grandchildren and residue to wife and children with vesting on death without informal writings clause

STYLE 5   Liferent of residue to spouse whom failing children with vesting postponed

STYLE 6   Liferent of house to mother, liferent of half residue to spouse whom failing children, half residue to children, with vesting on death

STYLE 7   Residue to wife whom failing children on accumulation and maintenance trust

STYLE 7A   Accumulation and maintenance trust for grandchildren

STYLE 8   Short form of will by husband in favour of wife whom failing children with short form accumulation and maintenance trust

STYLE 9   Two-year discretionary trust will

STYLE 10   Nil rate band discretionary trust will. Residue to wife whom failing children on accumulation and maintenance trust

STYLE 11   Short form of will by husband in favour of wife where no children at present and whom failing both spouses' siblings

STYLE 12   Short form of will by testator domiciled abroad of Scottish immoveable property

STYLE 13   Codicil to Style 2 will

STYLE 14   Codicil to Style 2 will

PRECIS OF STYLE 1

Short form of will by testator with no dependants excluding legacies

1. Revocation of prior wills

2. Executors

3. Provision for informal writings

4. Any legacies to be paid free of tax, expenses and interest

5. The residue is to pass to

6. The executors are given short powers of administration and management

7. Declaration of Scottish domicile

8. Declaration as to cremation

396

STYLE 1

Short form of will by testator with no dependants excluding legacies

I, A (design) in order to settle the succession to my estate after my death provide as follows:

S1.1   *Revocation*   (**ONE**)   I revoke all prior wills and testamentary writings.

S1.2   *Executors*   (**TWO**)   I appoint B (design) and C (design) to be my executors.

S1.3   *Informal writings*   (**THREE**) I direct my executors to give effect to any future writings subscribed by me however informal the same may be provided that in the opinion of my executors they clearly express my intentions.

S1.4   *Legacies*   (**FOUR**) Unless otherwise specified any legacy granted by any writing shall be paid or made over as soon as my executors consider practicable after my death free of government duties in respect of my death and of delivery expenses but without interest.

S1.5   *Residue*   (**FIVE**)   I direct my executors to make over the residue of my estate to D (design) whom failing to E (design).

S1.6   *Powers*   (**SIX**)   My executors shall have the fullest powers of retention, realisation, investment, appropriation, transfer of property without realisation, and management of my estate/

estate as if they were absolute beneficial owners; and shall have power to resign office and to appoint one or more of their own number to act as solicitor or agent in any other capacity and to allow him or them the same remuneration to which he or they would have been entitled if not an executor or executors.

S1.7	*Domicile*	(**SEVEN**) I declare that my domicile is Scottish.
S1.8	*Funeral instructions*	(**EIGHT**) I wish my body to be cremated: IN WITNESS WHEREOF

STYLE 1

References

General		This brief, simple Style is not dealt with specifically as a complete document in the text. Its overall format is self-explanatory. See Chapters 1 and 9 and para 6.134. If any beneficiary lacks full capacity, provisions should be included to deal with this – see paras 6.46–6.51, 6.127–6.128.
Preliminary wording		See para 3.02 and on designation of the testator see para 9.10.
S1.1	*Revocation*	See paras 3.03–3.09 and on foreign aspects paras 2.67–2.70.
S1.2	*Executors*	See paras 3.10–3.30.
S1.3	*Informal writings*	See paras 3.31–3.36.
S1.4	*Legacies*	See paras 3.37–3.41. On interest see paras 4.46–4.47. On delivery expenses see paras 4.58–4.60.
S1.5	*Residue*	See Chapter 5 and on destinations-over paras 5.26–5.27.
S1.6	*Powers*	See paras 7.01–7.02 and 3.19–3.25.
S1.7	*Domicile*	See paras 2.60–2.77.
S1.8	*Funeral instructions*	See paras 3.42–3.62.

PRECIS OF STYLE 2

Short form of will by testator with no dependants including legacies

1. Revocation of prior wills

2. Executors

3. Legacy to executor

4. Provision for informal writings

5. Any legacies to be paid free of tax, expenses and interest

6. Pecuniary legacy

7. Charitable legacy

8. Legacy of painting (bearing tax)

9. Legacy of furniture and effects

10. Legacy of animal

11. Legacy of house

12. Legacy evacuating special destination

13. Legacy of in hand farm

14. Legacy of farm tenancy

15. Legacy of croft tenancy

16. Legacy of private company shares (bearing tax)

17. Legacy of partnership interest

18. Legacy of business

19. Legacy of Lloyd's interest

20. Legacy writing off loan

21. Legacy of annuity

22. Legacy of timeshare

23. The residue is to pass to

24. The executors are given short powers of administration and management

25. Declaration of Scottish domicile

26. Funeral instructions (body for medical research/spare part surgery)

STYLE 2

Short form of will by testator with no dependants including legacies

I, A (design) in order to settle the succession to my estate after my death provide as follows:

S2.1 *Revocation* (**ONE**) I revoke all prior wills and testamentary writings.

S2.2 *Executors* (**TWO**) I appoint B (design) and C AND CO. (TRUSTEES) LIMITED, incorporated under the Companies Acts and having its registered office at (address) to be my executors.

S2.3 *Legacy to executor* (**THREE**) I direct my executors to pay to the said B if he shall accept office as executor the sum of ONE THOUSAND POUNDS.

S2.4 *Informal writings* (**FOUR**) I direct my executors to give effect to any future writings subscribed by me however informal the same may be provided that in the opinion of my executors they clearly express my intentions.

S2.5 *Legacies* (**FIVE**) Unless otherwise specified any legacy granted by any writing shall be paid or made over as soon as my executors consider practicable after my death free of government duties in respect of my death and of delivery expenses but without interest.

S2.6/

S2.6	*Pecuniary legacy*	**(SIX)** I direct my executors to pay:

(1) To my godson D (design), the sum of ONE THOUSAND POUNDS;

(2) To my housekeeper E (design), the sum of FIVE THOUSAND POUNDS provided she is in my employment at the time of my death; and

(3) To my gardener and friend F (design), whom failing to his son G (design), the sum of FIVE HUNDRED POUNDS.

S2.7	*Charitable legacy*	**(SEVEN)** I direct my executors to pay:

(1) To H Charity (address), the sum of TEN THOUSAND POUNDS.

(2) To the Fabric Fund of St. I's Church of Scotland (address), the sum of FIVE THOUSAND POUNDS; and

(3) To the Faculty of Medicine at the University of J, the sum of ONE HUNDRED THOUSAND POUNDS for research into Acquired Immune Deficiency Syndrome;

Declaring that:

(a) if any legatee has changed its name or has amalgamated with or transferred its assets to any other body or has been wrongly designed then my executors shall give effect to such legacy as if it had been made to such body with similar purposes as my executors may in their sole discretion decide; and

(b)/

(b)   the receipt of an authorised official of any body shall be a sufficient discharge to my executors.

S2.8   *Legacy of painting (bearing tax)*   (**EIGHT**)   I direct my executors to make over to K (design), my painting of 'Spotty the Dog' by Sir Henry Raeburn R.A. and I declare that while this painting is presently on temporary loan to The National Gallery, London and is the subject of an undertaking in terms of Section 31 of the Inheritance Tax Act 1984, this legacy is to bear its rateable proportion of any government duties in respect of my death.

S2.9   *Legacies of furniture and effects*   (**NINE**)   I direct my executors to make over:

(1)   to L (design), an item of my jewellery of her choice, to be made within six months of my death; and

(2)   to M (design) and N (design), equally between them and to the survivor of them all my articles of personal, domestic, household, garage, garden or leisure use, ornament or consumption and my motor vehicles and that in such way as they may agree or failing such agreement as my executors in their sole discretion shall consider approximately equal and fair.

S2.10   *Legacy of animal*   (**TEN**)   I direct my executors to make over my dog 'Spotty' or any other dog owned by me together/

together with the sum of ONE THOUSAND POUNDS to O

(design), provided he accepts responsibility for its welfare

for the remainder of its natural life.

S2.11 *Legacy of*   (**ELEVEN**)   I direct my executors to make
       house

over to P (design), my interest in any house occupied as

my normal residence at the time of my death, free of all

expenses of transfer, heritable debts and securities, and

other capital burdens affecting my interest in the house at

the time of my death.

S2.12 *Legacy*   (**TWELVE**)   I direct my executors to make
       evacuating
       special   over to Q my interest in the house known as 4 Blackacre
       destination

Street, Edinburgh, which house is held by myself and AA

on a special destination contained in the disposition by BB

in favour of myself and the said AA and the survivor of us

dated 5th April 1991 and recorded in the Sasine Register

for the County of Midlothian on 1st May 1991, and which

destination I hereby evacuate.

S2.13 *Legacy of in* (**THIRTEEN**)   I direct my executors to make
       hand farm

over to R (design), the farm and lands of Lochbarr,

Taynuilt, Argyll, including the farm house and other farm

buildings, free of all expenses of transfer, heritable debts

and securities, and other capital burdens affecting the

farm at the time of my death, together with the whole

stock/

stock (whether living or dead), crops (whether growing or harvested including timber standing or fallen), unexhausted manures, seeds, fertilizers and other farm stores, farm vehicles, machinery and implements, and all other corporeal moveables used in the business of farming and my rights in all premiums, subsidies and quotas, all in so far as belonging to me at the time of my death.

S2.14 *Legacy of farm tenancy* (**FOURTEEN**) I direct my executors to make over to S (design), my interest in the tenancy of the farm and lands of Biggarshiels, by Haddington, East Lothian, free of all expenses of transfer, heritable debts and securities, and other capital burdens affecting my interest at the time of my death, together with the whole stock (whether living or dead), crops (whether growing or harvested, including timber, standing or fallen), unexhausted manures, seeds, fertilizers and other farm stores, farm vehicles, machinery and implements and all other corporeal moveables used in the business of farming, and my rights in all premiums, subsidies and quotas, all in so far as belonging to me at the time of my death.

S2.15 *Legacy of croft tenancy* (**FIFTEEN**) I direct my executors to make over my tenancy of the croft at Greater Dalgleish, South Uist, to my nephew T (design).

S2.16/

S2.16	*Legacy of private company shares (bearing tax)*	**(SIXTEEN)** I direct my executors to make over to U (design), all my shares and stock of whatever classes in Spotty Pooper Scoopers Limited (Company number 100101) or such other shares or stock as may represent the same at the time of my death as a result of any amalgamation takeover or reorganisation of this Company as to which my executors shall be the sole judges, and I declare that this legacy is to bear its rateable proportion of any government duties in respect of my death.
S2.17	*Legacy of partnership interest*	**(SEVENTEEN)** I direct my executors to make over to V (design), my whole interest of whatever kind in the firm of Stevens' Festival Souvenirs as it is presently constituted or as it may be constituted at the time of my death.
S2.18	*Legacy of business*	**(EIGHTEEN)** I direct my executors to make over to W (design), my business presently carried on under the name Intercontinental Garden Gnomes at (address) together with the whole property, plant and machinery, stocks, contracts, book debts, bank or other accounts, goodwill and liabilities relating thereto as to all of which my executors shall be the sole judges, and subject to such discharges and indemnities as my executors may require.

S2.19/

S2.19 *Legacy of*   **(NINETEEN)**   I direct my executors to make
Lloyd's
interest   over to X my whole interest in Lloyd's of London

including all income and gains in respect thereof received

after my death, all profits of my underwriting accounts

open at the time of my death, my deposits and reserves,

any property given as security for a guarantee to support

my membership of Lloyd's, the benefit of any policy of

insurance taken out to protect my estate against loss

occurring as a result of my membership, but subject to all

losses liabilities and expenses referable to this interest

including income tax and capital gains tax, and subject to a

rateable proportion of any government duties in respect of

my death, and I declare that my executors' decision as to

the property covered by this legacy shall be conclusive.

S2.20 *Legacy*   **(TWENTY)**   I direct my executors to make
writing
off loan   over to Y the balance including interest if any remaining

outstanding of the loan of £5,000 which I made to him.

S2.21 *Legacy of*   **(TWENTY ONE)**   I direct my executors to pay to Z
annuity

(design) an annuity of TWO THOUSAND POUNDS during his

life, payable subject to income tax at such intervals not

being greater than one year as my executors may decide,

declaring that my executors may provide for the payment

of the annuity:

(1)/

(1)   by setting aside and retaining as a separate fund such part of my estate as they may in their sole discretion consider sufficient for the payment of the annuity, declaring that:

(a)   the annuity shall be a charge on the capital of this fund if the income thereof should be insufficient, but that it shall not be a charge on the residue of my estate;

(b)   they shall not distribute any surplus income but shall accumulate it with the capital of the fund during the period of twenty-one years after my death (although they may resort to such accumulated income for payment of the annuity for future years if required);

(c)   they shall have power to commute the annuity at any time with the consent in writing of the said Z by paying to him such capital sum from the fund as they in their sole discretion decide is reasonable in all the circumstances and on such commutation Z shall have no further claim in respect of the annuity; and

(d)   the separate fund on the termination of the annuity, or any balance on its commutation, or any surplus income arising more than twenty-one years after my death shall be distributed as part of the residue of my estate; or

(2)/

(2)   by purchase in their names of an annuity payable to them from any life office or other provider thereof in such amount as they in their sole discretion shall consider sufficient for the payment of the annuity to the said Z for his alimentary use; declaring that they may authorise the provider of the annuity to pay it directly to the said Z.

S2.22   *Legacy of timeshare*   (**TWENTY TWO**)   I direct my executors to make over to CC (design) my whole interest of whatever kind in the timeshare at The Smart Club, Back O'Beyond, Inverness-shire, as it is presently constituted or as it may be constituted at the time of my death.

S2.23   *Residue*   (**TWENTY THREE**) I direct my executors to make over the residue of my estate to DD (design), whom failing to EE (design).

S2.24   *Powers*   (**TWENTY FOUR**)   My executors shall have the fullest powers of retention, realisation, investment, appropriation, transfer of property without realisation, and management of my estate as if they were absolute beneficial owners; and shall have power to resign office and to appoint one or more of their own number to act as solicitor or agent in any other capacity and to allow him or them the same remuneration to which he or they would have been entitled if not an executor or executors.

S2.25/

S2.25 *Domicile* (**TWENTY FIVE**)   I declare that my domicile is

Scottish.

S2.26 *Funeral*   (**TWENTY SIX**)   I direct my executors to offer my
instructions
(body for   body, or any part thereof, to any hospital or University
medical
research/spare Faculty of Medicine for the purposes of spare part surgery
part surgery)
or medical research, training or education and in the event

of this offer not being taken up or my remains subsequently

being released I wish to be cremated: IN WITNESS WHEREOF

STYLE 2

References

General		This Style while very long in the form presented, is only an extended version of Style S1, including a range of legacies. General matters relating to legacies are dealt with in Chapters 4, 5 and 6. If any beneficiary lacks full capacity, provisions should be included to deal with this – see paras 6.46–6.51, 6.127–6.128.
Preliminary wording		See para 3.02 and on designation of the testator see para 9.10.
S2.1	*Revocation*	See paras 3.03–3.09 and on foreign aspects para 2.67–2.70.
S2.2	*Executors*	See paras 3.10–3.30.
S2.3	*Legacy to executor*	See paras 6.149–6.156. On conflict of interest see paras 7.18–7.19. On conditional legacies see paras 5.37–5.51.
S2.4	*Informal writings*	See paras 3.31–3.36.
S2.5	*Legacies*	See paras 3.37–3.41. On interest see paras 4.46–4.47. On delivery expenses see para 4.58–4.60.
S2.6	*Pecuniary legacy*	See para 4.34–4.37. On the legacies to employed persons see para 5.47 and especially 6.135–6.136. On conditional legacies see paras 5.37–5.51.
S2.7	*Charitable legacy*	See paras 6.141–6.146.
S2.8	*Legacy of painting (bearing tax)*	See paras 4.58–4.62. On the tax point, see para 3.41.
S2.9	*Legacies of furniture and effects*	See paras 4.48–4.57.
S2.10	*Legacy of animal*	See para 4.67–4.70.
S2.11	*Legacy of house*	See paras 4.71–4.72, 4.76–4.81.
S2.12	*Legacy evacuating special destination*	See paras 2.25–2.30.

S2.13	*Legacy of in hand farm*	See paras 4.82–4.84, 4.90–4.93.
S2.14	*Legacy of farm tenancy*	See paras 4.75, 4.85–4.86, 4.90–4.93.
S2.15	*Legacy of croft tenancy*	See paras 4.88, 4.90–4.93.
S2.16	*Legacy of private company shares*	See paras 2.19, 4.90–4.93, 4.102–4.105, 4.107.
S2.17	*Legacy of partnership interest*	See paras 2.19, 4.90–4.93, 4.99–4.101.
S2.18	*Legacy of business*	See paras 2.19, 4.90–4.93, 4.96–4.98.
S2.19	*Legacy of Lloyd's interest*	See paras 4.126–4.127.
S2.20	*Legacy writing off loan*	See para 4.117–4.118.
S2.21	*Legacy of annuity*	See paras 4.129–4.135.
S2.22	*Legacy of timeshare*	See para 4.89.
S2.23	*Residue*	See Chapter 5 and on destinations-over paras 5.26–5.27.
S2.24	*Powers*	See paras 7.01–7.02 and 3.19–3.25.
S2.25	*Domicile*	See paras 2.60–2.77.
S2.26	*Funeral instructions*	See paras 3.42–3.62, in particular 3.56–3.61

PRECIS OF STYLE 3

Short form of will by husband in favour of wife whom failing children with vesting on death

1. Revocation of prior wills

2. Executors

3. Provision for informal writings

4. Any legacies to be paid free of tax, expenses and interest

5. The residue is to pass to the testator's spouse

6. If the spouse does not survive for 30 days then the residue passes to the testator's children equally with the children of any predeceasing children taking their parent's share

7. The executors are given wide powers to deal with funds falling to beneficiaries lacking capacity

8. The executors are given short powers of administration and management

9. Declaration of Scottish domicile

10. Guardians to children

11. Declaration as to cremation

STYLE 3

Short form of will by husband in favour of wife whom failing children with vesting on death

I, A (design) in order to settle the succession to my estate after my death provide as follows:

S3.1 *Revocation* (**ONE**)   I revoke all prior wills and testamentary writings.

S3.2 *Executors* (**TWO**)   I appoint my wife B, residing with me, and C (design) to be my executors.

S3.3 *Informal writings* (**THREE**)   I direct my executors to give effect to any future writings subscribed by me however informal the same may be provided that in the opinion of my executors they clearly express my intentions.

S3.4 *Legacies* (**FOUR**)   Unless otherwise specified any legacy granted by any writing shall be paid or made over as soon as my executors consider practicable after my death free of government duties in respect of my death and of delivery expenses but without interest.

S3.5 *Residue to wife* (**FIVE**)   I direct my executors to make over the residue of my estate to my wife B if she survives for thirty days after my death.

S3.6 *Residue to children* (**SIX**)   If my wife B does not survive me for thirty days, but in such event only, I direct my executors to make over/

over the residue of my estate to such of my children D, E and F and any other children of mine as shall survive me equally among them if more than one, declaring that should any of my children predecease me leaving issue (including adopted issue) who shall survive me each member of a generation of issue of such predeceasing child shall share equally in the part of my estate, both original and accresced, which would have fallen to its parent if in life.

S3.7 *Beneficiaries lacking capacity*

(**SEVEN**) If any part of my estate is held for a beneficiary who lacks full legal capacity my executors shall have full power either to pay or apply the whole or any part of the income or capital falling to such beneficiary for his or her benefit in any manner my executors think proper, or to retain the same until such capacity is attained, or to pay over the same to the legal guardian or the person for the time being having the custody of such beneficiary whose receipt shall be a sufficient discharge to my executors.

S3.8 *Powers*

(**EIGHT**) My executors shall have the fullest powers of retention, realisation, investment, appropriation, transfer of property without realisation, and management of my estate as if they were absolute beneficial owners; and shall have power to resign office and to appoint one or more/

more of their own number to act as solicitor or agent in any other capacity and to allow him or them the same remuneration to which he or they would have been entitled if not an executor or executors.

S3.9 *Domicile* (**NINE**) I declare that my domicile is Scottish.

S3.10 *Guardians* (**TEN**) In the event of my said wife so failing to survive me I appoint my brother and sister-in-law G (design) and H (design) to be guardians to my children.

S3.11 *Funeral instructions* (**ELEVEN**) I wish my body to be cremated: IN WITNESS WHEREOF

STYLE 3

References

General		This is a short family will. Provision for the testator's family is dealt with generally in Chapter 6. See in particular para 6.112 and see also Chapter 9.
Preliminary wording		See para 3.02 and on designation of the testator see para 9.10.
S3.1	*Revocation*	See paras 3.03–3.09 and on foreign aspects paras 2.67–2.70.
S3.2	*Executors*	See paras 3.10–3.30.
S3.3	*Informal writings*	See paras 3.31–3.36.
S3.4	*Legacies*	See paras 3.37–3.41. On interest see paras 4.46–4.47. On delivery expenses see paras 4.58–4.60.
S3.5	*Residue to wife*	See Chapter 6 generally, especially paras 6.02–6.09, 6.29 and 6.112. On survivorship, see paras 5.15–5.19. See also paras 9.16–9.22.
S3.6	*Residue to children*	See Chapter 6 generally, especially paras 6.11–6.12, 6.29, 6.33–6.51, 6.112, 6.114, 6.118–6.119, 6.122. On destinations-over and division among beneficiaries see paras 5.02–5.14, 5.26–5.27. See also paras 9.16–9.19.
S3.7	*Beneficiaries lacking capacity*	See paras 6.46–6.51, 6.127–6.128.
S3.8	*Powers*	See paras 7.01–7.02 and 3.19–3.25.
S3.9	*Domicile*	See paras 2.60–2.77.
S3.10	*Guardians*	See paras 6.86–6.111.
S3.11	*Funeral instructions*	See paras 3.42–3.62.

PRECIS OF STYLE 4

Short form of will by husband with legacy to grandchildren and residue to wife and children with vesting on death without informal writings clause

1. Revocation of prior wills

2. Executors

3. Legacy of £100,000 to grandchildren who survive testator to be paid free of tax

4. The residue is to pass half to the testator's spouse and half, or the whole if the spouse does not survive for 30 days, to the testator's children equally with the children of any predeceasing children taking their parent's share

5. Lifetime gifts are to be brought into account in calculating a beneficiary's share of residue

6. The executors are given wide powers to deal with funds falling to beneficiaries lacking capacity

7. The executors are given short powers of administration and management

8. Declaration of Scottish domicile

9. Guardians to children

10. Declaration as to cremation

STYLE 4

Short form of will by husband with legacy to grandchildren and residue to wife and children with vesting on death without informal writings clause

I, A (design) in order to settle the succession to my estate after my death provide as follows:

S4.1	*Revocation*	(**ONE**) I revoke all prior wills and testamentary writings.

S4.2 *Executors* (**TWO**) I appoint my wife B, residing with me, and C (design) and either of whom failing D (design) to be my executors.

S4.3 *Legacy to grandchildren* (**THREE**) I direct my executors to pay the sum of ONE HUNDRED THOUSAND POUNDS to such of my grandchildren as shall survive me equally among them if more than one, declaring that should any of my grandchildren predecease me leaving issue who shall survive me each member of a generation of issue of such predeceasing grandchild shall share equally in the part, both original and accresced, which would have fallen to its parent if in life, payable as soon as my executors consider practicable after my death free of government duties in respect of my death but without interest.

S4.4 *Residue to wife and children* (**FOUR**) I direct my executors to make over the residue of my estate one half to my wife B if she survives for/

for thirty days after my death and one half, or the whole if she does not so survive, to such of my children E, F, G and any other children of mine as shall survive me equally among them if more than one, declaring that should any of my children predecease me leaving issue (including adopted issue) who shall survive me each member of a generation of issue of such predeceasing child shall share equally in the part of my estate, both original and accresced, which would have fallen to its parent if in life.

S4.5 *Lifetime advances* (**FIVE**) I direct my executors in calculating the amount of residue to take into account any advances made by me to any beneficiary and to deduct such advances from the share of residue due to such beneficiary or his or her issue, and my executors shall be the sole judges as to the calculations required by this direction.

S4.6 *Beneficiaries lacking capacity* (**SIX**) If any part of my estate is held for a beneficiary who lacks full legal capacity my executors shall have full power either to pay or apply the whole or any part of the income or capital falling to such beneficiary for his or her benefit in any manner my executors think proper, or to retain the same until such capacity is attained, or to pay over the same to the legal guardian or the person for the time/

time being having the custody of such beneficiary whose receipt shall be a sufficient discharge to my executors.

S4.7 *Powers* (**SEVEN**)   My executors shall have the fullest powers of retention, realisation, investment, appropriation, transfer of property without realisation, and management of my estate as if they were absolute beneficial owners; and shall have power to resign office and to appoint one or more of their own number to act as solicitor or agent in any other capacity and to allow him or them the same remuneration to which he or they would have been entitled if not an executor or executors.

S4.8 *Domicile* (**EIGHT**)   I declare that my domicile is Scottish.

S4.9 *Guardians* (**NINE**)   In the event of my said wife so failing to survive me I appoint my brother and sister-in-law H (design) and I (design) to be guardians to my children.

S4.10 *Funeral instructions* (**TEN**)   I wish my body to be cremated: IN WITNESS WHEREOF

STYLE 4

References

General		This Style is another family will, incorporating a division of the estate over two generations and involving a pecuniary legacy as well as fractional shares. The issues addressed are dealt with generally in Chapters 5 and 6.
Preliminary wording		See para 3.02 and on designation of the testator see para 9.10.
S4.1	*Revocation*	See paras 3.03–3.09 and on foreign aspects paras 2.67–2.70.
S4.2	*Executors*	See paras 3.10–3.30, and in particular 3.26–3.30.
S4.3	*Legacy to grandchildren*	On pecuniary legacies, see paras 4.34–4.37. On division between beneficiaries and destinations-over, see paras 5.02–5.27. On legacies to grandchildren, see paras 6.115–6.117, 6.123–6.124.
S4.4	*Residue to wife and children*	See Chapter 6 generally, especially paras 6.02–6.12, 6.29–6.52, 6.112–6.122 and on destinations-over, survivorship and the division among beneficiaries, see paras 5.02–5.27. See also paras 9.13–9.19.
S4.5	*Lifetime advances*	See paras 4.28–4.33.
S4.6	*Beneficiaries lacking capacity*	See paras 6.46–6.51, 6.127–6.128.
S4.7	*Powers*	See paras 7.01–7.02 and 3.19–3.25.
S4.8	*Domicile*	See paras 2.60–2.77.
S4.9	*Guardians*	See paras 6.86–6.111.
S4.10	*Funeral instructions*	See paras 3.42–3.62.

PRECIS OF STYLE 5

Liferent of residue to spouse whom failing children with vesting postponed

1. Revocation of prior wills

2. Executors and trustees

3. Provision for informal writings

4. Any legacies to be paid free of tax, expenses and interest

5. Legacy of furniture and personal effects to spouse

6. Liferent of whole residue to spouse

7. At the end of the liferent the capital passes to the testator's children then alive with the children of any predeceasing children taking their parent's share

8. The trustees can distribute capital to the testator's children with the liferenter's consent, or to the liferenter

9. Apportionment of income is excluded

10. The trustees are given wide powers to deal with funds falling to beneficiaries lacking capacity

11. If any beneficiary renounces any benefit then that benefit passes to the beneficiaries who would have been entitled if the original beneficiary had predeceased

12. The trustees are given wide and flexible powers of administration and management

13. Usual trustees' immunities

14. Declaration of Scottish domicile

15. Guardians to children

STYLE 5

Liferent of residue to spouse whom failing children with vesting postponed

I, A (design) in order to settle the succession to my estate after my death provide as follows:

S5.1 *Revocation* (**ONE**) I revoke all prior wills and testamentary writings.

S5.2 *Executors and trustees* (**TWO**) I appoint B (design), my wife C, residing with me, and D (design) to be my executors and trustees (who along with any other persons who may be appointed or assumed are referred to as 'my Trustees').

S5.3 *Informal writings* (**THREE**) I direct my Trustees to give effect to any future writings subscribed by me however informal the same may be provided that in the opinion of my Trustees they clearly express my intentions.

S5.4 *Legacies* (**FOUR**) Unless otherwise specified any legacy granted by any writing shall be paid or made over as soon as my Trustees consider practicable after my death free of government duties in respect of my death and of delivery expenses but without interest.

S5.5 *Personal effects to wife* (**FIVE**) I direct my Trustees to make over to my wife C if she survives for thirty days after my death all my articles of personal, domestic, household, garage, garden or/

or leisure use, ornament or consumption and my motor vehicles.

S5.6 *Liferent to wife* (**SIX**)   I direct my Trustees to hold the residue of my estate in liferent for my wife C provided that she survives for thirty days after my death.

S5.7 *Termination of liferent* (**SEVEN**)   On the failure termination or renunciation in whole or in part of the foregoing liferent, I direct my Trustees to make over the whole or such part of the residue to such of my children E, F, G and any other children of mine as shall survive the date or dates of vesting equally among them if more than one, declaring that should any of my children predecease those dates leaving issue (including adopted issue) who shall survive those dates each member of a generation of issue of such predeceasing child shall share equally in the part of my estate, both original and accresced, which would have fallen to its parent if in life, and in every case vesting shall be postponed until the date or dates of failure, termination or renunciation of the foregoing liferent.

S5.8 *Distributions from capital* (**EIGHT**)   My Trustees may make distributions out of the residue of my estate to any beneficiary or prospective beneficiary and including the liferenter provided that:

(1)/

(1) any distributions made to any prospective bene-

ficiary shall not be made without the consent of my wife;

(2) any distributions made to or for behoof of any pros-

pective beneficiary shall be taken into account in calcu-

lating the amount of residue and be deducted without

interest from the share of residue to which such pros-

pective beneficiary is or would have been entitled; and

(3) any distributions shall vest on payment.

S5.9   *No*   (**NINE**)   There shall be no apportionment as
        apportionment
                            between capital and income on any occasion.

S5.10   *Beneficiaries*   (**TEN**)   If any part of my estate is held for a
        lacking
        capacity   beneficiary who lacks full legal capacity my Trustees shall

                            have full power either to pay or apply the whole or any part

                            of the income or capital falling to such beneficiary for his

                            or her behoof in any manner my Trustees may think

                            proper, or to retain the same until such capacity is attained

                            accumulating income with capital, or to pay over the same

                            to the legal guardian or the person for the time being

                            having the custody of such beneficiary whose receipt shall

                            be a sufficient discharge to my Trustees.

S5.11   *Renunciation*   (**ELEVEN**)   In the event of any benefit conferred by
        of benefit
                            this will being renounced in whole or in part the benefit or

                            such part or parts thereof shall pass to the beneficiary or

                            beneficiaries/

beneficiaries who would have been entitled and on the terms and conditions which would have applied had the beneficiary so renouncing predeceased me.

S5.12 *Trustees' powers* (**TWELVE**)   My Trustees shall have the fullest powers of and regard to retention, realisation, investment, appropriation, transfer of property without realisation, and management of my estate as if they were absolute beneficial owners; and shall have power to do everything they may consider necessary or expedient for the administration of the trust; and in particular and without prejudice to these general powers my Trustees shall have power:

retention etc (1)   to retain, sell, purchase, lease or hire the estate or any part thereof;

investment (2)   to invest the whole or any part of the estate in heritable and leasehold property, investments, securities, insurance policies, deposits and other assets of whatever description, whether producing income or not, whether or not falling within the class of investments authorised for trust funds, whether or not payable to bearer, and wherever situated;

insurance policies (3)   to effect, maintain and acquire policies of insurance of whatever description; and to insure any property on whatever terms they think fit including on a first loss basis;

management/

management of (4)   to administer and manage any heritable or real
heritage

property forming part of the estate; to repair, maintain,

renew and improve the same and to erect additional

buildings and structures; to grant, vary and terminate

leases and rights of tenancy or occupancy; to plant, thin

and cut down timber; to work or let minerals; all as my

Trustees may think proper and as if they were absolute

owners of the estate;

businesses   (5)   to continue or to commence any business, whether

alone or in conjunction or in partnership with any other

persons, or through any companies, for such period as my

Trustees may think proper; to appoint or employ any

trustee or any other person in any capacity in relation to

such business and to pay to them suitable remuneration

for services, including pension provisions for any

employees or their dependants; and to delegate or entrust

to any persons the control and management of such busi-

ness to such extent as my Trustees may think fit; and my

Trustees

(a)   may employ for the purposes of such business such

part of the income or capital as they think proper;

(b)   shall exercise only such control or supervision of

such business as they shall think fit;

(c)/

(c)   shall be entitled to be relieved from the estate from all personal responsibility for any loss arising from such business operations; and

(d)   shall be entitled to retain personally any remuneration for their services;

borrow and lend   (6)   to borrow or lend with or without security; and to grant or continue any guarantee or indemnity for the benefit of any beneficiary actual or prospective;

occupation by beneficiaries   (7)   to lend or allow to be used the whole or any part of the estate at such rate of interest or rent as they may consider appropriate, or free of interest or rent, to or by any person who is for the time being entitled to payment of a share of the income of the estate or to whom or for whose benefit the income may be paid or applied in the exercise of a discretion then available to my Trustees;

nominees   (8)   to allow the estate or any part thereof to be registered in the names of or held or the documents of title to be held by any person, firm, corporation or other body as nominee of my Trustees;

delegation of investment management   (9)   revocably to delegate any power or powers of making, managing, realising or otherwise dealing with any investment or deposit comprised in the estate to any person or persons upon such terms as to remuneration or otherwise/

otherwise as my Trustees may think fit and no trustee shall
be responsible for the default of any such agent if the
trustee in question employed him in good faith;

additions   (10)   to accept as an addition to my estate any other
property which may be made over to them;

allocation   (11)   to decide what is capital and what is income and the
between capital
and income   proportion in which expenses are to be charged against
capital and income respectively;

appropriation   (12)   to set apart and appropriate specific property of any
description to represent the whole or part of the share,
prospective or otherwise, of any beneficiary at such
valuation as my Trustees shall determine, so that thereafter the particular share or part shall have the full
benefit and whole risk of the appropriated investments or
assets;

settlement   (13)   to settle with any beneficiary entitled to any part of
the estate by conveying to him or her in satisfaction
thereof either specific property or money, or partly one
and partly the other, as to my Trustees shall seem proper
and at such valuation as they shall determine and to
compel acceptance accordingly;

conflict of   (14)   to enter into any transaction or do any act otherwise
interest
authorised by law or by this deed notwithstanding that any
trustee/

trustee is or might be acting as *auctor in rem suam* or with a conflict of interest between such trustee and himself as an individual or as trustee of any other trust or any partnership of which a trustee is a partner or any company of which a trustee is a shareholder or director or in relation to any combination of these capacities provided that the trustee or trustees with whom there is or may be any such conflict is or are not the sole trustee or trustees;

participation in discretion (15) to participate in the exercise of any discretion granted to my Trustees notwithstanding that a trustee is or may be a or the sole beneficiary in whose favour the discretion is then exercised provided that there is at least one trustee not so favoured;

resignation (16) to resign office notwithstanding any benefit hereunder;

agents (17) to appoint one or more of their own number to act as solicitor or agent in any other capacity and to allow him or them the same remuneration to which he or they would have been entitled if not a trustee or trustees;

non-resident trustees (18) to appoint any one or more trustees resident out of the United Kingdom and themselves to resign office;

administration abroad (19) to carry on the administration of the trust hereby created in some place out of the United Kingdom;

(20)/

renunciation (20) to renounce for themselves and their successors in
of powers
office the power to exercise any of the foregoing powers in

this purpose as if the same were vested in them beneficially

and not as trustees.

S5.13 *Immunities* (**THIRTEEN**) My Trustees shall not be liable for

depreciation in value of the property in my estate, nor for

omissions or errors in judgement, nor for neglect in man-

agement, nor for insolvency of debtors, nor for the acts,

omissions, neglects or defaults of each other or of any

agent employed by them.

S5.14 *Domicile* (**FOURTEEN**) I declare that my domicile is Scottish.

S5.15 *Guardians* (**FIFTEEN**) In the event of my said wife so failing to

survive me I appoint my brother and sister-in-law H

(design) and I (design) to be guardians to my children: IN

WITNESS WHEREOF

STYLE 5

References

General		This Style is dealt with at paras 5.74–5.80. On liferent trusts in general, see paras 5.62–5.67. On vesting, see paras 5.28–5.36.
Preliminary wording		See para 3.02 and on designation of the testator see para 9.10.
S5.1	*Revocation*	See paras 3.03–3.09 and on foreign aspects paras 2.67–2.70.
S5.2	*Executors and trustees*	See paras 3.10–3.30.
S5.3	*Informal writings*	See paras 3.31–3.36.
S5.4	*Legacies*	See paras 3.37–3.41. On interest see paras 4.46–4.47. On delivery expenses see paras 4.58–4.60.
S5.5	*Personal effects to wife*	See para 5.75. On the items contained within this legacy, see paras 4.48–4.57.
S5.6	*Liferent to wife*	See para 5.76. On issues relating to the meaning of 'wife', see paras 6.02–6.09. On survivorship, see paras 5.15–5.19. See also paras 9.16–9.19.
S5.7	*Termination of liferent*	See para 5.77. On issues relating to children, see paras 6.11–6.12, 6.29–6.52, 6.112–6.122. On destinations-over and the division among beneficiaries, see paras 5.02–5.14, 5.26–5.27. On renunciation, see paras 5.20–5.25. See also paras 9.16–9.22.
S5.8	*Distribution from capital*	See paras 5.78–5.80. On vesting, see paras 5.28–5.36.
S5.9	*No apportionment*	See para 7.28.
S5.10	*Beneficiaries lacking capacity*	See paragaphs 6.46–6.51, 6.127–6.128.
S5.11	*Renunciation of benefit*	See paras 5.20–5.25.
S5.12	*Trustees' powers*	See paras 7.03–7.27 and 3.19–3.25.
S5.13	*Immunities*	See para 7.29.
S5.14	*Domicile*	See paras 2.60–2.77.
S5.15	*Guardians*	See paras 6.86–6.111.

PRECIS OF STYLE 6

Liferent of house to mother, liferent of half residue to spouse whom failing children, half residue to children, with vesting on death

1. Revocation of prior wills

2. Executors and trustees

3. Provision for informal writings

4. Any legacies to be paid free of tax, expenses and interest

5. Liferent of house to mother

6. Legacy of furniture and personal effects to spouse

7. Liferent of half residue to spouse

8. Half of the residue passes to the testator's children equally with the children of any predeceasing children taking their parent's share

9. At the end of each liferent the capital passes to the testator's children alive at the testator's death with the children of any predeceasing children taking their parent's share

10. Apportionment of income is excluded

11. The trustees are given wide powers to deal with funds falling to beneficiaries lacking capacity

12. If any beneficiary renounces any benefit then that benefit passes to the beneficiaries who would have been entitled if the original beneficiary had predeceased

13. The trustees are given wide and flexible powers of administration and management

14. Usual trustees' immunities

15. Declaration of Scottish domicile

16. Guardians to children

STYLE 6

Liferent of house to mother, liferent of half residue to spouse whom failing children, half residue to children, with vesting on death

I, A (design) in order to settle the succession to my estate after my death provide as follows:

S6.1   *Revocation*   (**ONE**)   I revoke all prior wills and testamentary writings.

S6.2   *Executors and trustees*   (**TWO**)   I appoint B (design), my wife C, residing with me, and D (design) to be my executors and trustees (who along with any other persons who may be appointed or assumed are referred to as 'my Trustees').

S6.3   *Informal writings*   (**THREE**)   I direct my Trustees to give effect to any future writings subscribed by me however informal the same may be provided that in the opinion of my Trustees they clearly express my intentions.

S6.4   *Legacies*   (**FOUR**)   Unless otherwise specified any legacy granted by any writing shall be paid or made over as soon as my Trustees consider practicable after my death free of government duties in respect of my death and of delivery expenses but without interest.

S6.5   *Liferent for mother*   (**FIVE**)   I direct my Trustees to hold the house owned by me at (address) or such other house occupied by her/

her but not by me, or the property representing such house following a sale after my death in liferent for my mother E (design).

| S6.6 | *Personal effects to wife* | **(SIX)** I direct my Trustees to make over to my wife C if she survives for thirty days after my death all my articles of personal, domestic, household, garage, garden or leisure use, ornament or consumption and my motor vehicles. |

| S6.7 | *Liferent of half residue to wife* | **(SEVEN)** I direct my Trustees to hold one half of the residue of my estate in liferent for my wife C provided that she survives for thirty days after my death. |

| S6.8 | *Half residue to children* | **(EIGHT)** I direct my Trustees to make over one half of the residue of my estate to such of my children F, G, H and any other children of mine as shall survive me declaring that should any of my children predecease me leaving issue (including adopted issue) who shall survive me each member of a generation of issue of such pre-deceasing child shall share equally in the part of my estate, both original and accresced, which would have fallen to its parent if in life. |

| S6.9 | *Termination of liferents* | **(NINE)** Subject to the foregoing liferents, I direct my Trustees to make over the parts of my estate which were or would have been liferented to such of my children/ |

children F, G, H and any other children of mine as shall survive me, declaring that should any of my children predecease me leaving issue (including adopted issue) who shall survive me each member of a generation of issue of such predeceasing child shall share equally in the part of my estate, both original and accresced, which would have fallen to its parent if in life.

S6.10   *No apportionment*   **(TEN)**   There shall be no apportionment as between capital and income on any occasion.

S6.11   *Beneficiaries lacking capacity*   **(ELEVEN)**   If any part of my estate falls to a beneficiary who lacks full legal capacity my Trustees shall have full power either to pay or apply the whole or any part of the income or capital falling to such beneficiary for his or her behoof in any manner my Trustees may think proper, or to retain the same until such capacity is attained accumulating income with capital, or to pay over the same to the legal guardian or the person for the time being having the custody of such beneficiary whose receipt shall be a sufficient discharge to my Trustees.

S6.12   *Renunciation of benefit*   **(TWELVE)**   In the event of any benefit conferred by this will being renounced in whole or in part the benefit or such part or parts thereof shall pass to the beneficiary or beneficiaries who would have been entitled and on the terms/

terms and conditions which would have applied had the beneficiary so renouncing predeceased me.

S6.13 *Trustees' powers*

(**THIRTEEN**) My Trustees shall have the fullest powers of and in regard to retention, realisation, investment, appropriation, transfer of property without realisation, and management of my estate as if they were absolute beneficial owners; and shall have power to do everything they may consider necessary or expedient for the administration of the trust; and in particular and without prejudice to these general powers my Trustees shall have power:

retention etc

(1) to retain, sell, purchase, lease or hire the estate or any part thereof;

investment

(2) to invest the whole or any part of the estate in heritable and leasehold property, investments, securities, insurance policies, deposits and other assets of whatever description, whether producing income or not, whether or not falling within the class of investments authorised for trust funds, whether or not payable to bearer, and wherever situated;

insurance policies

(3) to effect, maintain and acquire policies of insurance of whatever description; and to insure any property on whatever terms they think fit including on a first loss basis;

management/

management
of heritage

(4) to administer and manage any heritable or real
property forming part of the estate; to repair, maintain,
renew and improve the same and to erect additional
buildings and structures; to grant, vary and terminate
leases and rights of tenancy or occupancy; to plant, thin
and cut down timber; to work or let minerals; all as my
Trustees may think proper and as if they were absolute
owners of the estate;

businesses

(5) to continue or to commence any business, whether
alone or in conjunction or in partnership with any other
persons, or through any companies, for such period as my
Trustees may think proper; to appoint or employ a trustee
or any other person in any capacity in relation to such
business and to pay to them suitable remuneration for
services, including pension provisions for any employees
or their dependants; and to delegate or entrust to any
persons the control and management of such business to
such extent as my Trustees may think fit; and my Trustees

(a) may employ for the purposes of such business such
part of the income or capital as they think proper;

(b) shall exercise only such control or supervision of
such business as they shall think fit;

(c) shall be entitled to be relieved from the estate from
all/

all personal responsibility for any loss arising from such business operations; and

(d) shall be entitled to retain personally any remuneration for their services;

borrow and lend (6) to borrow or lend with or without security; and to grant or continue any guarantee or indemnity for the benefit of any beneficiary actual or prospective;

occupation by beneficiaries (7) to lend or allow to be used the whole or any part of the estate at such rate of interest or rent as they may consider appropriate, or free of interest or rent, to or by any person who is for the time being entitled to payment of a share of the income of the estate or to whom or for whose benefit the income may be paid or applied in the exercise of a discretion then available to my Trustees;

nominees (8) to allow the estate or any part thereof to be registered in the names of or held or the documents of title to be held by any person, firm, corporation or other body as nominee of my Trustees;

delegation of investment management (9) revocably to delegate any power or powers of making, managing, realising or otherwise dealing with any investment or deposit comprised in the estate to any person or persons upon such terms as to remuneration or otherwise as my Trustees may think fit and no trustee shall be/

be responsible for the default of any such agent if the

trustee in question employed him in good faith;

additions   (10)   to accept as an addition to my estate any other

property as may be made over to them;

allocation   (11)   to decide what is capital and what is income and the
between
capital and   proportion in which expenses are to be charged against
income
                    capital and income respectively;

appropriation   (12)   to set apart and appropriate specific property of any

description to represent the whole or part of the share,

prospective or otherwise, of any beneficiary at such

valuation as my Trustees shall determine, so that there-

after the particular share or part shall have the full

benefit and the whole risk of the appropriated investments

or assets;

settlement   (13)   to settle with any beneficiary entitled to any part of

the estate by conveying to him or her in satisfaction

thereof either specific property or money, or partly one

and partly the other, as to my Trustees shall seem proper

and at such valuation as they shall determine and to

compel acceptance accordingly;

conflict of   (14)   to enter into any transaction or do any act otherwise
interest
                    authorised by law or by this deed notwithstanding that any

trustee is or might be acting as *auctor in rem suam* or with a

conflict/

conflict of interest between such trustee and himself as an individual or as trustee of any other trust or any partnership of which a trustee is a partner or any company of which a trustee is a shareholder or director or in relation to any combination of these capacities provided that the trustee or trustees with whom there is or may be any such conflict is or are not the sole trustee or trustees;

participation in discretion (15) to participate in the exercise of any discretion granted to my Trustees notwithstanding that a trustee is or may be a or the sole beneficiary in whose favour the discretion is then exercised provided that there is at least one trustee not so favoured;

resignation (16) to resign office notwithstanding any benefit hereunder;

agents (17) to appoint one or more of their own number to act as solicitor or agent in any other capacity and to allow him or them the same remuneration to which he or they would have been entitled if not a trustee or trustees;

non-resident trustees (18) to appoint any one or more trustees resident out of the United Kingdom and themselves to resign office;

administration abroad (19) to carry on the administration of the trust hereby created in some place out of the United Kingdom; and

renunciation/

renunciation
of powers

(20)   to renounce for themselves and their successors in office the power to exercise any of the foregoing powers in this purpose as if the same were vested in them beneficially and not as trustees.

S6.14   *Immunities*   (**FOURTEEN**) My Trustees shall not be liable for depreciation in value of the property in my estate, nor for omissions or errors in judgement, nor for neglect in management, nor for insolvency of debtors, nor for the acts, omissions, neglects or defaults of each other or of any agent employed by them.

S6.15   *Domicile*   (**FIFTEEN**)   I declare that my domicile is Scottish.

S6.16   *Guardians*   (**SIXTEEN**)   In the event of my said wife so failing to survive me I appoint my brother and sister-in-law I (design) and J (design) to be guardians to my children: IN WITNESS WHEREOF

STYLE 6

References

General		This Style is dealt with at paras 5.81–5.86. On liferent trusts in general, see paras 5.62–5.67. On vesting see paras 5.28–5.36.
Preliminary wording		See para 3.02 and on designation of the testator see para 9.10.
S6.1	*Revocation*	See paras 3.03–09 and on foreign aspects paras 2.67–2.70.
S6.2	*Executors and trustees*	See paras 3.10–3.30.
S6.3	*Informal writings*	See paras 3.31–3.36.
S6.4	*Legacies*	See paras 3.37–3.41. On interest see paras 4.46–4.47. On delivery expenses see paras 4.58–4.60.
S6.5	*Liferent for mother*	See paras 5.81–5.82. On trusts for specific assets, see paras 4.136–4.137. On the subject of the legacy, see paras 4.71–4.74 and 4.76–4.81. On the issue of relationship between the testator and the beneficiary, see Chapter 6 generally.
S6.6	*Personal effects to wife*	See paras 5.75 and 5.83. On the items contained in this legacy, see paras 4.48–4.57.
S6.7	*Liferent of half residue to wife*	See paras 5.76 and 5.84. On issues relating to the meaning of 'wife', see paras 6.02–6.09. On survivorship, see paras 5.15–5.19. See also paras 9.16–9.22.
S6.8	*Half residue to children*	See para 5.85. On issues relating to children, see paras 6.11–6.12, 6.29–6.52, 6.112–6.122. On destinations-over and the division among beneficiaries, see paras 5.02–5.14, 5.26–5.27. On survivorship see paras 5.15–5.19. See also paras 9.16–9.22.
S6.9	*Termination of liferent*	See para 5.86. On issues relating to children, see paras 6.11–6.12, 6.29–6.52, 6.112–6.122. On destinations-over and the division among beneficiaries, see paras 5.02–5.14, 5.26–5.27. On survivorship, see paras 5.15–5.19. See also paras 5.17–5.18.
S6.10	*No apportionment*	See para 7.28.
S6.11	*Beneficiaries lacking capacity*	See paras 6.46–6.51, 6.127–6.128.

S6.12   *Renunciation*   See paras 5.20–5.25.
          of benefit

S16.13   *Trustees*   See paras 7.03–7.27 and 3.19–3.25.
          powers

S6.14   *Immunities*   See paras 7.29.

S6.15   *Domicile*   See paras 2.60–2.77.

S6.16   *Guardians*   See paras 6.86–6.111.

PRECIS OF STYLE 7

Residue to wife whom failing children on accumulation and maintenance trust

1. Revocation of prior wills

2. Executors and trustees

3. Provision for informal writings

4. Any legacies to be paid free of tax, expenses and interest

5. The residue is to pass to the testator's spouse

6. If the spouse does not survive for 30 days then the residue passes to the testator's children equally with the children of any predeceasing children taking their parent's share

7. If any beneficiary is under 25 then the trustees are to hold the funds for that child on attaining that age. Until then the trustees can accumulate the income until a beneficiary attains age 21. Between ages 21 and 25 the trustees are to distribute a proportionate share of the income to that child. The trustees have power to advance income and capital before these ages

8. The trustees are given wide powers to deal with funds falling to beneficiaries lacking capacity

9. If any beneficiary renounces any benefit then that benefit passes to the beneficiaries who would have been entitled if the original beneficiary had predeceased

10. The trustees are given wide and flexible powers of administration and management

11. Usual trustees' immunities

12. Declaration of Scottish domicile

13. Guardians to children

AND STYLE 7 ALTERNATIVE

Accumulation and maintenance trust for grandchildren

6. If the spouse does not survive for 30 days then the residue passes to all of the testator's grandchildren born before the youngest one in life becomes 25. Each grandchild is entitled to an equal share of the residue according to the number of grandchildren in life either at the testator's date of death or the time when the grandchildren subsequently become 25.

STYLE 7

Residue to wife whom failing children on accumulation and maintenance trust

I, A (design) in order to settle the succession to my estate after my death provide as follows:

S7.1 *Revocation* (**ONE**) I revoke all prior wills and testamentary writings.

S7.2 *Executors and trustees* (**TWO**) I appoint B (design), my wife C, residing with me and D (design) to be my executors and trustees (who along with any other persons who may be appointed or assumed are referred to as 'my Trustees').

S7.3 *Informal writings* (**THREE**) I direct my Trustees to give effect to any future writings subscribed by me however informal the same may be provided that in the opinion of my Trustees they clearly express my intentions.

S7.4 *Legacies* (**FOUR**) Unless otherwise specified any legacy granted by any writing shall be paid or made over as soon as my Trustees consider practicable after my death free of government duties in respect of my death and of delivery expenses but without interest.

S7.5 *Residue to wife* (**FIVE**) I direct my Trustees to make over the residue of my estate to my wife C if she survives for thirty days after my death.

S7.6/

S7.6   *Residue to*   (**SIX**)   If my wife C does not survive me for
       children
thirty days, but in such event only, I direct my Trustees to

make over the residue of my estate to such of my children

E, F, G and any other children of mine as shall survive me

equally among them if more than one, declaring:

(1)   that should any of my children predecease me leaving

issue (including adopted issue) who shall survive me each

member of a generation of issue of such predeceasing child

shall share equally in the part of my estate, both original

and accresced, which would have fallen to its parent if in

life, and

(2)   that if any part of the residue of my estate falls to a

beneficiary who has not attained the age of twenty five

years my Trustees shall hold the same in accordance with

purpose (SEVEN).

S7.7   *Residuary*   (**SEVEN**)   I direct my Trustees to hold any part of
       beneficiaries
       under 25   the residue of my estate held for a beneficiary under the

age of twenty five years (which is referred to as 'the Trust

Fund') for the following purposes:

contingent   (1)   for such beneficiaries contingently on their attaining
entitlement
a vested interest as after provided for;

accumulation   (2)   to accumulate the income arising from the Trust

Fund by investing all surplus thereof and the resulting

income/

income therefrom in accordance with the powers hereafter
conferred until such beneficiaries respectively attain the
age of twenty one years;

income   (3)   for payment of the income of the share of the Trust
Fund to which any of such beneficiaries is prospectively
entitled to such beneficiary from the attainment by him or
her of the age of twenty one until he or she attains a vested
interest as provided for in the immediately succeeding
paragraph;

capital   (4)   for payment of an equal share of the capital of the Trust
Fund and the income accumulated prior to his or her acquir-
ing a vested interest in the income to such beneficiaries on
their respectively attaining the age of twenty five years and
subject as aftermentioned the said capital and accumulated
income shall not vest in any of such children or issue until the
date of payment of his or her share;

failure   (5)   if any of such beneficiaries fail to attain a vested
interest by reason of his or her predeceasing leaving issue
(including adopted issue), each member of a generation of
issue of such predeceasing beneficiary as survives and
attains the age of twenty five years shall share equally in
the share of the Trust Fund, both original and accresced,
which would have fallen to its parent if in life; and if any of
such/

such beneficiaries fail to attain a vested interest as before provided for leaving no issue who survive and attain the age of twenty five, to hold the share of the Trust Fund and any income accumulated at the date of such failure for behoof of the beneficiaries who would have been entitled if such beneficiary had never existed;

prohibited accumulations (6) if any accumulation of income of the Trust Fund is prohibited by law by reason of any event the income affected by such prohibition shall be paid or applied to or for such beneficiaries for the time being presumptively entitled to the capital of the Trust Fund or that part thereof from which such income arose;

payments (7) my Trustees may apply for the maintenance education or benefit of any beneficiary of a share of the Trust Fund (a) the income thereof including accumulated income in whole or in part and (b) the capital thereof in whole or in part, and such advances shall vest on payment or such application;

advance of entitlement (8) my Trustees may appoint at any time or times and in whole or in part that the age at which a beneficiary would otherwise become entitled to a share of the capital of the Trust Fund or to a right to the income thereof shall be advanced to such earlier age as they may decide, and if any such/

such appointment is revocable it shall unless earlier revoked become irrevocable when and to the extent that it shall become operative;

resettlement (9)   my Trustees shall have power, in relation to any part of the Trust Fund of which a beneficiary is then entitled to the income, to appoint that such part of the Trust Fund or any part or parts of the income or capital thereof shall be held for such trust purposes, together with such limitations, conditions and provisions for accumulation, maintenance, education and advancement for the benefit of such beneficiary alone or of such beneficiary's issue or the spouses of any of these persons, or of any other person or persons whom such beneficiary desires to be included as beneficiaries, or of him or her and them, and generally with such powers and discretions exercisable by my Trustees or by any other person or persons and on such terms as my Trustees shall think fit;

no (10)   there shall be no apportionment as between capital
apportionment and income on any occasion.

S7.8   *Beneficiaries* (**EIGHT**)   If any part of my estate is held for a
lacking
capacity beneficiary who lacks full legal capacity my Trustees shall have full power either to pay or apply the whole or any part of the income or capital falling to such beneficiary for his or/

or her behoof in any manner my Trustees may think proper, or to retain the same until such capacity is attained accumulating income with capital, or to pay over the same to the legal guardian or the person for the time being having the custody of such beneficiary whose receipt shall be a sufficient discharge to my Trustees.

S7.9   *Renunciation of benefit*   (**NINE**)   In the event of any benefit conferred by this will being renounced in whole or in part the benefit or such part or parts thereof shall pass to the beneficiary or beneficiaries who would have been entitled and on the terms and conditions which would have applied had the beneficiary so renouncing predeceased me.

S7.10   *Trustees' powers*   (**TEN**)   My Trustees shall have the fullest powers of and in regard to retention, realisation, investment, appropriation, transfer of property without realisation, and management of my estate as if they were absolute beneficial owners; and shall have power to do everything they may consider necessary or expedient for the administration of the trust; and in particular and without prejudice to these general powers my Trustees shall have power:

retention etc   (1)   to retain, sell, purchase, lease or hire the estate or any part thereof;

investment/

investment   (2)   to invest the whole or any part of the estate in heritable and leasehold property, investments, securities, insurance policies, deposits and other assets of whatever description, whether producing income or not, whether or not falling within the class of investments authorised for trust funds, whether or not payable to bearer, and wherever situated;

insurance policies   (3)   to effect, maintain and acquire policies of insurance of whatever description; and to insure any property on whatever terms they think fit including on a first loss basis;

management of heritage   (4)   to administer and manage any heritable or real property forming part of the estate; to repair, maintain, renew and improve the same and to erect additional buildings and structures; to grant, vary and terminate leases and rights of tenancy or occupancy; to plant, thin and cut down timber; to work or let minerals; all as my Trustees may think proper and as if they were absolute owners of the estate;

businesses   (5)   to continue or to commence any business, whether alone or in conjunction or in partnership with any other persons, or through any companies, for such period as my Trustees may think proper; to appoint or employ any trustee or any other person in any capacity in relation to such business and to pay to them suitable remuneration for/

for services, including pension provisions for any employees or their dependants; and to delegate or entrust to any persons the control and management of such business to such extent as my Trustees may think fit; and my Trustees

(a)   may employ for the purposes of such business such part of the income or capital as they think proper;

(b)   shall exercise only such control or supervision of such business as they shall think fit;

(c)   shall be entitled to be relieved from the estate from all personal responsibility for any loss arising from such business operations; and

(d)   shall be entitled to retain personally any remuneration for their services;

borrow and lend   (6)   to borrow or lend with or without security; and to grant or continue any guarantee or indemnity for the benefit of any beneficiary actual or prospective;

occupation by beneficiaries   (7)   to lend or allow to be used the whole or any part of the estate at such rate of interest or rent as they may consider appropriate, or free of interest or rent, to or by any person who is for the time being entitled to payment of a share of the income of the estate or to whom or for whose benefit the income may be paid or applied in the exercise of a discretion then available to my Trustees;

nominees/

nominees   (8)   to allow the estate or any part thereof to be registered in the names of or held or the documents of title to be held by any person, firm, corporation or other body as nominee of my Trustees;

delegation of investment management   (9)   revocably to delegate any power or powers or making, managing, realising or otherwise dealing with any investment or deposit comprised in the estate to any person or persons upon such terms as to remuneration or otherwise as my Trustees may think fit and no trustee shall be responsible for the default of any such agent if the Trustee in question employed him in good faith;

additions   (10) to accept as an addition to my estate any other property which may be made over to them;

allocation between capital and income   (11) to decide what is capital and what is income and the proportion in which expenses are to be charged against capital and income respectively;

appropriation   (12) to set apart and appropriate specific property of any description to represent the whole or part of the share, prospective or otherwise, of any beneficiary at such valuation as my Trustees shall determine, so that thereafter the particular share or part shall have the full benefit and the whole risk of the appropriated investments or assets;

settlement/

settlement   (13)   to settle with any beneficiary entitled to any part of the estate by conveying to him or her in satisfaction thereof either specific property or money, or partly one and partly the other, as to my Trustees shall seem proper and at such valuation as they shall determine and to compel acceptance accordingly;

conflict of   (14)   to enter into any transaction or do any act otherwise
interest   authorised by law or by this deed notwithstanding that any trustee is or might be acting as *auctor in rem suam* or with a conflict of interest between such trustee and himself as an individual or as trustee of any other trust or any partnership of which a trustee is a partner or any company of which a trustee is a shareholder or director or in relation to any combination of these capacities provided that the trustee or trustees with whom there is or may be any such conflict is or are not the sole trustee or trustees;

participation (15)   to participate in the exercise of any discretion
in discretion granted to my Trustees notwithstanding that a trustee is or may be a or the sole beneficiary in whose favour the discretion is then exercised provided that there is at least one trustee not so favoured;

resignation   (16)   to resign office notwithstanding any benefit hereunder;

agents/

agents (17)   to appoint one or more of their own number to act as solicitor or agent in any other capacity and to allow him or them the same remuneration to which he or they would have been entitled if not a trustee or trustees;

non-resident trustees (18)   to appoint any one or more trustees resident out of the United Kingdom and themselves to resign office;

administration abroad (19)   to carry on the administration of the trust hereby created in some place out of the United Kingdom; and

renunciation of powers (20)   to renounce for themselves and their successors in office the power to exercise any of the foregoing powers in this purpose as if the same were vested in them beneficially and not as trustees.

S7.11 *Immunities* (**ELEVEN**)   My Trustees shall not be liable for depreciation in value of the property in my estate, nor for omissions or errors in judgement, nor for neglect in management, nor for insolvency of debtors, nor for the acts, omissions, neglects or defaults of each other or of any agent employed by them.

S7.12 *Domicile* (**TWELVE**)   I declare that my domicile is Scottish.

S7.13 *Guardians* (**THIRTEEN**)   In the event of my said wife so failing to survive me I appoint my brother and sister-in-law H (design) and I (design) to be guardians to my children: IN WITNESS WHEREOF

STYLE 7

References

General		This Style is dealt with at paras 6.63–6.80. On accumulation and maintenance trusts in general, see paras 6.53–6.58. On vesting, see paras 5.28–5.36.
Preliminary wording		See para 3.02 and on designation of the testator see para 9.10.
S7.1	*Revocation*	See paras 3.03–3.09 and on foreign aspects paras 2.67–2.70.
S7.2	*Executors and trustees*	See paras 3.10–3.30.
S7.3	*Informal writings*	See paras 3.31–3.36.
S7.4	*Legacies*	See paras 3.37–3.41. On interest see paras 4.46–4.47. On delivery expenses see paras 4.58–4.60.
S7.5	*Residue to wife*	See Chapter 6 generally, especially paras 6.02–6.09. On survivorship see paras 5.15–5.19. See also paras 9.16–9.22.
S7.6	*Residue to children*	See para 6.64, and Chapter 6 generally on issues relating to children. On destinations-over and division among beneficiaries, see paras 5.02–5.14, 5.26–5.27. See also paras 9.16–9.22.
S7.7	*Residuary beneficiaries under 25*	See paras 6.65–6.80.
S7.8	*Beneficiaries lacking capacity*	See paras 6.46–6.51, 6.127–6.128.
S7.9	*Renunciation of benefit*	See paras 5.20–5.25.
S7.10	*Trustees' powers*	See paras 7.03–7.27 and 3.19–3.25.
S7.11	*Immunities*	See para 7.29.
S7.12	*Domicile*	See paras 2.60–2.77.
S7.13	*Guardians*	See paras 6.86–6.111.

STYLE 7 ALTERNATIVE

Accumulation and maintenance trust for grandchildren

S7A.6   *Residue to grandchildren*   (**SIX**) If my wife C does not survive me for thirty days, but in such event only, I direct my Trustees to hold the residue of my estate for such of my grandchildren as shall be born prior to the youngest of my grandchildren in life attaining the age of twenty five years equally among them if more than one, declaring:

predecease   (1) that should any of my grandchildren predecease me leaving issue who shall survive me each member of a generation of issue of such predeceasing grandchild shall share equally in the part of my estate, both original and accresced, which would have fallen to its parent if in life,

grandchildren over 25   (2) that where any of my grandchildren or issue representing predeceasing grandchildren has attained the age of twenty five at my death he or she shall be entitled outright to an equal share according to the number of grandchildren then in life together with the number of grandchildren who have predeceased me leaving issue then in life, and

grandchildren under 25   (3) that where any of my grandchildren or issue representing predeceasing grandchildren has not attained the age of twenty five at my death my Trustees shall hold the/

the part of the residue to be held for them and any
subsequently born grandchildren in accordance with
purpose (SEVEN), but

(a)   the share to which any of such beneficiaries is from
      time to time prospectively entitled shall be calculated
      by reference to the number of grandchildren (or issue
      as representing predeceasing grandchildren) then in
      life whose age does not exceed twenty five and whose
      shares have not previously been wholly advanced or
      appointed under paragraph (9), and the share of any
      such beneficiary shall be fixed indefeasibly when and
      to the extent that vesting of capital occurs in such
      beneficiary or the time when and to the extent that an
      appointment is made under paragraph (9);

(b)   any advances of capital or partial appointments
      under paragraph (9) shall be taken into account in
      such way as my Trustees in their absolute discretion
      shall determine; and

(c)   in the event of any part of the Trust Fund remaining
      unvested or unappointed under paragraph (9) when
      the youngest grandchild in life (or issue then in life as
      representing predeceasing grandchildren) attains the
      age of twenty five years, such remaining part shall
      then vest in him or her indefeasibly.

STYLE 7A

References

S7A.6   *Residue to*   See paras 6.81–6.84. On provisions for grandchildren
           grandchildren   generally, see paras 6.115–6.116 and 6.123–6.126.

PRECIS OF STYLE 8

Short form of will by husband in favour of wife whom failing children with short form accumulation and maintenance trust

1. Revocation of prior wills

2. Executors

3. Provision for informal writings

4. Any legacies to be paid free of tax

5. The residue is to pass to the testator's spouse

6. If the spouse does not survive for 30 days then the residue passes to the testator's children equally with the children of any predeceasing children taking their parent's share

7. Residue falling to beneficiaries under age 18 is to be held by the executors until they become 18. The executors have power to advance income or capital

8. The executors are given wide powers to deal with funds falling to beneficiaries lacking capacity

9. The executors are given short powers of administration and management

10. Declaration of Scottish domicile

11. Guardians to children

12. Declaration as to cremation

STYLE 8

Short form of will by husband in favour of wife whom failing children with short form accumulation and maintenance trust

I, A (design) in order to settle the succession to my estate after my death provide as follows:

S8.1	*Revocation*	(**ONE**)	I revoke all prior wills and testamentary writings.

S8.2	*Executors*	(**TWO**)	I appoint my wife B, residing with me, and C (design) to be my executors.

S8.3	*Informal writings*	(**THREE**)	I direct my executors to give effect to any future writings subscribed by me however informal the same may be provided that in the opinion of my executors they clearly express my intentions.

S8.4	*Legacies*	(**FOUR**)	Unless otherwise specified any legacy granted by any writing shall be paid or made over as soon as my executors consider practicable after my death free of government duties in respect of my death and of delivery expenses but without interest.

S8.5	*Residue to wife*	(**FIVE**)	I direct my executors to make over the residue of my estate to my wife B if she survives for thirty days after my death.

S8.6	*Residue to children*	(**SIX**)	If my wife B does not survive me for thirty days, but in such event only, I direct my executors to make over/

over the residue of my estate to such of my children D, E, F and any other children of mine as shall survive me equally among them if more than one, declaring that should any of my children predecease me leaving issue (including adopted issue) who shall survive me each member of a generation of issue of such predeceasing child shall share equally in the part of my estate, both original and accresced, which would have fallen to its parent if in life.

S8.7 *Residuary beneficiaries under 18*

(**SEVEN**) (1) Any share of the residue of my estate falling to a beneficiary who is under the age of eighteen years shall be held by my executors in trust for this beneficiary until the age of eighteen years is attained when the share will vest;

(2) income arising from such share shall be accumulated but my executors may apply all or part of the income or capital of this share for the maintenance, education or benefit of this beneficiary; and

(3) if this beneficiary does not attain the age of eighteen years then the share with any accumulated income shall be held for the beneficiaries who would have been entitled if the beneficiary had predeceased me.

S8.8 *Beneficiaries lacking capacity*

(**EIGHT**) If any part of my estate is held for a beneficiary who lacks full legal capacity my executors shall have/

have full power either to pay or apply the whole or any part of the income or capital falling to such beneficiary for his or her benefit in any manner my executors think proper, or to retain the same until such capacity is attained, or to pay over the same to the legal guardian or the person for the time being having the custody of such beneficiary whose receipt shall be a sufficient discharge to my executors.

S8.9   *Powers*   (**NINE**)   My executors shall have the fullest powers of retention, realisation, investment, appropriation, transfer of property without realisation, and management of my estate as if they were absolute beneficial owners; and shall have power to resign office and to appoint one or more of their own number to act as solicitor or agent in any other capacity and to allow him or them the same remuneration to which he or they would have been entitled if not an executor or executors.

S8.10   *Domicile*   (**TEN**)   I declare that my domicile is Scottish.

S8.11   *Guardians*   (**ELEVEN**)   In the event of my said wife so failing to survive me I appoint my brother and sister-in-law G (design) and H (design) to be guardians to my children.

S8.12   *Funeral*   (**TWELVE**)   I wish my body to be cremated: IN WITNESS
         instructions   WHEREOF

STYLE 8

References

General		This Style is dealt with at para 6.85. On accumulation and maintenance trusts in general, see paras 6.44–6.58. On vesting, see paras 5.28–5.36.
Preliminary wording		See para 3.02 and on designation of the testator see para 9.10.
S8.1	*Revocation*	See paras 3.03–3.09 and on foreign aspects paras 2.67–2.70.
S8.2	*Executors and trustees*	See paras 3.10–3.30.
S8.3	*Informal writings*	See paras 3.31–3.36.
S8.4	*Legacies*	See paras 3.37–3.41. On interest see paras 4.46–4.47. On delivery expenses see paras 4.58–4.60.
S8.5	*Residue to wife*	See Chapter 6 generally, especially paras 6.02–6.09. On survivorship, see paras 5.15–5.19. See also paras 9.16–9.22.
S8.6	*Residue to children*	See Chapter 6 generally on issues relating to children. On destinations-over and division among beneficiaries, see paras 5.02–5.14, 5.26–5.27. See also paras 9.16–9.22.
S8.7	*Residuary beneficiaries under 18*	See para 6.85.
S8.8	*Beneficiaries lacking capacity*	See paras 6.46–6.51, 6.127–6.128.
S8.9	*Powers*	See paras 7.01–7.02 and 3.19–3.25.
S8.10	*Domicile*	See paras 2.60–2.77.
S8.11	*Guardians*	See paras 6.86–6.111.
S8.12	*Funeral instructions*	See paras 3.42–3.62.

466

PRECIS OF STYLE 9

Two-year discretionary trust will

1. Revocation of prior wills

2. Executors and trustees

3. Provision for informal writings

4. Any legacies to be paid free of tax, expenses and interest

5. Two-year discretionary trust. The trustees are to hold the residue for such one or more of the testator's spouse, children and remoter issue and any trust for the benefit of any of these people in such shares as the trustees may decide at any time within two years of the testator's death. The trustees can set up new trusts and have power to accumulate income. If the trustees fail to make a decision within this time limit then the discretionary fund is to be held for

6. The trustees are given wide powers to deal with funds falling to beneficiaries lacking capacity

7. If any beneficiary renounces any benefit then that benefit passes to the beneficiaries who would have been entitled if the original beneficiary had predeceased

8. The trustees are given wide and flexible powers of administration and management

9. Usual trustees' immunities

10. Declaration of Scottish domicile

11. Guardians to children

STYLE 9

Two-year discretionary trust will

I, A (design) in order to settle the succession to my estate after my death provide as follows:

S9.1	*Revocation*	(**ONE**) I revoke all prior wills and testamentary writings.
S9.2	*Executors and trustees*	(**TWO**) I appoint B (design), my wife C, residing with me and D (design) to be executors and trustees (who along with any other persons who may be appointed or assumed are referred to as 'my Trustees').
S9.3	*Informal writings*	(**THREE**) I direct my Trustees to give effect to any future writings subscribed by me however informal the same may be provided that in the opinion of my Trustees they clearly express my intentions.
S9.4	*Legacies*	(**FOUR**) Unless otherwise specified any legacy granted by any writing shall be paid or made over as soon as my Trustees consider practicable after my death free of government duties in respect of my death and of delivery expenses but without interest.
S9.5	*Residue*	(**FIVE**) I direct my Trustees to hold the residue of my estate for such one or more of (1) my wife C (2) my issue (including adopted issue) (3) any person who is or

was/

was a spouse of any of such issue and (4) any trust established by any person for the benefit (whether of an income a capital or a discretionary nature) of any one or more of the foregoing persons (all of whom are referred to as 'the beneficiaries'), and in such shares or proportions, as my Trustees may by minute or minutes at any time or times within two years of my death determine, declaring:

(1) that my Trustees may by such minute or minutes grant legacies, shares of residue, interests in income or prospective or contingent interests of any kind in the whole or any part or parts of the residue subject to such provisions as they may determine, including but without prejudice to the foregoing generality provisions as to the accumulation of income, the vesting of capital in any beneficiary, the granting to any beneficiary or any other person of powers to appoint rights to income or capital, and the continuation of their discretionary powers;

(2) that my Trustees may renounce for themselves and their successors in office the power to exercise any of the foregoing powers as if the same were vested in them beneficially and not as trustees;

(3) that during the period of two years from the date of my death, or until the date or dates when any such determination/

determination or determinations take effect or the power to make a determination is renounced by them, my Trustees shall pay and apply the whole of the income of the residue without any apportionment being made to or for behoof of any one or more of the beneficiaries in such shares or proportions and in such manner as they may determine;

(4) that my Trustees may provide that, in the event of failure of all of my issue before the whole of the residue has vested, the class of beneficiaries shall be extended to include those who would be included if the class had been defined by reference to each of my grandparents [OR my children's grandparents] rather than by reference to me; and

(5) that in the event of my Trustees having failed to make a determination taking effect in relation to the whole or any part of the residue before the expiry of two years from the date of my death or having renounced the power to make such a determination, they shall on and from the expiry of the said period or the date of such renunciation hold the whole or such part of the residue absolutely for E.

S9.6   *Beneficiaries lacking capacity*   (**SIX**)   If any part of my estate is held for a beneficiary who lacks full legal capacity my Trustees shall have full power either to pay or apply the whole or any part of the/

the income or capital falling to such beneficiary for his or
her behoof in any manner my Trustees may think proper,
or to retain the same until such capacity is attained accumulating income with capital, or to pay over the same to the
legal guardian or the person for the time being having the
custody of such beneficiary whose receipt shall be a sufficient discharge to my Trustees.

S9.7 *Renunciation* (**SEVEN**)   In the event of any benefit conferred by this
      of benefit
                      will being renounced in whole or in part the benefit or such
                      part or parts thereof shall pass to the beneficiary or bene-
                      ficiaries who would have been entitled and on the terms
                      and conditions which would have applied had the bene-
                      ficiary so predeceased me.

S9.8 *Trustees'*   (**EIGHT**)   My Trustees shall have the fullest powers of
      powers
                      and in regard to retention, realisation, investment, appro-
                      priation, transfer of property without realisation, and
                      management of my estate as if they were absolute bene-
                      ficial owners; and shall have power to do everything they
                      may consider necessary or expedient for the administra-
                      tion of the trust; and in particular and without prejudice to
                      these general powers my Trustees shall have power:

      retention etc (1)   to retain, sell, purchase, lease or hire the estate or any
                      part thereof;

      investment/

investment   (2)   to invest the whole or any part of the estate in heri-

table and leasehold property, investments, securities,

insurance policies, deposits and other assets of whatever

description, whether producing income or not, whether or

not falling within the class of investments authorised for

trust funds, whether or not payable to bearer, and

wherever situated;

insurance   (3)   to effect, maintain and acquire policies of insurance
policies
of whatever description; and to insure any property on

whatever terms they think fit including on a first loss basis;

management   (4)   to administer and manage any heritable or real
of heritage
property forming part of the estate; to repair, maintain,

renew and improve the same and to erect additional

buildings and structures; to grant, vary and terminate

leases and rights of tenancy or occupancy; to plant, thin

and cut down timber; to work or let minerals; all as my

Trustees may think proper and as if they were absolute

owners of the estate;

businesses   (5)   to continue or to commence any business, whether

alone or in conjunction or in partnership with any other

persons, or through any companies, for such period as my

Trustees may think proper; to appoint or employ any

trustee and any other person in any capacity in relation to

such/

such business and to pay to them suitable remuneration for services, including pension provisions for any employees or their dependants; and to delegate or entrust to any persons the control and management of such business to such extent as my Trustees may think fit; and my Trustees

(a)   may employ for the purposes of such business such part of the income or capital as they think proper;

(b)   shall exercise only such control or supervision of such business as they shall think fit;

(c)   shall be entitled to be relieved from the estate from all personal responsibility for any loss arising from such business operations; and

(d)   shall be entitled to retain personally any remuneration for their services;

borrow and lend   (6)   to borrow or lend with or without security; and to grant or continue any guarantee or indemnity for the benefit of any beneficiary actual or prospective;

occupation by beneficiaries   (7)   to lend or allow to be used the whole or any part of the estate at such rate of interest or rent as they may consider appropriate, or free of interest or rent, to or by any person who is for the time being entitled to payment of a share of the income of the estate or to whom or for whose benefit the/

the income may be paid or applied in the exercise of a discretion then available to my Trustees;

nominees (8) to allow the estate or any part thereof to be registered in the names of or held or the documents of title to be held by any person, firm, corporation or other body as nominee of my Trustees;

delegation of investment management (9) revocably to delegate any power or powers of making, managing, realising or otherwise dealing with any investment or deposit comprised in the estate to any person or persons upon such terms as to remuneration or otherwise as my Trustees may think fit and no trustee shall be responsible for the default of any such agent if the trustee in question employed him in good faith;

additions (10) to accept as an addition to my estate any other property which may be made over to them;

allocation between capital and income (11) to decide what is capital and what is income and the proportion in which expenses are to be charged against capital and income respectively;

appropriation (12) to set apart and appropriate specific property of any description to represent the whole or part of the share, prospective or otherwise, of any beneficiary at such valuation as my Trustees shall determine, so that thereafter the particular share or part shall have the full benefit/

benefit and the whole risk of the appropriated investments

or assets;

settlement   (13)   to settle with any beneficiary entitled to any part of the

estate by conveying to him or her in satisfaction thereof either

specific property or money, or partly one and partly the other,

as to my Trustees shall seem proper and at such valuation as

they shall determine and to compel acceptance accordingly;

conflict of   (14)   to enter into any transaction or do any act otherwise
interest

authorised by law or by this deed notwithstanding that any

trustee is or might be acting as *auctor in rem suam* or with a

conflict of interest between such trustee and himself as an

individual or as trustee of any other trust or any part-

nership of which a trustee is a partner or any company of

which a trustee is a shareholder or director or in relation to

any combination of these capacities provided that the

trustee or trustees with whom there is or may be any such

conflict is or are not the sole trustee or trustees;

participation   (15)   to participate in the exercise of any discretion
in discretion

granted to my Trustees notwithstanding that a trustee is or

may be a or the sole beneficiary in whose favour the

discretion is then exercised provided that there is at least

one trustee not so favoured;

resignation   (16)   to resign office notwithstanding any benefit hereunder;

agents/

agents (17) to appoint one or more of their own number to act as solicitor or agent in any other capacity and to allow him or them the same remuneration to which he or they would have been entitled if not a trustee or trustees;

non-resident trustees (18) to appoint any one or more trustees resident out of the United Kingdom and themselves to resign office;

administration abroad (19) to carry on the administration of the trust hereby created in some place out of the United Kingdom; and

renunciation of powers (20) to renounce for themselves and their successors in office the power to exercise any of the foregoing powers in this purpose as if the same were vested in them beneficially and not as trustees.

S9.9 *Immunities* (**NINE**) My Trustees shall not be liable for depreciation in value of the property in my estate, nor for omissions or errors in judgement, nor for neglect in management, nor for insolvency of debtors, nor for the acts, omissions, neglects or defaults of each other or of any agent employed by them.

S9.10 *Domicile* (**TEN**) I declare that my domicile is Scottish.

S9.11 *Guardians* (**ELEVEN**) In the event of my said wife failing to survive me I appoint my brother and sister-in-law F (design) and G (design) to be guardians to my children: IN WITNESS WHEREOF

STYLE 9

References

General		This Style of discretionary trust is dealt with at paras 5.87–5.92. Discretionary trusts in general are dealt with at paras 5.68–5.72. See also para 6.61.
Preliminary wording		See para 3.02 and on designation of the testator see para 9.10.
S9.1	*Revocation*	See paras 3.03–3.09 and on foreign aspects paras 2.67–2.70.
S9.2	*Executors and trustees*	See paras 3.10–3.30.
S9.3	*Informal writings*	See paras 3.31–3.36.
S9.4	*Legacies*	See paras 3.37–3.41. On interest see paras 4.46–4.47. On delivery expenses see paras 4.58–4.60.
S9.5	*Residue*	See paras 5.88–5.92. On issues relating to who may be included among beneficiaries, see Chapter 6 generally. See also paras 9.16–9.17 and 9.20.
S9.6	*Beneficiaries lacking capacity*	See paras 6.46–6.51, 6.127–6.128.
S9.7	*Renunciation of benefit*	See paras 5.20–5.25.
S9.8	*Trustees' powers*	See paras 7.03–7.27 and 3.19–3.25.
S9.9	*Immunities*	See paras 7.29.
S9.10	*Domicile*	See paras 2.60–2.77.
S9.11	*Guardians*	See paras 6.86–6.111.

PRECIS OF STYLE 10

Nil rate band discretionary trust will residue to wife whom failing children on accumulation and maintenance trust

1. Revocation of prior wills

2. Executors and trustees

3. Provision for informal writings

4. Any legacies to be paid free of tax, expenses and interest

5. Nil rate band discretionary trust. The trustees are to hold the amount of the nil rate band less the amount of any taxable lifetime gifts, taxable legacies and legal rights claims for such one or more of the testator's spouse, children and remoter issue and any trust for the benefit of any of these people in such shares as the trustees may decide at any time within two years of the testator's spouse's death. The trustees can set up new trusts and have power to accumulate income. If the trustees fail to make a decision within this time limit then the discretionary fund is to be held as part of residue

6. The residue is to pass to the testator's spouse

7. If the spouse does not survive for 30 days then the residue passes to the testator's children equally with the children of any predeceasing children taking their parent's share

8. If any beneficiary is under 25 then the trustees are to hold the funds for that child on attaining that age. Until then the trustees can accumulate the income until a beneficiary attains age 21. Between ages 21 and 25 the trustees are to distribute a proportionate share of the income to that child. The trustees have power to advance income and capital before these ages

9. The trustees are given wide powers to deal with funds falling to beneficiaries lacking capacity

10. If any beneficiary renounces any benefit then that benefit passes to the beneficiaries who would have been entitled if the original beneficiary had predeceased

11. The trustees are given wide and flexible powers of administration and management

12. Usual trustees' immunities

13. Declaration of Scottish domicile

14. Guardians to children

STYLE 10

Nil rate band discretionary trust will residue to wife whom failing children on accumulation and maintenance trust

I, A (design) in order to settle the succession to my estate after my death provide as follows:

S10.1	*Revocation*	**(ONE)** I revoke all prior wills and testamentary writings.
S10.2	*Executors and trustees*	**(TWO)** I appoint B (design), my wife C, residing with me, and D (design) to be my executors and trustees (who along with any other persons who may be appointed or assumed are referred to as 'my Trustees').
S10.3	*Informal writings*	**(THREE)** I direct my Trustees to give effect to any future writings subscribed by me however informal the same may be provided that in the opinion of my Trustees they clearly express my intentions.
S10.4	*Legacies*	**(FOUR)** Unless otherwise specified any legacy granted by any writing shall be paid or made over as soon as my Trustees consider practicable after my death free of government duties in respect of my death and of delivery expenses but without interest.
S10.5	*Discretionary fund*	**(FIVE)** If my wife C survives me for thirty days, but in such event only, I direct my Trustees to hold such a sum/

sum (or property to such value) as will exhaust the nil rate band of inheritance tax as set out in Schedule 1 to the Inheritance Tax Act 1984 or any similar statutory successor, after taking into account (1) lifetime gifts made by me which are for Inheritance Tax purposes aggregable with or deemed to be part of my executry estate, (2) legacies other than those exempt from inheritance tax, (3) funds in trusts which are aggregable for inheritance tax purposes with my executry estate other than those exempt from inheritance tax and (4) any claims to legitim except claims discharged without consideration after my death, as to all of which my Trustees shall be the sole judges (which sum or property is referred to as 'the Discretionary Fund') for such one or more of (1) my wife C, (2) my issue (including adopted issue), (3) any person who is or was a spouse of any of such issue, and (4) any trust established by any person for the benefit (whether of an income or a capital or a discretionary nature) of any one or more of the foregoing persons (all of whom are referred to as 'the beneficiaries'), and in such shares or proportions, as my Trustees may by minute or minutes at any time or times within two years of my wife's death determine; declaring

(1)/

(1)   that my Trustees may by such minute or minutes grant legacies, shares of residue, interests in income or prospective or contingent interests of any kind in the whole or any part or parts of the Discretionary Fund subject to such provisions as they may determine, including but without prejudice to the foregoing generality provisions as to the accumulation of income, the vesting of capital in any beneficiary, the granting to any beneficiary or any other person of powers to appoint rights to income or capital, and the continuation of their discretionary powers;

(2)   that my Trustees may renounce for themselves and their successors in office the power to exercise any of the foregoing powers as if the same were vested in them beneficially and not as trustees;

(3)   that until the expiry of the period of two years from the date of my wife's death, or until the date or dates when any such determination or determinations take effect or the power to make a determination is renounced by them, my Trustees shall pay and apply the whole of the income of the Discretionary Fund without any apportionment being made to or for behoof of any one or more of the beneficiaries in such shares or proportions and in such manner/

manner as they may determine with power during the said period or until the said date or dates to accumulate the income for twenty one years; and

(4)   that in the event of my Trustees having failed to make a determination taking effect in relation to the whole or any part of the residue before the expiry of two years from the date of my wife's death or having renounced the power to make such a determination they shall on and from the expiry of the said period or the date of such renunciation hold the whole or such part of the Discretionary Fund as part of the residue of my estate as if my wife had predeceased me.

S10.6   *Residue to wife*   (**SIX**)   I direct my Trustees to make over the residue of my estate to my wife C if she survives for thirty days after my death.

S10.7   *Residue to children*   (**SEVEN**)   If my wife C does not survive me for thirty days, but in such event only, I direct my Trustees to make over the residue of my estate to such of my children E, F, G and any other children of mine as shall survive me equally among them if more than one, declaring

(1)   that should any of my children predecease me leaving issue (including adopted issue) who shall survive me each member of a generation of issue of such predeceasing child shall/

shall share equally in the part of my estate, both original and accresced, which would have fallen to its parent if in life, and

(2) that if any part of the residue of my estate falls to a beneficiary who has not attained the age of twenty five years my Trustees shall hold the same in accordance with purpose (EIGHT).

S10.8 *Residuary beneficiaries under 25*

(**EIGHT**)   I direct my Trustees to hold any part of the residue of my estate held for a beneficiary under the age of twenty five years (which is referred to as 'the Trust Fund') for the following purposes:

contingent entitlement

(1) for such beneficiaries contingently on their attaining a vested interest as after provided for;

accumulation

(2) to accumulate the income arising from the Trust Fund by investing all surplus thereof and the resulting income therefrom in accordance with the powers hereafter conferred until such children or issue respectively attain the age of twenty one years;

income

(3) for payment of the income of the share of the Trust Fund to which any of such beneficiaries is prospectively entitled, to such beneficiaries from the attainment by him or her of the age of twenty one until he or she attains a vested interest as provided for in the immediately succeeding paragraph;

capital/

capital (4) for payment of an equal share of the capital of the Trust Fund and the income accumulated prior to his or her acquiring a vested interest in the income to such beneficiaries on their respectively attaining the age of twenty five years and subject as aftermentioned the said capital and accumulated income shall not vest in any of such children or issue until the date of payment of his or her share;

failure (5) if any of such beneficiaries fail to attain a vested interest by reason of his or her predeceasing leaving issue (including adopted issue), each member of a generation of issue as survives and attains the age of twenty five years shall share equally in the share of the Trust Fund, both original and accresced, which would have fallen to its parent if in life; and if any of such beneficiaries fail to attain a vested interest as before provided for leaving no issue who survive and attain the age of twenty five years, to hold the share of the Trust Fund and any income accumulated at the date of such failure for behoof of the beneficiaries who would have been entitled if such beneficiary had never existed;

prohibited accumulations (6) if any accumulation of income of the Trust Fund is prohibited by law by reason of any event the income affected/

affected by such prohibition shall be paid or applied to or for such children or their issue for the time being prospectively entitled to the capital of the Trust Fund or that part thereof from which such income arose;

payments   (7) my Trustees may apply for the maintenance education or benefit of any beneficiary of a share of the Trust Fund (a) the income thereof including accumulated income in whole or in part and (b) the capital thereof in whole or in part, and such advances shall vest on payment or such application;

advance of   (8) my Trustees may appoint at any time or times and in
entitlement   whole or in part that the age at which a beneficiary would otherwise become entitled to a share of the capital of the Trust Fund or to a right to the income thereof shall be advanced to such earlier age as they may decide, and if any such appointment is revocable it shall unless earlier revoked become irrevocable when and to the extent that it shall become operative;

resettlement   (9) my Trustees shall have power, in relation to any part of the Trust Fund of which a beneficiary is then entitled to the income, to appoint that such part of the Trust Fund or any part or parts of the income or capital thereof shall be held for such trust purposes, together with such limitations/

limitations, conditions and provisions for accumulation, maintenance, education and advancement for the benefit of such beneficiary alone or of such beneficiary's issue or the spouses of any of these persons, or of any other person or persons whom such beneficiary desires to be included as beneficiaries, or of him or her and them, and generally with such powers and discretions exercisable by my Trustees or by any other person or persons and on such terms as my Trustees shall think fit;

no apportionment

(10)   there shall be no apportionment as between capital and income on any occasion.

S10.9   *Beneficiaries lacking capacity*

(**NINE**)   If any part of my estate is held for a beneficiary who lacks full legal capacity my Trustees shall have full power either to pay or apply the whole or any part of the income or capital falling to such beneficiary for his or her behoof in any manner my Trustees may think proper, or to retain the same until such capacity is attained accumulating income with capital or to pay over the same to the legal guardian or the person for the time being having the custody of such beneficiary whose receipt shall be a sufficient discharge to my Trustees.

S10.10   *Renunciation of benefit*

(**TEN**)   In the event of any benefit conferred by this will being renounced in whole or in part the benefit or

such/

such part or parts thereof shall pass to the beneficiary or beneficiaries who would have been entitled and on the terms and conditions which would have applied had the beneficiary so renouncing predeceased me.

S10.11 *Trustees' powers*

(**ELEVEN**)   My Trustees shall have the fullest power of and in regard to retention, realisation, investment, appropriation, transfer of property without realisation, and management of my estate as if they were absolute beneficial owners; and shall have power to do everything they may consider necessary or expedient for the administration of the trust; and in particular and without prejudice to these general powers my Trustees shall have power:

retention etc

(1)   to retain, sell, purchase, lease or hire the estate or any part thereof;

investment

(2)   to invest the whole or any part of the estate in heritable and leasehold property, investments, securities, insurance policies, deposits and other assets of whatever description, whether producing income or not, whether or not falling within the class of investments authorised for trust funds, whether or not payable to bearer, and wherever situated;

insurance policies

(3)   to effect, maintain and acquire policies of insurance of whatever description; and to insure any property on whatever/

whatever terms they think fit including on a first loss basis;

management of heritage (4) to administer and manage any heritable or real property forming part of the estate; to repair, maintain, renew and improve the same and to erect additional buildings and structures; to grant, vary and terminate leases and rights of tenancy or occupancy; to plant, thin and cut down timber; to work or let minerals; all as my Trustees may think proper and as if they were absolute owners of the estate;

businesses (5) to continue or to commence any business, whether alone or in conjunction or in partnership with any other persons, or through any companies, for such period as my Trustees may think proper; to appoint or employ any trustee or any other person in any capacity in relation to such business and to pay to them suitable remuneration for services, including pension provisions for any employees or their dependants; and to delegate or entrust to any persons the control and management of such business to such extent as my Trustees may think fit; and my Trustees

(a) may employ for the purposes of such business such part of the income or capital as they think proper;

(b)/

(b)   shall exercise only such control or supervision of such business as they shall think fit;

(c)   shall be entitled to be relieved from the estate from all personal responsibility for any loss arising from such business operations; and

(d)   shall be entitled to retain personally any remuneration for their services;

borrow and lend   (6)   to borrow or lend with or without security; and to grant or continue any guarantee or indemnity for the benefit of any beneficiary actual or prospective;

occupation by beneficiaries   (7)   to lend or allow to be used the whole or any part of the estate at such rate of interest or rent as they may consider appropriate, or free of interest or rent, to or by any person who is for the time being entitled to payment of a share of the income of the estate or to whom or for whose benefit the income may be paid or applied in the exercise of a discretion then available to my Trustees;

nominees   (8)   to allow the estate or any part thereof to be registered in the names of or held or the documents of title to be held by any person, firm, corporation or other body as nominee of my Trustees;

delegation of investment management   (9)   revocably to delegate any power or powers of making, managing, realising or otherwise dealing with any/

any investment or deposit comprised in the estate to any person or persons upon such terms as to remuneration or otherwise as my Trustees may think fit and no trustee shall be responsible for the default of any such agent if the trustee in question employed him in good faith;

additions   (10)   to accept as an addition to my estate any other property which may be made over to them;

allocation between capital and income   (11)   to decide what is capital and what is income and the proportion in which expenses are to be charged against capital and income respectively;

appropriation   (12)   to set apart and appropriate specific property of any description to represent the whole or part of the share, prospective or otherwise, of any beneficiary at such valuation as my Trustees shall determine, so that thereafter the particular share or part shall have the full benefit and the whole risk of the appropriated investments or assets;

settlement   (13)   to settle with any beneficiary entitled to any part of the estate by conveying to him or her in satisfaction thereof either specific property or money, or partly one and partly the other, as to my Trustees shall seem proper and at such valuation as they shall determine and to compel acceptance accordingly;

conflict/

conflict of interest (14)　to enter into any transaction or do any act otherwise authorised by law or by this deed notwithstanding that any trustee is or might be acting as *auctor in rem suam* or with a conflict of interest between such trustee and himself as an individual or as trustee of any other trust or any partnership of which a trustee is a partner or any company of which a trustee is a shareholder or director or in relation to any combination of these capacities provided that the trustee or trustees with whom there is or may be any such conflict is or are not the sole trustee or trustees;

participation in discretion (15)　to participate in the exercise of any discretion granted to my Trustees notwithstanding that a trustee is or may be a or the sole beneficiary in whose favour the discretion is then exercised provided that there is at least one trustee not so favoured;

resignation (16)　to resign office notwithstanding any benefit hereunder;

agents (17)　to appoint one or more of their own number to act as solicitor or agent or any other capacity and to allow him or them the same remuneration to which he or they would have been entitled if not a trustee or trustees;

non-resident trustees (18)　to appoint any one or more trustees resident out of the United Kingdom and themselves to resign office;

administration/

administration abroad (19) to carry on the administration of the trust hereby created in some place out of the United Kingdom;

renunciation of powers (20) to renounce for themselves and their successors in office the power to exercise any of the foregoing powers in this purpose as if the same were vested in them beneficially and not as trustees.

S10.12 *Immunities* (**TWELVE**) My Trustees shall not be liable for depreciation in value of the property in my estate, nor for omissions or errors in judgement, nor for neglect in management, nor for insolvency of debtors, nor for the acts, omissions, neglects or defaults of each other or of any agent employed by them.

S10.13 *Domicile* (**THIRTEEN**) I declare that my domicile is Scottish.

S10.14 *Guardians* (**FOURTEEN**) In the event of my said wife so failing to survive me I appoint H (design) and I (design) to be guardians to my children: IN WITNESS WHEREOF

STYLE 10

References

General		This Style is discussed at paras 5.96–5.107. Discretionary trusts in general are dealt with at paras 5.68–5.72.
Preliminary wording		See para 3.02 and on designation of the testator see para 9.10.
S10.1	*Revocation*	See paras 3.03–3.09 and on foreign aspects paras 2.67–2.70.
S10.2	*Executors and trustees*	See paras 3.10–3.30.
S10.3	*Informal writings*	See paras 3.31–3.36.
S10.4	*Legacies*	See paras 3.37–3.41. On interest see paras 4.46–4.47. On delivery expenses see paras 4.58–4.60.
S10.5	*Discretionary Fund*	See paras 5.98–5.104, 4.38–4.40.
S10.6	*Residue to wife*	See para 5.105 and Chapter 6 generally, especially paras 6.02–6.09. On survivorship, see paras 5.15–5.19. See also paras 9.16–9.22.
S10.7	*Residue to children*	See Chapter 6 generally on issues relating to children. On destinations-over and division among beneficiaries see paras 5.02–5.14, 5.26–5.27.
S10.8	*Residuary beneficiaries under 25*	On the accumulation and maintenance, trust provisions, see paras 6.65–6.80.
S10.9	*Beneficiaries lacking capacity*	See paras 6.46–6.51, 6.127–6.128.
S10.10	*Renunciation of benefit*	See paras 5.20–5.25.
S10.11	*Trustees powers*	See paras 7.03–7.27 and 3.19–3.25.
S10.12	*Immunities*	See para 7.29.
S10.13	*Domicile*	See paras 2.60–2.77.
S10.14	*Guardians*	See paras 6.86–6.111.

PRECIS OF STYLE 11

Short form of will by husband in favour of wife where no children at present and whom failing both spouses' siblings

1. Revocation of prior wills

2. Executors

3. Provision for informal writings

4. Any legacies to be paid free of tax, expenses and interest

5. The residue is to pass to the testator's spouse

6. If the spouse does not survive for 30 days then the residue passes to the testator's children equally with the children of any predeceasing children taking their parent's share

7. If there are no children or issue then if the testator has inherited his spouse's estate the combined estate passes half to the testator's siblings and half to the testator's spouse's siblings, but otherwise the testator's estate passes to his siblings

8. The executors are given wide powers to deal with funds falling to beneficiaries lacking capacity

9. The executors are given short powers of administration and management

10. Declaration of Scottish domicile

11. Declaration as to cremation

STYLE 11

Short form of will by husband in favour of wife where no children at present and whom failing both spouses' siblings

I, A (design) in order to settle the succession to my estate after my death provide as follows:

S11.1   *Revocation*   (**ONE**)   I revoke all prior wills and testamentary writings.

S11.2   *Executors*   (**TWO**)   I appoint my wife B, residing with me, and C (design) to be my executors.

S11.3   *Informal writings*   (**THREE**)   I direct my executors to give effect to any future writings subscribed by me however informal the same may be provided that in the opinion of my executors they clearly express my intentions.

S11.4   *Legacies*   (**FOUR**)   Unless otherwise specified any legacy granted by any writing shall be paid or made over as soon as my executors consider practicable after my death free of government duties in respect of my death and of delivery expenses but without interest.

S11.5   *Residue to wife*   (**FIVE**)   I direct my executors to make over the residue of my estate to my wife B if she survives for thirty days after my death.

S11.6   *Residue to children*   (**SIX**)   If my wife B does not survive me for thirty days, but in such event only, I direct my executors to make over/

over the residue of my estate to such of any children I may have as shall survive me equally among them if more than one, declaring that should any of my children predecease me leaving issue (including adopted issue) who shall survive me each member of a generation of issue of such predeceasing child shall share equally in the part of my estate, both original and accresced, which would have fallen to its parent if in life.

S11.7   *Failure*   (**SEVEN**)   If I am not so survived by my said wife or children or issue then:

(1)   in the event of my having inherited the residue of the estate of my wife B (as to which my executors shall be the sole judges) I direct my executors to make over the residue of my estate one-half to such of my brothers and sisters as shall survive me and the other half to such of my wife B's brothers and sisters as shall survive me; or

(2)   in any other case I direct my executors to make over the residue of my estate to such of my brothers and sisters as shall survive me;

declaring that should any of such brothers and sisters predecease me leaving issue (including adopted issue) who shall survive me each member of a generation of issue of such predeceasing brother or sister shall share equally in the/

the part of my estate, both original and accresced, which

would have fallen to its parent if in life.

S11.8 *Beneficiaries*   (**EIGHT**)   If any part of my estate is held for a bene-
       lacking capacity
                            ficiary who lacks full legal capacity my executors shall

have full power either to pay or apply the whole or any part

of the income or capital falling to such beneficiary for his

or her benefit in any manner my executors think proper,

or to retain the same until such capacity is attained, or to

pay over the same to the legal guardian or the person for the

time being having the custody of such beneficiary whose

receipt shall be a sufficient discharge to my executors.

S11.9 *Powers*   (**NINE**)   My executors shall have the fullest powers

of retention, realisation, investment, appropriation,

transfer of property without realisation, and management

of my estate as if they were absolute beneficial owners; and

shall have power to resign office and to appoint one or

more of their own number to act as solicitor or agent in any

other capacity and to allow him or them the same

remuneration to which he or they would have been

entitled if not an executor or executors.

S11.10 *Domicile*   (**TEN**)   I declare that my domicile is Scottish.

S11.11 *Funeral*   (**ELEVEN**)   I wish my body to be cremated: IN WITNESS
        instructions
                            WHEREOF

STYLE 11

References

General		This Style is dealt with at paras 6.25–6.28.
Preliminary wording		See para 3.02 and on designation of the testator see para 9.10.
S11.1	*Revocation*	See paras 3.03–3.09 and on foreign aspects paras 2.67–2.70.
S11.2	*Executors*	See paras 3.10–3.30.
S11.3	*Informal writings*	See paras 3.31–3.36.
S11.4	*Legacies*	See paras 3.37–3.41. On interest see paras 4.46–4.47. On delivery expenses see paras 4.58–4.60.
S11.5	*Residue to wife*	See Chapter 6 generally, especially paras 6.02–6.09. On survivorship, see paras 5.15–5.19. See also paras 9.16–9.22.
S11.6	*Residue to children*	See Chapter 6 generally on issues relating to children. On destinations-over and division among beneficiaries, see paras 5.02–5.14, 5.26–5.27. See also paras 9.16–9.22.
S11.7	*Failure*	See para 6.27.
S11.8	*Beneficiaries lacking capacity*	See paras 6.46–6.51, 6.127–6.128.
S11.9	*Powers*	See paras 7.01–7.02, 3.19–3.25.
S11.10	*Domicile*	See paras 2.60–2.77.
S11.11	*Funeral instructions*	See paras 3.42–3.62.

PRECIS OF STYLE 12

Short form of will by testator domiciled abroad of Scottish immoveable property

1. Executors

2. Legacy of house

3. The executors are given short powers of administration and management

STYLE 12

Short form of will by testator domiciled abroad of Scottish immoveable property

I, A (design) in order to settle the succession to my heritable estate in Scotland after my death provide as follows:

S12.1 *Executors* (**ONE**) I appoint B (design) and C (design) to be my executors.

S12.2 *Legacy of house* (**TWO**) I direct my executors to make over to D (design) whom failing to E (design) the dwellinghouse and grounds belonging to me known as 'Tayview', Glensporran, Perthshire.

S12.3 *Powers* (**THREE**) My executors shall have the fullest powers of retention, realisation, investment, appropriation, transfer of property without realisation, and management of my estate as if they were absolute beneficial owners; and shall have power to resign office and to appoint one or more of their own number to act as solicitor or agent in any other capacity and to allow him or them the same remuneration to which he or they would have been entitled if not an executor or executors: IN WITNESS WHEREOF

STYLE 12

References

General		This Style is dealt with at paras 2.78–2.82. See also paras 2.21–2.22, 2.60–2.77.
Preliminary wording		See para 3.02 and on designation of the testator see para 9.10.
S12.1	*Executors*	See paras 2.78–2.80 and 3.10–3.30.
S12.2	*Legacy of house*	See paras 2.79, 4.71–4.72 and 4.76–4.81.
S12.3	*Powers*	See paras 2.78–2.80, 3.19–3.25 and 7.01–7.02.

PRECIS OF STYLE 13

Codicil to Style 2 will

1. Substitution of executors
2. Changes in legacies in will
3. Substitution of subject of legacy
4. New legacy
5. New pecuniary legacy

STYLE 13

Codicil to Style 2 will

I, A (design) formerly of (old address) and now of (new address) make the following codicil to my will dated (date):

S13.1 **(ONE)** I revoke the appointment of B as executor and appoint FF (design) as executor as if he had originally been appointed in my will.

S13.2 **(TWO)** With reference to purpose (SIX) of my will:

(1) I increase the legacy to my godson D to THREE THOUSAND POUNDS; and

(2) I record that my former housekeeper E has now died.

S13.3 **(THREE)** I revoke the legacy in purpose (NINE) (1) of my will to L of an item of my jewellery of her choice and instead direct my executors to make over to her my gold Omega wristwatch and all my cameras and other photographic equipment.

S13.4 **(FOUR)** I direct my executors to make over to M my collection of Wemyss-ware plates.

S13.5 **(FIVE)** I direct my executors to pay to my friend GG (design) the sum of FIVE THOUSAND POUNDS as a token of my appreciation of her help to me over many years: IN WITNESS WHEREOF

STYLE 13

References

General	This Style is dealt with in Chapter 8.
Preliminary wording	See Chapter 8 and paras 3.02 and 9.10.
S13.1	See para 8.04 and on executors generally see paras 3.10–3.30.
S13.2	See para 8.05 and on the subjects of legacy Chapter 4.
S13.3	See para 8.05 and on the subjects of legacy paras 4.48–4.62.
S13.4	See para 8.05 and on the subjects of legacy paras 4.48–4.62.
S13.5	See para 8.05 and on pecuniary legacies paras 4.34–4.37.

PRECIS OF STYLE 14

Codicil to Style 2 will

1. Substitution of executors
2. Legacy to new executor

STYLE 14

Codicil to Style 2 will

I, A (design) make this codicil to my will dated (date):

I revoke purposes (TWO) and (THREE) of my will and substitute for them the following purposes:

S14.1   '(**TWO**)   I appoint FF (design) and GG (design) to be my executors.

S14.2   (**THREE**)   I direct my executors to pay to the said FF if he shall accept office as executor the sum of FIVE HUNDRED POUNDS.': IN WITNESS WHEREOF

STYLE 14

References

General	This Style is dealt with in Chapter 8.
Preliminary wording	See Chapter 8 and paras 3.02 and 9.10.
S14.1	See para 8.04 and on executors generally see paras 3.10–3.30.
S14.2	See para 8.05. On pecuniary legacies paras 4.34–4.37, on legacies to executors paras 6.149–6.156, 7.18–7.19, and on conditional legacies paras 5.37–5.39.

INDEX

Abatement
demonstrative legacy, 4.09
generally, 4.07
preferential legacy, 4.12
specific legacy, 4.10
tax and expenses, due to, 4.09
testator's power to regulate, 4.08, 4.11, 4.12
See also ADEMPTION, LEGACY
Acceptance of office of executor, *see* EXECUTORS
Accretion of legacies, 5.03, 5.04, 5.06, 5.07, 5.09, 6.33
Accumulation and maintenance trust
accumulation period, 6.67, 6.72, 6.85
apportionment between capital and income, *see*
    TRUST
beneficiaries –
    failure of, 6.70, 6.71
    future born, 6.81, 6.82
    generally, 6.64, 6.65
    grandchildren, 6.81, 6.82, 6.84
capital –
    advance of, 6.74, 6.77, 6.78, 6.83, 6.85
    application of, 6.74–6.76, 6.85
    discretion as to, 6.76
    generally, 6.69
conditional legacy, alternative to, 5.54
generally, 1.01, 6.53, 6.54, 6.63
income –
    advance of, 6.74, 6.77, 6.85
    application of, 6.73–6.75, 6.85
    generally, 6.68, 6.69, 6.72
new trust purposes, 6.79
short form, 6.85
subject of –
    business interests, 9.25
    residue, 6.64, 6.65
    specific assets, 4.137
taxation –
    capital gains tax, 6.58
    generally, 6.54, 6.55, 6.62
    income tax, 6.57
    inheritance tax, 6.54, 6.56
vesting, 6.66, 6.69, 6.84, 6.85
Accumulation of income
restrictions on, 5.69, 5.93, 6.53, 6.67, 6.72
Additions, *see* ALTERATIONS
Ademption
bank etc accounts, 4.119
clauses regulating, 4.16, 4.17
generally, 4.15

Ademption – *contd*
shares, 4.15, 4.16, 4.102, 4.103, 4.120
stock, 4.123
See also ABATEMENT, LEGACY
Administration of estates
foreign rules, 2.76
Adopted as holograph will
execution of, 2.58
meaning, 2.32
probativity of, 2.33
when to use, 2.58
Advance
lifetime, *see* COLLATION
Advance health care directive, *see* LIVING WILLS
Age
legacy conditional upon, 5.41–5.43
legal capacity, of, *see* CHILDREN
majority, of, meaning, 5.41, 6.46, 6.67, 6.95
testamentary capacity and, 2.02
Agricultural property relief, *see* INHERITANCE
    TAX
Aide memoire
use of, 9.02, 9.08
Alimentary liferent, *see* LIFERENT TRUST
Alterations
authentication of, 2.39, 2.44
forms –
    additions, 2.47
    erasures and deletions, 2.46
    errors in testing clause, 2.48
    names and signatures, 2.45
generally, 2.44
unauthorised,
    measures to combat, 1.04, 1.05, 2.44
Animal
destruction of, legacy conditional on, 4.69
legacy of –
    associated trust, 4.68, 6.148
    generally, 4.67
    problems, 4.68
    racehorse, 4.70
legacy to, competency, 4.67, 6.148
Annuity
legacy in form of –
    commencement and dates of payment, 4.130
    commutation, 4.133
    examples of uses, 4.68
    funding, 4.131, 4.132, 4.134
    generally, 4.129, 5.55
    purchase annuity, 4.134

518 INDEX

Step-parents
beneficiaries, as, 6.120
Stocks
jointly owned, 2.25
legacy of –
 ademption, 4.15, 4.123
 classification, 4.03
 generally, 4.123
Styles
generally, 1.01–1.08
trusts, 5.73 ff, 6.63 ff
use of, 1.09
See also CLAUSES
Substitution, *see* DESTINATION-OVER
Substitutional legacy, *see* LEGACY
Superannuation scheme, *see* PENSION SCHEME
Survivorship
clauses, 5.15–5.17, 5.19, 5.76, 5.104, 5.106,
 6.03, 6.26
destination, *see* DESTINATION-OVER, SPECIAL
 DESTINATION
presumption of, 5.16–5.18, 6.26
Suspensive condition, *see* CONDITIONAL LEGACY

Taking instructions
aide memoire, 9.08
considerations –
 annuities, 4.129–4.131, 4.134
 beneficiaries, generally, 9.13
 business interests, 2.19, 4.92, 4.97, 4.100,
  4.105, 6.140, 9.24, 9.25
 capacity, 9.11
 conditional legacy, 5.39
 description of legacies, 4.59
 designation,
  beneficiaries, 9.13
  testator, 9.10
 destruction of prior wills, 3.04
 domicile, 9.11
 donation of body for medical purposes, 3.58–
  3.60
 estate planning, 2.82, 9.12
 executors and trustees, suitability of, 9.27
 explanation of terms of will, 9.28
 foreign domiciled testator, 2.57, 2.72, 2.74,
  2.78–2.82, 9.11, 9.15
 foreign property, 2.22, 2.65, 2.73, 2.74, 2.76,
  2.77, 2.81, 2.82, 4.89, 9.15
 foreign resident legatees, 4.37
 foreign rules of administration, 2.76, 2.81,
  2.82
 foreign taxation, 2.77
 form of execution, 2.73
 form of will, 2.72, 2.80, 2.81
 funeral instructions, 3.42, 3.47, 3.58
 guardianship of children, 6.103
 heritable property, 4.71, 4.80
 informal writings, 3.33, 3.35
 inheritance tax reliefs, 4.92, 4.93
 intestate succession, 6.31, 9.03, 9.06, 9.07,
  9.16, 9.18
 legacies,
  property not owned by testator, 4.18

Taking instructions – *contd*
considerations – *contd*
 legacies – *contd*
  very large, 4.12
 legal rights, 9.03, 9.05, 9.09
 lifespan of will, 9.23, 9.29
 lifetime gifts, 4.33, 4.45
 living wills, 3.67
 Lloyd's interests, 4.126, 4.127
 multiple wills, 3.07
 mutual wills, 3.09, 9.26
 pension scheme benefits, 2.16
 pre-existing foreign will, 2.68–2.70
 prior rights, 6.31, 9.03, 9.04, 9.07, 9.16, 9.18
 review of will, 9.29
 second families, 9.22
 shares, quoted, 4.120
 special destinations, 2.26, 2.28, 2.29, 3.03
 state of mind, 2.03, 9.11
 tax, expenses and interest, 3.37, 3.38, 3.41,
  4.46, 4.47, 4.60
 timeshare interests, 4.89
 undue influence, 2.08, 9.11
generally, 1.09, 9.01, 9.02
interview format, 9.08, 9.30
Tax, expenses and interest, *see* CLAUSES
Tenancy, *see* LEASE
Testamentary capacity, *see* CAPACITY TO MAKE WILL
Testator
capacity, *see* CAPACITY TO MAKE WILL
change of name, 9.10
comprehension of will terms, importance of,
 1.02, 9.28
designation, 9.10
domicile, *see* DOMICILE
nationality, *see* NATIONALITY
Testing clause
errors in, 2.48
forms –
 docquet, 2.43, 2.44
 English, 2.57
 full, 2.41
 generally, 2.40
 short, 2.42
generally, 2.39
See also ALTERATIONS
Timeshare
legacy of, 4.89
Tombstone, *see* FUNERAL INSTRUCTIONS
Trade mark
legacy of, 4.113
Transplants, *see* DONATION OF BODY FOR MEDICAL
 PURPOSES
Trees, *see* WOODLANDS
Trust
accumulation and maintenance, *see*
 ACCUMULATION AND MAINTENANCE TRUST
accumulation of income, *see* ACCUMULATION OF
 INCOME
animal, to ensure welfare of, 4.68
apportionment between capital and income –
 exclusion of, 5.77, 6.80, 6.85
 generally, 7.28